SUPREME LAW OF THE LAND?

How do treaties function in the American legal system? This book provides a comprehensive analysis of the current status of treaties in American law. Its ten chapters examine major areas of change in treaty law in recent decades, including treaty interpretation, federalism, self-execution, treaty implementing legislation, treaty form, and judicial barriers to treaty enforcement. The book also includes two in-depth case studies: one on the effectiveness of treaties in the regulation of armed conflict and one on the role of a resurgent federalism in complicating U.S. efforts to ratify and implement treaties in private international law. Each chapter asks whether the treaty rules of the 1987 Third Restatement of Foreign Relations Law accurately reflect today's judicial, executive and legislative practices. This volume is original and provocative, a useful desk companion for judges and practicing lawyers, and an engaging read for the general reader and graduate students.

Gregory H. Fox is Professor of Law and Director of the Program for International Legal Studies at Wayne State University. He is the author of numerous publications, including Humanitarian Occupation (Cambridge, 2008) and Democratic Governance and International Law (with Brad R. Roth, Cambridge, 2000).

Paul R. Dubinsky is Professor of Law at Wayne State University, Vice-President of the International Law Association (U.S. branch), and book review editor of the American Journal of Comparative Law. His publications have appeared in the American Journal of Comparative Law, the Michigan Law Review, the Stanford Journal of International Law, the Yale Journal of International Law, Civil Litigation in a Globalizing World (2012) and International Law in Domestic Legal Systems (2011).

Brad R. Roth is Professor of Political Science and Law at Wayne State University. He is the author of Governmental Illegitimacy in International Law, Sovereign Equality and Moral Disagreement, and numerous other publications on sovereignty, constitutionalism, human rights and democracy, as well as the co-editor (with Gregory H. Fox) of Democratic Governance and International Law (Cambridge University Press, 2000).

Supreme Law of the Land?

DEBATING THE CONTEMPORARY EFFECTS OF TREATIES WITHIN THE UNITED STATES LEGAL SYSTEM

GREGORY H. FOX
Wayne State University School of Law

PAUL R. DUBINSKY
Wayne State University School of Law

BRAD R. ROTH
Wayne State University School of Law

CAMBRIDGE
UNIVERSITY PRESS

CAMBRIDGE
UNIVERSITY PRESS

University Printing House, Cambridge CB2 8BS, United Kingdom

One Liberty Plaza, 20th Floor, New York, NY 10006, USA

477 Williamstown Road, Port Melbourne, VIC 3207, Australia

314-321, 3rd Floor, Plot 3, Splendor Forum, Jasola District Centre, New Delhi - 110025, India

79 Anson Road, #06-04/06, Singapore 079906

Cambridge University Press is part of the University of Cambridge.

It furthers the University's mission by disseminating knowledge in the pursuit of education, learning and research at the highest international levels of excellence.

www.cambridge.org
Information on this title: www.cambridge.org/9781107689015
DOI: 10.1017/9781107588974

First published 2017
First paperback edition 2018

A catalogue record for this publication is available from the British Library

Library of Congress Cataloging in Publication data
NAMES: Dubinsky, Paul R., editor. | Fox, Gregory H., 1961– editor. | Roth, Brad R., editor.
TITLE: Supreme law of the land? : debating the contemporary effects of treaties within the United States legal system / edited by Paul R. Dubinsky, Gregory H. Fox, Brad R. Roth.
DESCRIPTION: Cambridge [UK] ; New York : Cambridge University Press, 2017. | Includes bibliographical references and index.
IDENTIFIERS: LCCN 2017032124 | ISBN 9781107066601 (hardback)
SUBJECTS: LCSH: Treaties. | United States. Congress – Powers and duties. | Treaty-making power – United States. | United States – Foreign relations – Treaties. | BISAC: LAW / International.
CLASSIFICATION: LCC KF4989 .S87 2017 | DDC 342.7302/4–dc23
LC record available at https://lccn.loc.gov/2017032124

ISBN 978-1-107-06660-1 Hardback
ISBN 978-1-107-68901-5 Paperback

For Gillian and Eleanor – GHF
For Eileen Dubinsky and in memory of Stanley Dubinsky – PRD

Contents

Contributors

Gary B. Born is a leading authority on international arbitration and litigation. He is the author of *International Commercial Arbitration* (2nd edn. 2014), *International Arbitration: Law and Practice* (2nd edn. 2015) and numerous other works on international dispute resolution. Mr. Born is the Chair of the International Arbitration Practice Group at Wilmer Cutler Pickering Hale and Dorr LLP and has been ranked for the past twenty years as one of the world's leading international arbitration practitioners. He has served as Counsel in more than 650 international arbitrations, including several of the largest ICC arbitrations and most significant ad hoc arbitrations in recent history. He is President of the Singapore International Arbitration Centre (SIAC) Court of Arbitration and serves in an advisory capacity at other institutions around the world. He is an Honorary Professor of Law at the University of St. Gallen in Switzerland and Tsinghua University, Beijing, and teaches regularly at law schools in Europe, Asia, and North and South America.

Dru Brenner-Beck is a retired U.S. Army Lieutenant Colonel and consultant on international law currently in private practice in Denver, Colorado. In the U.S. Army, she served as a military intelligence officer and military attorney, and after retirement as a law clerk to the Honorable Carlos F. Lucero, US. Court of Appeals for the Tenth Circuit. She is the author of "Accountability for Battlefield Misconduct" in *The Laws of War and the War on Terror* (2nd edn.), "War Crimes Trials at Guantanamo Bay: Key Developments in 2014" in *The War Report: Armed Conflict in 2014*, and "International Law and Detention at Guantánamo Bay" in *The Guantánamo Bay Reader* (forthcoming). She is also President of the National Institute of Military Justice.

Geoffrey S. Corn is Professor of Law at South Texas College of Law in Houston Texas, and a retired U.S. Army Lieutenant Colonel. His Army career included service as both an intelligence officer and a military attorney. His last position with the Army was as senior law of war expert advisor for the Judge Advocate General and Chief of the Law of War Branch. He is the lead author of *The Law of Armed Conflict: An Operational Perspective*, *The Laws of War and the War on Terror* (2nd edn.), and *National Security Law and The Constitution* (forthcoming).

Paul R. Dubinsky is Professor of Law at Wayne State University Law School. He has served as Director of Graduate Studies at Wayne Law, Associate Director of the Orville H. Schell, Jr. Center for International Human Rights at Yale Law School, and as an International Affairs Fellow of the Council on Foreign Relations. His works have appeared in the *American Journal of Comparative Law*, the *Michigan Law Review*, the *Stanford Journal of International Law*, the *Yale Journal of International Law*, *Civil Litigation in a Globalizing World* (Asser Press) and *International Law in Domestic Legal Systems* (Oxford University Press). Professor Dubinsky serves as Vice President of the American Branch of the International Law Association and as book review editor of the *American Journal of Comparative Law*. He has taught at the Benjamin Cardozo School of Law, Georgetown University Law Center, and Yale Law School.

Gregory H. Fox is Professor of Law and Director of the Program for International Legal Studies at Wayne State University School of Law. He has visited or held fellowships at Syracuse Law School, the Universidad Iberoamericana in Mexico City, the Lauterpacht Research Centre for International Law at Cambridge University, the Max Planck Institute for Comparative Public Law and Public International Law in Heidelberg, Germany and the Schell Center for Human Rights at Yale Law School. He is the author or editor of numerous works including *Humanitarian Occupation* (Cambridge 2008), *Democratic Governance and International Law* (Cambridge 2000) (with Brad Roth), and *International Law Decisions in National Courts* (Transnational 2005) (with Thomas M. Franck).

Mark Janis is William F. Starr Professor of Law at the University of Connecticut and Visiting Fellow, formerly Reader in Law, at the University of Oxford. A graduate of Princeton, Oxford, and Harvard, he is the author of several student books, including *International Law* (Aspen 7th edn. 2016), and, with John Noyes, *International Law Cases and Commentary* (West 5th edn. 2014), and the intellectual history, *America and the Law of Nations 1776–1939* (Oxford University Press 2010). Besides his appointments at Connecticut and Oxford, he has taught as a visitor at Cornell, UCLA, and Paris I, and is a member of the Council on Foreign Relations.

Margaret E. McGuinness is Professor of Law at Saint John's University School of Law, where she serves as Co-Director of the Center for International and Comparative Law and faculty director of the LLM in Transnational Legal Practice. Her research focuses on international law in the U.S. legal system, the regulation of international security, and U.S. human rights policy. Professor McGuinness graduated from Stanford Law School with distinction. Prior to her career in law, Professor McGuinness was a Foreign Service Officer with the U.S. State Department. She is a co-founder and contributor to *Opinio Juris*, the leading international law blog.

Michael D. Ramsey is Professor of Law and Director of International and Comparative Law Programs at the University of San Diego School of Law. He is the author of *The Constitution's Text in Foreign Affairs* (Harvard University Press 2007), co-author of *Transnational Law and Practice* (Wolters Kluwer 2015), and co-editor of *International Law in the U.S. Supreme Court: Continuity and Change* (Cambridge University Press 2011).

Brad R. Roth is Professor of Political Science and Law at Wayne State University. His scholarly work applies legal and political theory to problems in international and comparative public law. He is the author of *Governmental Illegitimacy in International Law* (Oxford University Press, 1999), winner of the 1999 Certificate of Merit from the American Society of International Law as "best work in a specialized area," and of *Sovereign Equality and Moral Disagreement* (Oxford University Press, 2011). He is also the co-editor (with Gregory H. Fox) of *Democratic Governance and International Law* (Cambridge University Press, 2000), and the author of over thirty journal articles, book chapters, and scholarly commentaries dealing with questions of sovereignty, constitutionalism, human rights, and democracy.

David P. Stewart is Professor from Practice of International and Transnational Law, Georgetown University Law Center. He is the President of the American Branch of the International Law Association, a member of the Inter-American Juridical Committee, and co-reporter of the ALI Restatement (Fourth) of Foreign Relations Law of the United States. He was previously an Assistant Legal Adviser at U.S. Department of State. David is co-editor of the *Digest of U.S. Practice in International Law* (1989–2003), co-author (with Judge Thomas Buergenthal and Prof. Dinah Shelton) of the *Nutshell on International Human Rights* (4th edn. 2009), and co-author (with Professors Luban and O'Sullivan) of *International and Transnational Criminal Law* (2nd edn. 2014).

Noam Wiener received a B.A. and LL.B from Tel-Aviv University and an LL. M. and S.J.D. from the University of Michigan. He is currently a Legal Officer at the United Nations Office for Legal Affairs. Dr. Wiener has clerked for Judge Bruno Simma at the International Court of Justice and practiced law in Tel-Aviv and New York. The views expressed in his chapter are his own and do not necessarily reflect the views of the United Nations.

Ingrid Wuerth holds the Helen Strong Curry Chair in International Law and is the Director of the International Legal Studies Program at Vanderbilt Law School. Professor Wuerth sits on the board of editors of the *American Journal of International Law*, is a member of the State Department's Advisory Committee on Public International Law, and serves as a Reporter for the Restatement (Fourth) of the Foreign Relations Law of the United States. She has received numerous honors and fellowships, including the Morehead Scholarship at the University of North Carolina at Chapel Hill, a Fulbright Senior Scholar award, the German Chancellor's Fellowship, election to the German Society of International Law, election to the Order of the Coif, and several teaching awards.

Acknowledgments

We are indebted to Zachary van Horn, Rachel Capler, Shahar ben Josef, Elaina Bailey, Kanika Suri, and Tanzania Jaysura for exceptional research assistance in preparing this manuscript and for the expert secretarial assistance of Olive Hyman. Michelle Lalonde of the Wayne Law School Library provided assistance at critical moments, and we are grateful for her exceptional work.

We thank the Program for International Legal Studies at Wayne Law School for hosting the authors' conference that launched this project.

We would also like to thank the Harvard Journal of Law and Public Policy for granting permission to reprint a modified version of Geoffrey S. Corn & Dru Brenner-Beck, *Exploring U.S. Treaty Practice through a Military Lens*, 38 HARV. J. L. & PUB. POL'Y 547 (2015).

Introduction

Gregory H. Fox, Paul R. Dubinsky, and Brad R. Roth

Imagine a claim brought in a U.S. federal court involving the violation of a treaty. The plaintiff asserts that she enjoys rights under a treaty ratified by the United States, that state-level officials have violated those rights and that the court should grant her relief. In the early twenty-first century, the road to litigating such a claim to conclusion will be a rocky one indeed. The court may dismiss the claim because the Senate, as part of its approval package, declared the treaty to be non-self-executing.[1] Even absent such a declaration, the court may on its own inquiry find the treaty to be non-self-executing.[2] Or the court may find that the treaty creates no individual rights.[3] Or it may find that the treaty or legislation implementing the treaty impinges upon exclusive state prerogatives protected by the Tenth Amendment to the Constitution.[4] Or the court may determine that the claim presents a non-justiciable political question.[5] Even if all these procedural hurdles are

[1] *See* Sosa v. Alvarez-Machain, 542 U.S. 692, 735, 124 S. Ct. 2739, 159 L. Ed. 2d 718 (2004) ("[T]he United States ratified the Covenant [on Civil and Political Rights] on the express understanding that it was not self-executing and so did not itself create obligations enforceable in the federal courts"); David P. Stewart, *United States Ratification of the Covenant on Civil and Political Rights: The Significance of the Reservations, Understandings, and Declarations*, 42 DEPAUL L. REV. 1183 (1993).

[2] *See* Medellin v. Texas, 542 U.S. 491, 512–13, 128 S. Ct. 1346, 170 L. Ed. 2d 190 (2008).

[3] *Ibid.* at 506 n. 3 ("Even when treaties are self-executing in the sense that they create federal law, the background presumption is that '[i]nternational agreements, even those directly benefiting private persons, generally do not create private rights or provide for a private cause of action in domestic courts'"); David Sloss, *When Do Treaties Create Individually Enforceable Rights? The Supreme Court Ducks the Issue in* Hamdan *and* Sanchez-Llamas, 45 COLUM. J. TRANSNAT'L L. 20 (2006–2007).

[4] *See* Bond v. United States, 134 S. Ct. 2077, 189 L. Ed. 2d 1 (2014) (employing statutory construction to sidestep a challenge on this basis); Curtis A. Bradley, *Current Developments: Federalism, Treaty Implementation, and Political Process: Bond v. United States*, 108 AM. J. INT'L L. 486 (2014).

[5] *See* Made in the USA Found. v. United States, 242 F.3d 1300 (11th Cir. 2001) (dismissing claim that NAFTA should have been approved as an Article II treaty because such a claim is

surmounted and the court reaches the merits of the claim, the court may accord special deference to the Executive branch's adverse interpretation of the treaty.[6] Or it may reach essentially the same unfavorable outcome through an inquiry of its own that is based solely on U.S. sources and ignores the views of other states parties to the treaty and the decisions of international tribunals.[7] Finally, the court may find the treaty contravened by a U.S. statute enacted after the treaty was ratified and give preference to the statute.[8]

If the claim fails in court for one or more of these reasons, the plaintiff might instead turn to the Executive branch for assistance. Surely an executive order requiring state officials to implement a federal treaty obligation would prevail over contrary state law. The Supremacy Clause provides that "the Constitution, federal laws made pursuant to it, *and treaties made under its authority*, constitute the supreme law of the land" and that "the Judges in every State shall be bound thereby, any Thing in the Constitution or Laws of any State to the Contrary notwithstanding."[9] In fact, however, such an executive order would not be effective; if the treaty is non-self-executing, its obligations would not come within the ambit of the Supremacy Clause, so the Executive would have no federal law to enforce against the state.[10] Moreover, if the Senate had approved the treaty as non-self-executing, efforts to enforce the treaty against a state would be deemed an assertion of Executive authority against the will of Congress, a category of Executive action that rarely survives judicial scrutiny.[11]

Many of these grounds for dismissing treaty claims or filtering them through the policy preferences of the Executive branch have deep roots in American

a non-justiciable political question); David J. Bederman, *Deference or Deception: Treaty Rights as Political Questions*, 70 U. COLO. L. REV. 1439 (1999).

6 *See, e.g.*, Sumitomo Shoji Am., Inc. v. Avagliano, 457 U.S. 176, 184–5, 102 S. Ct. 2374, 72 L. Ed. 2d 765 (1982) ("[T]he meaning attributed to treaty provisions by the Government agencies charged with their negotiation and enforcement is entitled to great weight"); Robert M. Chesney, *Disaggregating Deference: The Judicial Power and Executive Treaty Interpretations*, 92 IOWA L. REV. 1723 (2007).

7 *See, e.g.*, Medellin, 542 U.S. at 508–11 (interpreting meaning of Article 94 of the UN Charter without reference to any non-U.S. sources); Paul R. Dubinsky, *International Law in the Legal System of the United States*, 58 AM. J. COMP. L. 455, 470 (2010).

8 *See, e.g.*, Breard v. Greene, 523 U.S. 371, 376, 118 S. Ct. 1352, 140 L. Ed. 2d 765 (1998) (articulating last-in-time rule); Julian G. Ku, *Treaties as Laws: A Defense of the Last-in-Time Rule for Treaties and Federal Statutes*, 80 IND. L.J. 319 (2005).

9 U.S. Const., art. VI, cl. 2 (emphasis added).

10 Medellin, 542 U.S. at 504 ("This Court has long recognized the distinction between treaties that automatically have effect as domestic law, and those that – while they constitute international law commitments – do not by themselves function as binding federal law.")

11 *Ibid.* at 527 (stating that when the President seeks to enforce a non-self-executing treaty unilaterally "he acts in conflict with the implicit understanding of the ratifying Senate").

history. But their number and scope have expanded substantially in recent years. In just the last decade, three major Supreme Court decisions crystallized treaty-claim limitations based on non-self-execution,[12] on the last-in-time rule,[13] and on resistance to treaty interpretations originating from abroad.[14] The result of these and other judicial decisions, taken in combination with congressional and executive actions, appears to be a substantial diminution of treaties as a source of law within the U.S. legal system. As David Sloss has concluded, these doctrines "effectively shield government actors from accountability for treaty violations."[15]

To be sure, the prospects are much less bleak if treaty-based rights are asserted not against state or federal officials but rather against private parties. Some private law treaties – for example, the New York Convention on the Recognition and Enforcement of Foreign Arbitral Awards[16] – have been fully incorporated into statutory schemes and are regularly invoked with few procedural limitations.[17] The reason for their more favorable reception is likely that private law treaties are much less likely than their public law counterparts to challenge American laws or policies based on non-American norms. Instead, the private law treaties ratified by the U.S. seek to enhance transnational judicial cooperation in cases in which the parties typically are private and the underlying claims are grounded in domestic law.[18] Nonetheless, as the chapters that follow show, the treaty limitations discussed above may well be applied to private law treaties in the future. In addition, the more favorable treatment of private law treaty claims has not been uniform. In the *Schlunk*[19] and *Aerospatiale*[20] cases, for example, the Supreme Court declined to make resort to the Hague Service and Evidence Conventions mandatory, thereby

12 *Ibid.* at 512–13. 13 Breard, 523 U.S. at 376.

14 Sanchez-Llamas v. Oregon, 548 U.S. 331, 352–7, 126 S. Ct. 2669, 165 L. Ed. 2d 557 (2006).

15 David L. Sloss, *Treaty Enforcement in Domestic Courts: a Comparative Analysis*, in The Role of Domestic Courts in Treaty Enforcement: A Comparative Study, 25 (David L. Sloss, ed. 2009).

16 New York Convention on the Recognition and Enforcement of Foreign Arbitral Awards (1958), 21 U.S.T. 2519, 9 U.S.C.S. § 201.

17 The New York Convention is part of the Federal Arbitration Act. *See* 9 U.S.C. §§ 201–208. The Hague Service Convention is incorporated into U.S. procedural law at Fed. R. Civ. P. 4 (f), (h)(2). The Hague Child Abduction Convention is implemented by the International Child Abduction Remedies Act, 102 Stat. 437, 42 U.S.C. § 11601 et seq.

18 One might argue that the New York Convention is an exception, since the enforcement of a foreign arbitration award is a free-standing claim, separate and apart from the claim pursued in the arbitration itself.

19 Volkswagen Aktiengesellschaft v. Schlunk, 486 U.S. 694, 108 S. Ct. 2104, 100 L. Ed. 2d 722 (1988).

20 Societe Nationale Industrielle Aerospatiale v. U.S. Dist. Court for the S. Dist. of Iowa, 482 U.S. 522, 107 S. Ct. 2542, 96 L. Ed. 2d 461 (1987).

substantially undercutting the value of these treaties to many foreign litigants in U.S. courts.

The central question to be explored in this volume is whether these limitations have made the U.S. legal system less receptive to the enforcement of treaty claims. Additional questions follow. Do the limitations discussed above represent a break with past practice or continuity with preexisting trends? Do constraints on the implementation of U.S. international obligations reflect views embedded in the Constitution and in the assumptions of the founding era, or are they of a more recent vintage? Are such limitations motivated by an aversion to treaty-based claims, by hostility to the incorporation of international law more generally, by a belief that certain types of treaties (more prevalent in recent decades) threaten the integrity of national values and institutions, or by some other concerns?[21]

The answers to these questions will turn to a large extent on the historical baseline used to measure change in the domestic status of treaties. As Mark Janis and Noam Wiener demonstrate in their historical review in Chapter 1, treaties in American law have been profoundly affected by the political debates and geopolitical challenges of different eras. As those debates evolve and new challenges appear, treaties take on new roles. Measuring evolution from the founding era or from the immediate post–World War II period, for example, would yield very different conclusions about the nature and extent of change.

The present volume is not a general history of treaties in American law and so will not attempt to chart their ebb and flow across all of American legal history. We seek instead to assess treaties' contemporary status within the U.S. legal system. We have therefore chosen a relatively recent baseline – the treaty rules set out in the Restatement (Third) of Foreign Relations Law of the United States, published in 1987.[22] Each of the authors will ask whether developments since 1987 have affirmed the Restatement rules, modified them in some discernible fashion, or abandoned them altogether. We have chosen the Third Restatement as a baseline for four interrelated reasons. First, it is the most recent and most comprehensive codification of rules related to treaties in American law. As Chapter 2 of this volume will discuss, the Restatement took eight years to produce and each of its treaty provisions was subject to detailed

[21] The creation of barriers to incorporating ratified treaties into American law is distinct, of course, from reticence about entering into multilateral instruments in the first place. *See* Jessica T. Matthews, *The Death of Our Treaties*, 63 N.Y. *REV. BKS*, No. 5, March 24, 2016, at 28 (describing U.S. failure to ratify most recent multilateral agreements).

[22] RESTATEMENT (THIRD) OF THE FOREIGN RELATIONS LAW OF THE UNITED STATES, (AM. LAW INST. 1987) [hereinafter THIRD RESTATEMENT].

examination both within the American Law Institute (ALI), its institutional home, and in outside fora such as the Annual Meetings of the American Society of International Law.

Second, as Chapter 2 again demonstrates, the treaty norms of the Third Restatement were almost entirely uncontroversial during their drafting and were received largely without critical rebuke by federal courts or leading scholars. The Restatement rules, in other words, were the subject of little or no criticism that they misrepresented the law of the time. Other parts of the Third Restatement were highly controversial and led to a year-long standoff between the ALI and the State Department, which had strong objections to provisions related to customary international law, expropriation, the extraterritorial application of U.S. law, and the act of state doctrine.[23] But the Restatement's treaty rules faced no such pushback. If the intervening decades demonstrate a departure from the Restatement rules, therefore, one can be reasonably confident that the departure is also from the underlying law that the Restatement codified.

Third, in the period between the Second and Third Restatements (1965 to 1987) the United States began to consider, and in some cases ratify, multilateral agreements that would generate a large body of domestic jurisprudence on treaty issues. In the area of private law, the United States ratified the Hague Service Convention in 1967,[24] the New York Convention in 1970,[25] the Hague Evidence Convention in 1972,[26] and the Hague Convention on the Legalization of Foreign Public Documents in 1981.[27] The Hague Convention on Child Abduction was under consideration while the Third Restatement was being drafted and was ratified the year after its publication.[28] In the area of human rights, the United States was considering the Genocide

[23] *See, e.g.*, Benedict Tai, *A Summary of the Forthcoming Restatement of the Foreign Relations Law of the United States (Revised)*, 24 COLUM. J. TRANSNAT'L L. 677, 680 (1985–1986); John B. Houck, *Restatement of the Foreign Relations Law of the United States (Revised): Issues and Resolutions*, 20 INT'L L. 1361, 1361 (1986); Malcolm R. Wilkey, *Sections of the Revised Restatement Arousing Interest, Comment and Controversy*, 77 AM. SOC. INT'L L. PROC. 77 (1983).

[24] Hague Convention on the Service Abroad of Judicial and Extrajudicial Documents in Civil or Commercial Matters, Nov. 15, 1965, 20 U.S.T. 361, T.I.A.S. No. 6638, 658 U.N.T.S. 103.

[25] New York Convention, *supra* note 16.

[26] Hague Convention on the Taking of Evidence Abroad in Civil and Commercial Matters, *opened for signature* Mar. 18, 1970, 23 U.S.T. 2555.

[27] Convention Abolishing the Requirement of Legalisation for Foreign Public Documents, *opened for signature* Oct. 5, 1961, T.I.A.S. No. 10,072, 527 U.N.T.S. 189.

[28] Hague Convention on the Civil Aspects of International Child Abduction, Oct. 25, 1980, T.I.A.S. No. 11, 670, 1343 U.N.T.S. 49.

Convention, which it eventually ratified in 1988.[29] The Carter Administration had submitted four major human rights treaties to the Senate in 1978.[30] While these instruments were not acted upon before 1987, their pendency generated discussion in the Third Restatement[31] and all four treaties were ratified soon after the Third Restatement's publication.[32] Perhaps in part as a result of this treaty activity, the period immediately before and after 1987 saw an increase in the attention paid in law school casebooks and treatises to the role of treaties in international civil litigation and in foreign relations law.[33] The Third Restatement thus appeared at a time when American courts were increasingly in need of guidance on the domestic status of treaties. It is noteworthy that the Third Restatement overall was cited 96 times by federal courts in the five years following its publication, as compared to 16 citations to the Second Restatement in the same period following its publication in 1965.[34]

Fourth, in 2012 the American Law Institute began preparations on a Fourth Restatement of Foreign Relations Law,[35] with treaty norms an early part of that effort.[36] The conclusions reached in the chapters of this volume – whether the rules of the Third Restatement remain good law and, if not, how they have

29 Convention on the Prevention and Punishment of the Crime of Genocide, Dec. 9, 1948, 102 Stat. 3045, 78 U.N.T.S. 277.

30 President's Human Rights Treaty Message to the Senate, 14 WEEKLY COMP. OF PRES. DOC. 395 (Feb. 23, 1978).

31 *See* THIRD RESTATEMENT, *supra* note 22, Part VII, Introduction, § 701, cmt. e & rptr. n. 7.

32 The United States ratified the Convention on the Prevention and Punishment of the Crime of Genocide in 1988, the International Covenant on Civil and Political Rights in 1992, the International Convention on the Elimination of All Forms of Racial Discrimination in 1994 and the Convention Against Torture and Other Cruel, Inhuman or Degrading Treatment or Punishment in 1994. University of Minnesota Human Rights Library, Ratification of International Human Rights Treaties – USA, available at http://www1.umn.edu/humanrts/research/ratification-USA.html. *See generally*, Curtis A. Bradley, *The United States and Human Rights Treaties: Race Relations, the Cold War, and Constitutionalism*, 9 CHINESE J. INT'L L. 321 (2010).

33 *See, e.g.*, FOREIGN AFFAIRS AND THE U.S. CONSTITUTION (LOUIS HENKIN, MICHAEL J. GLENNON & WILLIAM D. ROGERS, ED. 1990); MICHAEL J. GLENNON, CONSTITUTIONAL DIPLOMACY (1990); HAROLD HONGJU KOH, THE NATIONAL SECURITY CONSTITUTION (1990); GARY B. BORN & DAVID WESTIN, INTERNATIONAL CIVIL LITIGATION IN UNITED STATES COURTS (1989); THOMAS M. FRANCK & MICHAEL J. GLENNON, FOREIGN RELATIONS AND NATIONAL SECURITY LAW (1987).

34 These numbers are based on a Lexis/Nexis search of the Federal Courts Combined Library for the two time periods. The search for citations to the Third Restatement excludes citations to non-final drafts produced prior to May 14, 1987.

35 *See* Layla Nadya Sadat, *The Proposed Fourth Restatement of the Foreign Relations Law of the United States: Treaties – Some Serious Procedural and Substantive Concerns* (Aug. 2015), available at http://papers.ssrn.com/sol3/papers.cfm?abstract_id=2650528.

36 *See* FOURTH RESTATEMENT OF THE FOREIGN RELATIONS OF THE UNITED STATES (Treaties – Council Draft No. 2) (Dec. 6, 2016).

changed – will, it is hoped, inform the choices to be made by the ALI in crafting the Fourth Restatement. This volume may serve in effect as a scholarly companion to the upcoming debate over treaty rules in the new Restatement and a reference work for courts and others seeking to understand those rules in the context of past practice for the sake of deciding whether ALI's forthcoming work should be followed.

With the 1987 baseline in place, how should one characterize the Third Restatement's approach to treaties? At the risk of oversimplification, one might describe it as seeking accommodation between the external obligations imposed by treaties themselves and the internal demands of a fluid and often rancorous federal system, one in which struggle over foreign relations power occurs both vertically (between the states and the federal government) and horizontally (between the Executive branch, the Congress, and the courts). When doctrines of U.S. law threatened to put the United States in breach of its treaty obligations, the Third Restatement sought wherever possible to shape the former in order to avoid the latter. Thus, while the Third Restatement's Reporters acknowledged that "[i]nternational law and the domestic law of the United States are two different and discrete bodies of law," they cautioned against devaluing international law on that basis. Lawful domestic acts can have internationally unlawful consequences:

> When international law is not given effect in the United States because of constitutional limitations or supervening domestic law, the international obligations of the United States remain and the United States may be in default.[37]

In the case of treaties, even if U.S. law prevailed domestically in conflicts with treaty obligations, "the United States remains bound internationally."[38] Repeating a principle of the international law of state responsibility, the Reporters explained that the United States (or any state) "cannot adduce its constitution or its laws as a defense for failure to carry out its international obligation."[39] In order to minimize U.S. violations of international law, the Third Restatement sought to overcome barriers to incorporation of treaty norms, sometimes in clever and farsighted ways.[40]

This spirit of accommodation appeared in each critical area of treaty law. Finding a treaty non-self-executing might well cut off an important means of

37 THIRD RESTATEMENT, *supra* note 22, ch. 2, Introductory Note, at 40. 38 *Ibid.*

39 *Ibid.*, § 115, cmt. b.

40 *Cf.* Peter J. Spiro, *Sovereigntism's Twilight*, 31 BERKELEY J. INT'L LAW. 307, 307 (2013) (noting the "conventional wisdom of the Third Restatement of Foreign Relations Law… that was receptive to the incorporation of international law.").

implementation or enforcement, leading to the international law violations about which the reporters warned. The Restatement fully accepted that if a treaty text clearly indicates that it is non-self-executing or if the Senate upon consent to ratification declares that intention, the courts are bound to give effect to those determinations. But absent such clear evidence, the Restatement articulated a presumption *in favor* of self-execution.[41] The reason again was the danger of non-compliance with international law: "Since generally the United States is obligated to comply with a treaty as soon as it comes into force for the United States, compliance is facilitated and expedited if the treaty is self-executing."[42] On the issue of treaty interpretation, the Restatement noted that American courts have been more willing to consult *travaux preparatoires* than the Vienna Convention on the Law of Treaties permits and that this difference in interpretive method could result in U.S. judicial decisions being viewed as breaches of American treaty obligations.[43] On the question of federalism limitations on the treaty power – or on Congressional authority to legislate pursuant to a treaty – the Restatement wholly agreed with Justice Holmes's opinion in *Missouri v. Holland*[44] and found only marginal instances in which exclusive state authority might preclude the federal government from legislating pursuant to a previously ratified treaty.[45] Finally, the likelihood of the United States undertaking an international treaty obligation at all is substantially affected by the domestic approval process deemed to be required – whether by a supermajority vote in the Senate (as provided by Article II of the Constitution), by a majority vote in both Houses of Congress, or by the President's signature alone. Not surprisingly, the Restatement adopted an exceptionally broad range of options, asserting that Article II treaties and congressional-executive agreements are fully interchangeable.[46]

41 Third Restatement, *supra* note 22, § 111, rptr. n. 5 ("[T]here is a strong presumption that the treaty has been considered self-executing by the political branches and should be considered self-executing by the courts.").

42 *Ibid.*

43 *Ibid.*, § 325, cmt. g. The Restatement attempted to downplay this possibility by asserting that the results of the VCLT approach and U.S. treaty interpretation doctrine tend to yield the same result, *ibid.*, though the Restatement did not cite any cases in support of this assertion.

44 Missouri v. Holland, 252 U.S. 416, 40 S. C. 382, 64 L. Ed. 641 (1920).

45 Third Restatement, *supra* note 22, § 302. The two instances mentioned were when a treaty is not "validly made" (i.e., a "sham" treaty designed to circumvent otherwise-applicable constitutional provisions) or when a treaty contravenes specific constitutional limitations, specifically those in the Bill of Rights. For a more detailed discussion of § 302, *see* Margaret McGuinness, "Treaties, Federalism, and the Contested Legacy of *Missouri v. Holland*," Chapter 5 of this volume.

46 Third Restatement, *supra* note 22, § 303, cmt. e.

The chapters that follow will assess how this accommodationist view of treaties has fared since 1987. The first two chapters set the stage for later discussions of specific treaty law issues. In Chapter 1, Mark Janis and Noam Wiener explore the history of treaties in the U.S. legal system since the founding era. Whereas later chapters review the political and judicial histories of particular issues, Janis and Wiener's broad historical overview reveals patterns of treaty embrace and rejection that cut across doctrinal categories. They conclude that for much of U.S. history – and notably with respect to the Bricker Amendment controversy of the 1950s – the domestic politics of race lurked behind many treaty controversies. Chapter 2 reviews the drafting and subsequent reception of treaty provisions in the Third Restatement. As noted above, unlike other provisions of the Restatement that provoked rancorous debate, the treaty sections were almost wholly uncontroversial during the drafting process. In the years following the Restatement's appearance, few courts or scholars of foreign relations law criticized the treaty sections or found them inconsistent with prevailing law.

The volume then moves from these general assessments to a discussion of how six specific areas of U.S. treaty law have fared since the Restatement's publication. Paul Dubinsky examines treaty interpretation in Chapter 3 and concludes that in the past three decades, judicial deference to executive interpretations of treaties has increased, with the result that the U.S. legal system as a whole has become less receptive to foreign views of a treaty's meaning than in the past. Chapter 3's innovative approach to this set of issues is to focus not on categories of agreements or on traditional canons of construction. Rather, Professor Dubinsky examines how models and analogies have guided the American approach to treaty language. Well before the Restatement era, and for much of American history, treaties were analogized to contracts. Courts following this approach would consult a variety of sources in order to reach the overarching goal of determining the treaty parties' mutual intent. By the late nineteenth century, a second model of treaties as analogous to statutes began to emerge. This brought with it a decline in efforts to seek the mutual intent of treaty parties in favor of ascertaining only the views of the United States as expressed during Senate (or, in the case of Congressional-Executive agreements, Congressional) approval of an agreement. The Third Restatement did not choose between these approaches but seemed to embrace both. It also confirmed that both were to be applied with some deference to the views of the Executive branch. As Chapter 3 reveals, in the post-Restatement period, the extent of executive deference has increased substantially, a development accentuated by the appearance of a third model of interpretation – the treaty as delegation. With this model, implementing legislation is regarded as a delegation of interpretive authority to executive departments and agencies, whose views are entitled not just to "one voice" deference but to *Chevron* deference, at least where a treaty relates to complex regulatory matters.[47]

In Chapter 4, Ingrid Wuerth addresses self-execution, perhaps the most widely debated doctrine concerning treaties' susceptibility to judicial application. The Third Restatement, departing from the Second, articulated a presumption in favor of self-execution, reasoning that it would facilitate treaty compliance. This argument echoed the Reporters' repeated link between domestic treaty application and compliance on the international plane. But as Wuerth details, the presumption did not take hold in the federal courts, and in its pivotal 2008 opinion in *Medellin v. Texas*, the Supreme Court arguably posited a presumption *against* self-execution.[48] *Medellin* also adopted the most far-reaching consequence of characterizing a treaty provision as non-self-executing: rather than merely limiting judicial enforcement of the provision, the Court altogether denied such a provision the status of "domestically enforceable federal law."[49] Moreover, the *Medellin* court appeared to agree with the Third Restatement that the question of whether or not a treaty is self-executing should be determined primarily by reference to the views of the President and the Senate at the time of the treaty's ratification. In his majority opinion, Justice Roberts notably did not consult any foreign or multilateral sources. Given that the treaty provision in question was an article of the United Nations Charter, to say that such sources existed in abundance is a vast understatement.

In Chapter 5, Margaret McGuinness considers issues of federalism. As in other areas of law in which the states and federal government compete for plenary authority, the question of Congress's capacity to legislate pursuant to treaties was thought to be essentially settled for most of the twentieth century. *Missouri v. Holland*, decided in 1920, not only declined to place meaningful limits on the subject matter of treaties, but also validated, as "necessary and

47 The Supreme Court frequently asserts that the United States must speak with "one voice" to the international community and has used this idea as a basis for deferring to the foreign policy judgments of the Executive branch. *See* David H. Moore, *Beyond One Voice*, 98 MINN. L. REV. 953 (2014). *Chevron* deference involves courts deferring to interpretations of statutes by Executive branch agencies charged with their implementation. *See* Chevron, U.S.A., Inc. v. Nat. Res. Def. Council, 467 U.S. 837, 104 S. Ct. 2778, 81 L. Ed. 2d. 694 (1984).

48 Medellin, 552 U.S. at 526 (2008) (treaty to be regarded as non-self-executing if it was "ratified without provisions clearly according it domestic effect"); *but see* Carlos Manuel Vazquez, *Treaties as Law of the Land: the Supremacy Clause and the Judicial Enforcement of Treaties*, 122 HARV. L. REV. 599, 652 (arguing against reading *Medellin* to say that "a treaty is non-self-executing unless its text clearly specifies that it has the force of domestic law").

49 Medellin, 552 U.S. at 534.

proper" to a treaty's execution implementing legislation not otherwise within the scope of Congressional authority (that is to say, beyond the scope of the Article I commerce or taxation powers).[50] It was testimony to the opinion's significance that, in the mid-1950s, Senator Bricker felt it necessary to propose a constitutional amendment designed to prevent human rights treaties from enhancing the federal government's authority to encroach on traditional state prerogatives. The Third Restatement unequivocally endorsed the *Holland* rule.[51] But as Professor McGuinness demonstrates, publication of the Third Restatement in 1987 was shortly followed by a revival of federalism limitations on the Commerce Clause power, leading inevitably to efforts to overturn *Holland* as inconsistent with newly invigorated claims of reserved state authority. While the Supreme Court declined to overrule *Holland*, when presented with the opportunity in *Bond v. United States*,[52] the majority opinion and several vigorous concurring opinions made clear that the matter was hardly settled.

In Chapter 6, David Stewart undertakes one of the first comprehensive examinations of treaty implementing legislation. His noteworthy conclusions serve to reframe much of the debate around the direct effect of treaties, which has often assumed a rather binary divide between instruments intended to be self-executing, which may be given direct effect by courts, and those not so intended, which may or may not be the subject of implementing legislation. In fact, as Stewart demonstrates, most recent U.S. treaties, whether initially self-executing or not, coexist with some form of implementing legislation. The legislation may have existed prior to the treaty or may have been enacted contemporaneously with the treaty's adoption. Implementing legislation is rarely enacted after treaty adoption. As a result, in recent years the question of whether treaty enforcement will occur through U.S. courts or regulatory agencies turns less on the direct effect of treaties themselves than the extent to which implementing legislation faithfully replicates a treaty's obligations. Stewart argues that there is little support for the commonly held view that self-executing treaties are more likely to be enforced than non-self-executing treaties. Chapter 6 thus registers a potentially optimistic note on the future of U.S. treaty observance in the era after *Medellin*.

In Chapter 7, Michael Ramsey addresses treaty form, the area in which American treaty practice has most dramatically departed from constitutional text. The Constitution sets out only one form, providing in Article II that the President shall submit an agreement to the Senate for its approval by a two-

50 Holland, 252 U.S. at 433. 51 Third Restatement, *supra* note 22, § 302.
52 Bond, 134 S. Ct. at 2077.

thirds vote. From the beginning of the Republic, however, Presidents have effectuated international agreements by other means: submitting agreements to both houses of Congress for approval by simple majorities (Congressional-Executive agreements) or binding the United States through the President's signature alone (sole Executive agreements). The Third Restatement proposed formalizing Congressional-Executive agreements as fully coequal alternatives to Article II treaties. Professor Ramsey shows that this offer of "interchangeability" has not been fully taken up by Presidents in the post–Third Restatement period. Many areas of treaty-making, such as private international law, have remained the province of Article II agreements. The only area in which Congressional-Executive agreements predominate is trade. Sole executive agreements have proliferated but in quite restricted areas and not beyond the limits prescribed by the Third Restatement.

Yet Professor Ramsey also shows that in the post-Restatement period these three traditional categories have become inadequate as a full typology of U.S. treaty-making. With increasing frequency, Presidents have entered into agreements with other nations pursuant to various forms of explicit or implicit statutory authorization. Sometimes these "preauthorized" agreements are nonetheless submitted to both Houses of Congress and sometimes they are not. While these "authorized" sole executive agreements can undoubtedly bind the United States under international law, their equivalency to Article II treaties in U.S. law is still open to question.[53]

In Chapter 8, Roger Alford builds on Professor Wuerth's chapter on self-execution by examining several doctrines that prevent courts from adjudicating the merits of treaty claims: lack of standing, lack of a private right of action, the last-in-time rule, the political question doctrine and Congressional imposition of "reservations, understandings, and declarations." All but the last are judicially created, highlighting the extent to which, in the post-Restatement period, courts have served as gatekeepers for the domestic application of United States treaty obligations. The Third Restatement addressed each doctrine, though some indirectly, and generally charted a middle course between the nineteenth-century tradition of a strong judicial role in monitoring treaty compliance and a growing twentieth-century skepticism of judicial involvement in matters of foreign relations. In the decades after publication of the Third Restatement, a number of scholars and litigants urged courts to expand these doctrines and further reduce occasions for the judiciary to consider

53 *See generally*, MICHAEL JOHN GARCIA, CONG. RESEARCH, SERV., INTERNATIONAL LAW AND AGREEMENTS: THEIR EFFECT UPON U.S. LAW (Feb. 18, 2015), available at https://fas.org/sgp/crs/misc/RL32528.pdf.

the merits of treaty claims. As Alford recounts, federal courts for the most part rejected these invitations, most notably in regard to the political question doctrine. But the Supreme Court has said little about how these doctrines apply specifically to treaty claims. At the same time, courts have shown little inclination to retreat from the Third Restatement's acceptance of these doctrines, which have become firmly entrenched.

The volume's final chapters present case studies of how the doctrines and processes examined earlier in the book have fared in two distinct categories of treaties: those concerned with the law of armed conflict (LOAC) and those relating to private international law. In Chapter 9, Geoffrey Corn and Dru Brenner-Beck ask how courts addressing LOAC treaties have dealt with many of the thematic questions addressed in earlier chapters. The record in the post-Restatement era is a mixed one, with legislation providing the vehicle for such judicial implementation of LOAC treaty obligations as has taken place. Most remarkably, the Supreme Court in the 2006 case of *Hamdan v. Rumsfeld* deemed the Uniform Code of Military Justice to incorporate by reference a fair trial provision of Common Article 3 of the 1949 Geneva Conventions and went on to reject a forcefully put Executive branch interpretation.[54] Congress responded to *Hamdan* with a statute stripping federal courts of jurisdiction over Geneva Convention-based claims,[55] reflecting a broader tendency to thwart judicial recourse.

From Chapter 9's consideration of the most public of public international law subjects, Chapter 10 moves to private international law. Paul Dubinsky focuses on the underappreciated extent to which federalism has shaped and ultimately limited U.S. participation in private international law treaties. This chapter offers perhaps the strongest evidence for a retreat from the Third Restatement's accommodationist stance. As Dubinsky recounts, in the 1960s and 1970s, the United States joined international bodies engaged in codifying principles of transnational judicial cooperation. The most prominent developments included ratification of three Hague Conference treaties (the Hague Service and Evidence Conventions and the Hague Child Abduction Convention) and two UNCITRAL conventions (the New York Convention on the Enforcement of Foreign Arbitral Awards and the UN Convention on the International Sale of Goods). All of these were Article II treaties, and the Senate raised virtually no concerns that these treaties might impinge on traditional state prerogatives, though arguments of this sort were clearly

54 Hamdan v. Rumsfeld, 548 U.S. 557, 126 S. Ct. 2749, 165 L. Ed. 2d 723 (2006).

55 *See* Military Commissions Act of 2006, P.L. 109–366, 120 Stat. 2600, *codified at* 10 U.S.C. 948a et seq. (2006).

available and had been made in the past. The law of child custody, for example, was (and still is) almost exclusively state law. But with the "new federalism" of the 1980s, U.S. participation in Hague Conference instruments slowed and then stalled. Efforts to secure U.S. acceptance of judgment recognition conventions were thwarted twice, in part by federalism objections. Thus, at a time when U.S. participation in the global economy requires enhanced transnational legal cooperation, the United States is being held back by domestic legal concerns.

The ten chapters of this book, which are synthesized in Gary Born's conclusion, offer the reader an opportunity to ask questions about the contemporary status of treaties. Do the treaty rules of the Third Restatement still reflect the consensus they appeared to embody in 1987? Have the contours of doctrines changed at the margins but not in their essence? Has the prevalence of implementing legislation for self-executing and non-self-executing treaties alike effectively rendered moot the question of a treaty's direct domestic effect? Are there any circumstances in which U.S. courts will hold governmental actors – state or federal – to account for treaty violations? To what extent have federalism concerns impeded American efforts to help unify private international law and improve transnational judicial cooperation? When courts interpret U.S. treaties, is their goal to determine the mutual intent of the parties, the subjective understanding of U.S. actors upon ratification, or something else?

These questions and others take on an added significance in light of the Fourth Restatement project now underway. It is to be expected that questions about the influence, workability, and datedness of the Third Restatement rules will be raised not only by the reporters for the Fourth Restatement project but also by the broad community of lawyers, academics, and government officials who will comment on each new draft. In order for that community to forecast the impact of various proposals, it needs to be reminded of the trends and problems that brought the United States to the Third Restatement. It needs to be reminded of what was proposed and rejected in previous eras. It needs to have before it as complete a record as possible of the Third Restatement's impact or lack thereof during the past three decades. This volume seeks to contribute to that record.

1

Treaties in U.S. Law from the Founding to the Restatement (Third)

Mark Weston Janis and Noam Wiener

This essay on historical background explores the role of treaties in United States law from the founding era to the publication of the Restatement (Third). At various stages in U.S. history, key stakeholders varied their view of treaties depending on issues sometimes only tangentially related to international law. Most importantly, attitudes were swayed over time by competing theories of states' rights and federalism.

We begin with the Framers of the Constitution, both before and at the Philadelphia convention and in the ratification debates. We then examine the profound effect of treaties on the states' rights versus federal power controversy as the nation fell into Civil War. We then turn to Reconstruction and the optimistic spirit that prevailed in the "Gilded Age" at the turn of the century. Finally, we turn to the period from 1914 to the 1980s, and argue that the changing nature of international law and the rise of the United States as a superpower in a bipolar world affected the treatment of treaties in U.S. law.

I THE FOUNDING: INTERNATIONAL LAW AS NATURAL LAW AND EARLY TREATIES

It is difficult to overestimate the importance of the law of nations and treaties to the founding generation. Ousting a legally constituted regime, American revolutionaries appealed to a higher set of laws, the law of nations, to justify their insurrection.[1]

The views expressed in this chapter by the authors are their own and do not necessarily reflect the views of the United Nations.

[1] Jesse S. Reeves, *The Influence of the Law of Nature upon International Law in the United States*, 3 *A.J.I.L* 547, 550–1 (1909).

Several passages in Blackstone's *Commentaries* about the law of nations probably influenced the first generation of U.S. politicians.[2] The law of nations was "a set of rules deducible by natural reason and established by universal consent among the civilized inhabitants of the world."[3] Jefferson, who drafted the Declaration of Independence, relied considerably on the law of nations.[4] A high regard for the law of nations and treaty obligations, however, soon clashed with local interests, as the new republic attempted to represent the collective interest.[5] Under the Articles of Confederation, the United States did not have an executive, albeit the states in Congress appointed a Minister to represent their combined interests vis-à-vis the European powers. The first such Minister, John Jay, was frustrated by the inability of the Union to compel individual states to comply with the 1783 Treaty of Paris with the United Kingdom ending hostilities.[6]

Two opposing forces pulled against each other from the start. On the one hand, the need to establish international status required recognition by the European Powers[7] – recognition that could be at great risk if the confederated government could not keep the obligations it took upon itself in treaties. On the other hand, the thirteen states, wary of the very concept of central authority and direly in need of the cash and resources, were loath to abide by U.S. measures that denied them and their citizens ownership of property confiscated from Tory loyalists.[8]

[2] Mark Weston Janis, America and the Law of Nations 1776–1939, 9 (2010).

[3] William Blackstone, Commentaries, Volume IV, Chapter 5 (1765).

[4] Copies of the works of Blackstone, Grotius, Pufendorf, and Vattel were found in the libraries of the founders and were cited by them in their various publications. Reeves, *supra* note 1, at 550.

[5] James J. Lenoir, *International Law in the Supreme Court of the United States*, 7 Mississippi L. J. 327, 331 (1935).

[6] John Jay, *Report of Secretary Jay on Mr. Adams Letter of 4th March, 1786*, in The Diplomatic Correspondence of the United States of America, Vol. 2, 592 (1837).

[7] Lenoir, *supra* note 5, at 331.

[8] David M. Golove, *Treaty-Making and the Nation: The Historical Foundations of the Nationalist Conception of the Treaty Power*, 98 Mich. L. Rev. 1075, 1137 (2000). *See, e.g.*, The Statutes at Large of South Carolina (Thomas Cooper and David J. McCord eds.) Vol. 4(2), *Estate Confiscation Act of 26 February 1782* 516–23, which authorized the state to seize the property of British Loyalists and sell it. See also the preconstitutional Respublica v. Gordon, 1 U.S. (1 Dall.) 233 (Pa. 1788) and Camp v. Lockwood, 1 US (1 Dall.) 393, (Pa. Ct. C.P. 1788), in which State courts examined the validity of Pennsylvanian bills of attainder that confiscated the land of loyalists and the Virginia Statute eventually contested in Ware v. Hylton, 3 U.S. 199, 200 (1796), which provided that debts owed to British subjects could be discharged by paying a fraction of the debt to the state treasury.

Critically, the reluctance of individual states to abide by the Treaty of Paris, ending hostilities between the British Empire and the United States,[9] severely hampered the ability of the United States to move past the Revolutionary War. At the request of John Adams, then the United States representative to the United Kingdom, John Jay prepared a report in 1786 detailing the violations of the Treaty of Paris by the two parties.[10] Although Jay recorded a long list of infractions by both sides, he concluded that British refusal to evacuate military outposts on U.S. territory was justifiable in light of state statutes that consistently violated articles of the Treaty requiring the return of property confiscated from British subjects and repayment of debts.[11] Jay recommended that the Continental Congress declare treaties to be "part of the law of the land."[12]

II THE CONSTITUTIONAL CONVENTION

Whatever the merits of Jay's recommendation, the road to treaty supremacy over state laws was neither certain nor easy. Two questions on treaty power were of central concern to the Framers of the Constitution: (1) who would have the power to conclude treaties, and (2) how would treaties bind the individual states?

At the Constitutional Convention, the delegates had at least two models on the question of authority to conclude treaties: the direct and the indirect methods. According to the direct method, common among the European Powers, the ability to conclude treaties was reserved to the monarch. Under this system, a monarch would typically appoint plenipotentiary envoys (ambassadors) to negotiate and sign treaties.[13] The treaties would then be sent back to the monarch for ratification.[14] Since this system was common in an era in which monarchs were both creators and executors of the law, ratification by the monarch sufficed to make treaties the law of the land.[15]

This model, however, was inapposite if there was a formal division between executive and legislative functions. Parliaments with legislative powers were fearful that monarchs might circumvent their authority.[16] Thus, a second,

[9] Definitive Treaty of Peace, U.S.-Great Britain, Sept. 3, 1783 8 Stat. 80 ("Paris Treaty").

[10] NORMAN A. GRAEBNER, RICHARD DEAN BURNS & JOSEPH M. SIRACUSA, FOREIGN AFFAIRS AND THE FOUNDING FATHERS, FROM CONFEDERATION TO CONSTITUTION 1776–1787, 85–7 (2011).

[11] Jay, *supra* note 6, at 659. [12] *Ibid.* [13] L. OPPENHEIM, INTERNATIONAL LAW 507 (1905).

[14] *Ibid.* at 532. [15] THE FEDERALIST NO. 69 (Alexander Hamilton).

[16] OPPENHEIM'S INTERNATIONAL LAW, 9th ED. 60 (Robert Jennings and Arthur Watts Eds.) (1992); IAN BROWNLIE, PUBLIC INTERNATIONAL LAW, 6TH ED., 44–5 (2003).

indirect model emerged, most prominently in the United Kingdom, by which parliaments took the additional step of passing implementing legislation, following executive ratification, in order for the treaty to become the law of the land.[17] A problem with the indirect method, however, was that while parliaments might be "honor bound"[18] to respect treaties signed by the executive, a risk always existed that legislative assemblies would refrain from enacting treaties. The two steps necessitated by the indirect model threatened international stability, seriously jeopardizing the ability of the executive to make credible international commitments necessary for the maintenance of peace and guaranteeing profitable commercial relations among sovereign states.

The indirect method had advocates among the delegates in Philadelphia. For example, on August 15, 1787, John Mercer of Maryland suggested that although the power to conclude treaties should be given to the executive, treaties should not become law until ratified by the legislature.[19] Similarly, on August 23 of that same year, Gouverneur Morris of Pennsylvania suggested that no treaty would be enforceable by the courts unless "ratified by a law," that is, passed by Congress.[20] However, the United States could ill afford the instability that would arise in case of ratification by the executive not honored by legislation.

Consequently, a third model incorporating elements from both the direct and indirect models was considered. This third model would not require incorporation by legislation of treaties into local law. Ratification would be the only necessary step required for the treaty to become law, somewhat diminishing the risk of noncompliance. To check the power of the executive to conclude treaties, the legislature would become involved in the process of ratification.[21]

This modified direct incorporation scheme was advocated by the authors of the Federalist Papers, who sought to consolidate the power to negotiate treaties in the federal government. They also supported granting the executive branch the power to negotiate and conclude treaties that would be binding internally, albeit subject to the consent of the Senate.[22] Perhaps surprisingly, the

17 We are using very broad terms here, since the identity of the agencies vary from country to country, and as many models exist of governments, so do the systems for incorporation of treaty law into local law. *See* MALCOLM N. SHAW, INTERNATIONAL LAW, 6TH ED., 129–95 (2008).

18 *See, e.g., Ware, supra* note 8, at 255; Edye v. Robertson (Head Money Cases), 112 U.S. 580, 598 (1884).

19 JAMES MADISON, NOTES OF DEBATES IN THE FEDERAL CONVENTION OF 1787, 461 (1966) (1787).

20 Notes from the Constitutional Convention, Thursday 23 August, available at the Yale Law School Avalon Project at http://avalon.law.yale.edu/18th_century/debates_823.asp.

21 SHAW, *supra* note 17, at 148–94.

22 *See* THE FEDERALIST NO. 3 (John Jay), THE FEDERALIST NO. 42 (James Madison), THE FEDERALIST NO. 53 (James Madison), THE FEDERALIST NO. 80 (Alexander Hamilton).

Anti-Federalist "Federal Farmer," who published a series of letters opposing the Federalists and who was extremely suspicious of the Senate, supported this regime. He extolled a senatorial check on the executive body, agreeing that the House of Representatives was an improper forum for the discussion of treaties.[23]

The Anti-Federalists were concerned with the amount of power that the direct method (albeit including a check by the Senate) granted the executive. The constitutional debate that took place in Virginia on June 18, 1788 provides an insight into these views. Ironically, those participants who most wished to limit the treaty power ascribed to it, perhaps in hyperbole, the greatest breadth, while those who supported it presented a much more moderate view.[24] (This debate should thus raise doubts about the citation of political statements as a source for "original intent.") George Mason raised concerns about the ability of the president to sign treaties that would surrender the territory of a state with the help of a minimal quorum of senators from the North.[25] Patrick Henry argued that under the treaty clause, "if any thing should be left to us, it would be because the President and the senators were pleased to admit it," and that the Constitution granted treaties power greater than in any country in Europe.[26]

Ultimately, the Constitution was ratified including the Treaty and Supremacy clauses with which we are familiar. Section 2 of Article II empowers the president to conclude treaties, with the advice and consent of two-thirds of the senators present, and Article VI makes treaties the "Supreme law of the land."[27]

[23] Federal Farmer, Letter XI, January 10, 1788, available at the Constitution Society webpage at www.constitution.org/afp/fedfar11.txt.

[24] Debate in Virginia Ratifying Convention, 18–19 June 1788 (Elliot 3:499–515), available at the University of Chicago press at http://press-pubs.uchicago.edu/founders/documents/a2_2_2-3s10.html.

[25] *Ibid.*

[26] *Ibid.*, meaning that the executive could effectively take over the legislator by the way of creating treaty obligations.

[27] At issue at the time of the framing were partisan issues. Specifically, of utmost interest to the delegates of the southern states in Philadelphia, was the possibility that a treaty with Spain would limit in some manner navigation rights on the Mississippi river (as was attempted by the Jay-Gardouqui treaty, which the Confederate Congress did not ratify). The two-thirds requirement ascertained that a majority based on the votes of the northern states would not be able to infringe on the interests of the South. *See* Joseph Ralston Hayden, The Senate and Treaties, 1789–1817, 54 (1920). See also the concerns raised by George Mason at the Constitutional convention on August 15th. Madison, *supra* note 19 at 461; Mason and Henry's comments at the Debate in Virginia Ratifying Convention, June 18–19, 1788 (Elliot 3: 499–515), available at the University of Chicago press at http://press-pubs.uchicago.edu/founders/documents/a2_2_2-3s10.html.

III THE NEW REPUBLIC

As the U.S. republic took form, the new branches of government began filling the provisions of the Constitution with practical content. The period between 1776 and 1830 was marked by a series of international agreements designed to achieve two purposes. One set of treaties regulated the relationship between the United States and other sovereign states while the other helped form and expand the borders of the new nation.[28] The first set of treaties provided the United States with the international recognition (and therefore legitimacy) it needed to engage in global politics. In a period when international law did not guarantee the basic rights of foreigners, treaties of amity and commerce provided aliens the right to own real and personal property and the protection of the law. Treaties of this sort were concluded, for example, with the Netherlands in 1782,[29] the King of Prussia in 1799,[30] and the King of Sweden and Norway in 1816.[31]

The second set of treaties helped define and expand the borders of the United States. The Treaty of Amity, Commerce and Navigation, Between His Britannic Majesty and The United States of America – more commonly known as the Jay Treaty – resolved border disputes between Great Britain and the United States left over from the 1783 Treaty of Paris.[32] The Louisiana Purchase Agreement, negotiated with France in 1803 during Thomas Jefferson's administration, added vast territories to the United States.[33] Another treaty concluded in 1819 with Spain added Florida to the United States and demarcated a clear line between Spanish New Mexico and the United States' Missouri Territory.[34]

While the federal government entered into these treaties to protect national interests, the economic and social pressures that caused the states to circumvent national obligations before 1789 persisted under the new Constitution. Early treaty law jurisprudence confronted two questions raised by state resistance to treaties that have persisted to this day: first, when does the federal government have the power to enforce treaty provisions against recalcitrant

[28] Charles Henry Burr, *The Treaty-Making Power of the United States and the Methods of Its Enforcement as Affecting the Police Powers of the States*, 51 PROCEEDINGS OF THE AMERICAN PHILOSOPHICAL SOCIETY, 270, 293 (1912).

[29] *See, e.g.*, Treaty of Amity and Commerce with the Netherlands, U.S.-Netherlands, Oct. 8, 1782, 8 Stat. 32.

[30] Treaty of Amity and Commerce, U.S.-Prussia, July 11, 1799, 8 Stat. 162.

[31] Treaty of Friendship and Commerce, U.S.-Sweden and Norway, Sept. 4, 1816, 8 Stat. 232.

[32] Treaty of Amity, Commerce, and Navigation, U.S.-Great Britain, Nov. 13, 1794, 8 Stat. 116.

[33] Treaty, U.S.-France, April 30, 1803, 8 Stat. 202.

[34] Treaty of Amity, Settlement, and Limits, U.S.-Spain, Feb. 22, 1819, 8 Stat. 252.

states, and second, when are treaties self-executing and when do they require additional legislation?

The early case of *Ware v. Hylton*[35] (1796) was one of a series of cases concerning Virginia's debt forgiveness legislation. As previously noted, Virginia enacted a statute confiscating debts owed by Virginians to British creditors. These debts could be discharged by the debtors by paying a percentage of the original debt to the Virginia treasury.[36]

Such state statutes were of sufficient concern to Britain to warrant inclusion of a provision in the Treaty of Paris ensuring that "creditors on either side shall meet with no lawful impediment to the recovery of the full value in sterling money of all bona fide debts heretofore contracted."[37] Armed with this provision and the Supremacy Clause of the new Constitution, Ware, an agent for a deceased British creditor, demanded payment of his debt by Hylton, a Virginian who claimed that part of the debt had already been discharged to the Virginia government.

The two most expansive opinions in *Ware* were penned by Justices Chase and Iredell. Both conducted a law-of-nations analysis to determine whether Virginia was within her rights to confiscate private property. While Justice Chase focused more closely on the power of the federal government to override the laws and constitutions of the individual states, Justice Iredell examined how the Constitution approached the question of self-execution.[38] Justice Chase's opinion created a precedent easy to understand:

> It is the declared will of the people of the United States that every treaty made by the authority of the United States shall be superior to the constitution and laws of any individual state, and their will alone is to decide. If a law of a state, contrary to a treaty, is not void, but voidable only by a repeal or nullification by a state legislature, this certain consequence follows – that the will of a small part of the United States may control or defeat the will of the whole. The people of America have been pleased to declare that all treaties made before the establishment of the national Constitution or laws of any of the states contrary to a treaty shall be disregarded.[39]

Chase's opinion expressly states that State laws and constitutions are subordinate to international treaties. He says this is true for "every treaty."[40] He further explains that the Supremacy Clause is essential to presenting a united foreign policy to the rest of the world.[41]

35 Ware v. Hylton, 3 U.S. (3 Dall.) 199 (1796). 36 Ware, 3 U.S. at 201.
37 Paris Treaty, *supra* note 9, art. 4. 38 Ware, 3 U.S. at 272. 39 *Ware*, 3 U.S. at 237.
40 *Ibid.* 41 *Ibid.*

Justice Iredell's opinion explains how treaty provisions became binding law immediately upon ratification with no need for further legislation, that is, self-executing. Iredell noted that in Great Britain, although the King creates international obligations, they do not become binding internal law until adopted by Parliament.[42] In the United States, however, a new system has been introduced:

> Under this Constitution therefore, so far as a treaty constitutionally is binding, upon principles of moral obligation, it is also by the vigour of its own authority to be executed in fact. It would not otherwise be the supreme law in the new sense provided for, and it was so before in a moral sense.[43]

In other words, treaties ratified by the President with the advice and consent of a two-thirds majority of the Senate members present, as set forth by the Constitution, may be directly applied by the courts. Thus, Iredell sets forth a default rule of self-execution.

Though subtle precursors to the doctrine of self-execution can be found in earlier cases,[44] this doctrine was further formally articulated (though still without the use of the actual term "self-execution") in *Foster & Elam v. Neilson*.[45] Two parts of the same passage in *Foster* convey Chief Justice Marshall's understanding of the manner in which treaties should be implemented and integrated into local law under the Supremacy Clause.

In *Foster*, Marshall stated that a treaty is "in its nature a contract between two nations, not a legislative act. It does not generally effect, of itself, the object to be accomplished, especially so far as its operation is infra-territorial; but is carried into execution by the sovereign power of the respective parties to the instrument."[46] He continued, however, that in the United States, "a different

42 *Ibid.* at 274; Justice Iredell then follows with an example based on a treaty regulating wine tariffs signed by France and Great Britain.

43 *Ibid.* at 277.

44 In *Camp*, *supra* note 8, and *Gordon*, *supra* note 8, the judges discussed the difference between two articles of the Paris Treaty that rendered one article enforceable because it stated a complete rule, while another article was not enforceable because it required Congress to recommend to the state legislature means by which to create a right, and therefore did not create a fully executed obligation. Similarly, in *Ware*, Justice Iredell noted the difference between "executed" as opposed to "executory" obligations. This difference has been confused with self-execution doctrine by some consequent court decisions by lower instances as well as in academic writing. Executed obligations are obligations that are already complete in temporal terms, while executory obligations are such that have not gone into force yet and will do so at a future date. Thus, while non-self-executing obligations are obviously executory since they require action by the political branches to come into force, some self-executing obligations may also be executory, if the treaty stipulates they will only come into force at a given date. *Ware*, 3 U.S. at 272.

45 Foster v. Neilson, 27 U.S. 253 (1829).

46 *Ibid.* at 314.

principle is established. Our constitution declares a treaty to be the law of the land. It is, consequently, to be regarded in courts of justice as equivalent to an act of the legislature, whenever it operates of itself without the aid of any legislative provision."[47] Marshall followed the path set by *Ware v. Hylton* in this part of the opinion. He then, however, made the following, somewhat cryptic, statement:

> But when the terms of the stipulation import a contract, when either of the parties engages to perform a particular act, the treaty addresses itself to the political, not the judicial department; and the legislature must execute the contract before it can become a rule for the Court.[48]

This statement is not entirely clear: What is meant by "import a contract?" In analyzing the treaty clause in question, Marshall asks whether the parties' obligations are complete, setting out definite legal relations, or whether they are open-ended obligations that require the political branches take further action to complete the treaty's objectives. Marshall examined whether the treaty transferred grants made by the Spanish King to new owners of land in Florida, or whether it only created an obligation to do so at a later date (thus, being a contract rather than an actual transfer).[49] Based on the treaty language, Marshall concluded that it did not create an actual transfer, but only directed the political branches to put the transfer into effect.

However, the treaty provision itself seems to be self-executing, providing that the grants in question are meant to be given legal force. Indeed this part of the opinion was reversed shortly thereafter in *United States v. Percheman*,[50] which, looked at the Spanish version of the treaty and interpreted the wording of the same clause as effectuating a transfer of property.[51]

Other Supreme Court cases in the same period as Foster created a jurisprudence that emphasized the important role of the law of nations in creating obligations in U.S. federal and state law[52] and reiterated the supremacy of treaties over state law.[53]

47 *Ibid.*

48 *Ibid. See also* Chapter 3 of this volume by Paul Dubinsky on the power of the contract metaphor in the interpretation of treaties.

49 *Ibid.* at 314–15.

50 32 U.S. 51 (1832).

51 *Ibid.* at 89; *see also* David Sloss, *Non-self-executing Treaties – Exposing a Constitutional Fallacy*, 36 UC Davis L. R. 1, 20 (2002); Carlos Manuel Vazquez, *The Four Doctrines of Self-executing Treaties*, 89 A.J.I.L. 695, 701 (1995).

52 See, e.g., Marshall's comment that acts of Congress should not be construed to violate the laws of nations in Murray v. The Charming Betsey, 6 U.S. 2 Cranch 64, (1804).

53 *See, e.g.*, United States v. Schooner Peggy, 5 U.S. 103 (1801); and Chirac v. Lessee of Chirac, 15 U.S. 2 Wheat. 259 (1817).

Two other sources from the new republic help explain the role of treaties in national law – opinions of the Attorney General of the United States and scholarly commentaries. The Attorney General was, at times, solicited for legal opinions by the President and by secretaries of executive agencies. Two opinions, somewhat contradictory, by Attorney General William M. Wirt address the issue of treaty rights provided to foreigners.

The first, published in 1819, concerns the "Right of Aliens to Hold Property," and responded to questions submitted by the Swedish *chargé d'affaires*.[54] Attorney General Wirt opined that aliens may carry and dispose of personal property, but added that there is no "power in the general government, as I conceive, to alter, either by law or by treaty, the provisions of the particular States" in respect of real property.[55] Thus, it appears that Wirt believed that the federal government could not interfere with the laws of individual states in matters reserved to the states, such as the ownership and disposition of land, by the way of a treaty provision. The second, an opinion issued in 1821 on the "Validity of the South Carolina Police Bill" (further discussed below),[56] explained that because a treaty with Great Britain permitted commerce "without any restriction on the color of the crew," South Carolina's police law could not forbid that which the treaty authorized.[57] Wirt provided no explanation for the manifest difference between his two opinions.

Scholarly writing during this period appears to have supported a broad, almost unlimited view of the treaty power. Between 1826 and 1833, James Kent and Joseph Story published commentaries on U.S. law.[58] The most authoritative restatement-like account of U.S. law in the early republic was written by James Kent, Chancellor of the State of New York and professor of law at Columbia College.[59] Kent's monumental four volume work, based on his law school lectures, *Commentaries on American Law* (1826–1830), was the first "great U.S. law treatise".[60] Kent clearly favored the federal government's ability to force treaty implementation on the states, and he describes this power as one of the "principal motives to union."[61] Kent also embraced

54 1 Op. Att'y Gen. 275. 55 *Ibid.*

56 1 Op. Att'y Gen. 659. The Statute is alternatively called the "South Carolina Police" law and the "South Carolina Negro Seaman Act" in the sources and we use both names interchangeably.

57 *Ibid.* at 661.

58 Mark Janis, *Americans and the Quest for an Ethical International Law*, 190 W. VA. L. REV. 571, 573–4 (2007).

59 PERRY MILLER, THE LIFE AND MIND IN AMERICA FROM THE REVOLUTION TO THE CIVIL WAR 109, 145–6 (1965).

60 L.M. FRIEDMAN, A HISTORY OF AMERICAN LAW 290 (1974).

61 JAMES KENT, COMMENTARIES ON AMERICAN LAW, VOL I, 278 (2d ed., 1832).

President Washington's understanding of the Supremacy Clause, according to which treaties become law upon ratification and do not require additional incorporation by Congress.[62]

Story also supported an expansive view of treaty supremacy in his 1833 *Commentaries*.[63] He began his discussion of the treaty power by noting that one of the reasons for the creation of the Constitution and the abandonment of the Confederation was the inability of the central government to enforce treaties over the individual states.[64] The supremacy of the treaty power over the individual states was, to Story, one of the important achievements of the Constitution. On the question of the direct applicability of treaties into local law, Story noted that the President has greater powers than the British Monarch in that, unlike the latter, who required an act of Parliament to incorporate treaties into domestic law, no action by the legislative branch is required to carry treaties into effect under the Constitution.[65] Story also provided analysis on the scope of the treaty power. His view on the matter was based on the understanding that the ability to conclude treaties is rooted in the inherent sovereign power of the United States.[66] Thus, Story explained that the power to conclude treaties should not be limited to specific subject matters because that would tie down the government and limit its ability to negotiate with other sovereign states.[67]

The later years of the Marshall Court saw an important shift in the debate over the treaty power, as the nation began "foundering" on the "rock on which the union would eventually split" – slavery.[68] *Elkison v. Deliesseline*,[69] decided by Supreme Court Justice William Johnson while riding Circuit in South Carolina, provides a case in point. In 1822, reacting to fears of a slave insurrection, the southern states enacted laws designed to prevent free Blacks from spreading antislavery sentiment.[70] "An Act for the Better Regulation and government of Free Negroes and Persons of Color; and for Other Purposes,"[71]

62 James Kent, Commentaries on American Law 268 (1st ed., 1826).

63 Joseph Story, Commentaries on the Constitution of the United States (1833).

64 Story describes this aspect of the Confederation as "utter imbecility." *Ibid.* at 1501.

65 *Ibid.* at 1515. 66 *Ibid.* at 1503. 67 *Ibid.* at 1502.

68 Alexander Stephens, Vice President of the Confederacy attributed this prediction to Thomas Jefferson in his Cornerstone Speech, delivered in 1861, shortly after the Confederate States began to secede from the Union. Alexander H. Stephens, *Cornerstone Speech*, available at Teaching American History at http://teachingamericanhistory.org/library/document/cornerstone-speech/.

69 Elkison v. Deliesseline, 8 Fed. Cas. 493, no. 4, 366 (C.C.D.S.C., 1823).

70 Scott Wallace Stucky, *Elkison v. Deliesseline: Race and the Constitution in South Carolina, 1823*, 14 N. C. Cent. L.J. 361, 373 (1983).

71 The Statutes at Large of South Carolina, (David J. McCord, ed.) 461 (1840).

better known as the South Carolina Negro Seaman Act of 1822, provided that any free man of African descent who came to port in South Carolina aboard a trading vessel bearing the flag of a foreign sovereign would be seized and placed in jail until the vessel in which he arrived left port.[72] The Act provided further that the ship's captain was required to pay for the prisoner's upkeep and to escort him back to the ship upon its departure; otherwise the prisoner would be pressed into slavery.[73]

This legislation ran afoul of treaties of commerce and amity the United States had "concluded with a number of nations whose ships called at Charleston, South Carolina." The British Consul, for example, complained that the incarceration of British sailors violated an 1815 commerce convention.[74] Although Secretary of State John Quincy Adams had persuaded South Carolina to cease enforcement of the Act for a short time, it was soon revived.[75]

Justice Johnson's judgment in *Elkison*, 36 years after the Constitutional Convention, was based on much the same logic that guided the Framers who supported the Supremacy Clause, echoing Hamilton's Federalist No. 80, and rebuked South Carolina for violating national obligations.[76] Justice Johnson warned of the risk of confusion and even war arising from violating the rights of foreigners under the law of nations,[77] reflecting Jay's and Madison's admonitions to the Continental Congress about dangers of individual states' refusing to abide by the Paris Peace Treaty. Justice Johnson also noted that the treaty had not been made solely for the benefit of British sailors and that if the treaty were violated, American ships might, in turn, find themselves prevented from conducting commerce.[78] Justice Johnson finally noted that counsel for South Carolina had stated that he would rather see the state secede from the Union than allow the act to be repealed.[79]

South Carolina's opposition to enforcement of the treaty, in other words, was driven by a purely internal concern: slavery. It had nothing to do with animus toward the British or international commerce, or with any particular view of international law. Rather, as part of the battle on states' rights, debate on the domestic role of international law was embroiled in the political struggle over slavery.

IV LATER ANTEBELLUM YEARS

Ten years after *Elkison*, the United States was no closer to ending the internment of black sailors. Despite Justice Johnson's judgment, repeated

[72] *Ibid.* art. III. [73] *Ibid.* [74] Elkison, 8 Fed. Cas at 493, 495. [75] *Ibid.* at 494.
[76] *Ibid.* at 495. [77] *Ibid.* [78] *Ibid.* [79] *Ibid.* at 494.

remonstrations by northern states, and promises by successive Secretaries of State to foreign consuls, South Carolina and the other southern states continued their practices and simply ignored the Supreme Court. Thus, while the law in theory in the 1820s, as summarized by Kent in his *Commentaries*, was such that treaties duly made by the president and the Senate had become the law of the land,[80] in practice some states refused to recognize treaty obligations insofar as they affected race relations.[81]

It would be useful to briefly pull back from our focus on treaties, and note some changes that had occurred in U.S. politics. With the election of Andrew Jackson in 1828, the political climate changed significantly.[82] As the founding generation died out, the spirit of a joint destiny could no longer assuage the emerging social and economic differences between northern and southern states. One manifestation of this reshuffling came in the views of the eight new Justices appointed to the Supreme Court between 1828 and 1840 by Presidents Jackson and Van Buren.[83]

Jackson's executive branch reflected new views of the power of treaties under the Supremacy Clause. For example, legal opinions on the South Carolina Negro Police Law drafted by John Berrien and Roger Taney, Attorneys General under Jackson, addressed British complaints to the State Department.

Berrien's 1831 opinion came to an opposite conclusion than the one reached by Attorney General Wirt a decade earlier. Berrien agreed with Wirt that in cases of conflict between state law and treaty provisions, the latter is superior.[84] However, Berrien limited the superiority of treaties (and federal laws in general) to those that are "indispensable to the due execution of power intended to be carried into effect."[85] In all other cases, according to Berrien, when the execution of a federal power could be accomplished by a means that does not conflict with a state law, the state law will prevail.[86] Berrien held that the admission of black seamen into U.S. ports was a "matter rather of convenience than of necessity," and that commerce between Great Britain

80 KENT, *supra* note 62, at 268.

81 *See, e.g.*, COMPILATION OF THE LAWS OF THE STATE OF GEORGIA, 411 (1831). *An Act to amend an Act, entitled An Act supplementary to an Act more effectually to enforce an Act prescribing the mode of manumitting Slaves in this State; and also to prevent the inveigling and illegal carrying out of the State Persons of Color*, §5.

82 William N. Eskridge Jr. & John Ferejohn, *The Elastic Commerce Clause: A Political Theory of American Federalism*, 47 VANDERBILT L. REV. 1355, 1373 (1994).

83 David P. Currie, *The Constitution in the Supreme Court: Contracts and Commerce 1836–1864*, DUKE L. J. 471, 472 (1983).

84 2 Op. Att'y Gen. 431. 85 *Ibid*. at 434 86 *Ibid*.

and the United States could be conducted without conflicting with the police power of the states.[87]

Taney's 1833 opinion, available only in draft form, departed even more radically from Wirt's views. Taney argued unabashedly that the prior forty years of jurisprudence on federal supremacy (including treaty supremacy) had been wrongly decided, and asserted that South Carolina had the right to enforce its statute notwithstanding the treaty with Great Britain.[88] Taney's opinion clearly carved out subject matter that was beyond the reach of federal law and treaties.[89]

After his appointment to the Supreme Court, Taney advanced the jurisprudence of states' rights as Chief Justice. Though there is much disagreement as to the role and ideology of the Taney Court, the antebellum Supreme Court clearly adopted a Jeffersonian approach to states' rights consistent with Taney's opinion as Attorney General on the Carolina Police Law.[90] Namely, the view that the Constitution did not create a new nation where one did not exist before, dividing the powers of government between federal and state levels, but rather that the states, possessed of inherent sovereignty, granted limited power to the federal government. Those powers not explicitly relinquished in the text of the Constitution remained with the states. Thus, for example, when opining on obligations of the Governor of Ohio to act pursuant to his obligation to extradite an escaped individual to Kentucky, Taney ruled that because Ohio was a sovereign state, the federal government had no power to compel Ohio's governor to act.[91]

87 *Ibid.* at 436.

88 H. Jefferson Powell, *Attorney General Power and the South Carolina Police Bill*, available at www.greenbag.org/v5n1/v5n1_from_the_bag_powell.pdf. Powell edited the three extant drafts of Attorney General Taney's opinion into a single document.

89 *Ibid.*

90 *See* Charles Beard & Mary Beard, The Politics of the Economic Drift, 689 (1927). See Ralston Hayden, *The States' Rights Doctrine and the Treaty-Making Power*, 22(3) Am. Hist. Rev. 566, 566 (1917), who emphasized the Supreme Court's role in raising State sovereignty to a degree that brought the Union back in 1860 to the disunity it suffered in 1787. *But see* Felix Frankfurter, *Taney and the Commerce Clause*, 49 Harv. L. Rev. 1286, 1287–99 (1936), who argued ardently that Taney's characterization as an agrarian and proslavery jurist was a mistaken simplification of historical record. Frankfurter also argued that to depict the Taney Court as localist in the sense that it attempted to undermine the strength of the Union is to misrepresent the underlying principles that motivated the Court's opinions. The true guiding principle, Frankfurter argued, was the preservation of the Union.

91 Kentucky v. Dennison, 65 U.S. 66, 107 (1860). See *infra* notes 98–104 and accompanying text for the Taney Court's judgments in cases in which the supremacy of treaties over state laws was examined.

Taney and other states' rights advocates could not directly attack both the explicit text of the Supremacy Clause – which clearly grants supremacy to treaties – and forty years of Supreme Court jurisprudence affirming treaty supremacy. Instead, states' rights advocates chipped away at the scope and legitimacy of federal power by narrowly construing the scope of the enumerated powers granted to Congress and by emphasizing the plenary sovereign authority of the states to overrule national interests.

In an important 1917 article, Joseph Ralston Hayden explored how Taney's states' rights approach affected the incorporation of treaties into United States law.[92] Hayden's research focused on the many treaties of amity and commerce the United States signed during the formative years and in the period leading up to the Civil War. His findings note a marked difference in the text of the treaties regarding property rights.[93] Property rights provide a useful lens into the incorporation of treaty provisions into national law because, following the Treaty of Paris, these provisions were the subject of a number of cases in which the Supreme Court consistently ruled that state laws on foreign property ownership were limited by the federal government's treaty power. Property and contract regulations were then, as now, primarily regulated by state law. And yet, in none of the Supreme Court cases in which state property and contract laws were found inconsistent with treaty obligations did the Supreme Court entertain the possibility that these laws might not be subject to the Supremacy Clause because of their subject matter.[94]

Nonetheless, a mere fifty-five years after *Ware*, Secretary of State Fillmore explained to the Senate, when seeking its support for a treaty signed with Switzerland, that "States have, sometimes by general, sometimes by special laws, removed the disabilities attaching to foreigners not naturalized in regard to holding of land. *But this is not supposed to be a power properly to be exercised by the President and Senate in concluding and ratifying a treaty with a foreign state.*"[95] Fillmore's statement is especially fascinating considering that as the Secretary of State it was presumably in his interest to support the constitutionality of a treaty his own department had negotiated.

Hayden's research provides additional examples of treaties whose scope was limited by the Senate because senators thought international treaties could not regulate matters such as foreign ownership of real and personal property. David Golove challenged Hayden's conclusion that the Senate had in this way

92 Hayden, *supra* note 90. 93 *Ibid.*

94 *See, e.g.*, Gordon, *supra* note 8, Camp, *supra* note 8, Ware, *supra* note 8, Foster, *supra* note 45.

95 Journal of the Executive Proceedings of the Senate of the United States, Vol. 8, 289 (Feb. 12, 1851) (emphasis added).

effectively elevated States' rights over treaty supremacy.[96] One, however, does not need to agree wholly with Hayden or Golove in this debate in order to discern a notable shift in the Senate away from the nationalist to a states' rights perspective during this period.

The same was true for the Supreme Court.[97] For example, in *Mager v. Grima*,[98] the sister of a wealthy individual who passed away in Louisiana contested the right of the state to withhold a special 10 percent estate tax that was levied solely upon unnaturalized legatees not domiciled in the State. Chief Justice Taney disposed of the case by ruling that estate taxes are "nothing more than an exercise of the power which every state and sovereignty possess."[99] Article VII of the Treaty of Friendship and Commerce signed with France in 1800, which promised French citizens treatment equal to that given U.S. citizens in cases of inheritance,[100] so little impressed Justice Taney that the words "treaty" or "convention" do not even appear in the Court's two page opinion.

Prevost v. Greneaux was another case in which the same Louisiana estate tax for foreigners was contested.[101] This case, decided in 1856, arose following the ratification of a new treaty with France in 1853 that made significant concessions to states' rights.[102] Article VII of the treaty limited the application of the equal tax provisions to "the states of the Union whose laws permit it, so long and to the same extent that said laws shall remain in force."[103] Despite this apparent codification of the relationship between the treaty rule and contrary state laws, Taney went out of his way to explain that "a treaty subsequently made by the United States with France could not divest rights of property already vested in the state, even if the words of the treaty had imported such an intention."[104]

Mager and *Prevost* espoused the same restrictive view of federal treaty power that Taney had expressed in his Attorney General's opinion on the South Carolina police statute. As we have already noted, this mid-nineteenth-century version of Thomas Jefferson's nullification theory emphasized the independence of the states.[105] Underlying this antifederalism is a view of the Union as an amalgamation of sovereign entities who, at their own discretion, can

96 Golove, *supra* note 8, at 1234. 97 Hayden, *supra* note 90, at 582–3.
98 49 U.S. 490 (1850). 99 *Ibid.* at 494.
100 Treaty of Friendship and Commerce, U.S.-France, Sept. 30, 1800, 8 Stat. 178.
101 Prevost v. Greneaux, 60 U.S. 1 (1856).
102 Consular Convention, U.S.-France, Feb. 23, 1853, 10 Stat. 114. 103 *Ibid.* art. VII.
104 *Prevost*, 60 U.S. at 7.
105 See the Kentucky Resolutions of 1798 and 1799, originally composed by Jefferson during the Aliens and Sedition Acts crisis. ELLIOT'S DEBATES, 540–5 (1836).

determine whether the federal government has exceeded its authority.[106] This was also, to a large degree the reasoning Taney used in *Dred Scott* to invalidate the Missouri Compromise.[107]

David Golove argues that in the years following the Civil War, Taney's approach to commerce power (and thus to federalism) was "relegated to history's dustbin."[108] This may be going too far. Of course the Civil War proved, with devastating force, that the individual states had no right or power to secede from the Union. However, debate regarding the power of the federal government to preempt state acts erupted again in full force when racial tensions in the South once again rose to the fore of U.S. political discourse in the twentieth century. Let us first look at the return to the national paradigm, which took hold during the latter half of the nineteenth century and the beginning of the twentieth century.

V RECONSTRUCTION OF THE NATIONAL PARADIGM

In 1880, Thomas Cooley, Dean of the University of Michigan Law School, published his *General Principles of Constitutional Law in the United States*, continuing in Story and Kent's tradition. Unlike Story and Kent, however, who were deeply concerned with why the Framers chose to allocate certain powers to specific branches of government, Cooley approached the Supremacy Clause from a structural perspective. He was less concerned with the novelty of allocating the power to conclude treaties jointly to the legislative and executive branches, and more interested in the interplay of treaty-based obligations with statutes and residual state power.

Cooley believed that under the Supremacy Clause, federal laws and treaties are both sovereign acts that differ only in the "form and in the organ … through which the sovereign will is declared."[109] As equal sovereign pronouncements of the federal government, both laws and treaties were to supersede state law.[110] Cooley, however, argued that certain powers belong to the individual states, and that when the states exercise these powers, they are sovereign and independent.[111] Whether state powers are to be construed broadly (that is, through a strict interpretation of federal powers) or narrowly

106 *Ibid.* at 540.

107 Dred Scott v. Sanford, 60 U.S. 393, 438–40 (1857). *See* Mark W. Janis, *Dred Scott and International Law*, 43 COL. J. INT'L L. 763 (2005).

108 Golove, *supra* note 8, at 1247.

109 THOMAS M. COOLEY, THE GENERAL PRINCIPLES OF CONSTITUTIONAL LAW IN THE UNITED STATES OF AMERICA, 31 (2nd edn. 1891).

110 *Ibid.* 111 *Ibid.* at 34.

is a question for which, according to Cooley, there are "ample occasion for differences."[112]

When discussing the breadth of the subject matter that treaties may cover, Cooley suggested that it is limited only by the power of the Constitution itself, which can only be changed through its own procedure.[113] Pronouncing the law as developed by the Taney Court, Cooley described the breadth of the subject matter of treaties as being limited by the authority of the individual states.[114] Interestingly, Cooley based this assertion, in a single footnote, on a passage from Story's Commentary (§1508)[115] and on a passage from Tucker's Blackstone Notes,[116] both of which are dedicated to the treaty power but which say nothing about the relationship between the treaty power and the authority of the states or the existence of state authority that limits the subject matter of the treaty power.

The case law, however, was changing even as Cooley wrote. Also in 1880, the Supreme Court decided the important case of *Geofroy v. Riggs*.[117] Ralston Hayden convincingly argues that a comparison of Justice Fuller's opinion in *Geofroy* and Taney's opinion in *Prevost* demonstrates the changing attitude towards treaties in the United States Supreme Court.[118] The Geofroy brothers were French nephews of well-to-do Washington, D.C. resident T. Lawrason Riggs, who died intestate. Upon Riggs's demise, a dispute arose between his more distant relatives and his nephews' guardian as to whether the nephews, who were neither U.S. citizens nor domiciled in the United States, were permitted to inherit the estate. For our purposes, the specific reasoning used by the Court to determine who was to inherit the property is not important.[119] *Geofroy*'s critical broader holding is that, contrary to the views expressed by all three branches of government in the years preceding the Civil War, "the treaty power of the United States extends to all proper subjects of negotiation" between the United States and foreign sovereigns.[120] In other words, the idea that individual state sovereignty can supersede the Supremacy Clause was rejected by the Court. The *Geofroy* court went further and quoted Vattel, stating that treaties ought to be "interpreted in a manner that gives them

112 *Ibid.* at 33. 113 *Ibid.* at 32, 106. 114 *Ibid.* at 106. 115 Story, *supra* note 63, at § 1508.

116 St. George Tucker, 1 Blackstone's Commentaries, App. 332, available at http://press-pubs.uchicago.edu/founders/documents/a2_2_2-3s24.html.

117 Geofroy v. Riggs, 133 U.S. 258 (1890). 118 *Hayden, supra* note 90, at 584.

119 The Court examined whether the language of the treaty with France applied to Maryland law as it stood in 1791 when Maryland gave up part of its territory for the creation of the District of Columbia, or whether Maryland law should have been applied as it stood in 1853 when the treaty was signed.

120 Geofroy, 133 U.S. at 266.

effect"[121] rather than restrictively, thus demonstrating an understanding of treaties as valid and binding instruments on a par with congressional enactments.

Following *Geofroy* and the subsequent *Hausenstine* and *Keller* opinions,[122] the executive negotiated international treaties without clauses limiting their applicability to the laws of the individual states, and the Senate approved such treaties without restrictions based on the "reserved" powers of the states. For example, the immigration treaty signed with China in 1881 promised Chinese subjects the full protection of the law without any trace of the language subjecting these rights to the laws of the individual states.[123] In the Senate, the treaty was proposed and, with no comment on the limitation of powers, passed forty votes to three.[124]

The executive branch expressed a similar view of the power of the federal government to bind states through U.S. treaty commitments. In an opinion written for the Secretary of State on the question of the power of a treaty between the United States and Great Britain, demarcating the boundaries of fisheries between the United States and Canada, Attorney General John Griggs explained that the regulation of fisheries is commonly accomplished through international agreements, and that in the case of a conflict between treaty provisions and state law, the former shall supersede the latter.[125]

Following the Supreme Court, lower federal and state courts upheld the supremacy of treaty provisions over contrary state laws. For example, some states enacted measures discriminating against Asians contrary to treaties of friendship commerce and navigation with both Japan and China.[126] *In re Tiburcio Parrott*[127] concerned a quicksilver mine in California employing Chinese miners. In 1879, the California constitution was amended to provide that:

> No Corporation now existing, or hereafter formed under the laws of this state, shall, after adoption of this constitution, employ, directly or indirectly, in any capacity, any Chinese or Mongolians. The legislature shall pass such laws as shall be necessary to enforce this provision.[128]

[121] *Ibid.* at 270.
[122] Hausenstein v. Lynham, 100 U.S. 483 (1879); Keller v. United States, 213 U.S. 138, 145–8 (1909).
[123] Immigration Treaty, U.S.-China, May 9 1881, art. II, 22 Stat. 826.
[124] Journal of the Executive Proceedings of the Senate of the United States, 67 May 5, 1881.
[125] 22 U.S. Op. Atty. Gen. 214 (1898).
[126] *See, e.g.*, the California Alien Land Law, Cal. Stats. 1931 p. 206.
[127] In re: Tiburicio Parrott, 1 F. 481 (Circuit Court D. Calif. 1880).
[128] *Ibid.* at 499.

Pursuant to this provision, the California legislature criminalized the conduct mentioned, but Parrot, an employer, refused to comply with the law. The Court struck down California's constitutional amendment and the criminal statute on the grounds that they violated both the Fourteenth Amendment and the U.S.-Chinese "Burlingame Treaty." The court emphasized that the treaty granted Chinese immigrants the right to enjoy the same privileges and immunities enjoyed by the citizens of any nation that has most favored nation rights granted to it by a treaty with the United States.[129] Judge Hoffman in his concurring opinion did not shy away from expressing his view on Chinese immigration,[130] but nonetheless found state efforts to expel Chinese nationals in the Burlingame Treaty to be an "audacious defiance of the national authority."[131] Judge Sawyer noted that granting privileges and immunities to foreign citizens was commonplace in treaties in that era and was therefore within the federal treaty-making power and that "the treaty making power is conferred by the Constitution in unlimited terms."[132] This went well beyond Cooley's Commentary, which held the treaty-making power to be limited by powers reserved to the states.

During the late nineteenth century, as a spate of scholarly law journals began regular publication, academic discussions of the treaty power became more common.[133] Several leading commentators articulated a broad conception of the federal treaty power, both in relation to contrary state law and in regard to the issues legitimately addressed by treaties. In an article published in 1886 in the *American Law Review*, Simon Greenleaf Croswell explored whether treaties affecting the taxing power of the United States could be concluded by the president with the advice and consent of the Senate but without approval from the House of Representatives.[134] Croswell concluded

129 *Ibid.* at 485.

130 "[T]he unrestricted immigration of the Chinese to this country is a great and growing evil." *Ibid.* at 498.

131 *Ibid.*

132 *Ibid.* at 508. Judge Sawyer's decision is also interesting in that it included reciprocity as a justification for enforcing treaty rights. Judge Sawyer explained that the United States did not ratify treaty provisions out of altruism towards the rights of foreign citizens, but rather to ensure the reciprocal safety of its own citizens abroad. Consequently, Judge Sawyer recounted the riotous attacks by Chinese citizens against Americans, French, and Chinese in Tien-tsin in 1870, the justice that had been meted to the rioters who harmed foreigners, and the compensation that had been paid to those harmed. Judge Sawyer reminded San Franciscans, that if protection is to be afforded to American interests in China, such protection must be afforded to Chinese interests in the United States. *Ibid.* at 519.

133 Harvard published its first Law Review in 1887. Others followed suit.

134 Simon Greenleaf Croswell, *The Treaty-Making Power under the Constitution*, 20 AM. L. REV. 513 (1886).

that treaties of commerce, which were the subject of regular diplomacy, indeed regulated a type of duty, but that Article III of the Constitution nonetheless permitted their passage without the approval of Congress.[135] Selden Bacon, a well-regarded New York attorney, addressed the power of the United States to acquire territory by treaty in an article in the *Yale Law Journal* and concluded that treaties are superior to state laws.[136]

In an article published in 1910, George Sutherland, at the time still a U.S. Senator, expounded a theory that differentiated between a strict separation of powers respecting domestic affairs, and a nationalistic approach to international affairs.[137] Sutherland argued that while the Constitution divided the power to enact statutes between the federal government and the several states, it granted the federal government unlimited sovereign power to enact treaty obligations.[138]

However, the superiority of treaties to state law was not a view shared by all commentators. Henry St. George Tucker, a former Virginia Congressman and law professor, published an article in 1914 attacking the claim that California's attempt to prevent the purchase of land by Chinese noncitizen residents violated the United States' treaty obligations.[139] Tucker argued that the Supremacy Clause indeed provides the federal government with the ability to overrule state legislation, but only in those areas of the law in which the federal government was delegated authority. Tucker was evidently more concerned with states' rights and issues of race than international law when he wrote on the treaty-making power. For example, two years later at the Storrs Memorial Lecture at Yale, Tucker explained that women's suffrage should not be forced upon the individual states by constitutional amendment because it would infringe on states' rights to self-government.[140] The importance race played in Tucker's agenda can be inferred from his comments during the Storrs Lectures that suggested it was unwise to have forced the Fifteenth Amendment on the South without popular approval.[141]

Tucker's arguments are not dissimilar to the arguments made by Roger Taney some eighty-five years earlier in his opinions as Attorney General and Chief Justice.[142] Both held that the Supremacy Clause allows treaty provisions

[135] *Ibid.* [136] Selden Bacon, *Territory and the Constitution*, 10 YALE L.J. 99 (1901).

[137] George Sutherland, *The Internal and External Powers of the National government*, 191 N. AM. REV. 373 (1910).

[138] *Ibid.* at 374.

[139] Henry St. George Tucker, *The Treaty-Making Power under the Constitution of the United States*, 199 N. AM. REV. 560 (1914).

[140] HENRY ST. GEORGE TUCKER, WOMEN'S SUFFRAGE BY CONSTITUTIONAL AMENDMENT (1916).

[141] *Ibid.* at 76–7. [142] *See* notes 88–91, *supra*, and accompanying text.

to overrule state law but only when the subject matter of a treaty comes within the enumerated powers of the federal government. The residual powers of the states are not subject, according to Tucker, to federal legislation and *a fortiori* not to treaties.[143] Tucker claimed that any other interpretation would grant rights to foreigners not available to U.S. citizens. As an example, Tucker noted it would be unimaginable that an African American from New York would be forbidden to ride in a railroad car in Texas assigned to whites while "the negro from Hayti or the Congo may under a treaty be free to . . . ride in any coach on a railroad that may suit his tastes."[144]

Edward Corwin, a professor of jurisprudence at Princeton, responded to Tucker in the same volume of the *North American Review* in which Tucker's article on Chinese exclusion was published.[145] First, Corwin argued that one purpose of the Constitutional Convention of 1787 was precisely to prevent the states from being able to limit the power of the federal government from concluding international treaties.[146] Second, Corwin observed that Tucker's description of the Supremacy Clause was contradicted by the numerous treaties regulating matters otherwise within the reserved powers of the states.[147] Lastly, Corwin explained that Tucker's analysis contradicted decisions such as *Hausenstein* and *Geofroy* which held that state legislative competence does not limit the federal treaty power even when the subject matter of treaties concerns areas in which Congress cannot legislate.[148]

Perhaps because Tucker believed he was not given an adequate opportunity to respond to Corwin,[149] one year later he published a full book on the treaty power.[150] Not surprisingly, racial issues figured prominently in Tucker's arguments. He devoted an entire chapter to the issue of segregation of Asian children in California public schools.[151] In 1906, the San Francisco Board of Education required all "Chinese, Japanese, or Korean" children to go to the "Oriental School, situated on the south side of Clay Street."[152] This resolution violated an 1894 U.S.-Japanese treaty, which provided that "the citizens or subjects of each contracting party shall enjoy in the territories of the other

143 Tucker, *The Treaty-Making Power*, *supra* note 139, at 562. 144 *Ibid.* at 563.

145 Edward S. Corwin, *The Treaty Making Power: A Rejoinder*, 199 N. AM. REV. 891 (1914).

146 *Ibid.* at 898. 147 *Ibid.* 148 Corwin, *supra* note 145, at 897.

149 Tucker complained in a letter sent to the editor of the journal. *See* Tucker, *The Treaty-Making Power*, 200 N. AM. REV. 308 (1914).

150 HENRY ST. GEORGE TUCKER, LIMITATIONS ON THE TREATY-MAKING POWER UNDER THE CONSTITUTION OF THE UNITED STATES (1915).

151 *Ibid.*

152 Elihu Root, *The Real Questions under the Japanese Treaty and the San Francisco School Board Resolution*, 1 AM. J. INT'L L. 273, 275 (1907).

the same privileges, liberties and rights."[153] Following a petition by the Japanese ambassador and a flurry of diplomatic and political activity, the San Francisco Board of Education was successfully convinced to repeal the resolution.[154]

Tucker contested the view that the federal treaty power is not limited by the powers reserved to the states. He argued that the powers were reserved not by virtue of a constitutional grant, but rather by the historical fact that the states never relinquished them in the first place.[155] For example, Tucker noted that because the power to regulate education is not an enumerated federal power, it could not become the subject of regulation by treaty.[156] Tucker concluded that the separation of powers between the states and the federal government is as fundamental as the separation between the three federal branches, and that, therefore, taking power away from the states by virtue of a treaty is tantamount to the overturning of the constitutional order.[157]

One target of Tucker's attacks was Elihu Root, whose approach to the treaty power can be described as diametrically opposite to Tucker's. In an address to the first meeting of the American Society of International Law, Root argued that unlike legislative, executive, and judicial powers, which were "distributed" between the states and the federal government, the treaty making power was vested solely in the federal government.[158] Root explained that the United States functions as a single sovereign nation when interacting with other nations; an individual state could not enact laws that violated a treaty based grant of rights or immunities without severely limiting the ability of the United States to exercise its sovereign powers.[159]

VI THE INTERWAR PERIOD

The most famous treaty the United States never ratified was the Covenant of the League of Nations. It is well known that Woodrow Wilson staked both his health and his political legacy on ratification of the Covenant, but to no avail. First, his health collapsed: he suffered a career-ending stroke in Pueblo, Colorado, while on an exhausting nationwide whistle-stop tour boosting the League to the American people. And second, his legacy was severely damaged when the Senate twice rejected the League, on October 2 and November 19, 1919.[160]

153 Treaty of Commerce and Navigation, U.S.-Japan, November 22, 1894, 29 Stat. 848, Article 1.
154 Root, *supra* note 152, at 276. 155 Tucker, *supra* note 150, at § 356. 156 *Ibid.*
157 *Ibid.* at § 358. 158 Root, *supra* note 152, at 278. 159 *Ibid.* at 283.
160 Janis, *supra* note 2, at 167–75.

Henry Cabot Lodge, who famously led the opposition to the League in the Senate, expressly articulated, in an article published in *Foreign Affairs* in 1924, that it was not isolationism or antagonism towards international treaties that guided his opposition to the League in 1919.[161] Rather, Lodge recounted the United States' major involvement in international treaties in the Americas and in the Pacific,[162] and even expressed support for disarmament treaties.[163] Lodge also explained that his reluctance to join the League was due to its Eurocentric nature and the wish to avoid American entanglement in European political struggles.[164]

We can glean from the treaties negotiated by the executive at the time, by the tenor of the language of members of the legislature, and by the decisions of the courts, that treaties were considered an important source of law. The opposition to the League of Nations also demonstrates that treaties were taken very seriously, and that refusal to join the League on the grounds that it might embroil the United States in European conflicts was based on the assumption that if the United States did join the League, it would be bound to have had no option but to comply with the obligations set forth in the Covenant.

As in other eras, there were dissenting voices. As the Japanese and Chinese exclusion cases on the West Coast demonstrate, in certain instances local interests created resistance to the norms created by federally mandated treaties.[165] Meanwhile, legal academics such as Tucker published articles contesting the majority view on the grounds of the limitation of federal power.[166]

It is in this environment of general acceptance of the power of treaties to resolve disputes that transcend national boundaries on the one hand and competing local interests on the other hand, that the Supreme Court decided *Missouri v. Holland*,[167] its clearest guidance yet on the preemptive power of treaties.

The following discussion does not replicate the many able accounts of Justice Holmes's opinion in *Missouri*.[168] Instead, we explain the context of the case and

[161] Henry Cabot Lodge, *Foreign Relations of the United States, 1921–1924*, 4 FOREIGN AFFAIRS 525 (1924).

[162] *Ibid.* at 527, 530. [163] *Ibid.* at 528.

[164] *Ibid.* at 539. Historical scholarship suggests a more politically calculated approach by Lodge and his colleagues to the Covenant of the League of Nations.

[165] See *supra* notes 126–32 and accompanying text.

[166] *See, e.g.*, L. L. Thompson, *State Sovereignty and the Treaty-Making Power*, 11 CAL. L. REV. 242, 257 (1922); Tucker, *supra* note 143.

[167] *Missouri v. Holland*, 252 U.S. 416 (1920).

[168] *See, e.g.*, Louis Henkin, *The Treaty Makers and the Law Makers: The Law of the Land and Foreign Relations*, 107 U. PENN. L. REV. 903, 908 (1959); Curtis A. Bradley, *The Treaty Power and American Federalism*, 97 MICH. L. REV. 391, 423 (1998); Golove, *supra* note 8, at 1255–72.

then describe how the opinion set the next stage in the evolution of treaties in U.S. law: agreements regulating the rights of individuals.

The public policy question at issue in *Missouri* – the conservation of natural resources – was a matter of robust public debate in late nineteenth- and early twentieth-century America. By the 1880s, Americans were becoming ever more environmentally conscious and were increasingly concerned about the slaughter of migratory birds.[169] The hunting problem was exacerbated both by technological developments in weaponry and increased demand for slaughtered birds, not only for food but also for fashion.[170] Bird watchers, farmers who relied on birds to destroy pests, and sport hunters all joined forces in new conservationist organizations, notably the Audubon Society, founded in 1886, to battle against those they called "market hunters" and "game hogs" who were responsible for destroying migratory birds in large numbers.[171]

The conservationists' first success was in sponsoring state legislation making trade in hunted birds difficult or illegal. This state-level strategy was vindicated in 1896, when the Supreme Court upheld a Connecticut statute prohibiting the transport of protected game birds out-of-state in *Geer v. Connecticut*.[172] Ironically, *Geer* would soon become a stumbling block for the conservationists. Justice White's opinion, holding that Connecticut had sovereign police power over migratory birds only temporarily in the state, would stand as an obstacle to upholding federal regulation of the same birds.[173]

But migratory birds are by definition transitory, and the conservationists soon moved on to promote regulation on the federal level. Their first success came in 1900 with the Lacey Act, which provided for the labeling of packages with birds or bird parts to indicate their contents and origin.[174] In 1913, Congress passed the Weeks-McLean Act, which purported to assert exclusive national control over the killing of migratory birds.[175] Thirty-two conservationist organizations supported Weeks-McLean in testimony before Senate and House Committees.[176]

See also Oona A. Hathaway, Spencer Amdur, Celia Choy, Samir Deger-Sen, John Paredes, Sally Pei & Haley Nix Proctor, *The Treaty Power: Its History, Scope and Limits*, 80 CORNELL L R. 239, 253–7 (2013); Thomas Heally, *Is Missouri v. Holland Still Good Law? Federalism and the Treaty Power*, 98 COLUM. L. REV. 1726 (1998).

169 KIRKPATRICK DORSEY, THE DAWN OF CONSERVATION DIPLOMACY: U.S.–CANADIAN WILDLIFE PROTECTION TREATIES IN THE PROGRESSIVE ERA 167–91 (1998).

170 *Ibid.* 171 *Ibid.* 172 Geer v. Connecticut, 161 U.S. 519 (1896).

173 Geer, 161 U.S. at 532. 174 16 U.S.C. 3371 and following.

175 DORSEY, *supra* note 169, at 178–91. The Weeks-McLean Act, known as the "migratory birds provision," was part of the March 4, 1913 Appropriations Act of the Department of Agriculture, 37 Stat. 828, 847, c. 145.

176 *Ibid.* at 9.

Even among its advocates, there was doubt whether Weeks-McLean could be sustained as constitutional. Elihu Root suggested that Weeks-McLean could be constitutionally bolstered if it were supported by a U.S. treaty.[177] In January 1913, Root proposed a Senate resolution, ultimately not adopted, that "the President be requested to propose to the governments of other North American countries the negotiation of a convention for the mutual protection and preservation of migratory birds."[178] Such a treaty might have comforted President William Howard Taft, who was otherwise inclined to veto Weeks-McLean. However, a treaty at this stage proved unnecessary because Taft, seemingly by inadvertence, signed Weeks-McLean on his rushed last day in office.[179]

Fortunately for the conservationists, incoming President Woodrow Wilson was far keener to protect migratory birds. Worried that Weeks-McLean might be declared unconstitutional by the courts, Wilson's administration began exploring the possibility of negotiating international migratory bird agreements with Mexico and Canada. In the meantime, opponents of Weeks-McLean (and supporters of states' rights) began to launch legal challenges to the Act's constitutionality.[180]

Without a treaty yet in hand, conservationists were forced to defend Weeks-McLean as it stood. They immediately launched a publicity campaign to support the Act's constitutionality.[181] But Weeks-McLean was nonetheless struck down by lower federal courts as unconstitutional. In *United States v. Shauver*, a defendant successfully objected to his indictment for hunting in violation of Weeks-McLean.[182] Relying on *Geer*, District Judge Trieber held that "*animals ferae naturae*, denominated as game, are owned by the states, not as proprietors, but in their sovereign capacity as the representatives and for the benefit of all their people in common."[183] If it were useful for Congress to regulate migratory birds, the judge suggested, "[i]t is the people who alone can amend the Constitution," and it was "the duty of the court ... to declare the

177 *See* 49 Cong. Rec. 1494 (1913), Hathaway, *supra* note 168, at 254.

178 "A *Long Step Forward*", Forest and Stream, Feb. 1, 1913, Vol. LXXXX, 145.

179 Dorsey, *supra* note 169, at 187–88; John G. Phillips, Migratory Bird Protection in North America 11–13 (1934).

180 Dorsey, *supra* note 169, at 192–201.

181 In November 1913, the counsel to the American Game Protective Association, Walter S. Haskill, speaking to the American Ornithologist's Union, reported that he had "discussed the subject with several United States Supreme Court Judges, who said the courts would support it. I do not want to prophesy what will happen if we go to the Supreme Court. We do not wish litigation, but I think we shall be sustained if we are attacked." *Defends Federal Bird Law*, N.Y. Times, Nov. 14, 1913, at 8.

182 214 Fed. Rep. 154 (E.D. Ark. 1914).

183 *Ibid* at 157.

act void."[184] Similarly, in *United States v. McCullagh*, District Judge Pollack held that "the title and exclusive power of control over wild game coming within the borders of a state of this country resides in the state and not in the nation."[185]

Supporters of the Act were persuaded that they did not want either *Shauver* or *McCullagh* to reach the U.S. Supreme Court before a migratory bird treaty could be concluded. Along with Root, they came to believe that marrying a statute to an international agreement was the best way to ensure its constitutionality. Negotiations with Canada progressed and, on August 29, 1916, the Senate approved and President Wilson ratified the nation's first migratory bird treaty, the Convention on the Protection of Migratory Birds.[186] The *New York Times* reported: "The chief purpose of both the treaty and the regulations is to save from extinction the migratory game birds, and to protect those birds which help the farmer by eating the insects that prey upon his crops."[187] Congress passed an Enabling Act to implement the Convention, which President Wilson signed on July 3, 1918.[188] The new law limited the national hunting season of migratory birds to no more than three-and-a-half-months and strove to equalize hunting opportunities among the states.[189]

After 1918, therefore, the constitutionality of federal regulation of migratory birds *with* a treaty foundation could be tested. Enter *Missouri v. Holland*. On July 2, 1919, U.S. District Judge Van Valkenburgh issued the first opinion.[190] Pursuant to the new Enabling Act, George L. Samples and W. C. Lapp were indicted for hunting and killing migratory birds in Missouri. Judge Van Valkenburgh, citing *Geer*, *Shauver*, and *McCullagh*, held that "in the absence of treaty there appears to have been no delegation of paramount authority to the federal government."[191] Hence, "this act, in the absence of [a] treaty, would be unconstitutional, as exceeding the legitimate powers of Congress."[192] However, the U.S.-Canada Convention on the Protection of Migratory Birds transformed the constitutional situation: "That the power to make treaties is a substantial power of highest degree, delegated by the states to the federal government by the terms of the Constitution, is beyond controversy."[193] As an exclusive federal power, the validity of the act solely "depends upon whether this treaty was a valid exercise of federal

[184] *Ibid.* at 160. [185] 221 Fed. Rep. 288, 294 (D. Kan. 1915).

[186] Dorsey, *supra* note 169, at 200–1; Phillips, *supra* note 83, at 13–20. Convention on the Protection of Migratory Birds, U.S.-Great Britain (for Canada), Aug. 16, 1916, 39 Stat. 1702.

[187] "*Saving the Birds*," N.Y. TIMES, Sept. 2, 1916, at 6. [188] PHILLIPS, *supra* note 179, at 20.

[189] *Win Fight to Save Birds: House Passes Treaty Enabling Act for Protection of Migratory Game*, N.Y. TIMES, June 7, 1918, at 13.

[190] 258 Fed. Rep. 479 (W.D. Mo. 1919). [191] *Ibid.* at 481. [192] *Ibid.* [193] *Ibid.*

authority as delegated by the Constitution."[194] A treaty, so long as it does not contradict the Constitution, is valid if it "is a compact made between two or more nations, entered into for the common advancement of their interests and the interests of civilization."[195] Since the United States and Canada both were to benefit by the protection of migratory birds, "the subject-matter comes properly within the treaty making power."[196]

Nine months later, on April 19, 1920, Associate Justice Oliver Wendell Holmes, Jr., delivered the judgment of the Supreme Court in *Missouri v. Holland*.[197] Holmes's opinion, only five pages long, strikes a decisive blow in favor of the nationalist approach to the treaty power. Holmes initially noted that under the "Necessary and Proper" clause, Congress has the power to legislate the provisions of treaties into law.[198] Holmes then addressed the question of whether treaties may regulate subjects over which Congress is not explicitly granted power in the Constitution. He responded to this question with an argument similar to that made by Sutherland in the article discussed above.[199] Holmes argued that the power to enact treaties is one that flows from the power of the sovereign and that when the need arises to regulate national interests though a treaty, a sovereign must be able to conclude treaties lest it lose its ability to act on those interests.[200] Because the Constitution clearly denies treaty power to the states in the Compact Clause,[201] that power must reside with the federal government.

The rest of Holmes's opinion, as Golove notes, is devoted to rejecting the Jeffersonian concept of federalism in treaty affairs.[202] Holmes rejected the idea that the states, as sovereigns prior to adoption of the Constitution, reserved powers that were not explicitly granted to Congress. Holmes saw no subject matter as "reserved" to the states such that it was beyond the federal treaty power (though he mentioned constitutional limitations without further elaboration), as long as the treaty fulfills a national interest.[203]

In formal legal doctrine, *Missouri v. Holland* became the principal judicial precedent supporting the supremacy of treaties against contradictory state laws. As Chandler Anderson wrote in the *American Journal of International Law* the same year the case was decided, *Missouri v. Holland* showed "that the treaty-making power is a *national* rather than a *federal* power, and that this distinction measures the whole difference between its jurisdiction and the jurisdiction of Congress in relation to the so-called

[194] *Ibid.* at 482. [195] *Ibid.* [196] *Ibid.* at 484. [197] 252 U.S. 416 (1920).

[198] *Ibid.* at 432. [199] *See* Sutherland, *supra* note 137, and accompanying text.

[200] Missouri, 252 U.S. at 433, citing Andrews v. Andrews, 188 U.S. 14, 33 (1903).

[201] U.S. Const. Art. I Sec. 10. [202] Golove, *supra* note 8, at 1263–5.

[203] Missouri, 252 U.S. at 4.

reserved powers."[204] In 1924, the Supreme Court in *Asakura v. City of Seattle*, following *Missouri v. Holland*, employed a bilateral treaty with Japan to invalidate a discriminatory municipal ordinance depriving a Japanese immigrant of his pawnbroker license.[205] In 1937, in *United States v. Belmont*, the public policy of New York State gave way to an executive agreement accepting the nationalization of property in Russia:

> In respect of all international negotiations and compacts, and in respect of our foreign relations generally, state lines disappear. As to such purposes the State of New York does not exist. Within the field of its powers, whatever the United States rightfully undertakes, it necessarily has warrant to consummate. And when judicial authority is invoked in aid of such consummation, state constitutions, state laws, and state policies are irrelevant to the inquiry and decision. It is inconceivable that any of them can be interposed as an obstacle to the effective operation of a federal constitutional power. Cf. *Missouri v. Holland*, 252 U.S. 416; *Asakura v. Seattle*, U.S. 332, 341.[206]

Given its expansion of federal legislative authority, *Missouri v. Holland* was soon perceived as a source of power for legal reform. In 1924, a note in the *Michigan Law Review* argued that since labor regulation had become a regular topic of international agreements, *Missouri v. Holland* now permitted national regulation of labor conditions that would be otherwise unconstitutional under then-existing U.S. constitutional law.[207] As we have noted above, others, especially segregationists, expressed strong opposition to the Supreme Court's holding in *Missouri*.[208] Indeed, labor rights were the forerunners of the many individual rights that would soon become the subject matter of international treaties.[209] These treaties, which came about following the fundamental shift that international law underwent following the Second World War, are the subject matter of the last section of our survey.

204 Chandler P. Andersen, *The Extension of Congressional Jurisdiction by the Treaty-Making Power*, 14 AM. J. INT'L L. 400 (1920) (emphasis in the original).

205 Asakura v. City of Seattle, 265 U.S. 332, 341 (1924).

206 United States v. Belmont, 301 U.S. 324, 331–2 (1937).

207 Note and Comment, *Labor Legislation under the Treaty Power*, 22 MICH. L. REV. 457, 457–63 (1924).

208 *See, e.g.*, Charles Pergler, *Limitations of the Treaty-Making Power*, 98 CENT. L. J. 41, 44–5 (1925).

209 It is worth noting, however, that the U.S. has ratified very few International Labor Organization conventions, and until quite recently, limited ratification almost exclusively to those that concerned seafaring. *Compare* International Labor Organization, *Ratifications for United States*, available at www.ilo.org/dyn/normlex/en/f?p=NORMLEXPUB:11200:0::NO::P11200_COUNTRY_ID:102871 *with Up-to-date Conventions not ratified by United States*, available at www.ilo.org/dyn/normlex/en/f?p=1000:11210:0::NO:11210:P11210_COUNTRY_ID:102871.

In the 1930s, adding to the federalism controversies surrounding the power of treaties vis-à-vis the states such as *Missouri v. Holland* were newer issues involving the separation of powers within the federal government itself, that is, the balance of powers among the legislative, executive, and judicial branches. As international affairs became more complicated and more immediate, the president sought to act more rapidly and with greater nuance, posing challenges to the authority of Congress in foreign affairs. So, for example, in *United States v. Curtiss Wright*, President Roosevelt was granted extraordinary powers, at his determination, to impose an arms embargo against the South American states, Bolivia and Paraguay, fighting the Chaco War (1932–1935).[210] When FDR prohibited arms sales to the combatants, the U.S. aircraft company, Curtiss-Wright, simply avoided the prohibition, making illegal sales in what were called "sordid circumstances," providing the company with two-thirds of their foreign sales in 1933.[211] When prosecuted, Curtiss-Wright alleged that it was not they, but rather Congress and the president, who had broken the law, since it was unconstitutional for Congress to delegate to the president the power to enact an arms embargo. The Supreme Court disagreed, writing that ordinary domestic separation of powers limitations on the executive branch did not apply to international affairs. The Union was, even before the Constitution, "the sole possessor of external sovereignty," and the "investment of the federal government with the powers of external sovereignty did not depend upon the affirmative grants of the Constitution."[212] Moreover, they were dealing not only "with an authority vested in the President by an exertion of legislative power, but with such an authority plus the very delicate, plenary and exclusive power of the President as the sole organ of the federal government in the field of international relations."[213]

The interwar expansion of the President's independent treaty making powers was capped by the case that never was. Even the Senate did not challenge the exceptional Hull-Lothian Agreement of 1940, where President Roosevelt and his Secretary of State, Cordell Hull, agreed with the United Kingdom to trade fifty U.S. destroyers to battle Hitler's Atlantic blockade in exchange for control of several key British bases in the Bahamas and the Caribbean.[214] The pact was never submitted to the Senate. The Hull-Lothian

210 299 U.S. 304 (1936).

211 Robert A. Devine, The Case of the Smuggled Bombers, in John A. Garraty, ed., Quarrels that have Shaped the Constitution 210 (1964).

212 Curtiss-Wright, 299 U.S. at 317. 213 *Ibid.* at 319.

214 1940 Hull-Lothian Agreement, 55 Stat. 1560 (1941), *reprinted in* 12 Bevans, Treaties and Other International Agreements of the United States of America, 1776–1949, at 560 (1974).

Agreement was said by many to violate U.S. and international neutrality laws, but Hull argued that it was "the Axis dictators, who had wrecked the [neutrality] convention [who would] alone have a motive for questioning our transaction."[215] Hull was right in practice for both the Senate and the Supreme Court steered clear of questioning Hull-Lothian in a case at U.S. law.

VII POST–SECOND WORLD WAR

The Second World War brought about a sea change in international law. After witnessing endless atrocities committed against civilian populations, states began to draft treaties of a new kind, guaranteeing rights to individuals. Under the pre-1945 Westphalian paradigm of international law, protections for individuals under international law were few and mostly indirect. But following the Universal Declaration of Human Rights, processes were initiated to establish treaties obligating sovereign states to treat their own individual citizens in accordance with international standards.[216] Starting with The Convention on the Prevention and Punishment of the Crime of Genocide, a series of human rights treaties were negotiated, creating a new front in the debate between conservatives and liberals.[217]

Missouri and its progeny had put what appeared to have been the final nail in the coffin of the states' rights claim against treaty preemption via the Supremacy Clause.[218] Arguments based on federalism could no longer be used to prevent the federal government from enforcing treaty based obligations on the states.[219] But the postwar human rights treaties created new controversies about the subject. This section will first explore the nature of opposition to the new treaties and then examine the mechanisms used to oppose their incorporation into U.S. law.

Opponents of human rights treaties evinced two types of concerns. First, the critics expressed skepticism toward the liberal humanist ideology underlying the treaties; and second, they opposed United States involvement in new forms of international cooperation, in particular the alleged surrender of American sovereignty to international organizations.

215 Cordell Hull, The Memoirs of Cordell Hull 839–42 (1948).

216 Phillip Jessup, The Modern Law of Nations 9–16 (1948).

217 John W. Bricker, *Making Treaties and Other International Agreements*, 289 Ann. Am. Acad. Pol. Sci. 133, 138 (1953).

218 *See, e.g.*, Fuji v. State of California, 38 Cal. 2d 718 (1952); *Reid v. Covert*, 354 U.S. 1 (1957).

219 *But see* the treatment of *Missouri* by the Supreme Court in the 1990s and onwards Margaret McGuinness' Chapter 5 of this volume.

The critics employed several methods to thwart the treaties' incorporation. At first, an attempt was made to amend the Constitution to curtail the reach of the Supremacy Clause. After this failed, the constitutional debate moved to the issue of self-execution and the inclusion of reservations, understandings, and declarations by the Senate. The debate continues today.

A *Civil Rights, International Law, and Sovereignty*

Attitudes towards treaties during the second half of the twentieth century focused on two interconnected issues almost completely absent from debates earlier in the country's history. First, the social-democratic politics of Western Europe, the rise of international communism, and the international labor movement alarmed American conservatives. Leading figures such as Ohio Senator John Bricker and Frank Holman, President of the American Bar Association (ABA), emphatically opposed the civil rights agenda of human rights treaties.[220] These concerns dovetailed the views of Southern Democrats who (correctly) saw the treaties as a threat to the racial status quo in the South.[221]

The direct clash between the new human rights instruments and Jim Crow had the effect of changing and sharpening race-based objections to treaty incorporation. Once treaties dealt directly with issues of equality and civil rights, the segregationists ceased taking the indirect route of opposing treaties on the ground of their empowering the federal government at the expense of the states. Rather, they attacked the treaties directly as seeking to alter existing race relations.[222] The ABA's Frank Holman did not mince words when opposing the Genocide Convention and draft convention on civil and political rights, asserting that adoption of these treaties would require the end of antimiscegenation laws[223] and would force civil rights legislation on the states.[224] Under the law at the time, both these statements were probably correct.

It is important to note that race was not the only factor in the debate over human rights treaties. Opposition to the treaties was also grounded

220 Frank Holman, *Treaty Law-Making a Blank Check for Writing a New Constitution*, 36 ABA JOURNAL 719, 787 (1950).

221 Peter J. Spiro, *Treaties, International Law, and Constitutional Rights*, 55 STAN. L. REV. 1999, 2016 (2003).

222 M. Glen Johnson, *The Contributions of Eleanor and Franklin Roosevelt to the Development of International Protection for Human Rights*, 9 HUM. R. Q. 19, 41 (1987).

223 *Holman, supra* note 220, at 787. 224 *Ibid.* at 788.

in non-race-based conservatism.[225] Those who had opposed New Deal initiatives declared they did not want to see the same political agenda achieved by other means. As Senator Bricker put it: "I do not want any of the international groups, and especially the group headed by Mrs. Eleanor Roosevelt, which had drafted the covenant of Human Rights, to betray the fundamental, inalienable, and God-given rights of American citizens enjoyed under the Constitution."[226] Rhetorical flourishes aside, Senator Bricker simply stated that he did not wish to see international instruments replace conservative values with liberal ideals in the areas of economic, social, and cultural rights.

The second substantive objection to participation in the emerging multilateral treaties – exceptionalism – is tightly bound up in the conservative objection to the liberal humanistic ideals of the postwar treaties. That is, the opposition was not so much to the specific content of the treaties, but rather to the idea that any influence from outside the United States would affect the way Americans are governed. As can be seen in Bricker's language, the treaty opponents closely linked isolationism and exceptionalism.[227] Thus, treaty opponents criticized not only the liberal ideology of the new internationalism, but also its source – the international community, which they considered a danger to U.S. sovereignty. Similar fears of the international community preyed on the slave states before the Civil War when they resisted the new international law condemning slavery and the slave trade.[228]

The exceptionalist critique was not limited to conservative senators. Florence Ellinwood Allen, a judge for the U.S. Court of Appeals for the Sixth Circuit, dedicated an entire book to the dangers of international human rights treaties.[229] Allen's book, which gave judicial credence to Bricker and Holman's criticism, argued that multilateral treaties create a novel problem because they extend their influence beyond the relationships between states and instead regulate the relationship between a state and its

225 Cathal J. Nolan, *The Last Hurrah of Conservative Isolationism: Eisenhower, Congress, and the Bricker Amendment*, 22 PRESIDENTIAL STUDIES QUARTERLY 337, 340 (1992).

226 Congressional Record, 82nd Congress, 2d sess. 7 February 1952, vol. 98; pt. 1: 912.

227 Peter Spiro named the reemergence of this view of international treaties as "sovereigntism." *See* Peter J. Spiro, *The New Sovereigntists: American Exceptionalism and its False Prophets*, 96 FOR. AFF. 9, 9–10 (2000).

228 Mark W. Janis, *Dred Scott* and International Law, 43 COLUM. J. TRANSNAT'L L. 763 (2005).

229 FLORENCE ELLINWOOD ALLEN, THE TREATY AS AN INSTRUMENT OF LEGISLATION (1952). Allen's criticism was all the more surprising because, nominated by Franklin Roosevelt, she was the first woman to sit on a federal circuit court and a prominent member of the anti-war movement. *See, e.g.*, Florence Ellinwood Allen, *Peace Through Justice*, 17 U. CIN. L. REV. 244, 261 (1948), in which Allen calls for public support of the United Nations and the International Court of Justice to enable both institutions to succeed where the League of Nations had failed.

citizens.[230] For Allen, as for other critics of multilateral human rights conventions, this created a serious threat to U.S. sovereignty.[231]

The debate over the meaning and implications of sovereignty during the postwar period mirrored a larger debate in the United States about the merits of international law. To international law scholars like Phillip Jessup, sovereignty claims allowed states to exempt themselves from abiding by basic universal norms. In his 1948 book on the law of nations, Jessup described sovereignty as "the quicksand upon which the foundations of international law are built."[232] On the other side of the divide, Franklin Roosevelt's former aide, Donald Richberg, saw "starry eyed internationalism" as a risk to sovereignty on par with "insidious Communism."[233]

The debate over sovereignty vis-à-vis international treaties is also important because it demonstrates the shift that had occurred in American perception of itself in the international community. During the formative years of the Union, concluding international treaties was considered an affirmation of the United States' sovereignty because it signaled recognition by other sovereign states and acceptance of the United States as a sovereign power.[234] As time went by, the United States, secure and eventually claiming a place as a superpower, became less concerned with the opinions of and the acceptance by other states.

Critics of the treaty power recognized that the Constitution had a comparatively streamlined mechanism for incorporating treaty obligations into national law. They thus ventured several efforts to change that process. The first was a proposed constitutional amendment.

B The Bricker Amendment

As noted above, *Missouri* affirmed that treaty provisions exceeding the scope of Congress's enumerated legislative authority, as well as federal legislation in furtherance of those provisions, overrule contrary state law. After *Missouri*, states' rights advocates, unable to use the federal courts to thwart the preemptive effect of treaties, set out to change the Constitution.[235]

Senator Bricker introduced his "Proposed Constitutional Amendment Relative to Making of Treaties and Executive Agreements" (the Bricker

230 Allen, *supra* note 229, at 10. 231 *Ibid*. at xiv. 232 Jessup, *supra* note 216, at 2.

233 Donald R. Richberg, *The Bricker Amendment and the Treaty Power*, 39 VIRGINIA L. REV. 753, 763 (1953).

234 *See* THE FEDERALIST NO. 19 (JAMES MADISON WITH ALEXANDER HAMILTON).

235 John W. Bricker & Charles A. Webb, *The Bricker Amendment*, 29 NOTRE DAME L. REV. 529, 535 (1954).

Amendment) on September 14, 1951.[236] Following its introduction, the Bricker Amendment was advanced in various versions as it wound its way through the Senate Judiciary and Foreign Affairs Committees and was finally brought to the Senate floor.[237] The effort aimed to limit treaty incorporation in three ways.

The first was to prevent treaties from altering the constitutional system of government or from abridging the individual rights guaranteed by the Constitution. Supporters of the Amendment explained that this was necessary to prevent the executive branch from altering the Constitution by the way of a treaty.[238] Opponents pointed out that although individual scholars had suggested that the Constitution might be subordinate to international law, neither the Supreme Court nor any previous administration had ever suggested that the Supremacy Clause might accomplish this result.[239]

The second suggested limitation was to reverse *Missouri* and explicitly restrict the subject matter of treaties to the federal powers enumerated in the Constitution. Proponents believed this limitation would shield Jim Crow legislation in the South against treaty-based preemption.[240]

A third limitation would have required all treaties to be enacted into legislation by Congress before becoming binding domestic law. This would have changed the constitutional regime from a system of direct incorporation into one of indirect incorporation. As noted earlier, during the Constitutional Convention, the idea of indirect incorporation was raised by some of the delegates but subsequently rejected.[241] This provision of the Bricker Amendment raised the greatest opposition from the Eisenhower Administration. Both the Secretary of State and President Eisenhower himself argued that indirect incorporation would cripple the executive's ability to execute an effective foreign policy.[242]

236 Much scholarly writing has already been dedicated to the Bricker Amendment. For analyses published while the debates were ongoing see, e.g., Bricker, *Making Treaties*, *supra* note. 217; Bricker, *The Bricker Amendment*, *supra* note 235; Richberg, *supra* note 233; Arthur Dean, *The Bricker Amendment and Authority over Foreign Affairs*, 32 FOREIGN AFFAIRS 1 (1953). For historical analysis see, e.g., Nolan, *supra* note 225; Johnson, *supra* note 222; DUANE A. TANANBAUM, THE BRICKER AMENDMENT CONTROVERSY: TEST OF EISENHOWER'S POLITICAL LEADERSHIP (1988); Louis Henkin, *U.S. Ratification Human Rights Conventions: The Ghost of Senator Bricker*, 89 AM. J. INT'L L. 341 (1995), NATALIE HEVENER KAUFMAN, HUMAN RIGHTS TREATIES AND THE SENATE, A HISTORY OF OPPOSITION (1990).

237 See KAUFMAN, *supra* note 236, at Appendix A (collecting seven different versions of the amendment).

238 *Ibid.* at 96–7.

239 *See* testimony by Secretary of State John Foster Dulles before the Senate, cited in *ibid.* at 98.

240 Spiro, *supra* note 221, at 2016.

241 *See* notes 19–20, *supra*, and accompanying text.

242 Nolan, *supra* note 225, at 343.

Ultimately, after the Eisenhower Administration promised to refrain from adopting the emerging human rights treaties[243] – a promise that held until the 1948 Convention on the Prevention and Punishment of the Crime of Genocide was finally ratified in 1988[244] – a softened version of the Bricker Amendment failed to achieve the required two-thirds Senate majority by one vote. The concerns that Senator Bricker and his supporters raised did not vanish, however, and opposition to legal change via treaty took on new forms. Two are worthy of explanation: an enhanced doctrine of non-self-execution and a restrained approach to the adoption of implementing legislation that would rely for constitutional validation on the *Missouri* doctrine's Necessary and Proper Clause rationale. Both trends were manifested, inter alia, in the Senate's practice of attaching qualifications (packages of reservations, understandings, and declarations) to instruments of treaty ratification.

C *The Doctrine of Non-Self-Execution*

Where applied, the doctrine of non-self-execution accomplishes the Brickerite goal of restricting indirect incorporation through judicial determination. It provides that the ratification of certain treaty provisions does not result in their becoming "the law of the land," as mandated by the Supremacy Clause.[245] Rather, provisions which create rights and obligations inside the United States, while binding on the international plane, do not directly become justiciable as part of U.S. law. To become binding U.S. law, therefore, additional implementing legislation must be enacted. Thus, the doctrine of self-execution interposes a second step that is necessary in order to establish of a rule of decision for courts. Although the non-self-execution concept had been longstanding, the post-Bricker doctrine differed in important ways from its nineteenth century progenitors, more aggressively limiting treaties' incorporation into domestic law.

As discussed above, non-self-execution arose from *Foster v. Neilson* and its progeny.[246] In those cases, the Supreme Court held that courts should distinguish self-executing from non-self-executing treaty provisions: if treaty

[243] Henkin, *The Ghost of Senator Bricker*, *supra* note 236, at 348–9.

[244] David P. Stewart, *United States Ratifications of the Covenant on Civil and Political Rights: The Significance of the Reservations, Understandings, and Declarations*, 42 DEPAUL L. REV. 1183, 1202 (1992).

[245] U.S. Const. Art. VI Sec. 2.

[246] *See*, notes 50–53, *supra*, and accompanying text. *See also* Bartram v. Robertson, 122 U.S. 116 (1887); Whitney v. Robertson, 124 U.S. 190 (1888).

provisions anticipate implementation only upon occurrence of an additional step, then they are not self-executing. For example, in the 1887 *Bartram* case, the Court ruled that a treaty between the King of Hawaii and the United States was not self-executing because Article 5 of the treaty had explicitly provided that congressional action was required.[247]

Importantly, *Bartram* did not base its self-execution determination on the subject matter of the treaty; it suggested no distinction, for example, between treaties regulating relations among states and those addressing purely private rights. The same can be said for other cases decided in the first half of the twentieth century.[248] Indeed, in *De Lima*, a treaty that quite unambiguously pertained to a public, rather than private subject matter, was nonetheless treated by the Supreme Court as self-executing.[249] The treaty in question established Puerto Rico's legal status as a territory of the United States, from which followed the wrongfulness of the imposition of a tariff on imports therefrom.[250] Thus, the treaty could be invoked by a private litigant in aid of a claim, even though the treaty itself created no private right or private cause of action. Post-Bricker, however, the doctrine of non-self-execution has been greatly expanded so that treaties are presumed to be non-self-executing unless they expressly state otherwise.[251]

In addition, the executive and the Senate jointly adopted the practice of attaching to instruments of treaty ratification a package of qualifications that go beyond what international law acknowledges as "reservations," i.e., statements, however denominated, that purport to modify the terms of international obligations accepted upon ratification. These qualifications – known collectively as Reservations, Understandings, and Declarations (RUDs) – have included statements that do not seek to modify obligations on the international plane, but that pertain exclusively to domestic implementation. The best known of these is the declaration of non-self-execution contained in the RUDs attached to the 1992 U.S. ratification of the International Covenant on Civil and Political Rights (ICCPR).[252] Notwithstanding

247 Bartram, 122 U.S. at 119.

248 *See, e.g.*, Cook v. United States, 288 U.S. 102 (1933); Cameroon Septic Tank Company v. City of Knoxville Iowa, 277 U.S. 39 (1913); United States v. American Sugar Refining Company, 202 U.S. 563 (1909); Fok Yung Yo v. United States, 185 U.S. 296 (1902); De Lima v. Bidwell, 182 U.S. 21 (1901).

249 De Lima, 182 U.S. at 196. 250 *Ibid.*, at 199.

251 Medellin v. Texas, 552 U.S. 491 at 519 (2008).

252 International Covenant on Civil and Political Rights, adopted Dec. 19, 1966, S. Exec. Doc. E, 95–2 (1978), 999 U.N.T.S. 171 (entered into force Mar. 23, 1976); Reservations, Understandings, and Declarations, 138 Cong. Rec. S4781–01 (daily ed., April 2, 1992); *see*

scholarly objections that RUDs "subvert[] the constitutional treaty system,"[253] such non-self-executing declarations have uniformly been accorded legal effect, thus preempting any *Foster v. Neilson* analysis of the terms of any treaty to which such a declaration is attached.

D The Restrained Approach to Implementing Legislation Expanding Federal Power

The *Missouri* doctrine's narrow escape in the Bricker controversy formally preserved for Congress the Necessary and Proper Clause authority to pass legislation in aid of treaties that would otherwise be deemed beyond the scope of Congress's enumerated powers (and thus as encroachments on residual rights of the states under the Tenth Amendment). However, as pointed out below in Margaret McGuinness' chapter on federalism,[254] this authority has been invoked quite sparingly, undoubtedly with an eye to avoiding a Supreme Court revisitation of Holmes's blanket conclusion that "[i]f the treaty is valid, there can be no dispute about the validity of the statute under Article I, § 8, as a necessary and proper means to execute the powers of the Government."[255] Were the federal government to be seen as exploiting the treaty power to expand unilaterally the scope of its legislative authority at the expense of the states – perhaps adopting a tendentiously broad interpretation of what legislative measures are "necessary and proper" to the implementation of a treaty obligation – the *Missouri* Court's sweeping assertion might well be reconsidered.[256]

also United States Committee on Foreign Relations Report on the International Covenant on Civil and Political Rights (January 30, 1992) in 31 I.L.M. 645, 657 (1992).

253 Henkin, The Ghost of Senator Bricker, *supra* note 236, at 347. *See also* David Weissbrodt, *United States Ratification of the Human Rights Covenants*, 62 MINN. L. REV. 35, 73 (1978); Lori Fisler Damrosch, *The Role of the United States Senate Concerning "Self-Executing" and "Non-Self-Executing" Treaties*, 67 CHI.-KENT L. REV. 515, 532 (1991); M. Cherif Bassiouni, *Reflections on the Ratification of the International Covenant on Civil and Political Rights by the United States*, 42 DEPAUL L. REV. 1169, 1173 (1993); Jordan J. Paust, *Avoiding "Fraudulent" Executive Policy: Analysis of Non-Self-Execution of the Covenant on Civil and Political Rights*, 42 DEPAUL L. REV. 1257, 1283 (1993); Malvina Halberstam, *United States Ratification of the Convention on the Elimination of All Forms of Discrimination Against Women*, 31 GEO. WASH. J. INT'L L. & ECON. 49, 50 (1997); William A. Schabas, *Invalid Reservations to the International Covenant on Civil and Political Rights: Is the United States Still a Party?*, 21 BROOK. J. INT'L L. 277, 285 (1995). *But see* Carlos Manuel Vazquez, *Treaties as Law of the Land: The Supremacy Clause and the Judicial Enforcement of Treaties*, 122 HARV. L. REV. 599, 671 (2008) (arguing that the declaration is constitutional).

254 Margaret McGuinness, chapter 5 of this volume. 255 Missouri, 252 U.S. at 432.

256 As discussed by Professor McGuinness in Chapter 5 of this volume, a determined effort to revisit *Missouri* was sidestepped in Bond v. United States, 131 S. Ct. 2355 (2014).

Beyond this general reticence, the President and the Senate, in attaching RUDs to the ratification instruments of human rights treaties, have taken care to include an "Understanding" regarding the implementation of treaty provisions in light of the federal structure of the United States. The ICCPR federalism understanding's rather murky language[257] seemingly suggests that because of the division of power between the federal government and the individual states, the United States cannot guarantee treaty compliance by the individual states.[258] This understanding thus appears calculated to short circuit the holding of *Missouri*, by expressly providing that the treaty ratification does not augment Congressional authority vis-à-vis the states.[259]

Commentators who support the federalism understanding and the non-self-executing declaration argue that the primary norms set forth in human rights treaties and the norms enshrined in U.S. law are similar, and that the minor differences should be legislated locally rather than imported from the outside, thus respecting the federal system of government.[260] Other commentators have argued that these qualifications have permitted the United States to make commitments that they would not have been otherwise able to make because of national constitutional and political reasons.[261]

Whether viewing these RUDs in a positive or a negative light, all commentators agree that their purpose is to limit the force of international treaty norms in the United States. Thus, as pointed out by Louis Henkin, the aspirations of

257 *See* Reservations, Understandings, and Declarations, *supra* note 252 ("[T]he United States understands that this Covenant shall be implemented by the Federal Government to the extent that it exercises legislative and judicial jurisdiction over the matters covered therein, and otherwise by the state and local governments; to the extent that state and local governments exercise jurisdiction over such matters, the Federal Government shall take measures appropriate to the Federal system to the end that the competent authorities of the state or local governments may take appropriate measures for the fulfillment of the Covenant.").

258 *See, e.g., United States Committee on Foreign Relations Report on the International Covenant on Civil and Political Rights* (Jan. 30, 1992), *in* 31 I.L.M. 645, 657 (1992).

259 *See* Brad R. Roth, *Understanding the "Understanding": Federalism Constraints on Human Rights Implementation*, 47 WAYNE L. REV. 893, 904–7 (2001). Critical commentators have argued that the federalism understanding is problematic because it either repeats exactly the holding of Missouri, rendering it moot, *see, e.g.*, Weissbrodt, *supra* note 253, at 65–6, or because it attempts to supplant *Missouri* in which case it is constitutionally void, John Quigley, *The International Covenant on Civil and Political Rights and the Supremacy Clause*, 42 DEPAUL L. REV. 1287, 1302–4 (1993); Thomas Buergenthal, *Modern Constitutions and Human Rights Treaties*, 35 COLUM. J. TRANSNAT'L L. 211, 222 (1998).

260 Stewart, *supra* note 244, at 1206.

261 Curtis A. Bradley & Jack L. Goldsmith, *Treaties, Human Rights, and Conditional Consent*, 149 PA. L. REV. 399, 467–68 (2000).

Senator Bricker to limit the power of treaties to affect domestic law were achieved without the need to change the Constitution.[262]

VIII CONCLUSION

We began this chapter by surveying the debates of the founders over how treaty provisions would enter domestic law. We suggested that an impetus behind convening the Constitutional Convention was the risk posed by the refusal of the individual states to comply with treaty obligations. In the ensuing debate, the Convention emphatically rejected an indirect incorporation theory for treaties, instead denominating treaty obligations the supreme law of the law without qualification.

As we followed the course of history, we showed how the political climate that predominated in different eras in United States' history affected the incorporation and implementation of treaty obligations in domestic law. We discussed how the federalist sentiments of the Union's early years was challenged by a states' rights approach to the relations between the federal government and the states. The domestic power of treaties was eroded. We then examined the reconstruction and post reconstruction eras, to see how the power and legitimacy of the central federal government was bolstered in post-Civil War society and how, subsequently, international treaties were increasingly respected vis-à-vis state and federal law. Between 1919 and 1941, the foreign relations powers of the President and the role of treaties grew to meet the emergencies of the times. Finally, following World War II, the Congress acted in various ways to limit the domestic effect of the new human rights treaties.

[262] Henkin, *The Ghost of Senator Bricker, supra* note 236, at 349.

2

Treaties in the Third Restatement

Gregory H. Fox

This chapter introduces the baseline from which the remaining chapters in this volume measure evolution in the American law of treaties. The baseline chosen is the 1987 Restatement (Third) of Foreign Relations Law of the United States.[1] The chapter asks whether the Restatement's account represented a consensus view of how treaties functioned within the legal system of the United States. If the Restatement's portrayal was indeed accurate, then its rules are a sound point of departure for measuring whether current rules diverge from the baseline.

This chapter approaches the consensus question from three perspectives. First, it examines the Restatement's drafting history and ask whether its rules on treaties in U.S. law were the subject of debate and, if so, whether those debates were resolved by negotiation and compromise or by one view prevailing over another. Second, it asks how the Restatement's treaty rules were received by state and federal courts. Since I seek judicial reaction to the Restatement rules themselves and not those rules as later reinforced or modified by courts, I have limited the inquiry to decisions issued within roughly a decade of the Restatement's publication in 1987. Third, the chapter looks at how the treaty rules were received by legal scholars within a similar time frame.

This chapter is not a comprehensive examination of all debates surrounding the treaty rules. Later chapters examine both the historical development of treaty norms prior to 1987 and, in more detail, how those rules have fared in the years since then. This chapter treads lightly over these complex questions in

I am grateful to Michelle Lalonde of the Wayne State Law School Library for outstanding research on issues in this chapter.

[1] *Restatement (Third) of the Foreign Relations Law of the United States* (Am. Law Inst. 1987).

order to focus directly on how the relevant actors of the time – participants in the drafting process, federal judges and leading scholars of foreign relations law – reacted to the Restatement's articulation of treaty norms. That is, the chapter analyzes only explicit discussions of the Restatement itself as opposed to discussions of the substantive issues addressed by the Restatement.

I DRAFTING THE RESTATEMENT

A *Starting the Project*

The Third Restatement began as an effort to respond to the substantial growth in international law and U.S. foreign relations law since publication of the Second Restatement in 1965.[2] But the project quickly became mired in controversy. Chief Reporter Louis Henkin clashed repeatedly with the American Bar Association, the Office of the Legal Advisor to the State Department, and several prominent lawyers who opposed portions of his drafts.[3] The clashes resulted in publication being delayed a full year while the State Department sought to persuade the Reporters to change portions of the draft document.[4] In a remarkably candid moment at a meeting of the American Society of International Law, one scholar decried "the level of distrust that had developed over the years between the Reporters and government officials."[5]

As John Houck reported at the time, "these controversies centered around the treatment of customary international law, expropriation, extraterritorial application of U.S. law, and the act of state doctrine."[6]

[2] The volumes' designations often lead to confusion, since the Second Restatement was, in fact, the first Restatement the American Law Institute (ALI) published on U.S. foreign relations law. The "Second" designation was intended to distinguish that document from the first generation of Restatements, published in the 1920s and 1930s. By 1965 these had mostly been replaced by second editions.

[3] *See The Restatement of Foreign Relations Law of the United States, Revised: How Were the Controversies Resolved*, 81 ASIL Proc. 180, 183 (1987) (remarks of Professor Detlev Vagts).

[4] *See* Karl M. Meesen, *Forward, Special Review Essays: The Third Restatement of the Foreign Relations Law of the United States*, 14 Yale J. Int'l L. 433, 436 (1989).

[5] *The Restatement of the Foreign Relations Law of the United States, Revised, supra* note 3, at 181 (remarks of Professor Harold Maier).

[6] John B. Houck, *Restatement of the Foreign Relations Law of the United States (Revised): Issues and Resolutions*, 20 Int'l L. 136, 136 (1986). Houck was chair of a committee of the ABA Section on International Law charged with following the Restatement drafting process. At the 1982 Annual Meeting of the American Society of International Law, he discussed areas of the then-draft Restatement that his committee found problematic.

Notably they did not involve the Restatement's treaty provisions.[7] To be sure, the Third Restatement provisions on international agreements were occasionally criticized and debated.[8] But, relatively speaking, these debates about treaty law were on the margins and did not involve the most significant departures from the Second Restatement, such as eliminating the constitutional requirement that treaties be limited to "matters of international concern"[9] or the full interchangeability of Article II treaties and Congressional-Executive agreements.[10]

B The Reporter: Louis Henkin

The intellectual origins of the Third Restatement are closely associated with its Chief Reporter, Professor Louis Henkin, the person largely responsible for much of its shape and content.[11] Many of the Restatement rules echo positions Henkin had taken as a scholar; some that departed from the Second Restatement and later generated controversy are particularly

None involved international agreements. *See The Draft Restatement of the Foreign Relations Law of the United States (Revised)*, 76 ASIL PROC. 184, 194 (1982) (remarks of John B. Houck) (criticizing sections on customary international law, extraterritoriality and expropriation).

7 Former Legal Advisor to the State Department Monroe Leigh recounted in 1986 that the controversies concerned "the Reporters' proposed treatment of jurisdiction, extraterritoriality, Act of State, and expropriation as well as a general criticism that in many passages the text was not up to the high standards of the Institute with respect to drafting and craftsmanship." Monroe Leigh, *Private Investors Abroad – Problems and Solutions in International Business in 1985, reprinted from* PROCEEDINGS OF THE SOUTHWESTERN LEGAL FOUNDATION PRIVATE INVESTORS ABROAD—PROBLEMS AND SOLUTIONS IN INTERNATIONAL BUSINESS 2–3 (1986). *See also* Benedict Tai, A *Summary of the Forthcoming Restatement of the Foreign Relations Law of the United States (Revised)*, 24 COLUM. J. TRANSNAT'L L. 677, 680 (1985–1986) (while several additions and deletions were made to the Second Restatement's treaty rules, "[n]one raised any substantial controversy.").

8 *See, e.g.* Malcolm R. Wilkey, *Sections of the Revised Restatement Arousing Interest, Comment and Controversy*, 77 ASIL. PROC. 77, 78 (1983) (observing that the draft Restatement was unclear on whether "developing customary law overrides prior inconsistent treaties. This question is worthy of further discussion.").

9 THIRD RESTATEMENT, *supra* note 1, § 302 rptr note 2.

10 *Ibid.* § 303, cmt. e.

11 *See generally*, Paul B. Stephan, *Constitution, and Customary International Law: The Intellectual Origins of the Third Restatement of the Foreign Relations Law of the United States*, 44 VA. J. INT'L L. 33 (2003). Originally, Richard Baxter of Harvard Law School was the American Law Institute's (ALI) choice for Chief Reporter. He served for less than one year before he was elected to the International Court of Justice in 1978. Henkin replaced him and was assisted by Associate Reporters Andreas Lowenfeld, Louis Sohn, and Detlev Vagts. THIRD RESTATEMENT, *supra* note 2, at ix.

traceable to Henkin.[12] Some writers have described the document as "Henkin's Restatement."[13]

Louis Henkin was born in 1917 in what is now Belarus and immigrated with his family to the United States in 1923.[14] After attending Yeshiva University and Harvard Law School, where he was a member of the *Law Review*, he clerked for Judge Learned Hand on the Second Circuit Court of Appeals and then Supreme Court Justice Felix Frankfurter.[15] In between the two clerkships he served in the U.S. Army.[16]

After the war, Henkin served for one year as a consultant to the United Nations Legal Department and, from 1948–1956, as a lawyer in the Internal Organizations Bureau of the State Department.[17] In 1956, Henkin left the State Department for academia, first joining the University of Pennsylvania Law School and then Columbia Law School in 1962, where he remained for the rest of his career. Henkin also served as a leader in professional organizations, including as President of the American Society of International Law

[12] A useful example is the question of whether the Constitution requires that treaties address only matters of "international concern." The Second Restatement contained such a requirement. *See* RESTATEMENT (SECOND) OF THE FOREIGN RELATIONS LAW OF THE UNITED STATES ("SECOND RESTATEMENT") § 117(1) (Am. Law Inst. 1965) ("The United States has the power under the Constitution to make an international agreement if (a) the matter is of international concern"). Henkin lambasted this idea in a 1969 article in the American Journal of International Law, asserting that "the 'international concern' limitation may not in fact exist; that if there is some such limitation, it has been unduly and needlessly elevated to independent doctrine and its scope exaggerated; that, in any event, it is mislabeled and therefore likely to be misapplied." Louis Henkin, *"International Concern" and the Treaty Power of the United States*, 63 AM. J. INTL. L. 272, 273 (1969). Henkin repeated this argument in his 1972 treatise. LOUIS HENKIN, FOREIGN AFFAIRS AND THE CONSTITUTION 151–6 (1972). Not surprisingly, the Third Restatement also rejected "international concern" limitations on the treaty power. THIRD RESTATEMENT, *supra* note 1, § 302, rptr n. 2 ("[t]here is no principle either in international law or in United States constitutional law that some subjects are intrinsically 'domestic' and hence impermissible subjects for an international agreement."). But the question was not definitively settled by the vehemence of Henkin's views. Justice Thomas revived the idea in his concurrence in the Bond case, Bond v. United States, 134 S. Ct. 2077, 2102, 189 L. Ed. 2d 1 (2014) (Thomas, J, concurring), and recent scholarship has suggested that Henkin's historical arguments for rejecting the limitation were not wholly accurate. *See* Duncan B. Hollis, *The Treaty Power after Bond v. United States: An Intersubjective Treaty Power*, 90 NOTRE DAME L. REV. 1415 (2015).

[13] *See* Norman Silber & Geoffrey Miller, *Toward "Neutral Principles" in the Law: Selections from the Oral History of Herbert Wechsler*, 93 COLUM. L. REV. 854, 915 (1993); Lori Fisler Damrosch, *Louis Henkin (1917–2010)*, 105 AM. J. INT'L L. 287, 298 (2011).

[14] Damrosch, *supra* note 13, at 287. [15] *Ibid.*

[16] *Ibid.* Henkin emerged deeply affected by his war-time experience. He wrote to Judge Hand, "Ordinary suffering of unknown nature to anonymous human beings weighs on us like a dull inexplicable weight." *Ibid.* at 288.

[17] *Ibid.*

(1992–1994) and co-editor-in-chief of the American Journal of International Law (1978–1984).

Henkin started his academic career in the aftermath of the Bricker Amendment controversy, a debate merging the two fields that would become the primary focus of his scholarship – public international law and U.S. constitutional law.[18] Henkin wrote his first scholarly article about the Bricker controversy, *The Treaty Makers and the Law Makers*.[19] Henkin's next work, the book *Arms Control and Inspection in American Law*, also explored the intersection of these two fields.[20] His scholarship for the next decade, while wide ranging, focused increasingly on this area of law that did not yet have a name. It would later become known as United States Foreign Relations Law, in large part due to Henkin's own work.[21] His articles addressed such topics as the jurisdiction of federal courts in foreign relations cases,[22] the constitutional status of new human rights treaties then being drafted,[23] the Act of State Doctrine,[24] constitutional questions arising from the war in Vietnam,[25] and potential limitations on the scope of the treaty power.[26] Henkin also wrote extensively on human rights law on its own terms and was named the first director of the Lawyers Committee for Human Rights upon its founding in 1978.[27] Henkin's most prominent work of this period was his 1968 book *How Nations Behave*.[28] Henkin argued that contrary to much Realist thought at the time, compliance with international law is routine and violations

18 Henkin continued to write prolifically on these and other topics after completing work on the Third Restatement. This section highlights only his scholarship prior to his selection as Chief Reporter.

19 Louis Henkin, *The Treaty Makers and the Law Makers: The Niagara Reservation*, 56 COLUM. L. REV. 1151 (1956).

20 LOUIS HENKIN, ARMS CONTROL AND INSPECTION IN AMERICAN LAW (1958). *See also* Louis Henkin, *Arms Control and the Constitution*, 11 HASTINGS L.J. 267 (1959–1960).

21 *See* Louis Henkin, *"A More Effective System" For Foreign Relations: The Constitutional Framework*, 61 VA. L. REV. 751 (1975).

22 Louis Henkin, *Is There a Political Question Doctrine?*, 85 YALE. L.J. 597 (1975–1976); Louis Henkin, *The Foreign Affairs Power of the Federal Courts: Sabbatino*, 64 COLUM. L. REV. 805 (1964).

23 Louis Henkin, *Constitutional Rights and Human Rights*, 13 HARV. C.R.- C.L. L. REV. 593 (1978); Louis Henkin, *The United States and the Crisis in Human Rights*, 14 VA. J. INT'L L. 653 (1973–1974); Louis Henkin, *The Constitution, Treaties, and International Human Rights*, 116 U. PA. L. REV. 1012 (1968).

24 Louis Henkin, *Act of State Today: Recollections in Tranquility*, 6 COLUM. J. TRANSNAT'L L. 175 (1967).

25 Louis Henkin, *Viet-Nam in the Courts of the United States: Political Questions*, 63 AM. J. INT'L L. 284 (1969).

26 *"International Concern," supra* note 12.

27 Damrosch, *supra* note 12, at 296.

28 LOUIS HENKIN, HOW NATIONS BEHAVE (2nd edn. 1979) (1968).

exceptional. His dictum that "almost all nations observe almost all principles of international law and almost all of their obligations almost all of the time" is one of the most widely quoted in the field.[29]

In 1972 Henkin brought his experience and scholarship together in *Foreign Affairs and the Constitution*, one of the towering achievements in the field.[30] Henkin noted that his book was the first in fifty years to survey the broad range of constitutional issues bearing on foreign affairs.[31] The book explored the distribution of foreign affairs powers among the three federal branches and between the federal government and the states. It paid special attention to the role of courts in foreign affairs law. But Henkin recognized that many foreign relations issues had not and, for a variety of reasons, would likely never be addressed by courts, and the volume spent much time reviewing the outcome of political contests between the federal branches and the constitutional consequences of major foreign crises. One of the book's notable features was the breadth of authority Henkin assembled: the text was 281 pages and was followed by 218 pages of footnotes. The book received an enthusiastic reception.[32] When a second edition appeared in 1997, a reviewer in the *American Journal of International Law* recalled that the first edition's "lucidity, readability and balanced judgment quickly gave the book an authority unrivaled in the field."[33]

Foreign Affairs and the Constitution made clear that Henkin was firmly in the camp of liberal internationalism. In the book and in subsequent writing, he argued for the maximum possible incorporation of international norms

29 *Ibid.* at 47.

30 HENKIN, FOREIGN AFFAIRS, *supra* note 12. *See* CURTIS A. BRADLEY, INTERNATIONAL LAW IN THE U.S. LEGAL SYSTEM xiv (2nd edn. 2015) (discussing Henkin's "magisterial treatise").

31 HENKIN, FOREIGN AFFAIRS, *supra* note 12, at viii.

32 *See, e.g.* Stanley Futterman, LOUIS HENKIN, FOREIGN RELATIONS AND THE CONSTITUTION (1972), 7 *NYU J. INT'L L. & POL.* 203, 203 (1974) (book review) (Henkin's work "will be the first book anyone seriously interested in the constitutional law of foreign affairs will pull from the shelf"); Harold W. Chase, LOUIS HENKIN, FOREIGN RELATIONS AND THE CONSTITUTION (1972), 14 *HARV. INT'L L. J.* 641, 642 (1973) (book review) ("Professor Henkin provides a clear, systematic, concise and truly brilliant explication of the conduct of foreign affairs within the American constitutional system"); Victor G. Rosenblum, LOUIS HENKIN, FOREIGN RELATIONS AND THE CONSTITUTION (1972), 42 *U. CIN. L. REV.* 805, 805 (1973) (book review) ("Professor Henkin has produced a compelling, concise, meticulously organized and documented study"); Richard B. Bilder, LOUIS HENKIN, FOREIGN RELATIONS AND THE CONSTITUTION (1972), 21 AM. J. COMP. L. 786, 786 (1973) (book review) ("Professor Henkin's thoughtful, comprehensive and scholarly study of the constitutional law of American foreign affairs is likely to remain the leading work in this field for some time to come.").

33 Jules Lobel, LOUIS HENKIN, FOREIGN AFFAIRS AND THE CONSTITUTION (2nd ed. 1997), 91 AM. J. INT'L L. 556, 556 (1997) (book review).

into American law, decrying both the original Bricker movement and its subsequent iterations, for example U.S. reservations to human rights treaties.[34] He resisted a narrow understanding of the non-self-execution doctrine, arguing that a non-self-executing treaty still creates obligations for the Executive Branch and preemptive federal law vis-à-vis the states.[35] He rejected the widely held view that courts often employ the political question doctrine to abstain from examining the nature and extent of Presidential power in foreign affairs.[36] Writing in reaction to the *Garcia-Mir*[37] case and with respect to customary international law, Henkin defended the primacy of customary international law obligations over contrary executive acts:

> If I am correct, *Garcia-Mir* misinterpreted and misapplied *The Paquete Habana*. The court apparently considered any act of the President 'controlling' and extended that to include an act by the Attorney General. It took the view that the President – and the Attorney General – had power 'to disregard international law in service of domestic needs.' There is no such principle. The President cannot disregard international law 'in service of domestic needs' any more than he can disregard any other law.[38]

Supreme Court justices have frequently turned to Henkin's work in foreign affairs cases, including in such prominent decisions as *First National Citi Bank v. Banco Nacional de Cuba*,[39] *Dunhill v. Republic of*

34 *See* Louis Henkin, *U.S. Ratification of Human Rights Conventions: The Ghost of Senator Bricker*, 89 AM. J. INT'L L. 341 (1995).

35 Louis Henkin, *The Constitution and United States Sovereignty: A Century of Chinese Exclusion and its Progeny*, 100 HARV. L. REV. 853, 867 N. 5 (1987) (because a non-self-executing treaty is "an obligation of the United States, the treaty is law for the political branches, a binding obligation for the political branch that had the duty and the authority to carry it out on behalf of the United States. As national policy, it is law for the states and their governors, legislatures, and courts. And, where national public policy is relevant, it is law for all courts.").

36 Henkin, *Is There a Political Question Doctrine?*, *supra* note 22, at 610–12.

37 Fernandez-Roque v. Smith, 622 F. Supp. 887 (N.D. Ga. 1985), *rev'd in part sub nom.* Garcia-Mir v. Meese, 788 F.2d 1446 (11th Cir. 1986) (holding that an Executive Branch order superseded U.S. obligations under customary law concerning undocumented aliens).

38 Louis Henkin, *May the President Violate Customary International Law?: The President and International Law*, 80 AM. J. INT'L L. 930, 936 (1986). In the Paquete Habana, the Supreme Court famously stated that

> International law is part of our law, and must be ascertained and administered by the courts of justice of appropriate jurisdiction as often as questions of right depending upon it are duly presented for their determination. For this purpose, where there is no treaty and no controlling executive or legislative act or judicial decision, resort must be had to the customs and usages of civilized nations.

The Paquete Habana, 175 U.S. 677, 700 (1900).

39 First Nat'l City Bank v. Banco Nacional de Cuba, 406 U.S. 759, 776, 779 n. 4 (1972) (Brennan, J., dissenting).

Cuba,[40] *Dames & Moore v. Regan,*[41] *United States v. Alvarez-Machain,*[42] *Sale v. Haitian Centers Council*[43] *American Insurance Association v. Garamendi,*[44] *Sanchez-Llamas v. Oregon,*[45] *Bond v. United States,*[46] and *Zivitofsky v. Clinton.*[47]

C Finishing the Restatement

A full two years passed between ALI's decision to embark on a Third Restatement and the appearance of the first Preliminary Draft in September 1979. During that time, several leaders of the project made clear their priorities. None involved resolving major controversies in treaty law or progressively developing that law in new directions. The President and Director of ALI, for example, mentioned the need to take account of the Vienna Convention on the Law of Treaties, which had been finalized four years after the Second Restatement, as well as "such legislation as the Case Act and the Foreign Assistance Acts affecting the relationship between the executive and legislative branches in the making of international agreements and imposing limitations on executive action."[48] When Professor Baxter, the original Chief Reporter, described the major issues to be addressed at the 1978 ALI annual meeting, the only treaty questions he mentioned were the new Vienna Convention and the Case Act.[49]

From the first Preliminary Draft of September 1979 to the final draft of May 1986, the Third Restatement went through seven separate drafts. Each was discussed at the ALI annual meeting and, on several occasions, at the annual meeting of the American Society of International Law. We are left

40 Alfred Dunhill of London, Inc. v. Republic of Cuba, 425 U.S. 682, 715, 726 n. 11 (1976) (Marshall, J., dissenting).

41 Dames & Moore v. Regan, 453 U.S. 654, 679–80 (1981).

42 United States v. Alvarez-Machain, 504 U.S. 655, 670, 681 (1992) (Stevens, J., dissenting).

43 Sale v. Haitian Ctrs. Council, 509 U.S. 155, 196 n.6 (1993) (Blackmun, J., dissenting).

44 Am. Ins. Ass'n v. Garamendi, 539 U.S. 396, 415 (2003).

45 Sanchez-Llamas v. Oregon, 548 U.S. 331, 365, 383–4 (2006) (Breyer, J., dissenting).

46 Bond v. United States, 134 S.Ct. at 2100 (2014) (Scalia, J., concurring).

47 Zivitofsky v. Clinton, 132 S.Ct. 1421, 1429 (2012).

48 Memorandum from President and Director of the American Law Institute re: "Prepared Revision and Expansion of the Restatement of the Foreign Relations Law of the United States," at 6 (November 1977) (on file with authors).

49 *Statement of Professor Baxter*, 55 *ALI Proc.* 327, 328 (1978). Similarly, when newly appointed Chief Reporter Henkin addressed the 1979 ALI Annual Meeting, he said very little about treaties in describing the work ahead, the exception being the question of treaty termination which was then a hot topic because of Senator Goldwater's lawsuit challenging termination of the Taiwan defense treaty. *Statement of Professor Henkin*, 56 *ALI Proc.* 59, 60 (1979).

therefore with a remarkably complete record of the issues that were controversial and those that were not.

In the course of the drafting process, treaty issues were dispersed among three different parts of the Third Restatement: Section I dealing with international law and its relation to U.S. law generally, Section III dealing with international agreements and Section IX dealing with remedies for violations of international law.[50] The discussion below traces the drafting history of the major treaty law issues in each of these sections.

D *Treaty Issues in Part I*

Part I deals with international law and its relationship to U.S. law. The line between this section and Part III, which deals directly with international agreements, was not clear at the outset of the drafting process, and early on some issues initially dealt with in this more general section were moved to Part III, which is discussed below.

1 Self-Execution

The first Preliminary Draft of September 7, 1979, added a new section on self-execution. It defined a self-executing agreement as "one that takes effect as domestic law without the need of implementing legislation."[51] An agreement is considered non-self-executing "if it manifests an intention that it shall not become effective as domestic law of the United States without the enactment of implementing legislation."[52] If the text of an agreement is silent on its self-executing status, the draft's commentary explained, "account must be taken of any statement by the President in concluding the agreement or in submitting the agreement to the Senate or to the Congress as a whole, and of any expression of views by the Senate or the Congress in dealing with the agreement."[53]

The next iteration, the Council Draft of December 12, 1979, deleted the separate section on non-self-execution and incorporated that discussion into a more general section on "International Law and Agreements as Law of the United States" (§111 in the final draft). The Council Draft and

[50] In the SECOND RESTATEMENT, all issues related to treaties were grouped into Section III on International Agreements. Each treaty-law topic was in turn divided into provisions on "International Law" and provisions on the "Law of the United States."

[51] THIRD RESTATEMENT OF FOREIGN RELATIONS LAW OF THE UNITED STATES § 135(1) (Preliminary Draft No. 1, 1979).

[52] *Ibid.* § 135(2). [53] *Ibid.* cmt. d.

subsequent drafts changed little of substance from the Tentative Draft,[54] with the important exception of adding a presumption favoring self-execution in a reporter's note: "In general, agreements which can be readily given effect by executive or judicial bodies, federal or state, without further federal legislation, are deemed self-executing, unless a contrary intention is manifest."[55] The final version retained this presumption, though altering its justification somewhat, linking self-execution to ensuring U.S compliance with its treaty obligations.[56]

Remarkably, there was no discussion of self-execution at the two ALI annual meetings at which Part I of the Restatement was considered (1980 and 1985), or at the two ASIL meetings where Professor Henkin gave updates on the Restatement's progress (1982 and 1983).

2 Effect of Treaties on Inconsistent State Law

The Council Draft of December 12, 1979 combined two federalism provisions of the earlier Preliminary Draft, without substantive change, to create Section 135(1): "International law and international agreements of the United States are law of the United States and supreme over the law of the several states."[57] This rather absolute conception of treaty supremacy remained unchanged for the rest of the drafting process to become Section 111(1) of the final draft. Commentary added in 1980 made clear that sole executive agreements also prevailed over inconsistent state law.[58]

Tentative Draft 1 of April 1, 1980, however, limited the preemptive power of treaties to those that are self-executing, stating in a comment that a "non-self-executing treaty is not effective law in the United States until implemented by Congress, and then it would be the implementing legislation that effectively supersedes prior inconsistent federal or state law."[59] This

54 The final draft listed two additional categories of non-self-executing agreements: those explicitly denominated as such by the Senate at the time of ratification and those constitutionally required to be implemented through legislation. THIRD RESTATEMENT, *supra* note 1, § 111 (4) (b) & (c). Neither addition was inconsistent with the general principles in the Tentative Draft.

55 THIRD RESTATEMENT THE FOREIGN RELATIONS LAW OF THE UNITED STATES 131–61, rptr note 5 (Council Draft 1979).

56 *Ibid.* § 111, rptr note 5.

57 Council Draft, *supra* note 55, § 135(1).

58 THIRD RESTATEMENT THE FOREIGN RELATIONS LAW OF THE UNITED STATES § 135 cmt. a (Tentative Draft 1, 1980) ("[t]he President may make some agreements under his own constitutional authority... Such an international agreement concluded by the President prevails over inconsistent state law.")

59 *Ibid.*

language was removed from Tentative Draft 6 of April 12, 1985, and replaced with a comment that in a rather unclear fashion seemed to elevate the preemptive authority of non-self-executing treaties: "Even a non-self-executing agreement of the United States, not effective as law until implemented by legislative or executive action, may sometimes be held to be federal policy superseding State law or policy."[60] This comment was not explained further in the reporters' notes. It remained unaltered in the final draft.[61]

As with the non-self-execution provisions, the sections on treaties' effect on inconsistent state law were not the subject of discussion at ALI or ASIL meetings.

3 Treaties and Inconsistent Federal Law

All of the drafts contained a version of the familiar last-in-time rule and noted its deep roots in Supreme Court jurisprudence.[62] Although the rule was clear for Article II treaties, the rule for sole executive agreements was uncertain. The first Preliminary Draft (1979) wholly excluded from the last-in-time rule agreements made within the President's sole constitutional authority.[63] One year later, the black letter portion of Tentative Draft 1 (1980) seemed to eliminate the exception for sole executive agreements, applying the last-in-time rule broadly to an "agreement that becomes effective as law in the United States."[64] But commentary to that article stated that "[t]he effect of such an international agreement [*i.e.* one concluded on the President's own constitutional authority] on an earlier federal statute has not been established."[65] The final draft repeated this state of uncertainty, but appeared to reiterate the qualification of the first Preliminary Draft that a sole executive agreement concerning "a matter within the express

60 Third Restatement The Foreign Relations Law of the United States § 135 cmt. e (Tentative Draft No. 6, 1985). Professor Henkin appeared to support a relatively minor distinction between the preemptive authority of self-executing versus non-self-executing treaties when he stated at the 1982 ASIL Annual Meeting that "[t]he notion of having different degrees of federal law under the Constitution was one which he had never known in the U.S. system." 76 ASIL Proc., *supra* note 6, at 200.

61 Third Restatement, *supra* note 1 § 115, cmt. e.

62 *See, e.g.* Preliminary Draft No. 1, *supra* note 51, § 136(1); Tentative Draft 1, *supra* note 58, § 135; Third Restatement, *supra* note 1, § 115, cmt. c.

63 Preliminary Draft No. 1, *supra* note 51, § 136(1) (" A self-executing international agreement made on behalf of the United States, other than under the President's sole constitutional authority, supersedes inconsistent provisions of an earlier act of Congress").

64 Tentative Draft 1, *supra* note 58, § 135. 65 *Ibid.* cmt. a.

constitutional authority of Congress" would not prevail against an earlier inconsistent statute.[66]

There was brief discussion of the last-in-time rule at the 1980 ALI meeting, where Henkin reiterated the jurisprudential uncertainty on the preemptive authority of executive agreements.[67] The last-in-time rule was the subject of spirited debate at the 1982 ASIL panel on the draft Restatement, but almost wholly on the question of the relation between customary international law and earlier or later statutes.[68]

E Treaty Issues in Part III

Part III of the Restatement is focused specifically on international agreements. While the section made several important changes from the Second Restatement and dealt with issues of perennial controversy, the drafting process was remarkably tranquil. Most of the substantive doctrine contained in early drafts remained essentially unchanged in the final draft, though changes in wording and the placement of particular issues were made throughout.

1 The scope of international agreements

The Second Restatement contained a significant limitation on the scope of United States' international agreements: the subject matter must involve a "matter of international concern."[69] Henkin had addressed this question in *Foreign Affairs and the Constitution*, emphatically rejecting the proposition.[70] The first Preliminary Draft retained a much-weakened version of the idea, providing that the United States has the constitutional power to enter into an international agreement if it "serves a foreign policy purpose."[71] That phrase was not explained, but the Reporters' Notes strongly suggest it was a *de minimis* requirement.[72] At the 1980 ALI meeting, Henkin explained that the new

66 Third Restatement, *supra* note 1, § 115, cmt. c. Between publication of the First Tentative Draft and conclusion of the final draft, Robert Dalton, then Assistant Legal Advisor for Treaty Affairs, published a critique of § 135(1) making the point eventually adopted in the final draft. *See* Robert Dalton, *International Agreements in the Revised Restatement*, 25 Va. J. Int'l L. 153, 159–63 (1984–1985).

67 57 ALI Proc. 104–5 (1980). 68 76 ASIL Proc., *supra* note 6, at 189, 199–200.

69 Second Restatement, *supra* note 12, § 117(1)(a).

70 Henkin, Foreign Affairs *supra* note 12, at 151–6.

71 Preliminary Draft 1, *supra* note 51, § 304(a).

72 *Ibid.* § 304, rptr n. 1 (requirement that treaty serve some foreign policy interest or purpose of the United States "may very well be implied in the very word 'treaty' in the Constitution.").

language was not intended to put any widely subscribed treaties off limits to the United States, but instead to deal with the unlikely case of a (probably bilateral) treaty being used as a subterfuge to bind the United States to obligations unrelated to its foreign policy interests.[73]

The next draft (Council Draft 1 of December 12, 1979) dropped the requirement entirely from the black letter provision (Section 304 in that draft). A new comment – explaining that because international law did not limit the subject matter of treaties, neither should the law of the United States – remained essentially unchanged in the final draft.[74] The matter came up briefly at the 1980 ALI meeting, which considered Tentative Draft 1, and Henkin explained his views at length, essentially repeating his prior scholarship and the draft's reporters' notes.[75] At an ASIL meeting two years later, he noted that the "international concern" requirement had been an argument used by opponents of the United States entering human rights treaties, and scoffed at the claim, "as if there could be any doubt about the international concern with human rights or the foreign policy interest of the United States

[73] Henkin explained:

> I think this goes back, as you all know, to the whole history of the Bricker controversy. The fear was that a treaty would be used not for an international agreement but to what you might call a 'mock treaty.' You get some ambassador to sign something with you which has nothing to do with foreign policy or even international relations, but you go through the formality of a treaty when it is not a treaty. The difference is that the international concern concept was deemed to mean that certain subjects cannot be the subject of a treaty. We reject that. We were trying to take care of that hypothetical case, of the mock treaty, while making clear that anything can be the subject of a treaty if it is bona fide, if it has a foreign relations purpose. We were trying to take care of that hypothetical case, of the mock treaty, while making clear that anything can be the subject of a treaty if it is bona fide, if it has a foreign relations purpose.

57 ALI PROC., *supra* note 67, at 101.

[74] THIRD RESTATEMENT, *supra* note 1, § 302, cmt. c.

[75] Henkin explained:

> The old Restatement had picked up the suggestion that a treaty must deal with a matter of 'international concern.' Nobody quite knows what that means. But it has sometimes been interpreted, at least polemically, as meaning that there are some subjects on which you cannot make a treaty even though they are related to your foreign relations, and United States policy is to make some agreement with a foreign country on the subject. We think there never was any such rule. We think Charles Evans Hughes, to whom it is attributed, in a speech off the cuff at a meeting in Washington, never meant to articulate such a rule, and that to enshrine it in black letter is only to create confusion. There have been no cases which have made that point.

57 ALI PROC., *supra* note 67, at 98–9. While there was brief discussion about the nature of this important change, no participant voiced objections. The entire discussion takes up three pages in the ALI Proceedings. *Ibid.* at 98–101.

in that subject."[76] In any case, Henkin reported, eliminating the "matter of international concern" requirement had been supported by "our advisors, the ALI Council and the Institute."[77]

The first Preliminary Draft also contained a black-letter affirmation of the rule in *Missouri v. Holland*[78] that the United States could enter into an agreement "without regard to whether the Federal Government has power to deal with it under any constitutionally delegated power other than the treaty power."[79] A comment elaborated that "the Tenth Amendment reserving to the several states the powers not delegated to the United States does not limit the power to make treaties."[80] While subsequent drafts eliminated the Tenth Amendment issue from the black-letter provisions, the quoted sentence from Comment a remained and appears as comment d to the final version of Section 302. There was virtually no discussion of the issue at ALI meetings and none at the ASIL panels.

2 Treaty form

The first Preliminary Draft adopted the so-called interchangeability thesis that any topic legitimately the subject of an Article II treaty could also be addressed by a Congressional-Executive Agreement.[81] As a comment to that article explained, "[s]ince any agreement concluded as a Congressional-Executive agreement can also be concluded by treaty, the two methods are surely available alternatives in some cases; the prevailing view is that the Congressional-Executive Agreement can be used in all cases."[82] This view remained intact throughout the drafting process and, with some elaboration, entered the final draft.[83]

One prominent ALI member objected to the interchangeability thesis at the 1980 meeting, but Henkin was unmoved and no further discussion ensued.[84] The issue was not raised at the ASIL meetings.

As for sole executive agreements, Preliminary Draft 1 provided that "[a]n international agreement without reference to a treaty or act of Congress may deal with any matter that falls within the independent powers of the President under the Constitution."[85] Subsequent drafts involved progressively greater efforts to define the permissible scope of

76 76 ASIL PROC., *supra* note 6, at 188–9. 77 *Ibid.* at 189.
78 Missouri v. Holland, 252 U.S. 416 (1920). 79 Preliminary Draft 1, *supra* note 51, § 305.
80 *Ibid.* cmt. a. 81 Preliminary Draft 1, *supra* note 51, § 307. 82 *Ibid.* § 307, cmt. a.
83 *See* THIRD RESTATEMENT, *supra* note 1, § 303, cmt. e.
84 57 ALI PROC., *supra* note 67, at 106–7, 112 (statement of Dean Gerhard Casper).
85 Preliminary Draft No. 1, *supra* note 51, § 308.

executive agreements, though these efforts reached a natural limit resulting from a lack of case law on the subject. A Reporter's Note to the Preliminary Draft stated simply, "[r]epeated efforts to define the constitutional scope of" sole executive agreements "have not succeeded."[86] The final draft, which combined Section 308 and several related sections into an omnibus Section 303, retained the black letter rule with only minor changes.[87] The final comments to this provision gave several examples of areas frequently the subject of sole executive agreements and concluded that "[t]he great majority of sole executive agreements are of a routine character."[88]

Finally, all drafts provided that sole executive agreements prevail over contrary state law, though the rule migrated from the black letter provisions to a comment in the final draft.[89]

Apart from the brief discussion in the 1980 ALI meeting, there was no further discussion of executive agreements at ALI or ASIL meetings.

3 Reservations

The U.S. law provisions on reservations – in all drafts set out in a single section – were entirely uncontroversial. The first Preliminary Draft provided that if the Senate approved a treaty subject to a reservation or understanding, the President must, if he ratifies the treaty, do so based on the Senate's views.[90] These provisions were accepted in Section 314 of the final draft with only minor changes in wording. A black letter section requiring the President to give effect to the Senate's reservations to Executive Agreements made with

86 *Ibid.* § 308, rptr n. 1.

87 Third Restatement, *supra* note 1, § 303(4) ("the President, on his own authority, may make an international agreement dealing with any mater that falls within his independent powers under the Constitution.").

88 *Ibid.* § 303 cmt g. In response to a suggestion at the 1980 ALI meeting, the Reporters added language on the scope of executive agreements to what became § 311 on "Capacity and Authority to Conclude International Agreements." *See* 57 ALI Proc., *supra* note 67, at 108–9. Mirroring Article 46 of the Vienna Convention, § 311(3) of the final draft provides that a state may only invoke its violation of its own internal law as a basis for vitiating consent to an international obligation if that violation was "manifest." Reporters' Note c noted that "[s]ome agreements, such as the United Nations Charter or the North Atlantic Treaty, are of sufficient formality, dignity, and importance that, in the unlikely event that the President attempted to make such an agreement on his own authority, his lack of authority might be regarded as 'manifest.'"

89 Preliminary Draft 1, *supra* note 51, § 136(2); Third Restatement, *supra* note 1, § 303, cmt. j.

90 Preliminary Draft 1, *supra* note 51, § 323(1) & (2).

congressional approval was moved to the reporter's notes but was unchanged in substance.[91]

4 Treaty interpretation

Early drafts contained seven separate black letter sections on treaty interpretation.[92] Many reproduced portions of the Vienna Convention on the Law of Treaties almost verbatim. These sections were reduced to only two in the final draft, one on interpretation generally, focused mostly on rules of public international law, and one on U.S. law concerning the authority to interpret treaties.[93] But these substantial changes in form involved few changes in substance: many of the Vienna Convention provisions, for example, were moved to comments and reporters notes.

Most importantly, the Preliminary Draft's views on the differences between international tribunals' approaches to treaty interpretation and that of U.S. courts remained consistent. Article 329 of the first Preliminary Draft almost fully reproduced the rules on treaty interpretation in Article 31 of the Vienna Convention. The Reporters described this approach as rather "literal-minded" and observed that U.S. courts instead usually make "the attempt to 'ascertain the meaning intended by the parties' the primary object of interpretation."[94] But the Reporters also noted that while the Vienna Convention on the Law of Treaties and U.S. approaches may differ in their initial points of focus and sources consulted, the "difference in result between the international and the American approaches, however, should not be exaggerated."[95] While intervening drafts substantially limited the black letter language borrowed from the Vienna Convention and, as noted, collapsed many separate sections into two, commentary to final Section 325 agreed that the two approaches to interpretation would differ little in their results.[96]

One area that did change in the drafting process was the autonomy of courts in treaty interpretation. Here the drafters enhanced the primary of Executive

91 *Ibid.* § 323(4); THIRD RESTATEMENT, *supra* note 1, § 314, rptr n. a.

92 *See, e.g.*, Preliminary Draft No. 1, *supra* note 51, §§ 329–35.

93 THIRD RESTATEMENT, *supra* note 1, §§ 325–6.

94 Preliminary Draft No. 1, *supra* note 51, §329, cmt. a.

95 *Ibid.* Henkin remarked at the 1980 ALI Meeting that "despite the differences we describe between the American approach and the European or other approach, it turns out there are not any major differences in result." 57 ALI PROC., *supra* note 67, at 115. *See also* Dalton, *supra* note 66, at 168 ("it seems clear that the [Vienna] Convention's hierarchy of norms approach has had no adverse effect on the interpretive process of U.S. courts.").

96 THIRD RESTATEMENT, *supra* note 1, § 325, cmt. g ("[i]n most cases, the United States approach would lead to the same result" as that reached by an international tribunal).

Branch views but did not fully subordinate judicial interpretations. The Preliminary Draft provided that when interpreting treaties, U.S. courts should give "great weight to an interpretation made by the executive branch."[97] That language was retained in Section 326(2) of the final draft, but was preceded by the statement that "[c]ourts in the United States have final authority to interpret an international agreement for purposes of applying it as law in the United States."[98] That change would seem to reflect an enhanced role for the judiciary vis-á-vis the Executive from that described in previous drafts.

But the reporters also made interpretation by any branch of the U.S. government subject to authoritative international views. The first Tentative Draft (1980) added to a reporters' note the statement that "an interpretation of an agreement to which the United States is a party by an international body within the authority to interpret given that body by the agreement, is binding on the United States and its courts and agencies."[99] That language remained almost verbatim in the final draft.[100] This subordination of U.S. courts to international judicial interpretation of treaties would, of course, be famously rejected by the Supreme Court in the *Sanchez-Llamas* and *Medellin* cases.[101]

F Treaty Issues in Part IX

Remarkably, discussion of claims against the United States for violations of international agreements did not enter the drafting process until the fifth Tentative Draft of April 5, 1984. The version appearing there remained virtually unchanged in the final draft as section 907, which was not discussed at the final meeting.

This section is as notable for what it does not contain as for what it does. It provides that a "private person having rights against the United States under an international agreement may assert those rights in courts in the United States of appropriate jurisdiction either by way of claim or defense."[102] It notes that not all treaties create private rights and that sovereign immunity may pose a substantial hurdle to treaty claims reaching the merits in

97 Preliminary Draft No. 1, *supra* note 51, § 335.

98 Third Restatement, *supra* note 1, § 326(2).

99 Tentative Draft I, *supra* note 58, § 334, rptr n. 1.

100 Third Restatement, *supra* note 1, § 325, rptr n. 4.

101 Sanchez-Llamas v. Oregan, 548 U.S. at 331, 386 (2006); Medellin v. Texas, 552 U.S. 491, 505–11 (2008).

102 Third Restatement, *supra* note 1, § 907(1).

U.S. courts.[103] But the section does not address important procedural obstacles to treaty claims, such as lack of standing, the political question doctrine, etc.[104] Each of these judicially created hurdles had ample grounding in federal law at the time the Restatement was drafted, though none had been addressed by the Second Restatement either.

G *Conclusions: The Drafting Process*

The Third Restatement faced a great many controversial questions in updating and expanding its predecessor document, but the place of treaties in American law was not among them. Even substantial departures from the Second Restatement – such as eliminating the requirement that treaties address "matters of international concern" or affirming the preemptive authority of non-self-executing treaties and sole executive agreements – did not generate meaningful debate or revisions across the many drafts. Indeed, many provisions remained intact from their substance (if not always in their form) from the first drafts of 1979 until the final draft of 1986.

II RECEPTION OF THE RESTATEMENT IN FEDERAL AND STATE CASE LAW

A *Introduction*

In the roughly ten-year period following the publication of the Third Restatement, federal and state courts making express reference to the Restatement's treaty rules treated its provisions as highly persuasive authority. To be sure, courts were sometimes moved to highlight the Restatement's status as scholarly commentary rather than as a primary source of international law.[105] Notwithstanding occasional protestations that Restatement assertions – especially in the Comments and Reporters' Notes – represented efforts at progressive development rather than articulations of existing law, virtually all courts during this period accepted the Restatement's provisions as a guide to the prevalent approaches to treaty law. This positive treatment took a variety

103 *Ibid.*, cmt. a.

104 These and other procedural hurdles are discussed at length in Chapter 8.

105 *See, e.g.* United States v. Yunis. 327 F.2d 56, 99 (2d Cir. 2003) ("The Third Restatement, a kind of treatise or commentary, is not a primary source of authority upon which, standing alone, courts may rely for propositions of customary international law.").

of forms, from citation as sole definitive authority to citation as one of many authorities to quoting provisions extensively.[106]

Given the issue-specific nature of case law, there was seldom occasion for courts to address sweepingly the Restatement's treatment of the reception of treaties in U.S. law. Few, if any, courts entertained frontal challenges to the Restatement's treaty rules and weighed them against alternative readings of U.S. foreign relations law. The Restatement's subordinate status as legal authority most frequently led its provisions to be cited as part of a string of authorities, rather than emphasized as dispositive.[107] Courts did, however, make specific references to the Restatement in sorting out some of the more fraught treaty law issues.

The discussion below draws on a survey of decisions by federal and state courts that refer directly to the Restatement's treaty law sections.[108] The survey did not include decisions that address the substance of treaty issues covered by the Third Restatement but do not cite the Restatement itself.[109] Because I seek to understand whether courts regarded these sections as accurately embodying the law of the time, the inquiry is limited to cases decided in the ten years

[106] *See, e.g.*, U.S. v. Rezaq, 134 F.3d 112 (C.A.D.C. 1998) (citing Restatement §111 without comment); U.S. v. Caro–Quintero, 745 F.Supp. 599 (C.D. Cal. 1990) (extensive citation to Restatement on question of self-execution); In re AEG Acquisition Corp., 127 B.R. 34 (C.D. Cal. Bkrtcy Ct. 1991) (citation to §111 and its comment h as sole authority for legal propositions); Yapp v. Reno, 26 F.3d 1562 (11th Cir. 1994) (quoting several Restatement provisions on issue of treaty interpretation).

[107] *See, e.g.*, United States v. Davis, 767 F.2d 1025 (2d Cir. 1985); Barapind v. Reno, 72 F.Supp. 2d 1132 (E.D. Cal. 1999); Grynberg Production Corp. v. British Gas, 817 F.Supp. 1338 (E.D. Tex. 1993); U.S. v. Noriega, 808 F.Supp. 791 (S.D. Fla. 1992); Domingues v. State, 114 Nev. 783, 961 P.2d 1279 (Nev. 1998).

[108] The following search was performed in Westlaw's All State & Federal library: adv: "third restatement of foreign relations" OR restatement /s "foreign relations." The results were then narrowed for the relevant time period of May 14, 1987 (the publication date of the Third Restatement) to May 14, 1997. The results included a large number of "false hits," such as where the page number of a case cited within an opinion was the same as the Restatement section sought or where the opinion cited the Second and not Third Restatement. These were eliminated from the final results.

[109] Cases that do not cite the Restatement's treaty rules but agree with the substance of those rules are obviously not evidence of disagreement with the rules. Cases not citing the Restatement but which *do* disagree with the substance of its treaty rules might be understood as specifically rejecting those rules. But such a conclusion is at best conjecture. Courts might fail to cite the Restatement for any number of reasons, none of which can be ascertained with any certainty. One reason might be that it was never briefed by the parties. Another might be that courts felt no need to engage with a contrary source that carried no binding authority, much in the way that a lower federal court might not feel compelled to engage with every other lower federal court that disagrees with its legal conclusions on an issue not yet addressed by the Supreme Court. In my view, such "omission" cases do not present clear evidence of a court's view of Restatement sections one way or another.

following the Third Restatement's publication.[110] Later cases might criticize the Restatement as inaccurate because of developments substantially postdating its publication.

These decisions reveal little, if any criticism of the Restatement's U.S. treaty law provisions. The survey yielded a total of thirty state and federal cases citing sections relevant to international agreements decided in the ten years following the Restatement's publication.[111] Only one opinion directly questioned the Restatement's fidelity to U.S. law on treaties – Justice Scalia's 1989 concurring opinion in *United States v. Stuart*.[112] The rest of the citations were supportive.

The discussion that follows will not attempt to analyze all judicial decisions that make passing reference to the Restatement treaty rules, let alone to all cases dealing with the subject matter underlying those rules. Instead of such a frankly tedious effort to lay out all the evidence for a negative proposition – that virtually no state or federal courts pushed-back against the treaty provisions themselves – this section will discuss some of the more notable judicial reactions to the major treaty law issues addressed in depth by later chapters in this volume.

B *Judicial Treatment of Selected Restatement Topics*

1 Self-execution

Courts have used the Restatement as a guide to the distinction between self-executing and non-self-executing treaty provisions.[113] In so doing, courts upheld the effectiveness of non-self-executing declarations attached to instruments of ratification, as specified in § 111(4) (b).[114]

110 There were several areas of treaty law in which there were no reported decisions in the ten-year period. In these instances, I discuss cases decided after 1997.

111 These are §§ 111–15, 301–3, 311–314, 321–6, 331–9, 703, 713, 906–7. The cases under each section are cited in the relevant subject-matter discussion below. I note here three cases that referred to Restatement sections dealing with pure international treaty law: Greenpeace, Inc. (U.S.A.) v. State of France, 946 F. Supp. 773, 783 (1996) (§ 713 on remedies for injury to nationals of other states); Ilva U.S., Inc. v. M/V BOTIC, 1992 WL 296562, 1993 A.M.C. 240 (§ 323 on successive international agreements); Trans-Orient Marine Corp. v. Star Trading & Marine, Inc., 731 F. Supp. 619, 623 (S.D.N.Y. 1990) (§ 336 on fundamental change of circumstances).

112 United States v. Stuart, 489 U.S. 353 (1989).

113 *See, e.g.*, In re Erato, 2 F.3d 11, 15 (2nd Cir. 1993); U.S. v. Caro–Quintero, 745 F. Supp. at 606; Rainbow Nav., Inc. v. Department of Navy, 686 F. Supp. 354, 357 (D.D.C. 1988); Com. v. Judge, 591 Pa. 126, 146, 916 A.2d 511 (Pa. 2007).

114 § 111 was cited by the following courts: Comm. of U.S. Citizens Living in Nicaragua v. Reagan, 859 F. 2d 929 (D.C. Cir. 1988); In re AEG Acquisition Corp., 127 B.R. 34 (Bankr. C.D. Cal. 1991; In re Erato, 2 F. 3d at 11; United States v. Noriega, 808 F. Supp 791 (S.D. Fla.

Thus, in *Buell v. Mitchell*,[115] an appeal from the denial of a *habeas corpus* petition in a death penalty case, the Sixth Circuit relied on the Restatement in declining even to entertain challenges to the death penalty predicated on U.S. obligations under the International Covenant on Civil and Political Rights (ICCPR):

> [E]ven if the agreements were to ban the imposition of the death penalty, neither is binding on federal courts. 'Courts in the United States are bound to give effect to international law and to international agreements, except that a 'non-self-executing' agreement will not be given effect as law in the absence of necessary authority.' Restatement (Third) of Foreign Relations Law § 111 (1987). Neither the American Declaration nor the International Covenant is self-executing, nor has Congress enacted implementing legislation for either agreement.[116]

The *Buell* court did not dwell on the reason for the ICCPR's non-self-executing status: the non-self-executing declaration attached to the instrument of ratification.[117] The authoritativeness of such a declaration has not gone unquestioned. In his dissenting opinion in the First Circuit's decision in *Igartua-de la Rosa v. United States*,[118] Judge Howard, though himself making extensive use of the Restatement, opined that "a declaration by the Senate that a treaty is non-self-executing should not be dispositive," and that before reaching a conclusion on the point, "a court must conduct an independent and searching inquiry into the treaty's purpose."[119] He therefore would have preferred to "permit the parties to develop a record concerning the ICCPR."[120] This counterpoint to the Restatement approach, however, has never gained traction in the federal courts.

In regard to the determination of whether a treaty provision should be deemed self-executing in the absence of a declaration, a Restatement Reporters' Note indicates a presumption in favor of self-executing status, as follows:

1992). Relatedly, § 112 ("Determination and Interpretation of International Law: Law of the United States") was cited by Grynberg Prod. Corp. v. British Gas, P.L.C., 817 F. Supp. at 1338, and §114 ("Interpretation of Federal Statute in Light of International Law or Agreement") was cited by United States v. Vasquez- Velasco, 15 F. 3d 833 (9th Cir. 1994).

[115] Buell v. Mitchell, 274 F.3d 337 (6th Cir. 2001). [116] *Ibid.* at 372.

[117] 138 Cong. Rec. S4781, S4784 (daily edn., Apr. 2, 1992).

[118] Igartua-de la Rosa v. United States., 417 F.3d 145, 184–92 (1st Cir. 2005) (en banc) (Howard, J., dissenting).

[119] *Ibid.* at 189. This assessment was shared by one other member of the *en banc* court, Judge Torruella. *Ibid.* at 174.

[120] *Ibid.* at 192.

> [I]f the Executive Branch has not requested implementing legislation and Congress has not enacted such legislation, there is a strong presumption that the treaty has been considered self-executing by the political branches, and should be considered self-executing by the courts. (This is especially so if some time has elapsed since the treaty has come into force.)[121]

A few District Courts commented favorably on this language; the court in *Seguros Commercial American v. Hall* applied this "strong presumption."[122] Yet also in keeping with the Restatement (§ 907, comment a), the court denied that any presumption of private right of action under the treaty followed from the treaty's self-executing status.[123] This latter point has been emphasized in Court of Appeals decisions that have also cited the relevant Restatement provision.[124]

2 Effect of treaties on inconsistent state law

As noted above, *Buell v. Mitchell* refused to entertain a challenge to a state's death penalty statute on the basis of a non-self-executing treaty.[125] Thus, in keeping with the terms of the Restatement, the court considered the Supremacy Clause not to be implicated where the treaty provision was non-self-executing. Other courts faced with conflicts between self-executing treaties and state acts followed the Restatement rule and found the treaty dispositive.[126]

There remains a question of whether state courts themselves might render a non-self-executing treaty operative in state law. In *Kazi v. Dubai Petroleum Co.*,[127] the Texas Court of Appeals allowed an Indian national to bring a wrongful death action as a result of the mutuality of the obligations

121 Third Restatement, *supra* note 1, § 111, rptr n. 5.

122 Seguros Commercial American v. Hall, 115 F. Supp. 2d 1371, 1378 (M.D. Fla. 2000); *see also* McKesson Corporation v. Islamic Republic of Iran, 1997 U.S. Dist. LEXIS 8903, at 45 (D.D.C. 1997); Rainbow Nav., Inc. v. Dep't of Navy, 686 F.Supp. at 357 (citing presumption as described in Second Restatement Foreign Relations (Revised) Tentative Draft No. 1 (1980) § 131).

123 *Ibid.* at 1378. U.S. v. Marcos, 1990 WL 20160, at *7 (S.D.N.Y. 1990) also cited comment a to § 907 for the same proposition.

124 *See, e.g.*, United States v. Li, 206 F.3d 56, 67 (1st Cir. 2000) (en banc); United States v. Emuegbunam, 268 F.3d 377, 389 (6th Cir. 2001).

125 274 F.3d at 372.

126 *See* United States v. Palestine Liberation Org., 695 F. Supp. 1456, 1465 (S.D.N.Y. 1988); United States v. Georgescu, 723 F. Supp. 912, 921 (E.D.N.Y. 1989); In re Erato, 2 F.3d at 15.

127 Kazi v. Dubai Petroleum Co., 961 S.W.2d 313 (Tex. App. 1997).

of United States and India under the ICCPR. Citing the Restatement, the court acknowledged that non-self-executing treaty provisions "are not transformed into federal law by virtue of the Supremacy Clause" and of their own force establish no enforceable individual rights.[128] However, the court reasoned:

> [P]laintiff herein is not basing her action on a treaty between India and the United States but on a Texas statute: Tex. Civ. Prac. & Remedies Code Sec. 71.031(a). Since she is 'a citizen of another country,' she can only bring an action for wrongful death or personal injury under that statute if 'the (her) country has equal treaty rights with the United States on behalf of its citizens,' *ibid.* §71.031(a)(3).[129]

In the court's view, these "equal treaty rights" of Indian nationals were already being implemented by general U.S. law, without need for implementing legislation, and therefore the necessary treaty rights existed within the meaning of the pertinent Texas statute.[130] By this rationale, the court, while never contradicting the Restatement, found a means by which the non-self-executing treaty provision could be made effective through the vehicle of existing Texas law. The relevant ICCPR provision thus does not override, but rather activates, a provision of state law.

3 Treaties and inconsistent federal law

The last-in-time rule was among the least controversial of the Third Restatement's provisions, producing routine and uncritical citation by courts.[131] In *Committee of U.S. Citizens Living in Nicaragua v. Reagan*,[132] the District of Columbia Circuit determined that a federal statute authorizing military assistance to Nicaragua insurgents could not be invalidated on the basis of a decision against the United States by the International Court of Justice (ICJ), notwithstanding the U.S. obligation under Article 94 of the United Nations Charter to abide by the ICJ's decision. Without need of express reference to the Restatement, the court held that the relationship between the funding authorization and the Charter obligation was governed

128 *Ibid.* at 317. 129 *Ibid.* at 317. 130 *Ibid.* at 318.

131 *See generally* In re Erato, 2 F.3d at 15; Boureslan v. Aramco, 857 F.2d 1014, 1023 (5th Cir. 1988); United States v. Georgescu, 723 F. Supp. 912, 921 (E.D.N.Y. 1989); Am. Tel. & Tel. Co. v. M/V Cape Fear, 763 F. Supp. 97, 108 (D.N.J. 1991); In re Korean Air Lines Disaster, 814 F. Supp. 599, 604 (S.D.N.Y. 1993).

132 Comm. of U.S. Citizens Living in Nicaragua v. Reagan, 859 F. 2d at 929.

by the last-in-time rule[133] and further determined that Article 94 did not by its terms confer individual rights.[134]

The court then considered whether the Charter obligation of adherence to ICJ judgments qualified as a peremptory norm, a designation that hypothetically might, the court suggested (without deciding), establish for the obligation a higher rank in the hierarchy of domestic law. Citing Restatement § 331 comment e, the court noted that "doctrine of *jus cogens* is of such 'uncertain scope' that a 'domestic court should not on its own authority refuse to give effect to an agreement on the ground that it violates a peremptory norm.'"[135] This note of caution supported the court's conclusion that even if a *jus cogens* norm would have the effect of invalidating a later-in-time statute – a question postponed to another day – disobedience to an ICJ judgment did "not generate the level of universal disapprobation" to qualify as a *jus cogens* violation.[136]

4 The scope of international agreements

Whereas the Second Restatement had characterized the constitutional authority to conclude treaties as conditioned on the international agreement pertaining to a matter "of international concern,"[137] as discussed, the Third Restatement designedly rejected this condition.[138] While courts rarely mentioned this question in the Restatement's aftermath, the Second Circuit had occasion to address the issue in its 1997 decision in *United States. v. Lue*.[139]

133 *Ibid.* at 936 ("treaties and statutes enjoy equal status and therefore that inconsistencies between the two must be resolved in favor of the lex posterior"); *cf.* THIRD RESTATEMENT, *supra* note 1, § 115 ("An act of Congress supersedes an earlier . . . provision of an international agreement as law of the United States if the purpose of the act to supersede the earlier rule or provision is clear or if the act and the earlier rule or provision cannot be fairly reconciled . . ."). § 115 was favorably cited by Footwear Distributors & Retailers of Am. v. United States, 852 F. Supp. 1078 (Ct. Int'l Trade); United States v. Noriega, 808 F. Supp. 791; United States v. Palestine Liberation Org., 695 F. Supp. 1456.

134 Comm. of U.S. Citizens Living in Nicaragua v. Reagan, 859 F. 2d at 938.

135 *Ibid.* at 941.

136 *Ibid.* at 942. § 331 was also favorably cited by Comm. of U.S. Citizens Living in Nicaragua v. Reagan, 859 F. 2d 929; First Fid. Bank, N.A. v. Gov't of Antigua & Barbuda–Permanent Mission, 877 F.2d 189 (2d Cir. 1989).

137 SECOND RESTATEMENT, *supra* note 12, § 117(1) (Constitution conveys the power "to make an international agreement if (a) the matter is of international concern . . .")

138 THIRD RESTATEMENT, *supra* note 1, § 302, cmt. c. ("Contrary to what was once suggested, the Constitution does not require that an international agreement deal only with 'matters of international concern.'")

139 United States. v. Lue, 134 F.3d 79 (2nd Cir. 1997). *Lue* is the only reported decision in the ten years after the Restatement's publication citing Section 302, comment h, and addressing the

In *Lue*, the defendant had been convicted under the Hostage Taking Act[140] – a statute implementing the Hostage Taking Convention[141] – for an attempted abduction that was purely domestic and nonpolitical in nature. The defendant contended that the Convention, in regulating such matters, exceeded the scope of the treaty power. The court rejected this contention as too heavily reliant "on a dichotomy between matters of purely domestic concern and those of international concern, a dichotomy appropriately criticized by commentators in the field," invoking verbatim a comment to §302 of the Third Restatement:

> Contrary to what was once suggested, the Constitution does not require that an international agreement deal only with 'matters of international concern.' The references in the Constitution presumably incorporate the concept of treaty and of other agreements in international law. International law knows no limitations on the purpose or subject matter of international agreements, other than that they may not conflict with a peremptory norm of international law. States may enter into an agreement on any matter of concern to them, and international law does not look behind their motives or purposes in doing so. Thus, the United States may make an agreement on any subject suggested by its national interests in relations with other nations.[142]

The court further noted that where a treaty is constitutionally valid, the Necessary and Proper Clause validates legislation that is "plainly adapted" to the treaty's implementation. The court determined that this standard requires only "that the effectuating legislation bear a rational relationship to a permissible constitutional end … The Act here plainly bears a rational relationship to the Convention; indeed, it tracks the language of the Convention in all material respects."[143]

"matters of international concern" question. § 302 was also favorably cited by Fernandez v. Fernandez, 208 Conn. 329. Relatedly, § 301, defining an "international agreement" was favorably cited by First Fid. Bank, N.A. v. Gov't of Antigua & Barbuda–Permanent Mission, 877 F.2d at 189; Von Dardel v. Union of Soviet Socialist Republics, 736 F. Supp. 1 (D.D.C. 1990); In re Manuel P., 215 Cal. App. 3d 48, 263 Cal. Rptr. 447 (Ct. App. 1989); and Wolf v. Fed. Republic of Germany, No. 93 C 7499, 1995 WL 263471 (N.D. Ill. May 1, 1995).

140 Hostage Taking Act, Pub. L. No. 98–473, 98 Stat. 1837, *codified at* 18 U.S.C. § 1203 (1984).

141 International Convention Against the Taking of Hostages, Dec. 17, 1979, 1316 UNTS 205, T.I.A.S. No. 11081, 18 ILM 1456 (1979).

142 Lue, 134 F.3d at 83, *quoting* Third Restatement, *supra* note 1, § 302, cmt. c.

143 *Ibid.* at 84. Questions about the scope of the treaty power under United States law do not implicate an agreement's binding force in international law. Restatement § 321 on the "Binding Force of [an] Agreement" was favorably cited by Footwear Distributors & Retailers of Am. v. United States, 852 F. Supp. at 1078 . Relatedly, one court favorably cited § 324 on the "Effect of [an] International Agreement for Non-Party States." Carbotrade SpA v. Bureau Veritas, No. 92 CIV. 1459 (RPP), 1992 WL 367133 (S.D.N.Y. Nov. 20, 1992).

5 Treaty form

The Restatement asserted as the "prevailing view . . . that the Congressional-Executive agreement can be used as an alternative to the treaty method in every instance."[144] The issue rarely arose in the decade after the Restatement, with only two reported cases citing the Restatement, both favorably.[145]

In *Ntakirutimana v. Reno*,[146] the Fifth Circuit upheld the surrender of a criminal suspect to the International Criminal Tribunal for Rwanda (ICTR) pursuant to a Congressional-Executive Agreement. Ntakirutimana argued that by not requiring an Article II treaty, the court below had "read the treaty-making power out of the Constitution."[147] The Court of Appeals, in rejecting this assertion, quoted a comment to Restatement § 303 as follows: "Which procedure should be used is a political judgment, made in the first instance by the President, subject to the possibility that the Senate might refuse to consider a joint resolution of Congress to approve an agreement, insisting that the President submit the agreement as a treaty."[148]

In *Made in the USA Foundation v. United States*, the Eleventh Circuit, faced with a challenge to the constitutionality of the North American Free Trade Agreement, held that "with respect to international commercial agreements such as NAFTA, the question of just what constitutes a 'treaty' requiring Senate ratification presents a nonjusticiable political question."[149] In support of its holding, the court quoted favorably a Restatement Reporters' Note observing that "Congressional-Executive agreements have in fact been made on a wide variety of subjects, and no such agreement has ever been effectively challenged as improperly concluded."[150]

144 Third Restatement, *supra* note 1, § 303, cmt. e.

145 The District Court in the *Made in the USA* case also cited the interchangeability thesis in § 303, comment e. Made in the USA Found. v. United States, 56 F. Supp. 2d 1226, 1292–3 (N.D. Ala. 1999).

146 Ntakirutimana v. Reno, 184 F.3d 419 (5th Cir. 1999). 147 *Ibid.* at 427.

148 *Ibid.* (quoting Third Restatement, *supra* note 1, § 303, cmt. e).The dissent expressly rejected this position: "If the Treaty Clause is to have any meaning there is some variety of agreements which must be accomplished through the formal Article II process. Otherwise, the heightened consideration dictated by Article II could be avoided by the President and a majority of Congress simply by substituting the label of 'executive agreement' for that of 'treaty.'" *Ibid.* at 435–6 (DeMoss, J., dissenting). § 303 was favorably cited by New York Chinese TV Programs, Inc. v. U.E. Enterprises, Inc., No. 88CIV.4170(JMW)(KAR), 1989 WL 22442 (S.D.N.Y. Mar. 8, 1989).

149 Made in the USA Foundation v. United States, 242 F.3d 1300, 1302 (11th Cir. 2001) *cert. den. sub nom.* United Steelworkers of America, AFL-CIO, CLC v. United States, 534 U.S. 1039 (2001).

150 *Ibid.* at 1305 n.12 (quoting Third Restatement, *supra* note 1, § 303, rptr n. 8).

6 Reservations and understandings

In keeping with the Restatement, Understandings attached by the Senate to the instrument of ratification have been held to govern a treaty's interpretation in U.S. courts.[151] In *Auguste v. Ridge*,[152] the Third Circuit, in applying the Torture Convention's implementing legislation, the Foreign Affairs Reform and Restructuring Act (FARRA),[153] declined to offer protection from extradition under the Convention Against Torture to a Haitian national convicted of drug offenses in the United States. In assessing the contention that the conditions of the Haitian prisons constituted torture under the Convention (CAT) and FARRA, the court looked to the Understanding attached to the instrument of CAT ratification, which stated that "in order to constitute torture, an act must be specifically intended to inflict severe physical or mental pain or suffering."[154]

The court rejected the petitioner's alternative interpretation of the Convention standard. "Auguste's claim that a specific intent standard is in conflict with what he perceives to be the prevailing international consensus," the court held, "misses the point." Notwithstanding concern for "the shared expectations of the contracting parties," the court insisted that "where the President and the Senate express a shared consensus on the meaning of a treaty as part of the ratification process, that meaning is to govern in the domestic context."[155] The court explained:

> We find support for this position in the Restatement (Third) of the Foreign Relations Law of the United States, a persuasive authority. Section 314(2) of the Restatement states: When the Senate gives its advice and consent to a treaty on the basis of a particular understanding of its meaning, the President, if he makes the treaty, must do so on the basis of the Senate's understanding. *See* Restatement (Third) of the Foreign Relations Law of the United States § 314 (2004). Comment d to § 314 further states: 'A treaty that is ratified or acceded to by the United States with a statement of understanding becomes effective in domestic law subject to that understanding.' *See* § 314 cmt. d. Thus, we hold that, for purposes of domestic law, the understanding proposed by the President and adopted by the Senate in

[151] A number of federal courts favorably cited the Restatement's general provision on treaty interpretation, § 325. One court favorably cited § 326 on the "Authority to Interpret [an] International Agreement: Law of the United States." *See* Juda v. United States, 13 Cl. Ct. 667 (1987).

[152] Auguste v. Ridge, 395 F.3d 123 (3d Cir. 2005).

[153] Foreign Affairs Reform and Restructuring Act ("FARRA"), Pub. L. No. 105–227, Div. G., Title XXII, § 2242, 112 Stat. 2681, 2681–822, codified as note to 8 U.S.C. § 1231 (2012).

[154] 136 CONG. REC. S17, 486, S17491–2 (daily ed. 1990).

[155] Auguste, 395 F.3d at 143.

> its resolution of ratification are the binding standard to be applied in domestic law.[156]

This Restatement section led other circuits to reach the same conclusion.[157]

7 Treaty interpretation

The most significant controversy to arise within the federal courts directly over the Third Restatement's treaty law provisions concerned interpretive method. At issue was the role extrinsic evidence can properly play in the interpretation of treaty provisions that, on their face, are unambiguous in their application to the facts at hand. In *United States v. Stuart*,[158] the Supreme Court adopted the Restatement's inclusive approach, over Justice Scalia's vigorous objection in his separate concurrence.

In *Stuart*, a double taxation treaty between the United States and Canada obligated the Internal Revenue Service to supply to its Canadian counterpart requested taxpayer information that the IRS is "in a position to obtain under [U.S.] revenue laws."[159] The taxpayer contended that because the IRS "would not be able, under American law, to issue an administrative summons to gather information for use by the Government once a Justice Department referral was in effect, the IRS is not in a position to obtain such information once Canadian authorities have reached a corresponding stage in their investigation."[160] Both the majority and the concurrence rejected the taxpayer respondent's analogical reasoning, noting that the treaty's text did not call for any such limitation by analogy.

The dueling opinions, however, took different positions on what evidence, beyond the treaty text, could properly be brought to bear on the question. The majority went on to note that "[n]ontextual sources that often assist us in 'giving effect to the intent of the Treaty parties' . . . such as a treaty's ratification history and its subsequent operation, further fail to sustain respondents' claim," citing with respect to ratification history the Committee Report and the "brief floor debate in the Senate."[161] The Court justified the invocation of these materials as follows:

156 *Ibid.* at 142.

157 *See* Pierre v. Attorney General, 528 F.3d 180, 187 (3d Cir. 2008) (citing *Auguste* as authority for following the Restatement in this regard); Cherichel v. Holder, 591 F.3d 1002, 1012 (8th Cir. 2010) (same).

158 United States v. Stuart, 489 U.S. 353 (1989).

159 Convention between the United States and Canada Respecting Double Taxation, Mar. 4, 1942, 56 Stat. 1405–6, T. S. No. 983, Art. XIX.

160 United States v. Stuart, 489 U.S. at 404.

161 *Ibid.* at 405.

> Nor is reliance on the Senate's preratification debates and reports improper. As Justice Scalia acknowledges, the American Law Institute's most recent Restatement counsels consideration of such materials. See Restatement (Third) of Foreign Relations Law of the United States § 314, Comment d (1987) ("indication that ... the Senate ascribed a particular meaning to the treaty is relevant"); *ibid.*, § 325, Reporters' Note 5 ("A court ... is required to take into account ... (i) Committee reports, debates, and other indications of meaning that the legislative branch has attached to an agreement ...")[162]

Justice Scalia objected that "using every string to one's bow in this fashion has unfortunate implications," namely the suggestion that "*had* the extrinsic evidence contradicted the plain language of the Treaty it would govern."[163] Moreover, even if the treaty's language were to be deemed ambiguous, use of the Senate's preratification debates and reports rather than the negotiating record would be, in Justice Scalia's view, "rather like determining the meaning of a bilateral contract between two corporations on the basis of what the board of directors of one of them thought it meant when authorizing the chief executive officer to conclude it."[164] Justice Scalia dismissed the majority's invocation of the Restatement as follows:

> The American Law Institute's Restatement of the Foreign Relations Law of the United States would permit the courts to refer to materials of the sort at issue here. See Restatement (Third) of Foreign Relations Law of the United States § 314, Comment d (1987); *ibid.*, § 325, Reporter's Note 5. But despite the title of the work, this must be regarded as a proposal for change rather than a restatement of existing doctrine, since the commentary refers to not a single case, of this or any other United States court, that has employed the practice.[165]

Although Justices Kennedy and O'Connor, finding the treaty text fully dispositive, would have stopped short of the majority's resort to extratextual sources, neither saw fit to join Justice Scalia's concurrence. Moreover, as Detlev Vagts, one of the Third Restatement's associate reporters, subsequently pointed out in a rather sharp response to the Scalia concurrence, the Restatement position on the use of Senate preratification materials actually had considerable grounding in Supreme Court precedent.[166]

162 *Ibid.* at 405 n. 7. 163 *Ibid.* at 372 (Scalia, J., concurring). 164 *Ibid.*at 374.

165 *Ibid.* at 375.

166 *See* Detlev F. Vagts, *Senate Materials and Treaty Interpretation: Some Research Hints for the Supreme Court*, 83 AM. J. INT'L L. 546, 547–8 (1989) (referring to cases decided before

C *Conclusions: The Restatement as Persuasive Authority for U.S. Courts*

Although U.S. courts' reception of the Third Restatement's treaty law provisions as a whole does not admit of a comprehensive generalization, it is fair to say that courts in the ensuing period made considerable use of the Restatement as persuasive authority in this area, sometimes relying principally on its provisions and otherwise invoking it as further support for a proposition independently established by case law. Opinions calling into question the relationship between the Restatement approach and existing U.S. law were relative rarities, and outright judicial rejections of the Restatement's treatment of treaties are difficult to find.

III SCHOLARLY RECEPTION OF THE RESTATEMENT

A *Introduction*

The Restatement's reception by scholars was mostly unremarkable. Scholars by in large supported the Restatement as a whole, and their invocation of particular provisions largely supported the Restatement's conclusions. As a group of prominent European scholars (one of the rare overall assessments of the undertaking) indicated in their joint review of the project:

> In general, the statements in the Restatement reflect prevailing views and positions, and one can normally be sure that nothing is said that either does not meet the approval of the greater part of the legal community or is totally unacceptable. The negative aspect is that thought-provoking and unfamiliar considerations that raise new questions and put traditional answers in doubt can seldom be found.[167]

Notwithstanding some misgivings about "the national approach to international law,"[168] these reviewers took little exception to the Restatement. Not all commentators, however, were so approving of the nature of the project as a whole. In the words of one of the nation's leading international law scholars of the day, Stefan Riesenfeld of the University of California at Berkeley, "the law of foreign relations seems to be too complex to be subject to a Restatement

publication of the Third Restatement, especially Immigration & Naturalization Service v. Stevic, 467 U.S. 407, 417–18 (1984)).

167 Rudolf Bernhardt, Ulrich Beyerlin, Karl Doehring & Jochen Frowein, RESTATEMENT OF THE LAW THIRD: THE FOREIGN RELATIONS LAW OF THE UNITED STATES, 86 AM. J. INT'L L. 608, 609 (1992) (book review).

168 *Ibid.* at 620.

and the ordinary processes of the American Law Institute and too serious to be left to the generalists."[169]

Although law review articles in the decade following the Restatement's publication most frequently cited the Restatement uncritically as a reflection of established law or predominant jurisprudential opinion, commentators occasionally spoke to the merits of particular Restatement propositions. But few scholars engaged in extensive assessments of whether the treaty rules accurately reflected current law. Although it would be both impractical and unedifying to catalog all of the fragmented references comprehensively, a small sampling of the more extensive scholarly reactions, arranged by topic, follows below.

B *Scholarly Comments on Selected Restatement Topics*

1 Self-execution

The Restatement designates three circumstances in which a treaty may be non-self-executing: manifest unilateral intention of the United States, the attachment of a non-self-executing declaration, or a constitutional requirement of implementing legislation.[170] These qualifications to the Supremacy Clause's apparent conferral upon treaties of direct effect in U.S. courts came in for considerable criticism from some quarters.

Carlos Vazquez objected to the treaty-by-treaty analysis of U.S. intent, on the ground that while international law may not require treaty provisions to be directly effective in court proceedings, the question of U.S. intent cannot be unmoored from the Supremacy Clause: "we are interpreting the provision of the U.S. Constitution by which the Framers determined how the United States would carry out its international treaty obligations."[171] Vazquez, among others, also cast doubt on the capacity of a non-self-executing declaration to

[169] Stefan A. Riesenfeld, THIRD RESTATEMENT OF THE FOREIGN RELATIONS LAW OF THE UNITED STATES, 14 YALE *J.* INT'L L. 455, 467 (1989) (book review).

[170] THIRD RESTATEMENT, *supra* note 1, § 111(4) (treaty non-self-executing (a) if "the agreement manifests an intention that it shall not become effective as domestic law without the enactment of implementing legislation, (b) if the Senate in giving consent to a treaty, or Congress by resolution, requires implementing legislation, or (c) if implementing legislation is constitutionally required.").

[171] Carlos Manuel Vazquez, *The Four Doctrines of Self-Executing Treaties*, 89 AM. J. INT'L L. 695, 707–08 & n. 59 (1995), criticizing § 111 cmt. h, as well as § 314 cmt. d ("A treaty ratified or acceded to by the United States with a statement of understanding becomes effective in domestic law ... subject to that understanding") and § 303 cmt. d (characterizing non-self-executing declarations as "presumably not improper").

control the treaty's domestic legal status in contradiction to the implications of the treaty language itself.[172] And Jordan Paust characterized as a red herring the supposed constitutional requirement that international obligations touching on particular subject matter be given effect only by means of implementing legislation.[173]

On the other hand, the Reporters' Note asserting a presumption in favor of self-executing status for negative obligations – the duty to refrain from particular actions, or to undertake them only as specified – was invoked favorably to support the justiciability of treaty provisions where raised as defenses against governmental action.[174]

2 Effect of treaties on inconsistent state law

There remained ambiguity about the Supremacy Clause implications of the Restatement's assertion that "a 'non-self-executing' agreement will not be given effect as law in the absence of necessary implementation."[175] In particular, there is continuing discord over whether a ratification instrument's declaration of non-self-executing status impedes a treaty from preempting inconsistent provisions of state law. David Sloss argued at length that the Restatement approach to this and related questions was flawed.[176] Contrary to the view expressed by supporters of the non-self-executing declarations that the Senate attached to the ratifications of human rights conventions,[177] Sloss insisted on Supremacy Clause grounds that "the treaty

172 *Ibid.* at 708; *see also* Stefan A. Riesenfeld & Frederick M. Abbott, *The Scope of U.S. Senate Control over the Conclusion and Operation of Treaties*, 67 CHI.-KENT L. REV. 571, 641 (1991) ("The Senate may not legislate outside the confines of the treaty instrument. A declaration inconsistent with the treaty is ineffective as a matter of international and municipal law."); John Quigley, *The International Covenant on Civil and Political Rights and the Supremacy Clause*, 42 DEPAUL L. REV. 1287, 1304 (1993) ("since a qualification statement other than a reservation is not part of the treaty, the Senate's statement was not the 'law of the land'").

173 Jordan Paust, *Self-Executing Treaties*, 82 AM. J. INT'L L. 760, 775 (1988) (rejecting "completely the current insistence that certain treaties are inherently non-self-executing because legislative power exists, for example, to regulate commerce, to define and punish crimes, and to appropriate money").

174 Thomas Michael McDonnell, *Defensively Invoking Treaties in American Courts – Jurisdictional Challenges under the U.N. Drug Trafficking Convention by Foreign Defendants Kidnapped Abroad by U.S. Agents*, 37 WM. & MARY L. REV. 1401, 1428 n.126 (1995–1996) (citing THIRD RESTATEMENT § 111 rptr n. 5).

175 THIRD RESTATEMENT, *supra* note 1, § 111(3).

176 David Sloss, *Non-Self-Executing Treaties: Exposing a Constitutional Fallacy*, 36 U.C. DAVIS L. REV. 1 (2002).

177 *See, e.g.*, Curtis A. Bradley & Jack L. Goldsmith, *Treaties, Human Rights, and Conditional Consent*, 149 U. PA. L. REV. 399, 446–7 (2000).

makers cannot, by means of an NSE declaration, prevent a treaty from invalidating a conflicting state law."[178] Sloss rejected the suggested analogy to "a federal statute [that] specifies that it is not intended to preempt state law"; whereas such a statute "is simply clarifying that Congress chose not to exercise its power of field preemption," the Supremacy Clause imposes "conflict preemption" wherever terms of a treaty are inconsistent with state laws.[179]

3 Treaties and inconsistent federal law

The Restatement's position on the last-in-time rule and other aspects of the role of self-executing treaties in the hierarchy of federal law does not appear to have been controversial. More controversial was the Restatement's assertion of the unilateral Presidential authority, as an incident of the foreign relations power, to terminate a treaty in accordance with its terms.[180] Professor Riesenfeld, though previously of another view, came to embrace the Restatement's conclusion "that the President may act alone, if the treaty provides for termination by denunciation."[181]

4 The scope of international agreements

The issue of a subject-matter limitation on treaties (to "matters of international concern") and its relationship to federalism considerations remains contested. Contrary to the Restatement position, Curtis Bradley deduced from "the core assumptions of the Founders" that the treaty power was understood to be "limited either by subject matter, by the reserved powers of the states, or both."[182] He further invoked the Bricker Amendment debates of the 1950s, during which Secretary of State John Foster Dulles gave assurance that treaties could not reach matters "which do not essentially affect the actions of nations in relation to

[178] Sloss, *supra* note 176, at 42. [179] *Ibid.*

[180] THIRD RESTATEMENT, *supra* note 1, § 339 cmt. a n. 58. *See also* Michael J. Glennon, *The Constitutional Power of the United States Senate to Condition Its Consent to Treaties*, 67 CHI.-KENT L. REV. 533, 557 (1991) (distinguishing Presidential authority to terminate or suspend treaties in accordance with their terms from abrogation, a power not ordinarily regarded as within the President's unilateral authority).

[181] Riesenfeld & Abbott, *supra* note 172, at 584.

[182] Curtis A. Bradley, *The Treaty Power and American Federalism*, 97 MICH. L. REV. 390, 417 (1998–1999). Bradley acknowledged that the Restatement's "rejection of subject-matter limitation on the treaty power now appears to be the accepted view, at least among academic commentators." *Ibid.* at 433.

international affairs, but are purely internal."[183] Bradley thus complained: "In what has become a rather disturbing phenomenon in the development of American foreign affairs law, the new *Third Restatement* position, adopted without authority, is now being treated as if it were black-letter law."[184]

5 Treaty form

A similar complaint of opponents about the unreflective acceptance of the Restatement position could be heard in regard to the project's endorsement of the interchangeability of Article II treaties and Congressional-Executive agreements.[185] As the most elaborate scholarly statement in opposition to the passage of the North American Free Trade Agreement (NAFTA) lamented, "The Restatement expresses the widely prevailing view."[186]

6 Reservations and understandings

One controversy within international law that was touched upon in the Restatement was the severability of invalid reservations. Where a given reservation is deemed to contradict the object and purpose of a multilateral treaty, the offending reservation either vitiates the state's consent to the treaty as a whole or, as some have contended, is properly severed from the ratification

[183] *Ibid.* at 430 (citing Treaties and Executive Agreements: Hearings on S.J. Res. 1 Before a Subcommand. of the Senate Comm. on the Judiciary, 84th Cong. 183 (1955)).

[184] *Ibid.* at 432–3.

[185] THIRD RESTATEMENT, *supra* note 1, § 303(2). *See also ibid.* § 303 cmt. e (elaborating on interchangeability).

[186] Bruce Ackerman & David Golove, Is NAFTA Constitutional?, 108 *HARV. L. REV.* 799, 805 n.12 (1995) (citing LOUIS HENKIN, FOREIGN AFFAIRS AND THE CONSTITUTION 173–6 (1972)); *see also*, Phillip R. Trimble & Jack S. Weiss, *The Role of the President, the Senate and Congress with Respect to Arms Control Treaties Concluded by the United States*, 67 *CHI.-KENT L.REV.* 645, 650–3; Memorandum from Monroe Leigh, Legal Adviser to the State Department (Sept. 24, 1975), reprinted in 121 CONG. REC. 36,718, 36,721 (1975); CONGRESSIONAL RESEARCH SERV., LIBRARY OF CONGRESS, TREATIES AND OTHER INTERNATIONAL AGREEMENTS: THE ROLE OF THE UNITED STATES SENATE 58–9 (Comm. Print 1993). Ackerman and Golove also cited dissenting opinions. *See, e.g.*, THOMAS M. FRANCK & EDWARD WEISBAND, FOREIGN POLICY BY CONGRESS 141–5 (1979); MICHAEL J. GLENNON, CONSTITUTIONAL DIPLOMACY 183 (1990); Memorandum from Michael J. Glennon, Assistant Counsel, Office of the Legislative Counsel, to Sen. Dick Clark (Sept. 24, 1975), *reprinted in* 121 CONG. REC. 36,724, 36,726 (1975). Although acknowledging the interchangeability view as the dominant one since the New Deal, Ackerman and Golove regarded it as historically inauthentic. *See* Ackerrman & Golove, *supra*, at 807 ("Leading critics like Edwin Borchard were on solid ground in emphasizing the gap between older practices and the emerging doctrine of interchangeability").

instrument, with the effect of binding a state to the very obligation which the state had expressly refused to accept. The topic subsequently became the subject of a vigorous 1995 exchange between the State Department Legal Adviser's Office (taking the former position) and the Human Rights Committee established to implement the International Covenant on Civil and Political Rights.[187]

According to the Reporters' Notes, "In some cases it might be argued that, under the rules relating to separability (§ 338, comment e), the impermissible reservation was ineffective and the state is bound by the agreement without that reservation."[188] This view anticipated the Human Rights Committee's position in 1995 and was well-received by the above-mentioned group of European scholars reviewing the Restatement for the *American Journal of International Law* (Bernhardt, *et al.*).[189] Stefan Riesenfeld and Frederick Abbott spoke to this point as follows: "The Restatement view, though perhaps confusing, appears to support the conclusion that only a reservation which is valid and effective under rules of international law is part of a treaty and thus the law of the United States. It is essential that this conclusion be clarified."[190]

7 Treaty interpretation

As noted above, the Restatement invoked favorably the approach to interpretation adopted in Articles 31 and 32 of the Vienna Convention on the Law of Treaties – one that, at least in principle, limits resort to extrinsic evidence of the states parties' intent. This method contrasted with the typical U.S. judicial approach to treaty interpretation, which at that time permitted considerable inquiry into the negotiating record. A Restatement comment warned that although "[i]n most cases, the United States approach would lead to the same result, ... an international tribunal using the approach called for by this section might find the United States interpretation erroneous and United States action pursuant to that interpretation a violation of the agreement."[191]

[187] *See* Human Rights Committee, General Comment 24 (52), U.N. Doc. CCPR/C/21/Rev.1/Add.6 (1994); Letter from Conrad Harper, U.S. State Department Legal Adviser, to Francisco Jose Aguilar-Urbina, Chairman, U.N. Human Rights Committee (Mar. 28–29, 1995), available at www.un.org/documents/ga/docs/50/plenary/a50-40.htm.

[188] Third Restatement, *supra* note 1, § 313, rptr n. 4.

[189] Bernhardt, Beyerlin, Doehring & Frowein, *supra* note 167, at 610–11.

[190] Riesenfeld & Abbott, *supra* note 172, at 597.

[191] Third Restatement, *supra* note 1, § 325, cmt. g.

This observation has drawn favorable comment from scholars seeking to harmonize the U.S. approach with that of international jurists.[192] At the same time, it has been criticized by those partial to the U.S. courts' characteristic methods:

> Unfortunately, the Restatement (Revised) does not accurately describe the current American law or international law of treaty interpretation. Further, section 325 promotes an unnecessarily vague methodology derived from a treaty the Senate has refused to ratify. In light of both the Supreme Court's strong position on the essentials of interpreting international agreements, and the jurisprudential defects in the Restatement's current position, the American Law Institute should reformulate Restatement (Revised) section 325.[193]

Notwithstanding its "internationalist" take on interpretive methods in general (§ 325), the Restatement reflected the U.S. courts' tendency to accord "great weight to an interpretation made by the Executive Branch."[194] Even more provocatively, it posited as binding, for purposes of domestic law, the "particular understanding" of a treaty's meaning on which the Senate's advice and consent was based.[195] These assertions drew predictable criticism from commentators of an internationalist bent.[196]

C Conclusions: The Restatement as a Mainstream Account of the Role of Treaties in U.S. Law

The reactions listed above in no way reflect the full range of scholarly engagements with the positions taken in the Restatement's treaty provisions, but they give some indication of how the Restatement figured in the ensuing debates over the relationship between treaties and U.S. law. By and large, scholars tended to accept the Restatement as a generally accurate account – both

192 *See, e.g.*, Perry S. Bechky, *Mismanagement and Misinterpretation: U.S. Judicial Implementation of the Warsaw Convention in Air Disaster Litigation*, 60 J. AIR L. & COM. 455, 476–7 (1994–1995).

193 James C. Wolf, *Comment: The Jurisprudence of Treaty Interpretation*, 21 U.C. DAVIS L. REV. 1023, 1069 (1987–1988).

194 THIRD RESTATEMENT, *supra* note 1, § 326(2). 195 *Ibid.* § 314(2) & cmt. d.

196 *See, e.g.*, Riesenfeld & Abbott, *supra* note 172, at 608 ("The combined view of the political branches may be close to determinative, but since this view is not part of the express terms of the treaty and is not independent domestic legislation with the force of law, it remains for the courts under Article III of the Constitution to determine the meaning of the treaty in accordance with applicable rules of construction"); Riesenfeld, *supra* note 169, at 461–2 ("a treaty should have the same effect domestically as it has internationally"), 466 ("despite the views expressed in the Restatement, it is questionable whether the Senate can bind the courts by appending an understanding to its resolution of advice and consent").

for better and for worse – of the law as it was and of extrapolations that could be derived with reasonable caution. Indeed, as noted above, critical commentators were less likely to disparage the weight of the Restatement's claims than to complain of the project's influence in consolidating emerging doctrines that they regarded unfavorably. Debates about particular provisions reflected the live controversies about international law and its reception in U.S. law that raged at the time of the Restatement's promulgation, but the Restatement was quintessentially a mainstream project – one almost as likely to be criticized from either side of the typical divide between those more and less friendly to American exceptionalism.

IV CONCLUSIONS

The answer to the question posed by this chapter – whether the treaty rules of the Third Restatement accurately reflected law at the time of its publication – appears to be "yes." With some notable exceptions, the Third Restatement was not undertaken primarily to address perceived deficiencies in the treaty provisions of the Second Restatement. Instead, as ALI officials noted at the time, the project was more a response to new developments (such as the Vienna Convention on the Law of Treaties and the Case Act) since publication of the Second Restatement. The substance of the treaty rules proposed by the Reporters in 1979 at the outset of the drafting process largely survived the seven drafts and multiple public debates to appear in the final document. In the succeeding decade, courts addressing treaty issues were rarely critical of the Restatement and indeed most frequently treated it as a persuasive source to be included in string citations. Not surprisingly, critical comments did appear in academic reactions. But the Restatement provisions subject to scholarly critique were ones in which the law had been in flux for some time and were already the subject of debate. Critical scholarship represented less an indication that the Restatement had ignored or misstated clear law of the period than a dissatisfaction with the Reporters taking a side in ongoing and unresolved debates.

3

Competing Models for Treaty Interpretation

Treaty as Contract, Treaty as Statute, Treaty as Delegation

Paul R. Dubinsky

Americans have been interpreting treaties for more than two centuries. In recent decades, a cottage industry of sorts has arisen among legal scholars seeking to identify patterns in treaty cases and trends that look behind what courts say they are doing when they interpret treaties.[1] This chapter explores what courts actually say that they are doing in interpreting treaties and

With heartfelt thanks to Bethany Berger, Kirsten Carlson, John Dolan, Duncan Hollis, and Mathias Reimann.

[1] This literature is extensive. Recent contributions point to trends based on whether the United States is a party to litigation involving a treaty, see David Sloss, *Judicial Deference to Executive Branch Treaty Interpretations: A Historical Perspective*, [Judicial Deference] 62 N.Y.U. ANN. SURV. AM. L. 497 (2007) (using a sample of nineteen Supreme Court treaty cases from 1789 to 1838) or on whether the agreement at issue is a public law treaty or a private law treaty, *See, e.g.*, Paul B. Stephan, "Treaties in the Supreme Court: 1946–2000," in INTERNATIONAL LAW IN THE SUPREME COURT: CONTINUITY AND CHANGE (David L. Sloss, Michael D. Ramsey & William S. Dodge, eds. 2012) ["CONTINUITY AND CHANGE"] (based on analysis of 130 cases during the period from 1946 to 2000). The late David Bederman concluded that the best explanation of outcomes in treaty cases during the early years of the Rehnquist Court was the position advocated by the Executive branch in its submission to the Supreme Court. *See* David Bederman, *Revivalist Canons and Treaty Interpretation*, [Revivalist Canons] 41 *UCLA L. REV.* 943 (1994). Some years later, Professor Bederman noted that clashes among justices of the Supreme Court with respect to textualism in statutory cases had carried over to treaty interpretation cases. *See* David Bederman, Medellin's *New Paradigm for Treaty Interpretation*, [New Paradigm] 102 AM. *J. INT'L L.* 529 (2008). Very recently, a group of scholars has explored whether broad trends in the "normalization" or "domestication" of foreign relations law explain the outcomes in judicial treaty interpretation. *See* Harlan Grant Cohen, *The Death of Deference and the Domestication of Treaty Law*, 2015 *BYU L. REV.* 1467 (2015); Ganesh Sitaraman and Ingrid Wuerth, *The Normalization of Foreign Relations Law*, 128 HARV. L. REV. 1897 (2015); Curtis A. Bradley, *Foreign Relations and the Purported Shift Away from "Exceptionalism,"* 128 HARV. L. REV. F. 294 (2015); Carlos M. Vazquez, *The Abiding Exceptionalism of Foreign Relations Doctrine*, 128 HARV. L. REV. F. 305 (2015); Stephen I. Vladeck, *The Exceptionalism of Foreign Relations Normalization*, 128 HARV. L. REV. F. 322 (2015).

determining their effects within the legal system of the United States.[2] In particular, this chapter's focus will be on the use of models, analogies, metaphors, and other figures of speech. These have been a mainstay of American judicial treaty discourse continuously from the Founding to the present. The first claim of this chapter is that, for a long period of time, U.S. treaty interpreters making comparisons between treaties and other legal instruments have imported into the American law of treaty interpretation cannons of construction that originated in other bodies of law.[3] This practice began in the earliest years of the Republic and endures up to the present, throughout a range of treaty-making eras, and with varying degrees of success.[4] For most of this period, the dominant analogies have been what will here be referred to as the "treaty-as-contract" and the "treaty-as-statute" models.

This approach to treaty interpretation was never static. Over the span of the nineteenth century, when the treaty-as-contract analogy was dominant, there was a process of continuity and change in employing and explicating these analogies. For present purposes, this chapter makes a second claim about this process of continuity and change; for much of American legal history, change was gradual and largely organic. For American courts in the nineteenth century, there was substance to the treaty-as-contact analogy. Case-by-case interpretation of international agreements was driven, at least in part, by the contemporary understanding of the nature of and the law of private law contracts.

2 Treaties to which the United States is a party have effect within the domestic U.S. legal system and also outside that system. For example, treaties can be the subject of dispute resolution in international tribunals or arbitral bodies, in the context of state-to-state negotiation or litigation in the courts of other countries. Treaty interpretation also plays a role in influencing legislative or executive actions by other countries or by international institutions. The focus of the current effort is limited to the impact of U.S. treaties within the domestic legal system of the United States. That impact can be found in legislative choices made by Congress, in actions by the Executive branch, in adjudicated outcomes in courts, and in action or inaction at the state or municipal level in the shadow of preemption. With such a wide canvas of potential impact by treaties, the present work concentrates on the interpretation of treaties in the context of adjudication within the U.S. and interpretation by the Executive branch.

3 This is not to suggest that employing analogies in treaty interpretation is a uniquely American practice. Comparisons between contract interpretation and treaty interpretation, for example, are common in other legal systems and also in international law. *See generally* Omar M. Dajani, *Contractualism in the Law of Treaties*, 34 MICH. J. INT'L L. 1 (2012).

4 For recent literature on the importance of metaphor and analogy in interpretive method in different fields of law, *see, e.g.*, Vicki Jackson, *Constitutions as "Living Trees"? Comparative Constitutional Law and Interpretive Metaphors*, 75 FORDHAM L. REV. 921 (2006); Thomas W. Joo, *Contract, Property, and the Role of Metaphor in Corporations Law*, 35 U.C. DAVIS L. REV. 779 (2002) (using the "contractarian metaphor" to examine the internal working of the firm); Thomas Ross, *Metaphor and Paradox*, 23 GA. L. REV. 1053 (1989).

That model was dominant for more than a century, by which time a model that conceived of treaties as akin to statutes began to appear with frequency in judicial opinions. For decades, the two models coexisted. Both were adapted organically as the United States accumulated a growing assortment of treaties, as statutes came to play a large role in the domestic legal system and as the law of contracts became systematized in treatises and statutes.

During this era, courts applying one model or the other periodically rejected executive branch treaty interpretations without according them high levels of deference. Courts understood one of their key constitutional roles to be steering the country away from result-oriented and short-term thinking in interpreting international agreements. Judges regarded themselves as guardians of the country's reputation for reliability in international affairs. Another judicial motivation was promoting and then preserving the reputation of American courts as unbiased fora for resolving transnational disputes.

As with the other chapters in this volume, the Third Restatement will serve as this chapter's point of reference. In the years since publication of the Third Restatement, judicial deference to executive branch treaty interpretation has increased. Although such deference already had been on an upward trajectory for decades, the trend not only continued in the 1990s and 2000s; it did so in ways that the Restatement's authors had not anticipated. Most notably, wider trends in U.S. law (especially administrative law) brought forth proposals for a new model – what one might call the "treaty-as-delegation model." The label is a reference to the impact that *Chevron v. Natural Resources Defense Council*[5] has had beyond the confines of U.S. administrative law, extending even to international law. As the last section of this chapter shows, *Chevron* has made tentative inroads in the way that the Executive branch and a minority of courts approach treaty interpretation. These inroads are apparent in extraordinary forms of judicial deference to agency interpretations of treaties. The agency expertise to which the model defers originates in delegations of authority from Congress. In sum, *Chevron* deference, if widely adopted, would substantially reduce the role of the judiciary in interpreting the nation's treaties. This development also would be a major departure from the Third Restatement.

In contrast with the contract model, the "treaty as delegation" model does not have roots in the conception of treaties that prevailed in the Founding Generation. Nor has it developed gradually and organically as the contract and statutory models have. Rather, the delegation model is partly a product of

5 Chevron, U.S.A., Inc. v Nat. Res. Def. Council, Inc., 467 U.S. 837, 104 S. Ct. 2778, 81 L. Ed. 2d 694 (1984).

the technical and regulatory nature of some contemporary treaties, though countries similar to the United States and party to these same treaties adhere to traditional modes of treaty analysis, such as those in the Vienna Convention on the Law of Treaties (VCLT). Rather, the spread of the delegation model owes much to the writings of a small group of contemporary international and administrative law scholars, whose writings support a highly centralized view of executive power not only in the realm of treaties but in other aspects of international law and foreign relations law. Following this academic lead, some federal courts have begun applying *Chevron* to treaties with implementing legislation.

I argue that the delegation model seeks to loosen the connection between U.S. treaty interpretation and its traditional anchors in contract interpretation, statutory interpretation, and Articles III and IV of the U.S. Constitution.[6] Those anchors are part of a tradition that extolls the position of courts in relation to treaties as different from that of the political branches. The former interpret texts that they did not negotiate, that they have no stake in affirming or invalidating, and with respect to which they stand at least one step removed from the short-term international and domestic political consequences of interpretation. At the core of the treaty-as-delegation model, in contrast, is discomfort with judicial incursion into foreign relations, even if the incursion is for no purpose other than to declare what the law is.[7]

In examining models of treaty interpretation and the recently proposed turn toward exceptionally high levels of judicial deference to the Executive branch, this chapter proceeds in three stages. First, it demonstrates the influence exerted on U.S. treaty interpretation from 1787 to 1987 by the "treaty-as-contract" and the "treaty-as-statute" models. The former was dominant in the U.S. throughout the nineteenth century and remains part of the American law of treaty interpretation. The latter's influence grew throughout the twentieth century. Since then, these two models have coexisted. Both are regularly applied by courts and occasionally by Congress and the Executive branch. Both models have their imperfections. Their coexistence can be chaotic. However, both have proven useful in guiding the United States toward abiding by its treaty obligations.

The second stage of the analysis focuses on the period after 1987; that is, after publication of the Third Restatement. This section charts the decline in dominance of the contract and statute models. It also shows the lack of

6 This is not to say that all provisions of the Constitution are justiciable or to deny that enforcement of statutory norms is sometimes difficult.

7 *See infra* section VI.

influence of the treaty sections of the Third Restatement, which attempted to codify those models. This decline is reflected in court opinions that employ these analogies with decreasing frequency; in opinions that invoke these analogies in shallow ways that do not drive the court's analysis; in Executive branch treaty-making practice, and in new forms of treaty implementation.

The third stage of the analysis grapples with post-Restatement efforts to bring about ahistorically high levels of judicial deference to executive branch treaty interpretation. Although some level of executive deference has long been part of the U.S. treaty regime, *Chevron* deference is different in extent and rationale from traditional forms of deference. The Third Restatement's position on judicial deference was articulated with reference to agency expertise, the possibility that executive interpretation of treaties can be informed by understandings and broad foreign policy strategies not known to courts, and the principle that the country should speak with "one voice" in foreign policy. Limitations on deference, according to the Third Restatement view, were required by the stature of the judiciary as a coequal branch, by differences in treaty interpretation in domestic fora and international fora, and by the essential judicial role in protecting individual rights through judicial review. In contrast, those advocating a delegation model of deference – one premised on analogizing treaties and their implementing legislation to regulatory statutes – promote a very different view of deference, one premised on default rules, inferred legislative intent, and the immediate needs of the administration in power.

I PREFACE

At the outset, it may be useful to make three observations. First, in a volume concerned with so many aspects of American treaty law and practice, the topic of interpretation is the thread that runs through all the chapters. Whether legal change in the United States can be brought about by treaty is an inquiry typically conducted in relation to a proposed treaty text, a text that must be interpreted. Determining whether some or all of a treaty is self-executing requires a method for determining whether it was the intent of the Executive branch, the Senate, and perhaps the House of Representatives[8] for the treaty's norms to enter the U.S. legal system directly, without need for implementing legislation. Whether a treaty trumps federal or state legislation turns on how the treaty's scope is understood. In drafting implementing

[8] The intent of the House would be relevant if the treaty were a Congressional-Executive Agreement or if one were interpreting implementing legislation.

legislation, Congress needs to understand the relationship between the treaty text and existing U.S. law.[9] In short, the question asked in each chapter of this volume presupposes an act of treaty interpretation. In order to avoid redundancy, this chapter will borrow data from other chapters and consider treaties from a range of fields and time periods in order to present trends in the enterprise of interpretation.

Second, this chapter asks how U.S. courts, legislatures, and Executive branch officials ascribe meaning to international agreements. There is a large body of public international law on how treaties are to be interpreted in international fora.[10] Some of this law influences how interpretation takes place within the legal system of the United States. Also, treaty interpretation is a comparative subject; countries other than the United States have legislation, traditions, and constitutional provisions pertaining to treaties.[11] It should be made clear at the outset that treaty interpretation outside the United States is only a peripheral concern of this chapter.

Third, treaty interpretation in the United States involves many different actors providing input at different stages: from the assessment of an instrument's potential to change an existing legal regime to the negotiation of a specific text, which is then examined during the processes of ratification and implementation to, finally, interpretation in a specific, factually rich dispute.[12] Assessment precedes the chain of events that launches the Executive

9 David Stewart makes this point in Chapter 6 when he analyzes different paths to implementing legislation, including preimplementation. *See* David Stewart, "Recent Trends in U.S. Treaty Implementation," Chapter 6 of this volume.

10 Since 1969, the Vienna Convention on the Law of Treaties (VCLT) has been at the center of that body of law, though it is supplemented by rules of customary international law (CIL) and general principles of law. *See* Vienna Convention on the Law of Treaties, *opened for signature* May 23, 1969, *entered into force* January 27, 1980, 1155 U.N.T.S. 331. Currently, 114 countries are parties to the VCLT. Fifteen countries, including the United States, have signed but not ratified the treaty. The International Court of Justice (ICJ) has characterized the VCLT rules of interpretation as reflecting customary international law. *See, e.g.*, Case Concerning Avena and Other Mexican Nationals (Mex. v. U.S.) 2004 I.C.J. 37, 39–44 (Mar. 31, 2004). On many occasions, the United States has stated that it regards "many provisions" of the VCLT as codifying customary international law. *See* United States Department of State, "The Vienna Convention on the Law of Treaties," available at www.state.gov/s/l/treaty/faqs/70139.htm; Brief for the United States as Amicus Curiae Supporting Petitioner at 9 n.6, *Abbott v. Abbott*, 560 U.S. 1 (No. 08–645), 2009 WL 3043970, at *9 n. 6.

11 *See generally*, National Treaty Law and Practice (Duncan B. Hollis, Merritt R. Blakeslee & L. Benjamin Ederington, eds. 2005).

12 For a detailed look at treaty actions within the Executive branch, *see* Robert E. Dalton, "United States" in *ibid.* at 765. For a study of the historical role of the U.S. Senate in approving and rejecting proposed treaties, see Cong. Research Serv., S. Rpt. 106–71, Treaties and Other International Agreements: The Role of the United States Senate: A Study (2001), prepared for the Committee on Foreign Relations, United States Senate. A less lengthy

branch as treaty negotiator. A department or agency, in confronting a policy problem, must determine if existing treaties address the problem at hand, whether a new treaty would be more effective, and whether bilateral or multilateral treaty negotiations would be most fruitful. Before pursuing negotiations toward a new treaty, agencies will need to research how existing treaties have been understood by the Executive branch, Congress, by courts, by other countries, and by officials of state governments in the United States. In seeking the consent of the Senate (Article II treaties) or Congress as a whole (Congressional-Executive agreements), the Executive branch will make representations to Congress about what the treaty commits the United States to do and what benefits the United States stands to gain. The Executive branch may also need to interpret the treaty in the context of working with Congress and stakeholders in drafting implementing legislation and in promulgating regulations and guidelines for the treaty's enforcement. After the treaty enters into force for the United States, agencies and departments of the Executive branch will interpret the treaty in the context of civil, criminal, or administrative litigation.

Congress also interprets treaties. The Senate does so when it receives agreements negotiated by the Executive branch requiring its advice and consent[13] and in deciding whether or not to attach reservations, understandings, or declarations (RUDs). The House and the Senate do so when voting on implementing legislation and on whether to appropriate funds for implementation. They also do so as part of the process of legislating, which may require knowledge of whether a proposed statute is consistent with existing or contemplated treaties. Congress also interprets treaties as part of overseeing whether the Executive branch is carrying out its duties under the Take Care Clause.

Finally, courts interpret treaties. Much of this chapter is an analysis of treaty interpretation by U.S. courts. Focusing on judicial interpretation has advantages and disadvantages. An advantage is that courts, unlike other interpreters, regularly give us detailed written analyses of the meaning of treaties and the process of reasoning that led them to ascribe that meaning. Among the disadvantages of focusing primarily on judicial opinions is that the analysis is based on a small subset of all the interpretive activity taking place within the

overview can be found on the Senate's website, available at www.senate.gov/artandhistory/history/common/briefing/Treaties.htm (last visited Sep. 8, 2015). For a detailed exploration of the stages of treaty implementation, *see* John Norton Moore, The National Law of Treaty Implementation (2001).

13 *See* U.S. Constitution, Art. 2, sec. 2.

government. A more multi-sourced analysis, however, is beyond the ambitions of the current chapter.[14]

II TREATY AS CONTRACT

In Chapter 1 of this volume, Mark Janis and Noam Weiner argue that U.S. treaty law in the nineteenth century was shaped by the nation's efforts to grapple with issues surrounding slavery and federal supremacy. Remarkably, these struggles did not significantly impact the methods employed by American courts in interpreting treaties at that time.[15] Why did the approach to treaty interpretation remain stable during such periods of political upheaval and later, as America's place in the world changed? One reason is the central role that comparisons played in U.S. treaty interpretation, especially in the country's early years. Repeatedly, judges and statesmen in the early decades of U.S. treaty interpretation examined international agreements as if they were not something foreign and unusual (as they usually were) but rather as though they were something familiar.

In reality, the nation's treaties at that time were few in number[16] and rarely gave rise to adjudicated disputes.[17] With the exception of cases in the U.S. Supreme Court, it was rare for a treaty to be at the center of a litigated dispute, certainly rare in comparison with contracts, wills, deeds, trusts, and other legal documents. In a dispute over the interpretation of a will, there was no need to interpret a bequest by analogizing the will to a contract, a statute, or some other legal document. Courts were familiar with wills, and there was a considerable body of law on how wills should be interpreted. With respect to treaties, however, courts were on unfamiliar ground. Interpretive rules that

[14] A more full-bodied understanding of treaty analogies would require data on the manner in which scores of federal and state officials approach treaties in the numerous day-to-day encounters that do not give rise to litigation. Also relevant would be the manner in which private actors (lawyers and their clients) shape their behavior based on anticipated actions by courts and the political branches.

[15] *Compare, e.g.*, Prevost v. Greneaux, 60 U.S. 1, 15 L. Ed. 572 (1856) *with* De Geofroy v. Riggs, 133 U.S. 258, 10 S. Ct. 295, 33 L. Ed. 642 (1890), two cases separated in time by the Civil War and grappling with the scope of the federal treaty power. Both cases turned on the interpretation of an 1853 bilateral agreement with France. Despite the difference in outcome, the Court's method is quite similar.

[16] *See* Library of Congress, "A Century of Lawmaking for a New Nation: U.S. Congressional Documents and Debates, 1774–1875," available at http://memory.loc.gov/cgi-bin/ampage?collId=llsl&fileName=008/llsl008.db&recNum=10 (containing List of Treaties Between the United States and Foreign Nations).

[17] *See* David L. Sloss, Michael D. Ramsey & William S. Dodge, *International Law in the Supreme Court, 1789–1860*, in ["CONTINUITY AND CHANGE"], *supra* note 1.

had been developed for nontreaty legal sources (mainly private-law contracts) were borrowed for treaty interpretation.

When the U.S. Supreme Court decided its first landmark treaty case, *Ware v. Hylton*,[18] none of the justices' opinions drew upon U.S. sources for rules of treaty interpretation. No such interpretive rules were to be found in the Constitution or in federal statutes. With a dearth of U.S. sources on such an important question,[19] courts in these early years looked at the writings of classical European authors and borrowed principles and precedents from various areas of nontreaty law, such as the jurisprudence relating to contracts. Reference to well-known European works conferred legitimacy on early U.S. treaty jurisprudence; courts drew upon widely influential authors respected across Europe. This may have allayed fears in Europe that the courts of the new country, a product of war and revolution, would not be law abiding.[20]

On important issues of treaty interpretation, the works of prominent European writers – mainly from civil law countries – and the Anglo-American common law of contracts, reinforced one another. As discussed below, classical authors repeatedly referred to treaties as a species of contracts. Treaty formation and breach were understood in contractual terms. And the considerable body of common law jurisprudence in Britain and the colonies interpreting private law contracts was general enough and adaptable enough to be applied to treaties. Citing frequently to Vattel[21]

18 Ware v. Hylton, 3 U.S. 199, 1 L. Ed. 568 (1796). *Ware* was the first case in which the new Court struck down a state statute; the grounds were that the statute conflicted with the Treaty of Paris.

19 The Federalist Papers expressed the view that treaties should be interpreted like contracts, but none of the opinions in *Ware* cited the *Federalist* or other sources from the Constitutional Convention or the state ratification conventions. *See* THE FEDERALIST NO. 64 (John Jay) ("[T]reaties are made, not by only one of the contracting parties, but by both"); THE FEDERALIST NO. 75 (Alexander Hamilton) (characterizing treaties as contracts with foreign nations and not as "rules prescribed by the sovereign to the subject").

20 British common law was received into the legal systems of the states by state constitutions or by so-called "reception statutes." The existing British law and practices on treaties and their interpretation, however, were not immediately received into the U.S. legal system. One possible reason for this disparity may be that the written Constitution of the United States, with its Supremacy Clause, stood in contrast to British dualism in regard to treaties and the domestic legal order. In other words, the new American conception of treaties and their relationship to domestic law was, from the start, critically different from the British tradition. Additionally, in the first decades, the most important treaties to be interpreted by American courts were treaties with Great Britain. It would have been odd, perhaps objectionable, to have adopted British rules of treaty interpretation in such a context.

21 *See, e.g.*, United States. v. Arredondo, 31 U.S. 691, 752, 8 L. Ed. 547 (1832) (citing Vattel for the proposition that interpreting treaties, like contracts, starts with the intent of the parties); Holmes v. Jennison, 39 U.S. 540, 572, 10 L. Ed. 579 (1840) (relying on Vattel to interpret the

and Grotius,[22] seventeenth- and eighteenth-century courts in the United States proceeded on the assumption that treaties did not require their own set of interpretive rules. Their meaning could be determined through a familiar set of assumptions and precedents.

Influential early American treatise writers also believed that courts interpreting treaties should borrow the approach to construing private law contracts.[23] In both settings, the goal was to find the mutual intent of the parties to an agreement. The text of the agreement was evidence of that intent but not conclusive evidence. Inferences often employed in contract law could guide the interpreter of a treaty. Default rules from the law of contracts could be enlisted as well.[24]

The apparent soundness of this approach was reinforced by the stature of the cited authorities. Among these, Hugo Grotius and Emerich de Vattel were especially familiar to well-read American lawyers, judges, and statesmen.[25] For

compact clause of the U.S. Constitution); De Geofroy v. Riggs, 133 U.S. at 270 (relying on Vattel for the proper approach to treaty interpretation).

22 *See, e.g.*, Rex v. Booth, 2 Haw. 616, 641 (1863) (citing Grotius for the principle that "[t]reaties and other contracts are to be construed according to their intent"); Comegys v. Vasse, 26 U.S. 193, 209, 7 L. Ed. 108 (1828) (referring extensively to Grotius in interpreting the U.S.-Spain treaty ceding Florida to the U.S.); Com. v. Deacon 1823 WL 2218, *2 (Pa. 1823) (relying on Grotius to interpret extradition treaty).

23 *See, e.g.*, JAMES KENT, COMMENTARY ON INTERNATIONAL LAW 392 (2nd edn. 1878) (the "meaning [of treaties] is to be ascertained by the same rules of construction and course of reasoning which we apply to the interpretation of private contracts") (citing Vattel). For a discussion of Kent's substantial influence on early American legal thought, see John Langbein, *Chancellor Kent and the History of Legal Literature*, 93 COLUM. L. REV. 547, 552 (1993) (noting that Kent's views on treaties were significantly influenced by those of Alexander Hamilton). For Hamilton's characterization of treaties in contractual terms, *see* FEDERALIST NO. 75, *supra* note 19.

24 *See, e.g.*, United States. v Percheman, 32 U.S. 51, 68, 8 L. Ed. 604 (1833) (stating that ambiguities in treaties, like ambiguities in contracts, should be construed against the promissor rather than the promissee and citing Vattel).

25 *See, e.g.*, Thomas Jefferson, *Opinion on the Treaty With France*, (Apr. 28, 1793) *in* 25 PAPERS OF THOMAS JEFFERSON (Bond, ed. 1961) (relying heavily on Grotius, Vattel, and Samuel von Pufendorf); David Armitage, FOUNDATIONS OF MODERN INTELLECTUAL THOUGHT 201 (2013) (recounting that Benjamin Franklin obtained copies of the 1775 edition of Vattel's *Droit des Gens* and distributed them to the Harvard College Library, the Library Company of Philadelphia, and to the Continental Congress and stating that the book was used by John Adams in drafting model treaties); JAMES KENT, COMMENTARIES ON AMERICAN LAW 18 (1826) ("The international jurist most widely cited in the first 50 years after the Revolution was Emmerich de Vattel."); JAMES KENT, KENT'S COMMENTARY ON INTERNATIONAL Law 36 (1878 ed.) ("[Vattel's book] has been cited more freely than that of any other public jurist, and is still the statesman's manual and oracle."); F. Wharton, UNITED STATES REVOLUTIONARY DIPLOMATIC CORRESPONDENCE 64 (1889) (quoting Benjamin Franklin as stating that Vattel's *Droit des Gens* "has been continually in the hands of the members of our Congress now sitting").

Grotius, the law applicable to agreements between sovereigns was a subset of the law that applied to private contracts. In both settings, agreements consisted of an exchange of promises, the promise was backed not only by a moral or honor-based duty to perform but also a legal duty, and the meaning of the agreement resided in the mutual intent of the parties, as supplemented by various rules that were part of the law of nations.[26] Similarly, Vattel's *Droit des Gens (Law of Nations)*,[27] published in 1758, emphasized the "dignity and equality of nations" as constituting the foundation of the international legal order and as central to the formation and interpretation of agreements among nations.[28] Just as consent was central to private lawmaking, the consent of nations was essential to the international system of lawmaking through treaties. In Chapter XVII, Vattel articulated a list of rules and presumptions for interpreting treaties, many of which were similar to the domestic contract law of that era.[29]

In addition to enjoying the support of classical sources, the contract analogy had pragmatic benefits for a young nation. If treaties were contracts, then parties to treaties, like those to contracts, were in positions of formal equality with one another, regardless of their actual bargaining power and stature.[30] With the Treaty of Paris, the disparity in stature, economic resources, and military power between the United States and Great Britain was substantial, but examining the treaty in contractual terms tended to obscure these

26 *See* HUGO GROTIUS, DE JURE BELLI AC PACES, 176–77 (FRANCIS W. KELSEY TRANS., 1925) ("It is a right, which natural reason dictates, that everyone who receives a promise, should have the power to compel the promisor to do what a fair interpretation of his words suggests.").

27 *See* EMMERICH DE VATTEL, THE LAW OF NATIONS ON PRINCIPLES OF THE LAW OF NATURE APPLIED TO THE CONDUCT AND AFFAIRS OF NATIONS AND SOVEREIGNS, INTRODUCTION, § 24 (CHARLES D. FENWICK TRANS., 1916) ("States, like individuals, can acquire rights and contract obligations by express promises, by compacts and by treaties, from which there results a *conventional* Law of Nations particular to the contracting parties" [emphasis in original]).

28 *See ibid.* §§ 35, 173.

29 *See, e.g., ibid.* § 265 ("In the interpretation of treaties, compacts, and promises, we ought not to deviate from the common use of the language, unless we have strong reasons for it"), § 271 (ambiguities can be interpreted to the detriment of the party who had an opportunity to clarify).

30 Equality of stature was important. The "Thirteen united States of America" had proclaimed not only their independence from Britain but also their "separate and equal station" among "the powers of the earth." U.S. Declaration of Independence at ¶1. This aspiration ran through the constitutional drafting period. *See, e.g.*, DEBATES ON THE FEDERAL CONSTITUTION 506 (J. Elliot, 2nd edn. 1863) (James Wilson) ("[I]n their nature treaties originate differently from laws. They are made by equal parties, and each side has half of the bargain to make . . ."); DONALD S. LUTZ, THE ORIGINS OF AMERICAN CONSTITUTIONALISM 16–17 (1988) (to the Framers' generation, "[a] contract usually implied an agreement that had mutual responsibilities on a specific point").

disparities. When the laws of some U.S. states blocked British creditors from collecting on unpaid prewar debts to Americans, Great Britain allowed the matter to be treated as a legal dispute. The treaty required British creditors to bring their claims to U.S. courts and plead their right to recovery. This process elevated the stature of American courts and placed U.S. citizens and British subjects on equal footing. Final word thus rested, or appeared to rest, with an American court and not with the British navy. That preserved American dignity while at the same time vindicating the treaty rights of British creditors.[31]

In *Ware v. Hylton*, which held state legislation preempted by the Treaty of Paris, several of the opinions employed contract-associated terms such as "reciprocity"[32] and "promise."[33] In the view of Justice Patterson, the treaty's drafters, in using the words "it is agreed," meant that the United States "had expressly contracted" to confer rights on British creditors, rights that were to be enforced in U.S. courts and not solely by negotiation between the two countries.[34] For Justice Iredell, the law of nations functioned as a kind of common law of contracts in treaty cases by incorporating customs and principles of reciprocity.[35] Significantly, and in stark contrast to later cases, all of the opinions in *Ware* relied in part on non-U.S. legal sources.[36] None made reference to the views of the Executive branch or Congress.[37] Rather, the opinions of the justices were grounded in the writings of European scholars maintaining that treaties created contractual obligations.[38]

Over the course of the nineteenth century and into the twentieth, state and federal courts regularly used the contract metaphor, either explicitly or implicitly, in interpreting treaties. In the early 1800s, courts did so on the strength of

[31] All of which is not to say that the possibility of resort to force did not hover over the case. *See* Ware, 3 Dal. at 261 (Iredell, J.) ("The peace of mankind, the honour of the human race, the welfare, perhaps the being of future generations, must in no inconsiderable degree depend on the sacred observance of national conventions"), *ibid.* at 256 (referring to the "uncommon magnitude of the subject" matter of the case).

[32] *Ibid.* at 253–4. [33] *Ibid.* at 272 (Iredell, J.) [34] *Ibid.* at 240 (Patterson, J.).

[35] *Ibid.* at 261 (Iredell, J.).

[36] *See* Carlos Vazquez, *The Supremacy Clause and the Judicial Enforcement of Treaties*, 122 HARV. L. REV. 599 (2008).

[37] Iredell was emphatic in stating that treaty interpretation is in the final analysis a judicial duty. To him there was a clear body of law, the law of nations, to which courts were to turn in interpreting treaties. *Ibid.* at 261 ("The Judiciary is undoubtedly to determine in all cases in law and equity, coming before them concerning treaties.").

[38] The opinions in *Ware* cite to Grotius, Vattel, Samuel von Puffendorf, and Cornelis van Bynkershoek.

Ware v. Hylton[39] and European authors.[40] Later, they did so on the strength of other precedents, especially *Foster v. Nielson*, a case involving competing claims to land in Florida under a peace treaty between the United States and Spain. Justice Marshall famously began his opinion in *Foster* by declaring that "[a] treaty is in its nature a contract between two nations, not a legislative act,"[41] a sentence that since then has been cited repeatedly (albeit in slightly different wording) by lower federal courts and state courts as the basis for using contractual tools to interpret treaties.[42] Even though in *Foster* the sentence served to interpret a specific facet of treaties: whether they are self-executing (intended to have immediate legal effects within the U.S. legal system) or whether the treaty's norms enter the domestic U.S. legal system only

39 The U.S. Supreme Court cited *Ware* 14 times over the course of the nineteenth century. *See* Westlaw list of citing references for the case (last visited Jan. 2, 2016).

40 Familiarity with Grotius and Vattel eventually decreased. A smaller proportion of American judges were proficient in French and other continental European languages. Increasingly, international law came to them, if at all, through treatises written by American authors. *See* HENRY WHEATON, ELEMENTS OF INTERNATIONAL LAW (1836); FRANCIS WHARTON, THE OFFICE OF LEGAL ADVISOR, DIGEST OF THE INTERNATIONAL LAW OF THE UNITED STATES (1886); SAMUEL B. CRANDALL, TREATIES: THEIR MAKING AND ENFORCEMENT (1904); GEORGE B. DAVIS, ELEMENTS OF INTERNATIONAL LAW (1900).

41 Foster v. Neilson, 27 U.S. 253, 314, 7 L. Ed. 415 (1829). Today the statement is most often associated with the non-self-executing treaty doctrine. In *Medellin v. Texas*, Chief Justice Roberts quoted Marshall as a basis for concluding that Article 94 of the United Nations Charter imposed obligations on the United States and that those obligations became law within the domestic legal system only if Congress chose to implement the Charter by legislation. *See* Medellin v. Texas, 552 U.S. 491, 504–05, 128 S. Ct. 1346, 170 L. Ed. 2d 190 (2008). Throughout the nineteenth century and well into the twentieth, however, Marshall's declaration was cited as a rule of treaty interpretation that required courts to seek out the mutual intent of the contracting parties. *See* Worcester v. State of Ga., 31 U.S. 515, 581, 8 L. Ed. 483 (1832) (stating that a treaty is a "compact formed between two nations or communities"); Whitney v. Robertson, 124 U.S. 190, 194, 8 S. Ct. 456, 31 L. Ed. 386 (1888) ("A treaty is primarily a contract between two or more independent nations, and is so regarded by writers on public law"); Fourteen Diamond Rings v. United States, 183 U.S. 176, 22 S. Ct. 59, 46 L. Ed. 138 (1901) (a treaty "[i]n its essence ... is a contract. It differs from an ordinary contract only in being an agreement between independent states instead of private parties"); Jordan v. K. Tashiro, 278 U. S. 123, 49 S. Ct. 47, 73 L. Ed. 214 (1928) (courts must consider the interests and intentions of both parties to a treaty in order to secure "reciprocity between them"); Santovincenzo v. Egan, 284 U.S. 30, 40, 52 S. Ct. 81, 76 L. Ed. 151 (1931) ("Treaties are contracts between independent nations"); Bd. of Cty. Comm'rs v Aerolineas Peruanasa, S.A., 307 F.2d 802, 806 (5th Cir. 1962) ("[I]n construing [a] treaty, as other contracts, we give consideration to the intent of the parties so as to carry out their manifest purpose"); Marks v. United States, 12 U.S. Cust. App. 110, 112 (Ct. Cust. App. 1924) (stating that treaties must be interpreted "by the same process of reasoning and by the same rules of construction as are applied to the interpretation of contracts between individuals").

42 A Westlaw search of that sentence reveals its being cited directly or indirectly and with slightly different wording in at last 50 cases from 1829 to 1899.

through implementing legislation.[43] The contract analogy stuck, even as the number of U.S. treaties increased and the purposes of such treaties became more varied than just the pursuit of reciprocal bargains.

This use of the contract analogy had identifiable consequences. With it came the fundamental duty of the interpreter to discover the *mutual* intent of the parties to the agreement. Just as commercial contracts consisted of the terms on which both or all parties agreed, the same was true of treaties; a treaty's terms could not be divined from the objectives of just one party.[44] A court could not rest its interpretation on pre-treaty writings or post-treaty actions by the United States alone. For treaties authenticated in more than one language and containing translation discrepancies, courts were required to look beyond the English version.[45] Treaty interpreters, like contract interpreters, were not confined to the text; the search for mutual intent could lead to context, custom, course of dealing, and the postagreement behavior of both parties.[46]

The contract analogy, when faithfully applied, brought a measure of evenhandedness to interpreting treaties. It did so at a time when U.S. courts were eager to acquire a reputation abroad for being fair to foreign litigants and a reputation at home for being guardians of the nation's long-term interest in

43 *See* Ingrid Wuerth, "Self-Execution," Chapter 4 of this volume.

44 *See, e.g.*, Washington v. Washington State Passenger Fishing Vessel Ass'n, 443 U.S. 658, 675, 99 S. Ct. 3055, 61 L. Ed. 2d 823 (1979) ("[I]t is the intention of the parties, and not solely that of the superior side, that must control any attempt to interpret the treaties."); Seufert Bros. Co. v. United States, 249 U.S. 194 (1919) (inquiring into "[h]ow the Indians understood this proviso we are considering").

45 *See, e.g.*, United States v. Arredondo, 31 U.S. at 753 (concluding that a discrepancy in the English and Spanish treaty texts required "an inquiry into the intention and understanding of the parties who negotiated the treaties"); Percheman, 32 U.S. at 68 ("There is a difference between the English and the Spanish versions of the eighth article. Both are equally originals, but surely the justice and liberality of the United States will extend to the claimants the full benefit of either."); Gen. Elec. Co. v. Robertson, 25 F.2d 146, 152 (D. MD. 1928) (consulting the German version of the 1921 peace treaty between the U.S. and Germany in a patent dispute). For recent examples, see Eastern Airlines, Inc. v. Floyd, 499 U.S. 530, 535, 111 S. Ct. 1489, 113 L. Ed. 2d 569 (1991) ("Because the only authentic text of the Warsaw Convention is in French, the French text must guide our analysis"); Air France v. Saks, 470 U.S. 392, 105 S. Ct. 1338, 84 L. Ed. 2d 289 (1985) (interpreting both the English and French versions of the Warsaw Convention); Sale v. Haitian Centers Council, Inc., 509 U.S. 155, 180–83, 113 S. Ct. 2549, 125 L. Ed. 2d 128 (1993) (noting different English translations of the French verb *refouler* in the 1951 United Nations Convention Relating to the Status of Refugees).

46 *See, e.g.*, O'Connor v. United States, 479 U.S. 27, 107 S. Ct. 347, 93 L. Ed. 2d 206 (1986) ("The course of conduct of parties to an international agreement, like the course of conduct of parties to any contract, is evidence of its meaning,"*citing* Uniform Commercial Code § 2–208(1)).

keeping its promises.[47] An important result of the contract analogy, one that figures importantly in the next section of this chapter, is that during the early decades of the Republic, the views of the Executive branch regarding a treaty's meaning were not especially influential with American courts. Sometimes courts did not refer to the executive branch's position at all. When they did, it was not accompanied by special hesitation to reject a State Department view, even in cases taking place in a national security setting.[48] It was the emergence of noncontractual analogies for treaties that increased the extent of judicial deference to executive branch views.

III TREATY AS STATUTE

The contract analogy was dominant for more than a century. Thereafter, while its use continued, its dominance declined.[49] A second analogy, the treaty as legislative act or statute, ascended. For long stretches of time, the two

47 *See* Jonathan I. Charney, *Judicial Deference in Foreign Relations*, 83 AM. J. INT'L L. 805, 806 (1989) ("The Founding Fathers sought to establish the United States as a trustworthy member of the international community.").

48 *See, e.g.*, The Amiable Isabella, 19 U.S. 1, 2, 5 L. Ed. 191 (U.S. 1821) (rejecting U.S. government's argument and holding that a ship was immune from capture because of a treaty with Spain). Writing for the Court, Justice Story said that judicial interpretation of treaties had to be "observe[d] with the most scrupulous good faith," even in a military context, and that good-faith interpretation was a duty of the judiciary regardless of actions or positions taken by Congress and the Executive branch. *See also* United States v. Laverty, 26 F. Cas. 875, 875–6 (D. La. 1812) (interpreting Treaty of Paris and rejecting U.S. government's view that defendant was an "alien enemy").

49 As explained later in this section, the contract analogy remained in use in the United States in the twentieth century, though its application was sporadic and inconsistent. In some cases, courts invoked common law principles of contract law, but these principles did not strongly influence the court's interpretation of the treaty. For example, in Sullivan v. Kidd, 254 U.S. 433, 41 S. Ct. 158, 65 L. Ed. 344 (1921), the Court began its analysis as follows: "Writers of authority agree that treaties are to be interpreted upon the principles which govern the interpretation of contracts." *Ibid.* at 438 (*citing* 5 Moore International Law Digest 249). From there, however, the Court failed to apply this principle to the treaty at issue, an 1899 bilateral treaty with Great Britain granting British nationals a right to inherit land in the U.S. Some contemporary U.S. legal scholarship continues to argue in favor of applying some aspects of contract law to treaty interpretation. *See e.g.*, Robert Anderson IV, *"Ascertained in a Different Way;" The Treaty Power at the Crossroads of Contract, Compact, and Constitution*, 69 GEO. WASH. L. REV. 189 (2000–2001); Sital Kalantry, *The Intent-to-Benefit: Individually Enforceable Rights Under International Treaties*, 44 STAN. J. INT'L L. 63 (2008); Justin Lowe, Note: *What Would Grotius Do? Methods and Implications of Incorporating the Contract Law Doctrine of Illusory Promises into the Law of Treaty Interpretation*, 6 WASH. U. GLOBAL ST. L. REV. 703 (2007); Curtis J. Mahoney, Note: *Treaties as Contracts: Textualism, Contract Theory, and the Interpretation of Treaties*, 116 YALE L. J. 825 (2006–07); Jared Wessel, *Relational Contract Theory and Treaty Interpretation: End-Game Treaties v. Dynamic Obligations*, 60 N.Y.U. ANN. SURV. AM. L. 149 (2004–2005).

analogies coexisted in case law, with the choice of metaphor sometimes related to aspects of the treaty in question, such as whether the treaty was bilateral or multilateral, whether the text used words of promise, and whether the treaty related to a field of law in which prior treaties repeatedly had been analogized to contracts.

Several developments contributed to the contract analogy's decline. One was a change in the structure and level of detail of the nation's international agreements. By the twentieth century, an increasing proportion of U.S. treaties no longer resembled private-law contracts. For example, the Friendship, Commerce and Navigation treaties of the twentieth century were more detailed and covered a wider scope of economic relationships than the trade agreements of the nineteenth century.[50] Though the FCN's were framed and drafted as reciprocal arrangements, they had somewhat of a legislative character, for example, in elevating the concept of most favored nation and the principle of nondiscrimination to international norms and not just bargained-for outcomes.

Relatedly, over the course of the nineteenth century, courts in the United States became accustomed to working with statutes. Once a rare wave in a common law sea, statutes eventually became common fare.[51] Congress and the judiciary could see the similarities between statutes and treaties once they had gained experience drafting and construing legislative texts, becoming used to legislative history, and the process of amending and revisiting legislation.

A second development was the rise of "liberal interpretation," often in the context of the adjudication of disputes with Native American tribes in the nineteenth century. At the core of these disputes were agreements between the tribes and the United States. This litigation made up a large portion of U.S. treaty litigation at that time.[52] Although these agreements were called

[50] *See* John F. Coyle, *The Treaty of Friendship, Commerce and Navigation in the Modern Era*, 51 *Colum. L. Rev* 302 (2013).

[51] *See* Grant Gilmore, The Ages of American Law 86 (1977) ("Between 1900 and 1950 the greater part of the substantive law, which before the 1900s had been left to the judges for decision in light of common law principles, was recast in statutory form"); Guido Calabresi, A Common Law for the Age of Statutes 95 (1982) (referring to the large volume of statute making that took place during this time period).

[52] The pattern of managing U.S.-tribal relations by treaty came to an end (at least prospectively) in 1871. *See* Indian Appropriation Act of Mar. 3, 1871, 25 U.S. Code §71, 16 Stat. 566, *codified at* Revised Statutes §b 2079 ("No Indian nation or tribe within the territory of the United States shall be acknowledged or recognized as an independent nation, tribe, or power with whom the United States may contract by treaty; but no obligation of any treaty lawfully made and ratified with any such Indian nation or tribe prior to March 3, 1871, shall be hereby invalidated or impaired.").

"treaties" and required the advice and consent of the Senate, they were not analyzed using a pure contract model. Unlike agreements with foreign nations, land cession agreements with Indian tribes in the nineteenth century often were not a product of genuine negotiation.[53] They could consist of one party (the United States) regulating the conduct of the other party rather than entering into an agreement based on reciprocity.[54] Many of these treaties involved a tribe ceding land to the United States.

When claims under such treaties arrived in U.S. courts, the treaties were interpreted using a modified form of the traditional contract analogy. Formally, these documents were referred to as "treaties" and judicial opinions adjudicating tribal claims occasionally cited precedents involving treaties with foreign countries. In *Worcester v. Georgia*,[55] the Supreme Court crafted a new variation on the traditional contract analogy:

> The language used in treaties with the Indians should never be construed to their prejudice. If words be made use of which are susceptible of a more extended meaning than their plain import, as connected with the tenor of the treaty, they should be considered as used only in the latter sense.[56]

For decades after *Worcester*, this new way of talking about this narrow category of treaties grew. These treaties were thought to be reflective of a special relationship between the United States and Indian tribes, one that created an implied duty of good faith interpretation by U.S. courts, which were the exclusive forum for adjudicating disputes arising under these agreements.[57] This manner of interpreting agreements that were not the product of arms' length bargaining typical of (or thought to be typical of) U.S. treaties with other sovereigns, came to be called "liberal interpretation."[58] It was

[53] Earlier "peace and friendship" treaties more often were the product of genuine reciprocity.

[54] Sometimes the agreement was drafted in a manner suggesting a reciprocal exchange of benefits. Often, these descriptions were illusory; the tribe was not choosing to move from one piece of land to another; it was being ousted. *See* Siegfried Wiessner, *American Indian Treaties and Modern International Law*, 7 ST. THOMAS L. REV. 567 (1995).

[55] Worcester v. State of Ga., 31 U.S. 515 (1832). [56] *Ibid.* at 582.

[57] In modern parlance, one might consider nineteenth-century U.S. treaties with Indian tribes as incorporating choice of forum and choice of law clauses, both of them in favor of the United States, with the sole authentic version of the treaty being in English and the only forum for dispute resolution being courts of the United States. It is difficult to find an example of such a one-sided array of procedural provisions among sovereign states, even in the case of peace treaties in which one party was vanquished by the other. By comparison, the Treaty of Versailles was authenticated in German and it provided that disputes were to be resolved by arbitration.

[58] *See, e.g.*, Tulee v. State of Washington, 315 U.S. 681, 684–5, 62 S. Ct. 862. 86 L. Ed. 1115 (1942); United States v. Shoshone Tribe of Indians of Wind River Reservation in Wyoming,

liberal in the sense that courts liberally recognized private rights recognized by the treaty.[59]

The extensive application of liberal interpretation to Indian treaties made inroads in the contract analogy. Judicial references to tribes as "wards of the nation,"[60] and as "unlettered people,"[61] in need of "protection" by the federal government sullied the illusion of contractual equality. In reality, some of the treaties that the United States imposed on native Americans functioned more like statutes than contracts. Depending on the specific tribe, circumstance, and treaty wording, these treaties functioned like statutes in that they were not based on reciprocity; they deprived the tribe of adjudicative jurisdiction over U.S. citizens committing offenses on tribal lands; they regulated aspects of daily life for members of the tribes; and they were regarded by U.S. courts as part of a regime by which the federal government extended protective responsibility to the tribes and their members.[62] In 1871, Congress enacted legislation stripping Indian tribes

304 U.S. 111, 116, 58 S. Ct. 794, 82 L. Ed. 1213 (1938); Choctaw Nation v. United States, 119 U.S. 1, 28, 7 S. Ct. 75, 30 L. Ed. 306 (1886). Liberal interpretation of treaties can be traced even earlier – to Justice Joseph Story's opinion in Shanks v. DuPont, 28 U.S. 242, 7 L. Ed. 666 (1830). *Shanks* involved an interpretation of Jay's Treaty. Story stretched principles of contract interpretation in order to permit a British plaintiff to inherit in South Carolina notwithstanding obstacles under state law. In reaching this result, Story queried: "If the treaty admits of two interpretations, and one is limited, and the other liberal; one which will further, and the other exclude private rights; why should not the most liberal exposition be adopted?" *Ibid.* at 249. As employed by Story, liberal interpretation involved being generous in extending rights to nationals of U.S. treaty partners, perhaps in the hope of avoiding conflict with European powers over relatively minor treaty matters and with the effect of asserting federal power to invalidate state legislation that interfered with the domestic enforcement of treaties.

59 *See, e.g.*, Beecher v. Wetherby, 95 U.S. 525, 24 L. Ed. 440 (1877); Leavenworth, L. & G.R. Co. v. United States, 92 U.S. 733, 23 L. Ed. 634, 747 (1875). Notwithstanding the new and benign sounding characterization, the results often were not favorable to the tribes. *See, e.g.*, Lone Wolf v. Hitchcock, 187 U.S. 553, 566, 23 S. Ct. 216, 47 L. Ed. 299 (1903) (making reference to the "moral obligation" of Congress to act in "good faith" in carrying out such treaties but ruling against tribal claims based on the U.S. government's "plenary authority" over tribal relations and right to enact statutes in conflict with Indian treaties). *Lone Wolf* draws an express comparison between treaties with Indian tribes and those "made with foreign nations," and concludes that Congress in either situation can enact subsequent statutes in conflict with the treaty. *Id.* at 565. *See also* The Cherokee Tobacco, 78 U.S. 616, 621–2, 20 L. Ed. 227 (1870) (holding that considerations of "humanity and good faith" in U.S. treaties with Indian tribes do not bar such treaties from being superseded by federal statute).

60 *See* United States v. Kagama, 118 U. S. 375, 383, 6 S. Ct. 1109, 30 L. Ed. 228 (1886).

61 *See* Worcester v. State of Ga., 31 U.S. at 580 ("How the words of the treaty were understood by this unlettered people, rather than their critical meaning, should form the rule of construction.").

62 *See generally* Francis Paul Prucha, American Indian Treaties: The History of a Political Anomaly (1994).

prospectively of their status as independent nations with which the United States had to enter into treaties.[63]

Outside the context of tribal litigation, liberal interpretation came to refer to the willingness of courts to go beyond the four corners of the treaty in carrying out interpretation.[64] Although the term "liberal interpretation" of U.S.-Indian treaties rarely led to judicial investigation into Native-American sources or interpretations, "liberal interpretation" of U.S. treaties with foreign countries did authorize investigation into documents that today would be characterized as part of either the *travaux preparatoire* or legislative history. A good example is Justice Brandeis's opinion in *Cook v. United States*, which involved interpretation of a 1924 bilateral treaty with Great Britain.[65] The case concerned the right of the U.S. Coast Guard to stop and search British ships in order to enforce the Prohibition laws. Brandeis's majority opinion uses a wide range of interpretive tools found outside the four corners of the treaty. He begins by examining the treaty's "history" in relation to stopping ships suspected of smuggling.[66] He summarizes opposing points of view about the law enforcement activities that the United States can perform in its territorial waters. Having examined the treaty's context, the opinion then concludes that the agreement was a compromise designed to avoid U.S.-British conflict. Finally, Brandeis explains what the American side and the British side understood to be the nature of the compromise.[67]

A third development that impacted the dominance of the contract model took place in the early decades of the twentieth century. By then, scholarly treatises for decades had incorporated the assumption of similarity between contracts and treaties. Now, that assumption came under criticism from a new generation of scholars less interested in the roots of U.S. treaty practice than in some of the ambitious international goals that treaties could help accomplish

63 *See* Indian Appropriation Act, *supra* note 52. However, treaties that had been entered into before 1871 typically remained in force and thus could be the subject of litigation and treaty interpretation by U.S. courts long after 1871. *See* cases summarized in *supra* note 58 and 59.

64 As noted above, contract interpretation in the 1800s focused on the search for mutual intent, which was not always encapsulated in the text of the agreement. It was not unusual to examine the context in which the agreement had been reached; the manner in which the parties dealt with one another after the agreement was in place; and any customary ways of behaving that the parties may have incorporated implicitly into the written agreement. *See generally* Samuel Williston, WILLISTON ON CONTRACTS (1st edn. 1920).

65 Cook v. United States, 288 U.S. 102, 53 S. Ct. 305, 77 L. Ed. 641 (1933). 66 *Ibid.* at 107.

67 The United States secured "a definite fixing of the zone of legitimate seizure of British" vessels. *Ibid.* at 118. Great Britain secured the right of British ships to travel through U.S. territorial waters for the purpose of transporting intoxicating liquors between ports outside the United States, provided the merchandise was sealed. *Ibid.* at 120–1. The Court found the treaty to be self-executing. *Ibid.* at 119.

in the future. One ambition was for the United States to enter into a network of multilateral treaties that would accomplish global aims in a quasi-legislative fashion. Aims such as removing obstacles to global commerce or stamping out evils such as the global white slave trade seemed to lie beyond a contractual model of treaties. [68]

For these reasons (treaty form, liberal interpretation, and scholarly debate), and perhaps others, American courts shifted away from what had been their exclusive reliance on the contractual model. But this shift was not a complete departure from the past. The rise of the statute analogy did not bring about the end of the contract analogy. The two coexisted.[69]

As with the absorption of contract rules of interpretation, the turn to statutes required the interpreter to work with a set of tools created for other purposes. The fit was not at all perfect. Treaties are not statutes nor are they contracts. One key difference between employing a statutory analogy rather than a contractual one lies in the source of obligation. The source of statutory obligations is voting; some views prevail over others. When treaties are the product of majority voting rather than consensus, the search for meaning is the search for the views that prevailed. In contrast, the source of contractual obligation is mutual assent. The interpreter of contractual treaties must reject proposed "terms" that were not mutually agreed upon.[70] As a practical matter, this understanding of treaty formation, like contract formation, requires the interpreter to examine the text (and sometimes sources outside the text) from two independent perspectives. In contrast, statutes often can be interpreted without dwelling at length on the losers' point of view, except to the extent that it sheds light on how those who prevailed understood a given provision. Of course a "losing" country in treaty negotiations can choose not to ratify the treaty. It is not bound to accept the treaty as law in the way that the losing faction in a legislative debate is bound by the result.[71]

68 So when Hersch Lauterpacht, in 1927, put forward a full-throated defense of the contract analogy, his effort received a cool reception in the United States It arrived at a time when "[twentieth-century publicists emphasise[d] the profound difference between" treaties and contracts. *See* Hersch Lauterpacht, PRIVATE LAW SOURCES AND ANALOGIES OF INTERNATIONAL LAW 155 (1927).

69 Sometimes they coexist in the same case. In *Medellin v. Texas*, 552 U.S. 491 (2008), Chief Justice Roberts's majority opinion purports to operate on the UN Charter as if it were a statute. *See* 552 U.S. 506 ("The interpretation of a treaty, like the interpretation of a statute, begins with its text."). Justice Breyer's dissenting opinion regards the contract analogy as more helpful. *See* 552 U.S. at 556–7.

70 *See, e.g.*, U.C.C. § 2–207(2) (preventing the inclusion of additional terms in an acceptance if those terms materially change the offer).

71 Since the 1960s, interim obligations have become an important feature of treaty law. Under article 18 of the VCLT, states that have signed a treaty have a legal duty to refrain from

Employing a statutory model, therefore, can be an invitation to examine a treaty text unilaterally, or at least more unilaterally than if examined with a contract model. During the first half of the nineteenth century in particular, courts following the contract analogy were serious about pursuing mutual intent and not solely the intent of U.S. negotiators. Those courts stated repeatedly that a treaty's terms were to be found in the express words of the agreement and in terms that could be inferred by applying the principle of good faith.[72] Courts were not to rewrite the agreement from a U.S. perspective nor were they to rely on the postratification views of the Executive branch. They were to be attentive to differences in meaning between the English and non-English versions.[73] This period of case law was remarkable in deciding some important cases against U.S. litigants.[74]

Statutes are also different from contracts with regard to those who are subject to their terms. Statutes are the means by which communities regulate the activities of their members and prescribe rules of general application. Contracts typically bind a limited number of individuals or entities regulating themselves in ways that may depart greatly from the general norms of the community. Important distinctions follow from this observation. Statutes in the United States are produced by electoral majorities, often over the strenuous objections of electoral minorities. It is the task of statutory drafters to

defeating the object and purpose of the treaty prior to its entry into force. *See* David Moore, *The President's Unconstitutional Treatymaking*, 59 *UCLA L. Rev.* 598 (2012); David C. Scott, *Presidential Power to "Un-sign" Treaties*, 69 *U. Chi. L. Rev.* 1447 (2002); Edwart T. Swaine, *Unsigning*, 55 *Stan. L. Rev.* 2061 (2003). It is difficult to square the existence of such interim obligations – duties that arise before the agreement is ratified – with a contractual model of treaties, especially when in practice such interim obligations can exist for considerable periods of time. *See* Moore, *supra* at Appendix (providing a chart of the length of interim obligations of the United States under various unratified treaties).

72 *See generally* Michael P. Van Alstyne, *The Death of Good Faith in Treaty Jurisprudence and a Call for Resurrection*, 93 Geo. L. J. 1885, 1907–16 (2005) (collecting cases and arguing that the good faith cannon functionally died a silent death before World War II). Professor Van Alstyne proposes a limited resurrection of the good faith cannon as a means of restoring the internationalist perspective to U.S. treaty interpretation and as a necessary constraint on the power of the Executive branch in construing treaties. *Ibid.*

73 *See* Restatement (Third) of the Foreign Relations Law of the United States (Am. Law Inst. 1987), § 325, cmt. f (stating that when there is a difference in meaning between two or more authenticated versions of a treaty, the task of a court in the United States is to choose a meaning "that best reconciles the texts").

74 In addition to *Ware v. Hylton*, *see, e.g.*, United States v. Arredondo, 31 U.S at 729–30 (ruling in favor of recipient of grant of land from Spain and against the U.S. government); Cook v. United States, 288 U.S. 102 (ruling in favor of British ship owner and against U.S. government). *See generally* Duncan B. Hollis, *Treaties in the United States Supreme Court, 1860–1900*, *in* International Law in the U.S. Supreme Court 55 (David L. Sloss, Michael D. Ramsey & William s. Dodge, eds. 2011).

package the views of the majority voting bloc. Those interpreting statutes often must discern the details of the position agreed upon within that bloc. Statutes in the United States are the result of a process that is at least partially public and leaves a paper trail of prior drafts, related statutes, public hearings, committee reports, and other documents that shed light on interpretive disputes. In contrast, classic two-party contracts (like bilateral treaties) record the compromises reached between two main interests. The dispute between those adjudicating a contract dispute revolves around a document that embodies, at least in parts, opposing points of view that, through negotiations, were reconciled by compromises thought to bring overall benefits to the contracting parties.[75]

In sum, the adoption of the statutory analogy reflected a shift in basic assumptions during a period in which, increasingly, more of American law consisted of statutes. But the statutory model also provided interpretive constraints and predictability, just as the contract model had done. Treaty interpretation remained primarily a lawyerly endeavor. There were new documents to bring into the interpretive task – preliminary drafts of multilateral treaties, the explanatory reports of international organization sponsoring treaty conferences, floor discussion, Senate reports and hearings that resembled legislative history – but the new tools were ones that had domestic legislative analogues. They were not the source of unbounded manipulation. The diligent judge, aided by capable lawyers and in search of a treaty's purpose, had much to peruse.[76] For UN-sponsored treaties, an extensive and accessible *travaux* often is available. That trove of documents likely contains the initial description of the treaty project, which country or countries proposed it, and an articulation of the goals to be pursued. If the treaty is

75 After all, either or both parties can walk away from a deal that is disadvantageous, either in the context of that particular document, in the context of its wider relationship with the other party, or its wider set of relationships within a particular industry or political community. The fact that negotiations resulted in agreement indicates that both sides assessed the contract as a whole as better than the next best alternative.

76 *See* Charney, *supra* note 47, at 809 (arguing that "if one examines the negotiating records of treaties, it becomes apparent that they do not differ significantly from legislative histories of domestic statutes."). This statement reflects a common view of treaty documentation but glosses over significant differences between treaty documentation and statutory documentation. The former typically is produced over a longer period of time (sometimes decades) in multiple languages, in a context in which new States may enter in the middle of ongoing negotiations, and in which some States are party to the VCLT and some are not. *See* Paul R. Dubinsky, *Adventures in Treaty Interpretation*, 57 AM. J. COMP. L. 745 (2009). In addition, the complications associated with treaty ratification do not have a clear counterpart in U.S. legislation: Treaties enter into force for states parties at different points in time, and some states ratify subject to reservations, understandings, and declarations.

concluded under the auspices of a specific international organization (e.g., UNIDROIT), the organization's main *raisons d'être* can be found in its governing statute. Moreover, there is cause for construing words or phrases found in one UNIDROIT treaty in light of how the same words or phrases are understood in other UNIDROIT treaties.

Of course there also are documents unilaterally generated by the United States. These include U.S. proposals, oral statements at treaty conferences, negotiating positions, and papers that the U.S. delegation receives from interest groups before or during the negotiations. After the treaty text is finalized, there are other documents that may reflect a unilateral U.S. perspective. Such documents include the testimony of delegation members or experts before Congress, Congressional committee reports, RUDs voted on by the Senate, and treaty implementing legislation. The foregoing list is "unilaterally generated by the United States" in the sense that these documents are generated as part of the U.S. domestic political process. Some sources are also unilateral in the sense that they are produced after the treaty drafting process has been concluded – that is, after there is an agreed upon text. If a member of a U.S. treaty delegation testifies to the Senate Foreign Relations Committee that a proposed treaty does not require any changes in existing U.S. law, that statement is made at a time and in a forum in which there is unlikely to be the opportunity for the articulation of foreign opposition to this position.[77]

From a reliability and accuracy point of view, there are two main problems with interpretations arrived at using the statutory analogy and tools of statutory construction. The first is selectivity. Like contemporary legislative histories, the *travaux* associated with contemporary multilateral treaties can be voluminous.[78] As with statements made on the Senate floor, it can be difficult years later for an adjudicator to ascertain the significance of a particular statement or

[77] The fact that an interpretation is unilaterally generated does not automatically make it of low value; that depends on the interpretive issue that it addresses. With respect to interpreting whether or not a U.S. treaty is self-executing, for example, Professor Bradley stresses that foreign treaty negotiators typically do not form an intent with respect to whether a given treaty will be self-executing within the U.S. legal system. *See* Curtis A. Bradley, *Intent, Presumptions, and Non-Self-Executing Treaties*, 102 AM. J. INT'L L. 540 (2008).

[78] For example, the HCPIL Judgments Project negotiations, which began in 1992 as an effort to produce an ambitious treaty providing for the international recognition of a broad swath of civil judgments, have now consumed twenty-five years of effort as of this writing. Along the way, these negotiations have yielded a Hague Choice of Court Convention that is very limited in scope. The *travaux* associated with the Choice of Court Convention potentially includes the work of several diplomatic conferences, and many more working sessions, formal and informal. The interpretive situation is further complicated by major changes in the direction of the project and in its fundamental goals, as well as long hiatuses. Moreover, the membership of the HCPIL changed several times during the project. For commentary on the

document. It may be difficult to ascertain who was present when the statement was made or precisely when a given document was circulated.

The second problem is that among the trove of documents potentially to be consulted is a subset that an intellectually honest interpreter would have to characterize as suspect. Suppose, for example, that in testimony to the Senate Foreign Relations Committee the State Department Legal Advisor represents that nothing in the proposed treaty requires that any change be made to current U.S. law. What weight should such a statement be given in Congressional or judicial interpretation of the treaty? Is the statement a representation that a majority of the countries that participated in the negotiations even understood what it would mean for the treaty to be in harmony with U.S. law as it existed at a specific point in time? Does the statement mean that U.S. consent to the treaty was conditioned on none of its provisions requiring any change in U.S. law?

In sum, much about the statutory model for interpreting treaties, like the contractual one, is lawyerly work. In that respect, the statutory model imposed constraints on interpretation. As with the contract model, the statutory model was understood as involving lawyerly tools, work that did not bring with it an unquestioning deference to executive branch views. The statutory model, however, created new temptations to bring unilateralism to the interpretation of treaties. This was especially so to the extent that Senate reports and hearings became an important set of interpretive materials, to the extent that the focus of interpretation moved away from course of dealing and other actions to statements and documents, and to the extent that the search for mutual assent and the overall purpose of the agreement was replaced by marshalling statements made at treaty conferences.

IV TREATY INTERPRETATION AND THE THIRD RESTATEMENT

Both the contract and the statutory analogies found their way into the American Law Institute's Second (1965) and Third (1987) Restatements of the Foreign Relations Law of the United States. Both documents were created for the purpose of being major resources for executive branch negotiators, Congressional oversight committees, and courts. For present purposes, the Third Restatement's treaty interpretation sections can be seen to stress three major themes. First, in regard to analogies, the Third Restatement had to deal with a body of contract precedents and statutory

interpretive difficulties associated with such complications, *see* Dubinsky, *Adventures in Treaty Interpretation*, *supra* note 76.

precedents that were inconsistent and, in the day-to-day planning of transnational transactions, prone to unpredictability. At that time, there seemed to be no *ex ante* way of predicting whether a court would regard a treaty as similar to a statute and delve into *travaux* or as similar to a contract, requiring (perhaps) a focus on the treaty-making history of the parties, the relationship between their various treaties and their mutual intent. Sometimes courts had referred to neither model.[79] The text of section 325 of the Third Restatement – in referring to good faith, context, subsequent agreements, and post-agreement practice – bowed to the continuing influence of the contract model.[80] Reporters' note 5 to that section, on the other hand, essentially laid out the treaty-as-statute model: courts in the United States had to consult committee reports and "other indications of meaning that the legislative branch has attached to an agreement." They also were to consult "unilateral statements of intention" of the Executive branch and "internal official correspondence and position papers prepared for use of the United States delegation in the negotiation."

This latter statement in the reporters' note clearly is in tension with the text of section 325; the internal correspondence of the U.S. delegation – correspondence not shared with other delegations – is off-limits from a contract interpretation perspective. The Restatement's solution to this apparent contradiction was to conclude that U.S. law on treaty interpretation had incorporated more than one analogy (which was true), that these analogies coexisted at the time of the Restatement's drafting (also true) and that the clue to why courts' turned to one analogy rather than another was that certain analogies fit some factual contexts better than others.[81] On this last point, the notes to section 325 offer a sketchy attempt to categorize a seemingly haphazard practice of employing comparisons by dividing the universe of treaties into a list of categories, a list that is incomplete: tools of contract interpretation are to be applied to treaties involving a single transaction, such as the transfer of territory.[82] Other treaties regulate ongoing behavior. In this they resemble

79 There were cases in which the Supreme Court had referred to neither the contract model nor the statute model, even though these analogies seemed to be appropriate in light of prior case law. *See, e.g.*, Clark v. Allen, 331 U.S. 503 (1947) (interpreting 1923 bilateral Friendship, Commerce, and Consular Rights Treaty with Germany with respect to the ability of foreign nationals to inherit property).

80 These are all facets of treaty interpretation emphasized in judicial opinions following the contract view.

81 *See* Third Restatement, *supra* note 73, § 325, cmt. d ("Different approaches to interpretation have developed for particular categories of agreements.").

82 *Ibid.* (stating that these agreements "should be construed like similar private contracts between private parties" and that "[d]ifferent types of agreements may call for different approaches").

statutes.[83] Yet other treaties create international organizations designed to engage in lawmaking of their own. According to the Restatement, such treaties have a "constitutional quality."[84]

Although there was some descriptive accuracy and plausibility to these attempts at categorization, the section as a whole, along with its notes and comments, did not offer much guidance. To some degree, the lack of guidance was a function of the underlying case law, which had become chaotic by the time of the Third Restatement drafting process. Courts had continued to say that treaties were contracts, but often there was no longer any interpretive bite to this characterization.[85] Sometimes courts imported tools of statutory interpretation. Sometimes they announced that deference was owed to the Executive branch's views but then engaged in a *de novo* review of the treaty anyway. And sometimes courts actually did extend deference. The Restatement acknowledged this reality, attempted to offer a rationale for the seeming chaos, and then suggested a categorization anchored partly in the existing case law and partly in a normative view of the respect due particular treaties, such as the UN Charter.

The second theme of the Third Restatement's approach pertained to the relationship between the U.S and the international law of treaty interpretation. Here, the Restatement leaned toward aligning the former with the

83 *Ibid.* § 325, rptr. note 1 ("United States courts, accustomed to analyzing legislative materials, have not been hesitant to resort to *travaux préparatoires*.").

84 *Ibid.* § 325, cmt. d ("Agreements creating international organizations have a constitutional quality, and are subject to the observation in McCulloch v. Maryland, 17 U.S. (4 Wheat.) 316, 407, 4 L.Ed. 579 (1819) that 'we must never forget that it is a constitution that we are expounding . . .'"). For this suggestion, the Restatement offered no example of a U.S. interpreter (court, legislator, or executive branch official) ever having actually applied this analogy. In the years leading up to the Third Restatement, the European Court of Justice had begun referring to the Treaty of Rome as having constitutional qualities and purposes and as creating a "new legal order" by which sovereign States had ceded part of their sovereignty to that new order. *See* Paul R. Dubinsky, *The Essential Function of Federal Courts: The European Union and the United States Compared*. 42 AM. J. COMP. L. 295 (1994). It is hard to imagine that those who drafted the Third Restatement were unfamiliar with this development, though it is difficult to discern whether comment d to § 325 was, in effect, a place holder for the anticipated future interpretation of treaties by which the United States would cede significant sovereignty to international institutions. In 2008, the Supreme Court declined to take into account the constitutional qualities to treaties such as the UN Charter and the Statute of the International Court of Justice. *See* Medellin v. Texas, 522 U.S. 491, 506 (2008).

85 The Court in Coplin v. United States, 6 Cl. Ct. 115, 125–6 (1985) began its analysis by stating that "[t]reaties and other international agreements are contracts between sovereign states." It specifically rejected the model of treaties as "international legislation." *Id.* at 126 (*citing* Bishop, *Reservations to Treaties*, 103 Recueil des Cours 245, 255 (1962)). *Coplin* then went deep into the negotiating history of the Panama Canal treaty in a manner resembling statutory interpretation rather than contract interpretation.

latter. It did so through receptiveness to the VCLT, which the United States had not ratified and which differed in critical ways from the traditional U.S. approach. The reporters' notes to section 325 emphasized commonality in stating (without example) that often the two routes will lead to the same result.[86] The Third Restatement's internationalist orientation is also evident in its position on the decisions of international tribunals. Reporters' note 4 states: "The United States and its courts and agencies ... are bound by an interpretation of an agreement of the United States by an international body authorized by the agreement to interpret it." In support, the note cited only one source, a decision of the Federal Communication Commission, which did not in fact provide the support needed.[87] Furthermore, section 325(2) and VCLT article 31(2) both incorporate a standard tool of contract interpretation: using subsequent agreements and practices among treaty parties as a means of understanding the intent of those parties at the time of treaty formation. But the reporters hastened to point out that use of *travaux* by American courts could be quite extensive, more extensive than contemplated by the VCLT.[88]

[86] THIRD RESTATEMENT, *supra* note 73, § 325, rptr. note 4.

[87] The case cited is Matter of International Bank for Reconstruction and Development, 17 F.C.C. 450, 461 (1953). The Reporters argued that U.S. courts are obliged to treat as precedent the treaty interpretations of international courts, such as the International Court of Justice, a position eventually rejected in Medellin v. Texas, 522 U.S. 491, 506 (2008).

The problems with citing *Matter of International Bank for Reconstruction and Development* in 1987 for this proposition were many: It was not a judicial decision. It was not recent. Most importantly, the decision did not say what the Reporters' Note implied. At most, the decision stood for the uncontroversial proposition that when the United States is party to a treaty, the text of which sets out rules of interpretation, the United States has a duty to apply those treaty rules:

> By virtue of its membership in the Fund and Bank, the United States is obliged to conform to the provisions of the respective Articles of Agreement, including the provisions of the respective Articles relating to interpretation of the Articles. As a consequence, the United States is obliged to carry out the Articles of Agreement as interpreted in accordance with the provisions of the Articles.

Ibid. at 461–2. The last sentence is ambiguous. The phrase "as interpreted in accordance with the provisions of the Articles" fails to specify whose interpretation must be followed by the United States and whether this duty is self-executing. The extent to which this one citation was offered in support of the proposition that courts in the United States are "bound" by the treaty interpretations of international tribunals illustrates the extent to which the Third Restatement's treaty sections, commentary, and notes lean against unilateral interpretation of treaties.

[88] *See* THIRD RESTATEMENT, *supra* note 73, § 325, comment g ("This section suggests a mode of interpretation of international agreements somewhat different than that ordinarily applied by courts in the United States. Courts in the United States are generally more willing than those of other states to look outside the instrument to determine its meaning."). Recently, Professor Julian Mortenson has argued that articles 31 and 32 of the VCLT permit greater use of *travaux*

The third theme of the Third Restatement's approach to treaty interpretation is deference to the Executive branch. Like the Second Restatement, the Third articulated as law the position that courts should accord "great weight" to the interpretations arrived at by the Executive branch.[89] Like the Second, it also failed to acknowledge that such a rule was contrary to judicial practice during the decades immediately after the Founding and through the nineteenth century, when the contract model was predominant. Both Restatements also failed to note that the extent of deference to the views of the Executive branch, even late in the twentieth century, was variable and often not outcome-determinative.[90] The justification for deference was that executive departments and agencies possessed special expertise in treaty affairs.[91]

Despite these flaws in its treatment of the subject of deference, the Third Restatement nonetheless was able to draw on a series of Supreme Court cases that employed the "great weight" doctrine. Among them was *Kolovrat v. Oregon*, decided in 1961, in which the Court struck down an Oregon law prohibiting non-U.S. citizens from inheriting property in that state.[92] This result followed, in substantial part, from post-ratification diplomatic correspondence from the State Department pertaining to an 1881 bilateral treaty with Serbia (a predecessor to Yugoslavia) that, in the view of the Executive branch, was intended to confer inheritance rights on Serbian nationals.[93] In

than traditionally thought. *See* Julian Mortenson, *The Travaux of Travaux: Is the Vienna Convention Hostile to Drafting History?* 107 AM. J. INT'L L. 780 (2013).

89 THIRD RESTATEMENT, *supra* note 73, § 326, cmt. b; RESTATEMENT (SECOND) OF THE FOREIGN RELATIONS LAW OF THE UNITED STATES § 152 (1965). Surprisingly, § 152 of the Second Restatement did not refer to case law in support of the "great weight" duty of deference, even though such support was available, and it ignored early twentieth-century cases that had characterized the level of deference differently. *See, e.g.*, Charlton v. Kelly, 229 U.S. 447, 468 (1913) ("much weight").

90 *See, e.g.*, The Amiable Isabella, 19 U.S. at 2 (rejecting U.S. government's argument and holding that a ship was immune from capture because of a treaty with Spain). For the Court, Justice Story wrote that judicial interpretations of treaties had to be "observe[d] with the most scrupulous good faith," even in a military context, and that good-faith interpretation was a duty of the judiciary regardless of actions or positions taken by Congress and the Executive branch. *See also* U.S. v. Laverty, 26 Fed. Cas. at 875–6 (interpreting Treaty of Paris and rejecting U.S. government's view that defendant was an "alien enemy").

91 *See* Richard B. Bilder, *The Office of the Legal Adviser: The State Department Lawyer and Foreign Affairs*, 56 AM. J. INT'L L. 633, 674 (1962) ("The reason for the 'great weight' doctrine is essentially that of 'agency expertise' – a recognition of the Department's special experience in such areas, its frequent role as negotiator of such agreements, and its access to confidential facts.")

92 Kolovrat v. Oregon, 366 U.S. 187, 81 S. Ct. 922, 6 L. Ed. 2d 218 (1961).

93 *Ibid.* at 194 ("While courts interpret treaties for themselves, the meaning given them by the departments of government particularly charged with their negotiation and enforcement is

the succeeding decades, *Kolovrat* was cited repeatedly as a principal authority for deferring to the Executive branch, though at times the citing court employed variations on the term "great weight."[94]

Despite the Third Restatement's adopting the "great weight" formulation, section 326(2) reiterates the traditional view that the judiciary has final word on a treaty's meaning for purposes of applying the treaty as law within the legal system of the United States.[95] This position implies that any interpretive deference to the Executive branch must fall short of total unquestioning acceptance.[96] The notes to section 326(2) attempt to clarify "great weight," suggesting its meaning is not identical in all cases. Courts are especially likely to defer to an Executive branch interpretation that was articulated prior to litigation. Similarly, there is deference to an interpretation that has been articulated in the context of diplomatic interchange with other countries.[97] Courts are less likely to defer when individual rights are at stake.[98] The duty of deference is less, according to the Restatement, when the executive's position on the treaty is articulated for the first time in the very litigation that is before the court.[99]

Overall, the Third *Restatement* conveyed a complicated and not entirely coherent depiction of American treaty interpretation. No attempt was made to square the deference principle with the contract and statute metaphors. But, crucially, the Restatement did codify the contract and statute models; it did fix a standard for judicial deference; and it did offer rationales for that deference.

given great weight."). While *Kolovrat* was decided on treaty interpretation grounds, the factually similar and subsequent case of *Zschernig v. Miller* held that state laws discriminating against foreign nationals were preempted by federal supremacy in foreign affairs. *See* Zschernig v. Miller, 389 U.S. 429, 436–49, 88 S. Ct. 664, 19 L. Ed. 2d 683 (1968).

94 *See, e.g.*, El Al Israel Airlines, Ltd. v. Tsui Yuan Tseng, 525 U.S. 155, 119 S. Ct. 662, 671, 142 L. Ed. 2d 576 (1999) ("Respect is ordinarily due the *reasonable views* of the Executive Branch concerning the meaning of an international treaty.") (emphasis added); Chan v. Korean Airlines, Ltd., 490 U.S. 122, 109 S. Ct. 1676, 104 L. Ed. 2d 113 (1989); Sumitomo Shoji America, Inc. v Avagliano, 457 U.S. 176, 102 S. Ct. 2374, 72 L. Ed. 2d 765 (1982).

95 Note 5 to § 325 uses the word "required." The text of section 326(2) says that courts "will" give great weight to executive branch interpretations, perhaps suggesting something different than "required."

96 Third Restatement, *supra* note 73 § 326(2) ("Courts in the United States have final authority to interpret an international agreement for purposes of applying it as law in the United States, but will give great weight to an interpretation made by the Executive Branch."); *see also* § 326, cmt. b. Of course, in some circumstances courts may be prevented from adjudicating the merits of treaty claims because of lack of standing, the need to apply the political question doctrine, or other impediments. In such instances, the executive branch's interpretation may be final for practical purposes because it is not subject to judicial review.

97 *Ibid.*, rptr. note 2. 98 *Ibid.* 99 *Ibid.*

V THE THIRD RESTATEMENT IGNORED

Shortly after publication of the Third Restatement, the Supreme Court decided in rapid succession five treaty cases that showed the limited influence of the Restatement's treaty interpretation rules. Despite its recent publication under the leadership of Louis Henkin,[100] the majority opinions in these cases did not mention the Second or Third Restatements, suggesting that what had appeared to be a broad consensus about the domestic law of treaty interpretation was, in fact, not particularly strong.

The first of these five cases was *Societe Nationale Industrielle Aerospatiale v. U.S. District Court*,[101] in which the Court interpreted the Hague Evidence Convention,[102] a multilateral treaty to which the United States had become a party in 1972. The second was *Volkswagenwerk Aktiengesellschaft v. Schlunk*,[103] which involved the 1965 Hague Service Convention that had entered into force for the United States in 1969.[104] The third case, *United States v. Stuart*,[105] centered on a bilateral Canada-U.S. tax treaty[106] in which a disagreement surfaced among members of the Court over the permissible use of *travaux*. The fourth case, *U.S. v. Alvarez-Machain*,[107] required the Court to interpret the 1978 bilateral extradition treaty between the United States and Mexico.[108] The fifth case, *Sale v. Haitian Centers Council*,[109] centered on the

100 Chapter 1 of this volume discusses the Supreme Court's frequent citation of Henkin's scholarship, both before and after the Third Restatement. *See* Mark Janis & Noam Wiener, "Treaties in U.S. Law from the Founding to the Third Restatement," Chapter 1 of this volume.

101 Societe Nationale Industrielle Aerospatiale v. U.S. Dist. Court, 482 U.S. 522, 107 S. Ct. 2542, 96 L. Ed. 2d 461 (1987).

102 Convention on Taking of Evidence Abroad in Civil or Commercial Matters, March 18, 1970, T.I.A.S. No. 7444, available at www.hcch.net/index_en.php?act=conventions.text&cid=82 [hereinafter the Hague Evidence Convention].

103 Volkswagenwerk Aktiengesellschaft v. Schlunk, 486 U.S. 694, 108 S. Ct. 2104, 100 L. Ed. 2d 722 (1988).

104 *See* Convention on Service Abroad of Judicial and Extrajudicial Documents in Civil and Commercial Matters, Nov. 15, 1965, 20 U.S.T. 361, T.I.A.S. No. 6638, available at www.hcch.net/en/instruments/conventions/full-text/?cid=17.

105 United States v. Stuart, 489 U.S. 353, 109 S. Ct. 1183, 103 L. Ed. 2d 388 (1989).

106 The Convention & Protocol between Canada and the United States of America for the Avoidance of Double Taxation and the Prevention of Fiscal Evasion in the Case of Income Taxes, March 4, 1942, 56 Stat. 1399, T.S. No. 983.

107 United States v. Alvarez-Machain, 504 U.S. 655, 112 S. Ct. 2188, 119 L. Ed. 2d 441 (1992).

108 Extradition Treaty, United States-United Mexican States, May 4, 1978, 31 U.S.T. 5059, T.I.A.S. No. 9656.

109 Sale v. Haitian Centers Council, Inc., 509 U.S. 155 (1992).

interpretation of the 1967 Protocol[110] to the 1951 Convention on the Status of Refugees.[111]

Taken together, these five treaty interpretation cases – decided by the Supreme Court in a span of six years immediately after publication of the Third Restatement – did much to expose the fragmentation of judicial treaty interpretation in the United States and to foreshadow future fragmentation. The future was to be one in which the Third Restatement's provisions on interpretation would have little influence on the courts or the Executive branch. All five cases received substantial criticism from scholars but few wrote about how the Court had ignored the Third Restatement and its attempt to make sense of analogies in treaty law.

The five cases build on one another and share common features: (1) the Court ignores the Restatement's rules on treaty interpretation; (2) the Court rejects or bypasses the contract analogy in favor of the statutory analogy without explanation; (3) the Court's inquiry into *travaux* or legislative history elevates U.S. sources and treaty objectives above non-U.S. sources and above the objectives of other States party to the treaty; (4) the Court largely adopts the interpretation put forward by the Executive branch, whether appearing before it as a party or as amicus,[112] states that it defers to these views but does not indicate the degree of deference or the reason for doing so. In three of the cases – *Aerospatiale, Schlunk*, and *Alvarez-Machain* – the mode of interpretation leads to the conclusion that the treaty is merely an optional means of achieving a result (e.g., serving process, obtaining evidence, securing jurisdiction over a criminal suspect) and that U.S. courts or executive branch officials are not precluded from pursuing the same result solely through domestic law.[113]

Aerospatiale held that the Hague Evidence Convention's central authority mechanism – the judicial assistance process by which litigants in one country seek discovery materials located in other countries – is not exclusive; rather, it is a "permissive supplement" and not a "replacement" for direct discovery

110 Protocol Relating to the Status of Refugees, October 4, 1967, 606 U.N.T.S. 267.

111 Convention Relating to the Status of Refugees, July 28, 1951, 19 U.S.T. 6259, 6276, T.I.A.S. No. 6577.

112 The U.S. government was a party in the *Alvarez-Machain, Sale* and *Stuart* cases. It submitted amicus briefs in *Aerospatiale* and *Schlunk*.

113 In other words, in three of the cases, the Court's handiwork produces a result somewhat similar to that of some RUDs. As explained by Roger Alford in Chapter 8 of this volume, a common use of RUDs in post–Third-Restatement treaty practice is to make sure that entry into treaty relations does not bring about significant changes in domestic U.S. law. *Aerospatiale* and *Schlunk* have a similar effect. *See* Roger Alford, "Judicial Barriers to the Enforcement of Treaties", Chapter 8 of this volume.

under U.S. statutes and rules of civil procedure.[114] In remanding, the Court essentially left lower federal courts and state courts to interpret the requirements of the Convention on a case-by-case basis,[115] a result widely criticized in other Hague Conference member states.[116] In nearly three decades of applying *Aerospatiale*, state and federal courts have overwhelmingly concluded that discovery can proceed via the Federal Rules of Civil Procedure backed up by an American court's sanction powers under Rule 37 or its state-court counterpart. Litigants rarely are required to proceed through the treaty mechanism.[117]

In reaching this result, the majority began by stating that treaties are "in the nature of a contract between nations," to which "general rules of construction apply."[118] From there, however, the Court ignored its own contract-analogy precedents. It switched to the statutory analogy in summarizing the history of the negotiations leading to the Convention. This summary had a unilateral quality to it. The Court focused overwhelmingly on statements made by U.S. participants and an analysis of Convention objectives that gave weight to U.S. aims but was dismissive of those of other Convention countries.[119] Overall, the opinion tracked the recommendations in the U.S. Government brief.

114 Aerospatiale, 482 U.S. at 536.

115 Among the factors to be weighed by trial courts in determining whether to require litigants to proceed by way of the Convention are the extent of the intrusiveness of unilateral U.S. discovery mechanisms and the likelihood that the Convention will be used for discovery abuse, such as delay or undue expense. *Ibid.* at 546–7.

116 *See* Permanent Bureau, Hague Conference on Private International Law, "The Mandatory/Non-Mandatory Character of the Evidence Convention" (2008), available at https://assets.hcch.net/upload/wop/2008pd10e.pdf (summarizing extensive discussion of the *Aerospatiale* decision at the 1989 Hague Special Commission meeting examining the operation of the Evidence Convention and at subsequent Special Commission meetings).

117 For analyses of lower court cases, *see* Patrick J. Borchers, *The Incredible Shrinking Hague Evidence Convention*, 38 Tex. J. Int'l L.J. 73 (2003); Construction and Application of the Convention, 1 A.L.R. Int'l 289 (2010); Kathleen Braun Gilchrist, *Rethinking Jurisdictional Discovery Under the Hague Evidence Convention*, 44 Vand. J. Transnat'l L. 155 (2011). In U.S.-based litigation, the treaty is typically used to obtain discovery from nonparties. *See, e.g.*, In re Baycol Products Litig., 348 F. Supp. 2d 1058 (D. Minn. 2004); Tulip Computers Int'l B. V. v. Dell Computer Corp., 254 F. Supp. 2d 469, 474 (D. Del. 2003).

118 Aerospatiale, 482 U.S. at 533 (citing *Ware v. Hylton* and other cases).

119 In amicus briefs, several states parties to the Evidence Convention articulated their view of the Convention's central objectives, some of which differed from those emphasized in the U.S. Government brief. The amicus briefs submitted by France, Germany, and Switzerland argued that the Convention embodied reciprocity: countries without broadly permissive discovery standards triggered by litigants had agreed to provide some support for U.S.-style discovery in litigation pending in U.S. courts provided that these countries received something in return – a process by which the discovery demands of U.S. litigants would be judicially mediated before becoming required of litigants domiciled outside the United States. The Court's majority opinion never really responded to this argument. *See* Brief for

The *Schlunk* case also involved a treaty resulting from early U.S. participation in the Hague Conference. As in *Aerospatiale*, the majority in *Schlunk* interpreted the convention without referring to the Third Restatement. Its conclusion severely undercut the Convention's central authority mechanism that had been, from the standpoint of many other states, a key part of the bargain reached during negotiations. In *Schlunk*, the principal treaty provision at issue was Article 1, which states that: "The present Convention shall apply in all cases, in civil or commercial matters, where there is *occasion to transmit a judicial or extrajudicial document for service abroad*."[120] What if U.S. law deems service complete when some agent of the defendant, one located within the U.S., is served in the forum state? The Court in *Schlunk* concluded that under these circumstances there is no "occasion to transmit" a judicial document for service abroad. As a result, the applicability of the treaty is determined not only by the law of the United States, but by the law of a particular U.S. state, and that the treaty did not apply because the Illinois statute in *Schlunk*, designated an agent for receipt of process on behalf of a foreign corporation.

Justice O'Connor's opinion in *Schlunk* fixes on the term "service of process"[121] even though the English version of the Convention employs the phrase "service of judicial documents." The Court's opinion implicitly concludes that the text of the treaty is somehow unclear.[122] It then goes on

the Federal Republic of Germany as Amicus Curiae in Support of Petitioners,1986 WL 727492; Brief of Government of Switzerland as Amicus Curiae in Support of Petitioners,1986 WL 727499 (U.S.); Brief of Amicus Curiae the Republic of France in Support of Petitioners, 1986 WL 727501.

120 Hague Service Convention, *supra* note 104, Art. 1 (emphasis added).

121 Schlunk, 486 U.S. at 700 (relying on *Black's Law Dictionary*, *Wright & Miller on Federal Practice and Procedure* and an American-authored treatise on international judicial assistance). A search of Lexis and Westlaw does not reveal any amicus briefs having been filed by any states parties to the Convention, nor does it reveal whether the Supreme Court or the U.S. Government invited other countries to clarify such terms with reference to the French text. It is also not clear which Hague countries were aware of the *Schlunk* litigation and whether those countries became aware of it in time to file amicus briefs.

122 The Court never says why the text is unclear. Such a determination should have been made and explained in order to overcome the inference that a treaty with a detailed list of acceptable methods of service implicitly excludes other methods. *See* Hague Service Convention, *supra* note 104, at Art. 3 & 10. Courts in the United States have long applied the rule of construction that if a contract or a statute or a treaty provides an explicit list, then the list either must be deemed to be exclusive or the document can be interpreted only as permitting additional items similar to items on the list. *See* Antonin Scalia & Bryan A. Garner, READING LAW: THE INTERPRETATION OF LEGAL TEXTS (2012). Service within the United States on a statutorily designated agent of a defendant is not at all similar to the four methods of service listed in the Hague Service Convention.

to rely wholly on U.S. sources to define the former phrase and applies a "liberal" method of interpretation by consulting the Convention's context, its *travaux*, and its relation to two prior Hague treaties. In carrying out this legislative-history type inquiry, the Court gives an incomplete description of the purposes of the Convention. It ignored a fundamental goal of many non-U.S. states parties: assuring that efforts to gather evidence in a coercive manner be filtered through the central authority of the requested state, which determines whether requests fall within the scope of the treaty. Instead, the Court examines the Convention's purposes exclusively from a U.S. point of view.[123]

The practical result in the *Schlunk* case is that successful service on a foreign litigant can turn on state statutes and state procedural rules. This outcome was roundly criticized abroad. So was the Supreme Court's method.[124] As Professor Stephen Burbank aptly explained: "Even if the Court reached the correct treaty interpretations in *Schlunk* and *Aerospatiale*, it employed reasoning that could deny to treaties regulating procedure in international civil litigation the power to constrain unilateral action."[125]

The *Stuart* case further wandered from the Third Restatement, in particular its position on travaux and legislative history. In *Stuart*, all members of the Court agreed that a 1942 double taxation treaty authorized the IRS to provide assistance to Canadian tax authorities. Justice Brennan's majority opinion went a step further; it tried to show that the legislative history of the Senate's consent to ratification supported the same result. Justice Brennan's foray into the Executive branch's representations to the Senate and the latter's deliberations prompted three justices to take the majority to task for

[123] Schlunk, 486 U.S. at 698 (characterizing those purposes as "provid[ing] a simpler way to serve process abroad, ... assur[ing] that defendants sued in foreign jurisdictions would receive actual and timely notice of suit, and ... facilitat[ing] proof of service abroad."). No reference was made to the role that central authorities can play in providing uniform interpretation of the treaty in the requested state, assuring that documents are translated, and protecting domiciliaries of the state from being harassed by requests that clearly fall outside the scope of the Convention.

[124] *See* Report on the Operation of the Hague Service Convention and the Hague Evidence Convention, 28 I.L.M. 1556, 1560–1 (1989) (singling out for criticism *Aerospatiale* and *Schlunk*). Periodic reports like this on the operation of one or more existing Hague conventions can affect the assessments of Hague Conference countries regarding whether the United States can be counted on to live up to future treaty obligations. *See* Lawrence Collins, *The Hague Evidence Convention and Discovery: A Serious Misunderstanding?* 35 INT'L & COMP. L. Q. 765, 783 (1986).

[125] Stephen Burbank, *The Reluctant Partner: Making Procedural Law for International Civil Litigation*, 57 L. & CONTEMP. PROBS. 103, 137 (1994).

straying from the treaty text.[126] When the meaning of a treaty text is clear, they argued, going outside that text risks muddying an agreed-upon method of treaty interpretation.[127]

The Court decided the fifth case, *Alvarez-Machain*, one year after *Stuart*. The case focused on a 1978 extradition treaty with Mexico, which set out in detail the range of criminal offenses that can become the subject of extradition requests and the procedures by which the government of one country can request that authorities in the other proceed with extradition. In contrast to *Stuart* (in which Chief Justice Rehnquist voted with the majority), Justice Rehnquist's opinion for the Court in *Alvarez-Machain* showed great reluctance to dive deeply into *travaux*. It also confusingly moved from the statutory model to the contract model without explaining why such a switch within the same case and with respect to the same treaty is coherent.

Alvarez-Machain first expressly invoked the treaty-as-statute model,[128] leading to an exploration of the text. That text says much about extradition procedures and extraditable offenses but nothing about abduction. So how is one to determine whether a self-help mechanism (extraterritorial abduction) is lawful when the treaty says nothing about abduction or other nontreaty mechanisms? The majority put forward two answers to this question. The first was to deploy a presumption against exclusivity; the default rule of interpretation must be that the treaty's means of securing jurisdiction over the defendant was not intended to be the exclusive means of obtaining jurisdiction. In the absence of treaty language rebutting such a presumption, one should not

[126] Justice Scalia was the most adamant: "Here the implication is that, had the extrinsic evidence contradicted the plain language of the Treaty it would govern. That is indeed what we mistakenly said in the earlier case that the Court cites as authority for its approach." Stuart, 489 U.S. at 371 (Scalia, J., concurring) (citing *Sumitomo Shoji Am., Inc. v. Avagliano*, 457 U.S. 176). The Restatement squarely weighed in on the side of consulting pre-ratification Senate materials. *See* THIRD RESTATEMENT, *supra* note 73, § 314, cmt. d. For one scholar's tutorial on how to use Senate materials in treaty interpretation, *see* Detlev F. Vagts, *Senate Materials and Treaty Interpretation: Some Research Hints for the Supreme Court*, 83 AM. J. INT'L L. 546 (1989).

[127] This debate was replayed in Medellin v. Texas, 552 U.S. 491 (2008), a case that turned in part on the interpretation of Article 94 of the UN Charter. Chief Justice Roberts's majority opinion equated treaties with statutes and then interpreted the Charter without reference to its *travaux* and historical background, over the objections of three dissenting Justices. Some commentaters have concluded that *Medellin* is an important victory for textualism. *See, e.g.*, David Bederman, New Paradigm, *supra* note 1. Note, however, that to the extent that the political branches post-*Medellin* are likely to require implementing legislation and not rely on self-execution, the frequency of judicial interpretation of treaty texts (as opposed to implementing statutes) may decrease.

[128] Alvarez-Machain, 504 U.S at 663 ("In construing a treaty, as in construing a statute, we first look to its terms to determine its meaning.").

conclude that the United States meant to relinquish unilateral mechanisms in entering into the treaty.[129] The majority, however, pointed to no basis in contract law, statutory construction, or the Court's treaty interpretation precedents for such a presumption.

Second, Justice Rehnquist drew a distinction between unlawful acts and acts that violate the extradition treaty. He conceded that officially sanctioned cross-border kidnapping may violate public international law[130] but nonetheless wrote that such illegality does not speak to whether the United States violated the bilateral extradition treaty. The main victims of this approach were the Third Restatement and an American history of treaty interpretation grounded in rule-of-law observance.[131]

The *Alvarez-Machain* majority does not rest this newly discovered presumption of exclusivity on the statutory model announced at the outset, perhaps because it makes little sense for a treaty implicitly to condone self-help measures when these measures undermine the treaty's purpose.[132] That purpose was to bring the transnational transfer of criminal suspects under a framework of mutual cooperation.[133] Thus when Justice Rehnquist switches

[129] The Court conflated two very different forms of nonexclusivity. The valid observation that a party to an extradition treaty may "voluntarily render an individual to the other country on terms completely outside of those provided in the treaty," *ibid.* at 667, did not in any way strengthen the argument for rendition that is *involuntary* and contrary to the will of the territorial state.

[130] Alvarez-Machain, 504 U.S at 667–9.

[131] It would be more consistent with traditional American concern for treaties, such as that typified by *Ware* and the post-Founding period, to presume that internationally unlawful acts are not to be construed as consistent with U.S. treaty obligations. *See* Murray v. The Schooner Charming Betsy, 6 U.S. 64, 2 L. Ed. 208 (1804) (defending cannon of statutory construction that U.S. statutes are presumed not to embody an intent by the political branches to violate international law). Some scholars who support the delegation model of treaty interpretation, *see infra* Section VI, also support a limited version of the *Charming Betsy* canon. *See, e.g.*, Bradley, *infra* note 186 at 536 ("the redefinition of federal court power after *Erie*" "compel[s] reexamination of the *Charming Betsy* canon); Daniel Abebe & Eric A. Posner, *The Flaws of Foreign Affairs Legalism*, 51 VA. J. INT'L L. 507, 510–511 (2011); *see also* Al-Bihani v. Obama, 590 F.3d 866, 880 (D.C. Cir. 2010) (Kavanaugh, J., dissenting from denial of rehearing en banc and *citing* Bradley).

[132] Strangely, the Court in *Alvarez-Machain* failed to cite *Aerospatiale* or *Schlunk* in support of a presumption against exclusivity. In both of these cases the Court held other mutual assistance treaties to be nonexclusive, though they were distinguishable in that actions by U.S. courts and litigants were not alleged to be violations of international law or foreign law.

[133] As the dissent argues, among the main goals of extradition treaties is to bring about the reliable, orderly, and nonviolent transfer of criminal suspects or convicted persons from one country to another, under judicial supervision. *Ibid.* at 670–88 (Stevens, J., dissenting). The forcible and unlawful kidnapping of a suspect, in the absence of judicial supervision, brings about the opposite of the treaty's goal. In other words, it may make sense to conclude that a treaty is nonexclusive with respect to nontreaty routes that are consistent with or supportive of

analogies in arguing that Mexico was on notice that U.S. courts had adjudicated and upheld jurisdiction in other instances of abduction,[134] this amounts to a switch from statutory analysis to contract analysis. The reasoning is as follows: if one country is aware (or should have been aware) that the other has a propensity to kidnap, then an implied permission to kidnap should be incorporated into the treaty, as might conceivably be the case in contract interpretation.[135] Such reasoning leaves us with an opinion comprised of a superficial statutory analysis and a disingenuous contract analysis.

In *Sale v. Haitian Centers Council*, the Court interpreted Article 33 of the 1951 Convention Relating to the Status of Refugees, a provision incorporated by reference in the 1967 Protocol Relating to the Status of Refugees. The United States is party to the latter, which is implemented by federal statute.[136] Under the Convention and Protocol, member states are obligated not to "expel or return" refugees to a country in which they fear persecution. Under the Court's 8–1 ruling, the treaty does not impose any such obligation on the United States when acting outside of its territory and territorial waters. The Court thus sustained the legality of the Bush and Clinton administrations' policy of interdicting Haitian refugees on the high seas, effectively preventing them from reaching a place where they could claim the protections of the treaty before being forcibly returned to Haiti.

Writing for the majority, Justice Stevens considered the French version of the Convention, and determined that the word "*refouler*" in Article 33 is not precisely equivalent to "return."[137] Ironically, the Stevens opinion interprets U.S. implementing legislation by reference to the treaty that it was designed to implement but does so precisely to undermine what would appear to be the plain meaning of the statute.[138] By seizing upon the treaty's use of the French

treaty procedures, but it hardly makes sense for countries to become party to treaties that leave them free to continue to pursue means that undermine the treaty.

134 The two cases are Ker v. Illinois, 119 U.S. 436, 7 S. Ct. 225, 30 L. Ed. 421 (1886) and Frisbie v. Collins, 342 U.S. 519, 72 S. Ct. 509, 96 L. Ed. 541 (1952). In the former, the kidnapping was from Peru to the United States. In the latter, the kidnapping was from Illinois to Michigan. In both cases, the Supreme Court adjudicated Due Process challenges to the resulting criminal trial and conviction. The Court's opinion in *Ker* makes no mention of any extradition treaty between the United States and Peru at that time.

135 Neither the majority opinion nor the dissent flags this move from statutory analogy to contract analogy.

136 *See* 8 U. S. C. § 1253(h) (1988 ed. and Supp. IV), *as amended by* § 203(e) of the Refugee Act of 1980, Pub. L. 96–212, 94 Stat. 107, sec. 243(h).

137 Sale, 509 U.S. at 180.

138 *See ibid.* at 188–89 (Blackmun, J., dissenting) ("Today's majority nevertheless decides that the forced repatriation of the Haitian refugees is perfectly legal, because the word 'return' does not mean return, because the opposite of "within the United States" is not outside the United

term "*refouler*" (which he translates as "'repulse,' "repel," "drive back," and even "expel"),[139] he succeeded both in depriving the statutory term "return" of its ordinary meaning and in circumventing the treaty regime's World War II/ Holocaust-inspired "object and purpose." He further delved into the Convention's *travaux* for the purpose of finding comments of state representatives to support an extraordinarily narrow interpretation of the provision's coverage, finding that the treaty did not impose extraterritorial obligations on states parties.[140] Refugees had to "arrive" in the United States in order to acquire the right not to be "returned."[141]

Sale would have been a more coherent opinion if the majority had engaged the Restatement. The treaty's context and its overriding objectives would have been a much better resource for reconciling its French and English versions than Justice Stevens's quick perusal of two French-English dictionaries. The majority's efforts to deal with bilingualism also would have benefitted from following the approach of the Restatement's section 325, which is to (1) reconcile the texts by choosing a meaning that, if possible, recognizes both versions as authentic and explores the full range of meanings of each in order to spot areas of overlap; and (2) carry out the process of reconciliation in light

States, and because the official charged with controlling immigration has no role in enforcing an order to control immigration" (citations omitted).

139 *Ibid.* at 181.

140 Justice Stevens places great emphasis on an exchange of floor statements by members of the Swiss, Dutch, and British delegations, almost as if these statements were the functional equivalent of speeches by members of Congress on a bill under consideration. *See ibid.* at 184–7. Extending the statutory analogy, Stevens deemed the silence of the other delegates to be evidence of their support for the Swiss and Dutch positions. *Ibid.* However, as Justice Blackmun pointed out in dissent, the majority's assumption that silence indicates consent does not function in the treaty context as it does in the domestic legislative context. *Ibid.* at 194–98 (Blackmun, J., dissenting). Indeed, one may go further than Justice Blackmun and point out that the statute analogy actually misleads: when a member of Congress debates and votes on legislation, he or she may have strong political incentives to go on record as opposing or supporting a proposal. He or she may want constituents or donors to know that their representative spoke up. Thus, on Capitol Hill sometimes silence supports an inference of acquiescence. Members of treaty delegations operate under different incentives. Typically, few delegates at multilateral treaty negotiations hold elected office. A number hold government posts in foreign ministries and other departments. In their line of employment, one gets into trouble by talking too much, especially if a position has not been cleared with superiors at home. Thus, in treaty negotiations, silence may indicate only that a delegate has concluded that the better part of wisdom is not to respond to every proposal and comment, especially if the proceedings are moving along at a glacial pace. To attach such importance to a few floor statements, as Justice Stevens does, rather than to focus more on the treaty's overall vision of a refugee regime and the extent of protection to be extended, represents a failure to appreciate the limitations of the statutory analogy.

141 *See ibid.* at 182 (affirming lower court's reading that "return" was intended to refer only to refugees already within the territory but not yet resident there).

of the treaty's object and purpose. Ultimately, under the Restatement approach, debate about linguistic tensions is subordinated to ascertaining the main objectives served by the treaty.[142] It is a weakness of the majority opinion in *Sale* that it ignores the Restatement's internationalist nuance on this score and allows itself to be driven by a mechanical and shallow wrestling with multilingualism.

Collectively, these five cases were evidence both of the Third Restatement's lack of influence and of a troubling chaos in American judicial method in treaty interpretation. The interpretive methods employed by the same court (indeed, sometimes by the same justice) over a short period of time were inconsistent. The traditional prioritizing of treaty observance and unbiased interpretation gave way to opinions driven by unilateral U.S. sources and U.S. policies, such as federalism. The newly published Restatement, the product of a decade of work by leading scholars, played no part in these opinions. One of the primary themes to emerge – that treaties are tools for multiplying the options available to the United States or its citizens without bringing about changes in U.S law or limiting resort to unilateral self-help – paralleled other post-Restatement developments toward unilateralism in other facets of U.S. treaty practice, such as frequent resort to reservations, understandings, and declarations ("RUDs").[143]

VI JUDICIAL DEFERENCE AND THE TREATY AS DELEGATION

The Executive branch's interpretations prevailed in *Aerospatiale, Schlunk, Stuart, Alvarez-Machain*, and *Haitian Centers Council*, but these decisions were not complete wins for the Executive. The Court had extended some deference to executive views,[144] but not the extent of deference that the

142 *See* Third Restatement, *supra* note 73, § 33:

> Except where a particular text prevails, when a comparison of the authentic texts discloses a difference of meaning which is not removed by resorting to the rules of interpretation stated elsewhere in this section, the meaning that best reconciles the texts, having regard to the object and purpose of the international agreement, is to be adopted.

143 *See* Roger Alford, "Judicial Barriers to the Enforcement of Treaties," Chapter 8 of this volume (noting U.S. treaty reservations, understandings, and declarations repeatedly used as a means of ensuring that the United States does not, by multilateral treaty, commit to make significant changes in its domestic law, especially not its domestic civil rights law).

144 *See, e.g.*, Aerospatiale, 482 U.S. at 562 n. 19 ("Our conclusion is confirmed by the position of the Executive Branch and the Securities and Exchange Commission, which interpret the 'language, history, and purposes' of the Hague Convention [and] is entitled to 'great weight.'").

Executive branch had urged.[145] The majority opinions had announced a duty of deference but then had operated at a level of detail inconsistent with a deferential stance. Justice Stevens in *Haitian Centers* and Justice Brennan in *Stuart* had delved deeply into *travaux* and legislative history, unwilling to rest their opinions on the Justice Department's brief.[146] In these and later cases, the term "great weight" was not used consistently[147] and, because the opinions had not referred to the Third Restatement, one could not be sure of the status of those parts of the Restatement that specifically suggested limits on the extent of deference.

In addition, during the same time period that some federal opinions described the judicial posture as deferential, other opinions continued to make use of the contract analogy in interpreting a range of treaties, not just instruments that the Third Restatement had deemed as agreements concerning "single transactions."[148] This was true in a series of cases interpreting the Warsaw Convention, a multilateral treaty regulating air carrier liability. In *TWA v. Franklin Mint*, the Court declared at the outset that a "treaty is in the nature of a contract between nations." [149] It then took up whether treaty breach was excused because of changed circumstances. In *Air France v. Saks*, Justice O'Connor had sought to give specific treaty words "a meaning consistent with the shared expectations of the contracting parties."[150] *Zicherman v. Korean Airlines* relied on another principle of contract interpretation: construing the document based on patterns of conduct and understandings that arose after the document had entered into force.[151] The opinion in *Eastern Airlines v. Floyd* also followed a contract interpretation approach.[152] In none of these did the Court clearly identify the perspective of the Executive branch in the case and indicate the weight that it should be given. This string of Warsaw

145 *See, e.g.*, McNary v. Haitian Centers Council, Inc., 1992 WL 541276 (U.S.), II (U.S. Pet. Brief, 1992) (arguing against any judicial review of INS action with respect to plaintiffs); U.S. v. Alvarez-Machain, 1992 WL 551127 (U.S.), 40 (U.S. Pet. Brief, 1992) ("[T]he determination of whether an extradition treaty violation should take precedence over the Nation's interest in enforcing our criminal laws is a policy judgment that is not for the courts to make.").

146 Alvarez-Machain and Haitian Centers can be regarded as different from the other cases in that the former required interpretation of treaties in the context of foreign policy crises: pursuing the war on drugs at its source and addressing political instability in Haiti.

147 *See, e.g.*, El Al Israel Airlines v. Tseng, 525 U.S. at 169 (1999) ("Respect is ordinarily due the *reasonable views* of the Executive Branch concerning the meaning of an international treaty.") (emphasis added).

148 Third Restatement, *supra* note 73, § 325, cmt. d

149 TWA v. Franklin Mint, 466 U.S. 243, 253 (1991).

150 Air France v. Saks, 470 U.S. at 399 (1985).

151 Zicherman v. Korean Airlines, 516 U.S 217 (1996).

152 Eastern Airlines, Inc. v. Floyd, 499 U.S. at 539 (referring to the "contracting parties").

Convention opinions – so different in their use of analogies, deference to Executive views, and tone than the five principal cases discussed in the previous section – seemed like a further sign of chaos.

Thus, for those seeking a strong view of Executive branch authority in treaty law, the Third Restatement turned out to be cold comfort.[153] It used the phrase "great weight" and gave more explanation of that term than the Second Restatement, but the Supreme Court in the late 1980s and the 1990s ignored section 325 of the Third Restatement. It did not even make reference to U.S. amicus briefs in important Warsaw Convention cases. And the string of Executive victories from *Aerospatiale* to *Haitian Centers Council* was not, in terms of interpretive method, enough. The government had won in *Haitian Centers* only after Justice Stevens had delved into French-English dictionaries, the statements of foreign delegations during the negotiations, and elements of the treaty's travaux and the statute's legislative history. Such extensive judicial inquiry into sources was difficult to square with "great weight."

A *Pre-*Chevron *History of Deference*

Deference to Executive branch treaty interpretations has a long and convoluted history. It can be traced to the Marshall court, well known for asserting judicial power against the political branches in constitutional cases but more cautious in asserting that power when interpreting treaties. In *Foster v. Neilson*,[154] widely cited for the non-self-executing treaty doctrine,[155] Marshall cast doubt on American courts' ability to function as neutral adjudicators in treaty disputes that pit the interests of the U.S. government against those of foreign sovereigns, at least in boundary disputes:

> In a controversy between two nations concerning a national boundary, it is scarcely possible that the courts of either should refuse to abide by the measures adopted by its own government. There being no common tribunal to decide between them, each determines for itself on its own rights.[156]

Few American courts in the nineteenth century echoed Marshall's articulation of early versions of the deference principle in such bare-knuckle

[153] Nevertheless, Professor Bederman argued that from 1986 to 1994, the interpretive position advocated by the Executive branch was the variable most predictive of the outcome in the Supreme Court. *See* Bederman, Revivalist Canons, *supra* note 1.

[154] Foster v. Neilson 27 U.S. (2 Pet.) 253 (1829).

[155] *See* Ingrid Wuerth, "Self-Execution," Chapter 4 of this volume.

[156] Foster v. Neilson, 27 U.S. at 307.

terms. Indeed, this aspect of *Foster* cut sharply against the arguments that had prevailed a generation earlier in favor of creating a federal judiciary with jurisdiction in cases requiring treaty interpretation.[157] It made little sense for Article III of the Constitution and § 25 of the Judiciary Act of 1789 to have conferred federal court jurisdiction if federal courts were no more credible as interpreters of treaties than state courts or, for that matter, the Secretary of State.[158] And if, as Marshall claimed, federal courts could not help but take sides in such cases, why had the Framers not chosen to preserve the integrity of the federal judiciary by channeling treaty cases away from federal courts?

The Third Restatement's drafters faced a complicated body of case law and tradition on the issue of deference: As Paul Stephan has noted, by the twentieth century,[159] the Restatement could not plausibly take the early nineteenth-century position that, across the board, treaty interpretation was purely a matter of textual deciphering and skillful search for the intent of the parties to the agreement. But neither could the Restatement, if it was to restate existing case law and executive practice, state a single formulation of deference. Even more problematic, in wading through many decades of treaty interpretation cases, one searches in vain for instances in which deference was decisive. Commonly, courts announce some variation of the deference principle, then discuss a variety of other factors – text, context, *travaux*, subsequent or prior behavior of the parties – and then reach a conclusion without explaining the extent to which deference influenced the outcome.

Thus in 1992, with *Haitian Centers* and the other four cases decided, it appeared that the executive branch's ability to influence judicial treaty interpretation was substantial but hardly conclusive. Subsequent developments in administrative law and academia would propel the efforts of the Executive branch to go beyond "great weight" and seek higher levels of deference.

157 *See* Judiciary Act of 1789, 1 Cong. ch. 20, September 24, 1789, 1 Stat. 73.

158 For a collection of early cases in which the Supreme Court ruled against the U.S. government's proffered interpretation of treaties, *see* David Sloss, *Judicial Deference to Executive Branch Treaty Interpretations: A Historical Perspective*, 62 N.Y.U. ANN. SURV. AM. L. 497 (2007). Professor Sloss maintains that the Supreme Court had a "zero deference approach in treaty interpretation cases in the late eighteenth and early nineteenth centuries." *Ibid.* at 499. Chief Justice Marshall's statement in *Foster*, however, suggests some level of deference, at least in boundary cases. See supra text accompanying note 156.

159 *See* Paul B. Stephan, "Treaties in the Supreme Court: 1946–2000," in CONTINUITY AND CHANGE, *supra* note 17 (arguing that after World War II period, the administrative state became more substantial and pervasive in many aspects of American law, including treaties).

B CHEVRON DEFERENCE

The first of these developments was Justice Stevens's 1984 opinion in *Chevron v. NRDC*, a case in which regulations of the Environmental Protection Agency were challenged as inconsistent with federal environmental legislation.[160] *Chevron* held that when statutory provisions are ambiguous, courts must defer to the views of the agency administering the statute, so long as the agency's interpretation is reasonable, even if, in the opinion of a reviewing court, other interpretations are more plausible.[161] The rationale for *Chevron* deference is that statutes incorporate more than substantive legal rules; they also incorporate delegations of authority running from Congress to federal agencies. The basis for deference under *Chevron*, is not limited to comparative expertise and other factors mentioned in pre-*Chevron* case law; rather courts must defer to agencies because Congress writes statutes intending to delegate interpretive authority to agencies.

Chevron's substantial impact on the enterprise of interpretation was not confined to administrative law. Its core principle – that interpretive authority can be delegated to the Executive branch – migrated into other fields. In the decade after publication of the Third Restatement, *Chevron* had impacted treaty interpretation. It had done so in three main areas: refugee law, conservation treaties, and Indian treaties.[162]

1 *Refugee treaties*

INS v. Cardoza-Fonseca[163] involved a challenge to an agency's interpretation of the 1951 United Nations Convention Relating to the Status of Refugees, which was implemented by the Refugee Act of 1980. The issue was whether the term "refugee" had the same meaning in the statute and the treaty. Writing for the majority, Justice Stevens (who wrote the majority opinions in *Chevron* and *Sale*) concluded that under *Chevron's* first prong, the INS's interpretation of the treaty implementing statute had been clearly incorrect.[164] *Cardoza-Fonseca*'s reliance on *Chevron* was remarkable for

160 Chevron U.S.A., Inc. v. Nat. Res. Def. Council, Inc., 467 U.S. 837 (1984).

161 *Ibid.* at 843–4. If the statute directly and specifically answers the legal question before the court, however, no deference is owed to the agency. *Ibid.* at 862.

162 In 2005, the Third Circuit stated that "Whether agencies are to be given *Chevron* deference when interpreting and implementing treaties is an unsettled topic." Auguste v. Ridge, 395 F.3d 123, 145 n. 22 (3rd Cir. 2005).

163 INS v. Cardoza-Fonseca, 480 U.S. 421, 107 S. Ct. 1207, 94 L. Ed. 2d 434 (1987).

164 *Ibid.* at 453–4.

several reasons: the Court did not explain why *Chevron* applied in the treaty context, did not refer to the just-published Third Restatement, and did not discuss any of the major treaty interpretation cases it had recently decided. The message of *Cardoza-Fonseca* seemed to be that the author of *Chevron* was so certain it applied to an agency's interpretation of treaty implementing legislation that it was unnecessary to spell out why this was so. A decade later, in *INS v. Aguirre-Aguirre*,[165] a case raising a different issue in connection with the same statute and treaty, the Supreme Court reaffirmed *Cardoza-Fonseca* and reversed the lower court for failing to apply *Chevron*.[166]

In 2009, the Court went a step further in solidifying *Chevron*'s application to adjudicating refugee claims. At issue in *Negusie v. Holder*[167] was whether the "persecutor bar" precludes refugee status even if the alien's assistance in carrying out acts of persecution was coerced. The majority held that the agency's interpretation of the 1980 version of the statute was flawed because it had relied upon a pre-1980 precedent that did not apply to the 1980 statutory amendment.[168] However, the agency was entitled, on remand, to pursue "additional investigation or explanation." This was so because ambiguities in statutes within an agency's jurisdiction are "delegations of authority to the agency to fill the statutory gap in a reasonable fashion."[169] For this proposition, the *Negusie* court cited a nontreaty *Chevron* case.[170]

In dissent, Justices Stevens and Breyer lamented that the Court had taken *Chevron* too far; *Chevron* had never been meant to move "pure question[s] of statutory construction" from courts to agencies,[171] nor to suggest that *Chevron* deference is "an all-or-nothing venture."[172] Thus, the state of discussion after *Negusie* did not concern whether *Chevron* deference applied to the 1967 Protocol to the Refugee Convention or why *Chevron* applied and the Third Restatement's "great weight" standard did not. The debate now was over how to apply *Chevron*, not only in the refugee context but across the board, with the author of *Chevron* urging narrow application and being on the losing end of that argument.

165 I.N.S. v. Aguirre-Aguirre, 526 U.S. 415, 424, 119 S. Ct. 1439, 143 L. Ed. 2d 590 (1999) ("It is clear the principles of *Chevron* deference are applicable to this statutory scheme.").

166 *Ibid.* at 430. In addition to *Chevron* deference, the INS was entitled to deference because of its "exercise [of] especially sensitive political functions that implicate questions of foreign relations." *Ibid.* at 425.

167 Negusie v. Holder, 555 U.S. 511, 129 S. Ct. 1159, 173 L. Ed. 2d 20 (2009).

168 *Ibid.* at 520.

169 *Ibid.* at 1167.

170 *Ibid.*, *citing* National Cable & Telecommunications Assn. v. Brand X Internet Services, 545 U.S. 967, 980, 125 S. Ct. 2688, 162 L. Ed. 2d 820 (2005).

171 *Ibid.* at 1170, 1172 (Stevens, J., dissenting).

172 *Ibid.* at 1173.

2 *Wildlife treaties*

In a series of cases relating to treaties that protect migratory birds, the D.C. Circuit Court of Appeals approached challenges to agency action through the lens of *Chevron*. *Hill v. Norton*,[173] is the most striking of these cases. In *Hill*, the court did something odd in terms of extending deference: it first applied *Chevron* and then also applied the "great weight" standard. The plaintiff challenged the Interior Department's decision not to include the mute swan on its *List of Migratory Birds* entitled to protection under the treaty and its implementing statute. Applying "the familiar *Chevron* analysis,"[174] the court found the agency's interpretation to be a "convoluted and strained attempt to find ambiguity where none appears."[175] Then, after giving the agency the benefit of the doubt on step 1 of the *Chevron* analysis, the court concluded under step 2 that the Department's decision was not based on a permissible construction of the statute.[176] Finally, and curiously, the Court then referred to the rule "that a court must pay 'great weight' to 'the meaning given [to treaties] by the departments of government particularly charged with their negotiation and enforcement.'"[177] In effect, this last move seemed to say that an agency interpretation that had failed the two-step test for *Chevron* deference still was entitled to the lower standard of deference articulated in the Third Restatement and in Supreme Court cases such as *Kolovrat* and *Sumitomo Shoji*.[178]

3 *Native American treaties*

In *Sohappy v. Hodel*,[179] a dissenting opinion strongly advocated *Chevron* deference in interpreting treaties between the United States and Native American tribes. The majority had ruled against the United States and struck down Bureau of Indian Affairs regulations as inconsistent with the applicable treaties and their implementing legislation.[180] In dissent, Judge Alex Kozinski

173 Hill v. Norton, 275 F.3d 98 (D.C. Cir. 2001). 174 *Ibid.* at 104. 175 *Ibid.*

176 *Ibid.* at 105. 177 *Ibid.* at 104, *citing* Kolovrat, 366 U.S. at 194.

178 *See supra* notes 92 and 94. In *Hill*, the Department's work was so misguided as not to be sustainable even under the "great weight" standard. More recently, the same statute and treaty were examined in *The Fund for Animals v. Norton*, 365 F. Supp. 2d 394 (S.D.N.Y. 2005), a case in which the Department's position was sustained as a reasonable interpretation of the implementing statute. The court ruled that it had to defer to the Agency's interpretation of the term "close season" and to its view that the statute applies to fewer than all migratory birds covered by the treaty, concluding that "[t]he court is not empowered to substitute its judgment for that of the agency." *Ibid.* at 414.

179 Sohappy v. Hodel, 911 F.2d 1312 (9th Cir. 1990). 180 *Ibid.* at 1318.

took the majority to task for "engaging in de novo interpretation of ambiguous treaty language,"[181] rather than deferring to "permissible" and "rational" agency interpretations pursuant to *Chevron*,[182] even though, at that time, no case or statute had established a rule entitling Bureau of Indian Affairs treaty interpretations to *Chevron* deference.[183] Subsequently, *Texas v. United States* adopted the reasoning of the *Sohappy* dissent as the majority rule for the 5th Circuit with respect to Indian treaties.[184]

C The Scholarly Debate

The second development affecting the extent of deference to executive treaty interpretations came from the academy. Curtis Bradley's 2000 article, *Chevron Deference and Foreign Affairs*, is especially important.[185] As with his work reevaluating the *Charming Betsy* canon of interpretation,[186] Bradley's work on treaty interpretation focuses on a reexplanation and recharacterization of a long-standing doctrine concerning assimilation of international law into the U.S. legal system. The result is an attempt to unify the confusing variety of judicial pronouncements on deference to executive branch treaty interpretation.[187] Bradley argued that many treaty deference

[181] *Ibid.* at 1321, 1329 (Kozinski, J., dissenting). [182] *Ibid.*

[183] The dissent cited two cases in support of what it said was an "established rule of treaty interpretation." *Ibid.* at 1329. In fact, there was no established rule at that time, and the two cases cited were inapposite. Neither Chem. Mfrs. Ass'n v. Nat. Res. Def. Council, Inc., 470 U.S. 116 (1985), nor Am. Paper Inst., Inc. v. Am. Elec. Power Serv. Corp., 461 U.S. 402 (1983) were treaty cases.

[184] Texas v. United States, 497 F.3d 491, 520 (5th Cir. 2007) ("IGRA contemplates that the Secretary of the Interior, and not the federal or state courts or a mediator, shall perform the task of interpreting state and federal laws and treaties to assure that a proposal or compact for Indian gaming complies with them.").

[185] Curtis A. Bradley, *Chevron Deference and Foreign Affairs*, 86 Va. L. Rev. 649 (2000).

[186] Curtis A. Bradley, *The* Charming Betsy *Canon and Separation of Powers: Rethinking the Interpretive Role of International Law*, 86 Geo. L.J. 479 (1998).

[187] Professor Bradley's assertion that "courts have given deference to the Executive Branch in foreign affairs *throughout* the nation's history," *ibid.* at 651 (emphasis added), does not acknowledge that, especially in the early years of the Republic, courts sometimes saw themselves as counterbalances to short-sighted and opportunistic treaty interpretation by the Executive branch. *See, e.g.*, the discussion of *Ware v. Hylton* in Section II, *supra*. As David Sloss has documented, in its early decades the Supreme Court frequently rejected treaty interpretations proposed by the Executive branch. *See* Sloss, *Judicial Deference, supra* note 2. The core premise of the treaty-as-contract model, as applied in the nineteenth century, was that treaty-related litigation typically presented courts with questions of law that could be resolved using familiar principles of contract interpretation. Even in landmark cases, such as *Ware v. Hylton*, the Supreme Court did not seek out the position of the Executive branch.

cases can be explained by presuming "that the United States treaty makers have delegated interpretive power to the Executive branch because of its special expertise in foreign affairs."[188] In contrast, the application of *Chevron* to treaty interpretation should be narrow with respect to treaty issues that are purely judicial in nature. One way in which Bradley's application of *Chevron* to treaties differs from the Third Restatement's great weight test is that in the former the judiciary is obliged to defer to current agency interpretations even if those interpretations are contrary to those of prior administrations. This is so because the basis for deference is Congressional delegation of interpretive authority; it is not based merely on an agency's accumulation of factual knowledge and expertise.

The coauthored work of Eric Posner and Cass Sunstein takes Bradley's perspective further. *Chevronizing Foreign Relations Law*[189] argues that the *Chevron* principle should permit agencies "to interpret statutory ambiguities so as to defeat" a wide range of foreign relations law principles, such as the *Charming Betsy* canon, the revenue rule, the presumption against extraterritoriality, the act of state doctrine, and the application of comity in general.[190]

Scholarship on treaties and *Chevron* is situated within the wider context of American foreign relations law. In Bradley's view, the "*Chevron* perspective" contrasts with the "pure rule of law perspective" or "*Marbury* perspective."[191] In that wider context, Bradley's criticism of the *Marbury* perspective has much in common with Daniel Abebe's and Eric Posner's critique of what they call "foreign affairs legalism."[192] Abebe's and Posner's target for criticism is an account of separation of powers that supports the premise that the judiciary has "an interest in" and a "capacity for restraining the executive's foreign affairs powers."[193] They address and support *Chevronizing* treaty interpretation as part of a wider critique of what they see as transfers of power over foreign relations decision making from the Executive to the judiciary.[194]

188 Bradley, *Chevron Deference*, *supra* note 185, at 702.

189 *See* Eric A. Posner & Cass R. Sunstein, *Chevronizing Foreign Relations Law*, 116 YALE L.J. 1170, 1205–7 (2007). Posner and Sunstein agree with Bradley that *Chevron* deference should apply to treaty interpretation where text is ambiguous. *Ibid.* At 1201 n. 100.

190 *Ibid.* at 1193. Posner and Sunstein do acknowledge, however, that "the deference principle is not unlimited." *Ibid.* at 1195.

191 Bradley, *Chevron Deference*, *supra* note 185, at 654–66.

192 Abebe & Posner, supra note 131. This article builds upon JACK L. GOLDSMITH & ERIC A. POSNER, THE LIMITS OF INTERNATIONAL LAW (2006).

193 Abebe & Posner, *supra* note 131, at 518.

194 *Ibid.* at 547.

As with Bradley's account, Abebe's and Posner's normative critique does not adequately address a stubborn fact: federal courts have been disagreeing with executive branch treaty interpretations for a very long time, often without significant pushback from the Executive branch. At the Founding, it was anticipated that the United States would enter into treaties and that American courts would adjudicate disputes relating to those treaties. Although neither the Constitution nor the Judiciary Act of 1789 specified the relationship between executive branch treaty interpretation and judicial interpretation, judicial behavior in the first decades of the Republic shows the extent to which judges regarded the unbiased interpretation of treaties as one of their most important duties. In cases such as *Ware v Hylton*, *The Amiable Isabella*, and others discussed in Section I of this chapter, the Supreme Court undertook this mission without much attention to the opinions of the political branches, and the available evidence suggests that the judiciary sustained little criticism from the political branches for its independence with respect to treaty interpretation. Thus any attack on "foreign affairs legalism" or the "Marbury Perspective" on treaties must explain not only the long lasting and pervasive use of the contract model and the statutory model in judicial treaty interpretation, but the near total absence of criticism of these legalistic models throughout the history of U.S. treaty practice.

D Deference After 9/11

The treaty-as-delegation model is a recent addition to the toolbox courts use to interpret treaties. In the span of two decades, this model has begun to exert an influence on how the Executive branch regards its treaty interpretation authority. At first glance, there would appear to be a trend toward marginalizing courts' role in treaty interpretation, at least for a substantial subset of treaties. A more careful look, however, reveals countercurrents. These were evident in the resounding defeat for the Executive branch in *Hamdan v Rumsfeld*.[195] The following discussion will assess *Hamdan*'s impact on treaty interpretation methods, asking whether it is a context-specific limitation on Executive deference or something more substantial and long lasting.[196]

Hamdan was quite an unusual case: an immensely high-profile political/legal confrontation that turned on the interpretation of a treaty.[197] The

195 Hamdan v. Rumsfeld, 548 U.S. at 557.

196 For a more detailed discussion, *see* Geoffrey S. Corn & Dru Brenner-Beck, "Case Study No. 1: Exploring U.S. Treaty Practice through a Military Lens," Chapter 9 of this volume.

197 The case also turned on the interpretation of a statute, the Uniform Code of Military Justice, and on the extent of the President's Article II powers.

elements of this confrontation were a treaty widely known to the public at large (the Third Geneva Convention);[198] a large number of American citizens in uniform and thus affected by that treaty; a war popularly supported at first but losing support by 2006; a Commander-in-Chief's interpretation of the treaty that had never been advanced by the United States in previous wars; actions by Congress designed to prevent adjudication of the treaty dispute;[199] and public revelations that grave offenses had been committed against detainees in U.S. custody. Despite the then-existing trend toward executive deference, five Justices disagreed with every aspect of the Government's position. Three dissenting Justices accused the majority of arrogating power to the judiciary and "openly flouting" its duty to defer to the President.[200]

Although the case formally turned on an article of the Uniform Code of Military Justice,[201] at the center of *Hamdan* were the four Geneva Conventions concluded in 1949 and ratified by the United States in 1955,[202] a common provision of which was deemed to have been incorporated into the statute by reference. The question was whether Common Article 3 of the four Conventions, a provision establishing minimum standards of treatment for enemy fighters detained in noninternational armed conflicts, was applicable to the U.S. conflict against al Qaeda and its associates, and if so, whether the military commissions that had been established by Presidential Order under President George W. Bush were consistent with Common Article 3.[203]

The majority held that Common Article 3 of the Conventions did apply to the commissions and that the commission procedures failed to meet Geneva

198 The Geneva Conventions have been ratified by 196 countries and are pillars of contemporary humanitarian law. They are taught to all members of the U.S. military and are widely referenced in popular culture. A 2011 survey by the International Committee of the Red Cross found that a large percentage of the American public considered themselves familiar with these treaties. *See* American Red Cross, Survey on International Humanitarian Law (2011) available at http://www.redcross.org/images/MEDIA_CustomProductCatalog/m12940087_Survey_on_International_Humanitarian_Law.pdf.

199 In the Detainee Treatment Act of 2005, Pub. L. No. 109–148, §§ 1001–1006 (2005), *available at* http://thomas.loc.gov/cgi-bin/cpquery/T?&report=hr359&dbname=109&, Congress sought to insulate actions by the military and the Executive branch from judicial review.

200 Hamdan, 548 U.S. at 678 (Thomas, J., dissenting).

201 Uniform Code of Military Justice, 64 Stat. 109, 10 U.S.C. §§ 836, 821.

202 *See, e.g.*, Geneva Convention Relative to the Treatment of Prisoners of War, August 12, 1949, T.I.A.S. 3364 (Feb. 2, 1956) [Geneva III].

203 The military commission at issue in *Hamdan* was created pursuant to the Executive Order of November 13, 2001 issued by President George W. Bush. *See* Detention, Treatment, and Trial of Certain Non-Citizens in the War Against Terrorism, 66 FR 57833. For statutory authority for that Order, *see* Authorization for the Use of Military Force, Pub. L. No. 107–40, September 18, 2001, 115 Stat. 224 *codified at* note following 50 U.S.C. §1541.

standards.[204] Justice Stevens's majority opinion made no reference to the Court's precedents according "great weight" to Executive treaty interpretations or to opinions he had authored (*Haitian Centers* and *Chevron*) extending much deference to the Executive branch. The opinion extended no deference at all. It engaged in a *de novo* analysis and completely rejected the Government's positions.[205] In sharp contrast, Justice Thomas's dissenting opinion applied an extraordinarily high degree of deference.[206]

Despite this chasm of disagreement, the majority and the dissent had two things in common: neither applied sections 325 or 326 of the Third Restatement, and neither drew upon the Court's many precedents conceiving of treaties as similar to contracts or statutes. Making an oblique reference to the delegation model, the dissent characterized the case in *Chevron* terms when it asked rhetorically how it made sense to extend *Chevron* deference to a recent Corps of Engineers decision regarding water drainage but not to the President's "wartime decisions."[207]

This question was appropriately put to Justice Stevens, who had authored the majority opinions in *Chevron* and *Haitian Centers* and whose administrative law jurisprudence strongly supported executive deference.[208] But the question drew no response. The majority explained why the Government was wrong but never explained what, if any, deference the Government's treaty interpretation was owed. Thus, a case with the potential to clarify much about U.S. treaty interpretation actually clarified very little. One thing was clear: the Third Restatement's complete lack of influence on the Court.[209] None of the opinions in *Hamdan* referred to it. The government's brief did not even discuss the treaty sections of the Third Restatement, relying instead on the

204 Hamdan, 548 U.S. at 629–33. 205 *Ibid.* at 576–81.

206 *Ibid.* at 678 (Thomas, J., dissenting). That deference was characterized in several different formulations: *Youngstown* deference, "great weight," "a heavy measure of deference," and the deference due the Commander-in-Chief. Justice Thomas made no attempt to differentiate among these formulations nor did he say that they were equivalent.

207 *Ibid.* at 706, *citing* Rapanos v. United States, 547 U.S. 715 (2006) (upholding administrative interpretation of the Clean Water Act under *Chevron* review). *Rapanos*, however, had involved statutory interpretation, not treaty interpretation.

208 *See* Deborah Pearlstein, *Justice Stevens and the Expert Executive*, 99 GEO. L. J. 1301, 1307 (2011) ("If the Court were serious about deferring to the Executive's legal interpretation anywhere, surely it would be here."); *see also* Dawn Johnsen, *"The Essence of a Free Society": The Executive Powers Legacy of Justice Stevens and the Future of Foreign Affairs Deference*, 106 NW. U. L. REV. 467 (2012).

209 The *Hamdan* case was an opportunity to take up the Third Restatement's suggestion that some treaties might be viewed as "constitutional." The universality of the Geneva Conventions and their relationship to customary international law might be thought to qualify them as constitutional treaties. None of the party briefs or opinions pursued this line of thought.

President's inherent Article II powers.[210] And the majority did not discuss the Court's *Chevron* precedents at all.

The lack of deference in the *Hamdan* majority opinion was striking, so striking as to prompt many commentators to wonder what it meant for treaty interpretation generally. Not only did the Court decline to defer to the President in a national security context, it also failed to cite or distinguish its many precedents calling for according "great weight" to the executive branch's views on a treaty's meaning. Justice Thomas's dissent alluded to *Chevron*, but Justice Stevens (the author of *Chevron*) did not. Was *Hamdan* to be understood as applying the brakes to interpretive trends in favor of ever increasing levels of deference and of an analogy supportive of that deference? Or was *Hamdan* the product of exceptional facts and the perceived need to defend the rule of law against unprincipled treaty interpretation by the Executive branch leading to a national embarrassment?[211] Had the jurisdiction-stripping provisions of the 2005 Detainee Treatment Act[212] complicated the application of deference precedents in the eyes of the *Hamdan* majority by attempting to prevent the judiciary from taking any part in interpreting treaties when the stakes are very high? Was *Hamdan* a temporary speed bump produced by exceptional circumstances and the expectation that judicial treaty interpretation would return to its pre-*Hamdan* deference trajectory?[213]

In several cases subsequent to *Hamdan*, the Court has returned to the treaty-as-contract model and also has shown relatively low levels of deference to the Executive branch. The Court decided *Abbott v. Abbott* [214] under a non-*Chevron* conception of deference that was just one of four factors, and Justice Breyer's dissenting opinion extended little deference at all. *BG*

210 The government's brief went far beyond deference or delegation. It bypassed the argument that the administration's interpretation of the Geneva Conventions was entitled to "great weight." It also eschewed reliance on the Authorization for the Use of Military Force (AUMF) enacted by Congress in September of 2001.

211 At that point, no federal court had been given the opportunity to adjudicate the Bush administration's other controversial treaty interpretations relating to the legality of preemptive self-defense under the UN Charter, the definition of torture under the Torture Convention, or the extraterritorial scope of U.S. obligations under human rights treaties.

212 The 2005 Detainee Treatment Act sought to bar, *inter alia*, "application[s] for a writ of habeas corpus filed by or on behalf of an alien detained by the Department of Defense at Guantanamo Bay, Cuba." *See* Detainee Treatment Act of 2005, *supra* note 199, § 1005(e)(1).

213 *See* Julian Ku and John Yoo, Hamdan v. Rumsfeld: *The Functional Case for Foreign Affairs Deference to the Executive Branch*, 23 *Const. Comment.* 179, 179 (2006) (predicting that "it is doubtful that the Court's opinion will have the long-term significance of a *Youngstown Sheet & Tube Co. v. Sawyer*").

214 560 U.S. 1 (2010).

Group v. Republic of Argentina[215] concerned first, an investment treaty between Argentina and the United Kingdom and, second, the duty of courts in the United States to recognize an arbitration award made pursuant to the investment treaty but allegedly infirm because of a failure to exhaust local remedies. The Court's decision – that under the New York Convention courts in the United States may not conduct de novo review of the decisions of arbitrators with respect to the treaty's exhaustion requirement – exhibited a sophisticated analysis of the contract analogy, one that probed both similarities and differences between treaties and private law contracts. In terms of deference, the Court pointedly rejected the Justice Department's analysis of the treaty.[216] In the same term, *Lozano v. Montoya Alvarez*[217] also exhibited a nuanced understanding of the relationship between treaties, statutes, and contracts. *Lozano* involved the relationship between state statutes of limitations and claims arising under the Hague Child Abduction Convention. The Court rejected the contention that the state law principle of equitable tolling could, in effect, be grafted onto the treaty's one-year statute of limitations.[218] The Court reached this result after investigating the course of performance of states parties under the treaty and recognizing that although federal legislation in the United States is drafted against a background of common law principles, the same is not generally true of treaties.[219]

Hamdan could mark a turning away from the delegation model and a return to traditional models with more modest levels of deference. Alternatively, the case could be a limited course correction and a reminder that now, as in earlier eras, the Court has a special role (a product of *Ware* and its early history) in preventing treaty interpretation and statute enactment by the political branches from endangering the rule of law and thoroughly sullying the nation's reputation for keeping its treaty commitments.

215 B.G. Group PLC v. Republic of Argentina, 134 S. Ct. 1198, 1208 (2014).

216 *Ibid.* at 1208–9 ("We do not accept the Solicitor General's view as applied to the treaty before us.").

217 Lozano v. Montoya-Alvarez, 134 S. Ct. 1224, 1232 (2014) (stating that treaties are "primarily compact[s] between independent nations," and that the court's duty is "to ascertain the intent of the parties by looking to the document's text and context.")

218 *See* Hague Child Abduction Convention, Art.12 (providing an exception to the duty to return a child when proceedings "have been commenced after the expiration of the period of one year" from the date of the wrongful removal).

219 Lozano, 134 S. Ct. at 1232 (noting that Congress legislates against a background of common law principles but the same is not true of treaty negotiators). *See also ibid.* at 1206:

> We shall initially treat the document before us as if it were an ordinary contract between private parties. Were that so, we conclude, the matter would be for the arbitrators. We then ask whether the fact that the document in question is a treaty makes a critical difference. We conclude that it does not.

VII CONCLUSION

Since the Founding, American treaty interpretation has been shaped by analogies. Its content has included doctrines and principles imported from other fields of law. The U.S. Supreme Court first embraced this use of metaphor in *Ware v. Hylton*, with its contractual understanding of American commitments toward Great Britain. In *Ware*, the Court was very much aware of and deliberate about the national purposes served by equating treaties with private-law contracts. The comparison established the law-abiding credibility of an upstart democracy. It elevated the stature of the new country by placing it in a posture of formal equality with European powers. The analogy also provided a compelling narrative for why, in the country's early decades, the judicial interpretation of treaties trumped the views of other federal and state actors. Treaties were cast as amenable to judicial tools in the same way as agreements for buying and selling goods.

In decades subsequent to *Ware*, treaty opinions reveal a judicial branch making regular use of the contract analogy and in tune with the purposes that it served. In nineteenth-century America, the contract analogy enabled the United States to accomplish a difficult task, devising a road map for internalizing treaty law. This was necessary because the Supremacy Clause hinted at the relationship between treaties and other sources of American law but did not spell out this relationship in detail. Nor did the Supremacy Clause indicate the manner in which externally made treaty commitments became law within the domestic legal system, the manner in which treaties should be interpreted, or the respective roles of the Executive branch, Congress, and the Judiciary in the process of interpreting treaties.

No comparison is perfect. An analogy is helpful to the extent it allows one to see the familiar in that which is (at least initially) unfamiliar. Analogies are unhelpful to the extent they obscure and divert one's attention from that which should drive analysis of a legal text. On those scales, the contract analogy was immensely helpful in the early decades of the United States. One indication of this success was the essentially universal manner in which it was accepted. But, in time, the imperfections of the analogy became apparent. With respect to treaties with Indian tribes, the analogy became distorted. Liberal interpretation, as carried out by courts, was an early attempt to correct for this failing. Later, Congress switched to something closer to a statutory model for the relationship between Indian tribes and the United States. In the twentieth century, with the gradual arrival of multilateral treaties, scholars and courts devised a statutory model for interpretation, borrowing from the domestic field of statutory construction. This was necessary because the contract analogy (with its focus on mutual assent and a remedy structure drawn from private law) did not map well onto new multilateral treaties, whose goals were legislative in character and whose provisions were not especially driven by reciprocity. Tools of statutory construction illuminated the role of interest groups, prolonged drafting processes and related treaty efforts in treaty formation.

The contract and statute analogies encounter challenges if our model of treaties shifts away from the private-law bargaining process or the interest-group laden legislative process. With the emergence of foreign relations law as a sprawling discipline, it becomes possible (and for some desirable) to carry out treaty-making and assessing treaty interpretation less with reference to Article II of the Constitution or tradition and more with reference to the wider and less textually bound goal of advancing the foreign policy goals formulated in the White House and the agencies that it controls. With this shift in viewpoint, interpretation can be less a matter of determining the meaning of a single document or a single provision in a single document and more a matter of understanding the treaty meaning that best fits within a broad foreign policy process – a process that involves executive orders, diplomatic positions, agency regulations, troop movements, intelligence gathering, and more. In short, a process of which treaties may constitute a small part. This shift to a treaty text that may be just one element of a far-ranging foreign policy, best explains the pace and argumentativeness of the current search for the right level of deference.

The latest iteration in this search for an appropriate level of deference is the "treaty-as-delegation" model. This model, like its predecessors, seeks to import doctrines from other bodies of law into treaty interpretation. In contrast to the Third Restatement, which acknowledged the influence of contract rules of interpretation and the body of U.S. law on statutory construction, the delegation model looks to U.S. administrative law and foreign relations law. The insights to be transplanted are that much of law is part of a complicated regulatory process, that this regulatory process increasingly is transnational and that we should presume that Congress often delegates the details of such regulation to executive agencies. Included within this delegation is the interpretation of treaties that are a part of this transnational regulatory process. These *Chevron*-based assumptions lead to the conclusion that a single treaty is like a thread woven into a large foreign policy garment; the Executive branch is best positioned to understand how the threads fit together in the garment as a whole. It is the Executive that is best positioned to assign meaning to an international agreement that is a part of an intricate network of bilateral and multilateral relationships.

But U.S. foreign policy is not a fabric, and individual treaties are not merely threads. This metaphor is an unhelpful way of approaching much of U.S. treaty law. It is unhelpful on several accounts. First, the *Chevron* approach to treaty interpretation is based on a fiction of Congressional delegation. Few implementing statutes contain an express delegation of interpretive authority to agencies or departments or even express statements with respect to deference. If Congress wanted courts to defer, it would be straightforward and clarifying for it to say so, especially in the context of many decades of court precedents (and two Restatements) that support something less than *Chevron* deference. In that absence of express legislative instructions, those who argue in favor of *Chevron* deference would have us risk frustrating the intent of Congress rather than implementing it.

Second, *Chevron* deference in the realm of treaties is profoundly ahistorical. As explained in Sections 1 and 2 of this chapter, for most of American history treaty interpretation has been regarded as a core Article III duty, one for which the interpretive constraints are legal rather than political in nature. There is a difference between a judicial interpretation being constrained by a rule of contract law or of statutory construction, on the one hand, and the foreign policy priorities of the Executive branch on the other. The Third Restatement attempted to codify a tradition of judicial deference, analogies, and legal constraint. In anchoring the delegation model to contemporary theories of administrative law and separation of powers, its proponents have ignored the Founding period and the first century of American treaty interpretation. It is not enough to say that contemporary treaties are different from treaties past; it is necessary to demonstrate how such differences necessitate a major departure from a long tradition in which treaties have been regarded as akin to legal documents (contracts, statutes) that hardly lack amenability to judicial interpretation.

Third, the case for *Chevronizing* treaty interpretation is an attack on the competency of courts. One strand of this argument is that courts are functionally ill-suited to interpreting highly technical regulatory treaties, just as they allegedly are ill-suited to interpreting similarly technical statutes. A second strand is that courts are ill-suited to making foreign policy or second-guessing the foreign policy decisions of other branches. Yet a third strand is a warmed-over version of the more general antimajoritarian attack on federal courts: Foreign policy decisions, once implemented, can be difficult to undo. Hence, judicial treaty interpretations, while theoretically subject to reversal by statute or by subsequent treaty, in practice can be irreversible.

All of these antijudicial strands of the delegation model face a basic problem: courts in the United States have been interpreting treaties for nearly

230 years. The practice began early in the nation's history, shortly after its war of independence had been won. Throughout the centuries to follow, courts have continued to perform this interpretive task, in cases involving critical legal and political issues. Courts have done so with, until recently, little pushback from Congress or the Executive. In short, a delegation model that fundamentally questions the judicial role in treaty interpretation seems more manufactured than organic.

The Third Restatement accurately codified the "great weight" standard repeatedly applied by the Supreme Court. That standard was based on a view of agency expertise and not a fiction of congressional delegation. That standard had emerged organically from changes in the subject-matter, level of detail, and multilateral dimension of treatymaking. That standard, when thoughtfully applied, could be reconciled with a long history of judicial treaty interpretation in which, from time to time, courts rejected the arguments of the Executive branch. The *Chevronizing* literature fails to show that the Restatement's view – itself quite skeptical of a plenary role for the judiciary – has led to costly mistakes meriting an even more diminished role for courts in treaty interpretation than that set out in the Restatement.

4

Self-Execution

Ingrid Wuerth

The Supremacy Clause of the Constitution provides that all treaties made by the United States "shall be the supreme Law of the Land." Under the Articles of Confederation, states' failures to comply with U.S. treaty obligations were a source of friction with foreign governments and of weakness when it came to efforts to negotiate new agreements. The Supremacy Clause was designed to resolve these problems by making treaties superior to state law. The 1796 case of *Ware v. Hylton*[1] provides an early example of the application of the Supremacy Clause. The Court held for a British creditor who had sued a Virginia debtor, reasoning that a Virginia statute was preempted by the 1783 Treaty of Peace ending the Revolutionary War. The treaty provided that prewar debts would be honored.[2]

The Treaty of Peace at issue in *Ware* was "self-executing" – meaning that it was directly enforceable in U.S. courts. Justice Marshall, in his 1829 opinion for the Court in *Foster v. Neilson*,[3] held that some treaty provisions are "non-self-executing" and cannot be enforced in U.S. courts absent implementing legislation by Congress. This distinction between self-executing and non-self-executing treaties has generated much scholarship as well as its share of confusion in the courts. It is the subject of this chapter.

The Restatement (Third) of the Foreign Relations Law of the United States addressed several important issues related to treaty self-execution. For example, it provided for a judicial presumption in favor of self-execution, it strongly suggested that Senate declarations of non-self-execution are valid, and it reasoned that the intent of U.S. treaty makers (rather than all of the parties to a treaty) should control the issue of self execution. The presumption in favor of self-execution would have tended to increase the domestic applicability of

[1] Ware v. Hylton, 3 U.S. (3 Dall.), 199 (1796). [2] *Ibid.*

[3] Foster v. Neilson, 27 U.S. 253 (1829).

treaties by rendering more of them self-executing. The second two features probably tended in the opposite direction: that is, to decrease domestic applicability of treaties by rendering fewer of them self-executing. The presumption as such has not withstood the test of time, while the second two provisions have been strengthened in years since the Third Restatement was adopted. Ironically enough, human rights litigation has, on the whole, shifted the U.S. courts toward less, rather than greater, application of treaties as domestic law. The current unanswered question is the extent to which the Supreme Court's hostility toward self-execution in the context of human rights related cases such as *Medellin v. Texas* will undermine the domestic enforcement of other categories of treaties long understood to be directly enforceable in U.S. courts.

I THE RESTATEMENT (THIRD) AND SELF-EXECUTION

The Third Restatement of the Foreign Relations Law of the United States provides in Section 111(3) that "Courts in the United States are bound to give effect to international law and to international agreements of the United States, except that a 'non-self-executing' agreement will not be given effect as law in the absence of necessary implementation." International agreements may be partly self-executing and partly non-self-executing.[4]

Section 111(4) provides that an international agreement is non-self-executing

(a) if the agreement manifests an intention that it shall not become effective as domestic law without the enactment of implementing legislation,
(b) if the Senate in giving consent to a treaty, or Congress by resolution, requires implementing legislation, or
(c) if implementing legislation is constitutionally required.

Controversy emerged during the drafting of the Third Restatement, especially around the topics of jurisdiction and the status of customary international law within the U.S. legal system.[5] Treaty self-execution generated less attention.[6]

The Third Restatement's treatment of self-execution generally favored the direct enforcement of treaties in U.S. courts. It did so most significantly

[4] Restatement (Third) of the Foreign Relations Law of the United States ("Third Restatement") § 111, cmt. h.

[5] *See* Davis R. Robinson, *Conflicts of Jurisdiction and the Draft Restatement*, 15 Law & Pol'y Int'l Bus. 1147, 1152 (1983); Harold G. Maier, *The Authoritative Sources of Customary International Law in the United States*, 10 Mich. J. Int'l L. 450 (1989).

[6] *Compare* Jordan Paust, *Self-Executing Treaties*, 82 Am. J. Int'l L. 760 (1988).

through the "strong presumption" in favor of self-execution. The Reporters' Notes also outlined the types of treaties that have generally been treated as self-executing with little or no discussion, and they rejected the argument that multilateral treaties are presumptively non-self-executing. The general approach to self-execution is consistent with the work of the Third Restatement as a whole.[7]

A *Presumption in Favor of Self-Execution*

Perhaps the most significant change from the Restatement (Second) is the language in the Third Restatement providing that treaties should be given effect by courts in the United States unless they are non-self-executing for one of the reasons set forth in Section 111(4).[8] The language and organization of Section 111 arguably create a background norm or presumption that treaties are self-executing absent evidence to the contrary, as stated more explicitly in the Reporters' Notes. Reporters' Note 5 provides that in the absence of implementing legislation (or a request by the executive branch for such legislation) "there is a strong presumption that the treaty has been considered self-executing by the political branches and should be considered self-executing by the courts."[9] The same note goes on to say that "[o]bligations not to act, or to act only subject to limitations, are generally self-executing."[10] By contrast, The Second Restatement, from 1965, provided that a treaty which manifests an intention that it "shall become effective as domestic law" is "self-executing while a treaty that does not manifest such an intention is non-self-executing."[11] The Second Restatement language does not suggest a presumption in favor of or against self-execution. Similarly, the Reporters' Notes to the Second Restatement did not include language about a presumption in favor or against self-execution.

What precipitated this change? The Reporters' Notes to the Third Restatement do not cite new cases stating that treaties are presumptively self-executing. Instead, they cite *United States v. Postal*,[12] which reasoned that

7 *See* Paul R. Dubinsky, Chapter 3 of this volume.

8 There was no Restatement (First) of Foreign Relations Law. *See* Gregory H. Fox, Chapter 2 of this volume.

9 The same note states that "a finding that a treaty is not self-executing is a finding that the United States has been and continues to be in default, and should be avoided." THIRD RESTATEMENT § 111, Reporters' Note 5.

10 *Ibid.*

11 RESTATEMENT (SECOND) OF THE FOREIGN RELATIONS LAW OF THE UNITED STATES (Hereinafter "SECOND RESTATEMENT") § 141(1)(A) and (2)(A).

12 United States v. Postal, 589 F.2d 862 (5th Cir. 1979).

multilateral treaties are presumptively *non*-self-executing.[13] The Reporters' Notes also defend a presumption in favor of self-execution on policy grounds: it facilitates prompt compliance with treaty obligations.[14] The change in approach in the Third Restatement thus appears to reflect not so much the direction of the case law since the Second Restatement, but instead the growing importance of self-execution to the judicial enforcement of treaties. Courts had long enforced treaties, especially those protecting property and commercial rights, without explicitly discussing self-execution, much less applying a presumption of any kind.[15] In describing the period between 1901 and 1945, Michael Van Alstine writes that "[t]he cases are legion in which the Supreme Court simply cited that constitutional status [as supreme Law of the Land] and then moved forward with an application of the terms of the treaty."[16] He goes on to observe that "the more surprising discovery from a canvass of the numerous treaty cases in the first half of the twentieth century is the absence of any detailed examination of the direct effect of treaties in domestic law."[17]

The Second Restatement appears to reflect this approach. By the time the Third Restatement was drafted, however, the issue of self-execution was clearly emerging as a limitation on the judicial enforceability of treaties, because of both the lower court cases raising the issue[18] and the declarations of non-self-execution proposed by the Carter administration when it transmitted several human rights treaties to the Senate. Although these limitations were most prevalent in human rights and other multilateral treaties that limited the actions of the federal government,[19] the Restatement language was couched in broad terms.

[13] THIRD RESTATEMENT § 111, Reporters' Note 5 (citing *Postal*, 589 F.2d 862). Other cases decided after the Second and before the Third Restatements have been criticized for holding treaties non-self-executing, and because they are arguably in tension with a presumption in favor of self-execution. *See* Carlos Manuel Vázquez, *The Four Doctrines of Self-Executing Treaties*, 89 AM. J. INT'L L. 695, 709 (1995) (criticizing *Mannington Mills, Inc. v. Congoleum Corp.*, 595 F.2d 1287, 1298 (3d Cir. 1979), *Handel v. Artukovic*, 601 F. Supp. 1421 (C.D. Cal. 1985) and Tel-Oren v. Libyan Arab Republic, 726 F.2d 774, 809 (D.C. Cir. 1984)).

[14] THIRD RESTATEMENT § 111, Reporters' Note 5.

[15] Michael P. Van Alstine, *Treaties in the Supreme Court, 1901–1945* in INTERNATIONAL LAW IN THE U.S. SUPREME COURT (David L. Sloss, Michael D. Ramsey, William S. Dodge, eds., 2011).

[16] *Ibid.* [17] *Ibid.*

[18] *See* David Sloss, *When do Treaties Create Individually Enforceable Rights? The Supreme Court Ducks the Issue in Hamdan and Sanchez-Llamas*, 45 COLUM. J. TRANSNAT'L L. 20, 106–110 (2006) (discussing Mannington Mills, Inc. v. Congoleum Corp., 595 F.2d 1287, 1298 (3d Cir. 1979), *Postal*, 589 F.2d at 876–84 (5th Cir. 1979) and *Tel-Oren*, 726 F.2d at 798 (D.C. Cir. 1984) (Bork, J., concurring)).

[19] *See* Paul B. Stephan, *Treaties in the Supreme Court, 1946–2000* in INTERNATIONAL LAW IN THE U.S. SUPREME COURT *supra* note 15.

B Determining Whether a Treaty is Non-Self-Executing

Section 111(4) of the Third Restatement provides three circumstances under which treaties are not self-executing: the agreement manifests such an intention; Congress or the Senate requires implementing legislation; or such legislation is constitutionally required. The subsection discusses the first and third; the next subsection discusses the second.

According to the Third Restatement, a treaty is not self-executing if it "manifests an intention that it shall not become effective as domestic law without the enactment of implementing legislation."[20] Comment h to this section asserts that it is the intention of the United States that is dispositive for the question of self-execution, rather than the collective intentions of the parties to the treaty. This comment also suggests that the text of the treaty is relevant to determining whether it is non-self-executing, as are any statements by the president when concluding the agreement or submitting it to the Senate, along with "any expression by the Senate or by Congress in dealing with the agreement."

Reporters' Note 5 further explains the distinction between self-executing and non-self-executing treaties. In *Foster v. Neilson*, Chief Justice Marshall reasoned based on the Supremacy Clause that a treaty is to be treated by the courts as equivalent to a statute whenever the treaty "operates of itself, without the aid of any legislative provisions."[21] By contrast, when the terms of the treaty "import a contract, when either of the parties engages to perform a particular act," then the treaty "addresses itself to the political, not the judicial department; and the legislature must execute the contract, before it can become a rule for the court."[22]

Determining whether a treaty is self-executing has proven to be an increasingly difficult task for the courts. Treaty text rarely says anything explicit about self-execution and it is not always obvious whether a treaty is a commitment addressed to the legislature or a commitment which should be immediately enforced by the courts. Certain categories of treaties, such as Friendship, Navigation and Commerce, bilateral extradition treaties, as well as agreements conferring property rights on foreign nationals, have historically been viewed as self-executing.[23] Although many of these treaties are bilateral, the Third Restatement rejected the suggestion that multilateral treaties are less likely than bilateral treaties to be self-executing.[24] The possibility that other

[20] THIRD RESTATEMENT § 111(4)(a).

[21] Foster v. Neilson, 27 U.S. 253, 314 (1829).

[22] THIRD RESTATEMENT Reporters' Note 5 (quoting Foster v. Neilson, 27 U.S. 253, 314 (1829)).

[23] *See, e.g.*, Ware v. Hylton, 3 U.S. 199 (1796); United States v. Rauscher, 119 U.S. 407 (1886); Asakura v. Seattle, 265 U.S. 332 (1924).

[24] THIRD RESTATEMENT Reporters' Note 5 (discussing United States v. Postal, 589 F.2d 862 (5th Cir. 1979)).

parties to a multilateral treaty might view it as non-self-executing was cited by one court to support a distinction between bilateral and multilateral agreements.[25] Reporters' Note 5 did not agree with this view, reasoning instead that few other countries distinguish between self-executing and non-self-executing treaties and that treaties are generally binding on state parties whether or not they are self-executing.

The cases decided between the Second and Third Restatements sometimes relied on a mixture of the foregoing factors – and others, such as the consequences of the self-execution determination – to ascertain if a treaty was self-executing.[26] In other cases, courts applied treaties as self-executing with little discussion,[27] a practice consistent with the courts' historical approach to many categories of treaties. Questions of treaty self-execution arose with increasing frequency in human rights cases; courts usually held those treaties non-self-executing. In part for this reason, treaty self-execution became increasingly unclear and contested.[28] In this context, the presumption of self-execution adopted by the Third Restatement had the potential to play a significant role in self-execution decisions.

Less significant as a practical matter are constitutional limitations dictating that some treaties cannot be self-executing and must have implementing legislation before courts can apply them. Comment i to Section 111 provides that implementation by Congress is constitutionally required if "the agreement would achieve what lies within the exclusive law-making power of Congress under the Constitution," including an agreement that would provide for payment of money and probably agreements that would bring the United States into a state for war or that would impose criminal liability on individuals.

C *Declarations of Non-Self-Execution*

During the late 1970s and 1980s, as work on the Third Restatement moved forward, the president and Senate began to consider the use of declarations of

[25] United States v. Postal, 589 F.2d 862 (5th Cir. 1979).

[26] *See, e.g.*, Frolova v. Union of Soviet Socialist Republics, 761 F.2d 370, 373 (7th Cir. 1985); *Tel-Oren*, 726 F.2d at 810 (D.C. Cir. 1984); *id.* at 808–10 (Bork, J. concurring); In re Alien Children Ed. Litig., 501 F. Supp. 544, 590 (S.D. Tex. 1980); People of Saipan, By & Through Guerrero v. U.S. Dep't of Interior, 502 F.2d 90, 101–2 (9th Cir. 1974) (Trask, C.J., concurring); United States v. Postal, 589 F.2d at 876 (5th Cir. 1979).

[27] *See, e.g.*, Trans World Airlines, Inc. v. Franklin Mint Corp., 466 U.S. 243 (1984) (holding Warsaw Convention self-executing); Fox v. Regie Nationale des Usines Renault, 103 F.R.D. 453 (W.D. Tenn. 1984) (holding the Convention on the Service Abroad of Judicial and Extrajudicial Documents in Civil or Commercial Matters self-executing).

[28] *See* Vázquez, *supra* note 13.

non-self-execution as part of the reservations, declarations, and understandings included with the ratification of human rights treaties. The Carter Administration proposed attaching declarations of non-self-execution to four human rights treaties transmitted to the Senate in 1978: the International Convention on the Elimination of all Forms of Racial Discrimination (Race Convention);[29] the International Covenant on Civil and Political Rights (ICCPR);[30] the International Covenant on Economic, Social and Cultural Rights (ICESCR);[31] and the American Convention on Human Rights (ACHR).[32] President Carter also sought ratification of the Convention on the Elimination of Discrimination against Women (CEDAW) in 1980, but without a declaration of non-self-execution.[33]

The text of the Third Restatement suggests that declarations or other statements of non-self-execution are valid. Section 111(4)(b) provides that an agreement is non-self-executing if "the Senate in giving consent to a treaty, or Congress by resolution, requires implementing legislation."[34] Comment d to section 303 of the Third Restatement is even more explicit, stating that "[t]he Senate may also give its consent on conditions that do not require change in the treaty but relate to its domestic application, e.g., that the treaty shall not be self-executing."[35] Despite this language, the Chief Reporter for the Third Restatement, Professor Louis Henkin, eventually argued against declarations of non-self-execution on legal and policy grounds.[36]

After the Third Restatement was published the Senate adopted the non-self-execution declarations for the ICCPR and the Race Convention, which were ratified in 1992 and 1994 respectively. The Convention Against Torture was also ratified in 1994, and it, too, included a declaration of non-self-execution.[37] No declaration of non-self-execution was adopted by the United States for the

29 International Convention on the Elimination of All Forms of Racial Discrimination, opened for signature Mar. 7, 1966, S. Exec. Doc. C, 95–2 (1978), 660 U.N.T.S. 195. The United States deposited its instrument of ratification on October 21, 1994

30 International Covenant on Civil and Political Rights, adopted Dec. 19, 1966, S. Exec. Doc. E, 95–2 (1978), 999 U.N.T.S. 171 (entered into force Mar. 23, 1976).

31 United Nations, International Covenant on Economic, Social and Cultural Rights, adopted Dec. 16, 1966, 993 U.N.T.S. 3 (entered into force Jan. 3, 1976).

32 O.A.S.T.S. No. 36 (entered into force July 18, 1978), 9 I.L.M. 673.

33 United Nations, Convention on the Elimination of All Forms of Discrimination Against Women, adopted Dec. 18, 1979, 1249 U.N.T.S. 13 (entered into force Sept. 3, 1981).

34 Third Restatement § 111(4)(b).

35 Third Restatement § 303, Reporters' Note 4 (citing to Section 111(4)).

36 *See infra* text at notes 59–61.

37 United Nations, Convention Against Torture and Other Cruel, Inhuman or Degrading Treatment or Punishment, adopted Dec. 10 1984, 1465 U.N.T.S. 85 (entered into force June 26, 1987).

Genocide Convention, which was ratified in 1988. The Senate resolution of ratification of the Genocide Convention did include a declaration that the president would not deposit the instrument of ratification until after implementing legislation had been enacted. The president complied. The Senate Foreign Relations Committee interpreted this declaration as showing that the Convention was not self-executing.[38]

The ratification of human rights treaties by the United States in the late 1980s and early 1990s followed many decades of stalemate and political conflict. For example, President Truman had submitted the Genocide Convention to the Senate in 1948. Opponents of ratification cited the potential domestic effects of the treaty, including potential claims that the treatment of African Americans and Native Americans constituted genocide. In light of the Supreme Court's decision in *Missouri v. Holland*, concerns also surfaced during this period about the enactment of statutes pursuant to treaties that would otherwise be beyond Congress' Article I powers. These resulted in proposals during the 1950s to amend the U.S. Constitution to make all treaties non-self-executing and to make clear that treaties were subject to federalism limitations. Generally known as the "Bricker Amendment" after Senator John Bricker of Ohio, these proposals were defeated, in part because the Eisenhower administration announced that it did not intend to sign or seek ratification of human rights treaties. Aside from seeking ratification of the Genocide Convention, subsequent Presidents largely followed suit until the Carter administration.[39]

Even after President Carter sought ratification of a broad set of human rights treaties, it was more than a decade before the Senate approved the four of them to which the United States is today a party. CEDAW, the ICESCR, and the ACHR still have not received the advice and consent of the Senate, nor have the Convention on the Rights of the Child (CRC) (entered into force in 1990, now with 196 state parties), and the Convention on the Rights of Persons with Disabilities (CRPD) (entered into force in 2008, now with 159 state parties).[40] The Senate Foreign Relations Committee voted favorably on

[38] David Sloss, *The Domestication of International Human Rights: Non-Self-Executing Declarations and Human Rights Treaties*, 24 YALE J. INT'L L. 129, 132–4, 163–4 (1999).

[39] *See* Janis & Wiener, Chapter 1 in this book and its discussion of *Missouri v. Holland*. The Senate did ratify a protocol to the Convention Relating to the Status of Refugees in 1968. Henkin suggests that perhaps this treaty was understood as relating largely to aliens rather than to domestic human rights issues. LOUIS HENKIN, FOREIGN AFFAIRS AND THE U.S. CONSTITUTION 477–8 n. 101 (2nd ed. 1996).

[40] U.N. Treaty Collection, Convention on the Rights of Persons with Disabilities 1, https://treaties.un.org/doc/Publication/MTDSG/Volume%20I/Chapter%20IV/iv-15.en.pdf (last visited Oct. 26, 2015).

CEDAW in 1994 and 2002, both times with a declaration of non-self-execution attached. CRPD received a favorable vote from the Senate Foreign Relations Committee in July 2012, again with a declaration of non-self-execution.[41]

D A *Presumption Against Private Rights and Private Causes of Action*

There was another important difference between the Second and Third Restatements. The Second Restatement did not explicitly address private rights and causes of action, but a comment – not the black letter – in the Third Restatement provides that "[i]nternational agreements, even those directly benefiting private persons, generally do not create private rights or provide for a private cause of action in domestic courts, but there are exceptions with respect to both rights and remedies."[42] Although private rights and private causes of action are distinct from treaty self-execution, as the Restatement also makes clear,[43] the three issues are closely related as a practical matter because all three help determine when individuals may invoke rights conferred by treaties and because there is some overlap in their content. A right that benefits an individual is a "private right." A private "right of action" or "cause of action" allows a private party to bring an action in court. If a treaty itself creates a private cause of action, it is self-executing and it creates a private right. If a treaty does not create a cause of action, but a cause of action is conferred by another source, then an individual can invoke the protections of the treaty assuming that that the treaty confers private rights and is self-executing.[44] Less clear in the years after the Third Restatement was adopted was whether a non-self-executing treaty could be applied as law by courts, assuming that a cause of action was supplied by another source. Some scholars have suggested or argued that non-self-executing treaties could be so applied,[45] while courts generally held that non-self-executing treaties could not be applied as law.[46]

Until the mid-twentieth century, the Supreme Court appears to have treated at least the issues of self-execution and private rights as one: treaties that related to the rights of individuals (especially in property or commerce)

41 S. COMM. ON FOREIGN RELATIONS, REPORT ON THE CONVENTION ON THE RIGHTS OF PERSONS WITH DISABILITIES, S EXEC. DOC. NO. 112–6 (2d Sess. 2012).

42 THIRD RESTATEMENT § 907, cmt. (a); *see also Ibid*. § 111, cmt. h.

43 *Ibid*. § 111, cmts. g and h.

44 *See* McKesson Corp. v. Islamic Rep. of Iran, 539 F.3d 485, 489–91 (D.C. Cir. 2008).

45 *See, e.g.*, Oona Hathaway *et al.*, *International Law at Home: Enforcing Treaties in U.S. Courts*, 37 YALE J. INT'L L. 51, 84, n. 214 (2012).

46 *See* United States, ex rel. Perez v. Warden, FMC Rochester, 286 F.3d 1059, 1063 (8th Cir. 2002); Wesson v. U.S. Penitentiary Beaumont, TX, 305 F.3d 343, 348 (5th Cir. 2002).

were treated as self-executing, generally as a matter of course and without resorting to an explicit discussion of presumptions. Writing about the period between 1901 and 1945, for example, Michael Van Alstine has concluded that "[the Supreme Court's] common practice when confronted with a treaty claim was simply to observe that treaties may function as federal law and to apply the treaty as such."[47] One might thus question – as Justice Breyer has – whether the Third Restatement's view that international agreements directly benefiting private persons generally did not create private rights actually corresponded with judicial practice when the Third Restatement was enacted.[48] In any event, the Third Restatement language explicitly identifying the three issues as distinct was the harbinger of things to come: as courts began to focus on the issue of self-execution, especially in human rights cases, they began to treat the creation of private rights and a private cause of action as separate, additional hurdles to the judicial enforceability of treaty norms.[49]

II ACADEMIC AND JUDICIAL RESPONSE TO THE RESTATEMENT (THIRD)

A *Academic Response*

The ratification of major human rights treaties with declarations of non-self-execution and the growing importance of self-execution in the courts generated significant academic commentary beginning in the early 1990s, just after the Third Restatement was finalized.[50] The Second Edition of Professor Louis Henkin's masterful book *Foreign Affairs and the U.S. Constitution* from 1996 illustrates the shift. The first edition, from 1972, devoted little attention to treaty self-execution and did not discuss a presumption in favor of self-execution or declarations of non-self-execution.[51] The second edition, which came out less

47 Van Alstine, *supra* note 15 at 203.

48 *See infra*, text at note 92 (discussing Justice Breyer's view); Hathaway *et al.*, *supra* note 45, at 66–7 (comparing cases involving commerce and property, which were generally held judicially enforceable and those involving sovereign relationships (such as the U.N. Charter), which were not treated as judicially enforceable).

49 Some courts even reasoned that treaties which did not explicitly create a cause of action were therefore also non-self-executing. *See, e.g., Tel-Oren*, 726 F.2d at 808 (Bork, J., concurring); United States v. Thompson, 928 F.2d 1060, 1066 (11th Cir.1991).

50 *See, e.g.*, Lori Fisler Damrosch, *The Role of the United States Senate Concerning "Self-Executing" and "Non-Self-Executing" Treaties*, 67 CHI.-KENT L. REV. 515 (1991); John Quigley, *The International Covenant on Civil and Political Rights and the Supremacy Clause*, 42 DEPAUL L. REV. 1287 (1993).

51 LOUIS HENKIN, FOREIGN AFFAIRS AND THE CONSTITUTION (1972).

than a decade after the Third Restatement,[52] devotes much more attention to these topics. It also states that there is a "strong presumption" in favor of self-execution, and that a "non-self-executing promise is highly exceptional."[53] Declarations of non-self-execution, the Second Edition states, are "'anti-Constitutional' in spirit and highly problematic as a matter of law," based in part on the Supremacy Clause.[54] Academic writing during most the 1990s echoed these themes.[55] Scholars, particularly Carlos Vázquez, argued that the Supremacy Clause presumptively makes all treaties self-executing based both on its text and on the Framers' goal of increasing U.S. compliance with treaties.[56]

The academic focus on self-execution and declarations of non-self-execution initially led to three lines of criticism of the Restatement, all suggesting that despite adopting a presumption in favor of self-execution, the Third Restatement approach nevertheless renders too many treaties non-self-executing. Professor Vázquez, writing in 1996, argued that the Restatement's language that "the intention of the United States determines whether an agreement is to be self-executing in the United States" was in "some tension with the text and apparent purposes of the Supremacy Clause."[57] He argued that the intent of the parties to the treaty, rather than the intent of U.S. treaty makers, should control, lest the unilateral actions of U.S. officials result in under-enforcement of the treaty and international friction.[58]

Other criticism focused on declarations of non-self-execution. Professor Henkin, without explicitly criticizing the Restatement, suggested that the Framers of the U.S. Constitution intended all treaties to be the law of the land, and that only a treaty that "undertook to do something in the future that could be done only by the legislature" could be non-self-executing, calling into question the constitutionality of declarations of non-self-execution.[59]

52 Henkin, *supra* note 39. 53 *Ibid.* at 200–4. 54 *Ibid.* at 202.

55 David Sloss, writing in 1999, remarked that "[v]irtually all of the commentators have criticized the NSE declarations on policy grounds. A few commentators have argued that the NSE declarations are invalid." David Sloss, *The Domestication of International Human Rights: Non-Self-Executing Declarations and Human Rights Treaties*, 24 YALE J. INT'L L. 129 (1999).

56 Carlos Manuel Vázquez, *The Four Doctrines of Self-Executing Treaties*, 89 AM. J. INT'L L. 695, 698–9 (1995); Carlos Manuel Vázquez, *Treaty-Based Rights and Remedies of Individuals*, 99 COLUM. L. REV. 1087–1102 (1992); *see also* John Quigley, *The International Covenant on Civil and Political Rights and the Supremacy Clause*, 42 DEPAUL L. REV. 1287 (1993).

57 *Ibid.* at 707–8 (citing cases from the 1970s and 1980s); *see also* David Sloss, *Non-Self-Executing Treaties: A Constitutional Fallacy*, 36 U.C. DAVIS L. REV. 1 (2002) (extensively criticizing the intent-based approach of the Third Restatement).

58 Vázquez, *supra* note 13.

59 Louis Henkin, *U.S. Ratifications of Human Rights Conventions: The Ghost of Senator Bricker*, 89 AM. J. INT'L L. 341, 346–7 (1995); *see also* Charles H. Dearborn III, *The Domestic Legal Effect of Declarations That Treaty Provisions Are Not Self-Executing*, 57 TEX. L. REV. 233, 236

Other scholars argued that declarations of non-self-execution are not themselves "treaties" and are thus beyond the power of the president and Senate to enact as law.[60] Professor David Sloss maintained that because of the constitutional problems they create, declarations of non-self-execution should be interpreted narrowly to mean only that the treaty does not create a cause of action.[61]

Third, Professor Jordan Paust argued in the late 1980s – also based in part on the text and history of the Constitution – that the class of treaties that are non-self-executing because they require implementation by Congress as a constitutional matter is very narrow, and does not include treaties imposing international crimes.[62] He criticized the Third Restatement language as suggesting that this class of treaties is broader.

The initial attacks on the Restatement's self-execution language thus came from the "left" – meaning here those in favor of broad treaty self-execution and the assertive enforcement of treaties in U.S. court. The general thrust of these attacks was consistent with broader trends in both the domestic enforcement of international law and law generally. Writing in 1991, Harold Koh pointedly linked the growing transnational human rights litigation to the rise of domestic public interest litigation and to "a growing acceptance by litigants of United States courts as instruments of social change."[63] As international human rights litigation gained traction in the United States, public interest organizations generally turned to law and litigation, rejecting the traditional tools of political change, such as elections."[64]

But beginning in the late 1990s, scholars from the "right" began to argue against self-execution and in favor of declarations of non-self-execution, for both constitutional and policy reasons. Professor John Yoo, for example, advanced a far-reaching argument against treaty self-execution. He argued that under the Supremacy Clause treaties cannot be directly enforced in courts if they regulate areas that fall within Congress's Article I, Section 8 powers. Yoo relied in part on historical materials showing that the drafters and ratifiers of the Constitution sought to separate legislative and executive power and did not want the executive power of treaty making to undermine Congress' law-making powers. As a matter of policy, Yoo argued that the

(1979) (arguing that declarations of NSE are not binding on the courts and should not be given effect).

60 Quigley, *supra* note 56, at 1303–5. 61 Sloss, *supra* note 55, at 143.

62 Jordan Paust, *Self-Executing Treaties*, 82 AM. J. INT'L L. 760 (1988).

63 Harold Hongju Koh, *Transnational. Public Law Litigation*, 100 YALE L.J. 2347, 2364 (1991).

64 *See* GORDON SILVERSTEIN, LAW'S ALLURE: HOW LAW SHAPES, CONSTRAINS, SAVES, AND KILLS POLITICS 9 (2009).

congressional implementation of treaties protects democratic principles by preserving a role for the House of Representatives, an especially important consideration given the increase in scope of treaties and the pace of globalization.[65] As a result, courts should presume that treaties are not self-executing – directly counter to the Restatement's approach.

Other scholars advanced a more modest argument in favor of declarations of non-self-execution, arguing that the Supremacy Clause does not limit the power of the treaty-makers to "define the domestic scope of the law they made," a position supported by the Third Restatement.[66] They also noted that declarations of non-self-execution serve an important policy function, in part because they (coupled with other RUDs) were politically necessary to ensure U.S. ratification of key human rights treaties.[67] The work of all of these scholars was part of broader trends in the burgeoning U.S. foreign relations scholarship of the late 1990s: a surge in work critical of international law, especially its direct incorporation into U.S. law, and a renewed focus on originalism and constitutional text and structure.

B *The Restatement (Third) in the Courts Before* Medellin

In the main, the academic debates about declarations of non-self-execution were neither generated by, nor reflected in the work of, the courts. Consistent with the Restatement, courts have uniformly given effect to declarations of non-self-execution, generally reasoning that the intent of the U.S. treaty makers controlled or at least informed the resolution of this issue,[68] although

65 John C. Yoo, *Globalism and the Constitution: Treaties, Non-Self-Execution and the Original Understanding*, 99 COLUM. L. REV. 1955 (1999); John C. Yoo, *Treaties and Public Lawmaking: A Textual and Structural Defense of Non-Self-Execution*, 99 COLUM. L. REV. 2218 (1999). Professors Vázquez and Flaherty wrote responses. *See* Carlos Vázquez, *Laughing at Treaties*, 99 COLUM. L. REV. 2154 (1999); Martin S. Flaherty, *History Right?: Historical Scholarship, Original Understanding, and Treaties as "Supreme Law of the Land,"* 99 COLUM. L. REV. 2095 (1999).

66 *See* THIRD RESTATEMENT § 303, Reporters' Note 4.

67 Curtis A. Bradley & Jack L. Goldsmith, *Treaties, Human Rights, and Conditional Consent*, 149 *U. PA. L. REV.* 399, 446, 458–9 (2000).

68 *See* Igartúa-de la Rosa v. United States, 417 F.3d 145, 150 (1st Cir. 2005) (ICCPR); Mironescu v. Costner, 480 F.3d 664 n.15 (4th Cir. 2008) (Convention Against Torture); Raffington v. Cangemi, 399 F.3d 900, 903 (8th Cir. 2005) (Convention Against Torture); Auguste v. Ridge, 395 F.3d 123, 132, n.7, 140 (3d Cir. 2005) (Convention Against Torture); Guaylupo-Moya v. Gonzales, 423 F.3d 121, 133, 137 (2d Cir. 2005) (ICCPR); Castellano-Chacon v. INS, 341 F.3d 533, 551 (6th Cir. 2003) (Convention Against Torture); Sosa v. Alvarez Machain, 542 U.S. 692, 735 (2004) (ICCPR not self-executing); United States v. Postal, 589 F.2d 862, 876 (5th Cir. 1979); Diggs v Richardson, 555 F.2d 848, 851 (D.C. Cir. 1976) ("In determining

a few judges have expressed concerns about this view.[69] What did change, as discussed above, was the political branches' use of declarations of non-self-execution in human rights treaties.

1 The presumption in favor of self-execution does not take hold

The courts' treatment of treaties *without* declarations of non-self-execution was more complex even prior to the Supreme Court's decision in *Medellin v. Texas*[70] (discussed in detail below). Although courts continued to apply many types of treaties as self-executing, they almost always did so without the benefit of a formal presumption.[71]

Only four courts appear to have actually applied the Third Restatement presumption and found a treaty self-executing.[72] In one of those cases, the very cursory treatment of self-execution was dicta, as the court went on to hold that

whether a treaty is self-executing courts look to the intent of the signatory parties as manifested by the language of the instrument.").

69 Igartua-de la Rosa v. United States, 417 F.3d 145 (Howard, J. dissenting); *Ibid.* (Torruella, J. dissenting); United States v. Li, 206 F.3d 56, 61 (1st Cir. 2000) (Torruella, J. dissenting). A case from 1957, before adoption of the Second Restatement, reasoned that a Senate declaration providing that the treaty would be implemented by Congress, might be unconstitutional because the treaty power does not extend to domestic issues – including the implementation of treaties by Congress. Power Auth. of N.Y. v. Fed. Power Comm'n, 147 F.2d 538 (D.C. Cir. 1957), vacated and remanded with directions to dismiss as moot sub nom., 355 U.S. 64 (1957).

70 Medellin v. Texas, 552 U.S. 491 (2008).

71 *See, e.g.*, El Al Israel Airlines, Ltd v. Tsui Yuan Tseng, 525 U.S. 155, 161–63 (1999) (Warsaw Convention); Cornejo v. County of San Diego, 504 F.3d 853, 857 (9th Cir. 2007) (Vienna Convention on Consular Relations); Jogi v. Voges, 480 F.3d 822 (7th Cir. 2007) (Vienna Convention on Consular Relations); McKesson Corp. v. Islamic Rep. of Iran, 271 F.3d 1101 (D.C. Cir. 2001) (Treaty of Amity); In re Erato, 2 F.3d 11 (2d Cir. 1993) (Treaty on Mutual Assistance in Criminal Matters); United States v. Lindh, 212 F.Supp.2d 541 (E.D.Va. 2002) (Geneva Convention Relative to the Treatment of Prisoners of War); Seguros Comercial America v. Hall, 115 F. Supp. 2d 1371, 1380 (M.D. Fl. 2000) (Convention Between the United States and the United Mexican States for the Recovery and Return of Stolen or Embezzled Vehicles and Aircraft); Consulate General of Mexico v. Phillips, 17 F. Supp. 2d 1318, 1332 (S.D. Fl. 1998) (Bilateral Consular Convention).

72 *See* Rainbow Nav., Inc. v. Dept. of Navy, 686 F. Supp. 354, 357 (D.D.C. 1988) (applying presumption from the SECOND RESTATEMENT (Revised) Tentative Draft No. 1 (1980) § 131); United States v. Noriega, 808 F. Supp. 791, 799 (S.D. Fla. 1992) ('Were this Court in a position to decide the matter, it would almost certainly find that Geneva III is self-executing"); United States v. Li, 206 F.3d 56 (2000) (en banc) (Vienna Convention on Consular Relations). In McKesson Corp v. Islamic Rep. of Iran, 1997 WL 361177 (D.D.C. 1997), the District Court applied the Restatement presumption, but the Court of Appeals decision that reversed in part did not. 271 F.3d 1101 (D.C. Cir. 2010). This analysis does not include treaties with Indian nations, which are generally understood as self-executing. *See* Seneca Nation of Indians v. New York, 206 F. Supp. 2d 448 (W.D.N.Y. 2002).

in any event the treaty could not provide the basis for the suppression of evidence or the dismissal of an indictment.[73] In another of those cases, the court, while apparently adopting the Restatement's presumption, characterized it as inconsistent with previous judicial practice reflecting a contrary presumption.[74] Other courts employed what sounds like a presumption of *non*-self-execution, sometimes without noting the Restatement as contrary authority. For example, in 1992 the Fourth Circuit reasoned [c]ourts will only find a treaty to be self-executing if the document, as a whole, evidences an intent to provide a private right of action.[75] The Fourth Circuit repeated this statement a decade later when it held the Geneva Conventions were non-self-executing.[76]

Presumptions and Senate declarations aside, courts have looked to a variety of factors to determine whether a treaty was self-executing. Consistent with language in the Third Restatement, courts considered whether the treaty provision is suitable for judicial application or whether it is best understood as directed to the political branches and thus non-self-executing. Treaty language that is broad, vague or only aspirational is not easily applied by the courts and is thus usually deemed non-self-executing.[77] Specific language meant to take immediate effect suggests, by contrast, that the provision is self-executing.[78] Treaties that appear to confer rights on individuals are often deemed self-executing especially in the contexts of commercial and property claims,[79] but also for extradition, service conventions, and aircraft liability treaties.[80] Treaty text itself (especially that of multilateral treaties) rarely addresses the issue of domestic enforceability, in part because different countries have different implementation systems. Even if treaties do address

[73] *Li*, 206 F.3d 56.

[74] *Noriega*, 808 F. Supp. at 798 (S.D. Fla. 1992); *see also* United States v. Lindh, 212 F. Supp. 2d 541, 554 (E.D. Va. 2002).

[75] Goldstar (Panama) v. United States, 967 F.2d 965, 968 (4th Cir.1992); *see also* United States v. Emuegbunam, 268 F.3d 377, 389 (6th Cir. 2001); Wier v. Broadnax, 1990 WL 195841 (S.D.N.Y. 1980).

[76] Hamdi v. Rumsfeld, 316 F.3d 450, 468–9 (4th Cir. 2003), *vacated*, 542 U.S. 507 (2004). The Supreme Court did not reach the issue.

[77] *See, e.g*, Frolova v. Union of Soviet Socialist Republics, 761 F.2d 370, 373–6 (7th Cir. 1985).

[78] *See, e.g.*, Asakura v. City of Seattle, 265 U.S. 332, 340–1 (1924).

[79] *See, e.g.*, Delchi Carrier SpA v. Rotorex Corp., 71 F.3d 1024, 1027–8 (2d Cir.1995) (Convention for the International Sale of Goods).

[80] *See, e.g.*, Factor v. Laubenheimer, 290 U.S. 276 (1933) (extradition); Cheung v. United States, 213 F.3d 82, 94–95 (2d Cir. 2000) (same); El Al Israel Airlines, Ltd. v. Tsui Yuan Tseng, 525 U.S. at 161–3 (Warsaw Convention); British Caledonian Airways, Ltd. v. Bond, 665 F.2d 1153, 1161 (D.C. Cir. 1981) (Chicago Convention on International Civil Aviation); Hornsby v. Lufthansa German Airlines, 593 F. Supp. 2d 1132, 1135 (C.D. Cal. 2009) (Montreal Convention).

domestic implementation and enforcement, this language is not dispositive as to self-execution in the U.S. legal system, which is an issue of U.S. domestic law.[81]

2 Private rights and causes of action

A presumption in favor of self-execution was also undermined by language in the Third Restatement that was understood as adopting a presumption against private rights and private causes of action even with respect to self-executing treaties.[82] This separate presumption (if it is a presumption) led some courts to reason or suggest a presumption against self-execution itself, which undermined the distinction between self-execution and private rights or private causes of action.[83] In other cases, the Restatement language about private rights of action provided courts with an additional basis for concluding that a treaty was not judicially enforceable.[84] These developments are consistent with the Court's reasoning in the context of statutory interpretation, where it has become increasingly reluctant to imply private causes of action.[85]

Four Justices of the Supreme Court appeared to disapprove of the Restatement comment on private rights and causes of action in a case entitled *Sanchez-Llamas v. Oregon*.[86] The majority opinion assumed but did not decide that the Vienna Convention on Consular Rights (VCCR) created individually enforceable rights.[87] Justice Breyer's dissenting opinion did, by contrast, reach the issue. He began by noting that the VCCR is self-executing and went on to explain that the lower courts are divided on whether it creates

81 *See* Trans World Airlines, Inc. v. Franklin Mint Corp., 466 U.S. 243, 252 (1984).

82 See Third Restatement of the Foreign Relations Law of the United States § 907, cmt. (a); *see also ibid.* at § 111, cmt. h.

83 *Goldstar (Panama) S.A. v. U.S.*, 967 F.2d 965 (4th Cir. 1992).

84 *See, e.g.*, United States v. Li, 206 F.3d 56 (2000) (en banc); Seguros Comercial America v. Hall, 115 F. Supp. 2d 1371 (2000); *Cornejo v. County of San Diego*, 504 F.3d 853 (2007).

85 *See, e.g.*, Middlesex Cnty. Sewerage Auth. v. Nat'l Sea Clammers Ass'n, 453 U.S. 1, 13–19 (1981) (same under the Federal Water Pollution Control Act, Pub. L. No. 92–500, 86 Stat. 816 (1972), and the Marine Protection, Research, and Sanctuaries Act of 1972, Pub. L. No. 92–532, 86 Stat. 1052 & 1061 (1972)); Touche Ross & Co. v. Redington, 442 U.S. 560, 562–79 (1979) (same under 15 U.S.C. § 78q(a) (1970) (current version at 15 U.S.C. § 78q(a) (2012)); *Cannon v. Univ. of Chi.*, 441 U.S. 677, 680–717 (1979) (same under Title IX of the Education Amendments of 1972 § 901, 20 U.S.C. § 1681 (1976) (amended 1986)); Cort v. Ash, 422 U.S. 66, 85 (1975) (holding no implied private right of action under the former 18 U.S.C. § 610 (1970) (current version at 52 U.S.C. § 30118 (2012)).

86 Sanchez-Llamas v. Oregon, 548 U.S. 331, 371–78 (2006) (Breyer, J. dissenting); *see also id.* at 360 (Ginsburg, J. concurring) (joining Part II of Justice Breyer's dissenting opinion, which reasoned that the VCCR created private rights).

87 *Sanchez-Llamas*, 548 U.S. at 343.

privately enforceable rights.[88] Justice Breyer's conclusion that the VCCR creates private rights was based in part on its text.[89] The obligations set forth in the Convention are the kind the courts commonly enforced by courts, and Article 36 itself refers to the "rights" of foreign nationals.[90] The government argued against a private right of action in *Sanchez-Llamas* based in part on the "long-established presumption that treaties and other international agreements do not create judicially enforceable individual rights."[91] In support, the government's brief cited the Third Restatement. Justice Breyer noted the government's argument but responded that "[t]he problem with that argument is that no such presumption exists."[92]

III MEDELLIN V. TEXAS

The Supreme Court issued its most extensive decision ever on treaty-self-execution in 2008. The case, *Medellin v. Texas*,[93] held judgments of the International Court of Justice non-self-executing in U.S. courts. The case and the mostly negative academic response to it are described in this section.

A *Case*

The *Medellin* decision is the Supreme Court's most important opinion on self-execution since its 1829 decision in *Foster v. Neilson*. The case involved José Ernesto Medellin, a Mexican national, who was sentenced to death in 1994 by a Texas court for his involvement in the rapes and murders of two teenage girls. Article 36 of the Vienna Convention on Consular Relations (Vienna Convention) required that Medellin be informed of his right to assistance from the Mexican consul. He was not informed of this right and Mexican authorities were not aware of his situation until 1997, by which time he had exhausted his direct appeals. Courts denied Medellin's petition for a writ of habeas corpus based on the Vienna Convention violation because he had defaulted on this claim by not raising it earlier.[94]

Article 36 violations were widespread in the United States; some of the aggrieved countries turned to the International Court of Justice (ICJ). Litigation focused largely on remedies and the consequences of breach; the violations of Article 36 itself were largely uncontested. In a 2001 case by

88 *Ibid.* at 371–8. 89 *Ibid.*

90 Vienna Convention on Consular Relations, adopted April 24, 1963, 596 U.N.T.S. 261 (entered into force Mar. 19, 1967), Art. 36.

91 *Sanchez-Llamas*, 548 U.S. at 376. 92 *Ibid.* 93 Medellin v. Texas, 552 U.S. 491 (2008).

94 *Ibid.* at 501.

Germany against the United States, the ICJ held that an individual denied his Article 36 right was entitled to "review and reconsideration" of his sentence, procedural default rules notwithstanding.[95] The United States argued that procedural default rules were permissible under the Vienna Convention based on Article 36(2), which provides that Convention rights "shall be exercised in conformity with the laws and regulations of the receiving state" as long as "said laws and regulations [] enable full effect to be given to the purposes for which accorded under this Article are intended." The International Court of Justice rejected this view.[96] In a subsequent habeas petition, Medellin argued that U.S. courts were bound by the ICJ's interpretation of the Vienna Convention, namely that procedural default rules could not prevent review and reconsideration of his sentence.[97] Medellin's case was not the subject of the ICJ's 2001 decision, however, which considered the case of two German nationals. The Supreme Court held in 2006 in *Sanchez-Llamas v. Oregon*[98] – which also involved the applicability of the ICJ judgments in distinct but similar cases – that the ICJ's decisions were entitled to "respectful consideration" but that the Vienna Convention was best read as permitting procedural default rules, the ICJ decision to the contrary notwithstanding.

Mexico had, in the meantime, brought its own case in the ICJ against the United States and won. The convictions of Medellin and other Mexican nationals were the basis for the *Case Concerning Avena and Other Mexican Nationals*.[99] The ICJ held the United States in breach of the Vienna Conventions, concluding that executive clemency did not give "full effect" to the Convention (contrary to the argument presented by the United States) and that Medellin was entitled to review and reconsideration of his sentence, apparently through a "judicial process."[100] Back in the U.S. courts, Medellin maintained that the *Avena* judgment was binding on the courts of Texas and obligated them to review and reconsider his sentence. The U.S. government argued that the ICJ judgment was not self-executing, but that Texas courts were obligated to give it effect based upon a memorandum from President Bush directing them to do so. The Texas courts rejected both arguments.[101]

95 LaGrand (Germany v. United States of America), Judgment, ICJ Reports 2001, 446, paras. 125–6.

96 *Ibid.* 97 *Ibid.* at 503–6. 98 *Sanchez-Llamas*, 548 U.S. 331.

99 Request for Interpretation of the Judgment of 31 March 2004 in the Case concerning Avena and Other Mexican Nationals (Mexico v. United States of America), Judgment, I.C.J. Reports 2009, 3.

100 *Ibid.* at para. 31. 101 *Medellin*, 552 U.S. at 538.

The Supreme Court granted certiorari and affirmed in a 6–3 decision. The majority opinion, authored by Chief Justice Roberts, held that although the United States was obligated under international law to comply with the ICJ's judgment in *Avena*, this obligation was not self-executing and thus did not automatically bind Texas.[102] The *Medellin* case thus turned not on the Vienna Convention itself, but instead on the direct enforceability of ICJ judgments in U.S. courts. The Optional Protocol to the Vienna Convention provides that disputes arising out of its interpretation come within the compulsory jurisdiction of the ICJ. But the obligation to *comply* with a judgment of the ICJ comes not from the Optional Protocol, the Court reasoned, but instead from Article 94 of the Charter of the United Nations.[103] Under Article 94(1), each member of the UN "undertakes to comply" with a decision of the ICJ in any case to which it is a party. The Court, following the argument of the Executive Branch, concluded that "undertakes to comply" contemplates not immediate legal effect in domestic courts but instead a commitment to take future action. The Court also considered the enforcement mechanism available under Article 94 for non-compliance with an ICJ judgment – reference to the U.N. Security Council – and concluded that it suggested diplomatic, not judicial, enforcement.[104] In response to the dissenting opinion by Justice Breyer, the Court rejected a multifactored judgment-by-judgment approach to self-execution as too indeterminate and affording the courts too much discretion.

The Court did not explicitly adopt a presumption in favor of either self-execution or non-self-execution, nor did it explicitly state whether the intent of U.S. treaty makers or the intent of the parties to the treaty controls the self-execution question. The Court's reasoning strongly suggests, however, that the intent of U.S. treaty makers should control the self-execution question (in keeping with the Third Restatement), and that there is no presumption in favor of self-execution (in contrast to the Third Restatement). Some have understood the Court as going further and implicitly adopting a presumption *against* self-execution. Justice Breyer's dissent suggests as much, when he argues that the Court is misguided to the extent that it erects a presumption against self-execution.[105] The majority opinion appeared to reject such a presumption, however, when it reasoned that no "talismanic words" are necessary to create self-executing treaties.[106] In light of the Court's reasoning about Article 94(1) of the U.N. Charter, judgments of the ICJ are unlikely to be

[102] *Ibid.* at 506. [103] *Ibid.* at 500. [104] *Ibid.* at 509–11.
[105] *Ibid.* at 546 (Breyer, J., dissenting). [106] *Ibid.* at 521.

deemed self-executing, whether or not a formal presumption against self-execution is applied.

Having concluded that the ICJ judgment was not directly enforceable in U.S. courts, the Supreme Court did not need to address whether the relevant treaties created private rights or private causes of action. But in a paragraph in footnote 3, apparently designed to distinguish these three issues, the Court sets out in dicta the language of the Third Restatement providing that even self-executing treaties that directly benefit private persons generally do not create private rights or a private cause of action.[107] Justice Breyer, writing in dissent in *Sanchez-Llamas*, had expressed in no uncertain terms his disagreement with the Restatement view, at least as articulated as a presumption. But the Third Restatement's language about private rights and causes of action – part of a comment, not the black letter of the Restatement – received a significant boost from footnote 3 of *Medellin*.

The Court also resolved some, but not all, uncertainties around the domestic status of non-self-executing treaties. Non-self-executing treaties, the Court reasoned, are not "domestically enforceable federal law."[108] This reasoning effectively forecloses the argument that courts may enforce non-self-executing treaties as long as the cause of action comes from a different source, such as the habeas statute or a criminal case.[109] However, *Medellin* leaves open the question of whether a non-self-executing treaty is just judicially unenforceable domestic law or whether it is not domestic law at all.[110] The distinction might matter for the executive branch, which might be bound or empowered by a non-self-executing treaty even if it is not enforceable in court. The language of Supremacy Clause, which provides that the "all treaties" are the supreme law of land supports this reading. Non-self-executing treaties remain "the law of the land" even if they cannot be judicially enforced.

The Court did make clear that the President cannot unilaterally enforce a non-self-executing treaty in court. As noted above, the United States government had argued that the courts must apply the *Avena* judgment not because it was self-executing, but instead based on President Bush's memorandum. The Court rejected this argument. The government defended the President's actions as implicitly authorized through the Optional Protocol and the U.N.

[107] *Ibid.* at 506 n. 3. [108] *Ibid.* at 534. (Stevens, J., concurring).

[109] See *supra* text at note 46.

[110] *Compare* Medellin v. Texas, 552 U.S. at 534 ("Conversely, a 'non-self-executing' treaty does not by itself give rise to domestically enforceable federal law. Whether such a treaty has domestic effect depends upon implementing legislation passed by Congress.") *with id.* at 504 (apparently equating non-self-execution with an international obligation which is "not binding federal law enforceable in United States courts.").

Charter.[111] The Court disagreed, based in part on the non-self-executing character of those agreements: "[T]he responsibility for transforming an international obligation arising from a non-self-executing treaty into domestic law falls to Congress, not the Executive."[112] The Court went on to say that "[a] non-self-executing treaty, by definition, is one that was ratified with the understanding that it is not to have domestic effect of its own force. That understanding precludes the assertion that Congress has implicitly authorized the President – acting on his own – to achieve precisely the same result."[113]

Justice Stevens concurred with the judgment in *Medellin*, but he wrote separately. He explicitly rejected a presumption against self-execution, but also did not adopt a presumption in favor of self-execution. The question of self-execution was for Justice Stevens more difficult than the majority allowed, especially the interpretation of "undertakes to comply," which (unlike the language of some treaties) does not foreclose self-execution. In the end, however, he found the majority's reasoning more convincing than that of the dissent. Justice Stevens also emphasized that Texas should act to bring the United States in compliance with the *Avena* judgment.[114] Justice Breyer dissented. His opinion begins with the Supremacy Clause and early cases interpreting it, and argues that as originally understood, the Clause gave domestic legal effect to treaties otherwise requiring implementing legislation. He correctly observes that the "Court has frequently held or assumed that particular treaty provisions are self-executing, automatically binding the States without more."[115] These cases, Justice Breyer argues, show that no particular language in the text of the treaty is necessary to render it self-executing. Moreover, treaties are very unlikely to include language about domestic implementation because such implementation varies from country to country, making it unsuitable for inclusion in the text of the treaty itself. Thus the majority was "misguided" insofar as it looked to the text of the treaty for a "clear statement" regarding domestic legal effect and implicitly adopted a presumption against self-execution.[116] As Justice Breyer put it, "the absence or presence of language in a treaty about a provision's self-execution proves nothing at all."[117] Justice Breyer proposed a context-specific, practical test for self-execution focusing on the language and subject matter of treaties, and how the courts have treated similar treaty provisions.

[111] Medellin, *supra* note 93, at 513. [112] *Ibid.* at 527.

[113] *Ibid.* at 527. The Court categorizes the President's action as falling within Youngstown category three. *Ibid.* For a criticism of this conclusion, see Ingrid Wuerth, Medellin, The New, New Formalism? 13 Lewis & Clark L. Rev. 1, 5–7 (2009).

[114] Medellin, *supra* note 93, at 533–7. (Stevens, J., concurring).

[115] *Ibid.* at 545 (Breyer, J., dissenting). [116] *Ibid.* at 546 (Breyer, J., dissenting).

[117] *Ibid.* at 549 (Breyer, J., dissenting).

B Academic Response

Much of the academic response to *Medellin* has been negative. The opinion is widely criticized for its lack of clarity about whether it adopts a presumption against self-execution, what language in treaties renders them self-executing or non-self-executing, and the status in domestic law of non-self-executing agreements.[118] Many find Chief Justice Roberts' reasoning in tension with the language and history of the Supremacy Clause. Professor Carlos Vázquez implausibly argues, for example, that the opinion should be read as concluding that the United States did not have a binding obligation to obey the ICJ judgment in *Avena*, because otherwise the Court's reasoning violates the Supremacy Clause.[119] Professor Oona Hathaway maintains that *Medellin* has impeded the enforcement of treaties in U.S. courts in ways that are inconsistent with the history and that "these trends in treaty interpretation resulting from *Medellin* should be deeply troubling."[120]

Professor David Sloss, another scholar critical of *Medellin*, argues for a two-step approach to the issue of self-execution.[121] The first question is one of treaty interpretation governed by international law: what does the treaty obligate the United States to do? The second question is one of domestic U.S. law: which government actors are responsible for domestic treaty implementation? This second question, Sloss argues, is almost never answered by the treaty itself and should not be addressed through a fictitious inquiry into the intent of the treaty makers, as the *Medellin* opinion does (and the Third Restatement endorses).[122] Not all concur in Sloss and Vázquez's reading of the Supremacy Clause, but they do overwhelmingly agree that treaty text rarely speaks to self-execution, rendering the majority's emphasis on text problematic – an issue insufficiently addressed by Chief Justice Roberts and likely to create confusion going forward. Finally, even those who agree with the outcome of *Medellin* tend to argue that the opinion should be construed narrowly and that it does not adopt any sort of presumption.[123]

118 *See, e.g.*, David Sloss, *Executing* Foster v. Neilson: *The Two-Step Approach to Analyzing Self-Executing Treaties*, HARV. INT'L L. J. 135, 184 (2012) (describing the Court's opinion in *Medellin* as "inscrutable"); *see also Self-Execution of Treaties*, 122 HARV. L. REV. 435 (2008) (similar); *cf.* Wuerth, *supra* note 113, at 5–7 (criticizing the *Medellin* opinion on other grounds); Jean Galbraith, *International Law and the Domestic Separation of Powers*, 99 VA. L. REV. 987, 1048 (2013) (arguing that some of the "reasoning in *Medellin* is brief, unsupported, and seemingly ignorant") and Andrew Tutt, *Treaty Textualism*, 39 YALE J. INT'L L. 283, 285 (2014) (noting that *Medellin* has been widely criticized).

119 *See* Carlos Manuel Vázquez, *Treaties as Law of the Land: The Supremacy Clause and the Judicial Enforcement of Treaties*, 122 HARV. L. REV. 599 (2008).

120 Hathaway, *supra* note 45, at 71. 121 Sloss, *supra* note 118. 122 *Ibid.*

123 John T. Parry, *Rewriting the Roberts Court's Law of Treaties*, 88 TEX. L. REV. 65, 67–9 (2010).

IV POST-*MEDELLIN*: COURTS AND THE SENATE

A *Courts*

The effect of *Medellin* in the lower courts has been threefold: to strengthen courts' applications of declarations of non-self-execution; to continue the trend away from a presumption in favor self-execution articulated by the Third Restatement; and to accord greater significance to the presumption against private rights and causes of action.

In the years since *Medellin*, lower courts have continued to enforce declarations of non-self-execution, consistent with the language in the Third Restatement and consistent with the reasoning in *Medellin* as well as most lower-court opinions prior to *Medellin*. At least one Court of Appeals has interpreted *Medellin* as strengthening the argument that declarations of non-self-execution should be enforced by the courts.[124]

For treaties lacking declarations of non-self-execution, courts have continued to enforce certain categories with little analysis of self-execution or private rights of action. These cases generally involve longstanding treaties with a history of direct domestic implementation, such as the Warsaw/Montreal Convention and the Convention on the International Sales of Goods.[125] The Conventions on the Privileges and Immunities of the United Nations has been held self-executing based on the text of the treaty and the views of the executive branch.[126]

124 Igartua v. U.S., 626 F.3d 592 (1st Cir. 2010); *see also* M.A. ex rel. P.K. v. Vill. Voice Media Holdings, LLC, 809 F. Supp. 2d 1041, 1058 (E.D. Mo. 2011); See v. McDonald, No. 1:10-CV -01520-AWI, 2013 WL 1281621, at *23 (E.D. Cal. Mar. 26, 2013).

125 *See, e.g*, Eid v. Alaska Airlines, Inc. 621 F.3d 858 (9th Cir. 2010) (apparently applying Warsaw convention without discussing self-execution); Lavergne v. ATIS Corp., 767 F. Supp. 2d 301 (D. Puerto Rico 2011) (applying Montreal Convention); Forestal Guarani S.A. v. Daros Intern., Inc. 613 F.3d 395 (3d Cir. 2010) (CISG vests private parties with a private right of action); Beth Schiffer Fine Photographic Arts, Inc. v. Colex Imaging, Inc. Slip Copy, 2012 WL 924380 D.N.J ("The CISG is a self-executing treaty that preempts contrary provisions of Article 2 of the UCC and other state contract law to the extent that those causes of action fall within the scope of the CISG. U.S. Const., Art. VI") (assuming CISG creates cause of action); In re Premises Located at 840 140th Ave. NE, Bellevue, Wash. 634 F.3d 557 (9th Cir. 2011) (holding MLAT with Russia self-executing w/o discussion). Riccitelli v. Elemar New England Marble & Granite, LLC, No. 3:08CV01783 DJS, 2010 WL 3767111, at *4 (D. Conn. Sept. 14, 2010); *see also* Peterson v. Islamic Republic of Iran, 758 F.3d 185, 189–90 (2d Cir. 2014) (holding Treaty of Amity, Economic Relations and Consular Rights between the United States and Iran self-executing); Petmas Investors Ltd. v. Sameiet Holbergs Gate 19, No. CIV. A. 13–6807 FLW, 2014 WL 6886028, at *6 (D.N.J. Dec. 4, 2014) (holding the Hague Service Convention self-executing).

126 Brzak v. United Nations, 597 F.3d 107 (2d Cir. 2010) (CPIUN self-executing) ("In determining whether a treaty is self-executing, we look to the text, the negotiation and drafting history, and the postratification understanding of the signatory nations. Medellin

No court since *Medellin* has applied a presumption in favor of self-execution, except perhaps in the context of interpreting nineteenth century treaties between Indian tribes and the United States.[127] A few courts have read *Medellin* as suggesting a presumption of non-self-execution. One court reasoned in dicta that after *Medellin* there is an "emerging presumption against finding treaties to be self-executing."[128] Another understood *Medellin* as adopting a "clear statement" rule to the effect that a treaty is self-executing only if it explicitly states as much.[129] Some courts appear to confuse the presumption against private rights and private causes of action (discussed below) and the presumption of non-self-execution.[130]

Nevertheless, most cases to date that have held treaties non-self-executing are consistent with pre-*Medellin* case law.[131] An arguable exception is Judge Kavanaugh's opinion in *Bihani v. Obama* reasoning that the Geneva Conventions are non-self-executing,[132] contrary to some (although not all)

v. Texas, 552 U.S. at 506–7. Additionally, the executive branch's interpretation of a treaty "is entitled to great weight." *Ibid.* at 513 (quoting Sumitomo Shoji America, Inc. v. Avagliano, 457 U.S. 176 (1982)). Based on these criteria, we have little difficulty concluding that the CPIUN is self-executing ... Consequently, we hold that the CPIUN is self-executing and applies in American courts without implementing legislation"; *see also* Georges v. United Nations, No. 13-CV-7146 JPO, 2015 WL 129657, at *1 (S.D.N.Y. Jan. 9, 2015).

127 Jones v. Norton, No. 2:09-CV-730, 2013 WL 1336125, at *3 (D. Utah Mar. 29, 2013) (the "broad presumption courts use when interpreting Indian treaties, indicates that the portion of the Ute Treaty in question was self-executing"); *but see* Robinson v. Salazar, 885 F. Supp. 2d 1002 (E.D. Cal. 2012).

128 ESAB Group, Inc. v. Zurich Ins. *PLC*, 685 F.3d 376, 387–88 (4th Cir. 2012); *see also* Safety Nat'l Casualty Corp v. Certain Underwriters at Lloyd's London, 587 F.3d 714, 737 (5th Cir. 2009) (Clement, C.J., concurring in the judgment) (reasoning that the treaty is self-executing but noting that "there may be a growing judicial consensus that multilateral treaties are presumptively non-self-executing.").

129 M.C. v. Bianchi, 782 F. Supp. 2d 127 (E. D. Pa. 2011).

130 *See, e.g.*, M.A. ex rel. P.K. v. Vill. Voice Media Holdings, LLC, 809 F. Supp. 2d 1041, 1058 (E.D. Mo. 2011).

131 *See, e.g.*, Yuen Jin v. Mukasey 538 F.3d 143 (2d Cir. 2008) (Convention Against Torture); United States v. Bahel, 662 F.3d 610 (2d Cir. 2011) (Dues provision of U.N. Charter); Khan v. Holder, 584 F.3d 773 (9th Cir. 2009) (1967 United Nations Protocol Relating to the Status of Refugees); Belmora LLC v. Bayer Consumer Care AG, No. 1:14-CV-00847-GBL, 2015 WL 518571, at *15 (E.D. Va. Feb. 6, 2015) (Article 6b is of the Paris Convention); Abbas v. U.S., No. 10-CV-0141S, 2014 WL 3858398, at *4 (W.D.N.Y. Aug. 1, 2014) (U.N. Convention Relating to the Status of Refugees); *see also* United States v. Kelly, 676 F.3d 912 (9th Cir. 2012) (suggesting but not holding that the 1907 Hague Convention Respecting the Laws and Customs of War on Land is not self-executing); Alaska v. Kerry, 972 F. Supp. 2d 1111, 1113 (D. Alaska 2013) (parties agree that the International Convention for the Prevention of Pollution from Ships is non self-executing).

132 Al-Bihani v. Obama, 619 F.3d 1, 10 (D.C. Cir. 2010) (opinion of Kavanaugh, J., concurring in denial of rehearing en banc). Another new holding post-Medellin is Doe v. Holder, 763 F.3d

earlier precedent.[133] Judge Kavanaugh suggests that bilateral treaties might be presumptively self-executing and that multilateral treaties might be presumptively non-self-executing,[134] but his opinion does not specifically apply a presumption, and it notes some important self-executing multilateral treaties. The opinion relies on the Supreme Court's textual analysis from *Medellin* to conclude that the Geneva Conventions' language "undertakes to respect" rendered them non-self-executing.[135]

Medellin may turn out to have the most immediate effect with respect to private rights and private causes of action. As described above, the opinion quotes in dicta the Third Restatement's language that treaties, even those benefiting private persons, generally do "not create private rights or provide for a private cause of action in domestic courts."[136] Lower courts have relied on *Medellin* and applied a presumption against private rights even with respect to treaty agreements that benefit individuals. In some of these cases, even where the cause of action is supplied by a source other than the treaty (such as a Section 1983 action or a habeas petition), courts have refused to judicially enforce treaties, even those that are self-executing and that benefit individuals, based on the presumption that they "do not create private rights" enforceable by individual litigants.[137] An example is litigation based on the Vienna Convention on Consular Relations (VCCR). In *Mora v. New York*, for example, a case brought in part under 48 U.S.C § 1983, the Second Circuit reasoned based on *Medellin*'s footnote 3 that although the VCCR benefited individuals and although the plaintiffs had a cause of action from an independent source, plaintiffs could not rely on the treaty because it did not create "private rights."[138] The Second Circuit reached this conclusion without deciding whether the VCCR was self-executing.[139] Although most courts had reached the same result in VCCR cases even before *Medellin* was decided,[140] footnote 3 of the *Medellin* opinion bolstered the Second Circuit's conclusion that there was no private right of action, as the *Mora* opinion itself reasoned.

251, 253 (2d Cir. 2014) (holding some provisions of the United Nations Convention against Transnational Organized Crime are not self-executing).

133 United States v. Noriega, 808 F. Supp. 791 (S. D. Fl. 1992); United States. v. Lindh, 212 F. Supp. 2d 541(E.D.Va. 2002); *but see* Hamdi v. Rumsfeld, 316 F.3d 451, 468–69 (4th Cir. 2003), vacated on other grounds by Hamdi v. Rumsfeld, 542 U.S. 507 (2004).

134 *Al-Bihani*, 619 F.3d at 15–16; *see also* United States v. Postal, 589 F.2d at 878.

135 *Al-Bihani*, 619 F.3d at 20–1.

136 Third Restatement § 907, cmt. (a).

137 *See, e.g.*, Loza v. Mitchell, 766 F.3d 466, 499 (6th Cir. 2014) (Vienna Convention on Consular Relations); Gandara v. Bennett, 528 F.3d 823, 827 (11th Cir. 2008) (same); Cornejo v. County of San Diego, 504 F.3d 853, 872 (9th Cir.2007) (same).

138 *Mora v. New York*, 524 F.3d 183 (2d Cir. 2008).

139 *Ibid.* at 193 n. 16.

140 *See, e.g.*, Cornejo v. County of San Diego, 504 F.3d 853, 859–64 (9th Cir. 2007).

Another potentially significant example is *McKesson Corp. v. Islamic Rep. of Iran*, involving the Treaty of Amity between the United States and Iran.[141] The D.C. Circuit held that that the treaty is self-executing but nonetheless refused to enforce it on the grounds that it does not create a private cause of action. Unlike the plaintiffs in *Mora*, the *McKesson* plaintiffs relied upon the treaty itself to supply the cause of action. Citing the Restatement and *Medellin*'s footnote 3, the D.C. Circuit held that the Treaty of Amity created no private cause of action. The D.C. Circuit had reached the opposite conclusion before *Medellin* was decided, suggesting that *Medellin* had precipitated the change, in this context in a commercial case.[142] As Professor Hathaway has argued based in part on *McKesson*: "*Medellín* has changed the nature of U.S. courts' treaty analysis, leading them increasingly to adopt a strong presumption that treaties are neither self-executing nor protective of private rights and thus do not give rise to private rights of action. This shift is evident in the lower federal courts' decisions in the nearly four years since the Supreme Court's decision."[143] Hathaway's argument might be something of an overstatement, because the outcomes of pre- and post-*Medellin* cases are largely consistent.[144] In *McKesson* itself, the D.C. Circuit relied not only on the intervening decision in *Medellin*, but also on the change of views of the Executive Branch as the *McKesson* litigation progressed. The government eventually argued that the treaty created no private cause of action, and the D.C. Circuit so held, citing (in addition to *Medellin*) the proposition that the government's interpretation of a treaty should be accorded "great weight" by the courts.[145]

Ironically, the Third Restatement's greatest impact on domestic enforceability of treaties may come from the language of Section 907, comment a, on private rights and private causes of action. Generally, the Third Restatement was geared toward increasing the applicability of international law in U.S. courts,[146] but this comment is increasingly used to limit the application of treaties by U.S. courts. The limitations are particularly clear and

[141] McKesson Corp. v. Islamic Republic of Iran, 539 F.3d 485, 488 (D.C. Cir. 2008).

[142] Hathaway, *supra* note 45, at 71–6 (2012) (describing cases in detail).

[143] Hathaway, *supra* note 45.

[144] See Vienna Convention on Consular Relations Cases above. *See also* Gross v. German Found. Indus. Initiative, 549 F.3d 605, 615 (3d Cir. 2008) (affirming a pre-Medellin decision by District Court holding that the treaty did not create private rights).

[145] McKesson Corp. v. Islamic Republic of Iran, 539 F.3d 485, 491 (D.C. Cir. 2008).

[146] *See* Paul B. Stephan, *Courts, the Constitution, and Customary International Law: The Intellectual Origins of the Third Restatement of the Foreign Relations Law of the United States*, 44 VA. J. INT'L L. 33, 59 (2003) (arguing that one goal of the THIRD RESTATEMENT was to "encourage the penetration of international law into federal law").

pronounced in human rights related cases such as *Medellin*. Especially with the boost from footnote 3 of *Medellin*, such limitations may migrate from human rights cases to cases involving commercial and property law.[147] A Restatement drafted with an eye towards advancing human rights[148] may have, at least in this context, not only failed to advance human rights but also undermined international law more generally.

B *Senate Advice and Consent to Treaties post-*Medellin

As of October 2015, the U.S. Senate had given its advice and consent to ninety-four treaties since the beginning of 2008.[149] Five treaties do not include declarations of self-execution or non-self-execution. Seven treaties have some articles or provisions that are self-executing and some articles that are not. Eighty-two have unqualified declarations of self-execution (sixty-eight) or non-self-execution (fourteen).[150] These numbers appear to reflect a growth in the use of declarations of self-execution. The Senate Foreign Relations Committee noted in 2008 the benefits of using declarations of self-execution in the wake of *Medellin*.[151]

147 *See* Hathaway, *supra* note 45; see Sloss, *supra* note 55.

148 *See* Ernest A. Young, *Universal Jurisdiction, the Alien Tort Statute, and Transnational Public-Law Litigation after Kiobel*, 64 DUKE L.J. 1023, 1050 (2015).

149 This figure includes Protocols and Amendments to existing treaties. *See Treaty Documents*, CONGRESS.GOV, available at www.congress.gov/treaties (Oct. 28, 2015).

150 For those treaties since 2008 that the Senate has declared to be self-executing, *see* S. EXEC. REP. NO. 112–3, at 6 (2011); S. EXEC. REP. NO. 111–4, at 4 (2010); S. EXEC. REP. NO. 111–3, at 6 (2010); S. EXEC. REP. NO. 111–1, at 5 (2009); S. EXEC. REP. NO. 110–22, at 13–14 (2008); S. EXEC. REP. NO. 110–17, at 7 (2008); S. EXEC. REP. NO. 110–16, at 8 (2008); S. EXEC. REP. NO. 110–15, at 10 (2008); S. EXEC. REP. NO. 110–14, at 6 (2008); S. EXEC. REP. NO. 110–13, at 11–21 (2008); S. EXEC. REP. NO. 110–12, at 10–20 (2008). For those the Senate has declared to be non-self-executing, *see* S. EXEC. REP. NO. 113–4, at 6 (2014); S. EXEC. REP. NO. 113–3, at 6 (2014); S. EXEC. REP. NO. 113–2, at 7 (2014); S. EXEC. REP. NO. 113–1, at 6 (2014); S. EXEC. REP. NO. 111–5, at 34 (2010); S. EXEC. REP. NO. 111–2, at 9 (2010); S. EXEC. REP. NO. 110–20, at 10 (2008); S. EXEC. REP. NO. 110–19, at 10 (2008); S. EXEC. REP. NO. 110–28, at 20–22 (2008); S. EXEC. REP. NO. 110–18, at 13–14 (2008). For treaties that have some articles or provisions the Senate has declared to be self-executing and others the Senate has declared to be non-self-executing, *see* S. EXEC. REP. NO. 112–2, at 13 (2011); S. EXEC. REP. NO. 110–26, at 10 (2008); S. EXEC. REP. NO. 110–25, at 16, 18 (2008); S. EXEC. REP. NO. 110–24, at 12 (2008); S. EXEC. REP. NO. 110–23, at 9 (2008); S. EXEC. REP. NO. 110–22, at 14. For those treaties that the Senate has not declared to be either self-executing or non-self-executing, *see* S. EXEC. REP. NO. 111–6, at 100–10 (2010); S. EXEC. REP. NO. 110–27, at 6–8 (2008); S. EXEC. REP. NO. 110–11, at 13 (2008); S. EXEC. REP. NO. 110–10, at 7 (2008).

151 *See, e.g.*, S. Exec. Rep. No. 110–12, at 9–10 (2008); *see also* Vázquez, *supra* note 13, at 695.

Scholars have questioned the constitutionality of declarations of self-execution, just as they have questioned the constitutionality of declarations of non-self-execution. Both permit the Senate and president to make a legally significant declaration that goes beyond the scope of the treaty itself.[152] This arguably permits lawmaking outside the constitutionally prescribed methods of making domestic law – through statutes or treaties. The constitutional problem may be more significant with respect to declarations of self-execution, however, because they implement otherwise non-self-executing treaties into domestic law through non-constitutionally-prescribed channels.[153] Declarations of non-self-execution, by contrast, simply prevent treaty language from having domestic legal effect, arguably less of an expansion of power as against the states and the House of Representatives.

The Senate's increased use of declarations of self-execution is an interesting development, suggesting that the political branches may in the future be more explicit about self-execution. The Senate's recent practice may also suggest that *Medellin* was successful as an information-forcing mechanism.[154] The increased use of declarations of self-execution and the continued use of declarations of non self-execution may in time reduce not only the significance of presumptions, but also the role of the courts in determining whether a treaty is self-executing. Of course, even if future treaties include such declarations, many of the treaties already in force do not. Many of the treaties already in force fall into categories that courts have treated as self-executing (and also at times as conferring private rights of action and even private causes of action). The most important question about self-execution today is whether courts will take the language and reasoning of *Medellin* and use it to deem commercial and property-related treaties as non-self-executing or otherwise not enforceable.

V THE RESTATEMENT (FOURTH)

As of 2017, substantial work has been done on the Treaties section of the Fourth Restatement of the Law: The Foreign Relations Law of the United

152 Such declarations go beyond the scope of the treaty because the treaty does not address self-execution.

153 Vázquez, *supra* note 13, at 685–94.

154 For an overview of the theory of information-forcing court decisions, see generally Einer Elhauge, *Preference-Eliciting Statutory Default Rules*, 102 COLUM. L. REV. 2162 (2002).

States.[155] Council Draft No. 2 was submitted and approved by Council of the American Law Institute in January, 2017. Final approval of the treaties sections is expected in May, 2017.

Like the Third Restatement, and like the Supreme Court's decision in *Medellin*, draft language in § 110 of the Fourth Restatement (Council Draft No. 2, Treaties) defines the self-execution inquiry in terms of the intent (or understanding) of the U.S. treaty makers.[156] The draft language of the Fourth Restatement also provides, more clearly than the Third Restatement, that courts will defer to Senate declarations (in the resolution of advice and consent) of self-execution and non-self-execution.[157] Contrary to some language in the Third Restatement, the draft Fourth Restatement does not adopt a presumption in favor of self-execution; it also does not adopt a presumption against self-execution.[158] The first Reporters' Note to § 110 acknowledges that "the Court has recognized a wide variety of treaty provisions as directly enforceable, across a range of subject matters" including the recovery of monetary debts, the rights of aliens, property claims from territorial acquisition, extradition treaties, civil air-carrier liability, trademark rights and international civil discovery rules." Comment d to § 110 provides that courts may use the subject matter or type of treaty as a relevant consideration in the self-execution inquiry.[159]

Private rights of action and related issues are given an entire section in the Fourth Restatement. The new § 111, "Private Rights of Action Under Treaties," limits the purported presumption against private rights of action, discussed above in Sections II.B.2 and IV.A., to a presumption against conferring "on private parties *a right to seek damages*."[160] Language in the Third Restatement and dicta in *Medellin* suggested, by contrast, that there is a general presumption that treaties do not create *private rights*. The distinction is important. Under the *Medellin* dicta, lower courts held that even if a treaty is self-executing, and even if a statute provides a cause of

[155] The author of this Chapter is a Reporter (Sovereign Immunity) for the FOURTH RESTATEMENT OF THE FOREIGN RELATIONS LAW OF THE UNITED STATES (Hereinafter "FOURTH RESTATEMENT").

[156] FOURTH RESTATEMENT, Council Draft No. 2, Treaties, § 110(2). [157] *Ibid.*

[158] FOURTH RESTATEMENT, Council Draft No. 2, Treaties, § 110, Reporters' Note c3, entitled "Lack of presumption for or against self-execution."

[159] FOURTH RESTATEMENT, Council Draft No. 2, Treaties, § 110, cmt. d and R.N. 10 ("... treaty provisions addressing the same subject matter, or of a recurring type, are often treated similarly for purposes of self-execution either because the relevant considerations point toward the same conclusion or because U.S. treatymakers were likely to have understood them in light of past practice.").

[160] FOURTH RESTATEMENT, Council Draft No. 2, Treaties, § 111(1) (italics added).

action, there is nevertheless a presumption that treaties do not confer rights on individuals. The Restatement limits that presumption to situations in which the individual is seeking a damages remedy. It does not apply when the treaty is invoked as a defense in litigation or when equitable relief is sought.

VI CONCLUSION

Overall, the efforts to enforce international human rights treaties directly in U.S. courts have largely backfired. During the 1980s, as the United States became party to human rights treaties, promoters of human rights began also to focus on the enforcement of those conventions in U.S. courts. Courts upheld declarations of non-self-execution, which were often attached to human rights treaties. This development was consistent with the Third Restatement. Courts did not, however, employ a presumption in favor of self-execution, putting their approach in tension with the Third Restatement. Initially, these roadblocks mostly limited the direct enforcement of human rights treaties in U.S. courts. Over time, however, courts have begun to apply language and reasoning from human rights cases to other cases in order to preclude or call into question the direct judicial enforcement of a growing body of international commitments, based in part on the Third Restatement's language suggesting a presumption against private rights of action. The Supreme Court's decision in *Medellin*, a human rights-related case, reinforced and likely accelerated these trends, even though the language about a presumption against private rights and causes of action was dicta relegated to a footnote. *Medellin* did not employ a presumption for or against self-execution, but it did focus on the text of the treaty on the intent of the U.S. treaty-makers as the touchstone of the judicial inquiry on self-execution. Critics, and the dissenting opinion by Justice Breyer, argue that treaty text is a very poor tool for determining self-execution in the U.S. courts. Some also questioned the relationship between *Medellin*'s approach to self-execution and the Supremacy Clause.

Today, the Third Restatement's language on private rights of action, as repeated in *Medellin*, is being used to call into question the judicial enforcement of treaties even in the context of property, contract, and commercial rights. It is unclear how far this development will go. Lower courts since *Medellin* appear to usually reach the same outcome in particular cases as they did before *Medellin*, and treaties which have long been interpreted as self-executing are likely to continue to be interpreted that way by lower courts going forward. Especially, however, for new treaties or treaties which have been applied only infrequently by the lower courts, it is increasingly likely that they will be deemed non-self-executing (except insofar as the Senate has begun to declare treaties as self-executing as part of the advice and consent process). Since *Medellin*, the vast majority of treaties have included either a declaration of self-execution or declaration of non-self-execution, reducing the role of courts in making treaty-by-treaty (or clause-by-clause) determination of self-execution.

Finally, declarations of non-self-execution have limited the enforcement of treaties in U.S. courts and for that reason were a source of criticism of the Third Restatement. It is easy to forget today, but one of most significant changes in U.S. treaty-practice since the Third Restatement is the U.S. ratification of major human rights treaties. Declarations of non-self-execution appear to be part of what convinced the Senate to finally give its advice and consent to these instruments. Moreover, in practice, declarations of non-self-execution vary in importance from treaty to treaty. For treaties that have been implemented through legislation, declarations on non-self-execution are of little practical significance. Overall, declarations of non-self-execution, which have been the basis for several lines of criticism directed at the Third Restatement, have at least arguably played a positive role in terms of facilitating greater acceptance by the United States of human rights instruments.

5

Treaties, Federalism, and the Contested Legacy of *Missouri v. Holland*

Margaret E. McGuinness

This chapter will examine the effect of federalism on the making and enforcement of treaties in the United States. For the United States, federalism – a system of government that recognizes dual sovereigns, one at the state and the other at the national level – is central to the constitutional order, to the nation's self-conception of limited government, and to the particularly American view of democracy and liberty. As Justice Kennedy recently underscored, "[t]he federal system rests on what might at first seem a counterintuitive insight, that 'freedom is enhanced by the creation of two governments, not one.'"[1] The United States is also a nation founded on the idea that, when it comes to international relations, the federal government, not the states, speaks for the nation. These two founding ideals, both central to the constitutional order, are in some tension with one another. Federalism presents a particular challenge to questions of how and under whose authority the United States can engage in international law-making through treaty.

The 1920 case *Missouri v. Holland*[2] has long stood for the twin propositions that the federal treaty power operates independently of the limits of Article I, § 8, and that when the federal government enters into a valid treaty, Congress has the concomitant power to enact legislation to enforce the subject matter of that treaty as domestic law. As Chief Justice Holmes pronounced in *Holland*, "[I]f the treaty is valid there can be no dispute about the validity of the statute under Article I, Section 8, as a necessary and proper means to execute the powers of the Government."[3] Holmes therefore dismissed any suggestion that treaty-implementing legislation on a subject beyond the constitutionally

Thanks to Kathleen Scahill, Enisa Dervisevic, Kathryn Schwimm, and Paul Brown for research assistance.

1 Bond v. United States, 131 S. Ct. 2355, 2364 (2011) (citing Alden v. Maine, 527 U.S. 706, 758 (1999)).

2 Missouri v. Holland, 252 U.S. 416 (1920). 3 *Ibid.* at 430.

enumerated powers of Congress "is forbidden by some invisible radiation from the general terms of the Tenth Amendment."[4]

Following the logic of *Holland*, the 1987 Restatement (Third) of Foreign Relations ("Third Restatement") concluded that the subject matter of valid treaties the United States may "make" pursuant to its constitutional authority is not limited.[5] But the Third Restatement also noted that, while the Tenth Amendment placed no restrictions on the treaty power, the Supreme Court had, in the time since the decision in *Holland*, struck down Congressional and Executive efforts to enforce treaty provisions that limit constitutionally protected individual rights. The Reporter's notes to Section 302 of the Third Restatement stated: "Treaties and other international agreements are subject to the prohibitions of the Bill of Rights and other restraints on federal power, such as those relating to suspension of the writ of habeas corpus or prohibiting the grant of titles of nobility."[6]

Since the publication of the Third Restatement, the Supreme Court's federalism jurisprudence has shifted, away from upholding federal assertions of power to legislate over a broad range of subjects, to reining in federal efforts to legislate pursuant to the interstate Commerce Clause and Section 5 of the Fourteenth Amendment.[7] This shift, toward a federalism that more narrowly defined the scope of national law-making prerogatives, has raised questions about federalism limitations on the treaty power that were thought to have been settled by *Holland*. During the same time, this "new federalism" has spurred the idea of state law-making power as a means of legal innovation.

4 *Ibid.* at 433–4. Holmes left open the narrower, but nonetheless important, question of whether implementing legislation is "necessary and proper" to giving effect to the U.S. obligation undertaken by a particular treaty. *See* Stewart, Chapter 6 in this book.

5 RESTATEMENT (THIRD) OF FOREIGN RELATIONS LAW OF THE UNITED STATES ("THIRD RESTATEMENT") § 302 Reporters' Note 1 (1987). The Third Restatement shifted slightly away from the formulation of 1965 Restatement (Second), which states in § 117(1)(a) that the United States may make a treaty on a "matter of international concern" that also does not contravene the Constitution. The Reporters' notes of the Second Restatement further explain that "matter of international concern" means an agreement "must relate to the external concerns of the national as distinguished from matters of a purely internal nature." SECOND RESTATEMENT FOREIGN RELATIONS LAW OF THE UNITED STATES §117 Reporters' Note 1, cmt. b. (1965). The Notes further explained, "Matters of international concern are not confined to matters exclusively concerned with foreign relations..." and "matters of international concerns have both international and domestic effects, and the existence of the latter does not remove a matter from international concern."

6 THIRD RESTATEMENT at § 302 cmt. b (1987). The comment goes on to note and cross reference a comment that the invalidity of the treaty provision as a matter of internal law may not excuse the obligation as a matter of international law. THIRD RESTATEMENT at § 311(3).

7 For an overview of what is sometimes referred to as the Rehnquist Court's "federalism revolution," see Erwin Chemerinsky, *Keynote Address*, 41 WILLAMETTE L. REV. 5 (2005).

This view of state and local law-making powers sees diversity among the states as a valuable feature of federalism in regulatory areas as distinct as environmental regulation and securities fraud. Under this view of federalism innovation, states and localities have acted in some instances to reject international norms and legal standards, and in others to embrace international norms, including those created by treaties. The Constitution prohibits states from entering into "any Agreement or Compact" with other states or foreign sovereigns absent Congressional approval. But states have increasingly pushed the boundaries of the Compacts Clause while also asserting their prerogative to adopt policies and laws that reflect international norms.

The resulting legal landscape is one that appears to reflect opportunistic and inconsistent international law-making at the federal and state levels. In the two decades since the Third Restatement, legal scholars have debated the proper balance between the national government's power to make domestic law through treaties and the states' power to make law in areas that, absent treaties, would be reserved to the states. One side of the debate argues that an aggressive application of the treaty power, such as that expressed in *Holland*, would supplant state and local police powers and thereby weaken the democracy- and liberty-enhancing values of federalism that the Constitution intended to promote. The other side argues that any federalism limitations on the national government's power to make and carry out treaty commitments would undermine the centralization of foreign policy that is essential to the constitutional order. Both concerns may be overstated, especially in light of constitutional practice.

The Supreme Court's 2014 decision in *Bond v. United States,*[8] left the central holding of *Holland* untouched, thus preserving the full potential of a robust national treaty power.[9] Restrained Executive and Congressional practice over the past three decades, combined with formal adoption of federalism "understandings" on several multilateral treaties as a condition to Congressional approval, has tempered enforcement of treaties on subjects that encroach on traditional state prerogatives – in particular, human rights treaties. These developments since the Third Restatement reflect the dynamic nature of dual sovereignty in the area of treaty-making, and suggest that U.S. practice will continue to be fluid and flexible, and that the balance between national and state prerogatives is more likely to be determined by practices in the political branches than in the Supreme Court. For U.S. treaty

8 Bond v. United States, 134 S. Ct. 2077 (2014).

9 As of the 2005 decision in *Gonzalez v. Raich*, 545 U.S. 1 (2005), the federalism revolution of the Supreme Court appears to have slowed. *Ibid.* at 9 (upholding a federal statute that criminalized the growing and possession of marijuana).

partners, federalism will therefore continue to present both challenges to and opportunities for bringing the United States into compliance with international treaty norms.

I CONSTITUTIONAL ORIGINS AND HISTORICAL PRACTICE

Article II of the Constitution states that the president "shall have Power, by and with the Advice and Consent of the Senate, to make Treaties, provided two thirds of the Senators present concur."[10] The power to "make" treaties is complemented by the president's power to receive and appoint ambassadors, which places the central functions of international diplomacy carried out by those ambassadors, *i.e.*, negotiation and agreement-making, in the Executive branch.[11] Article VI, the Supremacy Clause, gives treaties supremacy over state law:

> This Constitution, and the Laws of the United States which shall be made in Pursuance thereof; *and all Treaties made, or which shall be made, under the Authority of the United States, shall be the supreme Law of the Land*; and the Judges in every State shall be bound thereby, any Thing in the Constitution or Laws of any State to the Contrary notwithstanding.[12]

Further clarifying the exclusivity of the national government's power to "make Treaties," the Compacts Clause of Article I, Section 10 states that "No State shall enter into any Treaty, Alliance or Confederation,"[13] and goes on to prohibit states "without the consent of Congress" from "enter[ing] into any Agreement or Compact with another State, or with a foreign Power."[14] As a textual matter, the Constitution is clear that the national government, not the states, has the power, through the President, to "make treaties," and that treaties so "made," are supreme over any contrary state law.

As a means of enforcing the Supremacy Clause, Article III grants the federal courts power to decide over "all Cases … Arising under … treaties made."[15] Despite granting the federal courts jurisdiction over treaty disputes, the Constitution is less clear about the process through which treaty terms become domestic law. The Constitution is silent as to whether treaties are self-

[10] U.S. Const. art. II, § 2.

[11] U.S. Const. art. II, § 2, cl. 2. (the president "shall nominate, and by and with the Advice and Consent of the Senate, shall appoint Ambassadors, other public Ministers and Consuls…"); U.S. Const. art. II, § 3 ("[The President] shall receive Ambassadors and other public Ministers. …").

[12] U.S. Const. art. VI (emphasis added). [13] U.S. Const. art. I, § 10, cl. 1.

[14] U.S. Const. art. I, § 10, cl. 3. [15] U.S. Const. art. II, § 2, cl. 1.

executing or non-self-executing, which some observers conclude reflects an implicit assumption by the drafters that all treaties were self-executing.[16] Article I of the Constitution provides one key to implementation: the Necessary and Proper Clause.[17] The Third Restatement states in the Reporters Notes to Section 111:

> Under Art. 1 Section 8, of the United States Constitution, Congress has the power to 'make all laws which shall be necessary and proper for the carrying into Execution ... all other powers vested by this Constitution in the Government of the United States, or in any Department of officer thereof.' *Congress therefore has the power to enact legislation necessary and proper for carrying into execution a treaty properly made by the President with the consent of the Senate, or an executive agreement within the President's authority under the Constitution.*[18]

In addition to the treaty power, "all the other powers" encompasses other legislative powers, including the Foreign Commerce Clause,[19] and the Define and Punish Clause,[20] which may each offer separate constitutional bases for legislation enacted to comply with a particular treaty obligation.[21]

The language of the Necessary and Proper Clause leaves some room for debate whether Congress is limited to legislating only to the extent legislation is itself "necessary" to comply with the obligations created under the treaty, and also whether Congress itself may determine what is required to comply with a particular treaty.[22] This is a particularly challenging problem where

[16] *See* Wuerth, Chapter 4 in this book (discussing the academic debate over the meaning of the Supremacy Clause and whether the Founders intended treaties to be presumptively self-executing).

[17] U.S. CONST. art. I, § 8.

[18] THIRD RESTATEMENT at § 111 Reporters' Note 8 (emphasis added) (quoting U.S. CONST. art. I, § 8). This understanding of the Necessary and Proper Clause is broadly accepted in constitutional law treatises. *See* ERWIN CHEMERINKSY, CONSTITUTIONAL LAW: PRINCIPLES AND POLICIES 287 (4th edn. 2011).

[19] Congress shall have the power "To regulate *Commerce with foreign Nations*, and among the several States, and with the Indian Tribes." U.S. CONST. art. I § 8 cl. 3 (emphasis added).

[20] "The Congress shall have Power To ... *define and punish* Piracies and Felonies committed on the high Seas, and Offences against the Law of Nations ...." U.S. CONST. art. I § 8 cl. 10. (emphasis added).

[21] See Stewart Chapter 6 in this book for a discussion of the "Define and Punish" clause; Corn & Beck, Chapter 9 in this book for a discussion of how the Foreign Commerce Clause could be used to enact legislation giving effect to treaties. *See generally*, Scott Sullivan, *The Future of the Foreign Commerce Clause*, 83 FORDHAM L. REV. 1955 (2015).

[22] *See* Brad R. Roth, *Understanding the "Understanding": Federalism Constraints on Human Rights Implementation*, 47 WAYNE L. REV. 893, 899–900 (2001) (noting, in the context of

treaty language may be ambiguous and the treaty does not provide for a mechanism of definitive resolution of interpretive questions.[23]

The Bill of Rights to the Constitution restricts the powers of the national government to legislate in ways that impair those individual rights that the drafters saw as central to a government of limited powers.[24] Reflecting this constitutional commitment to a national government of limited powers, one that represents the dual sovereignty of the states and national government, the Tenth Amendment states that "[t]he powers not delegated to the United States by the Constitution, nor prohibited by it to the States, are reserved to the States respectively, or to the people."[25] The Treaty Clause, however, is silent as to any subject matter limits on treaties, leaving open the question whether any subject matter that is reserved for the states under the Tenth Amendment would be either off-limits for legislating pursuant to treaties or, in the case of self-executing treaties, enforceable as domestic law.

The potential textual and structural conflict is clear: if the treaty power is unlimited in scope and subject matter, then the powers of the national government expand vis-à-vis the states when it adopts treaties, to include areas that would otherwise be off-limits when the national government is acting to address purely domestic policy matters. A review of the early history of the treaty power and federalism is helpful to understanding how Holmes resolved the textual ambiguity to reach the broad holding in *Holland* – and why Louis Henkin strongly endorsed this view in the drafting of the Third Restatement – that the Tenth Amendment does not act as an independent restriction on the subject matter of treaties.

U.S. participation in human rights treaties, that the "real question" raised when Congress invokes the Necessary and Proper clause is "under what circumstance a Congressional interpretation of human rights treaty obligations can serve to extend federal authority over matters otherwise reserved to the states.").

[23] *Ibid.* at 900 (discussing how the lack of "authoritative interpretation at the international level" raises the question of whether the Court or Congress should have the final say of "reconciling federal foreign policy interests with the prerogatives of the states..."). The states may, of course, enact legislation or adjudicate claims in ways that are consistent with and give effect to national treaties, but there is no proscribed mechanism in the Constitution through which that occurs. *See* Julian G. Ku, *The State of New York Does Exist: How the States Control Compliance with International Law*, 82 N.C. L. Rev. 457, 476–99 (2004)(providing historical examples of the ways in which states give effect to rights created under treaties).

[24] *See* U.S. Const. Amend. I-X (limiting the powers of the Government to pass laws infringing upon certain individual rights).

[25] U.S. Const. Amend. X.

A *Nationalizing the Treaty Power and the Subject Matter of Treaties*

After the adoption of the Articles by the Continental Congress,[26] issues immediately arose concerning the power to make treaties, the scope of the subject matter of treaties to be concluded with foreign states, and the ability of the national Congress to enforce the terms of treaties on the states.[27] The national government was assigned the power to determine issues of war and peace, to send and receive ambassadors, and to enter into treaties and alliances.[28] However, as a result of limitations on the Continental Congress's power to pass legislation, the authority of Congress more generally to give effect to its foreign affairs powers – including treaties – was significantly curtailed. The national Congress had no ability to legislate, for example, in the area of foreign commerce.[29] But the states were restricted under the Articles from imposing taxes and duties that would interfere with treaties entered into or already proposed by the national government with France and Spain.[30] The ambiguities and contradictions of the Articles in the area of treaty-making prompted the assertion by the states that they retained the right to make treaties, to interpret the degree to which they were bound by national treaties, and to have their own voice in the foreign policy-making of the nation.[31] The result was legal uncertainty at home and diplomatic tensions

[26] For a summary of the history of the treaty power and its challenges during the Articles era, see David Golove, *Treaty-Making and the Nation: The Historical Foundations of the Nationalist Conception of the Treaty Power*, 98 MICH. L. REV. 1075, 1102–32 (2000). Examples included the problem of alien land ownership. *Ibid.* at 1104–15.

[27] *See id.* at 1102–4. *See also* Oona Hathaway et al., *The Treaty Power: Its History, Scope and Limits*, 98 CORNELL L. REV. 239, 245–53 (2012).

[28] *See* ARTICLES OF CONFEDERATION of 1781, art. IX. *See also* Golove, *supra* note 26, at 1104 n.66. One significant contradiction in the Articles was the right of the states to imposes taxes and duties and the provision that "no treaty of commerce shall be made, whereby the legislative power of the respective states shall be restrained from imposing such imposts and duties on foreigners as their own people are subjected to, or from prohibiting exportation or importation of any species of good or commodities whatsoever." ARTICLES OF CONFEDERATION of 1781, art. IX. *See* discussion in Golove, *supra* note 26, at 1108–9.

[29] Golove, *supra* note 26, at 1104 (note 66 and 67).

[30] *See* ARTICLES OF CONFEDERATION of 1781, art. VI. (prohibiting the states from "any imposts or duties which may interfere with any stipulations in treaties entered into by the United States, in Congress assembled, with any king, prince or state, in pursuance of any treaties already proposed by Congress to the court of France and Spain."); *See also*, Golove, *supra* note 26, at 1109 (describing art. VI as in contradiction with art. IX and permitting states – outside of the treaties with France and Spain – to be unrestrained from violating Congress's treaties).

[31] Golove, *supra* note 26, at 1102–4. Some examples of problems during the Articles era include the problem of land ownership in the United States by aliens and enforcement of the Treaty of Peace by the states. *Ibid.* at 1115–31. Article IX of the Articles gave the "sole and exclusive right and power of determining on peace and war," "of sending and receiving ambassadors" and also

abroad over the enforceability of the full scope of treaties,[32] leading ultimately to a "divide and conquer" strategy of negotiation of commercial agreements by the British government with the separate states.[33] The Articles era demonstrated the impossibility of coordinating treaty negotiations among the states[34] and laid the groundwork for an improved, national coordination mechanism in the new Constitution.[35]

Thus, the Founders saw this "nationalizing" of the treaty power – reflected in the Treaty Clause, the Compacts Clause and the Supremacy Clause – as essential to restoring the new nation's credibility and reliability as a treaty partner by ensuring the effective conduct of foreign affairs and state compliance with international obligations.[36] Together, these provisions removed ambiguity about the *exclusivity* of the treaty power resting in the national government and established that treaties were superior to state law.

The Necessary and Proper Clause further conferred on Congress the power to legislate in furtherance of treaty compliance. Professor Nicholas Rosenkranz has controversially argued that the Necessary and Proper Clause's assignment of the power to "carry into execution" the Article II power to "make treaties" authorizes only legislation to give effect to treaty-"making" (*e.g.*, the funding for diplomats and negotiations), and does not authorize legislation to execute the underlying treaty obligations.[37] Although

of "entering into treaties and alliances," to Congress. ARTICLES OF CONFEDERATION of 1781, art. IX.

32 *See* discussion of the Treaty of Amity and Commerce with France, Golove, *supra* note 26, at 1113–14.

33 *Ibid.* at 1127–30 (discussing Lord Sheffield's plan to discontinue treaties with the United States and instead to make them with the separate states).

34 The collective action problem was acute as foreign powers could engage the states in a "race to the bottom" on issues of trade and customs. The result was the states themselves became locked in "trade wars and conflicts." *Ibid.* at 1131.

35 Golove refers to the "grueling experience" under the Articles as leading to several lessons, including "maximizing the national government's influence in negotiations with foreign states." *Ibid.* at 1132. This argument is echoed in the modern debates of national power to enforce treaties – on any constitutional subject matter – against the states. *See* Brief for the United States in Opposition at 20–2, Bond v. United States, 134 S. Ct. 2077 (2014) (No. 12–158).

36 Professor David Golove has described three lessons the Founders gleaned from their experience with the Articles: [F]irst, that any rigid limitations on the treaty power in favor of the state created serious potential to embarrass the conduct of our foreign affairs with the most grave possible consequences; second, that the federal government had to have sufficient power to ensure that any obligations it undertook to foreign countries would be observed by the states; and third, that to ensure state compliance with the stipulations of treaties, it was essential that treaties supersede any conflicting provisions of state law. Golove, *supra* note 26, at 1103–4.

37 Nicholas Quinn Rosenkranz, *Executing the Treaty Power*, 118 HARV. L. REV. 1867, 1884 (2005).

adopted by Justice Scalia in his concurrence in *Bond*,[38] this interpretation is not widely supported and flies in the face of both constitutional practice and early Supreme Court jurisprudence.[39]

Because nothing in the Constitution defined or described the scope of the subject matter of treaties, scholars have looked to extrinsic sources to understand the intent of the drafters.[40] The ratification debates contain relatively little explicit discussion of the treaty power – and thus little analysis of the relationship between the treaty power and the states or of the subject matter of treaties.[41] The Founders assumed that the foreign affairs powers of the national government, including the exclusive power to make treaties, were powers inherent to sovereignty within the international system – an assumption that did not require articulation of the full scope of the treaty power.[42] While the Founders agreed that treaties should be more difficult to make than they had been during the Articles of Confederation period,[43] the only limitations on

38 *See* Bond v. United States, 134 S. Ct. 2077, 2099 (2014) (Scalia, J., concurring) ("[A] power to help the President make treaties is not a power to implement treaties already made.") (citing Nicholas Quinn Rosenkranz, *Executing the Treaty Power*, 118 HARV. L. REV. 1867, 1884 (2005)).

39 *See* Edward T. Swaine, *Federalism and International Law: Putting Missouri v. Holland on the Map*, 73 MO. L. REV. 1007, 1016–17 (2008) (refuting the supposed tension between the views of Hamilton, Madison, and Marshall on the Necessary and Proper Clause and rejecting Rosenkranz's textual interpretation of the treaty power as implausible). *See also* Jean Galbraith, *Congress's Treaty-Implementing Power in Historical Practice*, 56 WM. & MARY L. REV. 59, 75–7 (2014) (discussing how Rosenkranz's narrow textualist argument entirely dismisses historical practice).

40 Indeed, the drafters expressly sought not to define precisely what was meant by the treaty power for fear that such definition would prove "defective." James Madison stated "I do not think it is possible to enumerate all the cases in which such external regulations would be necessary. Would it be right to define all the cases in which such external regulations would be necessary? Would it be right to define all the cases in which Congress could exercise this authority? The definition might and probably would, be defective." *See* Hathaway et al., *supra* note 27, at 248, & n. 31 (citing the 3 DEBATES IN THE SEVERAL STATE CONVENTIONS ON THE ADOPTION OF THE CONSTITUTION AS RECOMMENDED BY THE GENERAL CONVENTION AT PHILADELPHIA IN 1787 (Jonathan Elliott ed., 2nd edn. 1859 at 514–15).

41 *See, e.g.*, Curtis A. Bradley, THE TREATY POWER AND AMERICAN FEDERALISM, 97 MICH. L. REV. 390, 410 (1998) (noting, "Neither the records of the Federal Convention nor the Federalist Papers contain much discussion of this issue."). *But see* Golove, *supra* note 26, at 1132 (noting that "it was the forcefulness with which these lessons [of the Articles era] had been brought to the attention of the Founders that accounts for the surprisingly minimal discussion of the scope of the treaty power both in Philadelphia and in the ensuing national debates from 1787–1789.").

42 Scholars are in general agreement that the Founders view of treaty subjects as "international" to mean that they saw treaties as part of foreign affairs and separate from domestic law-making and policy. *See* Bradley, *supra* note 41, at 411.

43 *See* Bradley, *supra* note 41, at 410–11. *See also*, LOUIS HENKIN, FOREIGN AFFAIRS AND THE UNITED STATES CONSTITUTION 442, n. 2 (2nd edn. 1996).

subject matter that can be inferred from the discussions in the ratification debates was that treaties be "international" in nature.[44] For the Founders, the "international" nature of treaties meant, at the very least, that they were agreements between sovereigns that would govern subjects of international relations.[45]

The treaty subject matter considered "international" in the late eighteenth century ranged from the high politics of interstate peace, to commerce, to the protection of individuals outside their home states from arbitrary treatment under foreign law, to the extradition of criminal defendants.[46] But scholars who have examined original understandings of the text are divided on whether that international conception of treaties means the Founders placed limits on the subject matter of treaties.[47] One group of scholars reads the near absence of a discussion of limits on the treaty power during the ratification debates and the use of the term "international" as support for their conclusion that Founders placed no limits on the subject matter of treaties.[48] Others take the view that the use of the term "international" limits the subject matter of treaties to the types of treaties entered into in the late eighteenth century – thus excluding the broad expansion of treaty-making that we have seen in the latter half of the twentieth century.[49] Historical originalism, as an interpretive

44 *See* Bradley, *supra* note 41, at 411 (quoting Alexander Hamilton in the Federalist that treaties are "not rules prescribed by the sovereign to the subject, but agreements between sovereign and sovereign.").

45 *See* Michael D. Ramsey, The Constitution's Text in Foreign Affairs 29 (Harvard Univ. Press, 2007) (discussing the assumption reiterated in *Curtiss-Wright* that "everyone thought that foreign affairs powers were inherently national, not possessed by the states.").

46 For examples from the preconstitutional era, *see* Treaty of Alliance Between the United States of America and His Most Christian Majesty, U.S.-Fr., Feb. 6, 1778, 8 Stat. 6 (mutual defense provisions) and Treaty of Amity and Commerce Between the United States of America and His Most Christian Majesty, U.S.-Fr., Feb. 6, 1778, 8 Stat. 12 (Consular protection and trade preference provisions). For an early example after the adoption of the Constitution, *see* Treaty of Amity, Commerce and Navigation, Between His Britannick Majesty; and the United States of America, by their President, with the Advice and Consent of their Senate, U.S.-U.K., Nov. 19, 1794, 8 Stat. 116 [hereinafter Jay Treaty] (containing in Article XXVII the first formal bilateral extradition agreement entered into by the United States).

47 *See* Bradley, *supra* note 41, at 411; Golove, *supra* note 26, at 1091–2. *See also* Ramsey, *supra* note 45, at 29 (noting that even if "everyone shared common understandings about the sources of foreign affairs powers, those assumptions might not show up in the text itself, nor – perhaps – even in contemporaneous commentary upon the text."); Gary Lawson & Guy Seidman, *The Jeffersonian Treaty Clause*, 2006 Ill. L. Rev. 1, 3–4 (2006) (proposing an "implementational theory" of the treaty power that posits a treaty power whose scope is limited to implementing through treaty only those powers of the national government enumerated elsewhere in the Constitution).

48 *See* Hathaway et al., *supra* note 27, at 245. *See also* Golove, *supra* note 26, at 1141.

49 *See* Bradley, *supra* note 41, at 411; *See* Rosenkranz, *supra* note 37.

method, has proved unhelpful in ascertaining clear subject matter limitations in the federalism context, with scholars tending to cherry-pick those materials that support their own reading of the text.[50]

A review of the drafting history is somewhat more helpful in uncovering state concerns over how the treaty power would be used and the clear concern by the Founders that treaties not be used in ways that would destroy the Constitution itself.[51] The record of ratification contains evidence that the Founders did not view the treaty power as permitting the national government to act in ways that would limit other constitutionally created rights.[52] Left unclear, and therefore open to debate, was whether federalism, as understood through the Tenth Amendment as a statement of an American type of subsidiarity, *i.e.*, treating the residual plenary powers of the states as superior to the powers of the limited national government, was included in the constitutional limitations on the treaty power.

B *Structural Federalism and the Process of Treaty-Making*

While there was little discussion in the ratification debates about the broader question of states' rights and the national power to legislate pursuant to treaty, prior to the adoption of the Tenth Amendment, the Founders discussed and adopted processes intended to both protect the federal constitutional structure and account for state concerns regarding the scope of treaties. Throughout the ratification debates, the creation of the Senate was viewed as the central safeguard to states' rights. Under the Constitution, treaties are to be made with two-thirds approval of the Senate, a body which was elected by the state legislatures and served as the

50 On the issue of subject matter limitations outside the federalism context, there has been little discussion. Rather, the discussions have focused on limitations not on treaty-making power, but the power to implement the treaties as domestic law. *See generally* Wuerth, Chapter 4 in this book.

51 For example, Patrick Henry raised the concern in the Virginia Ratifying Convention that the "President and Senate could 'make any treaty . . . from the paramount power given them," and that this power was therefore "dangerous and destructive." Hathaway et al., *supra* note 27, at 247 (citing THE DEBATES OF THE SEVERAL STATES CONVENTION ON THE ADOPTION OF THE FEDERAL CONSTITUTION AS RECOMMENDED BY THE GENERAL CONVENTION AT PHILADELPHIA IN 1787 504 (Jonathan Elliot ed., 2nd edn. 1937)).

52 Scholars who are divided over the scope of the subject matter limitations of treaties are in agreement on this point. *See* Golove, *supra* note 26, at 1148; *see* Bradley, *supra* note 41, at 413. *See also* Hathaway et al., *supra* note 27, at 248–9 (arguing that "supporters did not see the treaty power as unchecked" because they had put in place structural and procedural safeguards of the power).

central procedural protection for states interests in national law-making.[53] A supermajority of the Senate is required, not only for consent to treaties, but also for the appointment of Ambassadors and Ministers, a provisions that allows the states a larger voice in foreign affairs than in other areas of national law-making.[54] These structural safeguards were viewed by the Founders as adequate to prevent any danger that the national government would use the treaty power to undermine state or local prerogatives.[55] While procedural safeguards are not equivalent to clear subject-matter limitations, some scholars view the safeguards discussion as implying that the President and Senate can, together, make treaties on any subject.[56]

The procedural safeguard for adoption of treaties does not address the question of implementation of treaties. The implementation of treaties raises concerns about federalism because, while the Senate participates in the process of treaty-making, it does not have special textual authority to determine what effect a treaty has in domestic law. Under the Constitution, the Senate's role is to approve the treaties that are negotiated by the president. Whether the treaty becomes direct domestic law that could be enforced as a matter of domestic law largely depends on whether the treaty is deemed self-executing or non-self-executing. If a treaty is self-executing, no further action is required by Congress to make the treaty provisions directly enforceable as domestic law. If a treaty is non-self-executing, Congress must pass some form of implementing legislation to make the treaty provisions enforceable as a matter of domestic law.[57] As a matter of constitutional practice, however, the Executive has coordinated with the Senate in order to pave the way for approval or treaties it would like to ratify. This has led to the Executive drafting for Senate approved so-called reservations, understandings, and declarations (RUDs), including declarations of non-self-execution and understandings concerning federalism, to treaties that might encroach on state prerogatives. This has been a consistent pattern in human rights treaties, and the political branches have cooperated closely to work out the language of RUDs.[58]

53 *See* Hathaway et al., *supra* note 27, at 249–50.

54 U.S. Const. art. II, § 2, cl. 2. ("[The President] shall have Power, by and with the Advice and Consent of the Senate, to make Treaties, provided two thirds of the Senators present concur...).

55 *See* Hathaway et al., *supra* note 27, at 242. 56 *See, e.g.*, Golove, *supra* note 26, at 1090.

57 For a full discussion, see Wuerth, Chapter 4 in this book. Whether a non-self-executing treaty remains "supreme law of the land" binding on the states, remains uncertain after the *Medellin* opinion, which rendered non-self-executing treaties unenforceable against the states. *Ibid.* at 19–25.

58 Where the international agreement is adopted by the United States through an Executive Agreement, the President likely retains sole discretion to determine whether the agreement is

Legislation that implements a treaty is passed as any other legislation: by a simple majority of both houses of Congress. Thus, the procedural safeguards that serve as a break on the subject and scope of treaties follow from the power of the Senate to approve or disapprove of a treaty made by the president. Treaty-implementing legislation is subject to other political procedural protections, but the text of the Constitution provides no special procedural or structural impediment to its adoption, beyond the Necessary and Proper clause.

C Nineteenth-Century Practice and the First Wave of Globalized Treaty Subjects

For the first century or so of the Republic, there was little controversy over the federal government's exclusive power to carry out foreign relations, engage in international law-making through the Treaty Power, and to bind the states to treaty obligations through the Supremacy Clause.[59] In the absence of constitutional text on how and when treaties were to be implemented as domestic law, the Supreme Court stepped in. In *Foster v. Neilson*,[60] the Court made its first and most lasting pronouncement on the question of self-executing and non-self-executing treaties:

> Our Constitution declares a treaty to be the law of the land. It is consequently to be regarded in courts of justice as equivalent to an act of the legislature whenever it operates of itself, without the aid of any legislative provision. But when the terms of the stipulation import a contract, when either of the parties engage to perform a particular act, the treaty addresses itself to the Political, not the Judicial, Department, and the Legislature must execute the contract before it can become a rule for the Court.[61]

The Court addressed which kinds of treaties require implementing legislation and which can be given direct effect by the courts,[62] but it was up to

self-executing or non-self-executing, though *Medellin* has muddied the waters on this question as well. *See* Wuerth Chapter 4 (discussing Bihani v. Obama).

59 For case law of the early nineteenth Century, *see* Am. Ins. Co. v. 356 Bales of Cotton, 26 U.S. 511, 542 (1828) ("The Constitution confers absolutely on the government of the Union, the powers of making war, and of making treaties"); *see* Barron v. City of Baltimore, 32 U.S. 243, 249 (1833) ("A state is forbidden to enter into any treaty, alliance or confederation. If these compacts are with foreign nations, they interfere with the treaty-making power, which is conferred entirely on the general government"); *see* Holmes v. Jennison, 39 U.S. 540, 551 (1840) ("The powers of war and peace, and of making treaties, are conferred upon the general government; and at the same time, expressly prohibited to the states").

60 Foster v. Neilson, 27 U.S. 253 (1829). 61 *Ibid.* at 254.

62 *See* Medellín v. Texas, 552 U.S. 491 (2008) (applying a presumption of non-self-execution for the purpose of determining the applicability of the Optional Protocol of the Vienna Convention on Consular Relations).

Congress to determine how it would draft and pass legislation to execute treaties and whether the Necessary and Proper Clause imposed any limitations on the scope or subject matter of implementing legislation. In a review of nineteenth-century practice, Professor Jean Galbraith has concluded that Congress, cognizant and protective of its own role in making good on U.S. international commitments, viewed the treaty power as one that *expanded* Congress's power to legislate.[63] At a time when the enumerated powers of Congress to which the Necessary and Proper clause gave effect were considered rather narrow in scope, the power to execute treaties beyond those enumerated subjects was viewed as an essential check on the president's power to make treaties that might then be made binding domestic law without Congressional legislation.

Galbraith's review of Congressional practice further reveals that there was a consensus on this point: individual law makers who were generally opposed to a robust national treaty power nonetheless agreed with supporters of a strong treaty power that Congress possessed the constitutional authority, under the Necessary and Proper clause, to pass treaty-implementing legislation – including on subjects that went beyond Congress's enumerated legislative powers under Article 1.[64] Indeed, for lawmakers concerned that the treaty power might be used to create obligations that would be given direct effect as U.S. law (those that the Supreme Court would later call "self-executing"), the Necessary and Proper clause was invoked in support of their view that treaties *required* Congressional legislation to be made domestic law.[65] The broad power of Congress to implement treaties was in this way viewed a check on finding treaties self-executing, and a reassertion of Congressional power to define the full domestic legal effect of treaty rights and obligations. This practice and early understanding of the scope of Congress's treaty-implementing power is a strong refutation of Professor Rosenkranz's argument, adopted by Justice Scalia in *Bond*, that Congress's power to legislate treaties under the Necessary and Proper clause is limited to legislation about "making" treaties.[66]

This Congressional practice started first with those treaty subjects that fell squarely within Congress's enumerated powers, but continued to include passage of implementing legislation in areas that Congress believed, at the time, were beyond its authority to legislate in the absence of a treaty. For example, when the United States entered into the Jay Treaty with Great Britain in 1796, members of Congress argued that the Necessary and Proper

63 *See generally* Galbraith, *supra* note 39. 64 Galbraith, *supra* note 39, at 81–2.
65 *Ibid.* at 81–108. 66 See discussion of *Bond infra* p. 28.

clause showed that the Founders intended a role for Congress to implement treaties and that therefore the agreement with Great Britain could not be self-executing.[67] The opponents of the treaty pointed out that the power to regulate foreign commerce was an enumerated power of Congress, not the president. Thus, the Necessary and Proper Clause could be invoked to require implementing legislation before the commercial aspects of the treaty became domestic law under the Supremacy Clause.[68]

Later, the United States entered into territorial treaties, trademark treaties, and extradition treaties, to which Congress gave effect through implementing statutes.[69] This Congressional practice is important to understanding how the political branches viewed the gaps in the text of the Constitution, and supports the assumption, articulated later by Justice Harlan in *Neely v. Henkel* and by Justice Holmes in *Holland*, that the Necessary and Proper Clause gives Congress a role in implementing treaty obligations. This conclusion was reflected in leading legal treatises of the late nineteenth- and early twentieth centuries, which saw the Necessary and Proper Clause as empowering Congress to implement treaties.[70] Taken together with the procedural protections inherent in the requirement of senatorial approval of treaties, this practice suggests a robust national treaty power that encompasses both broad subject matter and Congressional power to give effect to treaties.

Further, the adoption after the Civil War of the Thirteenth, Fourteenth, and Fifteenth Amendments to the Constitution narrowed the scope of the Tenth Amendment, expressly placing power in the hands of Congress to enact legislation binding on the states in order to give effect within the states to the abolition of slavery and to the requirements of equal protection and due process.[71] The full scope of Congress's power to enforce these requirements through legislation impinging on state and local authority, however, remained

[67] As Galbraith notes, the term "self-executing" was not used in 1796, but the later-developed constitutional term serves as a useful label for the views of Congress at the time. Galbraith, *supra* note 39, at 82, n. 83.

[68] *Ibid.* at 83–4. [69] *Ibid.* at 93–104.

[70] The only legal treatise to oppose invoking the treaty power to upend understandings of state prerogatives was that written by George Tucker – who viewed the potential of treaties to extend rights to non-white foreigners, in conflict with segregationist laws of the states, as a danger to the constitutional order. *See ibid.* at 36–8 (discussing treatises by Butler and Tucker). Tucker's opposition to a broad treaty power not constrained by federalism reflected his concerns that international treaties might support integration of blacks and basic rights for women. *See ibid.* at 37 n. 138 (noting Tucker's opposition to racial integration and women's franchise).

[71] U.S CONST. amend. XIV, § 5 ("The Congress shall have the power to enforce, by appropriate legislation, the provisions of this article.").

contentious, and was the subject of subsequent Supreme Court challenges over the validity and application of certain federal civil rights statutes.[72]

By the close of the nineteenth century, America stood poised to grow in international stature and began to expand the reach of its global interests. The advances in transportation and manufacturing that came with the industrial revolution created new economic opportunities and an increasingly globalized marketplace for goods and labor that prompted nation states to look to international agreements and treaty-making as a means to formalize their rights and obligations as participants in the global market. International law-making during the nineteenth century had grown to include formal treaties on the laws of war,[73] and even agreement to abolish the slave trade[74] – two developments that served as precursors to human rights treaties.

Commensurate with its growing international stature, between 1895 and 1920, the United States entered into 303 treaties on subjects from water boundary rights, to the trade in fur seals, to trademark protections. Forty-five of these were multilateral agreements.[75] And while the United States failed to join the League of Nations, the creation of post–World War I international institutions, in particular the International Labor Organization and the Mandates system of the League, expanded and deepened the scope of treaties to include state obligations to observe and protect the rights of groups and individuals.

Given Congressional and executive practice over the course of the nineteenth century, as well as the dominant view of leading legal scholars of the time, Congress appeared well positioned to use its power under the Necessary and Proper clause to enact legislation to give effect to whatever new international legal agreements the United States might adopt to facilitate its more active role in global affairs. The Supreme Court seemed to agree. In the 1901 case of *Neely v. Henkel*, the Supreme Court made clear that Congress had the power to pass treaty-implementing legislation.[76] This is the setting against which the 1920 case of *Missouri v. Holland* was decided.

72 *See, e.g.*, Civil Rights Cases, 109 U.S. 3 (1883), and the recent cases discussed *infra* at notes 128–31

73 Convention for the Amelioration of the Condition of the Wounded in Armies in the Field, Aug. 22, 1864, 22 Stat. 940 [hereinafter Geneva Convention of 1864].

74 Treaty of Paris, Fr.-U.K., May 30, 1814, 1 B.S.P. 151 (in which France agreed with Great Britain to end the slave trade). During the first half of the nineteenth century, Great Britain entered into a series of other bilateral treaties with states abolishing the slave trade.

75 These data are derived from U.S. Treaties in Force, 1894 through 1920. Data on file with author.

76 Neely v. Henkel, 180 U.S. 109 (1901). *Neely* involved a statute implementing a peace treaty between Spain and the United States and the extradition of a criminal defendant to the newly established Republic of Cuba pursuant to that statute. Justice Harlan wrote the unanimous

II *MISSOURI V. HOLLAND* AND ITS LEGACY

In *Missouri v. Holland*, the Supreme Court upheld the constitutionality of a federal statute regulating bird hunting in Missouri on the ground that statutes enacted pursuant to the national treaty power were not subject to the federalism limitations of the Tenth Amendment. The case is often described as standing for the basic proposition that the national government can do through treaty what it otherwise may not do through national legislation.

The story behind the case begins with a classic collective action problem: regulating the hunting of migratory birds.[77] Prior to 1900, there were no federal laws regulating the capture of migratory birds; only a patchwork of state and territorial laws regulating hunting and resale of birds. The lack of coordinated regulation reduced the populations of many bird species, including insectivores essential to agriculture, to near extinction.[78]

The Lacey Act of 1900[79] attempted to overcome the tragedy of the commons by making it illegal to engage in interstate transport of birds or wildlife taken in violation of state or territorial law.[80] But its weak enforcement provisions proved inadequate to the task. Congress got tougher with the passage of the Weeks-McLean law of 1913, which deemed all migratory game and insectivorous birds that passed through the borders of any state or territory to be within the custody of the U.S. Government and prohibited the destruction or taking of those migratory species. As many of its proponents feared would happen, two federal courts declared the Weeks-McLean statute unconstitutional as outside Congress' enumerated powers, rejecting, in accordance with Court precedent at the time, the argument that regulation of game found within the

decision in which the Court held that the Necessary and Proper Clause "includes the power to enact such legislation as is appropriate to give efficacy to any stipulations which it is competent for the President by and with the advice and consent of the Senate to insert in a treaty with a foreign power." *Ibid.* at 121.

77 This discussion draws from Margaret E. McGuinness, *Foreword: Return to Missouri v. Holland: Federalism and International*, 73 MO. L. REV. 921 (2008). *See also* Charles Lofgren, *Missouri v. Holland in Historical Perspective*, 1975 SUP. CT. REV. 77, 78 (1975).

78 *A Guide to the Laws and Treaties of the United States for Protecting Migratory Birds*, U.S. FISH AND WILDLIFE SERVICE (last visited Jun. 19, 2015), www.fws.gov/Migratorybirds/Regulations Policies/treatlaw.html.

79 16 U.S.C. §§ 3371–8.

80 The Lacey Act currently covers, with the threat of strict penalties, the illegal taking of a wider array of wildlife, fish, and plants than any other wildlife protection law in the United States. *See* United States v. McNab, 331 F.3d 1228, 1238 (11th Cir. 2003) (discussing expansion of the Lacey Act by Congress in the early 1980s).

borders of a state could be accomplished through the Commerce Clause.[81] In reaction to these court decisions, the United States negotiated and the Senate approved the Migratory Bird Treaty with Great Britain (acting on behalf of Canada) in 1916. Congress passed the implementing statute, the Migratory Bird Treaty Act ("MBTA"), in 1918.[82]

After two local hunters were indicted in Jackson County Missouri under federal regulations implementing the MBTA, the State of Missouri sued in United States District Court for an injunction against further enforcement of the regulations by Ray P. Holland, the federal game warden.[83] The Judge dismissed the State's claim, finding that the Migratory Bird Treaty did not violate the Constitution and that it involved a matter of "mutual interest" between nations.[84] Missouri, of course, appealed to the Supreme Court.

The holding of *Holland* is, on its face, straightforward: If a treaty is valid, the statute implementing it is valid and can be enforced through the Supremacy Clause against the states.[85] The Tenth Amendment, Justice Holmes reasoned, does not provide some "invisible radiation" that limits the application of the treaty power in this case. On the difference between Congress acting pursuant to the treaty power or acting pursuant to its enumerated powers, Holmes noted:

> Acts of Congress are the supreme law of the land only when *made in pursuance of the Constitution*, while treaties are declared to be so when made *under the authority of the United States*. It is open to question whether the authority of the United States means more than the formal acts prescribed to make the convention. We do not mean to imply that there are no qualifications to the treaty-making power, but they must be ascertained in a different way.[86]

81 United States v. Shauver, 214 F. 154 (E.D. Ark. 1914); United States v. McCullagh, 221 F. 288 (D. Kan. 1915). By that time, Senator Elihu Root – who just a few years earlier had founded the American Society of International Law – had suggested the use of a treaty as a solution to any constitutional infirmities.

82 Lofgren, *supra* note 77, at 82. 83 *Ibid.* at 92.

84 United States v. Samples, 258 F. 479 (W.D. Mo. 1919).

85 On whether Congress could enforce the bird conservation treaty against the state, where it might not otherwise have been able to do so pursuant to its enumerated legislative powers, Justice Holmes stated:

> If the treaty is valid, there can be no dispute about the validity of the statute under Article I, § 8, as a necessary and proper means to execute the powers of the Government. The language of the Constitution as to the supremacy of treaties being general, the question before us is narrowed to an inquiry into the ground upon which the present supposed exception is placed.

Missouri v. Holland, 252 U.S. 416, 432 (1920).

86 *Ibid.* at 433. (emphasis added) (citation omitted). Holmes used the occasion of *Holland* to also express his view on the form of interpretation to be applied to the Constitution, looking beyond text:

Less clear from the case is what the actual structural limitations or these "qualifications" on the treaty power might be. Holmes stated that "matters of the sharpest exigency for the national wellbeing" or "national action" would be appropriate for handling through treaty and treaty implementing legislation.[87] But Holmes did not reach – and did not need to reach on the facts before him – the question of whether some treaty subjects concerning issues not of "national wellbeing" or not requiring "national action" would prohibit Congressional implementing legislation. Holmes concluded simply that the migratory bird treaty "does not contravene any prohibitory words to be found in the Constitution."[88] Holmes' failure to state precisely the limits of treaty subject matter, as well as his failure to note whether the Necessary and Proper clause limits Congress' power to those measures strictly necessary to comply with the treaty, makes *Holland* somewhat unsatisfactory. But Holmes was clear that broad federalism concerns – that is, taking into account state disagreement with the subject matter of treaties or objection to the preemption of state law by treaty obligations – did not present a constitutional obstacle to treaty-implementing legislation.

A *The Bricker Amendment Debates*

In the wake of *Missouri v. Holland*, the treaty power became the subject of intense debate and speculation. In the years after *Holland*, advocates of the ideal of a national government of limited, enumerated powers (leaving all other functions and powers to the states and the people), perceived threats to states' rights as emanating more from the treaty power than from the Commerce Clause (at least, until *Wickard v. Filburn*). Professor Forrest Revere Black, for example, laid out his concerns that American jurisprudence was on a course to erase, functionally, federalism from the books, and that *Holland* "enumerated a doctrine that will give aid and comfort to the

> [W]hen we are dealing with words that also are a constituent act, like the Constitution of the United States, we must realize that they have called into life a being the development of which could not have been foreseen completely by the most gifted of its begetters. It was enough for them to realize or to hope that they had created an organism; it has taken a century and has cost their successors much sweat and blood to prove that they created a nation. The case before us must be considered in the light of our whole experience, and not merely in that of what was said a hundred years ago.

Ibid.

87 *Ibid.*

88 *Ibid.*

advocates of unlimited power."[89] Drawing on the earlier work of George Tucker, Black and others argued that the treaty power could be employed to undermine the protection of individual rights and perhaps destroy the Constitution itself.[90]

On the other side were those who supported the ways in which *Holland* reaffirmed the exclusivity of the foreign affairs powers to the national government and in particular the pragmatism of Holmes' reasoning in areas where the collective regulation by the states had failed. For them, the decision in *Holland* offered a promising new avenue to bring American law more into line with what were seen as desirable aspects of other nations' laws.[91] The fears of those who saw *Holland* as a loophole through which all state power would be subsumed only heightened after World War II and the creation of the United Nations through a multilateral treaty. These fears inspired efforts by Frank Holman as president of the American Bar Association in the late 1940s later taken up by Senator John Bricker of Ohio, to amend the Constitution.[92] Those sounding alarm saw the sweeping precedent set by Justice Holmes as permitting international legal commitments to usurp completely the police powers of the states and to undermine any structural limitations on Congressional and presidential power.[93] Contrary to this scenario, more measured views on *Holland* and were also aired at the time. One commentator argued that

89 Forrest Revere Black, *Missouri v. Holland—A Judicial Milepost on the Road to Absolutism*, 25 ILL. L. REV. 912, 916 (1930–31).

90 *Ibid.* at 918–22 (arguing that creating federal law pursuant to treaty power could lead to extraconstitutional acts by the federal government).

91 Joseph P. Chamberlain, *Migratory Bird Treaty Decision and Its Relation to Labor Treaties*, 10 AM. LAB. LEGIS. REV. 133, 135 (1920) (arguing that *Missouri v. Holland* could justify the United States entering into treaties for international protection of labor).

92 Frank E. Holman, *Treaty Law-Making: A Blank Check for Writing A New Constitution* 36 A.B.A. J. 707, 739 (1950). *See also* Frank E. Holman, *An "International Bill of Rights": Proposals Have Dangerous Implications for U.S.*, 34 A.B.A. J. 984 (1948); Frank E. Holman, *Must America Succumb to Statism?* 35 A.B.A. J. 801 (1949). For a brief history of the maneuvering surrounding the Bricker Amendment, see also, Nelson Richards, *The Bricker Amendment and Congress' Failure to Check the Inflation of the Executive's Foreign Affairs Powers, 1951–1952*, 94 CAL. L. REV. 175 (2006).

93 *See, e.g.*, Eberhard P. Deutsch, *The Peril in the Treaty Making Power*, 37 A.B.A. J. 659 (1951); William Fleming, *Danger to America: The Draft Covenant on Human Rights*, 37 A.B.A. J. 739, 816 (1951). The concerns of the legal analysts found political bedfellows with those isolationists opposed more broadly to U.S. participation in the United Nations, as well as those states rights conservatives seeking to rein in national power that had expanded considerably during the New Deal era. *See* Cathal J. Nolan, *The Last Hurrah of Conservative Isolationism: Eisenhower, Congress and the Bricker Amendment*, PRESIDENTIAL STUDIES QUARTERLY, Vol 22, No. 2, 337–49 (1992).

adequate judicial tools existed to guard the Constitution against abuses of the treaty power in the form of what is now referred to as the "subject matter" limitation on the treaty power.[94]

These efforts to amend the Constitution from the late 1940s through the early 1950s sought to limit the scope of the treaty power and the use of executive agreements in order to prevent the president from committing the United States (and thus the states) to the broad post–World War II internationalist projects. The emerging international human rights treaty system, of which many of the practices of the states (including the persistence of Jim Crow segregation) would be found in violation, loomed large in the Bricker Amendment debates.[95] The amendments ultimately failed, but only after the Eisenhower administration dropped its effort for the United States to ratify the then-new Genocide Convention, and announced it would not seek to join any new human rights treaties.[96] Eisenhower's maneuver preserved the broad powers articulated in *Holland*, but the debate preserved the politically potent idea of American human rights exceptionalism and solidified the discomfort surrounding U.S. participation in treaty regimes that would give effect to individual rights that are grounded in texts outside the United States or state constitutions. The debate left open many questions surrounding what deeper and broader national engagement in the international legal order would mean for the value of federalism to the democratic order of the United States.

B *Henkin, The Restatement (Third), and the Defeasance Theory of* Missouri v. Holland

These concerns had not disappeared when in 1965, the American Law Institute addressed the Foreign Relations Law of the United States in the Restatement (Second), which stated in Section 118 that:

94 William S. Andrews, *Judicial Review and the Growth of the Treaty Power*, 3 SYRACUSE L. REV. 315 (1951–1952).

95 *See* Nolan, *supra* note 93, at 342 (quoting Senator Bricker's denunciation of the UN Human Rights Commission: "I do not want any of the international group, and especially the group headed by Mrs. Eleanor Roosevelt, which has drafted the Covenant of Human Rights, to betray the fundamental, inalienable, and God-given rights of American citizens enjoyed under the Constitution."). For a comprehensive treatment of the Bricker debates, see David L. Sloss, THE DEATH OF TREATY SUPREMACY, (Oxford University Press, 2017).

96 See Nolan, *supra* note 93, at 344–5. The United States finally ratified the Genocide Convention in 1988, during the administration of President Reagan.

(1) An international agreement made by the United States as a treaty may deal with any matter as to which the United States has the constitutional power to make an international agreement under the rules stated in § 117.
(2) The treaty power under Article II, section 2, of the Constitution is delegated to the United States *within the meaning of the Tenth Amendment and thus may deal with a matter described in subsection (1) above without regard to whether the United States has power to deal with it under any other constitutionally delegated power.*[97]

Section 117, referenced in Section 118, stated in full:
§ 117. Scope of International Agreements

(1) The United States has the power under the Constitution to make an international agreement if
 (a) the matter is of international concern, and
 (b) the agreement does not contravene any of the limitations of the Constitution applicable to all powers of the United States.
(2) The scope of international agreements made by different methods under the Constitution of the United States is indicated in §§ 118–21.[98]

The comments to Section 117 did little to clarify whether the constitutional limitations on treaty-making might include federalism limitations, but did note that the constitutional limitations such as those "contained in the Bill of Rights apply to action taken under the grant of the power to make international agreements just as to action taken under other grants of governmental power."[99]

Section 117 cited to *Missouri v. Holland* on the scope of subject matter, noting that the facts of *Holland* ("State A and the United States make a treaty providing for specified closed seasons and other measures of protection for migratory birds that fly over or live in both states") related to subject matter of "international concern" which rendered the treaty constitutional.[100] Section 118 cited *Holland* under comment b, addressing "Treaty power and the power of Congress compared":

> The treaty power of the United States is not limited by the extent of the powers delegated to Congress by the Constitution. This follows from the fact that the treaty power is itself an independent power granted to the President and the Senate under the Constitution.[101]

97 Second Restatement, *supra* note 5, at § 118 (emphasis added). 98 *Ibid.* at § 117.
99 *Ibid.* at § 117 cmt. d. 100 *Ibid.* at § 117 cmt. b(2).
101 *Ibid.* at § 118 cmt. b. Illustration one of the comment cited *Holland* as one of the cases that the Supreme Court upheld on the basis of the "'treaty power' without finding it necessary to

The Second Restatement could be read to imply no federalism constraints – whether through the structure of the Constitution or the Tenth Amendment. Because the international human rights project was in early infancy in the 1960s (the International Covenant on Civil and Political Rights, for example, would not come into force until 1976), the Second Restatement did not explicitly address whether human rights treaties would raise any constitutional objections on the basis that their subject matter is, largely, reserved to the states.[102]

To Professor Louis Henkin, the lead drafter of the 1987 Third Restatement, *Missouri v. Holland* made clear that treaty power could be used to "defease" state powers retained under the Tenth Amendment. The Third Restatement thus took a more robust and sweeping view of the national treaty power than did the Second Restatement. The Reporters of the Third Restatement underscored the foundational power of the Supremacy Clause by stating:

> International law and international agreements of the United States are law of the United States and supreme over the law of the several states.[103]

The Third Restatement continues in the Reporters Notes:

> Under Art. 1 Section 8, of the United States Constitution, Congress has the power to "make all laws which shall be necessary and proper for the carrying into Execution ... all other powers vested by this Constitution in the Government of the United States, or in any Department of officer thereof." *Congress therefore has the power to enact legislation necessary and proper for carrying into execution a treaty properly made by the President with the consent of the Senate, or an executive agreement within the President's authority under the Constitution.*[104]

The full scope of the international agreements is addressed later in the Restatement, under Section 302:

(1) The United States has authority under the Constitution to make international agreements.
(2) No provision of an agreement *may contravene any of the prohibitions or limitation so the Constitution applicable to the exercise of authority by the United States.*[105]

resolve doubts as to the power of Congress to deal with the subject on the basis of its own powers in the absence of a treaty."

102 *See ibid.* at § 118 Reporter's Note 1 (raising the issue that international human rights treaties have raised the concern that they address topics not of "international concern" but that the treaties would be stronger if the United States participated in them).

103 THIRD RESTATEMENT at § 111(1). 104 *Ibid.* at § 111 Reporters' Note 8 (emphasis added).

105 *Ibid.* at § 302.

To Henkin and the Restatement drafters, then, two limitations appear to apply to the national power to enact legislation to implement treaties: First, a treaty must be properly made, *i.e.*, must be a "valid" exercise of the treaty power, and second, a treaty must not violate limitations or prohibitions the that Constitution places on the "exercise of authority by the United States."

1 The "sham treaty" limitation

Under the first limitation, if the treaty was a "sham," that is, entered into not for the purpose of engaging another state on a subject matter of mutual interest and under which the United States and the counterparty would be undertaking obligations to one another, but rather entered into for the sole purpose of enacting otherwise impermissible legislation, the legislation could be considered unconstitutional if otherwise outside Congress' enumerated powers. According to the Third Restatement, any other treaty would be "valid."

As to subject matter limitations, the Restatement notes that the only limitation on the subject of treaties are those that arise under international law and that constitutional references to "treaties and to other agreement or compacts with foreign powers (Article I, Section 10; Article II, Section 2; Article VI)" fail to "define such agreement or intimate any limitations as regards their purpose or subject matter."[106] It continues, "States may enter into an agreement *on any matter of concern to them*, and international law does not look behind their motives or purposes in doing so. Thus, the United States may make an agreement on any subject suggested by its national interests in relations with other nations."[107] This formulation departs from the Second Restatement language that treaties address subjects of "international concern," suggesting a more expansive reading of *Holland*.

Henkin explained this shift to more expansive language at an ALI meeting in 1980:

> I think this goes back ... to the whole history of the Bricker controversy. The fear was that a treaty would be used not for an international agreement but to what you might call a "mock treaty." You get some ambassador to sign something with you which has nothing to do with foreign policy or even international relations, but you go through the formality of a treaty when it is not a treaty. The difference is that the international concern concept was deemed to mean that certain subjects cannot be the subject of a treaty. We reject that. We were trying to take care of that hypothetical case, of the mock treaty, while making clear that anything can be the subject of a treaty if

[106] *Ibid.* [107] *Ibid.* at § 302 cmt. e.

it is bona fide, if it has a foreign relations purpose. Since Hughes also used the language of foreign relations I thought the people who liked the original idea might be content with that.[108]

In addition to clarifying the consensus on preventing "sham" treaties, Henkin specifically rejected that the phrase "international concern," as included in Second Restatement §117, in comment c, represented limitation on subject matter:

The old Restatement had picked up the suggestion that a treaty must deal with a matter of "international concern." Nobody quite knows what that means. But it has sometimes been interpreted, at least polemically, as meaning that there are some subjects on which you cannot make a treaty even though they are related to your foreign relations, and United States policy is to make some agreement with a foreign country on the subject. We think there never was any such rule … There have been no cases which have made that point. As a result, we have not mentioned it in black letter and have made the explanation we have …[109]

Because the Migratory Bird Treaty was itself "bona fide," in that it created rights and obligations between the United States and Canada in an area of mutual concern and benefit (i.e., the protection of the birds), it likely would have survived Henkin's analysis under the Third Restatement, even though the treaty itself was pretextual. That is, the United States entered into the treaty for the purpose of ensuring the constitutionality of the statute implementing the treaty. The implication, however, is that a pretextual treaty passes the "sham" test because its subject is of "international concern," precisely the formulation of the Second Restatement. If the treaty had been about a human rights topic that addressed only internal policies (for example, a treaty prohibiting the application of the death penalty), entering into the treaty as a pretext for Congressional legislation would appear more objectionable, and therefore raise the question whether the treaty was a "sham."[110]

2 The constitutional prohibitions limitation

Under the second limitation, "constitutional limitations" on the treaty power, the Third Restatement notes:

108 57th A.L.I. Proc. 101 (1980) (emphasis added).

109 *Ibid.* at 98–9 (1980) (The Restatement section number to which Henkin refers, in this exchange (p. 86 in cmt.. c) was changed later in the drafting process.).

110 As Oona Hathaway has noted, "no scholar anywhere appears to openly admit that the treaty power can be lawfully used as a pretext to pass domestic legislation." Hathaway et al., *supra* note 27, at 290. (citation omitted)

> The view, once held, that treaties are not subject to constitutional constraints is now definitely rejected. Treaties and other international agreements are subject to the prohibitions of the Bill of Rights and other restraints on federal power, such as those relating to suspension of the writ of habeas corpus or prohibiting the grant of titles of nobility.[111]

Among the constitutional limitations, the Third Restatement notes that, after the 1957 decision in *Reid v. Covert*,[112] individual rights protected under the first eight amendments place limits on the subject matter of treaties. Henkin suggests that it is only the "prohibitory" language of the Constitution that limits the content of treaty obligations. That would include limitations on treaties that would "authorize what the Constitution forbids, or a change in the character of the government or in that of one of the States" including "cession of any portion of the territory of [a State] without its consent."[113]

Reid v. Covert did not specifically address federalism or any other limitations on the treaty power emanating from the Tenth Amendment. It merely reaffirmed that treaties could not contravene constitutionally created individual rights by holding that a U.S.-citizen spouse of a U.S. soldier stationed abroad was entitled to the full procedural rights of a civilian court, notwithstanding a U.S. executive agreement that agreed to try military personnel and their dependents through a court martial.[114] Indeed, the *Reid* court distinguished *Holland*:

111 Third Restatement, § 302 cmt. b. The comment goes on to note and cross reference a comment that the invalidity of the treaty provision as a matter of internal law may not excuse the obligation as a matter of international law. *See ibid.* at § 311(3).

112 Reid v. Covert, 354 U.S. 1 (1957) (holding that the treaty power cannot be used to limit the rights of individual U.S. citizen civilians to due process).

113 Third Restatement § 302 Reporters' Note 1. Reporters Note 3 addressed the particular problem posed by international boundary disputes that affect state boundaries:

> There are dicta suggesting particular hypothetical "States' rights" limitations on the subject matter of international agreements, e.g., that a treaty cannot modify a State's form of government or cede State territory without the State's consent. See De Geofroy v. Riggs, Reporter's Note 1. But a treaty resolving a boundary dispute is not deemed a cession of State Territory for this purpose. *See, e.g.*, the Chamizal Treaty of 1963, 15 U.S. T. 21, T.I.A.S. No. 5515, discussed in 109 Cong. Rec. 24851 (1963). However, the federal government has been sensitive to the interests of the States affected by boundary settlements.

Third Restatement, Reporters' Note 3.

114 The Court noted that the executive agreement in question, though not adopted as a formal treaty under Article II, operated as a treaty for the purposes of the bilateral agreement between the United States and the UK. *See* Reid v. Covert, 354 U.S. 1, 17 ("It would be manifestly contrary to the objectives of those who created the Constitution, as well as those who were responsible for the Bill of Rights – let alone alien to our entire constitutional history and

> There is nothing in *Missouri* v. *Holland*, 252 U. S. 416, which is contrary to the position taken here. There the Court carefully noted that the treaty involved was not inconsistent with any specific provision of the Constitution. The Court was concerned with the Tenth Amendment which reserves to the States or the people all power not delegated to the National Government. *To the extent that the United States can validly make treaties, the people and the States have delegated their power to the National Government and the Tenth Amendment is no barrier.*[115]

Reid thus confirmed the principle first discussed by the Framers that no treaties contravening the Constitution could be permitted. The problem for Henkin's analysis of the treaty power and federalism was that, just as the Third Restatement was being published, the line between what was constitutional and unconstitutional encroachment on state power by the federal government was beginning to shift dramatically.

C The "New Federalism" and Challenges to the Defeasance Theory of the Treaty Power

The ink was hardly dry on the Third Restatement when a new breed of legal scholars began to challenge its conclusions. Variously dubbed the "new sovereigntists"[116] or "new federalists,"[117] these scholars revived the Bricker-era skepticism about U.S. entanglements with international organization and law, and extended the states rights' revolution that had begun in the 1980s to the exercise of the national foreign affairs powers. On the issue of federalism and the treaty power, both *Missouri v. Holland* and the Third Restatement came under attack.[118] Underlying the sovereigntist critiques of the Third Restatement, and of Henkin's work in particular, was a deep skepticism of the power of international law to solve global problems, a rejection of at least some of the normative foundations of the international legal order, a concern about the antidemocratic nature of international law-making, and a view that international law-making could be used to dilute

tradition – to construe Article VI as permitting the United States to exercise power under an international agreement without observing constitutional prohibitions.").

115 *Ibid.* at 18 (emphasis added) (citing United States v. Darby, 312 U. S. 100, 124–25).

116 *See* Peter Spiro, *The New Sovereigntists – American Exceptionalism and Its False Prophets*, 79 FOREIGN AFF. 9 (2000).

117 *See* Duncan B. Hollis, *Executive Federalism: Forging New Federalist Constraints on the Treaty Power*, 79 S. CAL. L. REV. 1327 (2006).

118 For a framing of the discussion, *see* Curtis A. Bradley, *Federalism and the Treaty Power*, 98 AM. SOC'Y INT'L L. PROC. 341, 341 (2004); Duncan B. Hollis, *Introduction: (Re)Constructing the Treaty Power*, 98 AM. SOC'Y INT'L L. PROC. 339 (2004).

state and local power in ways that were offensive to constitutional structure and the ideals of federalism.[119]

Where the legal scholarship underpinning the return to federalism domestically relied on the ideology of smaller government and the democratic virtues of local control, the unifying theme of the sovereigntists was distrust of law-making and adjudication outside the United States and a distrust of any processes – including through the treaty power – that would bind the United States to any delegation of functions of governance or adjudication to international institutions.[120] Some sovereigntists reached their conclusions through an "originalist" construction to the Constitution that stood in opposition to the sort of "living constitutionalism" theory espoused in Holmes' *Holland* opinion and by Henkin.[121] Others were simply opposed to the United States constraining itself through international law in just about any way, and appeared to invoke constitutional restraints as the most effective means to block U.S. engagement in international law-making.[122]

Not all the federalism arguments were anti-internationalist in their goals; however, nor were they all representative of or wedded to any particular constitutional method.[123] In light of the potential expansion of U.S. commitments to international human rights treaties and other treaties whose subjects would fall squarely within traditional areas of state police powers, these commentators

[119] *See, e.g.*, Bradley, *supra* note 41 (reviving the question of federalism limitations on the Treaty power); Curtis A. Bradley, *The Treaty Power and American Federalism, Part II*, 99 MICH. L. REV. 98 (2000) [hereinafter Bradley II] (responding to Golove's historical critique of the new federalist conception of the treaty power); JACK L. GOLDSMITH AND ERIC A. POSNER, THE LIMITS OF INTERNATIONAL LAW (Oxford University Press, 2005)(presenting a broad critique of the effectiveness of international law). *See also*, Curtis A. Bradley and Jack L. Goldsmith, *Customary International Law and Federal Common Law: A Critique of the Modern Position*, 110 HARV. L. REV. 815 (1997) (arguing that federalism, *inter alia*, constrains the use of customary international law to displace contrary state law); John McGinnis and Ilya Somin, *Democracy and International Human Rights Law*, 84 NOTRE DAME L. REV. 1739 (2009) (criticizing the international human rights system as undemocratic).

[120] *See generally* JULIAN KU & JOHN YOO, TAMING GLOBALIZATION: INTERNATIONAL LAW, THE U.S. CONSTITUTION, AND THE NEW WORLD ORDER (2012).

[121] *See* Rosenkranz, *supra* note 37 (discussing the tension between the limited view of the powers of the legislature in the eyes of the Framers and the holding of *Missouri v. Holland*, which renders the "legislative power virtually without limit"). *See also* Seidman & Lawson, *supra* note 47 (describing their analytical approach as "reasonable-person originalism," and concluding that the Constitution limits the subject matter of treaties). For a view of historical textualism, *see* Ramsey, *supra* note 45.

[122] For a recent view, *see* KU & YOO, *supra* note 120, at 75–7 (discussing the constitutional restraint on delegating power to a body that is not responsible to Congress, such as an international organization created by treaty).

[123] *See* Bradley II, *supra* note 119 (responding to Golove's historical critique of the federalist/new sovereigntist conception of the treaty power).

wondered whether some federalism limits on the treaty power were warranted. At a time when the Rehnquist Court was trimming Congressional power to legislate under the interstate Commerce Clause, Professor Curtis Bradley claimed that, if federalism is a value to be protected, "there is no justification for giving the treaty power special immunity from such protection."[124] Instead, Bradley argued, the Court should apply the same federalism limitations that it applies when Congress legislates pursuant to the Commerce Clause and Fourteenth Amendments to legislation passed pursuant to treaties.[125] In areas where Congress does not have the power to legislate, the states serve as capable and proper enforcers of those treaty obligations.[126]

The new federalist critiques were built on the Rehnquist Court's new federalism jurisprudence, beginning with *United States v. Lopez* in the mid-1990s.[127] In *Lopez*, and later in *United States. v. Morrison*,[128] the Court struck down Congressional statutes that exceeded its power under the once seemingly limitless interstate Commerce Clause. In *New York* and *Printz*, the Court struck down as unconstitutional federal attempts to "commandeer" a state government's structures to implement federal law.[129] And in *City of Boerne v. Flores*, the Court rejected the argument that Section 5 of the Fourteenth Amendment could serve as the basis of Congressional power to

[124] Curtis Bradley claimed a sort of federalism "agnosticism": "I am not defending here the value of federalism, or judicial review of federalism . . ." in finding that no interpretive method and no interpretative materials "including text, history, structure and changed circumstances . . . justifies giving the treaty power special immunity from federalism limitations." Bradley, *supra* note 41, at 394.

[125] *Ibid. See also* Bradley II, *supra* note 119, at 111–18 (discussing the recent Supreme Court decisions that have limited Congress' legislative power under the Commerce Clause and Fourteenth Amendment).

[126] Bradley, *supra* note 41, at 393–4 (explaining that it is generally understood that the Tenth Amendment, which reserves those rights that are not expressly given to the United States to the several States, does not limit the power to make treaties or enter into other agreements) (quoting Third Restatement at § 302 cmt. d).

[127] United States v. Lopez, 514 U.S. 549, 561 (1995) (holding that Congress did not have the authority under the Commerce Clause to enact legislation regulating the possession of firearms near schools).

[128] United States v. Morrison, 529 U.S. 598, 627 (2000) (holding that Congress lacked the authority to enact a statute under the Commerce Clause or the Fourteenth Amendment). *See also* City of Boerne v. Flores, 521 U.S. 507, 518, 536 (1997) (striking down the Religious Freedom Restoration Act as outside Congress's remedial powers under the Fourteenth Amendment and reasoning that "'as broad as the congressional enforcement power is, it is not unlimited'") (quoting Oregon v. Mitchell, 400 U.S. 112, 128 (1970)).

[129] New York v. United States, 505 U.S. 144, 188 (1992) (holding that Congress and the Executive may not compel a state legislature to administer a federal program); Printz v. United States, 521 U.S. 898, 935 (1997) (holding that Congress cannot command state law enforcement officials to execute federal law).

enforce against the states a statute that purported to define the scope of individual religious liberty.[130] As a way to connect the treaty power with these federalism and anti-commandeering cases, the new federalists focused on the "subject matter" of treaties. As the international human rights system began to mature in the 1980s and 1990s, including with the establishment of a permanent International Criminal Court in 1998, the sovereigntists saw treaty-making as a potentially greater danger to state prerogatives than the Commerce Clause.

The new federalists' view of a changing conception of international treaty-making was not wrong. The post–World War II order was built distinctly on breaking down the traditional international law distinctions between inter-state subjects of international agreements and those topics that intruded more deeply into what had traditionally been with the realm of municipal or "local" law-making. The UN Charter is founded on the twin pillars of international security and the respect for human rights. Those human rights are secured in international covenants that get to the heart of the most local, intimate relationships between a state and its citizenry. The blurring of the line between the local and the global is the premise behind the expansion of universal jurisdiction in criminal law and the creation of new international crimes, the restrictions on local taxation and subsidies within the trade regime, and the deepening of international humanitarian law to govern internal conflicts and, in some instances, domestic law enforcement actions. It is not just that the world is less compartmentalized as a factual matter, but that the international legal order is quite *intentionally* premised on an expansion of the scope of subject matter to include the "local." The legitimacy of regulating such behavior through treaty is largely uncontested by UN member states across a wide range of subject matter.

At the heart of the sovereigntist critique, relying on theories of federalism that are grounded in a preference for a weaker national government and strong state and local control, is an adherence to rigid categorizations of the local, national, regional, and international. The sovereigntists explicitly reject more pluralistic understandings of how law operates and how law might be applied pragmatically – in ways that blur the categories of local,

130 City of Boerne v. Flores, 521 U.S. 507, 518, 536 (1997) (voiding the Religious Freedom Restoration Act as outside Congress's remedial powers under the Fourteenth Amendment and reasoning that "'as broad as the congressional enforcement power is, it is not unlimited'") (quoting Oregon v. Mitchell, 400 U.S. 112, 128 (1970)). For the argument that RFRA could, in principle, have been validated as an exercise of Congress's power to implement U.S. treaty obligations (specifically Art. 18 of the ICCPR), see Gerald L. Neuman, *The Global Dimension of* RFRA, 14 CONSTITUTIONAL COMMENTARY 33 (1997).

national, or international – to address global challenges. International treaty makers and the institutions that enforce treaties have grappled with issues of federalism and subsidiarity, and, contra the new federalists, have at times proved quite capable of accommodating these issues.[131] Human rights treaty bodies and courts, for example, have at times welcomed and encouraged subsidiarity or federal systems as a means of effective democratic governance.[132] At other times, however, independent policies by subnational governing units have been viewed as an obstacle to effective compliance with human rights treaty obligations.[133] In other areas of treaty law, enforcement of treaty terms through federal systems of government has been acknowledged and accommodated.[134]

The new federalists' opponents mounted a strong defense of *Holland* (which had never been overturned, nor modified), drawing on textual and historical support. Professor David Golove, for example, surveyed the founding documents to find originalist conceptions of the treaty power compatible with contemporary, expansive notions of the proper subject matter of treaties and supportive of Henkin's defeasance theory of the Tenth Amendment.[135] The nationalists saw *Holland* as correctly decided, and although not

131 For a discussion of the ways in which international law, including the foundational doctrine of *pacta sunt servanda*, accommodates federalism, see Edward T. Swaine, *Does Federalism Constrain the Treaty Power?*, 103 COLUM. L. REV. 403, 450–67 (2003).

132 This seeming contradiction – that global governance is more interested in applying substantive legal constraints on local behavior, but also welcomes local participation in law-making and enforcement – is not as paradoxical as it seems and allows for many forms of transnational law-making to occur, many of them outside traditional treaty-making. The European Court of Human Rights "margin of appreciation" doctrine is an example of how this is given effect in a regional human rights system. *See* Y. Shany, *Toward a General Margin of Appreciation Doctrine in International Law?* 16 EUR. J. INT'L LAW 907, 909–14 (describing the margin of appreciation as comprising (1) judicial deference, whereby international courts grant deference and respect for the ways in which national authorities execute their international obligations, and (2) normative flexibility, whereby norms subjected to the doctrine are characterized as unsettled or open-ended.). The Council of Europe itself sees the doctrine as crucial to maintaining state membership in the European Convention on Human Rights: "The margin of appreciation gives the flexibility needed to avoid damaging confrontations between the Court and the Member States and enables the Court to balance the sovereignty of Member States with their obligations under the Convention." The Margin of Appreciation: Introduction, at www.coe.int/t/dghl/cooperation/lisbonnetwork/themis/echr/paper2_en.asp, (downloaded July 30, 2015).

133 See discussion of criticisms of U.S. human rights practices (and explicit requests to remove federalism reservations the United States has attached to its human rights treaty ratifications) under the Universal Periodic Review process of the UN Human Rights Council *infra*, note 203.

134 *See* Ku, *supra* note 23, at 499–506.

135 Golove, *supra* note 26, at 1077. *See also* Carlos Manuel Vázquez, *Breard, Printz, and the Treaty Power*, 70 U. COLO. L. REV. 1317, 1320–1 (1999); Martin S. Flaherty, *Are We to be*

a thorough explication of the "constitutional prohibitions" restraint on the treaty power, at least a useful explanation of how foreign affairs generally, and the treaty power specifically, are different from other areas of dual sovereignty.[136]

D *The Underused Defeasance Power of* Missouri v. Holland

In the more than ninety years since *Holland*, the number of international treaties to which the United States is a party has grown exponentially. The subject matter of those treaties has also broadened to include those that require undertaking international obligations involving the protection of individual rights and the creation of individual liabilities. Yet for over ninety years, and despite the vigorous academic debate over the case, no challenge to *Holland* reached the courts. The reason for that absence is that the federal government has never fully embraced the full power that *Holland* appeared to hand it.[137] Rather than seize this seemingly limitless power that the critics of *Holland* warned against, practical politics and constitutional processes appear to have served as an effective break on the use of the treaty power to adopt domestic treaty implementing legislation that might "defease" states of power and alter the constitutional balance between the national and the local. This happened in two ways: through Executive branch restraint in entering into the treaties that caused the most concern, *i.e.*, international human rights treaties; and cooperation between the Executive and Congress to attach federalism "understandings" to any treaties that might potentially require the federal government to encroach on traditional state prerogatives. The effect of these practices, whether intended or not, was to keep the academic debate and any questioning of *Holland* and the Third Restatement's discussion of federalism out of the federal courts.

Since the failure of the Bricker amendment, constitutional practice has seemed to reflect a kind of assimilation of federalism within the Executive and Congress when it is engaged in treaty-making and treaty implementation.[138] Whether seen or unseen by U.S. treaty partners, this assimilation suggests that

a Nation? Federal Power vs. "States' Rights" in Foreign Affairs, 70 U. COLO L. REV. 1277, 1280 (1999).

136 *See* Flaherty, *supra* note 135.

137 *See* Peter J. Spiro, *Resurrecting Missouri v. Holland*, 73 MO. L. REV. 1029, 1030–31 (2008) ("The elastic terms of human rights regimes made Holland look like a loaded weapon, especially as the domestic civil rights movement started to gain traction.").

138 *Ibid.* at 1030 (arguing that the rejection of *Holland's* broad powers by the national government acts as a sort of "constitutional counter-norm").

U.S. negotiators come to the negotiating table with the values and structure of federalism already internalized, if not explicitly incorporated into their discussion drafts. Professor Duncan Hollis has observed that this implicit federalism has informed (some might say "infected") executive treaty negotiating practice for years.[139]

More explicit than this assimilation of federalism have been the formal efforts by the United States to limit its participation in international human rights treaties by attaching Reservations, Understandings, and Declarations (RUDs) that have the effect of making those commitments both non-self-executing and subject to the constraints of federalism.[140] The federalism "understanding" attached to the ICCPR reads:

> That the United States understands that this Covenant shall be implemented by the Federal Government to the extent that it exercises legislative and judicial jurisdiction over the matters covered therein, and otherwise by the state and local governments; to the extent that state and local governments exercise jurisdiction over such matters, the Federal Government *shall take measures appropriate to the Federal system* to the end that the competent authorities of the state or local governments may take appropriate measures for the fulfillment of the Covenant.[141]

139 *See* Hollis, *supra* note 117, at 1332–3 ("Apart from its domestic implications, Executive Federalism can also dramatically affect U.S. foreign relations. It can prevent some treaty-making altogether, constrain U.S. negotiating positions, impose extra costs for achieving U.S. negotiating goals, or complicate questions of U.S. compliance.").

140 *See, e.g.*, Convention Against Torture and Other Cruel, Inhuman or Degrading Treatment or Punishment, Dec. 10 1984, 1465 U.N.T.S. 85 (ratified by United States Oct. 21, 1994) [hereinafter CAT]; U.S. Senate Resolution of Advice and Consent to Ratification of the Convention Against Torture and Other Cruel, Inhuman or Degrading Treatment or Punishment, 136 Cong. Rec. S17491 (daily ed. Oct. 27, 1990) [hereinafter U.S. RUDS to Convention Against Torture]; International Covenant on Civil and Political Rights, Dec. 19, 1966, 999 U.N.T.S. 171 [hereinafter ICCPR]; U.S. Senate Resolution of Advice and Consent to Ratification of the International Covenant on Civil and Political Rights, 138 Cong. Rec. S4783 (daily ed. Apr. 2, 1992) [hereinafter U.S. RUDs to ICCPR]. *See also*, Curtis A. Bradley & Jack L. Goldsmith, *Treaties, Human Rights, and Conditional Consent*, 149 *U. Pa. L. Rev.* 399, 402 (2000); Louis Henkin, *U.S. Ratification of Human Rights Conventions: The Ghost of Senator Bricker*, 89 Am. J. Int'l L. 341, 348–9 (1995). *See also* Alford, Chapter 8 in this book.

141 U.S. Understanding attached to ICCPR. A similar understanding was attached to the CAT:

> That the United States understands that this Convention shall be implemented by the United States Government to the extent that it exercises legislative and judicial jurisdiction over the matters covered by the Convention and otherwise by the state and local governments. Accordingly, in implementing articles 10–14 and 16, the United States Government shall take measures appropriate to the Federal system to the end that the competent authorities of the constituent units of the United States of America may take appropriate measures for the fulfilment of the Convention.

The attachment of the federalism understanding, along with several other substantive reservations, understandings, and declarations regarding the content and implementation of the ICCPR, was a precondition to its approval by the U.S. Senate. It represented a historical follow-through from the Bricker-era commitments of the Eisenhower administration to limit U.S. engagement with international human rights treaties. The United States has subsequently attached RUDs of non-self-execution and federalism to all the major UN human rights treaties it has considered and ratified.[142] These RUDs signaled to U.S. treaty partners that, while the United States generally supported the normative commitments of the human rights agreements (with some substantive reservations, for example, on issues such as application of the death penalty), it would limit attempts to use the treaties themselves as the basis for domestic enforcement of the norms.[143] The attachment of RUDs meant the United States was still obligated to comply with the treaty as a matter of international law, but since most human rights treaties affected the balance of governmental and individual rights at the state level, the United States left resolution of the application of those treaty standards to domestic political processes. The Senate often had other, non-federalism concerns about implementation of human rights treaties, including resistance to altering rights at the federal level, and used the non-self-execution reservations attached to these ratifications to ensure that the treaties also did not create federal law.

Despite some success in using RUDs to gain senatorial support for joining human rights treaties, this device has not always overcome political opposition to any form of commitment to multilateral human rights regimes. The Convention on the Rights of Persons with Disabilities, for example, failed a Senate floor vote in 2012, even with U.S. RUDs for non-self-execution and

U.S. Understanding attached to the CAT. *See* 136 Cong. Rec. S17486–01 (daily ed., Oct. 27, 1990), available at www1.umn.edu/humanrts/usdocs/tortres.html (U.S. reservations, declarations, and understandings to the Convention Against Torture and Other Cruel, Inhuman or Degrading Treatment or Punishment).

142 Of the major UN human rights treaties, the United States is a party to the ICCPR; CAT; Convention on the Elimination of Racial Discrimination; Two optional protocols of the Convention on the Rights of the Child (though not the CRC itself); Optional Protocol on the Involvement of Children in Armed Conflict (2002); Optional Protocol on the Sale of Children, Child Prostitution and Child Pornography (2002). The United States has attached federalism understandings and other RUDs to each of these ratifications, with the notable exception of the child conflict Optional Protocol to the CRC. *See* United Nations High Commissioner for Human Rights, Status of Ratification, http://indicators.ohchr.org/.

143 Roth, *supra* note 22, at 894–5. *See also* Alford, Chapter 8 in this book (describing how RUDs have been used to avoid adjudication of claims in U.S. courts based on human rights treaty obligations).

federalism attached to the treaty.[144] But the inclusion of RUDs demonstrated that, in practice, the would-be treaty makers were not testing the limits of *Holland*.

The implicit and explicit restraints reflected in the Executive and Congressional practice serve as some evidence that the political safeguards on national power contemplated by the Constitution have operated to preserve the proper balance between state and national law-making, as well as ensure that the United States does not enter into treaties that do not enjoy broad support among the states. The requirement for a supermajority of the Senate to approve treaties has arguable served as an effective brake on any tendencies the Executive branch might have to push the bounds of its treaty power. U.S. treaty partners can observe how these constraints quite openly operate.

III *UNITED STATES V. BOND*: FEDERAL PROSECUTION OF A STATE CRIME OF INTERNATIONAL INTEREST

The Chemical Weapons Convention ("CWC") and its implementing legislation are not the kind of treaty and implementing legislation the critics of *Holland* feared. There is a clear international and national consensus on the need to control chemical weapons, heightened in the years following the attacks of 9/11, and general support for increased national powers (especially those that find a grounding in Congressional legislation) to address chemical and other weapons of mass destruction. The trade of chemical weapons and their precursors is a public safety problem that requires a coherent collective response and a centralized international bureaucracy to monitor and implement. Arms control, as part of a coherent national defense, falls well within the powers of the national government. But the specific controls that the CWC places on chemicals may effectively require that enforcement be carried out by local police and other nonnational authorities. And it was just such a law enforcement action by federal officials against an individual for acts that were concurrently violations of basic state criminal law that presented the Supreme Court with its first occasion to revisit *Missouri v. Holland*.

The facts of *Bond* offer a fascinating glimpse into how the subject matter of arms control treaties in an era of global terrorism may reach into many aspects of life that once would be construed as of strictly local concern. The *Bond* case involved a prosecution of a woman who had attempted to poison and do physical harm to another person (her husband's lover). Her

144 158 Cong. Rec. S7365–79 (daily ed. Dec. 4, 2012) (Executive Session).

acts came to the attention of federal law enforcement authorities because Bond had placed the harmful chemicals on, among other places, a mailbox, which triggered the law enforcement jurisdiction of the U.S. Postal Service. One feature of the sometimes overlapping nature of state and federal law enforcement is that federal prosecutors frequently cooperate with local and state prosecutors, and in some cases defer to state prosecution of crimes federal law enforcement has investigated. In *Bond*, the federal government decided to pursue the prosecution, arguing that Bond's possession and use of prohibited chemicals to harm another constituted federal crimes under the CWC Implementing Act.

Reflecting and drawing from the political and academic debates surrounding the Third Restatement, *Bond* represented the most direct challenge since *Holland* to the Congressional power to legislate pursuant to treaty. The Supreme Court granted *certiorari* on two questions, the first going to the heart of the potential textual and structural conflict between the Treaty Clause, the Necessary and Proper powers, and the Tenth Amendment:

> Do the Constitution's structural limits on federal authority impose any constraints on the scope of Congress' authority to enact legislation to implement a valid treaty, at least in circumstances where the federal statute, as applied, goes far beyond the scope of the treaty, intrudes on traditional state prerogatives, and is concededly unnecessary to satisfy the government's treaty obligations?[145]

This first question addressed whether the reasoning in *Holland* (and by implication the Third Restatement) could be extended to a criminal prosecution under a treaty-implementing statute for a local crime (poisoning by chemicals) that would otherwise not fall within the powers of Congress to regulate.[146] By asking whether Congress had the power to enact legislation that was "unnecessary" to satisfy the U.S. treaty obligation, it sought to clarify the full scope of the Necessary and Proper power when it is operating to execute the treaty power.

The second question presented a way to decide the case while avoiding those constitutional questions:

> Can the provisions of the Chemical Weapons Convention Implementation Act, codified at 18 U.S.C. § 229, be interpreted not to reach ordinary

[145] Petition for Writ of *Certiorari*, Bond v. United States., 2012 WL 3158880 (U.S.) at i.

[146] The United States waived any arguments that the CWC Act was an exercise of the interstate commerce clause. Bond v. United States, 134 S. Ct. 2077, 2087 (2014).

poisoning cases, which have been adequately handled by state and local authorities since the Framing, in order to avoid the difficult constitutional questions involving the scope of and continuing vitality of this Court's decision in Missouri v. Holland?[147]

In its opinion unanimously overturning Bond's conviction, six Justices agreed with Bond's argument under the second question, leaving the analysis of *Holland*, the Third Restatement, and the academic debates over the scope of federalism limitations on the treaty power, for discussion in three concurring opinions by Justices Scalia, Thomas, and Alito.

A *The Third Circuit to the Supreme Court: Time to Clarify* Holland

The Third Circuit below had ruled in favor of the government on both questions.[148] On Bond's federalism challenge to the statute itself, the Third Circuit held that *Holland* required it to uphold the statute as a necessary and proper means of implanting a valid treaty.[149] But the Third Circuit was eager for the Supreme Court to revisit and, perhaps, clarify *Holland*. Noting the Court's move toward a reinvigorated and expansive view of the Tenth Amendment – the limits that the Court had imposed on national lawmaking through the Commerce Clause and the Fourteenth Amendment, as well as on federal commandeering of the states to carry out national law – Judge Jordan expressed some sympathy for Bond's argument in favor of setting some limits on *Holland*:

> Cognizant of the widening scope of issues taken up in international agreements, as well as the renewed vigor with which principles of federalism have been employed by the Supreme Court in scrutinizing assertions of federal authority, *we agree with Bond that treaty-implementing legislation ought not, by virtue of that status alone, stand immune from scrutiny under principles of federalism*.[150]

Judge Jordan's view that *Holland* could not be said to remove *all* federalism limitations on the power to legislate pursuant to treaty did not, however, help

147 Petition for Writ of *Certiorari*, Bond v. U.S., 2012 WL 3158880 (U.S.) at ii.

148 Applying Section 229 of the statute, the Third Circuit held that Bond's use of "'highly toxic chemicals with the intent of harming Haynes' can hardly be characterized as 'peaceful' under that word's commonly understood meaning." Bond v. United States, 681 F.3d 149, 154 (3rd Cir. 2012) (citation omitted).

149 *Ibid.* at 163–5. The judges of the Third Circuit raised the problems that *Holland* might create for other treaties, discussing in detail the academic debates and critiques of the Third Restatement. *Ibid.* at 161–6.

150 *Ibid.* at 151.

Bond, because she was prosecuted under a statute implementing "an international agreement with a subject matter that lies at the core of the Treaty Power ... "[151] Jordan noted the *Holland* Court's failure to clarify what it referred to as "qualifications to the treaty-making power" and "somewhat obscure statement that they had to be found 'in a different way' than one might find limitations on other grants of power to the federal government."[152] In *Holland*, he noted, the treaty in question was found to be valid and did not do anything that contravened prohibitory words. Similarly, because the CWC Implementing Act implemented a valid treaty on a subject matter that the court concluded required national action, any potential limits on Congress' power to legislate were not applicable. The Third Circuit did not draw its own conclusions as to whether the legislation criminalizing particular behavior was "necessary" for the United States to comply with the CWC, but rather deferred to Congress' decision to pass the statute. Following Holmes in *Holland*, it held that, so long as the treaty was valid and addressed a question of national policy concern, the legislation implementing the treaty was valid.[153]

1 The Supreme Court avoids the constitutional question

The Supreme Court declined the Third Circuit's invitation to revisit *Holland*. In what Justice Roberts characterized as a "limited" ruling on the application of the statute to Bond's behavior,[154] six justices voted to reverse Bond's conviction under the federal statute on the grounds that, where Congress intends to create federal criminal liability of otherwise local conduct, the statute must be a "clear statement" that the statute intended to reach such conduct.[155] In striking down the conviction under the "clear statement rule," the justices adopted an arguably tortured interpretation of the CWC implementing statute, a statute crafted by Congress to reflect the

151 *Ibid.*

152 *Ibid.* at 156 (quoting Missouri v. Holland, 252 U.S. 416, 433 (1920)). He continued his lament, "[a]fter implying that Congress' powers are particularly sweeping when dealing with 'matters requiring national action,' the Court suggestion one limitation on the Treaty Power: If the implementation of a treaty 'contravene[s] any prohibitory words to be found in the Constitution,' then it may be unconstitutional." *Ibid.* (quoting 252 U.S. 416 (citation omitted)).

153 *Ibid.* at 166.

154 Bond v. United States, 134 S. Ct. 2077, 2093 (2014) ("This case is unusual and our analysis is appropriately limited.").

155 "We conclude that, in this curious case, we can insist on a clear indication that Congress meant to reach purely local crimes, before interpreting the statute's expansive language in a way that intrudes on the police power of the States." *Ibid.* at 2090 (citing *United States v. Bass*, 404 U.S. 336, 349 (1971)).

requirements of the underlying convention and which defined the term "peaceful" for the purposes of prosecutions under the statute.[156] Other than her personal motives for the crime, it is not at all clear that the prosecution of Bond for the possession and use of dangerous chemicals would not be precisely the type of prosecution the CWC contemplates in order to comply with its obligations. The CWC does not prescribe, however, that the prosecution be done at the federal level instead of the state level. The means through which a state party gives effect domestically to an international law obligation to comply are generally left to the state party itself. The Court left unresolved the issue of whether the Necessary and Proper clause limits the scope of implementing legislation to the minimum necessary to comply with the treaty.

The Court did not expressly predicate its holding on the constitutional avoidance principle, but its interpretation of the Section 229 of the Statute relied on the Court's consideration of federalism when interpreting federal criminal statutes, stating that "the background principle that Congress does not normally intrude upon the police power of the States is critically important."[157] This move to canons of statutory construction avoided deciding the constitutional question, while applying principles of federalism as a background constitutional norm. In striking down the federal prosecution under the CWC statute, the Court forces Congress to revise the legislation if it wishes to prosecute this kind of local behavior under the CWC in the future. Some observers might read this as an implicit limit on the Necessary and Proper power in the treaty context,[158] but it operates no differently than the clear statement rule as applied to other federal criminal statutes.

Along with Justices Thomas and Alito, Justice Scalia would have read the statute as applying to Bond's conduct, and would have found the application of the statute to her conduct unconstitutional.[159] Scalia saw the case an as

156 On the question of its statutory interpretation, Justice Scalia observed in his acerbic concurring opinion: "Today, the Court shirks its job and performs Congress's. As sweeping and settling as the Chemical Weapons Convention Implementing Act of 1998 may be, it is clear beyond doubt that it covers what Bond did; and we have no authority to amend it." *Ibid.* at 2094 (Scalia, J., concurring).

157 *Ibid.* at 2092. The Court also noted that "The Government's reading of section 229 would "'alter sensitive federal-state relationships,'" convert an astonishing amount of "traditionally local criminal conduct" into "a matter for federal enforcement," and "involve a substantial extension of federal police resources." *Ibid.* at 2091.

158 *See* Michael J. Glennon & Robert D. Sloane, *The Sad, Quiet Death of* Missouri v. Holland: *How* Bond *Hobbled the Treaty Power*, 41 YALE J. INT'L L. 51, 71–81 (2016).

159 Neither Alito nor Thomas joined Scalia's reasoning as to why the Act was unconstitutional.

occasion to clarify, if not fully overturn, *Holland*, which he noted contained an "unreasoned and citation-less sentence" which "purported to furnish the answer" to whether the Act was constitutional as applied to Bond.[160] Scalia's concurrence fully embraced the view of Professor Rosenkranz that the Necessary and Proper clause only empowers Congress to pass legislation that gives effect to the "making" of treaties, not the power to pass legislation implementing the treaty itself:[161]

> Once a treaty has been made, Congress's power to do what is "necessary and proper" to assist the making of treaties drops out of the picture. To legislate compliance with the United States' treaty obligations, Congress must rely upon its independent (though quite robust) Article 1, § 8, power.[162]

Justice Thomas would have gone further to limit the scope of the treaty power – and thus the powers under the Necessary and Proper clause to execute a treaty – to those "external" issues that were in the minds of the Founders.[163] His own survey of the constitutional practice since the ratification debates concluded that the "Treaty Power is limited to matters of international intercourse," and "[e]ven if a treaty *may* reach some local matters, it still *must* relate to intercourse with other nations."[164] Under his view, Thomas concluded that the Third Restatement deviates from historical practice – and by implication his own reading of *Holland* – when it declares "Contrary to what was once

160 Bond, 134 S. Ct. at 2098 (Scalia, J., concurring).

161 "[A] power to help the President make treaties is not a power to implement treaties already made." *Ibid.* at 2099 (Scalia, J., concurring) (citing Rosenkranz, *supra* note 37, at 1884).

162 *Ibid.* at 2099. Justice Thomas would also have reached the constitutional question, and concurred with Scalia's reasoning on the Necessary and Proper clause. This argument – seemingly unique to Rosenkranz (and now Scalia and Thomas) – has no support in the Founding documents, the historical practices of the political branches, or the Court's jurisprudence as articulated in the *Neely* and *Holland* cases. Justice Scalia attacked *Neely* and *Holland* as "unreasoned," but that is largely because the proposition that Congress had the power to enact legislation under the Necessary and Proper clause to give effect to valid treaties was, as commentators noted "uncontroversial (indeed, virtually uncontroverted)." *See* David Golove & Marty Lederman, *Stepping Back from the Precipice in Bond*, Opinio Juris (June 4, 2014), http://opiniojuris.org/2014/06/04/guest-post-stepping-back-precipice-bond/.

163 Bond, S. Ct. 134 at 2103 (2014) (Thomas, J., concurring) (describing the preconstitutional, Articles of Confederation practice that "reflect[ed] the use of treaty-making power only for matters of international intercourse; that practice provides not support for using treaties to regulate purely domestic affairs.").

164 *Ibid.* at 2108 (citation omitted). He reads *Holland* to be consistent with his view that "treaties by their nature relate to intercourse with other nations (including their people and property), rather than to purely domestic affairs." *Ibid.* As it upheld implementing legislation aimed at regulating migratory birds, which "were naturally a matter of international intercourse because they were creatures in international transit," *Holland* would have met the test. *Ibid.* at 2109. Citation omitted.

suggested, the Constitution does not require that an international agreement deal only with 'matters of international concern.'"[165] Thomas concluded that "the distinction between matters of international intercourse and matters of purely domestic regulation may not be obvious in all cases," but nonetheless suggested that "hypothetical difficulties in line-drawing are no reason to ignore a constitutional limit on federal power."[166]

Justice Alito concurred with Thomas, but would have further limited the scope of the treaty power in criminal prosecutions. He noted that, while the CWC addressed an issue of international concern, if the treaty is read to require the enactment of the federal criminal sanctions under which Bond herself was prosecuted, then the subject matter of the CWC exceeds the subject matter limits of the treaty power.[167] To Alito, Section 229 of the Statute cannot be regarded as "necessary and proper" to carry into execution the treaty power.[168] It is not clear whether Alito would hold more broadly that prosecution of local conduct is never a proper subject for a treaty, but by stating – in direct contradiction to the Third Restatement – that "the treaty power is limited to agreements that address *matters of legitimate international concern*,"[169] he leaves open the door to such a conclusion.

2 *Missouri v. Holland* survives

The decision in *Bond* left *Holland* intact and, by extension, the conclusions of the Third Restatement that relied on *Holland* and its reasoning. One might quibble that Chief Justice Roberts' downplaying of the severity of Bond's acts misunderstands the nature of the CWC treaty, creating a multilateral regime aimed at restricting the possession and trade in particular chemicals; it is quite possible that, motive aside, the ease with which Bond accessed the prohibited items calls for stronger, rather than weaker, national controls. But the decision is significant for not doing anything to diminish, dilute, or distinguish the holding in *Holland*.[170]

Within the majority opinion, however, are some indications of concern about what this treaty-implementing legislation and this prosecution did to the balance of federal and state power. The "clear statement" requirement espoused by the Court, developed for ordinary domestic legislation, now

[165] *Ibid.* at 2110 (quoting THIRD RESTATEMENT). THIRD RESTATEMENT, *supra* note 5, at § 302 cmt. c.

[166] *Ibid.* at 2111.

[167] *Ibid.* (Alito, J. Concurring) (joining in Scalia's statutory interpretation of the CWC statute, and also joined Thomas' reasoning on the scope of the treaty power).

[168] *Ibid.* [169] *Ibid.* [170] *See* Golove & Lederman, *supra* note 162.

applies to all treaty-implementing legislation. As Professor Curtis Bradley has noted, *Bond* – taken together with the Court's decision in *Medellin v. Texas*, rejecting the president's assertion of power to command a state to comply with an International Court of Justice judgment and implying a presumption in favor of non-self-execution of treaties, "signals more generally … that the Court will be attentive to federalism values even in cases involving foreign affairs."[171] Bradley sees virtue in this attentiveness, particularly in the area of treaty-implementing legislation, as it will require Congress to craft implementing legislation more precisely, and move away from the kind of broad copying of multilateral treaty language that appears to have been done in the CWC Implementing Act. To Bradley, the clear statement presumption is a useful check on Congress, requiring it to be clear about when it is "deliberately seeking to change the traditional balance of state and federal authority through its implementing legislation."[172]

Of course, by entering into the CWC treaty itself, the national government was already signaling that is was changing the "traditional balance" between state and federal authority – at least insofar as the prohibited chemicals were concerned. And direct copying of treaty language into the domestic law implementing a multilateral treaty commitment may be precisely what a treaty contemplates to bring a state party into compliance – particularly a treaty that prohibits reservations, as is the case with the CWC.[173] The main rationale for requiring that Congress adopt implementing legislation that is something "less than" a treaty text requires would be one rooted in the virtues of federalism, and the resulting diffusion of enforcement. This diffusion may be useful, or even necessary, in some treaty implementation where the mechanism of enforcement rests in traditional state court proceedings (for example, treaties addressing property rights and inheritance laws).[174] But arms control treaties seem unlikely subjects for such an approach, and do not generally contain federalism provisions themselves or permit federalism reservations.[175]

Only three justices voted to revisit *Holland* – and none of the other six even discussed or addressed *Holland*. That does not mean that Chief Justice

171 Curtis A. Bradley, Bond, Clear Statement Requirements, and Political Process, AJIL Unbound (June 3, 2014), www.asil.org/blogs/bond-clear-statement-requirements-and-political-process.

172 *Ibid.*

173 *See* Convention on the Prohibition of the Development, Production, Stockpiling and Use of Chemical Weapons and on Their Destruction, art. XXII, Jan. 13, 1993, 1974 U.N.T.S. 45 ("The Articles of this Convention shall not be subject to reservations.").

174 *See* Ku, *supra* note 23, at 476–98.

175 *See* Corn & Beck, Chapter 4 in this book (with reference to the Chemical Weapons Convention).

Roberts and Justice Kennedy – the two conservative justices joining with the four liberal justices to form a majority – find the Third Restatement's reading of *Holland* persuasive or that they would not revisit *Holland* on another occasion. Given the paucity of Congressional treaty-implementing statutes that go beyond enumerated powers of Art. I, § 8, such an occasion to revisit *Holland* seems unlikely to recur anytime soon.[176]

IV THE CONTINUING DYNAMISM OF INTERNATIONAL LAW-MAKING IN A FEDERAL SYSTEM

Proponents of federalism who seek to preserve state and local prerogatives in the face of increasing global commitments of the national government need not fear the implications of the judicial survival of *Holland*, for several reasons. First, the fallout from *Holland* and the battles over the Bricker amendment resulted in rather restrained behavior by the political branches in the process of making and implementing treaties. The Court has arguably played a democracy-reinforcing role in this area, indicating in the *Medellin* case, for example, a presumption against treaty self-execution.[177] But most of the action, as noted earlier, seems to be happening outside the courts, a development which may prove equally unsatisfying to the sovereigntists and to proponents of a more robust and exclusive use of the national treaty power.

Second, treaties, as understood by Article II of the Constitution, are no longer the exclusive or even central means through which the United States engages in international law-making. For many decades, the importance of treaties – whether self-executing or non-self-executing – has been diminishing as the United States has come to use executive agreements, Congressional-Executive agreements, and political commitments as alternative means to engage counterparties bilaterally and multilaterally.[178] In the case of non-Article II "treaties," the United States enters into agreements with international counterparts that are binding as a matter of international law, but which

[176] And as more than one commentator has observed, if the Court did not have five votes to overturn *Holland* in the *Bond* case and on the facts of that prosecution, it is unlikely to have a more attractive occasion to do so in the future. *See, e.g.*, Golove & Lederman, *supra* note 162 (discussing the significance of the fact that not one Justice in *Bond* argued in favor of overruling the part of *Holland* that held that the Article II treaty power is not limited to those subjects otherwise falling within the scope of Congress' Article I powers).

[177] *See* Wuerth, Chapter 4 in this book.

[178] *See* Oona Hathaway, *Treaties' End: The Past, Present and Future of International Law Making in the United States*, 117 YALE L. J. 1236 (2008); Duncan B. Hollis and Joshua J. Newcomer, *Political "Commitments" and the Constitution*, 49 VA. J. INT'L LAW 507 (2009).

may follow one of several different paths domestically: create no domestic legal rights, create fewer domestic legal rights than contemplated in the international agreement, or create comprehensive domestic legal rights under full Congressional legislation (as in the case of Congressional-Executive agreements, which are the vehicle by which most trade agreements are adopted). Political "commitments" – agreements with foreign states that fall short of formal international treaty status – can contain significant and robust obligations on the United States.[179] Each of these various approaches to international law-making are effectively driven and constrained by political processes, even where they are not constrained by the judiciary.

Third, the Compacts Clause does not fully constrain states from participating in the increasingly dynamic process of transnational law-making. Global disaggregation – of political preferences and affiliation, and of policy goals – has allowed states and localities in the United States to act on their own within a global system that enables subnational entities outside the United States to do the same.[180] So long as the actions taken by states and localities do not come into conflict with constitutionally valid policies and laws made pursuant to the foreign affairs powers of the federal government, and so long as they not constitute the entering into of impermissible international agreements, state and local governments have broad latitude to express their various policy preferences.

A *The Compacts Clause and the Rise of States as International Law Participants*

The Third Restatement Section 302 stated the largely uncontroversial view that "The United States has authority under the Constitution to make international agreements."[181] Under Comment f of Section 302, the Restatement underscored the prohibition of the Compacts Clause against states entering into any "Treaty Alliance of Confederation," and also, absent Congressional approval, entering into their own agreements with foreign states.[182] The Comment went on to conclude, "What distinguishes a treaty, which a State cannot make at all, from an agreement or compact, which it can make with Congressional consent, has not been determined" and would "probably be deemed a [non-justiciable] political question" by the courts.[183]

179 *See* Hollis & Newcomer, *ibid.* at 512 ("the international consequences of political commitments mimic those of treaty commitments.").

180 For a full discussion of this phenomenon see Peter J. Spiro, *Disaggregating U.S. Interests in International Law*, 67 LAW & CONTEMP. PROBS. 195 (Aut. 2004).

181 THIRD RESTATEMENT § 302 (1). 182 THIRD RESTATEMENT at § 302 cmt. f. 183 *Ibid.*

Despite the narrow space for international law-making by states granted by the Constitution and affirmed in the Third Restatement, states have reached beyond the strict textual limits of the Compacts clause to play a more active role on the international plane.[184] Since the Third Restatement, constitutional practice has consisted of a national government that underutilizes the defeasance powers over the states that *Holland* and the Restatement affirmed, while the states have pushed – and perhaps even exceeded – the limits of the Compacts Clause to become more active participants in the making and enforcement of international norms.

States have largely avoided any constitutional problems with the Compacts Clause by coordinating policy-making with foreign sovereigns through devices that fall short of formal agreements or treaties – even as international law has come to recognize the capacity of subnational governmental entities to enter into treaties and be bound by their terms.[185] The ways in which states have participated in international law-making have generally avoided formal agreements. Among the trends are local actions taken to comply with the Convention on the Elimination of Discrimination Against Women; state coordination with international targets to reduce greenhouse gas emissions targets; and the invocation of international standards when considering legislation to eliminate the death penalty.[186]

The states have encountered some judicial challenges to their international legal and policy initiatives in cases that raised general questions of the legislative authority of Congress (including unexercised dormant authority), the foreign affairs powers of the Executive, and the power of federal law or policy to preempt state actions. In the *Crosby* case in 2000, the Supreme Court struck down as unconstitutional a Massachusetts law creating a state procurement boycott against companies active in Burma on the ground that it conflicted with Congressional legislation that delegated to the president authority to enact trade and investment sanctions against the Burmese regime.[187]

184 Several scholars have chronicled this trend over the past few decades. *See, e.g.*, Richard B. Bilder, *The Role of States and Cities in Foreign Relations*, 83 AM. J. INT'L L. 821 (1989); Peter Spiro, *Foreign Relations Federalism*, 70 U. COLO. L. REV. 1223 (1999); and Duncan B. Hollis, *Unpacking the Compact Clause*, 88 TEX. L. REV. 741 (2010).

185 Duncan B. Hollis, *Unpacking the Compact Clause*, 88 TEX. L. REV. 741 (2010).

186 For a general discussion of these trends *see, e.g.*, Judith Resnik, *The Internationalism of American Federalism: Missouri and Holland*, 73 MO. L. REV. 1105 (2008); Peter J. Spiro, *The States Take on (Take in) International Law*, 20 WILLAMETTE J. INT'L L. & DISP. RESOL. 79 (2012).

187 Crosby v. National Foreign Trade Council, 530 U.S. 363 (2000). A treaty issue lurked behind the constitutional question ultimately decided in *Crosby*: whether the Massachusetts boycott statute violated U.S. obligations under the Government Procurement Agreement of the

In *Garamendi* in 2003, the Court struck down a California statute requiring insurance companies doing business in the state to disclose Holocaust-era accounts, where the federal government had reached a prior agreement with European states to deal with Holocaust-era insurance claims through an international settlement process.[188] Nonetheless, the opinions of the Office of Legal Counsel have tended to confirm the view that, despite some firm limits on state legislation that conflicts with contrary federal law or interferes with national foreign policy, states and localities may adopt policy positions and even laws that reflect foreign or international policy objectives.[189]

Accommodating state participation in international law-making, including through international agreements with national or subnational entities, adds a degree of complexity and uncertainty to international law-making. In some areas, states have been key players in giving effect to treaties and agreements the United States has entered, particularly where state law procedures provide the mechanism for carrying out the treaty provisions.[190] In other cases, states have proved an obstacle to meeting the treaty obligations of the United States, especially where domestic law provides no mechanism for the federal government to compel states to comply. And in cases where the states have sought to enter into binding legal agreements with foreign sovereigns (at the national and subnational level), Congress has played a diminishing role in reviewing the agreements, largely ceding this constitutional oversight role to the Executive branch.[191]

The 2008 *Medellin* case,[192] involving domestic enforcement of the 2004 International Court of Justice ruling in *Avena* that ordered the United States to give reconsideration of dozens of capital convictions obtained in violation of the Consular Convention, is a good example of the avenues and obstacles

General Agreement on Tariffs and Trade. *Ibid.* at 384 (Noting that the EU and Japan had filed a complaint against the United States at the World Trade Organization alleging that the Massachusetts statute violated the "certain provisions of the Agreement on Government Procurement."). The WTO complaint was one factor the court considered to support the U.S. government's claim that Massachusetts was interfering with Congress' intended policy vis-à-vis Burma. *Ibid.* at 384–5.

188 American Ins. Assn. v. Garamendi, 537 U.S. 1100 (2003).

189 *See* Department of Justice Office of Legal Counsel, Memorandum Opinion for the Associate Attorney General, "Constitutionality of South African Divestment Statutes Enacted by State and Local Governments," April 31, 1986, (www.justice.gov/sites/default/files/olc/opinions/1986/04/31/op-olc-v010-p0049.pdf).

190 Some examples include consular protections, trusts and estates and other transfers of property. *See* Ku, *supra* note 23. *See also* Swaine, *supra* note 131.

191 *See* Duncan B. Hollis, *Unpacking the Compact Clause*, 88 Tex. L. Rev. 741 (2010).

192 Medellin v. Texas, 552 U.S. 491 (2008).

states provide for treaty compliance.[193] In response to the ICJ decision, the president issued a memorandum stating that the United States would comply with the content of the ICJ's ruling. Texas challenged the applicability of the ICJ ruling as a matter of domestic law, and the constitutionality of the presidential memorandum. The Supreme Court held that the ICJ decision was not self-executing and therefore did not create binding domestic law that could compel Texas to reconsider the capital conviction.[194] The Court also rejected as a violation of separation of powers the president's attempt to give effect to the ICJ ruling through the memorandum. Congress, the Court concluded, not the president, could create federal law pursuant to treaty that would bind state courts.[195] The State of Oklahoma was affected by the same ICJ decision, but decided – even absent a federal statute – to grant clemency on the ground that the capital sentence was obtained in violation of the defendant's consular rights.[196] For the *Avena* claimants, federalism provided an obstacle to treaty compliance in the case of Texas, but also allowed an avenue, in the case of Oklahoma, for fulfilling a treaty obligation.

There are other ways beyond state court remedies in which federalism can enhance U.S. participation in international law-making – including crafting treaty norms and enforcement mechanisms. Professor Hollis has noted that state agreements with subnational foreign sovereigns "demonstrate the potential of these instruments to produce information and sharing and pooling of resources that would otherwise never occur" and "test an array of regulatory regimes for national governments to select from later in devising an international approach."[197] Professor Edward Swaine has argued that state compacts could be "employed in tandem with treaties as a vehicle for overcoming constitutional inhibitions on both the federal government and the states."[198] Such practice has been, and is likely to continue to be, accompanied by some

193 Avena and other Mexican Nationals (Mex. v. United States), 2004 I.C.J. 12 (Mar. 31).

194 For a full discussion of the case see Margaret E. McGuinness, *Medellin v. Texas: Supreme Court Hold ICJ Decision under the Consular Convention Not Binding Federal Law, Rejects Presidential Enforcement of ICJ Judgments over State Proceedings, ASIL Insights*, Vol. 12, issue 6 (Apr. 17, 2008).

195 Medellin, 552 U.S. 491, 529. Absent a federal court order, Texas rejected any further review of Medellin's claim and executed him. See *Medellin Executed for Rape, Murder of Houston Teens*, HOUSTON CHRON. Aug 5, 2008.

196 *See* Janet Levit, A *Tale of International Law in the Heartland: Torres and the Role of State Courts in Transnational Legal Conversation*, 12 TULSA J. COMP. & INT'L L. 163 (2004) (describing Oklahoma's compliance with the Avena Decision). Nevada also took note of the ICJ opinion in changing its behavior. *See* Duncan Hollis, Avena Lives! Supreme Court of Nevada Cites ICJ in Granting Gutierrez Evidentiary Hearing, Opinio Juris (Oct. 5, 2012, 9:16 PM), opiniojuris.org.

197 *Ibid.* at 796. 198 Swaine, supra note 131, at 413.

oversight by the federal government – increasingly the Executive branch. But it is unlikely to be subject to federal court review.

V CONCLUSION

Federalism, and the dynamism it promotes in U.S. policy-making, complicates U.S. participation in treaties. But notwithstanding certain notorious implementation gaps (as in *Medellin*), it is not clear that the peculiar features of federalism have made the United States a significantly less reliable treaty partner on the whole. The restrained behavior of the political branches in the area of treaty approval and treaty-implementing legislation reflects deference to the idea of dual sovereignty and a recognition that, at least in the American model, it strengthens rather than weakens democratic governance. In turn, strong democratic support for treaty obligations makes the United States a more reliable counterparty to its treaty partners.[199] Even federalism "understandings" on international human rights treaties have the value of keeping the United States in the tent of larger multilateral treaty regimes, where they might otherwise have resisted inclusion. Viewed from this perspective, the disaggregation of human rights enforcement mechanisms at the state level provides opportunities for more robust engagement with human rights norms, and a dynamic dialog between the federal government and states on human rights compliance.[200]

Treaty partners of the United States, particularly those within the multilateral human rights treaties, have at times objected strongly to U.S. reservations to these agreements, raising questions about U.S. compliance with the core commitments to those treaties.[201] These RUDs seemed less problematic in the immediate decade following the Third Restatement. They are viewed as significantly more problematic where non-self-execution declarations limit access

199 *See* Oona Hathaway, *Do Human Rights Treaties Make a Difference?*,111 YALE L.J. 1935, 1954 (2002) (arguing that human rights obligations undertaken by liberal states are more likely to be followed due to domestic pressure).

200 *See* Catherine Powell, *Dialogic Federalism: Constitutional Possibilities for Incorporation of Human Rights Law in the United States*, 150 U. PA. L. REV. 245 (2001).

201 *See, e.g.*, U.S. RUDs to Convention Against Torture, *supra* note 140 ([T]he United States considers itself bound . . . only insofar as the term "cruel, inhuman or degrading treatment or punishment" means the cruel, unusual and inhumane treatment or punishment prohibited by the Fifth, Eighth, and/or Fourteenth Amendments to the Constitution of the United States."). *See also* U.S. RUDs to ICCPR, *supra* note 140 ("[T]he United States reserves the right, subject to its Constitutional constraints, to impose capital punishment on any person (other than a pregnant woman) duly convicted under existing or future laws permitting the imposition of capital punishment, including such punishment for crimes committed by persons below eighteen years of age.").

to U.S. courts for claims relating to well-known treaty violations – of the Convention Against Torture and the International Covenant on Civil and Political Rights – by the United States in the years following the attacks of September 11, 2001.[202] Yet, despite obstacles that these U.S. RUDs pose to judicial redress in U.S. courts, they do not negate core U.S. obligations under these treaties as a matter of international law.[203] International treaty bodies and organs have been increasingly interested in the rights behavior of states and localities in the United States, and have not be reticent in shedding light on treaty violations, even where the only remedies to breach are political.[204] Under the recent Universal Periodic Reporting Process of the UN Human Rights Council, the United States must itself report on general human rights compliance at the federal, state and local level, and is subject to commentary of other UN member states, as well as by NGO observers to the Council.[205]

The international human rights regime presents a particularly complex picture of federalism and the treaty power, one that illuminates both challenges and opportunities for other treaty partners and human rights advocates seeking to bring U.S. behavior into compliance with its treaty commitments. While the values of federalism block some formal avenues for redress in federal courts, they open up channels at the local and state level for engagement politically and through civil society. The result is inconsistency on some core rights issues, as some states successfully assert prerogatives to resist compliance with treaty commitments, while others exceed the requirements of domestic law in bringing their policies into line with transnational norms.[206]

202 *See* 18 U.S.C. § 2340A (2015); Convention Against Torture, *supra* note 140.

203 *See, e.g.*, U.N. Human Rights Council, Universal Periodic Review, Report of the Working Group on the Universal Periodic Review: United States of America, p. 16, U.N. Doc. A/HRC/16/11 (Jan. 4 2011) [hereinafter UPR] (containing suggestions by numerous countries that the United States withdraw reservations on specific agreements, such as the ICCPR and Convention Against Torture, or withdraw reservations and declarations that undermine "the spirit of international human rights instruments").

204 *See, e.g.*, Report of the Special Rapporteur on Torture and Other Cruel, Inhuman or Degrading Treatment or Punishment, p. 8, U.N. Doc. A/HRC/28/68 (Mar. 5 2015) (discussing the fact that the United States is the only country to still imprison children for life without parole for committing homicide).

205 UPR, *supra* note 203.

206 *See, e.g.*, An Act to Eliminate the Death Penalty and Allow for Life Imprisonment Without Eligibility for Parole, Pub. L. No. 2007, c. 204 § 1 (codified at N.J. Stat. Ann. § 2C:11–3 (West Supp. 2008)) (establishing life without parole as the most severe punishment available in New Jersey, thereby abolishing the death penalty in that state).

6

Recent Trends in U.S. Treaty Implementation

David P. Stewart

The U.S. Supreme Court's decision in *Bond v. United States*[1] refocused attention on the challenges of effectively implementing international treaties in U.S. law. At issue in that case was the validity of a criminal prosecution brought under federal legislation implementing the Chemical Weapons Convention.[2] How the Court chose to dispose of the issue – by deciding that the implementing statute, unlike the treaty itself, must be read "consistent with principles of federalism inherent in our constitutional structure"[3] – illustrates one of the constraints the United States faces in giving domestic effect to detailed multilateral treaties.

More broadly, the decision highlighted several other trends in contemporary treaty practice: the increasing complexity of multilateral treaties generated in the international community, the resulting challenges to effective domestic compliance in the United States, and – most significantly for purposes of this volume – a growing reliance on implementing legislation by the United States to give effect to its international obligations.

The Court's earlier holding in *Medellin v. Texas*[4] reflected a strong doctrinal inclination towards a "dualist" approach to treaties (as well as decisions

The author gratefully acknowledges the research assistance of a number of Georgetown Law students, including Marie Greenman, Beth Palkovic, Igor Herbey, Sandor Callahan, Reilly Stephens, Erin Reynolds, and April Kent.

1 Bond v. United States, 134 S. Ct. 2077 (2014).

2 Convention on the Prohibition of the Development, Production, Stockpiling and Use of Chemical Weapons and on Their Destruction, *opened for signature* Jan. 13, 1993, S. Treaty Doc. No. 103–21, 1974 U.N.T.S. 317. The basis for Mrs. Bond's prosecution was 18 U.S.C. § 229 (2012). That provision was enacted as part of the Chemical Weapons Convention Implementation Act of 1998, Div. I, Pub. L. No. 105–277, 112 Stat. 2681, 268–856 (1998).

3 *Bond*, 134 S. Ct. at 2088.

4 Medellin v. Texas, 552 U.S. 491, 505 (2008) (treaties "are not domestic law unless Congress has either enacted implementing statutes or the treaty itself conveys an intention that it be 'self-

of international courts), placing it squarely at odds with the unmistakable support for self-execution reflected in the Restatement (Third) Foreign Relations Law, as Professor Wuerth demonstrates in Chapter 4. This chapter surveys U.S. treaty practice since the publication of the Third Restatement in 1986 to determine whether the Executive and legislative Congressional branches today share the *Restatement's* monist inclinations. It is clear that they do not.

In recent U.S. practice, very few treaties have been "self-executing" in the sense of being directly applicable as (or displacing existing) U.S. law. Nearly all have been legislatively implemented. It is difficult, however, to discern consistent patterns of legislative implementation.

I. THE ISSUE OF IMPLEMENTATION

The topic of legislative implementation has been largely overlooked (or at least under-explored) in the continuing academic debates over when treaties are (or are not) "self-executing" and whether the treaty power can effectively expand Congress' authority to enact statutes.[5] That should not surprise. Over the course of its history, the United States has become party to a vast number of treaties (estimated to exceed 10,000), and yet, in the absence of a comprehensive database, there is no simple way to determine which treaties have been implemented legislatively and which have not. Each treaty needs to be researched individually.[6]

This chapter aims to contribute to the discussion by reviewing: (i) when implementing legislation has been deemed to be required, (ii) what kind of legislation has been enacted, and (iii) what trends can be identified in the practice of legislative implementation. Adopting the topical approach of the authors of the Third Restatement, the chapter focuses on a selection of treaties

executing' and is ratified on these terms") (citing Igartua–De La Rosa v. United States, 417 F.3d 145, 150 (1st Cir. 2005)).

5 *See generally* Carlos M. Vázquez, *The Abiding Exceptionalism of Foreign Relations Doctrine*, 128 HARV. L. REV. F. 305 (2015); Michael Ramsey, *Congress's Limited Power to Enforce Treaties*, 90 NOTRE DAME L. REV. 1539 (2015); Jean Galbraith, *Congress's Treaty-Implementing Power in Historical Practice*, 56 WILLIAM & MARY L. REV. 59 (2014); *cf.* John Yoo, *Globalism and the Constitution: Treaties, Non-Self-Execution, and the Original Understanding*, 99 COLUM. L. REV. 1955 (1999). On the history and meaning of the treaty supremacy rule generally, see David Sloss, THE DEATH OF TREATY SUPREMACY: AN INVISIBLE CONSTITUTIONAL CHANGE (2016).

6 The State Department's *Treaties in Force* does not indicate the mode of implementation. One must refer to the website of the Senate Foreign Relations Committee and to other congressional resources in order to determine this information.

by categories, rather than an exhaustive survey. In other words, rather than simply asking whether Congressional implementation of treaties has increased since the 1980s, the chapter inquires what the specific practice has been in a number of substantive categories in order to discover whether any variations in approach can be identified.

Two notes of caution. First, this chapter does not address whether, in implementing a treaty, Congress can exercise greater legislative authority than it would be able to do in the absence of a treaty. This much-debated issue, familiar to all who have pondered the meaning of the Supreme Court's 1920 decision in *Missouri v. Holland*,[7] was deftly avoided in *Bond* but is discussed by Professor McGuiness in Chapter 5 of this volume.

Second, this chapter does not engage in the debate over whether some treaties are, by their very nature, "self-executing" while others are not.[8] Treaties in the former category are sometimes said intrinsically to be directly applicable in U.S. courts as federal law without need of legislative implementation, while those in the latter category must always be implemented legislatively.[9] In my view, this a priori approach is at best uninformative and confusing, and more importantly inconsistent with actual practice. As Professor Wuerth observes, a treaty is generally described as self-executing if it is deemed not to require implementing legislation and as non-self-executing if it does.[10] The term itself thus offers no guidance about when a particular treaty does or should fall into one category or the other. Rather, the distinction is a law-making one, properly made by the political branches.

In recent U.S. practice, the determination whether to implement a given treaty by legislation has generally been made when the president transmits the treaty to the Senate for advice and consent to ratification. If the Executive branch considers that a given treaty must (or should) be given effect in

7 Missouri v. Holland, 252 U.S. 416 (1920).

8 *See, e.g.*, Foster v. Neilson, 27 U.S. (2 Pet.) 253, 314 (1829); United States v. Percheman, 32 U.S. (7 Pet.) 51 (1833); *see also* Medellin v. Texas, 552 U.S. 491, 514 (finding it important to implement the "time-honored textual approach" of looking to the treaty language to see what it says about self-execution and how clearly it states it). This topic is addressed by Professor Wuerth in Chapter 4 of this volume.

9 Restatement (Third), Foreign Relations Law § 111(3) (Am. Law Inst. 1987) asserts categorically that "a 'non-self-executing' agreement will not be given effect as law in the absence of necessary implementation." *See also Medellin*, 552 U.S. at 516 ("The point of a non-self-executing treaty is that it addresses itself to the political, *not* the judicial department; and the legislature must execute the contract before it can become a rule for the Court." (quoting *Foster*, 27 U.S. 253 at 314 (1829)) (emphasis in original)).

10 In practice, "self-execution" is not an all-or-nothing proposition, as some provisions of a treaty may be self-executing while others are not. *See* Third Restatement, Foreign Relations Law § 111(3).

domestic law by implementing legislation, it will so indicate to the Senate and will frequently send a proposed bill at the same time the treaty is considered.[11] In such cases, ratification is normally deferred until the necessary legislation has been enacted in order to ensure that the United States has the ability to comply with its international obligations when the treaty comes into force for it.

Historically, however, the president and the Senate (the constitutional "treaty-makers") have not always followed this practice. As a result, the matter has occasionally had to be decided by the judiciary after ratification— – in litigation, for example, when one party challenges the direct application of the treaty in the absence of implementing legislation or, when legislation has been enacted, the interpretation or constitutionality of that legislation.[12] Since the U.S. Supreme Court's decision in *Medellin*, however, both the Executive branch and the Senate Foreign Relations Committee have taken pains to specify, at the "advice and consent" stage, whether or not the treaty requires new implementing legislation.[13]

[11] For example, see S. TREATY DOC. NO. 109–12, at V (2007), noting the Department of Commerce had submitted a draft "Patent Law Treaty Implementation Act," provisions of which were eventually included in the Patent Law Treaties Implementation Act of 2012, Pub. L. No. 112–211, 126 Stat. 1527 (2012) (codified at 35 U.S.C. §§ 381–90 (2012)). In a few cases, the Senate has been the one to determine (in its resolution of advice and consent) that the treaty should be implemented legislatively and to condition advice and consent on that ground. A recent illustration of the Senate's approach arose in connection with the Defense Trade Cooperation Treaties with the United Kingdom and Australia, discussed in greater detail *infra* at notes 139–141. Both treaties contained preambular statements that they would be self-executing in the United States. The Senate Foreign Relations Committee objected and, as a result, both treaties were ratified on a non-self-executing basis.

[12] The U.S. Supreme Court has addressed this issue infrequently. *See* David Sloss, *Non-Self-Executing Treaties: Exposing A Constitutional Fallacy*, 36 U.C. DAVIS L. REV. 1, 75 n.305 (2002).

[13] See, for example, the statement in the Senate Foreign Relations Committee report recommending that advice and consent be given to the bilateral investment treaty with Rwanda, S. REP. NO. 111–8, at 10 (2010):

> Following the Supreme Court's decision in Medellin v. Texas, 552 U.S. 491 (2008), the committee has taken special care to reflect in its record of consideration of treaties its understanding of how each treaty will be implemented, including whether the treaty is self-executing. As noted in Executive Report 110–25, the committee believes it is of great importance that the United States complies with the treaty obligations it undertakes. In accordance with the Constitution, all treaties – whether self-executing or not – are the supreme law of the land, and the President shall take care that they be faithfully executed. In general, the committee does not recommend that the Senate give advice and consent to treaties unless it is satisfied that the United States will be able to implement them, either through implementing legislation, the exercise of relevant constitutional authorities, or through the direct application of the treaty itself in U.S. law. That view largely coincides with the executive's long-standing position.

For present purposes, we can therefore leave aside the largely theoretical debate about whether some (or all) treaties are (or should be) presumptively self-executing.[14] Instead, this chapter aims to survey recent instances when implementing legislation has in fact been considered necessary (or not), to discern possible patterns of practice, and to suggest overall trends and reasons for those trends.[15]

What the current investigation demonstrates is that, for the United States, legislative implementation of multilateral treaties has clearly become the predominant practice. In fact, since the publication of the Third Restatement on the Foreign Relations Law of the United States, very few multilateral treaties can accurately be described as self-executing. Almost all treaties denominated "self-executing" have been bilateral but have actually rested on, and been effectively implemented by, existing legislation. Genuinely self-executing treaties (i.e., those that stand by themselves as directly applicable federal law and are not otherwise legislatively implemented) are unquestionably the rare exceptions.

At the same time, almost no treaties (whether bilateral or multilateral) are purely non-self-executing in the sense that they are not given effect by some aspect of U.S. law.[16] In short, almost all treaties (bilateral or multilateral) are in fact substantively implemented by positive legislative enactment of one type or another.

[14] In my view, whether a treaty requires implementing legislation, or alternatively is deemed directly applicable and enforceable in U.S. courts, is a "law-making" decision and therefore one properly made (in the United States, at any rate) by the political branches. It is not a matter of the treaty negotiators' intent or the specific treaty language, nor should it be left, at least in the first instance, to the judiciary. Here, I readily acknowledge disagreement with the position taken by my colleague Carlos Vázquez in *The Four Doctrines of Self-Executing Treaties*, 89 AM. *J.* INT'L *L.* 695, 707 (1995). The degree of deference to be accorded by the courts to the decision of the constitutional "'treaty-makers'" is still another question.

[15] Nor will this chapter discuss the questions related to the wisdom or validity of the various "conditions" – reservations, understandings, declarations – upon which the United States has occasionally based its ratification of multilateral human rights treaties (and other treaties as well). Whether and when such conditions are necessary to accommodate the requirements of the treaty in question to relevant U.S. law, and/or to obtain the Senate's advice and consent to ratification, is an important and complicated issue. It is unquestionably related to the issue of legislative implementation. But it speaks to the substantive obligations that the U.S. Government is prepared to accept under the treaty in question more than to the question of whether to implement those obligations directly or through legislation.

[16] I recognize that in *Medellin*, the Supreme Court defined "non-self-executing" to mean not directly applicable as law in domestic courts. In distinction to that judicially oriented view, my use of the term approaches the issue from the perspective of treaty implementation.

In consequence, the traditional distinction between treaties that are self-executing and those that are not appears outmoded and to a degree misleading. One might more accurately speak of several distinct categories:

(i) treaties that are not themselves directly effective as U.S. law ("non-self-executing"), which include those
  (a) that have no effect in domestic law (such as some disarmament and military cooperation agreements),
  (b) for which an adequate legislative basis already exists in U.S. law (sometimes described as "pre-implemented"), and
  (c) for which new legislation is required prior to ratification in order to assure U.S. compliance;
(ii) treaties that connect to existing legislation by making technical (often country-specific) adjustments to that legislation (such as bilateral tax and extradition treaties); and
(iii) a relatively small number of treaties that operate alone as U.S. law without regard to any implementing legislation.

Although treaties in the second and third categories are often combined for descriptive purposes, they operate quite differently; and only those in the last group can truly be considered "self-executing" in the sense the term is used in the Third Restatement and by the U.S. Supreme Court.

Regarding types of legislative implementation, it is difficult to discern any clear patterns in U.S. practice. Determining the form and content of that legislation appears to be ad hoc, reflecting the specific treaty requirements, the nature and content of existing legislation and relevant decisional law, and the prevailing practices in the relevant substantive area. Some representative approaches, however, are identified below, as are some suggestions for greater institutionalization of how these issues are handled within the Executive branch.

What might explain the strong current preference of the political branches for legislative implementation of treaties? One might ascribe it in part to a protective (even parochial) view of the national legislature, in order to maintain "democratic" control of domestic law-making (meaning, for some, a clear disinclination to change the law solely through the treaty power). A more discerning assumption could be that modern multilateral treaties, by virtue of their complexity and level of detail, pose more difficult problems than bilateral agreements for U.S. implementation, especially in view of the contemporary concepts of limited federal authority and the impact of the Tenth Amendment (or, to use the Court's formulation in *Bond*, "'principles of

Federalism'"[17]). A third perspective, for which there appears to be substantial supporting evidence, is that treaties today rarely write on a domestic *tabula rasa* but almost always address issues on which domestic law and legislation already exists, so that implementation entails adjustment and adaptation, rather than *de novo* enactment.

II. TRENDS IN U.S. TREATY- MAKING

In the decades after the United States was founded, treaties were comparatively rare, almost always bilateral, and far more limited in purpose and scope than today.[18] As Paul Dubinsky shows in Chapter 3, for much of the nineteenth19th century, treaties were reciprocal undertakings between two states, and many aspects of treaty law were treated as a subset of the private law of contracts. Most treaties served to end wars, settle boundaries, resolve international claims, establish friendly relations, secure trade relations, and establish obligations under which one government undertook, within its borders, to protect the citizens and interests of the other country.[19] In the absence of international organizations or regional structures, such agreements were of course a staple component of foreign relations. Not surprisingly, most did not require domestic implementation.[20]

As the world grew more complicated and the role of United States in the world matured, the pace of treaty-making increased, especially following World War II. In the fifty years between 1889 and 1939, the United States concluded only 524 Article II treaties[21] (or on average, about 11 per year between 1930 and 1945).[22] By comparison, during the 53 years between 1947

[17] Bond v. United States, 134 S. Ct. 2077, 2088 (2014).

[18] *See, e.g., ibid.* at 2100 ("[T]reaties were typically bilateral, and addressed only a small range of topics relating to the obligations of each state to the other, and to citizens of the other – military neutrality, for example, or military alliance, or guarantee of most-favored-nation trade treatment.")

[19] The categories of treaties mentioned by the Founding Fathers concerned issues like "war, peace, and commerce." *See* THE FEDERALIST NO. 64, at 390 (John Jay) (Clinton Rossiter ed., 1961).

[20] The early exceptions, of course, were treaties requiring the appropriation of funds. This is not to say that all or even most were "self-executing" in the sense of being directly applicable as federal law, since most in fact had no domestic application.

[21] *See* LOUIS FISHER, CONG. RESEARCH SERV., S. Prt. 106–71, *TREATIES AND OTHER INTERNATIONAL AGREEMENTS: THE ROLE OF THE UNITED STATES SENATE* 39 (2001) [hereinafter CRS Study].

[22] The mean average is based on data provided in the CRS Study, *supra* note 21, at 39.

and 2000, the U.S. Senate gave its advice and consent to 796 treaties[23] (averaging, 16.5 treaties per year between the years 1946 and 2001).[24]

A defining characteristic of post–World War II international law has been an extraordinary growth in the number, scope, and detail of multilateral conventions. The cause is no mystery. It is largely a function of the creation of international organizations created and empowered to address a wide array of issues (from criminal law, transportation, communications and culture, to environment, trade, health, labor law, and human rights) in the interests of the global community. The extent to which conventional international law today effectively "legislates" would simply astonish the Founding Fathers.

Based on information from the Library of Congress' Treaty Documents webpage, over the past forty years, the number of multilateral treaties under consideration by the Senate Foreign Relations Committee has significantly exceeded the number of bilaterals.[25] Virtually all of the bilaterals have been denominated "self-executing," while the vast majority of the multilaterals have been "non-self-executing" and resting on existing or proposed legislation.[26]

[23] David Auerswald & Forrest Maltzman, *Policymaking through Advice and Consent: Treaty Consideration by the United States Senate*, 65 *J. of Pol.* 1097, 1102 (2003). This figure does not include treaties that were still pending in the Senate or withdrawn from the Senate calendar at the time of the publication of Auerswald and Matlzman's text. Nor does it include trade and tariff agreements concluded between 1947 and 2000, which the United States views as Executive agreements, requiring a Joint Resolution for their implementation. *See id.* at 1102, n. 9.

[24] *See* Jeffrey Peake et al., *President Obama, the Senate, and the Polarized Politics of Treaty Making*, 93 *Soc. Sci. Q.* 1295, 1298 n.5 (2012) (citing CRS Study). Deviations from this upward trend in U.S. treaty-making do, however, exist. In select years before 1945, the United States concluded as many treaties as it did in years after 1945. For example, in the years 1930 and 1935, the United States concluded twenty-five treaties. CRS Study, *supra* note 21, at 39. Only in 1979, 1980, 1996, 1979, 1998, and 1999 did the United States sign twenty-five or more treaties. *Ibid.* By comparison, in select years after 1945, the United States concluded very few treaties. In 1960, the United States concluded five treaties. *Ibid.* In 1964, the United States concluded three treaties. *Ibid.* These low numbers better reflect pre-1945 trends. Despite the anomalous conclusion rates in 1930, 1935, 1960, and 1964, the United States has generally signed more treaties each year after 1945 on a fairly consistent basis. In 1996 and 1997 for example, the United States concluded forty-eight and forty treaties respectively. *Ibid.*

[25] *See Treaty Documents*, Libr. of Cong., https://www.congress.gov/treaties?loclr=bloglaw (last visited Feb. 1625, 20176). Counting treaties that had been received or were "under consideration" or "pending" in 1985 (99th Congress), the ratio was 32 bilaterals to 47 multilaterals. In 1995 (104th Congress), the numbers were 56 bilaterals to 48 multilaterals; in 2005 (109th Congress), 21 bilaterals to 55 multilaterals; and in 2015 (114th Congress) 16 bilaterals to 35 multilaterals.

[26] Most of the bilateral treaties concerned tax, extradition, mutual legal assistance, investment, FCN, or consular relations issues, discussed *infra*. Of course, "self-execution" is not an all-or-nothing proposition; it is not unusual for some provisions in a non-self-executing multilateral to be given direct effect (those, for example, addressing extradition and mutual legal assistance issues in a broader context of international criminal cooperation).

Recently, the overall pace of U.S. treaty-making has decreased sharply. According to data available on the Library of Congress' website, the Senate approved 182 resolutions of advice and consent during the 99th through the 106th Congresses (1985–2000) or about 11.4 per year, and 108 resolutions of advice and consent during the 107th to the 110th Congresses (2001–2008), or about 15.5 per year. By comparison, in the 111th through 114th Congresses (2009–2015), the number of approvals had fallen to 13 (2.2 per year).[27] The last group (2009–2015) included six multilaterals; the first (1985–2000) more than fifty. The Senate, of course, does not itself set the pace of treaty submissions; the Administrations of George W. Bush and Barack Obama have submitted far fewer treaties to the Senate than previous presidents.[28]

III. THE APPROACH OF THE RESTATEMENT (THIRD)

The effort to articulate objective criteria regarding the various modes of U.S. treaty implementation has been undertaken before, resting largely on existing precedent.[29] Perhaps the most authoritative statement to date was set out by the authors of the Third Restatement based on their review of historical practice over the previous 200 years.[30]

27 *See Treaty Documents*, *supra* note 25.

28 Peake, *supra* note 24, at 1299. The U.S. experience is not unique. Global bilateral treaty-making also surged after 1945. According to information from the World Treaty Index's electronic treaty database, the world's nations signed over 4,000 bilateral treaties between 1920 and 1939. In comparison, between 1960 and 1979, the number had risen to approximately 29,000 bilateral treaties. Bilateral treaty-making peaked in 1977, when 2,156 treaties were concluded. Since then, however, the number has declined. Between 1980 and 1999, the number of bilateral treaties concluded has dropped down to an average comparable to that of mid-1950s and early 1960s. *See* WORLD TREATY INDEX, http://worldtreatyindex.com (follow "WTI Bilateral Agreement Dataset" hyperlink) (current through 1999).

29 As one early twentieth century commentator said, "[i]n order to determine what treaty provisions require legislative execution, it is necessary to resort to legislative precedents, as the promptness with which Congress has usually met these obligations has quite removed the question from judicial determination." *See* SAMUEL B. CRANDALL, TREATIES, THEIR MAKING AND ENFORCEMENT 118 (1904).

30 Interestingly, the Restatement clearly adopts the view that once an international agreement has been concluded, it is normally for the president to decide whether that agreement is "self-executing" or requires further legislation. It acknowledges, of course, that Congress may also consider whether legislation is necessary and, if so, what it should provide, and that the issue may also become one for the courts if, in the absence of legislation, a litigating party seeks to invoke the agreement as law. *See* THIRD RESTATEMENT, FOREIGN RELATIONS LAW § 111 cmt. h. It thus seems to offer little theoretical support for those who contend that a treaty simply "is" or "is not" self-executing, as if that were an inherent quality (or perhaps a matter for the treaty's negotiators) rather than a political, law-making decision by duly empowered national authorities.

The Third Restatement leaned unmistakably in favor of self-execution. Reporters' Note 5 to section 111 confidently affirmed that:

> Self-executing treaties were contemplated by the Constitution and have been common. They avoid delay in carrying out the obligations of the United States. They eliminate the need for participation by the House of Representatives (which the Framers of the Constitution had excluded from the treaty process), and for going to the Senate a second time for implementing legislation after the Senate had already consented to the treaty by two-thirds vote.[31]

While the Reporters were staunch "internationalists" of monist inclinations, the approach they adopted in fact reflected a functionally and textually oriented view. Reporters' Note 5 took the position that treaties *are* self-executing, so that *no* implementing legislation is required or customarily enacted, *when* they "can be readily given effect by executive or judicial bodies, federal or State, without further legislation… unless a contrary intention is manifest."[32] Thus, "[o]bligations not to act, or to act only subject to limitations, are generally self-executing."[33] Finally, in the view of Third Restatement, treaties are presumptively self-executing when they confer "rights on foreign nationals, especially in matters ordinarily governed by State law," for example in provisions in treaties of friendship, commerce, and navigation.[34]

This view likely reflected the fact that historically, most U.S. treaties had in fact been self-executing, and that practice may well have been consistent with the Founders' expectations. No doubt it was also faithful to the Reporters' belief that self-execution offers a simpler, faster, and more reliable method of ensuring U.S. compliance with treaty obligations.

At the same time, the Reporters did recognize the possibility that some treaties might not be adopted on that basis. Thus, section 111(3) characterized non-self-executing treaties as an "exception" to the general rule that "[c]ourts in the United States are bound to give effect to international law and to international agreements of the United States."[35] More to the current point, section 111(4) (taken together with the associated Comments and

[31] Third Restatement, Foreign Relations Law § 111, Reporters' Note 5. [32] *Ibid.*

[33] *Ibid.* (citing United States v. Rauscher, 119 U.S. 407 (1886)).

[34] Third Restatement, Foreign Relations Law § 111, Reporters' Note 5. The Comment states categorically that "[t]his has been true from early in United States history," and cites a line of cases from Ware v. Hylton, 3 U.S. (3 Dall.) 199 (1796) and Fairfax's Devisee v. Hunter's Lessee, 11 U.S. (7 Cranch) 603 (1813) through Kolovrat v. Oregon, 366 U.S. 187 (1961) and Asakura v. Seattle, 265 U.S. 332 (1924).

[35] Third Restatement, Foreign Relations Law § 111(3) 5.

Reporters' Notes) suggested that U.S. practice reflects several principles for determining when implementing legislation is or may be required. In particular, it implied that legislative execution is *mandatory*: (1) when by its terms the agreement itself so specifies;[36] (2) when the Senate or the Congress so provides;[37] and (3) when the Constitution so requires.[38] These conclusions bear careful analysis.

(1) In fact, the first situation (treaty specification) has seldom arisen in U.S. practice, before or after enactment of the Third Restatement.[39] At the international level, the ordinary practice, of course, is to leave the modalities of implementation to each state party in accordance with its own internal law. Given the wide variations in practice around the world, it would be very difficult (and likely objectionable in the multilateral context) for the treaty negotiators to specify a particular mode of implementation for all states party to the treaty. In some domestic legal systems, all treaties are directly enforceable; in others, none are; in still others – like the United States – it depends.[40] In consequence, the treaties themselves almost never address the issue.

(2) The second case (decision by domestic treaty-makers) is surely the most common in U.S. practice and actually reflects prevailing contemporary practice. It is entirely proper for either the president or the Senate to propose that implementation of a particular treaty should be accomplished by way of legislation. When and why they make that determination, of course, is the open question.

36 More specifically, "if the agreement manifests an intention that it shall not become effective as domestic law without the enactment of implementing legislation." *Ibid.* at § 114(a). In practice, it is extremely rare for any treaty to make such a statement, if for no other reason than (1) how a particular treaty is implemented is generally considered to be a matter of domestic law, and (2) very few foreign legal systems make the distinction between treaties that become directly applicable upon ratification and those that require legislative implementation. It is not unusual, however, for a modern multilateral treaty (say, in the area of criminal law or human rights) to call upon states parties to take necessary legislative or other action appropriate to their domestic constitutional systems to give effect to its provisions. Such provisions in no way prejudge the form of implementation or require it when, for example, domestic law is already adequate to the treaty's requirements.

37 "[I]f the Senate in giving consent to a treaty, or Congress by resolution, requires implementing legislation." *Ibid.* at § 111(4)(b).

38 "[I]f implementing legislation is constitutionally required." *Ibid.* at § 111(4)(c).

39 For a unique recent example, see the Defense Trade Cooperation Agreements with the United Kingdom and Australia, discussed *infra* at notes 140–2.

40 By contrast, an obligation to adopt any legislation necessary to give effect to the treaty is common in those contemporary multilaterals that are intended to harmonize domestic practice among treaty partners.

(3) The third circumstance (constitutional requirement) has been the subject of differing interpretations over a long expanse of time and actually generated conflicting points of view within the text of the Third Restatement itself. The clearest statement is found in Comment (i) to Section 111, which asserts that "[a]n international agreement *cannot* take effect as domestic law without implementation by Congress if the agreement would achieve what lies within the exclusive law-making power of Congress under the Constitution."[41] The difficulty has been in knowing which treaties fall into this category.

Today it appears to be accepted, as a prudential matter if not as a clear constitutional imperative, that no international agreement requiring the expenditure of money by the U.S. Government should be concluded without prior Congressional approval.[42] Constitutionally, of course, appropriations are made by legislation originating in the House of Representatives.[43] Whether or not the treaty power might also be a basis for authorizing if not appropriating funds (as the Third Restatement seems to suggest[44]), there is a very strong and entirely understandable reluctance on the part of the Executive branch to assume international obligations for which the necessary legislative authority might not be forthcoming.[45]

Perhaps as a result of the debate over the Jay Treaty, the rule against authorization-by-treaty appears to have become the accepted view in the early years of the Republic.[46] In 1803, for example, president Jefferson consulted with the House prior to opening the negotiations with France (which ultimately led to the "Louisiana Purchase") and negotiations with Spain (for the purchase of Florida).[47] This view is not without its critics, however. In his

41 Third Restatement, Foreign Relations Law § 111 cmt. i (emphasis added).

42 *See, e.g., id.*; North Atlantic Treaty art. 11, Apr. 4, 1949, 63 Stat. 2241, 34 U.N.T.S. 243; United States v. Smith, 18 U.S. 153 (1820); United States v. Hudson, 11 U.S. 32 (1812).

43 U.S. Const. art. II, § 7.

44 "Under Congressional rules and practice … a treaty may serve as 'authorization' for the appropriation of funds, requiring only appropriation legislation." Third Restatement, Foreign Relations Law § 111, Reporter's Note 6.

45 Motivated, *inter alia*, by the Anti-Deficiency Act, Pub. L. No. 97–258, 96 Stat. 923 (1982) (codified at 31 U.S.C. § 1341 (2012)).

46 *See* Chapter 1 of this volume.

47 *Cf.* Turner v. American Baptist and Missionary Union, 23 F. Cas. (5 McLean) 344, 345–46 (Cir. Ct. Mich. 1852):

> [M]oney cannot be appropriated by the treaty-making power. This results from the limitations of our government. The action of no department of the government, can be regarded as a law, until it shall have all the sanctions required by the constitution to make it such. As well might it be contended, that an ordinary act of congress, without

1902 survey, Samuel Crandall sided against such a large role for the House of Representatives exercised through the medium of implementing legislation:

> To admit the necessity of the concurrence of the House in all such treaties [those requiring an appropriation] is to admit that body to an agency in the making of a large proportion of treaties concluded, and deny the efficacy of the treaty-making power as organized in the Constitution... If the concurrence of the House is necessary to the validity of the stipulation, its action should precede the final ratification; for the execution of a treaty cannot be with safety begun on our part, or requested by the other contracting power, if its validity is still dependent upon the action of an independent legislative body.[48]

Whether this proposition can be generalized to a principle that some treaties (or treaty provisions) are "constitutionally" non-self-executing (meaning that in all cases they require implementing legislation) is open to significant question. It is certainly unclear which subjects, beyond appropriations, might fall within that category. The Third Restatement did offer some possible examples: bringing the United States "into a state of war," creating an international crime (e.g., genocide), requiring punishment of certain actions (e.g., hijacking), or imposing a new tax or a new tariff (since under Article I, Section 7, "all bills for raising Revenue shall originate in the House of Representatives").[49] Yet Reporters' Note 6 unmistakably retreated from this position, stating explicitly that "[t]here is no definitive authority for the rule set forth in Comment i that agreements on some subjects cannot be self-executing... That a subject is within the legislative power of Congress does not preclude a treaty on the same subject ... No particular clause of the Constitution conferring power on the Congress states or clearly implies that the power can be exercised only by Congress and not by treaty" (meaning, of course, a self-executing treaty).[50]

Reporters' Note 5 suggested a fourth category when it referred (without detailed discussion) to judicial decisions holding treaties to be non-self-executing when they concern industrial property and conveyance of land to Indian nations. Still another category seems to be identified when Reporters' Note 5 states that agreements are more likely to be found non-self-executing

> the signature of the president, was a law, as that a treaty which engages to pay a sum of money, is in itself a law.

See generally David L. Sloss, Michael D. Ramsey & William S. Dodge, International Law in the Supreme Court to 1860, *in* INTERNATIONAL LAW IN THE U.S. SUPREME COURT: CONTINUITY AND CHANGE 7, 19 (David L. Sloss, et al., eds. 2011).

48 CRANDALL, *supra* note 29, at 131–2.

49 THIRD RESTATEMENT, FOREIGN RELATIONS LAW § 111 cmt. h.

50 *Ibid.* at § 111 Reporters' Note 6.

when they affect an area in which "Congress has already regulated extensively."[51]

The main difficulty with the approach of the Third Restatement is that it assumes all treaties (and therefore any particular treaty) must be either self-executing or else implemented by legislation or, turned around, that treaties not affirmatively implemented legislatively are therefore self-executing. Appealing as this binary approach might be, the Reporters in fact recognized an intermediate category: treaties that are neither self-executing nor legislatively implemented at the time of ratification but with which existing law is compliant. Comment h to section 111 noted that "[t]here can, of course, be instances in which the United States Constitution, or previously enacted legislation, will be fully adequate to give effect to an apparently non-self-executing international agreement, thus obviating the need of adopting new legislation to implement it."[52] In current parlance, these would be denominated "preimplemented" treaties.

In point of fact, even before *Medellin*, it seems clear that the pro-self-executing Restatement view had not found much support in the judiciary. While references to Comment h have not been uncommon (typically for explication of the self-execution/non-self-execution distinction),[53] the preference for self-execution expressed in Reporters' Note 5 has seldom been cited by any court.[54]

[51] *Ibid.* at § 111, Reporter's Note 5 (citing Robertson v. General Electric Co., 32 F.2d 495, (4th Cir. 1929), *cert. denied*, 280 U.S. 571 (1929) (peace-treaty-making undertaking regarding patents on industrial property)).

[52] Third Restatement, Foreign Relations Law § 111 cmt. h (citing Sei Fujii v. California, 217 P.2d 481 (Cal. App. 1950), *rehearing denied*, 218 P.2d 595 (Cal. Dist. Ct. App. 1950), *reversed on this question but affirmed on other grounds*, 242 P.2d 617 (1952)).

[53] *See* Gross v. German Found. Indus. Initiative, 549 F.3d 605, 613 (3d Cir. 2008); *In re* Erato, 2 F.3d 11, 15 (2d Cir. 1993); *cf.* Safety Nat. Cas. Corp. v. Certain Underwriters At Lloyd's, London, 587 F.3d 714, 726 (5th Cir. 2009) (dismissing § 111 as the work of "an advocate for the enforcement of implemented treaty provisions.")

[54] *But see* Beharry v. Reno, 183 F. Supp. 2d 584, 594 (E.D.N.Y. 2002) ("treaties are generally treated as self-executing, that is, they are enforceable in courts once signed and ratified"), *rev'd sub nom.* Beharry v. Ashcroft, 329 F.3d 51 (2d Cir. 2003); McKesson Corp. v. Islamic Republic of Iran, 1997 WL 361177, at *12 (D.D.C. June 23, 1997), *rev'd in part sub nom.* McKesson HBOC, Inc. v. Islamic Republic of Iran, 271 F.3d 1101 (D.C. Cir. 2001); *see also* Rainbow Nav., Inc. v. Dep't of Navy, 686 F. Supp. 354, 357 (D.D.C. 1988) ("A court interprets a treaty as self-executing unless 'the agreement manifests an intention that it shall not become effective as domestic law without the enactment of implementing legislation, or in those rare cases where implementing legislation is constitutionally required'") (quoting Restatement (Second) Foreign Relations § 131 (Am. Law Inst., Revised Tentative Draft No. 1, 1980)). Indeed, despite the admonition in comment h that "[w]hether a treaty is self-executing is a question distinct from whether the treaty creates private rights or remedies," many courts continued to treat the two enquires as essentially coextensive. "Courts generally hold a treaty is non-self-executing when ... the treaty provides no private right of action." Fund for Animals, Inc. v. Kempthorne, 472 F.3d 872, 881 (D.C. Cir. 2006)

In practice, this seems to have led to a preference *against* self-execution, as courts, relying on *The Head Money Cases*,[55] moved toward a strong presumption against such private rights (sometimes even demanding express language to overcome it).[56] This presumption is sometimes grounded in a citation to Third Restatement § 907, comment a, which states "[i]nternational agreements, even those directly benefitting private persons, generally do not create private rights or provide for a private cause of action in domestic courts . . ."[57]

In practice, of course, not all treaties are either legislatively implemented or self-executing, and in fact some have fallen into the intermediate ("neither/nor") group contemplated by the Third Restatement. A recent example is the 2014 UN Convention on Transparency in Treaty-Based Investor-State Arbitration, which was transmitted to the Senate on the basis that it would not be self-executing *and* would not require any implementing legislation.[58]

IV TREATIES BY CATEGORY

In the debate over self-execution vs. non-self-execution, the discussion often proceeds on the basis that certain categories of treaties have traditionally not required implementing legislation of any kind. Treaties in some substantive areas of the law are often said to be presumptively self-executing, including

(Kavanaugh, J, concurring) (citing, *inter alia*, Tel-Oren v. Libyan Arab Republic, 726 F.2d 774, 808 (D.C. Cir. 1984)); *see also* Hamdi v. Rumsfeld, 316 F.3d 450, 468 (4th Cir. 2003) *vacated*, 542 U.S. 507 (2004); Goldstar (Panama) S.A. v. United States, 967 F.2d 965, 968 (4th Cir. 1992) ("Courts will only find a treaty to be self-executing if the document, as a whole, evidences an intent to provide a private right of action"); United States v. Thompson, 928 F.2d 1060, 1066 (11th Cir. 1991) ("A treaty is self-executing if it creates privately enforceable rights.").

55 112 U.S. 580, 598 (1884).

56 *See* Medellin v. Texas, 552 U.S. 491, 506 n.3 (2008); United States v. Jimenez-Nava, 243 F.3d 192, 195 (5th Cir. 2001); United States v. Li, 206 F.3d 56, 60 (1st Cir. 2000); *Goldstar*, 967 F.2d at 968. The statement in Cook v. United States, 288 U.S. 102, 119 (1933) is sometimes cited to the contrary ("[In] a strict sense the Treaty was self-executing, in that no legislation was necessary to authorize executive action pursuant to its provisions"), but properly read it reflects the clear intent of the political branches regarding direct applicability.

57 Third Restatement, Foreign Relations Law § 907 cmt. a; *see Medellin*, 552 U.S. at 506 n.3; United States v. Emuegbunam, 268 F.3d 377, 389 (6th Cir. 2001). The untruncated paragraph of comment a, reproduced below, is more equivocal than the strong presumption for which it is being cited:

> International agreements, even those directly benefiting private persons, generally do not create private rights or provide for a private cause of action in domestic courts, but there are exceptions with respect to both rights and remedies. Whether an international agreement provides a right or requires that a remedy be made available to a private person is a matter of interpretation of the agreement. Where a remedy was intended, suit against a foreign state (or the United States) might nonetheless be barred by principles of sovereign immunity, unless such immunity is found to have been waived.

58 Adopted by UN General Assembly Res. 69/116 (Dec. 10, 2014); *signed by* the United States Mar. 17, 2015; *see* S. Treaty Doc. No. 114–15 (Dec. 9. 2015).

criminal law treaties (in particular those relating to extradition and mutual legal assistance), tax treaties, treaties of amity or friendship, commerce, and navigation (FCN), civil judicial assistance treaties (such as the Hague Service and Evidence Conventions), and commercial law treaties.[59]

To test that proposition, this chapter looks at recent U.S. practice in these and some other substantive areas in an effort to identify patterns of execution and to identify particular types of implementing legislation. This necessarily limited sampling (organized by topic category) suggests some overall contours of the field.

A *Extradition and Mutual Legal Assistance Treaties*

Extradition and mutual legal assistance are procedural mechanisms for the transfer of individuals and evidence across national borders for purposes of criminal prosecution. Most extradition and mutual legal assistance treaties are bilateral, and they are among the most numerous to be considered by the Senate Foreign Relations Committee in recent decades. Moreover, they are routinely denominated as "self-executing."[60]

Upon closer consideration, however, it becomes apparent that in fact these treaties do not function as self-contained stand-alone instruments but instead rely directly on existing federal statutory and decisional law developed over many decades. Indeed, the primary purpose of these treaties is to make the necessary technical adjustments so that the foreign legal system in question can connect to and function effectively with the existing U.S. legislative structure. In effect, these treaties serve as "connectors" or "adapter plugs" enabling a workable bilateral relationship between the United States and various foreign legal systems while obviating the need for a significant number of country-specific statutory amendments.

As the Senate Foreign Relations Committee noted a few years ago in giving advice and consent to ratification of the extradition treaty with the European Union as well as twenty-seven related bilateral extradition treaties:

59 *See, e.g.*, Michael Van Alstine, *Federal Common Law in An Age of Treaties*, 89 CORNELL L. REV. 892, 922–7 (2004).

60 The United States is also party to some twelve bilateral and two multilateral treaties providing for the transfer of sentenced persons ("prisoner transfer treaties"). They are designated self-executing but, like extradition treaties, take effect through specific domestic legislation enacted for this specific purpose. *See, e.g.*, Transfer of Offenders to or from Foreign Countries Act, Pub. L. No. 95–144, 91 Stat. 1212 (1977) (codified at 10 U.S.C. § 955; 18 U. S.C. 3244 §§ 4100–4115 (2012)); *see generally International Prisoner Transfer Program*, U.S. DEP'T OF JUST., www.justice.gov/criminal-oeo/international-prisoner-transfer-program (last visited Feb. 16, 2017); 7 FAM 480, U.S. DEP'T OF STATE, www.state.gov/documents/organi zation/86611.pdf; Bishop v. Reno, 210 F.3d 1295 (11th Cir. 2000).

> The legal procedures for extradition are governed by both federal statute and self-executing treaties. Subject to a contrary treaty provision, *existing* federal law implements aspects of these treaties. See 18 U.S.C. §§ 3181 to 3196. No *additional* legislation is needed for the United States to fulfill its obligations under these treaties.[61]

Similar statements are also made with respect to mutual legal assistance treaties. The Senate Foreign Relations Committee said, for example, regarding the mutual legal assistance treaties with the European Union and its member states: "These treaties, which are self-executing, will be implemented by the United States in conjunction with applicable federal statutes, including 18 [sic] U.S.C. § 1782. No *additional* legislation is needed for the United States to fulfill its obligations under these treaties."[62]

Again, the reason is simple: national criminal justice systems around the world often differ significantly in the details of their procedural operation and substantive content. The point of bilateral extradition and mutual legal assistance treaties is to establish functional arrangements for bilateral cooperation by overcoming specific obstacles and inconsistencies on the basis of negotiated arrangements. No single formula can possibly fit every situation. At the same time, it is impractical to adopt separate legislative provisions for each bilateral arrangement. Hence, the "self-executing" aspect of the treaties allows them to establish a functional bridge between the general legislation and the particular circumstances of the negotiated bilateral arrangement. The treaties rest on, and provide supplemental provisions for, existing legislation; without such legislation, they could not function.[63]

B Criminal Law

By distinction, in U.S. practice, international treaties adopting substantive criminal law provisions are typically not self-executing but have instead been

[61] S. Exec. Rep. No. 110–12, at 7 (2008) (emphasis added).

[62] S. Exec. Rep. No. 110–13, at 10 (2008) (emphasis added). The proper citation is to Title 28; *see also* Treaty with Jordan on Mutual Legal Assistance in Criminal Matters, S. Treaty Doc. No. 114–4 at V (2015)("The Treaty is self-executing and will not require *further* implementing legislation") (emphasis added).

[63] See, for example, S. Exec. Rep. No. 106–24, at 18 (2000), favorably reporting on the Mutual Legal Assistance Treaties with Cyprus, Egypt, France, Greece, Nigeria, Romania, South Africa, Ukraine and the Inter-American Convention on Mutual Legal Assistance in Criminal Matters with Related Protocol, in which, for each of the treaties, the Foreign Relations Committee noted that "For the United States, the Treaty is intended to be self-executing; no *new or additional* legislation will be needed to carry out the obligations undertaken" (emphasis added).

implemented by the adoption of new legislation. In fact, such treaties themselves generally require states party to take whatever domestic steps are necessary in order to be able to prosecute the specific crimes articulated in the treaties. For example, the 1948 Convention on the Prevention and Punishment of the Crime of Genocide, which defines the crime of genocide, also directs the contracting parties to adopt "necessary legislation to give effect to the provisions of the Convention and, in particular, to provide effective penalties for persons guilty of genocide."[64] Similar provisions can be found in many international criminal law conventions.

It is generally accepted today that in U.S. law, criminal offenses must be affirmatively enacted.[65] For federal purposes, the Congress possesses the exclusive power to define federal crimes. In the case of the Genocide Convention, therefore, the federal criminal code was amended to include the crime of genocide in accordance with the Convention definition.[66] Section 1091 of Title 18 incorporates the Convention's definition of genocide (as well as incitement, attempt, and conspiracy to commit genocide) and establishes the jurisdictional basis for federal prosecutions of those crimes (*inter alia*, when the offense is committed, in whole or in part, in the United States, or when committed by a U.S. national or permanent resident).

As reflected in *Bond*, federalism can be an important consideration in this area. In the U.S. system, the general "police power" rests with the individual states of the Union, and the ability of the federal legislature to adopt criminal law is limited (at least in theory) by its enumerated powers under the Constitution. Where existing state law is adequate to the treaty's requirements, there will be reluctance to adopt new federal law or procedures to implement the treaty. In the case of the Genocide Convention, this sensitivity was reflected in 18 U.S.C. § 1092, which provides that nothing in the implementing legislation for the Convention "shall be construed as precluding the

64 Convention on the Prevention and Punishment of Crimes against Internationally Protected Persons art. V, *opened for signature* Dec. 14, 1973, 28 U.S.T. 1975, 1035 U.N.T.S. 167; *see generally* Robert E. Dalton, *National Treaty Law and Practice: United States*, 30 STUD. TRANSNAT'L LEGAL POL'Y 189, 207–8 (1999).

65 In the United States, federal criminal law is statutory. The Supreme Court ruled long ago that no federal common law of crimes existed and that the national government could punish newspaper editors only pursuant to duly passed legislation by Congress. *See* United States v. Hudson & Goodwin, 11 U.S. (7 Cranch) 32 (1812). Most states follow the same approach, although in a few, common law principles relating crimes and criminal procedure have been recognized by the courts as still in force to the extent not abrogated or repealed, expressly or impliedly, by statute.

66 For implementation of the Genocide Convention, see Pub. L. No. 100–606, 102 Stat. 3045 (1988) (codified at 18 U.S.C. §§ 1091–93 (2012)).

application of State or local laws to the conduct proscribed by this chapter, nor shall anything in this chapter be construed as creating any substantive or procedural right enforceable by law by any party in any proceeding."

On occasion, federal interests will take precedence. For example, the 1973 Convention on the Prevention and Punishment of Crimes against Internationally Protected Persons, including Diplomatic Agents, which requires states parties *inter alia* to criminalize any "murder, kidnapping or other attack upon the person or liberty of an internationally protected person, or any violent attack upon the official premises, the private accommodation or the means of transport of an internationally protected person likely to endanger his person or liberty."[67] In almost all instances, such crimes would violate applicable state or local law. Because of the importance of these issues to the national government, however, federal law was amended to make it a federal crime to assault, strike, wound, imprison, or "offer violence to" a foreign official, official guest, or internationally protected person covered by the Convention.[68]

Implementing statutory enactments may also be found for the 1979 Convention Against the Taking of Hostages,[69] the 1997 U.N. Convention for the Suppression of Terrorist Bombings,[70] and the 1999 U.N. Convention for the Suppression of the Financing of Terrorism.[71] The 1992 Convention on the Prohibition of the Development, Production, Stockpiling, and Use of Chemical Weapons and on Their Destruction (the treaty at issue in *Bond*)[72] was implemented through the Chemical Weapons Convention Implementation Act of 1998,[73] a long and detailed statute. Section 201 of that Act specifies the civil and criminal penalties for violation of the treaty's requirements. The criminal provisions were codified at 18 U.S.C. §§

67 Those provisions were given effect in U.S. law by Pub. L. No. 94–467, 90 Stat. 1997 (1976), which amended 18 U.S.C. §§ 112, 878 and 1116 (2012).

68 18 U.S.C. § 112 (2012).

69 Pub. L. No. 98–473, 98 Stat. 1837 (1970) (codified at 18 U.S.C. § 1203 (2012)). The same title enacted the "Aircraft Sabotage Act," (codified at 18 U.S.C. § 31 (2012)), which gave effect to the criminal provisions of the Convention for the Suppression of Unlawful Acts Against the Safety of Civil Aviation, Jan. 26, 1973, 24 U.S.T. 564, 974 U.N.T.S. 177.

70 Jan. 12, 1998, S. Treaty Doc. No. 106–6, 2149 U.N.T.S 256, implemented by the Terrorist Bombings Convention Implementation Act of 2002, Pub. L. No. 107–197, 116 Stat. 721 (2002) (codified at 18 U.S.C. § 2332f (2012)).

71 Jan. 10, 2000, S. Treaty Doc. No. 106–49, 2178 U.N.T.S. 229, implemented by the Suppression of the Financing of Terrorism Convention Implementation Act of 2002, Pub. L. No. 107–97, 116 Stat. 724 (2002) (codified at 18 U.S.C. § 2339C (2012)).

72 Jan. 13, 1993, S. Treaty Doc. No. 103–21, 1974 U.N.T.S. 317.

73 Pub. L. No. 105–277, 112 Stat. 2681–856 (1998) (codified at 22 U.S.C. §§ 6701–71 (2012); 18 U.S.C. §§ 229–229F (2012)).

229–229(f). The specific provision at issue in Mrs. Bond's case, 18 U.S.C. § 229 (a)(1), makes it unlawful for any person knowingly to "possess, or use . . . any chemical weapon."[74]

Not every substantive criminal law treaty to which the United States is a party has been directly implemented through the adoption of a new federal statute. For example, the 2003 U.N. Convention against Corruption was the first multilateral treaty to target corruption on a global basis.[75] Among its many provisions are those obligating states party to criminalize certain forms of corruption-related misconduct: bribery of national public officials, bribery of foreign public officials or officials of public international organizations, embezzlement by public officials, and certain offenses related to money laundering and obstruction of justice. It also obligates parties to adopt measures to enable confiscation of proceeds of (or property of equivalent value to the proceeds) used in or destined for use in offenses established under the Convention.

Because the second Administration of President George W. Bush regarded the Convention's provisions (taking into account its proposed reservations) as consonant with existing U.S. law, it determined that no implementing legislation was necessary, and accordingly the treaty as a whole was considered non-self-executing.[76] However, giving full effect to the provisions in articles 44 and 46 regarding extradition and mutual legal assistance required them to be "self-executing" in order to connect them effectively to existing law. For this reason, U.S. ratification was subject to the following declaration:

> The United States declares that the provisions of the Convention (with the exception of Articles 44 and 46) are non-self-executing. None of the provisions of the Convention creates a private right of action. Article 44 and Article 46 of the Convention contain detailed provisions on extradition and legal assistance that would be considered self-executing in the context of normal bilateral extradition practice. It is therefore appropriate to except those

[74] 18 U.S.C. §§ 175–8 (2012), adopted by Pub. L. No. 101–298, 104 Stat. 201 (1990). Numerous other examples exist, including the 1982 Convention on the Physical Protection of Nuclear Material, *opened for signature* Mar. 3, 1980, T.I.A.S. No. 11,080, 1456 U.N.T.S. 101, *implemented by* the Convention on the Physical Protection of Nuclear Material Implementation Act of 1982, Pub. L. No. 97–351, 96 Stat. 1663 (1982) (codified at 18 U.S.C. § 831 (2012)); the 1988 Rome Convention for the Suppression of Unlawful Acts Against the Safety of Maritime Navigation, Mar. 10, 1988, S. Treaty Doc. No. 101–1, 1678 U.N.T.S. 201, *implemented by* Sec. 60019 of the Violent Crime Control and Law Enforcement Act of 1994, Pub. L. No. 103–322, 108 Stat. 1796 (1994), 18 U.S.C. § 2280 (2012).

[75] U.N. Convention Against Corruption, Dec. 11, 2003, S. Treaty Doc. No. 109–06, 2349 U.N.T.S. 41.

[76] S. Treaty Doc. No. 109–06, at 11 (2005).

provisions from the general understanding that the provisions of the Convention are non-self-executing.[77]

The same approach was proposed by the Executive branch in connection with the 2000 U.N. Convention against Transnational Organized Crime.[78] Because the requirements of that treaty could be carried out on the basis of existing legislation, the president proposed to declare the provisions of the Convention (with the exception of Articles 16 and 18) to be non-self-executing. Those two articles contain detailed provisions on extradition and legal assistance and, in a bilateral context, would normally be considered self-executing; the president therefore considered it appropriate to except those provisions from the general understanding that the provisions of the Convention are non-self-executing.

The Senate concurred in this view, noting that articles 16 and 18 would be self-executing and "implemented by the United States in conjunction with applicable federal statutes."[79] It further stated that "[a]n existing body of federal and state law will suffice" to implement the Convention. Accordingly, it gave advice and consent to ratification subject, *inter alia*, to a declaration that stated in part that "current United States law . . . fulfills the obligations of the Convention for the United States" and accordingly that the U.S. "does not intend to enact new legislation" to fulfill those obligations.[80]

Another variant is offered by the 1984 U.N. Convention Against Torture and Other Cruel, Inhuman or Degrading Treatment or Punishment,[81] article 2(1) of which requires each state party to take "effective legislative, administrative, judicial or other measures to prevent acts of torture in any territory under its jurisdiction." When the treaty was submitted for advice and consent, the Reagan Administration did not consider implementing legislation necessary since existing federal and state law already provided grounds for prosecuting anyone accused of committing an act within the scope of the term "torture" as

77 S. Exec. Rep. No. 109–6, at 21 (2005).

78 U.N. Convention against Transnational Organized Crime, art. xviii, Feb. 23, 2004, S. Treaty Doc. No. 108–16(A), 2225 U.N.T.S. 209.

79 S. Exec. Doc. No. 109–4, at 3 (2005).

80 *Ibid.* at 7. A similar declaration was attached to the Senate's resolution of advice and consent with respect to the Protocol to Prevent, Suppress and Punish Trafficking in Persons, Especially Women and Children, which was considered together with the Convention itself. S. Exec. Rep. No. 109–4, at 9 (2005); *see also* Council of Europe Cybercrime Convention, Nov. 23, 2001, S. Treaty Doc. No. 108–11, 2296 U.N.T.S. 161; The Inter-American Convention against the Illicit Manufacturing of Trafficking in Firearms, Ammunition, Explosives and Other Related Materials, Nov. 14, 1997, S. Treaty Doc. No. 105–49, O.A.S.T.S. No. 63.

81 Convention Against Torture and Other Cruel, Inhuman or Degrading Treatment or Punishment, Dec. 10, 1984, S. Treaty Doc. No. 100–20, 1465 U.N.T.S. 85.

defined by the Convention. When the Senate gave advice and consent in 1994, it agreed, declaring that "the provisions of Articles 1 through 16 of the Convention are not self-executing" but were in fact implemented by existing federal and state law. To this extent, the Torture Convention was in effect "preimplemented."[82]

At the same time, article 8 requires Convention offences to be extraditable for purposes of any extradition treaty existing between states parties. Article 5 further requires each state party to "take such measures as may be necessary to establish its jurisdiction over such offences in cases where the alleged offender is present in any territory under its jurisdiction and it does not extradite him pursuant to article 8." Because existing law would not have permitted U.S. prosecution of a non-U.S. offender alleged to have committed a covered offense abroad, a new provision was added to the federal criminal code to permit the United States to comply with its article 8 obligations. That provision made it a federal crime for anyone, acting outside the United States, to commit (or attempt to commit) torture as defined by the Convention.[83] The federal statute may be applied whenever the alleged offender is a national of the United States acting anywhere in the world and present anywhere or is an alien physically present in the United States.[84]

While perhaps not strictly considered a criminal law treaty, the 2005 UNESCO Convention Against Doping in Sport[85] offers yet another example of a treaty resting for its implementation on preexisting U.S. law. In recommending that the Senate give its advice and consent to ratification, the Senate Foreign Relations Committee said (without specifying whether the treaty was self-executing or not) that:

> U.S. ratification of the Convention would not require any changes to U.S. law, because the Convention's provisions are consistent with current U.S. law and practice, including the Controlled Substances Act, the Dietary Health Education Act of 1994, and the Federal Food, Drug, and Cosmetic Act. As a result, no additional implementing legislation will be necessary, should the United States become a party to the Convention.[86]

[82] But unlike the Corruption Convention, implementation in this case rested mostly on state rather than federal law.

[83] 18 U.S.C. § 2340A (2012). The criminal provisions were implemented by § 505 of the Foreign Relations Authorization Act for FY 1994 and 1995, Pub. L. No. 103–236, 108 Stat. 382 (1994), which added 2340, 2340A and 2340B to Title 18.

[84] 18 U.S.C. § 2340B (2012). The Convention's *non-refoulement* obligations were separately implemented. *See, e.g.*, 8 C.F.R. § 208.18 (2009).

[85] International Convention Against Doping in Sport, *adopted by* UNESCO on Oct. 19, 2005, S. TREATY DOC. NO. 110–14 (2008).

[86] S. EXEC. REP. NO. 110–11, at 11 (2008).

Overall, the practice in this area is clear: when a treaty requires the United States to prosecute a given offense not already criminalized by existing federal or state law, the adoption of new legislation has been considered necessary prior to ratification. When existing criminal law (state or federal) is adequate to the treaty's requirements, no new legislation is adopted, yet the treaty is nonetheless considered non-self-executing. Thus, the Genocide Convention required new federal legislation because of the specific substantive elements set forth in the treaty, while by distinction, existing federal and state law was considered adequate to meet the requirements of the Torture Convention. Clearly, while considerations of federalism form part of the analysis, the overriding issue is to assure U.S. compliance with its treaty obligations.

C *Commercial and Securities Law*

The United States is party to a comparatively small number of treaties (other than FCN's) dealing with commercial and securities law. Here, a predilection for self-execution – dating back to the time of the Third Restatement – is evident. Yet even within this limited set, the practice has varied.

For example, the 1980 U.N. Convention on the International Sale of Goods (CISG)[87] was ratified by the United States on December 11, 1986 and became effective on January 1, 1988. This convention aims to provide a modern, uniform and fair regime for the formation of contracts for the international sale of goods and to promote certainty in cross-border business-to-business dealings. Even though the treaty had broad support in the U.S. business community, its ratification proved controversial for several reasons, *inter alia* because of inconsistencies with the relevant parts of the Uniform Commercial Code and reluctance to "federalize" commercial law.[88] Nonetheless, it was ratified on a self-executing basis and, to the extent it applies in a given commercial context, therefore overrides inconsistent state law, including UCC Article 2.

In 2004, the United States ratified the Convention on International Interests in Mobile Equipment (known as the "Cape Town Convention") and its associated Protocol on International Interests in Mobile Equipment on Matters Specific to Aircraft Equipment.[89] Together, the Convention and Protocol establish an international legal framework for the creation, priority, and enforcement of security and leasing interests in the creation of

[87] United Nations Convention on Contracts for the International Sale of Goods, *opened for signature* Apr. 11, 1980, S. TREATY DOC. NO. 98–9, 1489 U.N.T.S. 31.

[88] *See, e.g.*, Peter Winship, *Congress and the 1980 International Sales Convention*, 16 GA. J. INT'L & COMP. L. 707 (1986).

[89] *Ratified* Oct. 28, 2004, S. TREATY DOC. NO. 108–10, 2307 U.N.T.S. 285.

a worldwide International Registry where interests covered by the Convention can be registered.[90] The Convention adopts "asset-based financing" rules already in place in the United States, enhancing the availability of capital market financing for air carriers at lower cost.

Because the finance provisions of the Convention and Protocol were deemed consistent with UCC Article 9, no implementing legislation was required, except for technical amendments to certain authorities relating to the filing of interests in registries through the Federal Aviation Administration. Otherwise, the UCC continues to apply, and no changes to it were required. The necessary technical amendments were adopted in the Cape Town Treaty Implementation Act of 2004[91] to make conforming changes to provisions of domestic law governing the registration of aircraft and the recordation of instruments.

By contrast, the Hague Convention on the Law Applicable to Certain Rights in Respect of Securities held with an Intermediary (2006) was recently ratified on a self-executing basis. It addresses the choice-of-law problem that often arises when interests in securities rapidly move electronically through intermediaries in high volume, across national borders, and through different legal systems. As the president's Transmittal indicated, "existing U.S. laws, including the Securities and Exchange Act of 1934, already provide to U.S. Government regulatory and supervisory authorities . . . [the necessary] authority to act in areas covered by the Convention."[92]

The recent transmittals of three other conventions in this area illustrate the diversity of approaches necessary to implement U.S. treaty obligations effectively and with due regard to the federal structure. The U.N. Convention on the Use of Electronic Communications in International Contracts sets forth uniform rules to facilitate electronic communications in international business by enhancing legal certainty and commercial predictability.[93] In the United States, those rules are codified in both federal and state law.[94] Although the treaty's provisions are substantially similar to existing U.S. law,

90 S. Treaty Doc. No. 108–10, at III (2000).

91 *See* Cape Town Implementation Act, Pub. L. No. 108–297, 118 Stat. 1095 (2004) (codified at 49 U.S.C. §§ 44101, 44107–08, 44113 (2012)).

92 S. Treaty Doc. No. 112–6, at VIII (2012). The Senate gave advice and consent to this Convention on Sept. 28, 2016. The treaty was ratified on Dec. 15, 2016 and accordingly entered into force on Apr. 1, 2017.

93 G.A. Res. 60/21 (Nov. 23, 2005).

94 *See* Electronic Signatures in Global and National Commerce ("E-Sign") Act, Pub. L. No. 106–229, 114 Stat. 468 (2000) (codified at 15 U.S.C. §§ 7001–06, 7021, 7031 (2012)); Unif. Electronic Transactions Act (Unif. Law Comm'n 1999), www.uniformlaws.org/Act.aspx?title=Electronic%20Transactions%20Act.

the Obama Administration stated its intent to propose separate implementing legislation.[95] Similarly, that Administration considered that implementing legislation would be required for the U.N. Convention on Independent Guarantees and Stand-by Letters of Credit,[96] which is substantively similar to (but not exactly the same as) the analogous provisions of the Uniform Commercial Code.[97] By contrast, the U.N. Convention on the Assignment of Receivables in International Trade,[98] which contains uniform rules to facilitate modern receivables financing practices, was proposed for ratification on a self-executing basis since its provisions "do not differ in any significant respect from those contained in existing U.S. law" (meaning article 9 of the Uniform Commercial Code).[99]

Somewhat paradoxically, the limited role of the federal government in the broad field of transactional commercial law appears to push in favor of self-execution (despite federalism concerns) because of the likely challenges of getting Congress to adopt legislation. At the same time, in the securities field, where federal authority is clear (but not exclusive), there is an apparent disinclination to intrude into areas considered state purviews.

D. *Intellectual Property*

In the United States, the intellectual property field is legislatively regulated, primarily by federal statutes but also by state trade secret laws. It is hardly surprising, therefore, that (as the Third Restatement recognized) the implementation of international treaties in the areas of patents, trademarks, and copyright has taken place through federal statutory enactments.

In 2013, the United States ratified the 2000 Patent Law Treaty (promulgated by the World Intellectual Property Organizations or WIPO). In recommending that advice and consent be given to this convention, the Senate Foreign Relations Committee stated clearly:

> Implementing legislation is required for this Treaty. It is expected, therefore, that the United States will not deposit its instrument of ratification until this legislative process is complete, so as to ensure that the United States is capable of complying with its obligations under the Treaty. Specifically, Title 35 of the United States Code must be amended in order to comply with the Patent Law Treaty. Implementing legislation will focus mainly on

95 S. Treaty Doc. No. 114–15, at III, V (2016).
96 *Adopted* Dec. 11, 1995, 2169 U.N.T.S. 163.
97 S. Treaty Doc. No. 114–9, at III, VI (2016).
98 G.A. Res. 56/81 (Dec. 12, 2001). 99 S. Treaty Doc. No. 114–7, at III, V (2016).

> amendments relating to the patent application filing date; relief in respect of time limits and reinstatement of rights due to an unintentional abandonment or delay; and restoration of priority rights due to an unintentionally delayed filing of a subsequent application. The Department of Commerce has submitted a draft bill to Congress entitled the "Patent Law Treaty Implementation Act" and it is currently under consideration by the Committees on the Judiciary of the House and Senate.[100]

The necessary legislation was adopted as the Patent Law Treaties Implementation Act of 2012 (PLTIA).[101]

The 1994 WIPO Trademark Law Treaty, which the United States ratified in 1998, was given effect by the Trademark Law Treaty Implementation Act.[102] That statute amended various provisions of the Trademark Act of 1946, to bring U.S. law into conformity with the treaty.[103]

Adherence by the United States to the Protocol Relating to the Madrid Agreement Concerning the International Registration of Marks, adopted at Madrid on June 27, 1989 (the "Madrid Protocol") was deemed not to require any substantive changes to U.S. trademark laws, but legislation was required to make necessary modifications in procedure.[104] The 1996 WIPO Copyright Treaty and the 1996 WIPO Performances and Phonograms Treaty[105] required legislation for certain provisions. The necessary provisions were adopted as part of the 1998 Digital Millennium Copyright Act.[106] The Agreement on Trade-Related Aspects of Intellectual Property Rights (TRIPS) is also non-self-executing, implemented by the Uruguay Round Agreements Act.[107]

Two more recent examples may be cited to the same effect: the 2012 Beijing Treaty on Audiovisual Performances[108] and the Marrakesh Treaty to Facilitate Access to Published Works for Persons Who Are Blind, Visually Impaired, or Otherwise Print Disabled.[109]

100 S. EXEC. REP. NO. 110–06, at 3–4 (2007).

101 Pub. L. No. 112–211, 126 Stat. 1527 (2012) (codified at 35 U.S.C. §§ 381–90 (2012)).

102 Pub. L. No. 105–330, 112 Stat. 3064 (1998).

103 15 U.S.C. § 1051, 1057, 1058–60, 1062, 1064, 1091, 1094, 1113–15, 1121, 1124, 1126 (2012).

104 See Madrid Protocol Implementation Act, § 13401 of the 21st Century Department of Justice Appropriations Authorization Act, Pub. L. No. 107–273, 116 Stat. 1913 (2002) (codified at 15 U.S.C. §§ 1141–1141n (2012)).

105 S. TREATY DOC. NO. 105–17(A) (1997) and S. TREATY DOC. NO. 105–17(B) (1997), respectively.

106 Title I, Pub. L. No. 105–304, 112 Stat. 2860 (1998) (codified at 17 U.S.C. § 101 (2012)).

107 Pub. L. No. 103–465, §§ 101–103, 108 Stat. 4809, 4814–19 (1994) (codified in scattered sections of 15 U.S.C. § 1052, 17 U.S.C. § 101, and 35 U.S.C. §§ 104, 154).

108 S. TREATY DOC. NO. 114–8 at III (2016) ("Proposed legislation is being submitted to both houses of the Congress in conjunction with this transmittal.").

109 S. TREATY DOC. NO. 114–6 at III (2016) (noting that legislation would be required).

E Family Law

In recent years, the United States has become party to several important treaties regarding parental rights in respect of children and is considering ratification of several others. Unsurprisingly, ratification of these treaties has generated federalism concerns, because most issues of family law in the United States remain a matter of state law. In addition, to the extent they contemplate the judicial resolution of transnational family disputes (in state and federal court), these treaties require legislative implementation (addressing both jurisdictional and substantive aspects).

For example, the 1980 Hague Convention on the Civil Aspects of International Child Abduction provides an internationally agreed upon and effective method for returning a child who has been abducted by a parent from one member country to another.[110] The United States ratified the treaty in 1988.[111] The Senate Foreign Relations Committee Report (and the resolution of advice and consent to ratification) did not explicitly specify whether the treaty should be considered non-self-executing, but it was implemented by the 1988 International Child Abduction Remedies Act ("ICARA").[112] That statute gives "[t]he courts of the States and the United States district courts . . . concurrent original jurisdiction of actions arising under the Convention" and authorizes a person who seeks a child's return to file a petition in state or federal court and instructs that the court "shall decide the case in accordance with the Convention."[113] If the child in question has been "wrongfully removed or retained within the meaning of the Convention," the child shall be "promptly returned," unless an exception is applicable.[114]

The 1993 Hague Convention on Protection of Children and Co-operation in Respect of Intercountry Adoption was ratified by the United States in 1998[115] on a non-self-executing basis[116] and implemented by the Intercountry Adoption Act of 2000.[117] That statute established an accreditation regime for

[110] Oct. 25, 1980, S. Treaty Doc. No. 99–11, 1343 U.N.T.S. 98 (*entered into force* for the United States, July 1, 1988).

[111] S. Treaty Doc. No. 99–11, (1986); *see also* Sean and David Goldman International Child Abduction Prevention and Return Act of 2014, Pub. L. No. 113–150, 128 Stat. 1807 (2014).

[112] Pub. L. No. 100–300, 102 Stat. 437 (1988) (codified at 42 U.S.C. § 11601 (2012)).

[113] *See* 42 U.S.C. § 11603(a)-(b), (d) (2012). Cases based on the Convention have now reached the Supreme Court in several instances. *See, e.g.*, Lozano v. Montoya Alvarez, 134 S. Ct. 1224 (2014); Abbott v. Abbot, 560 U.S. 1 (2010).

[114] 42 U.S.C. § 11601(a)(4) (2012).

[115] Mar. 31, 1994, S. Treaty Doc. No. 105–51, 1870 U.N.T.S. 167.

[116] S. Exec. Rep. No. 106–14, at 10–11 (2000).

[117] Pub. L. No. 106–279, 114 Stat. 825 (2000) (codified at 42 U.S.C. §§ 14901–54 (2012)).

persons in the United States who offer or provide adoption services in connection with a Convention adoption. Additional provisions are found in the Intercountry Adoption Universal Accreditation Act of 2012.[118] Federal regulations regarding the accreditation of agencies and approval of persons have also been adopted.[119]

In 2007, the United States signed the Hague Convention on the International Recovery of Child Support and Other Forms of Family Maintenance,[120] and the Senate Foreign Relations Committee reported the treaty favorably in 2010[121] on the basis that it would not be self-executing. This treaty addresses issues of domestic enforcement of foreign orders of support, and its obligations are accordingly addressed to governmental agencies as well as the courts. Although the Convention is considered largely consistent with current U.S. federal and state law and practice, implementation is being effected by adoption of an amended version of the Uniform Interstate Family Support Act (UIFSA)[122] by the individual states and other relevant jurisdictions, as well as through conforming amendments to Title IV of the Social Security Act, through which federal funding is supplied to state adoption agencies.[123]

F Arbitration/Dispute Settlement

A somewhat different mode of implementation was employed for one of the most important treaties from the perspective of private practitioners involved in transnational litigation and commercial dispute settlement, namely, the U.N. Convention on the Recognition and Enforcement of Foreign Arbitral Awards of 1958, commonly referred to as the "New York Convention."[124] In this instance, implementation was accomplished neither by self-execution nor the adoption of detailed legislation but rather through a hybrid

[118] Pub. L. No. 112–276, 126 Stat. 2466 (2013) (codified at 42 U.S.C. § 14925 (2012)).

[119] *See* 22 C.F.R. pt. 96 (2000). [120] S. TREATY DOC. NO. 110–21, at III (2007).

[121] S. EXEC. REP. NO. 111–02, at 8, 9 (2010), advice and consent to ratification given Sept. 29, 2010.

[122] Interstate Family Support Act Amendments (2008), 9 pt. 1 U.L.A. 121 (Supp. 1994); *see* UNIFORM LAW COMM'N, www.uniformlaws.org.

[123] Pub. L. No. 113–183, 128 Stat. 1919 (2014). The Instrument of Ratification was deposited on Sept. 7, 2016 and the Convention entered into force for the United States on Jan. 1, 2017.

[124] Convention on the Recognition and Enforcement of Foreign Arbitral Awards, June 10, 1958, 21 U.S.T. 2517, 330 U.N.T.S. 38. *See* Message from the President of the United States transmitting the Convention on the Recognition and Enforcement of Foreign Arbitral Awards, Exec. E., 90th Cong., 2d Sess. (1968).

mechanism: the Convention was itself enacted into federal law as Chapter Two of the Federal Arbitration Act.[125]

Ratification of this convention proved controversial from a federalism perspective, despite the fact that long-standing federal law (adopted in 1925) had endorsed arbitration as a method of dispute settlement and granted federal courts jurisdiction to enforce domestic arbitral agreements and awards. Because the federal courts had experience in this field, and the terms of the Convention were straightforward, direct incorporation of the treaty was both practicable and a way of diminishing the federalism issues (in comparison to self-execution).

Similarly, Chapter 3 of the Federal Arbitration Act incorporated the 1975 Inter-American Convention on International Commercial Arbitration (the so-called "Panama Convention"), providing for its direct enforcement in U.S. courts in accordance with that chapter.[126]

This mode of direct legislative incorporation has not been repeated in other areas. Even in the field of arbitration, direct legislative incorporation was not followed in the case of the 1965 Convention on the Settlement of Investment Disputes between States and Nationals of Other States (the so-called "Washington Convention"), to which the United States became a party in 1966.[127] The overall purpose of the International Center for the Settlement of Investment Disputes (ICSID) is "to provide facilities for conciliation and arbitration of investment disputes between Contracting States and nationals of other Contracting States in accordance with the provisions of [the] Convention."[128] ICSID's jurisdiction "extend[s] to any legal dispute arising directly out of an investment, between a Contracting State (or any constituent subdivision or agency of a Contracting State designated to the Centre by that State) and a national of another Contracting State, which the parties to the dispute consent in writing to submit to the Centre."[129] Pursuant to Article 54(1) of the Convention, "[e]ach Contracting State shall recognize an award rendered pursuant to th[e] Convention as binding and enforce the pecuniary

125 Pub. L. No. 91–368, 84 Stat. 692 (1970) (codified at 9 U.S.C. §§ 201–208 (2012)). Section 201 provides simply that "[t]he Convention on the Recognition and Enforcement of Foreign Arbitral Awards of June 10, 1958, shall be enforced in United States courts in accordance with this chapter."

126 9 U.S.C § 301 (1990) ("The Inter-American Convention on International Commercial Arbitration of January 30, 1975, shall be enforced in United States courts in accordance with this chapter."). Chapter 3 was added by Pub. L. No. 101–369, 104 Stat. 448 (1990).

127 ICSID Convention on the Settlement of Investment Disputes between States and Nationals of Other States, *opened for signature* Mar. 18, 1965, 17 U.S.T. 1270, 575 U.N.T.S. 159 (entered into force Oct. 14, 1966).

128 *Ibid.* at Art. 1(2). 129 *Ibid.* at Art. 54(1).

obligations imposed by that award within its territories as if it were a final judgment of a court in that State."

For purposes of U.S. law, the ICSID Convention was deemed non-self-executing. Accordingly, a new section was added to the U.S. Code providing that an award of an ICSID tribunal "shall create a right arising under a treaty of the United States" and the "pecuniary obligations imposed by such an award shall be enforced and shall be given the same full faith and credit as if the award were a final judgment of a court of general jurisdiction of one of the several States."[130]

As noted above, still a different approach was followed in respect of the 2014 UN Convention on Transparency in Treaty-Based Investor-State Arbitration, for which ratification was proposed on the basis that it would neither be self-executing nor require implementing legislation.[131]

G *Arms Control and Defense Cooperation*

The situation with respect to arms control and defense cooperation treaties is mixed. Many have not required any implementation in domestic law. For example, the 1991 START Treaty on the reduction and limitation of strategic offensive arms (START I) was ratified in 1994 without implementing legislation or even mention of its non-self-executing status.[132] The same was true of the START II Treaty in 1993[133] as well as the Treaty between the United States of America and the Russian Federation on Strategic Offensive Reductions, signed at Moscow on May 24, 2002 (the "Moscow Treaty"),[134] neither of which was implemented legislatively. As the Third Restatement recognized, when compliance with a treaty does not rest on or entail enforcement at the domestic level, no need exists for implementation (direct or otherwise).

More recently, the 2013 Arms Trade Treaty was transmitted to the Senate in December 2016 on a non-self-executing basis because the relevant "U.S. national control systems and procedures ... already met or exceed the

[130] Pub. L. No. 89–532, 80 Stat. 344 (1966) (codified at 22 U.S.C. § 1650a(a) (2012)).

[131] Note 58, *supra*.

[132] Treaty between the United States of America and the Union of Soviet Socialist Republics on the Reduction and Limitation of Strategic Offensive Arms (the START Treaty), U.S.-U.S.S.R., July 31, 1991, S. Treaty Doc. No. 102–20 (1991).

[133] Treaty with the Russian Federation on Further Reduction and Limitation of Strategic Offensive Arms (the START II Treaty), U.S.-Russ., Jan. 3, 1993, S. Treaty Doc. No. 103–1 (1993); *see* S. Exec. Rep. No. 104–10 (1995).

[134] Treaty Between the United States of America and the Russian Federation on Strategic Offensive Reductions, U.S.-Russ., May 24, 2002, S. Treaty Doc. No. 107–8 (2002); *see* S. Exec. Rep. No. 108–1 (2003).

requirements of the Treaty" and accordingly "no additional legislation or regulation is required to comply" with its provisions.[135]

On the other hand, the 1972 Convention on the Prohibition of the Development, Production and Stockpiling of Bacteriological (Biological) and Toxin Weapons and on Their Destruction ("Biological Weapons Convention"), which the United States ratified in 1975, did require domestic action. It was implemented by the Biological Weapons Anti-Terrorism Act of 1989.[136] That statute made it a federal crime knowingly to develop, produce, stockpile, transfer, acquire, retain, or possess any biological agent, toxin, or delivery system for use as a weapon, or knowingly to assist a foreign state or any organization to do so. It also authorized the Attorney General, *inter alia*, to seek warrants authorizing the seizure of any biological agent, toxin, or delivery system that "exists by reason of" such prohibited conduct.

The 1980 Convention on the Physical Protection of Nuclear Material, to which the United States became a party in 1982,[137] requires each state party to take "appropriate steps within the framework of its national law and consistent with international law" to ensure the protection of nuclear material within its territory, on board ships and aircraft subject to its jurisdiction, and otherwise "within its territory." It also requires states party, *inter alia*, to criminalize "[t]he intentional commission" of acts constituting the "receipt, possession, use, transfer, alteration, disposal or dispersal of nuclear material and which causes or is likely to cause death or serious injury to any person or substantial damage to property." The Convention also requires states party to criminalize theft or robbery of nuclear material, embezzlement or fraudulent obtaining of nuclear material, an act constituting a demand for nuclear material by threat or use of force or by any other form of intimidation, or a threat to use nuclear material to cause death or serious injury to any person or substantial property damage.[138] For the United States, the Convention was implemented by a statute establishing the required criminal provisions and penalties.[139]

The 1990 Treaty on Conventional Armed Forces in Europe (CFE), involving sixteen NATO members as well as the six Warsaw Pact states, was one of

[135] SEN. TREATY DOC. No. 114–14 at V (2016).

[136] Pub. L. No. 101–298, 104 Stat. 201 (1990) (codified at 18 U.S.C. §§ 175–8 (2012)).

[137] Nuclear Material Physical Protection Convention between the United States of America and Other Governments, Mar. 3, 1980, T.I.A.S. No. 11080, 1456 U.N.T.S. 101; *see* S. EXEC. REP. NO. 97–18 (1981).

[138] *Ibid.*

[139] Convention on the Physical Protection of Nuclear Material Implementation Act of 1982, Pub. L. No. 97–351, 96 Stat. 1663 (1982) (codified at 18 U.S.C. § 831 (2012)).

the most far-reaching and complex arms control treaties ever negotiated.[140] Among other things, it set agreed-upon troop and equipment ceilings, required the destruction of certain categories of equipment, and established mechanisms for information exchange, monitoring and oversight.[141] The United States became a party in 1991 and implemented the Convention through amendments to relevant federal law (specifically, the Arms Export Control Act and related authorities) to enable the president to transfer certain treaty-limited equipment to NATO member states.[142] Section 2 of the statute stated that "the authorities provided in this chapter shall be exercised consistent with the obligations incurred by the United States in connection with the CFE Treaty."[143]

Recently, the question of self-execution arose in connection with the bilateral Defense Trade Cooperation Treaties with the United Kingdom and Australia.[144] These agreements aimed to provide protections for U.S. defense articles and services exported to treaty partners under the Treaty through application of foreign law rather than through revisions to the U.S. export control regime. In an effort to circumvent certain provisions of the Arms Export Control Act and related ITAR regulations, both treaties included preambular "understandings" that they would be "self-executing in the United States." The Foreign Relations Committee objected, finding this statement to be "unprecedented in U.S. treaties," "problematic," and "substantively suspect in that it purported to rule out the use of legislation to make clear the federal government's authority to impose criminal or civil penalties for violations of the treaties, their implementing arrangements, and regulations issued to implement the treaties."[145] In response, the Senate's resolutions of advice and consent contained contrary declarations, making clear that the treaties are "not self-executing in the United States, notwithstanding the statement in the preamble to the contrary."[146]

140 Treaty on Conventional Armed Forces in Europe (CFE), Nov. 19, 1990, S. TREATY DOC. NO. 102–8, 30 I.L.M. 1.

141 *Ibid.*

142 Pub. L. No. 102–228, 105 Stat. 1691 (1991) (codified at 22 U.S.C. § 2799 (2012)).

143 22 U.S.C. § 2799(a) (2012).

144 Treaty between the Government of the United States of America and the Government of the United Kingdom of Great Britain and Northern Ireland Concerning Defense Trade Cooperation, U.S.-UK, June 21 and 26, 2007, S. TREATY DOC. NO. 110–7 (2007); Treaty between the Government of the United States of America and the Government of Australia Concerning Defense Trade Cooperation, U.S.-Austl., Sept. 5, 2007, S. TREATY DOC. NO. 110–10 (2007).

145 S. EXEC. REP. NO. 111–5, at 5, 11–12, 22, 34, 41 (2010).

146 *Ibid.* at 11.

H Human Rights Treaties

Over the past twenty-five years, the United States has ratified a number of international human rights treaties (beginning with the Genocide and Torture Conventions, discussed above by reason of their criminal provisions). Because existing law has been considered adequate to the requirements of the treaties (as accepted by the United States), they have generally been denominated as non-self-executing and, at the same time, as requiring no new legislation.[147]

For example, in 1992, the United States became a party to the International Covenant on Civil and Political Rights.[148] In giving advice and consent to ratification, the Senate Foreign Relations Committee agreed with the Administration's proposal that the substantive provisions of the Covenant should be considered "non-self-executing."[149] As the Administration explained, no implementing legislation was necessary since existing U.S. law "generally complies with the Covenant."[150] The "non-self-executing" declaration (virtually identical to the one taken with respect to the Torture Convention) was in part intended to signify that the Covenant would not create a cause of action in U.S. courts.[151]

147 Ample precedent for this approach existed in the long-standing practice followed with respect to the multilateral "labor law" conventions adopted by the International Labor Organization. Those treaties have traditionally been said to require no implementing legislation because relevant U.S. law and practice was sufficient for full U.S. compliance with the obligations in question. Thus, like some of the criminal law and commercial law treaties discussed above, they could be considered "pre-implemented" and therefore ratified on a non-self-executing basis. For example, when ILO Convention No. 111 (1958) concerning discrimination in employment and occupation was transmitted to the Senate, President Clinton stated that "U.S. law and practice fully comport with its provisions." Letter of Transmittal from President Clinton to the Senate, S. TREATY DOC. NO. 105–45, at III (1998). That conclusion was supported by a detailed legal analysis which concluded that "ratification of Convention 111 would not, in any way, change or require any change in current United States law and practice." *Ibid.* at 34. The same conclusion has been reached with respect to a significant number of other ILO conventions over the years. Other examples include the 1957 Abolition of Forced Labor Convention (ILO No. 105), ratified in 1991; the 1978 Labor Administration Convention (ILO No. 150), which the United States ratified in 1995 (S. TREATY DOC. NO. 103–26); the 1985 Labor Statistics Convention (ILO No. 160), ratified in 1990 (S. TREATY DOC. NO. 101–2); the 1995 Health and Safety in Mines Convention (ILO No. 176) ratified in 2001 (S. TREATY DOC. NO. 106–8); and the 1999 Convention on the Worst Forms of Child Labor (ILO No. 182) (S. TREATY DOC. NO. 106–5), ratified in 1999.

148 International Covenant on Civil and Political Rights, Dec. 16, 1966, 999 U.N.T.S. 171.

149 *See* S. EXEC. REP. NO. 102–23, at 19 (1992). For the full text of the Senate's resolution, see 138 CONG. REC. 8070 (1992).

150 *Ibid.* To the extent of a few variations with existing law, reservations were taken.

151 *Ibid.*

Similarly, the 1965 International Convention on the Elimination of All Forms of Racial Discrimination was ratified in 2002 on a non-self-executing basis for the same reason.[152]

In giving advice and consent to the Optional Protocol to the Convention on the Rights of the Child on the Sale of Children, Child Prostitution and Child Pornography,[153] the Senate Foreign Relations Committee noted that "the United States is already in a position to fulfill nearly all of the obligations of the Protocol, with one exception" (relating to jurisdiction over certain offenses committed in its territory or on board a ship or aircraft registered in the United States).[154] Accordingly, it proposed (and the Senate accepted) a declaration to the effect that the Protocol would not be self-executing (except for the provisions in Article 5, which concerned extradition for offences covered by Article 3(1)). Because "current law, including the laws of the states, adequately fulfills the obligations of the Protocol," no new legislation would be required to fulfill the U.S. obligations except for a minor change to federal law to satisfy its jurisdictional obligations regarding offenses on board U.S. ships and aircraft.[155]

Regarding the Optional Protocol to the Convention on the Rights of the Child on the Involvement of Children in Armed Conflict,[156] the Senate Foreign Relations Committee did not explicitly declare the treaty non-self-executing but merely observed that compliance with the treaty would not require significant changes in U.S. practice. Accordingly, no implementing legislation was proposed.[157]

In favorably reporting on the 2006 Convention on the Rights of Persons with Disabilities,[158] the Senate Foreign Relations Committee noted that the Convention is not considered self-executing and therefore its provisions

[152] For the text of the Senate's resolution, see 140 CONG. REC. S7634–02 (daily ed. June 24, 1994).

[153] Optional Protocol to the Convention on the Rights of the Child, on the Sale of Children, Child Prostitution, and Child Pornography, July 5, 2000, T.I.A.S. 13095, 2171 U.N.T.S. 227.

[154] *See* S. EXEC. REP. NO. 107–4, at 6 (2002).

[155] *Ibid.* at 10. While not strictly required by the Optional Protocol, the United States did adopt a provision (18 U.S.C. § 2423(c)) making it unlawful for any U.S. citizen (or alien admitted for permanent residence) who travels in foreign commerce or resides, either temporarily or permanently in a foreign country, to "engage in any illicit sexual conduct with another person." It has been upheld, in part, on the basis of the Optional Protocol. *See* United States v. Bollinger, 966 F. Supp. 2d 568 (W.D. N.C. 2013).

[156] Optional Protocol to the Convention on the Rights of the Child on the Involvement of the Children in Armed Conflict, *adopted* May 25, 2000, T.I.A.S. No. 13094, 2173 U.N.T.S. 222.

[157] *See* S. EXEC. REP. NO. 107–4, at 4 (2002).

[158] The United States signed this Convention on July 30, 2009. *See* S. TREATY DOC. NO. 112–7 (2012). Although it was favorably reported out by the Senate Foreign Relation Committee in 2014, it has yet to receive Senate advice and consent.

"cannot be directly enforced by U.S. courts or give rise to individually enforceable rights in the United States."[159] However, given the "comprehensive network of existing federal and state disability laws and enforcement mechanisms ... [i]n the large majority of cases, existing federal and state law meets or exceeds the requirements of the Convention."[160] Taking into account the reservations recommended in its resolution of advice and consent to address issues related to federalism and private conduct (in order to avoid altering the balance of power between the federal government and the states), no additional implementing legislation was deemed necessary with respect to the Convention.

Still another example of the preference for legislative implementation in this area is provided by the 1951 U.N. Convention on the Status of Refugees,[161] and more particularly by the 1958 Protocol to the Convention,[162] to which the United States became a party in 1980. The obligations assumed thereunder (in particular to grant asylum to an alien who meets the Convention's definition of a "refugee") were implemented by an appropriate amendment to the Immigration and Nationality Act.[163]

I Consular Conventions

Historically, bilateral consular conventions, which generally concern the prerogatives and functions of consulates and the protection of citizens of one state party in the territory of the other, have been self-executing in U.S. practice.[164] From the earliest days of the Republic, these treaties were intended to operate directly (which is to say preemptively) at the state and local (as well as federal) levels and to ensure equal (or non-discriminatory) treatment by governmental authorities.[165] Some sixty bilateral consular conventions still remain in force for the United States. For the most part, they appear to have operated as intended even though they are generally not considered a source of rights that can be directly invoked by individuals in U.S. courts.

[159] *See* S. TREATY DOC. NO. 112–7, at 2 (2012). [160] S. TREATY DOC. NO. 112–7, at 6 (2012).
[161] Convention Relating to the Status of Refugees, July 28, 1951, 189 U.N.T.S. 137.
[162] Protocol Relating to the Status of Refugees, Jan. 31, 1967, 19 U.S.T. 6223, 606 U.N.T.S. 267.
[163] *See* 1980 Refugee Act, Pub. L. No. 96–212, 94 Stat. 120 (codified at 8 U.S.C. § 1101(a)(42)(A) (2012)).
[164] For example, no implementing legislation was proposed with respect to the 1998 Protocol amending the 1950 Consular Convention between the United States and Ireland.
[165] *See, e.g.*, Asakura v. Seattle, 265 U.S. 332 (1924).

Following this practice, the 1963 Vienna Convention on Consular Relations was also ratified on a self-executing basis.[166] However, on several occasions over the past several years, U.S. compliance with the Convention has been challenged, in particular regarding the "consular notification and access" provisions of Article 36. Indeed, the United States has been found in breach of these obligations by the International Court of Justice because of its failure to provide consular notification rights to various foreign nationals who were subsequently convicted of murder and sentenced to death.[167]

That the Treaty has often been observed in the breach by the U.S. law enforcement community, despite the fact that it is self-executing, raises significant doubt about the Third Restatement rationale for favoring direct application. Lack of compliance has not resulted from lack of attention or commitment on the part of the federal government; in fact, the Executive branch has over the years made vigorous efforts to educate law enforcement authorities at all levels about its requirements. Neither can blame be attributed mainly to the lack of a "cause of action," since a judicial remedy would come only after a violation has occurred. More plausibly, the cause is simpler: absence of a clear and unambiguous direction to law enforcement authorities to provide the necessary notification at the time of arrest (perhaps at the same time as the *Miranda* warning). The remedy, therefore, could also be simple: enactment of straightforward federal (or uniform state) legislation. However, despite several efforts along these lines, no such legislation seems likely in the short run.[168]

J FCN Treaties/Treaties of Amity/Bilateral Investment Treaties

Like consular conventions, bilateral treaties of amity (also called treaties of friendship, commerce, and navigation, or "FCNs" for short) generally have been considered self-executing. As the Supreme Court observed in *Medellin*:

> Indeed, we have held that a number of the "Friendship, Commerce, and Navigation" Treaties . . . are self-executing – based on "the language of the[se] Treat[ies]." [Citing *Sumitomo Shoji America, Inc.*, 457 U.S. 176 (1982);

166 Vienna Convention on Consular Relations, Apr. 24, 1963, 21 U.S.T. 77, 596 U.N.T.S. 261. In view of the widespread acceptance of the Vienna Convention on Consular Relations, the United States no longer seeks to negotiate individual bilateral arrangements with other countries.

167 *See, e.g.*, Avena and Other Mexican Nationals (Mexico v. U.S.), Judgment, 2004 I.C.J. Rep. 12 (Mar. 31) and 2009 I.C.J. Rep. 3 (Jan. 19).

168 *See* David P. Stewart, *The Consular Notification Conundrum*, 21 TRANSNAT'L L. & CONTEMP. PROBS. 101 (2013).

> *Kolovrat v. Oregon*, 366 U. S. 187 (1961); and *Clark v. Allen*, 331 U.S. 503 (1947)] ... [N]either our approach nor our cases require that a treaty provide for self-execution in so many talismanic words ... Our cases simply require courts to decide whether a treaty's terms reflect a determination by the President who negotiated it and the Senate that confirmed it that the treaty has domestic effect.[169]

Thus, in approving of the 2001 Protocol to the 1951 Treaty of Friendship, Commerce and Navigation with Denmark, the Senate stated: "No further implementing legislation is required for the Protocol. Current law, specifically section 101(a)(15)(E)(ii) of the Immigration and Nationality Act, suffices to implement the Protocol."[170]

The many bilateral investment treaties ("BITs") which have replaced the Treaties of Amity appear to follow the same pattern. For example, in transmitting the 1995 Treaty between the Government of the United States of America and the Government of the Republic of Latvia Concerning the Encouragement and Reciprocal Protection of Investment (with Annex and Protocol), the president's message did not mention either the mode of implementation or the need for implementing legislation.[171]

However, in its proposed resolution of advice and consent to ratification of the Rwanda BIT, the Senate Foreign Relations Committee followed a bifurcated approach by declaring that specific articles would be considered self-executing, while the remainder of the treaty would not. It also declared that "[n]one of the provisions in this Treaty confers a private right of action."[172]

In so doing, the Committee expressed concern over whether, and how, the United States would ensure compliance with the non-self-executing provisions should it be found in breach by an arbitral panel.[173] Two of the treaty's most important provisions are among those declared non-self-executing. The first allows investors of one party to the Treaty to bring to binding arbitration claims that the government of the other party has breached

169 Medellin v. Texas, 552 U.S. 491, 521 (2008).
170 S. Exec. Rep. No. 110–1, at 2 (2007).
171 *See* S. Treaty Doc. No. 104–12 (1995).
172 S. Exec. Rep. No. 111–8, at 13 (2010) ("The advice and consent of the Senate under section 1 is subject to the following declaration: Articles 3 through 10 and other provisions that qualify or create exceptions to these Articles are self-executing. With the exception of these Articles, the Treaty is not self-executing. (None of the provisions in this Treaty confers a private right of action.) Arts. 3–10 pertain to governmental obligations with respect to ensuring national treatment, most-favored-nation treatment, the minimum standard of treatment, expropriation and compensation, transfers relating to a covered investment, performance requirements, appointment of senior management and directors, and publication of laws and decisions respecting investments.
173 S. Exec. Rep. No. 111–8, at 11 (2010).

specified provisions of the Treaty.[174] The other allows the two states party to submit disputes regarding the interpretation or application of the treaty to binding arbitration.[175] Noting that, apart from the New York and Washington (ICSID) Conventions, no existing treaty or statutory scheme governs the implementation in the United States of state-to-state arbitration awards, the Committee "urge[d] the executive branch to review its approach to ensuring compliance with adverse arbitral awards arising from non-self-executing treaties (including as it relates to compliance with the ICJ judgment in the *Avena* case) and to identify effective means to facilitate U.S. compliance with its treaty obligations."[176]

It is noteworthy that the Committee's concerns were not generated by the prospect of domestic litigation or an adverse decision by a U.S. court (it was careful to say, as the Administration did, that no provisions of the treaty would give rise to a private right of action) but rather the possibility that the United States might be found in violation of its treaty obligations by an international arbitral tribunal.

K *International Organizations*

Membership in public international organizations normally occurs by multilateral treaty and typically imposes both financial and substantive obligations on member states. When the organization will be based in the United States, specific arrangements are needed regarding the establishment and presence of the organization's headquarters and the missions representing other member states. Such treaties are not considered self-executing, and authorization for U.S. participation, including payment of financial contributions, is given by enactment of federal statutes.

For example, the U.N. Charter was one of the first multilateral treaties entered into by the United States following World War II. It is neither self-executing nor implemented by statute. However, U.S. involvement is authorized and regulated *inter alia* by the U.N. Participation Act,[177] the United Nations Headquarters Agreement,[178] and the International Organizations

[174] Investment Treaty with Rwanda, U.S.-Rwanda, art. 34, Feb. 19, 2008, S. Treaty Doc. No. 110–23 (2010).

[175] *Ibid.* at art. 37.

[176] S. Exec. Rep. No. 111–8, at V(B) (2010) ("Domestic Implementation of the Rwanda BIT").

[177] United Nations Participation Act of 1954, Pub. L. No. 79–264, 59 Stat. 619 (codified at 22 U.S.C. § 287e (2012)).

[178] Agreement between the United States and the United Nations regarding the Headquarters of the United Nations, June 26, 1947, 61 Stat. 3416, 11 U.N.T.S. 11 (*authorized by* S.J.Res. 144, 80th Cong., 1st Sess., Pub. L. No. 80–357, *set out in* 22 U.S.C. § 287 (2012)).

Immunities Act ("IOIA").[179] Similarly, the Charter of the Organization of American States is a non-self-executing treaty which has not been directly implemented by statute.[180] The Headquarters Agreement between the United States and OAS was legislatively implemented through the International Organizations Immunities Act.[181]

Where existing law does not provide a sufficient basis for participation in a specific international organization, special legislation may be needed. For example, in 1954, Congress authorized U.S. participation in the North Atlantic Treaty Organization (NATO) by statute.[182] Congress also authorized the appropriation of "such amounts as may be necessary from time to time for the payment by the United States of its share of the expenses of the Organization and all necessary salaries and expenses of the United States permanent representative to the Organization" as well as for persons appointed to represent the United States in NATO's subsidiary bodies or any multilateral organization that participates in achieving the aims of the North Atlantic Treaty.[183] It provides that the United States' permanent representative to the North Atlantic Treaty Organization shall be appointed by the president by and with the advice and consent of the Senate and that such representative shall have the rank and status of ambassador extraordinary and plenipotentiary.[184]

L *Environment/Conservation/Wildlife and Fisheries*

Treaties in these various categories, which have been frequently considered in the past thirty years, have been treated differently, depending on their specific provisions.

Many have required legislative implementation. One of the most significant recent instruments for achieving sustainable fisheries around the globe is the U.N. "Straddling Fish Stocks Agreement," concluded in 1995.[185] As a management regime, it sets out new principles for the conservation of straddling and

[179] 22 U.S.C. §§ 288–288f-7 (2012).

[180] Charter of the Organization of American States, Apr. 30, 1948, 2 U.S.T. 2394, 119 U.N.T.S. 3 (*as amended*, Feb. 27, 1967, 21 U.S.T. 607, T.I.A.S. No. 6849).

[181] Headquarters Agreement between the Organization of American States and the Government of the United States of America, May 14, 1992, S. Treaty Doc. No. 102–40 (1994); International Organizations Immunities Act, *supra* text accompanying note 164.

[182] North Atlantic Treaty Organization, ch. 937, Title IV, § 408, 68 Stat. 845 (1954).

[183] 22 U.S.C. § 1928 (2012). [184] *Ibid.*

[185] *See* Agreement for the Implementation of the Provisions of the United Nations Convention on the Law of the Sea of 10 December 1982 relating to the Conservation and Management of Straddling Fish Stocks and Highly Migratory Fish Stocks ("Straddling Fish Stocks Agreement"), Sept. 8, 1995, 2167 U.N.T.S. 88.

highly migratory fish stocks, including the precautionary approach, vessel monitoring systems, compatibility of conservation and management measures, transparency of activities within subregional and regional fishery management organizations, compliance of nonmember states with fishery management organizations' measures, high seas boarding and inspection, port state measures, and data collection and sharing standards. The agreement was implemented for the United States by the Fisheries Act of 1995.[186]

Similarly, the 1992 Convention for the Conservation of Anadromous Stocks in the North Pacific Ocean,[187] designed to protect certain migratory species, was implemented through new legislation that, *inter alia*, established federal enforcement authority, created a process for the appointment of U.S. commissioners, and repealed a preexisting statute that had governed the subject matter domestically.[188] While the Convention simply allocates three commission seats (and one vote) to each member country, the implementing legislation adds the requirement that two commissioners be citizens of particular states (Alaska and Washington), presumably due to the regional interest in the regulated fisheries.

Other conservation and environmental protection treaties have been implemented on the basis of existing legislative authority. For example, the 1989 Montreal Protocol on Substances that Deplete the Ozone Layer,[189] designed to phase out the use of chlorofluorocarbons (CFCs) and other compounds, followed on roughly a decade of U.S. domestic statutory law in the area of ozone depletion. In submitting the treaty, the Clinton Administration deemed that preexisting Clean Air Act authority regarding ozone protection (section 157 of the 1977 amendments) provided a sufficient basis for the EPA to promulgate the regulations necessary for implementation.[190] Similarly, the 1992 U.N. Framework Convention on Climate Change[191] was implemented on the basis of existing statutory authority without any additional legislation.[192]

186 Pub. L. No. 104–43, 109 Stat. 366 (1995) (codified at 16 U.S.C §§ 5501–09, 5601–10, 5701–09 (2012)).

187 Convention of Anadromous Stocks in the North Pacific Ocean, Feb. 11, 1992, T.I.A.S. 11465, S. Treaty Doc. No. 102–30 (1992).

188 16 U.S.C. §§ 1021–1035 (*repealed by* Pub. L. No. 102–567, Title VIII, 106 Stat. 4270 (1992) (codified at 16 U.S.C. §§ 5001–12 (2012)); Pub. L. No. 102–587, Title VIII, 106 Stat. 5039 (1992)).

189 Montreal Protocol on Substances that Deplete the Ozone Layer, Sept. 16, 1987, S. Treaty Doc. No. 100–10, 1522 U.N.T.S. 28.

190 S. Treaty Doc. No. 100–10, at VIII (1987).

191 United Nations Framework Convention on Climate Change, May 9, 1992, S. Treaty Doc. No. 102–38 (1992), 1771 U.N.T.S. 107.

192 S. Treaty Doc. No. 102–28, at VII (1992) ("The United States will implement this obligation through a variety of measures, including the Clean Air Act and its 1990 Amendments, the National Energy Strategy, and the Intermodal Surface Transportation Act of 1991."). At the

By contrast, many other treaties in this category have not been implemented legislatively. For example, when the 1916 bilateral treaty with Canada on protection of migratory birds (the treaty at issue in *Missouri v. Holland*) was amended in 1995,[193] no new legislation was required in light of the existing provisions of the Fish and Wildlife Improvement Act of 1978.[194] The 1994 U.N. Convention to Combat Desertification,[195] intended to combat land degradation and mitigate the effects of drought on arid, semi-arid, and dry sub-humid lands particularly in Africa, is aimed primarily at governmental policy and (from the U.S. perspective) at the goals and objectives of foreign assistance programs. Accordingly, it was adopted without any implementing legislation.[196]

Three wildlife and fisheries treaties were recently approved by the Senate on a non-self-executing basis (with an explicit statement that implementing legislation would be needed): the 2009 Convention on the Conservation and Management of High Seas Fishery Resources in the South Pacific Ocean, which established the South Pacific Regional Fisheries Management Organization (SPRFMO) to promote cooperation in conservation and management of high seas fishery resources in the South Pacific Ocean;[197] the 2012 Convention on the Conservation and Management of High Seas Fisheries Resources in the North Pacific Ocean, which established the North Pacific Fisheries Commission empowered to adopt and implement conservation and management measures for unregulated fish stocks in the high seas of the North Pacific Ocean;[198] and a 2007

time of ratification, both the Administration and the Senate took the position that any protocol following from the framework would itself have to be separately approved, and so, while theoretically legally binding, neither the framework nor any derivative has served as a basis for implementation of domestic emissions controls.

193 Protocol Amending the 1916 Convention for the Protection of Migratory Birds, U.S.-Can., Dec. 5, 1995, S. Treaty Doc. No. 104–28 (1995).

194 Pub. L. No. 95–616, 92 Stat. 3110 (1978) (codified at 16 U.S.C. § 712 (2012)).

195 U.N. Convention to Combat Desertification in those Countries Experiencing Serious Drought and/or Desertification, Particularly in Africa, Oct. 14, 1994, S. Treaty Doc. No. 104–29, 1945 U.N.T.S. 3. This convention sets forth four basic types of commitments for states parties: to adopt an integrated approach to desertification and to strengthen international cooperation; to have strategies to address desertification and to promote public awareness in this regard; (for developing-country Parties) to prepare National Action Programs identifying causes of, and measures to address, such desertification; and (for developed-country Parties) to provide support for developing-country efforts to combat desertification.

196 S. Treaty Doc. No. 104–29, at X (2000).

197 Convention on the Conservation and Management of High Seas Fishery Resources in the South Pacific Ocean, Nov. 14, 2009, S. Treaty Doc. No. 113–1 (2014); S. Exec. Rep. No. 113–2, at 6 (2014).

198 Convention on the Conservation and Management of High Sea Fisheries Resources in the North Pacific Ocean, May 2, 2012, S. Treaty Doc. No. 113–2 (2014); S. Exec. Rep. No. 113–3, at 5 (2014).

Amendment to the Convention on Future Multilateral Cooperation in the Northwest Atlantic Fisheries.[199]

Several other conservation treaties have received advice and consent with the express understanding that implementing legislation would be required: these included an Agreement with the Russian Federation on Management of the Alaska-Chukotka Polar Bear Population;[200] an Agreement with Canada relating to Albacore Tuna Vessels;[201] and a treaty on Fisheries with Certain Pacific Island States.[202]

M Tax Treaties

Bilateral tax treaties are among the most common treaties in U.S. practice. Together with extradition, mutual legal assistance, and bilateral investment treaties, they have made up nearly half of the treaties considered by the Senate in recent years. Tax treaties are typically described as "self-executing."[203] In point of fact, however, they rest upon and are implemented through relevant provisions of existing legislation (in this case, the Internal Revenue Code).

The principal aim of these bilateral treaties is to address issues of double taxation. Because the situations in question necessarily vary from country to country, as do the particular negotiated solutions, the arrangements embodied in the treaties must be directly effective. Amending the federal tax statutes for each bilateral arrangement would not be a plausible alternative. In operation then, bilateral tax treaties function as supplements to otherwise applicable tax code provisions and regulations. For this reason, the Senate Foreign Relations Committee typically notes, in recommending advice and consent to ratification, that no legislation is necessary to implement these agreements since they

[199] Amendment to the Convention on Future Multilateral Cooperation in the Northwest Atlantic Fisheries, *adopted on* Sept. 28, 2007, S. TREATY DOC. NO. 113–3 (2014); S. EXEC. REP. NO. 113–4, at 5 (2014).

[200] Agreement with the Russian Federation concerning Polar Bear Population, U.S.-Russ., Oct. 16, 2000, S. TREATY DOC. NO. 107–10 (2003).

[201] Agreement Amending Treaty with Canada concerning Pacific Coast Albacore Tuna Vessels and Port Privileges, U.S.-Can., May 26, 1981, S. TREATY DOC. NO. 108–1 (2003).

[202] Amendments to 1987 Treaty on Fisheries with Pacific Island States, April 2, 1987, S. TREATY DOC. NO. 108–2 (2003).

[203] *See, e.g.*, S. TREATY DOC. NO. 114–1, at V (2015), reporting on the Protocol Amending the Tax Convention with Japan, and S. TREATY DOC. NO. 113–4, at III (2014), reporting on the Protocol Amending the Convention between the United States of America and the Kingdom of Spain for the Avoidance of Double Taxation and the Prevention of Fiscal Evasion with respect to Taxes on Income and its Protocol, signed at Madrid on February 22, 1990.

build upon changes to U.S. income tax law made by the Tax Reform Act of 1986.[204]

Technically, it is accurate to say, as the Senate Foreign Relations Committee did (for example) when approving the bilateral Treaty (and accompanying Protocol) with Belgium for the Avoidance of Double Taxation and the Prevention of Fiscal Evasion with Respect to Taxes on Income, that "[a]s is the case generally with income tax treaties, the Protocol is self-executing and thus does not require implementing legislation for the United States."[205] The meaning is clear: because the Tax Code specifically recognizes the direct effect of such treaties,[206] no *new* legislation was required. But the bilateral treaty would not, in and of itself, provide a complete basis for resolving the issues.[207] Again, the "adapter plug" analogy is an apt description.

N *Judicial Assistance Treaties*

Another category of self-executing treaties are those multilateral agreements intended to assist parties in litigation with transnational elements. Although the United States (unlike many foreign countries) has no bilateral treaties regarding judicial assistance, it has long been a party to the two most important multilateral judicial assistance treaties: the 1965 Hague Convention on the Service Abroad of Judicial and Extrajudicial Documents in Civil or Commercial Matters[208] and the 1970 Hague Convention on the Taking of Evidence Abroad in Civil or Commercial Matters.[209] Both are denominated "self-executing" but build on, and supplement, existing domestic law in order to provide workable internationally agreed mechanisms of cooperation.

204 Pub. L. No. 99–514, 100 Stat. 2085 (1986); *see, e.g.*, S. TREATY DOC. NO. 101–10, at V (1989), reporting on the Convention with the Federal Republic of Germany on the Avoidance of Double Taxation and the Prevention of Fiscal Evasion with respect to Taxes on Income, with Protocol, signed at Bonn on Aug. 29, 1989.

205 S. EXEC. REP. NO. 110–2, at 6 (2007).

206 *See, e.g.*, 26 U.S.C. § 894(a)(1) (2012) ("The provisions of this title shall be applied to any taxpayer with due regard to any treaty obligation of the United States which applies to such taxpayer.").

207 Indeed, some have suggested that the self-executing status of tax treaties itself raises constitutional issues. *See* Rebecca M. Kysar, *On the Constitutionality of Tax Treaties*, 38 YALE J. INT'L L. 1 (2013) (arguing that tax treaties must not be self-executing but instead must be implemented through legislation passed by both houses or else be approved as Congressional-Executive agreements).

208 Convention on Service Abroad of Judicial and Extrajudicial Documents in Civil or Commercial Matters, *opened for signature* Nov. 15, 1965, 20 U.S.T. 361, 658 U.N.T.S. 163.

209 Convention on the Taking of Evidence Abroad in Civil or Commercial Matters, *opened for signature* Mar. 18, 1970, 23 U.S.T. 2555, 847 U.N.T.S. 231.

The Service Convention provides internationally agreed channels for transmitting requests for service of process of judicial documents from one "central authority" to another. For domestic purposes, it builds on existing rules regarding service, in particular Fed. R. Civ. P. Rule 4(f) (and the laws of individual states) and 28 U.S.C. § 1608. Like the Service Convention, the Evidence Convention establishes a Central Authority responsible for accepting and processing Letters of Request from other contracting States that seek various kinds of assistance, including the production of evidence. In specific cases, it rests on other provisions of federal law, including Fed. R. Civ. P. 28(b) and 28 U.S.C. §§ 1782–84, both of which predated the Convention.

V TYPES OF IMPLEMENTATION

As this review demonstrates, the often-used binary distinction between self-executing and non-self-executing treaties offers an inadequate, even misleading, description. The majority of treaties denominated "self-executing" actually rest upon, and are effectively implemented by, existing legislation. This is true, for example, of extradition, mutual legal assistance, and tax treaties, which together constitute the vast majority of bilateral treaties denominated "self-executing." Only a few multilateral treaties actually stand alone as directly applicable federal law in the United States (among the main examples are the Vienna Convention on Consular Relations and the CISG).[210]

At the same time, it is difficult to identify treaties labeled "non-self-executing" that lack any domestic implementing basis. Very few treaties are purely non-self-executing in the sense that they are not given effect by some aspect of U.S. law. In most instances, treaties have been substantively implemented by positive legislative enactment of one type or another. In a not-insignificant number of cases, no new legislative enactments have been needed since the treaty has rested on existing legislation deemed sufficient to satisfy the treaty requirements (which I have denominated the "preimplementation" category). In other cases, the necessary implementing provisions have been adopted before the treaty was ratified.

For these reasons, the self-executing/non-self-executing distinction has become strained and incomplete and may actually be confusing. Current U.S. practice is clearly marbled. A more accurate taxonomy would distinguish

[210] Others include the 1929 "Warsaw" Convention for the Unification of Certain Rules Relating to International Transportation by Air, *opened for signature* Oct. 12, 1929, 49 Stat. 3000, 137 L.N.T.S. 11, and the 1999 "Montreal" Convention for the Unification of Certain Rules for International Carriage by Air, art. 55, May 28, 1999, S. Treaty Doc. No. 106–45, 2242 U.N.T.S. 350.

between five different modes of implementation. Treaties which are labeled "non-self-executing" include three subsets:

(i) those for which no domestic implementation is contemplated or required (for example, arms control agreements or conventions which only address matters of policy);
(ii) those for which an adequate basis already exists in U.S. law (thus, the treaties can be termed "preimplemented," for example human rights treaties); and
(iii) those for which new legislation is required prior to ratification in order to assure U.S. compliance.

Treaties denominated "self-executing" likewise include two variants:

(iv) those which connect preexisting legislation by making country-specific adjustments to that legislation (such as bilateral tax and extradition treaties) and
(v) the relatively few that can be considered truly self-executing in that they operate by themselves as domestic law without regard to any implementing legislation (such as the CISG and the VCCR).

The vast majority of treaties ratified by the United States over the past three decades fall into the first three categories. In early periods of U.S. treaty history, a considerable number of treaties fell into Category v.[211]

Adopting this more precise typology will allow a more accurate evaluation of the relative frequency with which treaties are in fact adopted and implemented on one basis or another, and perhaps create a better picture of the relative merits and success of the different approaches to implementation.

With regard to the types and characteristics of implementing legislation, the descriptive task becomes far more difficult. Nothing in the Third Restatement spoke to this issue, nor does there seem to be any overall guidance from either the Executive or Congressional branches. While some patterns can be discerned regarding categories of treaties that generally are (or are not) legislatively implemented, as indicated in the previous section, decisions about the form and context of legislation appear to be ad hoc, reflecting the specific requirements of the treaty, the nature and content of any preexisting legislation, and the prevailing practices in the

[211] *See* Ingrid Wuerth, "Self-Execution," Chapter 4 of this volume; *see also* Michael P. Van Alstine, *Treaties in the Supreme Court, 1901–1945* in INTERNATIONAL LAW IN THE U.S. SUPREME COURT (Sloss, Ramsey, Dodge, eds. 2011).

given substantive area. There is no standard form and no central coordinating mechanism.[212]

One can, however, identify a number of representative approaches that have frequently been used.

Direct Legislative Incorporation. At one end of the spectrum is the direct or "short form" implementation, involving legislative incorporation of the treaty in its entirety. As indicated above, the main example is provided by the New York Convention, which was incorporated directly into federal law with a simple statement in 9 U.S.C. § 201: "The Convention on the Recognition and Enforcement of Foreign Arbitral Awards of June 10, 1958, shall be enforced in United States courts in accordance with this chapter." To be sure, subsequent provisions of Chapter 2 of the Federal Arbitration Act did supplement that statement by addressing a number of specific issues necessary to guide the courts in applying the Convention in specific cases (for example, by specifying when an agreement or award falls under the Convention, addressing issues of jurisdiction and venue, orders to compel, etc.) but the effect of the chapter was to make the treaty itself part of federal law.[213]

This approach may work well for treaties primarily intended for judicial interpretation and application, when (like the New York Convention) the text is relatively short and comparatively simple. It is not appropriate, however, in other situations, for example the 2005 Convention on Choice of Court Agreements, a longer and more complicated instrument which uses terminology not entirely consonant with U.S. practice and which (because it would apply to state courts) would likely raise difficult federalism concerns.[214]

Comprehensive Enactment. At the other end of the spectrum are instances in which the treaty's provisions have been legislatively "translated," supplemented and implemented in much greater detail than can actually be found in the treaty text itself. For example, the Chemical Weapons Convention

[212] Obviously, considerable experience and expertise about prior practice resides in the Legal Adviser's Office at the Department of State, as well as in the Senate Foreign Relations Committee, along with strong opinions about best approaches. But these are brought to bear on a case-by-case basis.

[213] Section 301 of Title IX does the same for the Inter-American Convention on International Commercial Arbitration of Jan. 30, 1975 (the "Panama Convention").

[214] For additional discussion of this treaty, see Paul R. Dubinsky, "Private Law Treaties," Chapter 10 of this volume and David P. Stewart, *Implementing the Hague Choice of Court Convention: The Argument in Favor of 'Cooperative Federalism,'* in FOREIGN COURT JUDGMENTS AND THE UNITED STATES LEGAL SYSTEM (Paul B. Stephan, ed., 2014).

Implementation Act of 1998,[215] a part of which was at issue in the *Bond* case, covered a significant range of subjects, including various required definitions, the establishment of a U.S. National Authority with a broad range of specific powers and duties including, for example, the conduct of inspections and submission of reports. It also provided for the imposition of criminal and civil penalties (including possible forfeiture) on violators, the imposition of sanctions on foreign companies and governments, and designated the Federal Court of Claims to hear cases involving claims of civil and criminal liability.[216]

Limited (Operational) Implementation. Between these two ends of the spectrum lie many examples of limited or tailored legislation designed to give effect only to those aspects of a treaty for which specific authority is required to ensure U.S. compliance.

For example, in giving effect to the Cape Town Convention on International Interests in Mobile Equipment, as modified by the Aircraft Equipment Protocol, the United States had to create the necessary domestic mechanisms to permit U.S. participation in the treaty scheme for registration of security interests in the equipment covered by the Protocol. The Cape Town Treaty Implementation Act[217] thus designated the Federal Aviation Administration's Civil Aviation Registry as the United States' "Entry Point to the International Registry" relating to civil aircraft of the United States (as well as aircraft for which a United States identification number has been assigned with regard to interests in aircraft engines). It required the FAA Administrator to establish a system for filing notices of prospective assignments and prospective international interests in, and prospective sales of, aircraft or aircraft engines under the Protocol.[218] Other provisions in the treaty did not require domestic implementation.

Obviously, the extent of required legislative implementation varies both with respect to the provisions of the treaty in question and the scope of existing law and governmental structures relevant to those provisions. Contrast the following examples.

The 1948 U.N. Genocide Convention reflected an international consensus, following the post–World War II war crimes trials, to establish a clear – and

[215] Pub. L. No. 105–277, 112 Stat. 2681–860 (1998) (codified at 22 U.S.C. §§ 6701–6771 (2012); 18 U.S.C. §§ 229–229F (2012)) (enacted as part of the Omnibus Consolidated and Emergency Supplemental Appropriations Act of 1998).

[216] Very few implementing statutes have been as detailed and lengthy as the Panama Canal Act of 1979, Pub. L. No. 96–70, 93 Stat. 452–500 (1979) (codified at 22 U.S.C. § 3601 (2012)), which took over one hundred sections to provide for the implementation of the bilateral Panama Canal Treaty of 1977, in particular the creation and functions of the Panama Canal Commission and related authorities.

[217] Pub. L. No. 108–297, 118 Stat. 1095 (2004).

[218] 49 U.S.C. § 44107 (2012).

broadly accepted – obligation among states to prosecute and punish individuals who commit a carefully defined category of the most heinous acts directed against members of national, ethnic, racial, or religious groups.[219] After the United States finally ratified the Convention (more than forty years after it had been submitted to the Senate), a new federal crime had to be enacted in order to meet U.S. obligations under the Convention. The Genocide Convention Implementation Act of 1987[220] created a new federal criminal offense of genocide based on the definitional and jurisdictional requirements of the treaty. The statute provides for the punishment of anyone who, whether in time of peace or in time of war, commits genocide as defined in the treaty, if the offense is committed within the United States or (wherever the offense is committed) if the offender is a U.S. national.[221] No other domestic legislation was required to satisfy U.S. undertakings.

Like the Genocide Convention Implementation Act, the Antarctic Conservation Act of 1978,[222] which implemented the Agreed Measures for the Conservation of Antarctic Fauna and Flora, consistent with the 1959 Antarctic Treaty,[223] also created a new federal offense (making it unlawful for U.S. citizens to tamper in certain ways with animals and plant life in Antarctica).[224] But this treaty required more, because it obligated the U.S. to regulate activities related to Antarctic fauna and flora. The statute thus broadly prohibited any U.S. citizen wherever located (and any foreign person within the United States) to possess, sell, transport, import, or export any native mammal or native bird taken in Antarctica or any native plant collected in any specially protected area. It also created a scheme for the National Science Foundation to license otherwise prohibited acts in the United States, and for the Secretary of State to regulate the relevant activities of U.S. citizens regarding expeditions to, and within, Antarctica.

Which method of legislative implementation is preferable? The Third Restatement did not speak to this question. From the international perspective, the answer is surely simple: the one that provides the most straightforward and faithful compliance with the obligations of the United States under the specific treaty in question. As a domestic matter,

219 Convention on the Prevention and Punishment of the Crime of Genocide, Dec. 9, 1948, S. Treaty. Doc. No. 91–12, 78 U.N.T.S. 277.

220 Pub. L. No. 100–606, 102 Stat. 3045 (1988) (the so-called Proxmire Act) (codified at 18 U.S.C. §§ 1001–93 (2012)).

221 18 U.S.C. §§ 1091–1903 (2012).

222 Pub. L. No. 95–541, 92 Stat. 2048 (1978).

223 Antarctic Treaty, Dec. 1, 1959, 12 U.S.T. 794, 402 U.N.T.S. 71. The aim of the treaty is the conservation and protection of the fauna and flora of Antarctica, and of the ecosystem upon which such fauna and flora depend.

224 16 U.S.C § 2403 (2012).

however, some would prioritize other desiderata, such as confining assertions of federal authority to those aspects of the treaty regime that clearly require affirmative enactment (new administrative structures or authorities, for example, or criminal or regulatory provisions). Courts, on the other hand, are most likely to appreciate clear statements of the rules to be applied in cases brought before them.

VI CONCLUSIONS AND FUTURE TRENDS

The foregoing indicates that the unmistakable leaning of the Third Restatement in favor of self-execution has not prevailed in U.S. treaty practice over the past thirty years. In fact, in the decades since the Third Restatement was published, the pendulum has swung decidedly in favor of legislative implementation. In the post–Third Restatement era, neither the courts nor the political branches have embraced the Third Restatement monist inclinations.

How is one to evaluate this evolution? Is legislative implementation (in any form) less likely than self-execution to ensure fidelity in the domestic application of treaty obligations? Put differently, what empirical support is there for the assertion in the Third Restatement that self-execution is the simpler, faster, and more reliable approach to ensuring U.S. compliance? The answer appears to be "not much at all."

While not having to wait for legislation to be drafted and enacted might seem "faster" and "simpler," self-execution alone does not necessarily mean more rapid Senate advice and consent. Moreover, as a matter of practice, treaties requiring implementing legislation are ratified (and enter into force) only after the necessary legislation has been adopted. As a result, there is in fact no difference in the rapidity with which the United States comes into compliance with its accepted obligations under the treaty in question. Much more importantly, recent practice fails to demonstrate that direct implementation of treaties (through "self-execution") is more likely to increase the prospects of U.S. compliance with treaty obligations. Neither guarantees compliance, and shortcomings are evident in both modes.

Some self-executing treaties do appear to work well from the perspective of compliance. Among the multilaterals, one can certainly point to the success of the 1999 Montreal Convention,[225] which, like its predecessor

[225] Convention for the Unification of Certain Rules for International Carriage by Air, *opened for signature* May 28, 1999, S. Treaty Doc. No. 106–45, 2242 U.N.T.S. 350 (*entered into force* for the United States Nov. 4, 2003); *see generally* J.C. Batra, *Modernization of The Warsaw System – Montreal 1999*, 65 J. Air L. & Com. 429 (2000); Sean Murphy, *Ratification of the 1999 Montreal Convention on Aviation Liability*, 98 Am. J. Int'l L. 177 (2004).

Warsaw Convention,[226] is directly applicable in U.S. courts without the aid of any legislation and has long been applied in U.S. litigation without generating much discernible judicial angst, much less international controversy or claims of breach.[227] Others, such as the CISG, have a less positive track record;[228] the Vienna Convention on Consular Relations has proved dysfunctional in significant respects.[229] Courts continue to struggle with The Hague Service and Evidence Conventions, particularly in the ways they connect to and interact with existing domestic law.[230]

By contrast, legislatively implemented multilaterals seem to have fared better, judging by the absence of international challenge or criticism. Here, one might look in particular to treaties in the fields of criminal law, intellectual property, family law, and conservation, and fish and wildlife fields. Even the New York Convention, incorporated directly into the Federal Arbitration Act, is generally viewed as working well.[231] As indicated above, the bulk of

226 Convention for the Unification of Certain Rules Relating to International Transportation by Air, Oct. 12, 1929, 49 Stat. 3000, 137 U.N.T.S. 11 *reprinted in* note following 49 U.S.C. § 40105, as amended by the Protocol Sept. 28, 1955, 478 U.N.T.S. 371 and the Montreal Protocol No. 4, Sept. 8, 1955, S. EXEC. REP. NO. 105–20, 2145 U.N.T.S. 36). *See generally* Andreas F. Lowenfeld & Allan I. Mendelsohn, *The United States and the Warsaw Convention*, 80 HARV. L. REV. 497, 498–9 (1967).

227 The Senate Foreign Relations Committee's report on the Montreal Convention explicitly concluded that the treaty provides the basis for a private right of action in U.S. courts and that no separate implementing legislation was required. *See* S. EXEC. REP. NO. 108–8, at 3, 6 (2003); *see also* 149 CONG. REC. S10,870 (daily ed. July 31, 2003) (statement of Sen. Biden); Hornsby v. Lufthansa German Airlines, 593 F. Supp. 2d 1132 (C.D. Cal. 2009); Baah v. Virgin Atlantic Airways Ltd., 473 F. Supp. 2d 591 (S.D.N.Y. 2007); Loryn B. Zerner, *Tseng v. El Al Israel Airlines and Article 25 of the Warsaw Convention: A Cloud Left Uncharted*, 14 AM. U. INT'L. REV. 1245 (1999).

228 *See, e.g.*, H. Allen Blair, *Hard Cases Under the Convention on the International Sale of Goods: A Proposed Taxonomy of Interpretive Challenges*, 21 DUKE J. COMP. & INT'L L. 269 (2011); Gilles Cuniberti, *Is the CISG Benefitting Anybody*, 39 VAND. J. TRANSNAT'L L. 1511 (2006). Paul Stephan, *The Futility of Unification and Harmonization in International Commercial Law*, 39 VA. J. INT'L L. 743 (1999).

229 *See. e.g.*, David P. Stewart, *The Consular Notification Conundrum*, 21 TRANSNAT'L L. & CONTEMP. PROBS. 101 (2013); Nicole M. Howell, *A Proposal for U.S. Implementation of the Vienna Convention's Consular Notification Requirement*, 60 UCLA L. REV. 1324 (2011); Yury A. Kolesnikov, *Meddling with the Vienna Convention on Consular Relations: The Dilemma and Proposed Statutory Solutions*, 40 MCGEORGE L. REV. 179 (2009).

230 *Compare* Volkswagenwerk Aktiengesellschaft v. Schlunk, 486 U.S. 694 (1988); Societe Nationale Industrielle Aerospatiale v. U.S. Dist. Court for Southern Dist. of Iowa, 482 U.S. 522 (1987). *See also* Menon v. Water Splash, Inc., 472 S.W.3d 28 (Ct. App. Texas 2015), cert. granted, 137 S.Ct. 547 (2016); John Coyle, *The Case for Writing International Law in the U.S. Code*, 56 B.C. L. REV. 433 (2015).

231 For an interesting discussion of the Convention, see S.I. Strong, *Beyond the Self-Execution Analysis: Rationalizing Constitutional, Treaty and Statutory Interpretation in International Commercial Arbitration*, 53 VA. J. INT'L L. 499 (2013).

"self-executing" bilateral treaties (extradition, mutual legal assistance, and tax treaties in particular) are in fact dependent on existing legislative structures for their operational effect. Here again, the lack of international challenges to U.S. compliance suggests that they are perceived as working reasonably well in the technical areas involved.

In the human rights area, criticism of the U.S. record is constant, of course, both because of alleged failures to accept all the obligations of the major multilateral treaties (by virtue of reservations) and because of alleged shortcomings in carrying out the obligations that have been accepted. Because human rights treaties are, at their core, aspirational and aimed at producing constant improvement, that criticism would likely continue no matter how the treaties were implemented.[232]

It may seem logical to expect that direct incorporation of treaty texts themselves, whether by legislation (as in the case of the New York Convention) or through self-execution (as in the case of the Vienna Convention on Consular Relations), is more likely to lead to compliance because it puts the precise obligations (as adopted by the international community) squarely in front of the domestic implementer (government official or court). That assumption, however, rests largely on faith in the ability of officials and judges to discern the meaning and intent of (often opaque) treaty language.

In some cases, where harmonizing the interpretation and application of treaty terms is important (as it is, for example, in the family law treaties), the assumption also depends on willingness (especially in the judiciary) to take into account relevant decisions by the courts of other states parties. When, as in the case of the Consular Relations Convention, the obligations are not codified in any form, the relevant domestic decision-maker may not always be aware that the United States has in fact undertaken the obligation in question.

Frequently, however, the language of the treaty is less than clear or precise, especially in the multilateral context when it has had to garner the acceptance of negotiators from many different countries and legal systems, not infrequently through compromise. Translating intensely negotiated formulations into language and concepts that are familiar to domestic authorities and consonant with U.S. legal concepts and constraints, while difficult, can clarify the judges' task. Leaving the task to courts on a case-by-case basis can risk inconsistent interpretations and possible noncompliance in the eyes of other states parties.

[232] *Compare* Ian Keysel, *Domesticating Human Rights Norms in the United States: Considering the Role and Obligations of the Federal Government as Litigant*, 46 GEO. J. INT'L L. 1009 (2015).

This concern would seem particularly important in light of the growing complexity of treaties (especially multilateral treaties) and the fact that they increasingly address issues on which U.S. law already exists. Treaties, in particular multilateral treaties, regularly deal with topics which, in earlier years, would have been considered in the United States to be exclusively matters of domestic (internal) competence and regulation. Indeed, it is challenging today to identify any major multilateral treaty that does not, to one degree or another, address issues on which a substantial body of U.S. domestic law already exists.[233] One of the main purposes of contemporary multilateral treaty-making is in fact to promote international standardization and harmonization in the way in which states parties address matters in their internal law. This makes negotiating treaties more challenging, since determining what content would be acceptable is not simply a matter of national policy but also a question of what domestic law already exists and whether (and how) it might need to be changed (or could not realistically be changed). The more detailed the treaty, the more difficult it is to find common ground among the negotiating states, especially those with differing legal cultures and traditions.

At the same time, contemporary multilateral treaty-making also poses growing challenges for U.S. implementation. Because domestic law almost always bears on the substantive provisions of the treaty, the "self-executing or not" question essentially becomes a decision whether to change the law directly through the treaty power (directly overriding duly enacted legislation and/or judicial decisions) or to utilize the normal legislative process (or, in rare cases, some combination of the two). That decision is also complicated by questions of federalism (for example, in the field of human rights and family law treaties, where many of the obligations touch on matters within state or local, not federal, purview). Concerns about issues of federalism inevitably form part of

[233] The few that do fall in this category typically concern mutual defense arrangements (such as NATO), multilateral arms control arrangements, and the structure and functioning of international organizations. See, for example, the Amendments to the Convention on the International Maritime Organization (Mar. 6, 1948), which, *inter alia*, increased the size of the IMO Governing Council and institutionalized the Organization's Facilitation Committee. Because these changes had no domestic impact, it is not surprising that the president's Transmittal did not refer to implementation of the treaty in U.S. law. *See* S. Treaty Doc. No. 104–36 (1996). See also S. Treaty Doc. No. 87–17, at 4 (1962) on ILO Convention (No. 116) concerning the partial revision of the conventions adopted by the ILO General Conference, including a letter from Labor Secretary Goldberg to Secretary of State Rusk: "Inasmuch as the convention does not directly affect U.S. law and practice, no enactment of legislation is required in its ratification." See also Protocols I and II to the African Nuclear Weapons Free Zone, S. Treaty Doc. No. 112–3 (2011) and Protocols 1, 2 and 3 to the South Pacific Nuclear Weapons Free Zone, S. Treaty Doc. No. 112–2 (2011) and other arms control agreements.

the Senate's evaluation but do not seem to focus in particular on the questions of implementation, leaving those issues to substantive experts in the area concerned.

The political branches clearly prefer to rely on the legislative process to change the law to conform to treaty obligations, rather than leaving the issue of compliance to the courts. In this regard, it is not enough simply to point to the number of treaties which have in recent years been denominated "self-executing" since most of them have in fact been legislatively implemented. The pertinent set includes those which have been approved as directly applicable in U.S. law without the aid of any legislation, and that number is comparatively small. Put differently, while it remains constitutionally permissible to do so, the political branches today do not favor use of the treaty power directly to effect changes in U.S. law.[234]

If there is no apparent reason to expect that future multilateral treaties will become less detailed or intrusive, neither is there any evident basis for anticipating that the domestic treaty makers will grow less inclined toward legislative implementation and more favorable to self-execution. The most obvious and compelling argument for such a change would be grounded in compelling evidence that self-execution enhances compliance with international obligations. Although such a claim is often put forward, the empirical case in support of it has yet to be made.

Finally, the search for consistency in the form and content of implementing legislation appears unavailing. In U.S. practice, before a treaty is submitted to the president for transmittal to the Senate, the treaty's substantive provisions are analyzed individually and in light of existing federal (sometimes state and local) law. For better or worse, this task is done on a piecemeal basis. Within the Executive branch, no central coordinating mechanism exists for the preparation or review of treaty-implementing legislation. When new statutory provisions are deemed necessary, they are drafted by the relevant Executive branch experts in light of existing law, coordinated by OMB, reviewed by the treaty experts in the Department of State's Office of the Legal Adviser, and considered by the appropriate congressional committees.

[234] It is not difficult to understand why the House of Representatives might have an institutional preference for implementation by means of legislation and against direct implementation of treaties, especially when treaties change the law. Interestingly, although direct implementation might be seen as maximizing the role of the Senate at the expense of the House, the same preference appears to be the general approach in the Senate. The reason may be that treaties follow a different pathway than legislation (the Foreign Relations Committee does not typically propose legislation) or because senators generally resist federal intrusion into state legal matters.

In terms of consistency, or lack thereof, often overlooked is the fact that proposed implementing legislation follows a different path toward becoming law than do the treaties that will require such implementation. Proposed legislation is considered by the relevant House and Senate committees, and (except in unusual cases) not by the Senate Foreign Relations Committee. In consequence, draft legislation is likely to follow the form and practices set by prior precedent in the particular field in question (environment, criminal, tax, etc.). In contrast, all proposed Article II treaties are subjected to review by the Foreign Relations Committee, which has its own practices and precedent.

To conclude with a recommendation, one useful step for the future might well be for the Executive branch to create a more vigorous interagency coordinating mechanism aimed at bringing greater consistency to the question of implementation. The Executive branch could also provide a needed means of postratification compliance monitoring. In an increasingly multilateral world, treaty compliance is an ongoing task, not a "one and done" undertaking that ends at ratification. If the United States truly desires to improve its record, then it must engage (to some degree) in continuous monitoring and assessment of treaty obligations with a view to improvement.

7

The Treaty and Its Rivals

Making International Agreements in U.S. Law and Practice

Michael D. Ramsey

Reading only the Constitution's text, one might suppose the constitutional regime for making international agreements in the United States to be quite straightforward. Article II, Section 2 states that the president has power to make treaties with the advice and consent of the Senate, provided two-thirds of the senators present concur. Article VI provides that all treaties made under the authority of the United States are the supreme law of the land. No provision of the Constitution's text directly mentions any power by the U.S. government to enter into any sort of international agreement apart from the "treaties" made according to Article II, Section 2 and having the force of Article VI.

For over one hundred years, the regime that appears on the face of the text roughly corresponded with reality. It never did so completely. Sometimes the president or the president's diplomatic agents made international agreements on minor matters without the Senate's advice and consent, especially in connection with military affairs and settlement of international claims. Sometimes Congress authorized the president in advance to make international agreements on minor matters without expressly requiring the supermajority consent of the Senate. Nonetheless, at least until the latter part of the nineteenth century, no international agreement of material consequence to U.S. foreign relations came about other than as specified in Article II, Section 2.

The next hundred years, however, transformed U.S. practice regarding international agreement-making to the extent that the Constitution's text and analyses based upon it wholly fail to capture what actually exists in modern practice. Conventionally, this transformation is described as the rise of two alternate forms of agreements: (1) the sole Executive agreement, done by the unilateral authority of the president in areas of the president's particular constitutional authority (whatever those may be); and (2) the Congressional-

Executive agreement, done with the approval of majorities of both Houses of Congress, and which is said to be fully interchangeable with the Article II, Section 2 treaty as a constitutional procedure. This modern account became the centerpiece of Section 303 of the Restatement (Third) of Foreign Relations Law, published by the American Law Institute in 1987.[1]

While accurate in some respects, even this conventional description fails to capture the complexity of modern agreement-making in the United States, and recent trends have contributed to the difficulty of providing a coherent legal and practical account. It is undoubtedly true that, simply as a numerical matter, Article II treaties have declined sharply as a percentage of U.S. international agreements. As described below, until the late nineteenth century, most U.S. international agreements (and all important ones) were approved as treaties. In contrast, today Article II treaties represent only a tiny fraction: a recent study found that between 1980 and 2000 the United States entered into a total of 375 Article II treaties and 2744 other agreements – that is, only 12 percent of agreements were concluded as treaties.[2] Practice since 2000 suggests an even smaller percentage.[3] And these studies count only binding agreements; much modern diplomacy is done through nonbinding agreements, so the numbers greatly understate the actual number of nontreaty agreements.

However, simply looking at reported numbers of treaties versus nontreaty agreements does not give a satisfactory account of U.S. practice for at least three reasons. First, nontreaty agreements have diverse and sometimes unclear sources of authority. In some cases, the president negotiates the agreement and submits it for approval by majorities of both Houses of Congress. For most agreements, the president makes them without any after-the-fact approval from Congress or the Senate. Within this latter category, the president may claim various sources of authority to enter into nontreaty agreements: express statutory authorization from Congress in advance; implied authority from Congress; express or implied authority from a prior treaty; or independent constitutional authority. As a practical matter, it may not always be easy – or even possible – to distinguish among some of these categories.[4] Increasingly,

[1] Restatement (Third) of the Foreign Relations Law of the United States, § 303 & comment e (1987) [hereinafter Third Restatement].

[2] Oona A. Hathaway, *Treaties' End: The Past, Present, and Future of International Lawmaking in the United States*, 117 Yale L.J. 1236, 1257–60 (2008) (collecting 1980–2000 statistics).

[3] *See infra* nn. 195–6 and accompanying text (indicating thirteen treaties and 233 other agreements, or 5.2% treaties, reported in a randomly selected year, 2009).

[4] Oona A. Hathaway, *Presidential Power over International Law: Restoring the Balance*, 119 Yale L.J. 140, 155 (2009) (estimating that approximately 20 percent of agreements between 1990 and

the president enters into international agreements on the basis of informal and often uncertain sources of authority, with uncertain legal effects.

Second, the numbers do not take into account the relative importance of treaties and other agreements. Treaties may remain well represented among important agreements, at least in some areas (although making that assessment seems challenging), despite their numerical decline. Likewise, agreements approved after-the-fact by Congress, although relatively small in number, include some of the United States' most important recent commitments in the area of international trade, including the North American Free Trade Agreement (NAFTA), the agreements establishing the World Trade Organization (WTO), and a range of bilateral free trade agreements. Agreements made by the president alone range from trivial diplomatic arrangements to ones of great consequence, including, for example, the Algiers Accords ending the 1980 hostage crisis with Iran.[5]

Third, there is no satisfactory explanation for why some agreements are made in one way and some in others. Undoubtedly, the vast expansion of U.S. diplomatic activity in modern times has encouraged greater presidential unilateralism and greater delegation to the president; individualized Senate approval of every U.S. agreement would hardly be possible, let alone practical. Complaints that the Article II process wrongly bypasses the House, the most democratically representative and accountable branch, may have particular force in areas of great domestic importance such as trade, while the difficulty of the Article II process may lead to concerns that useful and popular agreements can be defeated by a determined minority. At the same time, the Article II treaty, with the formalities and daunting supermajority hurdle described in the Constitution's text, has not withered away (as the Third Restatement seemed to predict and many academic commentators have wished). Instead, it remains a substantial force in U.S. foreign relations despite the rise of its rivals, although why that is the case, when easier alternatives appear to be commonly accepted, is puzzling.

Thus, even sorting out what is happening in modern practice, much less providing a theoretical account of it, may prove elusive. It does not appear that

2000 were sole executive agreements, with the remainder claiming some sort of congressional or treaty-based authorization).

5 *See ibid.* at 154 (noting range in importance of executive agreements from "mundane topics" to "issues that are significant to large numbers of Americans and might have been the subject of close congressional scrutiny had they been made public before they went into force").

either subject matter or importance – or indeed any other conclusive factor – determines how the United States' international agreements are made.[6]

In 2011, for example, President Barack Obama's administration signed the Anti-Counterfeiting Trade Agreement (ACTA), a multilateral agreement on intellectual property rights enforcement.[7] Initially, the Executive Branch argued that the agreement could be done on the president's independent authority as a sole Executive agreement. In part this argument rested on the proposition that ACTA would not require changes in U.S. law (and even at one point on the suggestion that it was nonbinding).[8] After substantial objections, including from members of Congress, the administration shifted ground to argue that Congress previously had approved the agreement implicitly in statutes authorizing the president to take action to prevent copyright abuse. This position also encountered sharp opposition, including from legal academics and commentators who argued that constitutionally the agreement should be approved either by two-thirds of the Senate or expressly by a majority of Congress.[9] Further complicating the picture was the fact that, with one notable exception, major intellectual property agreements had previously been approved as treaties through the Article II process – the exception being the Agreement on Trade-Related Aspects of Intellectual Property Rights (TRIPS), which was expressly approved after-the-fact by Congress.[10] As a result, the constitutional dimensions of U.S. entry into ACTA appeared, at minimum, uncertain.

6 Hathaway, *supra* note 2, at 1239 (concluding that "[a]lthough there are patterns to the current practice of using one type of agreement or another, those patterns have no identifiable rational basis"). The State Department, through a process known as the "Circular 175 Procedure," typically determines for Executive Branch what form an agreement should take, but that process contains substantial discretion. *See ibid.* at 1249–52.

7 Anti-Counterfeiting Trade Agreement, available at www.mofa.go.jp/policy/economy/i_property/pdfs/acta1105_en.pdf; *see* Office of the United States Trade Representative, Anti-Counterfeiting Agreement (ACTA), available at http://www.ustr.gov/acta.

8 Sean M. Flynn, *ACTA's Constitutional Problems: The Treaty Is Not a Treaty*, 26 AM. U. L. REV. 903, 903–4 (2011).

9 Letter from Margot Kaminski, et al., to U.S. Senate Committee on Finance, May 16, 2012, available at http://infojustice.org/wp-content/uploads/2012/05/Law-Professor-Letter-to-Senate-Finance-Committee-May-16-20122.pdf; Jack Goldsmith, *The Doubtful Constitutionality of ACTA as an Ex Ante Congressional-Executive Agreement*, LAWFARE (May 21, 2012), available at www.lawfareblog.com/2012/05/the-doubtful-constitutionality-of-acta-as-an-ex-ante-congressional-executive-agreement/. The ACTA enterprise was substantially undercut when the Parliament of the European Union refused post-signature consent. *See* Zack Whittaker, *"Last Rites" for ACTA? Europe Rejects Antipiracy Treaty*, July 4, 2012, available at http://news.cnet.com/8301-13578_3-57466330-38/last-rites-for-acta-europe-rejects-antipiracy-treaty/.

10 *See infra* Part III.

In a second recent example, the Obama Administration inherited from its predecessors the signed but unratified Law of the Sea (LOS) Convention.[11] Prior administrations had submitted the LOS Convention to the Senate under Article II, and although it had strong support from business and military leaders, the Senate had refused its consent.[12] President Obama put material effort into a renewed effort to secure Senate approval, but the treaty once again failed to gain the needed supermajority vote.[13] The assumption appears to remain (as it has been for the last twenty years) that the LOS Convention has for now been defeated (subject only to possible future revival in the Senate). That is, the assumption is that the supermajority Senate approval is the route the agreement must follow, and if it fails there, it fails. Yet why that should be so, when there are literally thousands of recent examples of international agreements approved other than by Senate supermajority consent, and when the constitutionality of these alternate routes is confidently affirmed by the Third Restatement, is at best a puzzle.

Thus, contrary to the plain formalism of the Constitution's text and the bland pragmatism of the Restatement, the ACTA and LOS Convention episodes reveal the U.S. agreement-making process to be fundamentally unsettled both as a theoretical and practical matter. It may appear unclear at best, even to the careful observer, whether an agreement must be approved and by what body; what constitutes the necessary approval; and what effect agreements made outside the Article II process have or should have in U.S. law.

This chapter assesses trends in U.S. agreement-making in the years since the Third Restatement's publication in an attempt to shed some light on modern practice. It proceeds as follows. Part I describes the Constitution's text and early practice regarding agreement-making. Part II describes the rise of agreement-making outside Article II, Section 2, culminating in Section 303 of the Restatement. Part III examines developments since the publication of the Restatement, including the continued importance of Article II treaties, the largely uncontroversial use of congressional approval in certain areas, and the sharp disputes over Executive agreements. Among other matters, this section

[11] Third United Nations Convention on the Law of the Sea, available at www.unlawofthesea treaty.org/.

[12] *See* Mark Landler, *Law of the Sea Treaty is Found on Capitol Hill, Again*, New York Times, May 23, 2012, available at www.nytimes.com/2012/05/24/world/americas/law-of-the-sea-treaty-is-found-on-capitol-hill-again.html.

[13] Kristina Wong & Sean Lengell, *DeMint: Law of the Sea Treaty Now Dead*, Washington Times, July 16, 2012, available at http://www.washingtontimes.com/news/2012/jul/16/demint-says-law-sea-treaty-now-dead/?page=all.

considers academic attempts to explain the modern practice of agreement-making, and that practice's resistance to theoretical explanation.[14]

I AGREEMENT-MAKING IN TEXT AND EARLY HISTORY

The Constitution's text appears to set forth a demanding regime for making and enforcing international agreements. Article II, Section 2 provides: "[the President] shall have Power, by and with the Advice and Consent of the Senate, to make Treaties, provided two thirds of the Senators present concur ..." Article VI provides that "all Treaties made, or which shall be made, under the Authority of the United States, shall be the supreme Law of the Land ..." The effect appears to be twofold. International agreements are difficult for the United States to make – especially compared to Americans' most immediate precedent, Britain, where the king could (at least in theory) make international agreements without parliamentary consent.[15] Only three other actions in the Constitution require supermajority approval: removing an official from office after impeachment, overriding a veto, and amending the Constitution.[16] At the same time, once approved, treaties appear to have a status in domestic law at least akin to statutes – again a radical departure from British law, in which in the ordinary course treaties were not in themselves part of domestic law and required implementing legislation.[17] In sum, the Constitution's text appears to say that treaties are hard to make but carry great force once made.

Both ideas reflect the concerns of the time. George Washington spoke for many Americans when, in his Farewell Address, he advised the nation to have "as little political connection as possible" with foreign nations.[18] In 1801

14 Leading modern treatments include Hathaway, *supra* note 2; Bradford Clark, *Domesticating Sole Executive Agreements*, 93 VA. L. REV. 1573 (2007); Peter J. Spiro, *Treaties, Executive Agreements, and Constitutional Method*, 79 TEX. L. REV. 961 (2001); John C. Yoo, *Laws as Treaties?: The Constitutionality of Congressional-Executive Agreements*, 99 MICH. L. REV. 757 (2001); Laurence H. Tribe, *Taking Text and Structure Seriously: Reflections on Free-Form Method in Constitutional Interpretation*, 108 HARV. L. REV. 1221 (1995); Bruce Ackerman & David Golove, *Is NAFTA Constitutional?*, 108 HARV. L. REV. 799 (1995). *See also* MICHAEL D. RAMSEY, THE CONSTITUTION'S TEXT IN FOREIGN AFFAIRS 135–54, 197–217 (2007); Michael D. Ramsey, *Executive Agreements and the (Non)Treaty Power*, 77 N.C. L. REV. 133 (1998).

15 *See* 1 WILLIAM BLACKSTONE, COMMENTARIES ON THE LAWS OF ENGLAND 242–50 (1765).

16 *See* U.S. CONST. Art. I, Sec. 3; Art. I, Sec. 7; Art. V.

17 *See* Ramsey, *Executive Agreements*, *supra* note 14, at 225–9 (discussing British practice).

18 *The address of General Washington to the people of the United States on His Declining of the Presidency of the United States*, Sept. 19, 1796, available at www.gpo.gov/fdsys/pkg/GPO-CDOC-106sdoc21/pdf/GPO-CDOC-106sdoc21.pdf.

Thomas Jefferson famously pledged in his First Inaugural Address to avoid "entangling alliances."[19] During the Articles of Confederation period, the sharply contested Jay-Gardoqui negotiations of 1785–1786, which would have traded U.S. claims to navigation of the Mississippi River for twenty years for Spain's concessions elsewhere, soured many people – especially in the critical state of Virginia – on treaty arrangements.[20] At the 1787 Constitutional Convention in Philadelphia, the debate over the Constitution's treaty-making provisions centered on whether to make treaty-making even harder (by requiring consent of three-fourths of senators, or two-thirds of all senators, not just of those present). It does not appear that there were many advocates for making it generally easier (other than for peace treaties), or for developing alternate forms of agreement-making. The president gained a role only late in the Convention, after Madison early on emphatically rejected presidential control over treaty-making. Congress as a whole was considered too unwieldy and insufficiently attuned to international affairs to be a serious contender for the treaty-making power. The atmosphere of the times was one of great caution regarding international commitments.[21]

But once treaties were made, Americans wanted them obeyed. The foreign policy of the Articles period notoriously suffered from states' failure to obey treaty obligations, most importantly the obligations of the 1783 peace treaty with Britain, but also obligations in commercial treaties with other important trading partners.[22] Not surprisingly for a weak nation facing powerful potential adversaries, the United States did not want to violate its treaty obligations. In the months leading up to the 1787 Convention, James Madison's influential essay *Vices of the Political System of Government in the United States* prominently identified U.S. inability to enforce treaties as a leading problem.[23] After the Convention Alexander Hamilton's *Federalist* 22 repeated the theme that "[t]he treaties of the United States under [the Articles] are liable to the

[19] Thomas Jefferson, *First Inaugural Address*, Mar. 4, 1801, available at www.bartleby.com/124/pres16.html.

[20] Charles Warren, *The Mississippi River and the Treaty Clause of the Constitution*, 2 GEO. WASH. L. REV. 271, 285 (1934); SAMUEL BEMIS, A DIPLOMATIC HISTORY OF THE UNITED STATES 73–81 (4th ed. 1955); Jack N. Rakove, *Solving a Constitutional Puzzle: The Treaty-Making Clause as a Case Study*, 1 PERSP. IN AMER. H. (N.S.) 233, 272–4 (1984).

[21] Warren, *supra* note 20, at 293–301; RAMSEY, CONSTITUTION'S TEXT, *supra* note 14, at 148–50; Rakove, *supra* note 20, at 275.

[22] *See* 31 JOURNALS OF THE CONTINENTAL CONGRESS 1774–1789, at 781–874 (John C. Fitzpatrick, ed., 1934) (Foreign Secretary John Jay's report on state treaty violations); FREDERICK MARKS, INDEPENDENCE ON TRIAL: FOREIGN AFFAIRS AND THE MAKING OF THE CONSTITUTION 3–95 (1973).

[23] James Madison, *Vices of the Political System of Government in the United States*, 9 PAPERS OF JAMES MADISON 348–49 (William Hutchinson et al., eds., 1962–1991) (1787).

infractions of thirteen different legislatures ... The faith, the reputation, the peace of the whole Union, are thus continually at the mercy of the prejudices, the passions, and the interests of every member of which it is composed."[24]

This situation might have been remedied just by giving Congress power to enforce treaties legislatively – a power the old Congress under the Articles did not have, and which had long been a power of Parliament. But at the Convention, delegates found the further step of equating treaties and statutes – that is, establishing international agreement-making as a form of domestic legislation – to be uncontroversial. As Hamilton explained, "Laws are a dead letter without courts to expound their true meaning and operation. The treaties of the United States, to have any force at all, must be considered as part of the law of the land."[25]

No other provision of the Constitution's text directly addressed any power by the national government to enter into international agreements. True, under Article II the president was Commander-in-Chief of the military and held the "executive Power" of the United States; the latter, under the understanding of the time, likely included some diplomatic functions.[26] And Article I, Section 8 gave Congress power to make all laws necessary and proper to carry into execution other powers conveyed in the document. These powers came to be relied on much later as possible bases of agreement-making authority outside of the Senate's supermajority consent. But text and history do not support them as broad grants of agreement-making power as an original matter.

As to the president, the grant of power to make treaties *with* Senate approval carries an inescapable negative implication that the president *cannot* make treaties on the president's own authority. Founding-era commentary strongly rejected a unilateral presidential authority over treaties (an authority, as noted, that was identified with the king's excessive power under the British system).[27] Moreover, the desire to guard against unwise treaties, a resilient theme reaching at least to the Jay-Gardoqui negotiations, suggests that any idea of general unilateral presidential power to make treaties would have met towering

[24] James Madison, Alexander Hamilton & John Jay, The Federalist Papers, No. 22 (Hamilton), at 177 (Isaac Kramnick, ed., 1987).

[25] *Ibid.* at 182. In the ratification debates, treaties' status as law proved much more divisive, especially in anti-treaty Virginia, where Patrick Henry seized on this provision as improperly bypassing the House. *See* Ramsey, Constitution's Text, *supra* note 14, at 164–5; Lance Banning, Virginia: Sectionalism and the General Good, in Ratifying the Constitution 261 (Michael Allen Gillespie and Michael Lienesch, eds., 1989).

[26] *See* Saikrishna B. Prakash & Michael D. Ramsey, *The Executive Power over Foreign Affairs*, 111 Yale L.J. 231 (2001); Ramsey, Constitution's Text, *supra* note 14, at 51–90.

[27] *See* Rakove, *supra* note 20, at 275.

resistance. As James Wilson explained: "Neither the President nor the Senate, solely, can complete a treaty; they are checks upon each other, and are so balanced as to produce security to the people."[28]

The idea of an alternate approval process through a majority of Congress is somewhat more plausible, as it would provide a check on treaty-making (and, being bicameral across two bodies elected in different ways, might be considered a sort of supermajority requirement).[29] But in the debates both in Philadelphia and around the nation, there was virtual unanimity on two points: (1) that Congress did not have any direct role in treaty-making (whether or not it should), and (2) that the dangers of ill-advised treaties were resolved (rightly or not) through the supermajority voting requirements in the Senate.[30]

One textual complication remains. Article I, Section 10 provides that "[n]o State shall enter into any Treaty, Alliance, or Confederation." But it goes on to say that no state shall "without the consent of the Congress ... enter into any Agreement or Compact with another State, or with a foreign Power ... " The implication is that some international agreements are not "treaties" (and states can make them, with congressional consent, even though states are flatly banned from making treaties).[31] If there are such "nontreaty" agreements, can the national government also enter into them? Presumably the states would not have more power than the national government in this regard. So if the national government has this power, which branch can exercise it and of what does it consist?

A plausible answer is as follows: at the national level this "nontreaty" agreement-making power falls within the president's executive power over foreign affairs (basically, the power to manage diplomacy).[32] As to content, the division between treaties and "Agreement[s] or Compact[s]" in Article I, Section 10 is also found in international law writing of the time, with which the Framers were familiar.[33] Unfortunately, within that writing the distinction

[28] *See* RAMSEY, CONSTITUTION'S TEXT, *supra* note 14, at 149–150 and n. 53.

[29] *See* Ackerman & Golove, *supra* note 14; David M. Golove, *Against Free-Form Formalism*, 73 NYU L. REV. 1791 (1998).

[30] *See* RAMSEY, CONSTITUTION'S TEXT, *supra* note 14, at 135–54; Ackerman & Golove, *supra* note 14, at 808–13.

[31] The Articles of Confederation, Article 6, had a similar distinction: states could not enter into "any conference, agreement, alliance, or treaty" with a foreign nation without Congress' consent, and states could not enter into "any treaty, confederation, or alliance" among themselves without Congress' consent (thus apparently "agreements" among states were permitted). *See* RAMSEY, CONSTITUTION'S TEXT, *supra* note 14, at 180.

[32] Ramsey, *Executive Agreements*, *supra* note 14, at 160–218.

[33] *See ibid.* at 165–171; Abraham Weinfeld, *What Did the Framers of the Federal Constitution Mean by "Agreements or Compacts"?*, 3 U. CHI. L. REV. 453, 454–6 (1936).

is not entirely clear or consistent, but it is clear enough that significant long-term agreements (at least) were called treaties. That distinction is consistent with how Article I, Section 10 describes state power: states were absolutely prohibited from making treaties but could make presumably less-important agreements with Congress' consent.[34] So while Article I, Section 10 suggests a slight qualification of Article II, Section 2's rule for agreement-making, it does not appear a large one, nor was it mentioned during the drafting and ratification process.

For the Constitution's first hundred years, agreement-making practice substantially followed what appears on the face of the text: the president made international agreements with the Senate's supermajority consent. With only a few ambiguities that were worked out early on, the practice changed relatively little across the Constitution's first century. That is not, as we will see, a complete description, but it captures the material practice.

An early ambiguity was whether Article II required the president to seek the Senate's "Advice" before negotiating a treaty, or just to seek the Senate's advice upon (together with consent to) the final product. As is well known, President Washington initially adopted the first approach and, finding it unhelpful, switched to the second; subsequent presidents followed his lead, and the practice soon became firmly entrenched.[35] Whether Washington had a constitutional obligation to obtain presignature advice remains doubtful, though academic accounts have argued that he did.[36] As a textual matter it seems adequate to get "Advice" upon a finalized proposal, and Article II, Section 2's coupling of advice with consent at a specified time (when senators are counted as "present") suggests that a single consideration by the Senate would suffice. Moreover, "Advice and Consent" in the appointments clause (in the same sentence of Article II, Section 2) appears to mean a yes-or-no vote upon a presidential nomination.[37] And prior to the Constitution, in states whose

34 Ramsey, *Executive Agreements, supra* note 14, at 194–200; *see also* Andrew T. Hyman, *The Unconstitutionality of Long-Term Nuclear Pacts That Are Rejected by over One-Third of the Senate*, 23 DEN. J. INT'L L. & POL'Y 313 (1995).

35 RAMSEY, CONSTITUTION'S TEXT, *supra* note 14, at 151–4.

36 *See* Arthur Bestor, *Separation of Powers in the Domain of Foreign Policy*, 5 SETON H. L. REV. 528 (1976); Arthur Bestor, *Respective Roles of the Senate and President in the Making and Abrogation of Treaties*, 55 WASH. L. REV. 1 (1979); Howard Sklamberg, *The Meaning of Advice and Consent: The Senate's Constitutional Role in Treatymaking*, 18 MICH J. INT'L L. 445 (1997).

37 U.S. CONST. Art. II, Sec. 2 ("[The President] shall nominate, and by and with the Advice and Consent of the Senate, shall appoint" officers of the United States); *see* RAMSEY, CONSTITUTION'S TEXT, *supra* note 14, at 139–40 (elaborating this argument); DAVID CURRIE, THE CONSTITUTION IN CONGRESS: THE FEDERALIST PERIOD 25 (1997) (noting that this is how appointments worked in early practice).

governors were required to take "advice" of a council before acting, there does not appear to have been an established practice that advice had to be taken continuously during the formation of a proposal as opposed to at a single sitting on a final proposal.[38] Whatever the merits of this debate, it soon became accepted as a practical matter that the president signed treaties and submitted the final product to the Senate for approval (or disapproval).

Another initial uncertainty was whether the Senate would (or should) play a meaningful role in checking presidential treaty-making. It is evident that the Framers generally envisioned an aggressive role for the Senate, and in practice that is the role the Senate played.[39] Early practice showed considerable Senate willingness to vote down treaties or (perhaps more significantly) parts of treaties. The hugely important 1794 Jay Treaty, which may have averted renewed war with Britain, passed the Senate without a vote to spare and only on the condition that one article be deleted.[40] Presidents surely understood from the outset that Senate approval was far from automatic.

A few exceptions to the necessity of Senate consent are worth noting, though they tend to confirm rather than undermine the rule. First, presidents made some international agreements without any participation by the Senate or Congress. The earliest one – at least the earliest in any official compilation of agreements – appears to be the "Wilmington Packet" agreement in 1799, when President John Adams' diplomatic agents settled a claim by private U.S. ship owners against the Netherlands.[41] With some ambiguities regarding the characterization of particular agreements, there were around fifty such Executive agreements prior to the Civil War.[42] But this practice never materially challenged the Senate's control over international agreement-making. The presidential agreements were all minor. Most were claims settlements done as exchanges of diplomatic notes; others involved temporary military matters or did not involve material obligations by the United States.[43] An entire diplomatic history of the United States could be written without mentioning most

[38] RAMSEY, CONSTITUTION'S TEXT, *supra* note 14, at 140–1. [39] *Ibid.* at 141–54.

[40] CURRIE, *supra* note 37, at 209–17. The Senate made its consent conditional upon removing one article of the treaty involving trade with the British West Indies. The British agreed to delete the article, and Washington declared the treaty approved. *Ibid.* at 211. Similarly, the Senate conditionally approved a treaty with Tunis in 1798, but on that occasion President Adams resubmitted the revised treaty for a second consent. *Ibid.* at n. 40. The Senate might also indicate rejection of a particular treaty provision through a declaration or reservation accompanying its consent.

[41] *See* 5 TREATIES AND OTHER INTERNATIONAL ACTS OF THE UNITED STATES OF AMERICA 1075 (Hunter Miller, ed., 1931–48) [hereinafter MILLER, TREATIES AND OTHER INTERNATIONAL ACTS].

[42] *See* Ramsey, *Executive Agreements*, *supra* note 14, at 174–83. [43] *Ibid.*

(or any) or them. Further, it is not clear that the practice was contrary to the Constitution's text. As discussed above, the text contemplates lesser agreements or compacts that are not treaties, and thus presumably not governed by Article II, Section 2; the president, acting through the "executive" diplomatic power, has a reasonable claim over them. The nineteenth-century Executive agreements did not need to have effect in domestic law, and at least the claims settlements (which were the most numerous in this period) seem encompassed by what eighteenth-century writers had called nontreaty "agreements."[44]

A second exception to agreement-making through the Senate was that Congress during this early period also occasionally authorized the Executive Branch to enter into international agreements. This practice may have begun even earlier than sole executive agreement-making. In 1792, Congress authorized the Postmaster General to enter into postal agreements with foreign officials regarding international mail delivery.[45] Whether these were understood as binding agreements under international law is unclear: they are not included in leading compilations of U.S. international agreements,[46] and Congress referred to them as "arrangements."[47] Apart from the postal agreements there were a few isolated episodes of Congressional approval. Perhaps most notably, in 1849 and 1851, Congress authorized the president to make an agreement with Britain regarding the construction of a lighthouse on Lake Erie: Britain ceded a small portion of land called Horseshoe Reef on the condition that the United States build a lighthouse on it.[48] But as with the sole

44 *Ibid.*; Hyman, *supra* note 34. As to effect in domestic law, the military agreements did not require any domestic legal effect as they could be implemented unilaterally by the president as Commander-in-Chief; settlement agreements also did not have domestic effect since at the time foreign sovereigns could not be sued in U.S. courts under any circumstances.

45 Act of February 20, 1792, § 26, 1 Stat. 236 (1792); *see also* Act of June 15, 1844, 5 Stat. 718 (1844) (authorizing Postmaster General to make arrangements with British government for delivery of mail between Boston and Canada); Ramsey, *Executive Agreements, supra* note 14, at 182–3.

46 *See, e.g.*, Miller, Treaties and Other International Acts, *supra* note 41 (compiling treaties and other international agreements made in the late eighteenth century but not listing the postal agreements made under the 1792 statute).

47 *See* Act of February 20, 1792, § 26, 1 Stat. 236 (1792) (Postmaster General authorized to "make arrangements with the postmasters in any foreign country" regarding foreign mail delivery); Act of June 15, 1844, 5 Stat. 718 (1844) (Postmaster General authorized "to make such arrangements as may be deemed expedient" with British government for the transmission of mail between Boston and Canada.).

48 *See* Protocol of the Cession of Horseshoe Reef, Dec. 9, 1850, U.S.-G.Br., 18(2) Stat. 325, 5. Miller, Treaties and Other International Acts, *supra* note 41, at 905, approved by Act of Mar. 3, 1849, 9 Stat. 38 (1849) and Act of Mar. 3, 1851, 9 Stat. 627 (1851). *See also* Wallace McClure, International Executive Agreements: Democratic Process under the Constitution of the United States 57–9 (1941) (noting other possible examples).

Executive agreements, none of these agreements was of any diplomatic or legal significance.

Two sometimes-misunderstood episodes merit further mention, although they actually confirm the dominance of the senatorial treaty-making model. In 1817, President James Monroe's administration negotiated the Rush-Bagot Agreement with Britain, limiting naval armaments on the Great Lakes.[49] Monroe at first was not inclined to submit the agreement to the Senate (presumably on the theory that it was made on his independent authority as Commander-in-Chief); he was persuaded to do so in part by his advisors and in part by the British, who wanted to be sure it was regarded as a binding agreement.[50] Ultimately, Monroe sent the agreement to the Senate with a note asking if this was the sort of agreement the Senate needed to approve, and the Senate voted a resolution of advice and consent without comment.[51] Unlike the nontreaty agreements noted above, the Rush-Bagot Agreement was a decisive episode in U.S. foreign relations, cementing the post-War of 1812 rapprochement with Britain and affirming the end of U.S. territorial ambitions in eastern Canada. Had it come out differently, it could rightly be seen as a constitutional breakpoint opening the way to substantial agreements done on the president's independent authority. As it was, it reinforced the stability of a system that remained in place almost to the dawn of the next century.

A second episode is sometimes read as a departure from the text's treaty-making prescriptions, but should not be so understood. In 1844, President John Tyler negotiated a treaty with the then-independent Republic of Texas under which Texas would be annexed and become a U.S. state. The Senate refused its consent, chiefly because northern senators opposed the admission of a new slave state.[52] Tyler then instead asked Congress to approve Texas' admission by majorities in each house, which Congress did.[53] At first glance this appears to be an end run around the treaty power, and in a sense it was. But, crucially, supporters of Texas statehood emphasized that admission

[49] Exchange of Notes Relative to Naval Forces on the American Lakes, Apr. 28–29, 1817, 18(2) Stat. 296, 2 Miller, Treaties and Other International Acts, *supra* note 41, at 645.

[50] *See* 2 Miller, Treaties and Other International Acts, *supra* note 41, at 647–8, notes.

[51] *Ibid.* at 645; 18(2) Stat. 296 (1818) (Senate resolution of advice and consent dated April 16, 1818); *see also* Ackerman & Golove, *supra* note 14, at 816–17 & n. 57.

[52] 4 Miller, Treaties and Other International Acts, *supra* note 41, at 699; *see ibid.* at 737–38 (discussing earlier attempts to gain approval); David Currie, The Constitution in Congress: Descent into the Maelstrom, 1829–1861, 92–7 (2005) [hereinafter Currie, Descent] (same).

[53] Joint Resolution of Mar. 1, 1845, 5 Stat. 797; Joint Resolution of Dec. 29, 1845, 9 Stat. 108; *see* 4 Miller, Treaties and Other International Acts, *supra* note 41, at 689–740; Currie, Descent, *supra* note 52, at 97–101.

need not be, and indeed probably should not be, done by an international agreement: once Texas was annexed, any treaty would cease to be in force internationally, and the terms on which Texas became a state (which were the substance of the proposed treaty) were really aspects of domestic law, not international law. As a result, Texas' supporters argued, approving admission by statute was the correct approach for what was fundamentally a domestic matter, and did not infringe the treaty-making power because it did not involve Congress approving an international commitment.[54] As a result, the Texas episode appears to confirm rather than undermine the dominance of the treaty-making clause during the period: the constitutional arguments made at the time in favor of Congress' action generally conceded rather than rejected the Senate monopoly over international agreement-making.[55]

In sum, until the late nineteenth century the overwhelmingly dominant form of U.S. international agreement-making was the Senate-approved Article II treaty. A scattering of minor agreements occurred outside Article II, Section 2, but their constitutional basis was not well understood or explained, and they never posed a serious challenge to the preeminence of the process laid out in the Constitution's text. Episodes that – had they developed differently – might have opened a path for rival processes, instead reaffirmed the role of the Senate: President Monroe did not insist on his unilateral authority to make the Rush-Bagot Agreement, and many supporters of Texas annexation denied that they were pursuing an alternative approach to treaty-making. As discussed in the next section, the story of the rivals begins in earnest as the end of the nineteenth century approached.

II THE RISE OF THE RIVALS, 1887–1987

The Constitution's second hundred years saw a transformation in the regime of international agreement-making in the United States. How complete a transformation occurred remains a difficult and contested question. But on any account, the practice at the end of the Constitution's second century differed substantially from that at the end of the first. At the beginning of that

54 *See* CURRIE, DESCENT, *supra* note 52, at 97–101. In particular, supporters of annexation pointed to Congress' express power to admit new states in Article IV, Sec. 3. *Ibid.* at 97–8. Some proponents argued that not all international agreements were treaties. *Ibid.* at 99. Opponents of the joint resolution strongly invoked the Senate's exclusive power to approve international agreements. *Ibid.* at 98.

55 A similar set of events transpired with respect to the annexation of Hawaii in 1898–1899. On the significance of the Texas and Hawaii episodes, see Ackerman & Golove, *supra* note 14, at 832–5.

period, Senate supermajority approval completely dominated agreement-making, with scattered and insignificant exceptions. By the end of that time, three great rivals had emerged, each with at least the potential to displace entirely the Article II, Section 2 process, and, at least numerically, Article II treaties represented only a small fraction of the U.S. international agreements.

The reasons for this transformation are no doubt complex and in any event their full exploration is beyond the scope of this chapter. But a brief comment on context is appropriate. The last decades of the nineteenth century brought enormous changes in U.S. foreign relations. The conclusion of the Civil War and the end of Reconstruction produced a newly powerful national government, freed of the debilitating struggle with slavery and sectionalism. Settlement of the West and a vast expansion of international commerce caused the United States to look abroad more than it had before, and its rising economic and military power gave the nation an international prominence it had previously lacked. At the turn of the century, the Spanish-American War and its aftermath, including the acquisition of substantial overseas territories, followed by the muscular diplomacy of President Theodore Roosevelt in Panama, the Caribbean, and elsewhere, confirmed the United States' new role as a global power. These trends accelerated in the twentieth century, compounded by a series of all-encompassing international crises: World War I, the international economic collapse of the 1930s, World War II, and the Cold War.

The new global U.S. roles and interests placed substantial pressures on the old constitutional forms of U.S. diplomacy. In particular, treaty-making under the Constitution's text, and as practiced for most of the nineteenth century, was difficult, time-consuming, and inflexible. Not surprisingly, new forms of agreement-making began to arise, often expressly linked to the need for speed and flexibility in the face of complex and dangerous global conditions. In particular, the problematic barrier of Senate supermajority approval was symbolized by the Senate's rejection in 1919 of President Wilson's signature foreign policy accomplishment, the post–World War I peace settlement and the League of Nations. Although Senate approval of treaties had never been automatic, the defeat of the League was a repudiation of the president that went far beyond earlier rejections.

The story of the second hundred years thus is the story of three new forms of agreement-making which began to displace the Article II, Section 2 treaty. First, the modern textbook alternative is the agreement negotiated by the president and approved after-the-fact by Congress in the manner of legislation. Under this method, consent of a majority of each of the two Houses of

Congress substitutes for consent of two-thirds of the Senate. The paradigmatic modern examples are trade agreements such as the North American Free Trade Agreement (NAFTA). Second, Congress has often granted the president authority to make international agreements in a particular area, without further congressional review or approval. The third form of agreement-making is that done by the president alone – an approach with long-standing roots in historical practice that increasingly expanded in the period we are considering. Further, the contours of presidential agreement-making became complicated by the rise of nonbinding agreements, under which presidents increasingly made substantial foreign policy commitments that purported not to bind the United States as a matter of international law, and by the increased acceptance of implied congressional approval of (or acquiescence in) presidential agreement-making.

A *Advance Approval by Congress*

Congress' role in approving major international agreements has roots in a series of innovations in international trade practice. Beginning in the early nineteenth century, Congress at times provided by statute that the United States would grant favorable tariff treatment to exports of a foreign country if that country granted favorable treatment to U.S. products. This practice of tariff reciprocity did not challenge the Senate's treaty-making power because it did not generate any formal agreements – the United States did not commit to continue favorable treatment in the future. But reciprocal trade legislation did lead to the practical innovation of Congress frequently delegating to the president the authority to determine whether other countries were offering the requisite reciprocal treatment and the power to adjust U.S. tariffs accordingly. In this system, the president's role naturally led to informal negotiation with foreign countries regarding what foreign trade practices the president would regard as sufficiently reciprocal.[56]

From this practice it was a short step to Congress saying overtly that the president could make agreements with other countries on tariffs, which Congress did in several trade statutes beginning in the late nineteenth century.[57] In a sense this was little more than statutory confirmation of an existing

[56] *E.g.*, 3 MILLER, TREATIES AND OTHER INTERNATIONAL ACTS, *supra* note 41, at 521 (agreement with Austria). *See* Ackerman & Golove, *supra* note 14, at 821–2; 2 CHARLES BUTLER, THE TREATY-MAKING POWER OF THE UNITED STATES 372 (1902).

[57] E.g., Act of Oct. 1, 1890, ch. 1244, Sec. 3, 26 Stat. 567, 612 (McKinley Tariff); Act of July 24, 1897, ch. 11, 30 Stat. 151 (Dingley Tariff). *See* Ackerman & Golove, *supra* note 14, at 821–2; Hathaway, *supra* note 2, at 1293–5.

practice. Importantly, Congress, the president, and academic accounts took the position that the president's reciprocal agreements were not binding international law, in the sense that Congress could override them at any time without violating any legal commitment made by the United States.[58] Thus they did not infringe the Senate's treaty-making power, which was the power to make *binding* international commitments.

But the new practice, and in particular its formal recognition and expansion, began to blur the traditional clear rule that treaties needed Senate supermajority approval. As one modern commentary describes, "the President . . . took the [tariff acts] as license to negotiate international agreements with foreign powers that looked so much like international treaties that they were frequently referred to as 'treaties' even though they were never submitted to the Senate."[59] However important the binding/nonbinding distinction was in diplomatic practice or constitutional theory, in the wider legal culture it likely had less resonance. What casual observers saw was that the president was making and Congress was approving trade agreements that looked like treaties. The impression was confirmed by the Supreme Court's 1912 decision *B. Altman & Co. v. United States*, which found that, for purposes of a jurisdictional statute, a reciprocal trade agreement – even though nonbinding – was a "treaty."[60]

As a result, when the executive branch abandoned the binding/nonbinding distinction (at least in the trade area) in the 1930s, it encountered little opposition. The legal culture at that point was accustomed to the president making trade agreements under prior statutory authority. The worldwide economic collapse – much of it blamed on high tariffs and other protectionist trade policies – contributed a sense of urgency. Franklin Roosevelt's Administration concluded international agreements directed toward stabilizing the prices of silver and wheat in 1933, with agreements on gold following in

58 *See* Ackerman & Golove, *supra* note 14, at 822–4. Contemporaneous academic accounts emphasized the distinction. *E.g.*, 2 BUTLER, *supra* note 56, at 372 n. 2 (reciprocal trade agreements not binding); 2 CHARLES C. HYDE, INTERNATIONAL LAW CHIEFLY AS INTERPRETED AND APPLIED BY THE UNITED STATES 229 (1905) (trade agreements "imposed no restriction on the United States").

59 Hathaway, *supra* note 2, at 1296.

60 B. Altman & Co. v. United States, 224 U.S. 583 (1912) ("While it may be true that this commercial agreement . . . was not a treaty possessing the dignity of one requiring ratification by the Senate of the United States, it was an international compact, negotiated between the representatives of two sovereign nations, and made in the name and on behalf of the contracting countries, and dealing with important commercial relations between the two countries . . . "). The Court had previously rejected a nondelegation challenge to the trade agreements in *Field v. Clark*, 143 U.S. 649 (1892).

later years. Shortly thereafter, Congress passed the 1934 Reciprocal Trade Agreements Act (RTAA), which adopted and expanded the earlier strategy of authorizing the president to make reciprocal trade agreements, and the Roosevelt Administration pursued an array of agreements lowering the ruinous tariffs of the early Depression years.[61]

None of these agreements was submitted to the Senate. In one sense that did not seem remarkable, because presidents had been doing something like this for at least forty years. But critically, Roosevelt's agreements – unlike the prior reciprocal trade agreements – were generally regarded as binding in international law.[62] As the Senate itself recognized in 1937 in reauthorizing the RTAA, trade agreements had now been taken out of Article II, Section 2.[63] The pattern continued after World War II, albeit in a somewhat ad hoc fashion. The centerpiece of the postwar order in trade was the General Agreement on Tariffs and Trade (GATT), designed to stop trade wars and introduce gradual negotiated reductions in tariffs. But the International Trade Organization (ITO), the international body envisioned to implement GATT, could not even gain a majority in Congress. So the Executive Branch under Presidents Truman and Eisenhower claimed delegated authority from a prior statute to negotiate tariffs under GATT, although the statute did not expressly provide it, and trade agreements proceeded under GATT without further direct domestic approval.[64] As described below, trade agreement practice eventually shifted to a different model, but advance approval by Congress remained a major (and numerically dominant) form of agreement-making as Congress increasingly passed statutes with transnational implications in other fields and increasingly adapted the trade agreement model to authorize the president to make agreements implementing those statutes.[65]

B Postsignature Approvals

The agreements made under delegated authority from Congress differed from traditional treaty approvals, not only in avoiding the supermajority requirement but also in dispensing altogether with after-the-fact legislative-branch approval. Of course that made them a powerful tool for the president, but they depended on Congress' willingness to delegate broad authority to the

61 Hathaway, *supra* note 2, at 1297. 62 Ackerman & Golove, *supra* note 14, at 845–7.

63 *See ibid.* at 851.

64 *See* John H. Jackson, *The General Agreement on Tariffs and Trade in United States Domestic Law*, 66 Mich. L. Rev. 249 (1967).

65 *See* Hathaway, *Presidential Power*, *supra* note 4, at 186–191 (describing post–World War II advance authorizations).

president (or, at least, on the president plausibly being able to claim authority from a prior statute). A more formidable rival to the Article II treaty might arise if Congress had the ability to approve agreements after-the-fact by majority vote.

In the most detailed telling of this part of the story, by Bruce Ackerman and David Golove, the dramatic point came at the end of World War II, as the United States contemplated a series of agreements to shape the postwar world order.[66] The roots of this form of agreement-making appear to extend a little earlier: a 1923 statute authorized the president to renegotiate Allied war debt arising from World War I[67] and Congress approved U.S. membership in the International Labor Organization (ILO) in 1934.[68] These were new ways to approve agreement-making, because in both cases Congress gave assent to existing agreements. Joining the ILO involved accepting the ILO constitution, which had been developed in the aftermath of World War I. The statute authorizing renegotiation of the war debts expressly required the president to bring the completed deals back to Congress for after-the-fact approval. As with the reciprocal trade legislation, these early developments did not directly challenge the Senate's general power of supermajority consent to treaties. The debt agreements were justified under Congress' power to dispose of U.S. property, and the ILO membership was defended (perhaps wrongly) on the ground that it imposed no binding obligations on the United States.[69] But, again like the reciprocal trade legislation, they began a blurring of categories that ultimately contributed to the collapse of Senate exclusivity.

As Professors Ackerman and Golove recount, by 1945, rightly or wrongly, conventional wisdom held that the Senate's rejection of the League and the consequent U.S. withdrawal from the affairs of Europe after World War I

[66] Ackerman & Golove, *supra* note 14, at 861–97. The question generated enormous academic literature at the time. *See, e.g.*, Myres S. McDougal & Asher Lans, *Treaties and Congressional-Executive or Presidential Agreement: Interchangeable Instruments and National Policy (parts 1 & 2)*, 54 YALE L.J. 181, 534 (1945) (arguing for the constitutionality of Congressional-Executive agreements); Quincy Wright, *The United States and International Agreements*, 38 AM. J. INT'L L. 341 (1944) (same); MCCLURE, *supra* note 48 (same); *Edward S. Corwin, The Constitution and World Organization* 31–54 (1944) (same); Edwin Borchard, *Shall the Executive Agreement Replace the Treaty?*, 53 YALE L.J. 664 (1944) (arguing for the exclusivity of Article II, Section 2); 2 CHARLES C. HYDE, INTERNATIONAL LAW CHIEFLY AS INTERPRETED AND APPLIED BY THE UNITED STATES 1416–18 (2d ed. 1945) (same); Herbert W. Briggs, *Treaties, Executive Agreements, and the Panama Joint Resolution of* 1943, 37 AM. POL. SCI. REV. 868 (1943) (same); Herbert W. Briggs, *The UNRRA Agreement and Congress*, 38 AM. J. INT'L L. 650 (1944) (same). *See* Ackerman & Golove, *supra* note 14, at 806–7 nn. 16–17.

[67] Act of Feb. 28, 1923, ch. 146, 42 Stat. 1325; *see* Ackerman & Golove, *supra* note 14, at 840–41.

[68] Joint Resolution of June 19, 1934, ch. 676, 48 Stat. 1182.

[69] *See* Ackerman & Golove, *supra* note 14.

had set the world on course for the World War II. The Executive Branch under Presidents Roosevelt and Truman was determined to move forward with the new postwar world order with or without the Senate. The two presidents thus presented a series of key agreements to Congress for postsignature majority approval, backed up by a proposed constitutional amendment in the House that would have eliminated the required Senate supermajority altogether.[70] The result was a potential constitutional crisis, resolved by a majority of the Senate approving the agreements as submitted to both houses without insisting on any special supermajority approval by the Senate.[71]

This outcome inaugurated a new model of agreement-making: postsignature approval by Congress. In the Ackerman/Golove account, it quickly became a usual procedure regarded as interchangeable with supermajority Senate consent as a means of constitutionally approving international agreements. As Ackerman and Golove quote President Truman in 1947, asking for Congressional consent to an agreement establishing U.S. trusteeship in the Pacific Islands territories:

> I have given special consideration to whether the attached trusteeship agreement should be submitted to the Congress for action by a joint resolution or by the treaty process. I am satisfied that either method is constitutionally permissible and that the agreement resulting will be of the same effect internationally and under the supremacy clause of the Constitution whether advised and consented to by the Senate or whether approval is authorized by a joint resolution.[72]

In 1954, apparently confirming the interchangeability of alternate approaches, Congress approved an agreement regarding construction of the St. Lawrence Seaway, which the Senate had earlier rejected when it had been presented for approval as a treaty.[73] Congress also began expressly authorizing the president to negotiate international agreements in particular areas subject to after-the-fact approval by Congress – notably in the Atomic Energy Act of

70 H.R. J. Res. 320, 78th Cong., 2d sess. (1944).

71 *See* Ackerman & Golove, *supra* note 14, at 861–89. The key approval was of the Bretton Woods agreements, establishing the International Monetary Fund and the World Bank, in 1945. *See* Bretton Woods Agreements Act, ch. 339, 59 Stat. 512 (1945). *See also* Ackerman & Golove, *supra* note 14, at 892 n. 425 (listing additional agreements, including approvals of U.S. membership in the U.N. Food and Agriculture Organization (1945), the U.N. Educational, Scientific and Cultural Organization (UNESCO) (1946), the International Refugee Organization (1947), the World Health Organization (1948) and the Caribbean Commission (1948), as well as approval of the United Nations Headquarters Agreement (1947) and the trusteeship agreement for the Pacific Islands (1947)).

72 H.R. Doc. No. 378, 80th Cong., 1st Sess. (1947); *see* Ackerman & Golove, *supra* note 14, at 896.

73 *See* Ackerman & Golove, *supra* note 14, at 893.

1954 and the Arms Control and Disarmament Act of 1961.[74] Later, Congress approved the 1972 Strategic Arms Limitation Treaty (SALT I) via the latter procedure,[75] confirming Congress' authority over agreements in a core area of national defense.

A more sophisticated version of this sort of authorization became the foundation for modern U.S. trade law in the Trade Act of 1974, which shifted trade agreements from their traditional procedure of advance authorization into a regime of after-the-fact approvals.[76] As discussed, the postwar innovation of after-the-fact congressional approval had not taken immediate hold in trade law because Congress was unwilling to approve the ITO, and the Executive Branch instead negotiated the initial GATT rounds under a claim of prior statutory approval. That pattern continued until the 1974 Act, which required after-the-fact approval, but also made the process more attractive by developing the "fast-track" procedure of mandating a vote within a specified time and without amendments.[77] Agreements approved under the Act's procedures included the Tokyo Round of GATT (the first GATT round subject to after-the-fact approval) and free trade agreements with Israel (1985) and Canada (1988).[78]

Thus, by the time the Third Restatement was published in 1987, the new form – increasingly called the "Congressional-Executive agreement" – appeared to be the emerging dominant approach. To be sure, the traditional Senate approval had not been wholly superseded, and Ackerman and Golove's account may overstate the extent to which the treaty-making clause was eclipsed.[79] Even in the immediate postwar period, some important international agreements had been approved under Article II, Section 2: in particular, the UN Charter, the North Atlantic Treaty Organization (NATO) Treaty, and other linchpins in the network of early Cold War security pacts. But momentum appeared to be on the side of the Congressional-Executive agreements, which not only moved into areas more traditionally associated with treaties (such as arms control), but also laid claim to areas typically handled through more open-ended prenegotiation approvals of executive action, such as trade. Moreover, no convincing theory seemed able to explain why some agreements were approved as Article II, Section 2 treaties and some as Congressional-Executive agreements, lending credence to the idea that either could be used

74 68 Stat. 919, 939–40 (1954) (authorizing president to enter into agreements on the peaceful use of nuclear energy); 75 Stat. 631, 634 (1961) (requiring arms control agreements to be approved by either the treaty-making power or by Congress).

75 Joint Resolution of Sept. 30, 1972, 86 Stat. 746.

76 88 Stat. 1978 (1975).

77 *See* Ackerman & Golove, *supra* note 14, at 904–6.

78 *Ibid.* at 906 & nn. 479–81.

79 *See* Spiro, *supra* note 14, at 981–93.

for any purpose. Not surprisingly, the Third Restatement affirmed the idea of interchangeability in Section 303: "The prevailing view is that the Congressional-Executive agreement can be used as an alternative to the treaty method in every instance."[80] "Interchangeability," Ackerman and Golove concluded, "had become part of the living Constitution."[81]

But this too was not the whole picture. First, by the 1980s the Senate was already beginning to fight back, particularly in the arms control area. Despite the precedent of SALT I, senators insisted that the controversial SALT II agreement be submitted under the treaty-making clause.[82] In approving the agreement on Intermediate-Range Nuclear Forces (INF) in 1987, the Senate added a declaration that seemed (despite some ambiguity) to call for future arms control agreements to be submitted under the treaty-making clause.[83] Second, there was another contender we have yet to consider: the sole Executive agreement, which had enjoyed a parallel rise to prominence – a part of the story taken up in the next subsection.

C *Agreement-Making by Presidential Authority*

As discussed, presidential agreement-making without formal congressional or Senate approval has roots going almost to the founding and in limited form may be defensible under the Constitution's text. But it has evolved from a minor diplomatic convenience principally directed to one-time claims settlements into a major element of U.S. foreign policy. This development has occurred in at least three ways: (a) the rise of sole Executive agreements; (b) the innovation of "nonbinding" agreements; and (c) increased claims of implicit congressional approval or acquiescence.

Sole Executive agreements' move to prominence roughly coincides with the historical pattern described above. In the post–Civil War era, presidents began making more significant agreements, especially in the military area. Several agreements with Mexico in the 1880s authorized each country's military forces to cross the border in pursuit of outlaws (a very significant concession, had it been expected that the Mexican Army would actually act upon it).[84] Executive agreements made up a substantial part of the interim

80 THIRD RESTATEMENT, *supra* note 1, § 303, cmt. e.

81 *See* Ackerman & Golove, *supra* note 14, at 896.

82 *See* Phillip Trimble & Jack S. Weiss, *The Role of the President, the Senate and Congress with Respect to Arms Control Treaties Concluded by the United States*, 67 CHI-KENT L. REV. 645, 661–2 (1991). The president ultimately withdrew the treaty after the Soviet invasion of Afghanistan.

83 *Ibid.* at 685–7.

84 *See* MCCLURE, *supra* note 48, at 242.

military and political arrangements after Spain's capitulation in the Spanish-American War.[85] By the early twentieth century it was probably no longer possible to say (as it had been earlier) that Executive agreements never covered matters of diplomatic consequence.

As with congressionally approved agreements, the biggest steps are associated with President Franklin Roosevelt. In 1933, Roosevelt controversially extended diplomatic recognition to the Soviet Union and negotiated a settlement of substantial outstanding claims between the two nations.[86] He avoided seeking any sort of congressional approval, likely the result of popular mistrust of the Communist regime at the time. Like other steps in our story, this was not in itself a big one: presidents had settled claims unilaterally before; diplomatic recognition was thought to be a core presidential power; and presidents were taking increasingly prominent roles in foreign affairs, including through the tariff negotiations discussed above and the nonbinding agreements discussed below.

But Roosevelt took the unusual step of trying to enforce his agreement as a matter of U.S. domestic law. Under the agreement, the Soviet Union assigned its claims against private parties in the United States to the U.S. government, and the United States filed suits to collect against private citizens. New York state law refused to recognize the validity of the Soviet claims to property located in New York, and Roosevelt sought to override the state law. Doing so meant insisting that the Executive agreement was a binding commitment under international law of equivalent status to a treaty under Article VI of the Constitution.[87]

In *United States v. Belmont*,[88] the U.S. Supreme Court upheld Roosevelt's position, ruling that he had power to enter into the recognition agreement and that the agreement overrode state law in the same manner as a treaty: "[W]hile this rule [supremacy over preexisting state law] in respect of treaties is established by the express language of cl. 2, Art. VI, of the Constitution, the same rule would result in the case of all international compacts and agreements."[89] Five years later, the Court reaffirmed its position in *United States v. Pink*.[90] If read broadly, these decisions might underwrite a dramatic shift of agreement-

[85] *See* Ackerman & Golove, *supra* note 14, at 818 & nn. 63–4. Ackerman and Golove's account, however, does not distinguish between agreements intended to be binding and agreements not intended to be binding.

[86] *See* Exchange of Notes at Washington Regarding General Relations, Nov. 16, 1933, U.S.-U.S.S.R., 11 International Agreements of the United States 1776–1949, at 1249 (Charles I. Bevans ed., 1971); Stephen Millet, The Constitutionality of Executive Agreements: An Analysis of United States v. Belmont 1–115 (1990).

[87] *See* Ramsey, *Executive Agreements*, *supra* note 14, at 145–54. [88] 301 U.S. 324 (1937).

[89] *Ibid.* at 331. [90] 315 U.S. 203 (1942).

making power to the president. At minimum, they contributed, along with parallel developments in congressionally approved agreements, to a blurring of categories surrounding agreement-making. Just as the treaty-making clause was losing its exclusivity as the way to make "treaties," Article VI appeared to be losing its exclusivity as the way agreements became "supreme Law of the Land."

Roosevelt followed up in 1940 with the important destroyers-for-bases agreement with Britain, also done on sole executive authority and a major step toward U.S. involvement in World War II.[91] Attorney General and future Supreme Court Justice Robert Jackson defended the agreement under the president's Commander-in-Chief power: while conceding that the president could not violate existing statutes, Jackson did not rest on any congressional authorization of the agreement.[92] Thus another avenue for agreement-making – at least in core executive areas – was becoming entrenched.[93]

Even before this time, a further potentially powerful executive form of agreement-making had emerged, this one associated with Franklin Roosevelt's cousin Theodore. An aggressive proponent of executive power, Theodore Roosevelt as president developed the idea of the "Gentlemen's Agreement" – that is, as he envisioned it, a diplomatic arrangement based on the good faith of particular leaders but not a formal binding agreement under international law.[94] Because they were not binding, these "agreements" were not "treaties" in the constitutional sense – the sine qua non of treaties

[91] Exchange of Notes at Washington Regarding Leasing of Naval Air Bases, Sept. 2, 1940, U.S.-U.K., 54 Stat. 2405.

[92] Acquisition of Naval and Air Bases in Exchange for Over-Age Destroyers, 39 Op. Att'y Gen. 484 (1940).

[93] The Destroyers-for-Bases agreement amounted to a substantial diplomatic event in a way most prior Executive agreements did not; however, it is possible to defend its constitutionality on the ground that it did not impose material on-going obligations on the United States. *See* Ramsey, *Executive Agreements, supra* note 14, at 237 n. 406.

Unlike Congressional-Executive agreements, sole executive agreements – at least outside the president's core constitutional powers – remained controversial. For example, beginning in 1972 the Senate has refused to approve the Vienna Convention on the Law of Treaties, an otherwise mostly uncontroversial agreement, because the Convention implies that the president could make agreements for the United States without Senate or congressional approval that would be treated as binding under international law. *See* CONGRESSIONAL RESEARCH SERVICE, TREATIES AND OTHER INTERNATIONAL AGREEMENTS: THE ROLE OF THE UNITED STATES SENATE 45–9 (2001).

[94] *See* Duncan Hollis & Joshua J. Newcomer, *"Political" Commitments and the Constitution*, 49 VA. J. INT'L L. 507, 563–6 (2009). On the international law and practice of nonbinding agreements, see Kal Raustiala, *Form and Substance in International Agreements*, 99 AMER. J. INT'L L. 581 (2005). On the constitutional aspects of nonbinding agreements, see Michael D. Ramsey, *Evading the Treaty Power?: The Constitutionality of Nonbinding Agreements*, 11 FIU L. REV. 371 (2016).

being their bindingness – and so no Senate approval was needed. So far this argument paralleled the contemporaneous view of reciprocal trade agreements discussed above. But Roosevelt went further in denying the need for congressional approval as well. The president's authority arose from the president's executive diplomatic power, which Roosevelt read expansively, and since (unlike the reciprocal trade agreements) he did not expect his promises to become part of U.S. law, he thought Congress had no role to play.[95]

Formally, Roosevelt may have been right,[96] and indeed the informal modus vivendi had long been an aspect of international diplomacy. But practically, his enhancement of the nonbinding agreement was substantial compared to earlier practice, as a sampling of these agreements suggests. For example, the 1907 "Gentlemen's Agreement" with Japan limited Japanese emigration to the United States;[97] the 1905 agreement with Santo Domingo – done in place of a treaty the Senate refused to approve – involved the United States taking over much of Santo Domingo's financial affairs.[98] President Woodrow Wilson followed Roosevelt's practice in the Lansing-Ishii Agreement regarding policy in the Far East.[99] In the World War II era, Franklin Roosevelt continued the practice, making far-reaching arrangements with the Allied Powers on his own authority without the use of binding agreements, as with the Atlantic Charter and the Yalta Agreement.[100]

Thus, by the end of World War II two forms of pure executive agreement-making had emerged (although the separation between them was not always clear), along with Congressional approval through either ex ante authorization or ex post consent. The distinctions became even less clear in the decades after the war, driven by a decline in formalism generally and by the pervasive influence of Justice Jackson's concurring opinion in the U.S. Supreme Court's seminal 1952 case *Youngstown Sheet & Tube Co. v. Sawyer*.[101]

95 No doubt earlier presidents had made such commitments, on a smaller, less public and more temporary basis. *See* Hollis & Newcomer, *supra* note 94, at 563–4 (discussing early practice). The modern, high-profile nonbinding agreement, however, appears to have begun with Theodore Roosevelt.

96 *See* Ramsey, *Evading the Treaty Power*, *supra* note 94, at 373–7 (reaching this conclusion); *but see* Hollis & Newcomer, *supra* note 94, at 569–78 (arguing for congressional involvement under some circumstances).

97 Notes Exchanged Between the United States and Japan Declaring Their Policy in the Far East, Nov. 30, 1908; *see* Hollis & Newcomer, *supra* note 94, at 564 & n. 253.

98 *See* Hollis & Newcomer, *supra* note 94, at 564 & n. 252; THEODORE ROOSEVELT, AN AUTOBIOGRAPHY 551 (1913).

99 Hollis & Newcomer, *supra* note 94, at 565 & n. 255.

100 *Ibid.* at 565.

101 343 U.S. 579 (1952).

Youngstown on its face had nothing to do with agreement-making, and Justice Hugo Black's formalist majority opinion did not offer much accommodation for executive actions not expressly authorized by statute or the Constitution.[102] But Jackson, who had defended the destroyers-for-bases deal as attorney general, outlined a more flexible approach, while agreeing with Black on the case's outcome. Separation of powers issues, Jackson wrote, could usefully be analyzed in a three-category framework: (1) where Congress had approved of a presidential action; (2) where Congress was silent; and (3) where Congress disapproved. In the first category, Jackson argued, presidential action would almost always be valid. Jackson made clear that congressional approval or disapproval could be informal or inferred from circumstances; in *Youngstown* itself, he found Congress's implied disapproval to be decisive.[103]

Though Jackson joined Black to rule against executive action in *Youngstown*, his opinion pointed the way for further expansion of executive power, including with respect to international agreements. If the executive branch could find an implicit congressional approval of its agreement-making, it would be in Jackson's category one, where its constitutionality seemed almost assured. GATT was an obvious example. Congress had voted down the ITO, but it had (sort of) authorized the president to negotiate a tariff regime apart from the ITO. As presidents pursued additional rounds of negotiations under GATT, Congress did not object, and indeed passed legislation assuming the validity of the GATT regime. And Jackson's structure could be pushed much further, depending on the extent to which generalized and informal congressional actions might be construed as consent.

This model of presidential agreement-making received a potentially broad endorsement from the Supreme Court in 1981 in *Dames & Moore v. Regan*. President Carter negotiated a deal with Iran to end the embassy hostage crisis; among other things, the Algiers Accords required that suits pending against Iran in U.S. courts be terminated and transferred to an international arbitral body. When President Reagan, succeeding Carter, sought to enforce the Accords, Dames & Moore (a claimant against Iran) objected. The Court, expressly embracing Jackson's *Youngstown* framework, found that Congress had "acquiesced" in presidential settlement of claims, a practice the Court traced back to the Wilmington Packet in 1799.[104]

102 *Ibid.* at 585–9. The case involved President Truman's seizure of private steel mills to assure supplies for the war effort in Korea; the Court invalidated the seizure, with Justice Black emphasizing that neither the Constitution nor any statute authorized it.

103 *Ibid.* at 635–40 (Jackson, concurring).

104 453 U.S. 654, 679 & n. 8 (1981).

Dames & Moore, if read broadly, was more radical than it sounded: the agreement in question was much more than the one-time settlement agreements of the nineteenth century, and in any event those agreements had never been seen as making domestic law.[105] By incorporating Jackson's flexible and informal requirements for approval, and arguably expanding them, *Dames & Moore* made it much easier for the Executive Branch to argue that it was making agreements with congressional approval. The need to seek formal approval, either through Article II, Section 2 or through Congress, correspondingly receded. On the other hand, *Dames & Moore* seemed to signal a retreat from sole Executive agreements of the *Pink/Belmont* variety. An aggressively pro-executive opinion could have cited *Pink* and *Belmont* prominently and exclusively, dispensing with the need to squeeze Congressional approval out of Congressional inaction. The Court's more prominent citation of Jackson's *Youngstown* concurrence pushed *Pink* and *Belmont*, and sole Executive agreements generally, to the background, and built up the need for some nominal tie to Congress for authority to make binding agreements. Whether for that reason or others, nonbinding agreements (which in practice did not purport to require any sort of congressional acceptance) continued to play a major role in U.S. diplomacy. Examples included President Kennedy's settlement of the Cuban Missile Crisis, President Nixon's diplomacy with China and his resolution of U.S. involvement in the Vietnam War, the Helsinki and Sinai Accords under President Ford, and various agreements under President Carter.[106]

These threefold developments left Executive agreements in a state of considerable uncertainty. As to any particular agreement, it might be very difficult to identify the claimed source of authority. For example, how could one tell if an Executive agreement was a "political" (nonbinding) commitment or a legal commitment? Some agreements, of course, might say so expressly: the 1975 Helsinki Final Act[107] expressly declared that it was nonbinding, while others recited that the parties intended to be legally bound. But others might be subject to substantial dispute as to their bindingness. Similarly, the idea of implicit Congressional approval or acquiescence made it difficult to tell, absent specific direction from the Executive Branch, whether an agreement should be categorized as done on presidential authority or done on authority provided by Congress.

[105] *See* Ramsey, *Executive Agreements*, *supra* note 14, at 218–35.

[106] *See* Hollis & Newcomer, *supra* note 94, at 565.

[107] Conference on Security and Cooperation in Europe: Final Act, Aug. 1, 1975, 73 Dep't St. Bull. 323 (1975).

D Conclusion: The Third Restatement and U.S. Agreement-Making in 1987

As the American Law Institute prepared the Third Restatement in the mid-1980s, the constitutional authority for international agreement-making in the United States was highly confused. At least five distinct alternatives to Article II, Section 2 treaty-making existed in theory and practice: express advance Congressional authorization; express postsignature Congressional approval; implicit Congressional approval; sole Executive agreements; and nonbinding agreements. No theory stood as a comprehensive explanation of them all, and practice appeared to adopt one or the other according to individual circumstances.

Perhaps understandably, the Restatement finessed the entire mess, making only two points. First, Congressional approval could substitute for supermajority Senate approval, and second, the president could make agreements independently in areas of the president's constitutional authority.[108] For the most part these assessments were not incorrect, just incomplete. The comments' assertion[109] of complete interchangeability between treaties and Congressional-Executive agreements, it is true, lacked full theoretical and practical support. A better answer would have been that no one could explain why some agreements took one form and some took the other, nor predict which form would prevail in an ongoing struggle that, at least in the arms control area, seemed to be reemerging. More broadly, the history of agreement-making in the Constitution's second hundred years reveals the shifting fortunes of various approaches, with none dominant in theory or practice. That pattern, as we will see, continued in the years after the Restatement.

III TREATIES IN THE POST-RESTATEMENT ERA, 1987–2015

A The Persistence of Treaties

Professor Edwin Borchard, in the midst of the World War II era debate over treaty-making power, asked "Shall the Congressional-Executive Agreement

108 Third Restatement, *supra* note 1, § 303 (noting that in addition to agreement-making with approval by the Senate, "the President, with the authorization or approval of Congress, may make an international agreement dealing with any matter that falls within the powers of Congress and of the President under the Constitution" and that "the President, on his own authority, may make an international agreement dealing with any matter that falls within his independent powers under the Constitution").

109 *Ibid.*, comment e (noting that "[t]he prevailing view is that the Congressional-Executive agreement can be used as an alternative to the treaty method in every instance. Which procedure should be used is a political judgment, made in the first instance by the President, subject to the possibility that the Senate might refuse to consider a joint resolution of Congress to approve an agreement, insisting that the President submit the agreement as a treaty").

Replace the Treaty?"[110] By the time of the Third Restatement, the consensus legal answer seemed to be that it could – that is, a Congressional-Executive agreement could do anything a treaty could.[111] And by the numbers, it may appear that the treaty has indeed been largely displaced: only a small fraction of U.S. international agreements are in modern practice approved through the Article II, Section 2 process.[112] Professor Oona Hathaway's 2008 academic study, fittingly titled *Treaties' End*, concluded that "Congressional-Executive Agreements have gradually eclipsed [the Treaty Clause] as the central method of international lawmaking in the United States."[113]

Yet the Article II, Section 2 treaty persists. The raw numbers hide a peculiar feature of modern practice. Despite the Third Restatement's declaration of "interchangeability," since its publication the treaty form has dominated the most important agreements in the most important areas of U.S. international relations. The only prominent exception is trade law, where the non–Article II approvals of NAFTA, the World Trade Organization (WTO), and various bilateral or regional free trade agreements stand not so much as a signal of treaties' decline, but rather a puzzling exception to an otherwise fairly consistent practice.

To begin, consider the range of subjects where treaties have dominated, and indeed in some cases reasserted their importance. In arms control, for example, the 1961 Arms Control Act expressly contemplated approval of arms control treaties outside Article II, and the path-breaking SALT I agreement with the Soviet Union was approved by Congress as a whole (albeit with the gesture of calling it an "interim" agreement).[114] But thereafter the focus shifted back to Article II, Section 2. As discussed, the pattern began even before the

[110] Borchard, *supra* note 66, at 664.

[111] *See* Third Restatement, *supra* note 1, § 303, cmt. e. The political question doctrine, as well as possible difficulties with finding plaintiffs with standing, likely account for a lack of judicial authority on the issue. A prominent lawsuit challenging NAFTA on the ground that it should have been approved as an Article II treaty was rejected by the court of appeals under the political question doctrine without reaching the merits of the question. *Made in the USA Foundation v. United States*, 242 F.3d 1300 (11th Cir. 2001). The district court had rejected the challenge on the merits. *Made in the USA Foundation v. United States*, 56 F. Supp. 2d 1226 (N.D. Ala. 1999).

[112] *See* Hathaway, *supra* note 2, at 1257–60 (finding in twenty-year period from 1980 to 2000 a total of 375 treaties and 2744 executive agreements – that is, only 12 percent of agreements were concluded as treaties).

[113] *Ibid.* at 1307.

[114] *See* Part II. However, as Professor Yoo notes, many significant arms control agreements prior to 1987 were done as Article II treaties, including the Limited Nuclear Test Ban Treaty (1963), the Threshold Test Ban Treaty (1974), the Anti-Ballistic Missile Treaty (1972), and the Nuclear Non-Proliferation Treaty (1968). *See* Yoo, *supra* note 14, at 804–5.

Third Restatement went to press, with SALT II in 1979 and the INF treaty in 1987.[115] The next two decades entrenched the treaty path: among others, the Strategic Arms Reduction Talks (START I) Treaty and the Treaty on Conventional Armed Forces in Europe (CFE) in 1991, START II in 1993, the Chemical Weapons Convention in 1997, the Comprehensive Nuclear Test Ban Treaty in 1999, the Moscow Treaty in 2003, and the New START Treaty in 2010 were all submitted to the Senate under the treaty-making clause.[116] No major arms control treaty was submitted or approved under Article I during this period. Moreover, after 1991 the Senate expressly used arms control to contest interchangeability, routinely attaching a declaration to its consent stating that arms control agreements should use the Article II supermajority process.[117] As a Senate report explained in 1999, "some in the executive branch persist in the mistaken belief that it is constitutionally acceptable to undertake militarily significant international accords by Executive agreement, approved by a simple majority vote of both Houses."[118]

The Article II, Section 2 approach has also dominated the U.S. approval of human rights agreements, despite the Senate's reluctance to give consent. During the Cold War era, the Senate declined to act on a series of important multilateral human rights agreements such as the 1948 Convention against Genocide (ultimately approved in 1986) and the 1966 International Covenant on Civil and Political Rights (ICCPR). The Senate approved the latter only in 1992, after the end of the Cold War, and made it subject to numerous reservations, understandings, and declarations – including a declaration that the Convention was not self-executing – that minimized its effect in the United States.[119] Other major human rights treaties submitted through the Article II, Section 2 process include the Convention Against Torture and

115 *See supra* notes 82–83.

116 *See* Spiro, *supra* note 14, at 996–8 (discussing practice to 2001).

117 In connection with the CFE treaty, the Senate declared "its intent to approve international agreements that would obligate the United States to reduce or limit the Armed Forces or armaments of the United States in a militarily significant manner only pursuant to the Treaty Power as set forth in Article II, Section 2, Clause 2 of the Constitution." S. Ex. Rep. No. 102–22, at 81 (1991). The Senate has repeated this declaration in subsequent treaties, in the words of Professor Spiro "to the point that it appears to have assumed the status of boilerplate." Spiro, *supra* note 14, at 997.

Interestingly, the most substantial challenge to this pattern came in 2002 when President Bush proposed making the Moscow Treaty a nonbinding arrangement, a proposal Russia rejected. But Bush's plan was not to shift approval from the Senate to Congress; rather, he would have bypassed approval altogether.

118 S. Exec. Rep. No. 106–2, at 18 (1999); *see* Spiro, *supra* note 14, at 997 n. 171.

119 *See* Curtis A. Bradley & Jack L. Goldsmith, *Treaties, Human Rights, and Conditional Consent*, 149 U. PA. L. REV. 399, 413–16 (2000).

the International Convention on the Elimination of All Forms of Racial Discrimination (both approved with reservations after long delays in 1994),[120] and conventions on the rights of women, children, and the disabled (which remain unapproved).[121] Despite difficulties in obtaining Senate approval, no major human rights agreement has been submitted or approved solely through Article I, even though Congress also implemented several of these treaties because they required enactment of criminal laws.[122]

A common generalization, in the face of the above practice, is that Congressional-Executive agreements dominate in economic matters while treaties are used elsewhere.[123] This is also not accurate. For example, in the early 1980s the U.S. State Department inaugurated a new program to provide legal protection for U.S. foreign investment, superseding the prior Friendship, Commerce, and Navigation (FCN) Treaties, which had been used until the 1960s. The new form, the Bilateral Investment Treaty (BIT), followed the old in its approval process under Article II, Section 2.[124] The United States is now party to over forty BITs, most negotiated since the 1980s and all approved under Article II, Section 2.[125] The only substantial modern investment agreement not approved through Article II, Section 2 is the Agreement on Trade-

120 *See* Yoo, *supra* note 14, at 807.

121 U.N. Convention on the Elimination of All Forms of Discrimination against Women (CEDAW), available at www.un.org/womenwatch/daw/cedaw; U.N. Convention on the Rights of Persons with Disabilities, available at www.un.org/development/desa/disabilities/convention-on-the-rights-of-persons-with-disabilities.html.

122 *E.g.*, the Convention on the Prevention and Punishment of the Crime of Genocide [hereinafter Genocide Convention], available at https://treaties.un.org/doc/publication/unts/volume%2078/volume-78-i-1021-english.pdf, and the Convention against Torture and Other Cruel, Inhuman or Degrading Treatment or Punishment, available at https://treaties.un.org/doc/Publication/UNTS/Volume%201465/volume-1465-I-24841-English.pdf.

123 *See* Yoo, *supra* note 14, at 811–12.

124 *See* Office of the U.S. Trade Representative, Bilateral Investment Treaties, available at www.ustr.gov/trade-agreements/bilateral-investment-treaties; Statement of the President accompanying U.S.-Bangladesh Bilateral Investment Treaty, available at http://tcc.export.gov/Trade_Agreements/All_Trade_Agreements/exp_002778.asp.

Notably, the president might plausibly have claimed statutory authorization for the BIT program. Section 601(b) of the Foreign Assistance Act, as then in force, provided: "In order to encourage and facilitate participation by private enterprise to the maximum extent practicable in achieving any of the purposes of this Act, the President shall ... accelerate a program of negotiating treaties for commerce and trade, including tax treaties, which shall include provisions to encourage and facilitate the flow of private investment to, and its equitable investment in, friendly countries and areas participating in programs under this Act." Foreign Assistance Act, available at https://legcounsel.house.gov/Comps/Foreign%20Assistance%20Act%20Of%201961.pdf.

125 *See* http://tcc.export.gov/Trade_Agreements/Bilateral_Investment_Treaties/index.asp (listing U.S. bilateral investment treaties).

Related Investment Measures (TRIMs), approved by Congress as part of the WTO agreements in 1995 (although congressionally approved trade agreements such as NAFTA often also include investor protection provisions similar to the BITs).[126]

Similarly, in the area of intellectual property, almost all major recent agreements have been approved by the Senate under the treaty-making clause, including all of the agreements administered by the World Intellectual Property Organization (WIPO).[127] Again the principal exception is a WTO-related agreement, the Agreement on Trade-Related Aspects of Intellectual Property Rights (TRIPS), which was approved by Congress.[128] Finally, tax treaties historically took the Article II approval route, and modern practice has showed no change in this pattern.[129]

In sum, the core pattern appears to be that, despite what Restatement Section 303 might seem to foreshadow, major international agreements (other than trade agreements) continue to be approved by the Senate through the Article II process.[130]

A second key point is that the Senate supermajority approval process did not become an automatic rubber stamp. If it had, one might argue that it persisted only because it lacked practical significance. But to the contrary, Senate opposition in a number of areas complicated presidential diplomacy. Some treaties were blocked or rejected. In 1999 the Senate voted down the

126 Agreement on Trade-Related Investment Measures (TRIMs), available at https://www.wto.org/english/docs_e/legal_e/18-trims.pdf. NAFTA, although principally a trade agreement, has an important section devoted to investment protection that parallels the usual BIT provisions; other bilateral and regional free trade agreements also include protections for investment. The 2016 Trans Pacific Partnership (TPP) Free Trade Agreement, which had been expected to be submitted as an ex post Congressional-Executive agreement until it was abandoned by the Trump Administration, had similar protections for investment.

127 *See* World Intellectual Property Organization, WIPO-Administered Treaties, available at www.wipo.int/treaties/en/.

128 Agreement on Trade-Related Aspects of Intellectual Property Rights (TRIPS), available at www.wto.org/english/tratop_e/trips_e/t_agmo_e.htm. The TPP Agreement, see *supra* n. 126, also included intellectual property protection.

129 *See* Yoo, *supra* note 14, at 811 n. 218.

130 To be clear, this is an impressionistic account. There is no comprehensive assessment of U.S. agreement-making practice in the modern era. The closest is Professor Hathaway's 2008 study *Treaties' End*, which found nontreaty agreements to dominate numerically. *See* Hathaway, *supra* note 2. However, she did not attempt to assess the relative importance of treaties and non-treaty agreements. Two other somewhat recent accounts, Professor Yoo's *Treaties as Laws?*, *supra* note 14, and Professor Spiro's *Treaties, Executive Agreements and Constitutional Method*, *supra* note 14, both published in 2001, generally support the account presented here, but they too do not purport to be comprehensive and of course do not address the practice since 2001.

Comprehensive Nuclear Test Ban Treaty despite heavy lobbying by President Clinton.[131] For many years the Law of the Sea Convention remained unapproved because it lacked the votes in the Senate.[132] President Obama made approval of that Convention a priority after 2008 but it again failed to obtain the needed supermajority, and in 2012, a prominent senator pronounced the Convention "dead" in light of thirty-four senators' commitments to vote against it.[133] Yet most of these agreements had the support of a majority of senators, and so might have been approved as Congressional-Executive agreements.

In other areas, the difficulty of obtaining Senate consent forced major changes or caused the agreements to languish unapproved. In 1997 the Senate made clear that it would not consent to the Kyoto Protocol on climate change.[134] As noted, approval of several key human rights treaties could only be obtained by the president accepting non-self-execution declarations (despised by the human rights community). Yet even with non-self-execution declarations attached, the Senate voted down the Convention on the Rights of Persons with Disabilities in 2012 (although a majority supported it) and refused even to vote on the Convention on the Elimination of all Forms of Discrimination against Women (CEDAW) despite the requests of multiple presidents.[135] The U.N. Arms Trade Treaty, which went into effect in 2014 without U.S. ratification, was so strongly opposed in the Senate that the President Obama did not even submit it for approval, although he signed it

[131] *See* Helen Dewar, *Senate Rejects Test Ban Treaty*, WASHINGTON POST, Oct. 14, 1999, available at www.washingtonpost.com/wp-srv/politics/daily/oct99/senate14.htm. The Obama Administration and various commentators subsequently urged that the Senate reconsider, but the Senate has not done so, and the assumption continues to be that Senate supermajority approval is the only option. *See* Mikhail Gorbachev, *The Senate's Next Task: Ratifying the Test Ban Treaty*, NEW YORK TIMES, Dec. 28, 2010, available at www.nytimes.com/2010/12/29/opinion/29gorbachev.html.

[132] In particular, President Bush pushed unsuccessfully for Senate consent in 2007. *See* President's Statement on Advancing U.S. Interests in the World's Oceans, May 15, 2007, available at https://georgewbush-whitehouse.archives.gov/news/releases/2007/05/20070515-2.html.

[133] Kristina Wong & Sean Lengell, *DeMint: Law of the Sea Treaty Now Dead*, WASHINGTON TIMES, July 16, 2012, available at www.washingtontimes.com/news/2012/jul/16/demint-says-law-sea-treaty-now-dead/?page=all.

[134] Helen Dewar & Kevin Sullivan, *Senate Republicans Call Kyoto Pact Dead*, WASHINGTON POST, Dec. 11, 1997, available at www.washingtonpost.com/wp-srv/inatl/longterm/climate/stories/clim121197b.htm.

[135] See *U.N. Treaty on Disabilities Falls Short in Senate*, CBS NEWS, Dec. 4, 2012, available at www.cbsnews.com/8301-250_162-57557077/u.n-treaty-on-disabilities-falls-short-in-senate/ (reporting 61–38 vote in favor of treaty); www.amnestyusa.org/sites/default/files/pdfs/cedaw_fact_sheet.pdf (discussing CEDAW).

and signaled his support.[136] And even where the Senate has given consent, it sometimes came only after a difficult campaign. Most prominently, the New START Treaty, a centerpiece of the Obama Administration's arms control policy, gained the requisite supermajority consent in 2010 only by a narrow margin after considerable suspense and debate.[137]

At the same time, the academic view of the Article II treaty underwent some adjustment. Whether or not the Third Restatement was entirely correct in saying that the conventional academic view accepted interchangeability in 1987, the next two decades witnessed substantial cracks in this supposed consensus. First, in connection with the approval of the WTO in 1994, several prominent academics, notably Laurence Tribe and Anne-Marie Slaughter, argued that supermajority Senate approval should be sought.[138] That provoked an extensive debate between Professors Ackerman and Golove on the one hand and Professor Tribe on the other in the *Harvard Law Review*, with Tribe making an extended textual case for the constitutional exclusivity of the Article II, Section 2 process.[139] Though the WTO was approved as a Congressional-Executive agreement (albeit with two-thirds of senators consenting), subsequent academic studies were not kind to interchangeability. Separate pieces in 2001 by John Yoo and Peter Spiro conceded the use of Congressional-Executive agreements in trade law but argued for Article II, Section 2 approval of major agreements

136 Arms Trade Treaty, available at http://treaties.un.org/doc/Treaties/2013/04/20130410%2012-01%20PM/Ch_XXVI_08.pdf#page=21; see Ramsey Cox, *Senate Votes 53–46 to Prevent U.S. from Joining UN Arms Trade Treaty*, THE HILL, Mar. 23, 2013, available at http://thehill.com/blogs/floor-action/senate/290001-senate-votes-to-stop-us-from-joining-un-arms-treaty (reporting Senate opposition); Pamela Falk, *US Wavers on Arms Trade Treaty at the UN*, CBS NEWS, June 3, 2013 (reporting Obama Administration's concern over Senate opposition to Arms Trade Treaty), available at www.cbsnews.com/8301-202_162-57587413/u.s-wavers-on-arms-trade-treaty-at-the-u.n/; Patrick Goodenough, *Unratified by US, Controversial UN Treaty Enters into Force*, CNS NEWS, Dec. 23, 2014, available at www.cnsnews.com/news/article/patrick-goodenough/unratified-us-controversial-un-arms-treaty-enters-force (noting continuing Senate opposition despite appeals by President Obama).

137 *See* James Oliphant & Michael Muskal, *Senate Passes New Start Treaty*, LOS ANGELES TIMES, Dec. 22, 2010, available at http://articles.latimes.com/2010/dec/22/news/la-pn-start-senate-20101223 (recording final vote of 71–26, a margin of seven votes); *New START Treaty: The Era of Magical Thinking*, THE ECONOMIST, Nov. 22, 2010, available at www.economist.com/blogs/democracyinamerica/2010/11/new_start_treaty (discussing opposition to the START treaty). During the debates, the treaty was regarded as "hanging by a thread." Gorbachev, *supra* note 131.

138 *See* GATT Implementing Legislation: Hearings on S. 2467 before the Senate Comm. on Commerce, Science and Transportation, 103d Cong., 2d Sess. 285–339 (1994) (statement of Laurence Tribe); Letter from Anne-Marie Slaughter to Sen. Ernest F. Hollings, Oct. 18, 1994, reprinted in *ibid.* at 286–90.

139 Ackerman & Golove, *supra* note 14; Tribe, *supra* note 14.

elsewhere.[140] Yoo followed up with a *New York Times* op-ed in 2009 (with John Bolton) expressly insisting on the exclusiveness of the treaty form for arms control agreements[141] – a prescription followed by the Obama Administration despite the near-defeat of the New START Treaty a year later. Even Professor Hathaway's 2008 antitreaty manifesto *Treaties' End* conceded that shifting the approval process entirely to Congress might require a constitutional amendment.[142]

Nonetheless, the Article II, Section 2 treaty cannot claim victory over the Restatement's "interchangeability" view, only survival. Its rivals also persist, and, as discussed below, to some extent have grown stronger. It remains true that at the level of routine diplomacy, the treaty has been largely "eclipsed" (Professor Hathaway's word)[143] by Executive agreements, which may or may not claim some sort of prior approval from Congress, and may or may not be formally binding in international law. Further, to the extent the claims for the Article II, Section 2 process rest upon a constitutional imperative, difficulty persists in reconciling text and practice. As Ackerman and Golove argued, Professor Tribe's uncompromising defense of Article II, Section 2 seemed to imply that almost the entirety of U.S. diplomatic practice was unconstitutional.[144] The more practical position, associated with Professor Slaughter, that major agreements require Senate supermajority consent, is difficult to reconcile with practice in the trade area and hampered by the extreme difficulty of defining the line between "major" and "minor." Neither Professor Yoo nor Professor Spiro, in their prominent attacks on interchangeability, managed successfully to tie their policy prescriptions to the Constitution's text (and indeed Spiro directly affirmed that difficulty).[145]

The result has been theoretical incoherence, but a reasonable degree of practical accommodation. Despite the Third Restatement's claim of interchangeability, almost all subsequent major international agreements have been submitted to the Senate through the Article II, Section 2 process, other than in the area of trade law, where postsignature approval by a majority of

140 Yoo, *supra* note 14; Spiro, *supra* note 14.

141 John R. Bolton & John Yoo, Restore the Senate's Treaty Power, New York Times, Jan. 4, 2009, available at www.nytimes.com/2009/01/05/opinion/05bolton.html.

142 Hathaway, *supra* note 2, at 1338. 143 *Ibid.* at 1307.

144 Ackerman & Golove, *supra* note 14, at 916–25.

145 *See* Yoo, *supra* note 14; Spiro, *supra* note 14. In particular, Professor Yoo argued that only matters closely related to textual authorities of Congress should be handled by Congressional-Executive agreement, but that theory seems inconsistent both with the submission of many major commercial agreements to the Senate and with Yoo's own insistence that arms control agreements (closely related to Congress' textual power to raise and support armies) be handled through Article II, Section 2. *See* Spiro, *supra* note 14, at 1003–9.

Congress has been entrenched as the standard approach. In contrast, minor agreements are rarely submitted to the Senate (or to Congress) for after-the-fact approval. There may be debates as to whether particular agreements conform to this pattern, but there seems little doubt that the pattern exists, just as there seems little theoretically satisfactory explanation for it.

B The Modern Scope of After-the-Fact Congressional Approval

The Congressional-Executive agreement, approved after signature by a majority of Congress, is the Article II treaty's greatest theoretical rival. As Professors Ackerman and Golove argued in 1995, and Professor Hathaway developed further in 2008, approval through Congress is most responsive to democratic and separation-of-powers values.[146] It retains a substantial check on executive power, vindicating the Framers' desire that treaty-making not be entrusted to the president alone. Yet it avoids the antidemocratic result that a small number of senators – perhaps, if they come from small states, representing only a tiny percentage of the population – might block agreements desired by broad majorities.

But despite its theoretical attractions, its academic supporters, and its validation by the Third Restatement, the formal ex post Congressional-Executive agreement has not prevailed in the last twenty-five years of practice. To be sure, it has become entrenched, far beyond where it was at the time of the Restatement, in the trade area. In 1993 NAFTA was approved as a Congressional-Executive agreement without serious constitutional objection, even though it was highly controversial as a policy matter and likely would not have carried two-thirds of the Senate.[147] In 1994 NAFTA's approval was overshadowed by the even more significant approval of the WTO, which itself involved an array of separate agreements covering almost all aspects of trade policy. As noted, unlike NAFTA the WTO did provoke some constitutional objections, but they failed to gain traction; the WTO package was approved by a wide margin. Then, as subsequent rounds of the WTO failed to produce further multilateral agreements, the United States devoted more effort to regional and bilateral free trade agreements – all of which were submitted to Congress as Congressional-Executive agreements. In 2002, Congress reauthorized the "fast-track" procedure for trade agreements until 2007,[148] and a new

[146] *See* Ackerman & Golove, *supra* note 14, at 916; Hathaway, *supra* note 2, at 1308–23.

[147] *See* Ackerman & Golove, *supra* note 14, at 802 n. 5 (noting that 38 senators voted against NAFTA).

[148] Trade Act of 2002, § 2103–05, 19 U.S.C. §§ 3803–05 (2002).

series of agreements were approved under this process, including the Dominican Republic-Central America Free Trade Agreement (CAFTA) and bilateral free trade agreements with Chile, Singapore, Australia, Morocco, Oman, Bahrain, and Peru.[149] Constitutional objections were negligible; the Ackerman-Golove/Tribe debate seemed to have run its course with Ackerman and Golove triumphant. The second Bush Administration's trade agreements were simply assumed to be destined for the Article I approval process, a pattern that continued in the Obama Administration with free trade agreements with Colombia, South Korea, and Panama.[150]

But Article I's victory in trade was not reflected elsewhere. As noted above, Congressional-Executive agreements lost out to treaties even in other economic areas, such as investment and intellectual property (except when considered in conjunction with trade), and tax. They did not become a realistic alternative elsewhere, even in areas where a minority of the Senate appeared especially hostile to agreement-making. For example, environmental organizations speculated that climate change agreements might be switched to the Article I process to ease approval, but no effort has been made in that direction. Though the Article I process for arms control remains on the books, no effort was made to use it to circumvent the Senate, even when the Senate blocked the Comprehensive Nuclear Test Ban treaty or threatened to block the New START Treaty. Indeed, in the modern era there has been no repetition of the St. Lawrence Seaway affair, the high-water mark of interchangeability, when the President submitted under Article I an agreement previously defeated under Article II.[151] Even as the Senate threatened (and ultimately blocked) at least four Obama Administration treaty priorities (the Law of the Sea Convention, the Arms Trade Treaty, CEDAW, and the Disability Rights Convention), and even when the President's party had majorities in both Houses, there was no material suggestion that these might be withdrawn and resubmitted through the Article I process.

Further, Congressional-Executive agreements, despite their democratic credentials, have been put on the constitutional defensive. The twenty-five years following the Third Restatement witnessed a revival of interest in formalism, textualism, original meaning, and Framers' values as modes of

[149] *See* http://trade.gov/fta/.

[150] *See President Obama Signs Trade Agreements and Trade Adjustment Assistance into Law*, available at https://ustr.gov/FTA. As noted, the Trans Pacific Partnership Free Trade Agreement was expected to be submitted as an ex post Congressional-Executive agreement.

[151] *See* Part II *supra*.

constitutional interpretation.[152] That development has been especially notable (although not uncontroversial) in foreign affairs law, where practicality and the needs of the Cold War had almost entirely displaced ordinary constitutional interpretation in prior years.[153] Among other things, it posed theoretical challenges for Congressional-Executive agreements because they are, despite their attractiveness, hard to reconcile with the formal Constitution.

This challenge was especially sharp in one area. Pure interchangeability, as pressed by the Restatement, proclaimed no limits on the subject matter of Congressional-Executive agreements.[154] Such a view might have been plausible at a time when conventional constitutional theory presumed essentially no limits on Congress' domestic legislative powers. But developments in constitutional theory in the late 1980s and 1990s attacked that presumption by returning to the Framers' idea of limited enumerated legislative powers. In *United States v. Lopez* in 1995 and *United States v. Morrison* in 2000, the Supreme Court established that Congress' legislative powers were not unlimited. Pure interchangeability could not accommodate that development, because it rested on Article I's grant of legislative power, and if that grant was not plenary, then Congressional-Executive agreements could not be plenary. So long as *Missouri v. Holland* remained good law, treaties appeared to have a wider scope.[155]

Even beyond the issue of enumerated powers, Congressional-Executive agreements lacked firm constitutional defenses, and the modern era did not produce any. Professors Ackerman and Golove may even have undermined Congressional-Executive agreements' standing by showing them to be largely a post–World War II innovation; their approach depended on a theory of

152 *See, e.g.*, THE CHALLENGE OF ORIGINALISM: THEORIES OF CONSTITUTIONAL INTERPRETATION (Grant Huscroft & Bradley W. Miller, eds., 2011).

153 *See* Ganesh Sitaraman & Ingrid Wuerth, *The Normalization of Foreign Relations Law*, 128 HARV. L. REV. 1897 (2015); Jack L. Goldsmith, *The New Formalism in United States Foreign Relations Law*, 70 U. COLO. L. REV. 1395 (1999). For criticism, see, e.g., Curtis A. Bradley, *Foreign Relations Law and the Purported Shift Away from "Exceptionalism,"* 128 HARV. L. REV. F. 294 (2015); Andrew Kent, *The New Originalism and the Foreign Affairs Constitution*, 82 FORDHAM L. REV. 757 (2013).

154 *See* THIRD RESTATEMENT, *supra* note 1, § 303, cmt. e.

155 *See* Missouri v. Holland, 252 U.S. 416 (1920) (finding that the scope of the treaty-making power was not limited to subjects within Congress' enumerated powers). Another aspect of the originalist revival was a challenge to *Missouri*, which in some versions proposed to limit the scope of the treaty-making power to Congress' enumerated powers, or to the types of treaties familiar in the eighteenth century. *See* Bond v. United States, 134 S. Ct. 2077, 2101 (2014) (Thomas, J., concurring in the judgment) (suggesting the latter proposed limitation); Michael D. Ramsey, *Missouri v. Holland and Historical Textualism*, 73 MO. L. REV. 969 (2008) (describing and criticizing the former proposed limitation).

informal constitutional amendment many people did not accept,[156] plus (as Professor Spiro argued in 2001)[157] a somewhat overblown account of post–World War II events. Subsequent scholarship did little to find a textual or historical basis for a broad Article I agreement power, although much of it accepted Article I approvals in particular areas.[158] Thus by the second decade of the twenty-first century, the NAFTA/WTO-type Congressional-Executive agreement in the trade area appeared (both practically and theoretically) as an anomaly, not as a model.

C Executive Agreements: The Dominant Form or a Footnote?

While much academic debate has focused on treaties and Congressional-Executive agreements, numerically speaking the vast majority of U.S. international agreements are made by the president without specific approval of either the Senate or Congress.[159] As noted, within this category are at least three distinct subcategories: areas where Congress has given express advance approval of presidential agreement-making; areas where the president claims some implicit or nonspecific advance approval from Congress or a prior Article II treaty; and agreements (either binding or nonbinding) made under the president's constitutional authority.[160]

At the outset, it should be noted that, as in prior times, it is often difficult to determine in which subcategory a particular agreement belongs. For example, the Anti-Counterfeiting Trade Agreement (ACTA), mentioned at the outset of this chapter, was signed by President Obama, and its particular terms were not directly approved by Congress or the Senate.[161]

156 *See* Ackerman & Golove, *supra* note 14, at 804 (tying defense of NAFTA to Professor Ackerman's broader theory of constitutional change presented in BRUCE ACKERMAN, WE THE PEOPLE (1991)); Spiro, *supra* note 14, at 970–1 (describing the Ackerman/Golove account).

157 *See* Spiro, *supra* note 14, at 981–1003.

158 *E.g.*, Hyman, *supra* note 34, at 320 (defending NAFTA on the grounds that it has a short termination period but generally opposing the constitutionality of Congressional-Executive agreements).

159 *See* Hathaway, *supra* note 2, at 1257–60 (finding that from 1980 to 2000 the United States concluded a total of 375 treaties and 2,744 executive agreements).

160 No comprehensive categorization of executive agreements in this regard is available (nor, perhaps, possible). Although the State Department is required to report non-treaty executive agreements to Congress pursuant to the Case Act, 1 U.S.C. § 112b(a), the Department does not identify the constitutional basis for each agreement. Further, the Department does not report nonbinding agreements.

161 Anti-Counterfeiting Trade Agreement, available at www.mofa.go.jp/policy/economy/i_property/pdfs/acta1105_en.pdf; *see* Office of the United States Trade Representative, Anti-Counterfeiting Agreement (ACTA), available at http://www.ustr.gov/acta.

Thus, in the terminology used here, it was an Executive agreement – but what sort? Initially, the Obama Administration claimed that it was made on the president's sole authority. At the same time, the administration suggested it was nonbinding, at least in the sense that it did not require any changes to U.S. law. After significant objections were raised in Congress and in commentary, the administration shifted ground and explained that the agreement was made under prior Congressional approval.[162] However, the new position did not rest on any specific delegation of agreement-making authority to the president, but rather upon statutory language expressing Congress' view that some (unspecified) actions should be taken to protect intellectual property abroad.[163] Given the various justifications, it seems difficult to say with confidence whether ACTA should be regarded as a sole Executive agreement or a congressionally approved Executive agreement. Indeed, given *Dames & Moore*'s emphasis on Congressional acquiescence to support a sole Executive agreement,[164] the categories may be too blurred to allow reliable categorization.[165]

Nonetheless, some generalizations may be suggested. First, nonbinding agreements remain an important if underexamined tool in U.S. agreement-making. They have begun to encounter some constitutional resistance, though only a little.[166] Second, sole Executive agreements received substantial judicial and academic attention during the modern period, with the ultimate result that they may appear weaker and more constitutionally suspect. Third, as foreshadowed by *Dames & Moore*, the congressionally authorized Executive agreement is the most consequential subcategory, at least in numerical terms, although it remains unclear how consequential this form is in terms of the overall direction of U.S. foreign relations.

162 *See supra* notes 7–9 and accompanying text. 163 *See* Flynn, *supra* note 8.

164 *See* Part II.C.

165 As a further example, in 2013, members of the WTO, including the United States, reached a series of agreements under the Doha Round of negotiations to expand and clarify certain WTO commitments. *See* World Trade Organization, *9th WTO Ministerial Conference, Bali, 2013 and After: Bali Package and 2014 Decisions*, available at www.wto.org/english/thewto_e/minist_e/mc9_e/balipackage_e.htm. The Obama Administration did not submit these agreements to Congress for approval, although it was unclear whether that was because they were implicitly approved by Congress as part of its prior approval of the WTO (which contemplated additional rounds of negotiation), because they were executive agreements within the president's sole power, or because they imposed no material binding duties on the United States. *See* Julian Ku, *Does the U.S. Congress Have to Approve the New WTO Agreement? Apparently Not*, Opinio Juris, Dec. 9, 2013, available at http://opiniojuris.org/2013/12/09/u-s-congress-approve-new-wto-agreement-apparently/#sthash.yDgVlUeY.dpuf.

166 *See* Hollis & Newcomer, *supra* note 94, at 575–81.

1 Nonbinding Agreements in the Modern Period

The modern period has seen a number of high-profile nonbinding agreements made by on the president's sole authority. Leading examples appear to include the 1997 NATO-Russia Founding Act on Mutual Relations; the 1988 Basel Accord on Capital Adequacy; and the 1992 Statement on Forest Principles.[167] As suggested by these examples, they span diverse subject matter. Indeed, it is unlikely that a comprehensive account of nonbinding agreements could be made: these agreements do not have to be published or reported to Congress and they can be negotiated in secret, or between lower-level agencies whose activities are difficult to monitor. Moreover, there is an uncertain line between nonbinding agreements and informal arrangements regarding diplomatic protocols and procedures that reflect an even lower level of formality.

In 2015, nonbinding agreements gained new attention when President Obama negotiated and signed a Joint Comprehensive Plan of Action (JCPOA) among the United States, Iran, the other permanent members of the U.N. Security Council, Germany, and the European Union regarding Iran's nuclear facilities.[168] Among other things, under the agreement the United States and the other signatory countries agreed to lift economic sanctions previously imposed on Iran and Iran agreed to certain procedures with respect to its nuclear programs designed to ensure that Iran did not develop nuclear weapons.[169] After some initial uncertainty, the Obama Administration appeared to describe the JCPOA as a nonbinding agreement that could be made on the president's independent authority.[170] Some language in the JCPOA's text supported this view,[171] although the

[167] *Ibid.* at 564–7; Raustiala, *supra* note 94, at 583–4. It may not always be clear when an agreement is nonbinding; hence some caution in making categorizations is required.

[168] Joint Comprehensive Plan of Action, signed at Vienna, July 14, 2015 [hereinafter JCPOA], available at http://eeas.europa.eu/statements-eeas/docs/iran_agreement/iran_joint-comprehensive-plan-of-action_en.pdf. See Ramsey, *Evading the Treaty Power, supra* note 94, at 377–381 (discussing constitutionality of the JCPOA).

[169] *See ibid.*, §§ 18–33 (sanctions); *ibid.* at §§ 1–17 (nuclear facilities).

[170] *See* Letter from Julia Frifield, Assistant Secretary, Legal Affairs, U.S. Department of State to Congressman Mike Pompeo, Nov. 19, 2015, available at https://www.scribd.com/document/291042867/Letter-from-State-Department-Regarding-JCPOA (describing the agreement as "not a treaty or an executive agreement" and as reflecting "political commitments"). Due to strong opposition by the Republican-controlled Congress, the Obama Administration wanted to avoid seeking Congress' approval. During the negotiations, Congress passed an act that gave Congress a period to review and potentially disapprove the JCPOA once it was finalized, but ultimately Congress was unable to pass the disapproving legislation due to a filibuster in the Senate.

[171] *See* JCPOA, *supra* note 169, preamble (reciting that "Iran and [the other parties to the JCPOA] will take the following voluntary measures within the timeframe as detailed in this JCPOA and its Annexes").

positions of the other signatories were not entirely clear. Assuming the JCPOA was properly characterized as a nonbinding agreement,[172] it represented an aggressive use of the president's independent authority over nonbinding agreements given its subject matter, specificity and duration.

Nonbinding agreements also began to receive some criticism in the modern period. President George W. Bush proposed to conduct significant relations with Iraq through nonbinding agreements, a course that provoked substantial skeptical comment and eventually a (slight) change in course by the Executive Branch.[173] President Bush also attempted to pursue arms control with Russia through a nonbinding agreement, but Russia refused to accept that route and Bush eventually submitted the final product under Article II, Section 2. A major academic study in 2009 by Duncan Hollis and Joshua Newcomer suggested some constitutional limits on nonbinding agreements that cover topics of substantial importance.[174] The 2015 JCPOA with Iran reignited this debate, as commentators and opposition politicians criticized President Obama for undermining the treaty-making power.[175] Others strongly defended the president's broad power to make nonbinding agreements, even on important matters such as Iran's nuclear ambitions.[176]

[172] Most U.S. commentators seemed to see it that way. *See, e.g.*, Marty Lederman, *Congress hasn't ceded any constitutional authority with respect to the Iran JCPOA*, BALKINIZATION, Aug. 8, 2015 (JCPOA is "a *nonbinding* 'political agreement.'"), available at http://balkin.blogspot.com/2015/08/congress-hasnt-ceded-any-constitutional.html; Julian Ku, *Those "Snap-Back" Sanctions in the Iran Deal Have a Pretty Big Loophole*, OPINIO JURIS, July 14, 2015 ("the Iran Deal is not a binding international agreement"), available at http://opiniojuris.org/2015/07/14/those-snap-back-sanctions-in-the-iran-deal-have-a-pretty-big-loophole/. *But see* Bruce Ackerman & David Golove, *Can the Next President Repudiate Obama's Iran Agreement?*, THE ATLANTIC, Sept. 10, 2015 (describing the JCPOA as a binding agreement approved by Congress), available at http://www.theatlantic.com/politics/archive/2015/09/can-the-next-president-repudiate-obamas-iran-agreement/404587/.

[173] Hollis & Newcomer, *supra* note 94, at 508–10. [174] *Ibid.*

[175] *See, e.g.*, David Rivkin & Lee Casey, *The Lawless Underpinnings of the Iran Nuclear Deal*, WALL STREET JOURNAL, July 26, 2015, available at http://www.wsj.com/articles/the-lawless-underpinnings-of-the-iran-nuclear-deal-1437949928.

[176] *See, e.g.*, Jack Goldsmith & Marty Lederman, *The Case for the President's Unilateral Authority to Conclude the Impending Iran Deal Is Easy because It Will (Likely) Be a Nonbinding Agreement under International Law*, LAWFARE, Mar. 11, 2015, available at www.lawfareblog.com/case-presidents-unilateral-authority-conclude-impending-iran-deal-easy-because-it-will-likely-be.

Also in 2015, the Paris conference on climate change produced a multilateral agreement which President Obama signed but did not submit to Congress or the Senate. A justification appeared to be that, at the United States' insistence, the agreement did not impose material binding obligations on the United States. *See* Marty Lederman, *The*

A further issue for nonbinding agreements highlighted by the 2015 JCPOA is the question of stability. Republicans in Congress generally took the position that the new president in 2017 need not honor the JCPOA, and several Republican presidential candidates in 2016 vowed to reject it.[177] Of course, presidents have also claimed power to terminate treaties, sometimes even in violation of the treaty's terms. The tenor of the 2015 debate, however, seemed to be that the JCPOA, as a nonbinding agreement, imposed even less constraint upon a new president.

From this record, one might say that nonbinding agreements sometimes, but not extensively, substitute for treaties in areas of substantial importance and are commonly employed at levels of routine diplomacy. Of course, measured in sheer numbers (if one were able to get an accurate count) they would surely outweigh treaties, and probably other forms of agreement-making as well. But it is hard to make the case that the course of U.S. foreign relations is substantially set by nonbinding agreements apart from a few noteworthy incidents. In particular, Russia's response to President Bush's nonbinding arms control initiative suggests that there are material nonconstitutional limits upon them.[178] However, the experience of the nonbinding JCPOA with Iran may set a precedent for expanded use of nonbinding agreements on important matters – in effect, as substitutes for treaties – in the future.

2 The Rise and Fall of Sole Executive Agreements?

A key question for sole Executive agreements is their status in domestic law. If a sole Executive agreement has domestic legal status, it is powerful – in effect,

constitutionally critical, last-minute correction to the Paris climate change accord, BALKINIZATION, Dec. 13, 2015, available at http://balkin.blogspot.com/2015/12/the-last-minute-correction-to-paris.html (recounting how U.S. negotiators required the agreement to use the word "should" rather than "shall" to maintain its nonbinding character); Ramsey, *Evading the Treaty Power, supra* note 94, at 381–7 (questioning constitutionality of the Paris agreement). However, other nonbinding agreements during this period attracted little attention or controversy. *See* Ramsey, *Evading the Treaty Power, supra* note 94, at 381 n. 42 (discussing the 2015 nonbinding agreement with China regarding cybersecurity).

177 *E.g.*, Jeffrey Goldberg, *How a President Rubio Would Undo the Iran Deal*, THE ATLANTIC, Aug. 6, 2015 (reporting presidential candidate Marco Rubio describing the JCPOA as a "political commitment" that as President he would not regard as binding); Senator Tom Cotton et al., *An Open Letter to the Leaders of the Islamic Republic of Iran*, Mar. 9, 2015 (letter on behalf of 46 Republican senators asserting that future presidents would not be bound by Obama Administration's deal with Iran), available at http://insider.foxnews.com/2015/03/09/sen-tom-cotton-and-46-colleagues-send-open-letter-iranian-leaders-nuclear-deal.

178 *See* Raustiala, *supra* note 94, at 584–6 (discussing factors involved in choosing nonbinding agreements).

it offers the president a way to make law without the participation of the legislative branch. If it does not have domestic legal status, a sole Executive agreement is less significant: if implemented by Congress, then it is effectively a Congressional-Executive agreement; if not implemented by Congress, then its effect would be limited to the international sphere.

In this regard, the modern era witnessed a sort of rise and fall of Executive agreements in a very short span. Earlier, *Dames & Moore* signaled that congressional approval, or at least acquiescence, plus a long history of executive action might be necessary to underwrite the domestic effect of Executive agreements. In 2003, the Supreme Court in *American Insurance Association v. Garamendi*[179] appeared to point the way to a more powerful and less constrained role – one that might extend as well to nonbinding agreements and even presidential statements of policy.

Garamendi turned on the effect of two Executive agreements President Clinton made with Germany and Austria relating to the settlement of Holocaust era disputes.[180] For the most part, the U.S. role was as facilitator of a settlement between Holocaust survivors and heirs and German and Austrian companies said to be responsible for Holocaust era injuries. The agreements bound the United States to do very little, and they did not purport to alter U.S. law directly. However, one impetus for the settlement was that litigation between the survivors and the European companies had arisen in U.S. courts, and the European companies wanted the settlement to stop the litigation. The U.S. government agreed to seek dismissal of the claims, although the agreements stopped short of promising that the litigation would be terminated.

Garamendi itself arose from a collateral issue: California passed a law requiring European insurers doing business in California to disclose insurance policies from the Holocaust era, with the likely intent that disclosure would facilitate litigation against the insurers in California court. (California also passed various measures to assist the litigation directly, although these were not the immediate subject of the *Garamendi* litigation.) Insurers challenged the California law as, among other things, inconsistent with the Executive agreements, and the Supreme Court agreed. Specifically, the Court held that the executive policy of settlement reflected in the Executive agreements conflicted with and thus preempted California's attempt to facilitate litigation rather than settlement.[181]

179 American Insurance Ass'n v. Garamendi, 539 U.S. 396 (2003).

180 *See* Brannon P. Denning & Michael D. Ramsey, *American Insurance Association v. Garamendi and Executive Preemption in Foreign Affairs*, 46 WM. & MARY L. REV. 825 (2004).

181 Garamendi, 539 U.S. at 410; *see* Denning & Ramsey, *supra* note 180, at 869–90.

Read broadly, that holding might have substantial consequences. First, it appeared to discard *Dames & Moore*'s reliance on Congressional acquiescence (since if anything Congress appeared to have acquiesced in the state's role). Second, unlike *Dames & Moore*, the opinion did not focus on the context of claims settlement; rather, it seemed to suggest that Executive agreements broadly would preempt state law. Third, it did not rest upon the legal effect of any specific language of the Executive agreements, but rather the policy they reflected – implying a broader swath of preemption surrounding an Executive agreement, and, potentially, executive policy not encompassed in a formal binding agreement.[182] For example, one might suppose, after *Garamendi*, that even a nonbinding agreement (or an agreement that would be considered non-self-executing were it a treaty) might by similar reasoning preempt state law.

Sole Executive agreements had also begun to come under new academic scrutiny[183] as a result of the formalist and originalist trends in constitutional theory and foreign relations law noted earlier. *Garamendi* stoked this critique, as commentators pointed out that it trampled on principles of federalism and separation of powers, enhancing executive power compared to both the states and Congress.[184] And indeed in a subsequent case, the executive branch under George W. Bush promptly seized on *Garamendi* to further expand executive preemption power.

The case was *Medellin v. Texas*,[185] which on its face had nothing to do with Executive agreements. The question was whether a treaty provision (Article 94 of the U.N. Charter) required Texas to give extra procedures to death row inmate José Medellín, as mandated by a ruling of the International Court of Justice (ICJ). The Bush Administration argued that the treaty was non-self-executing, and so Texas law was not affected by the treaty directly. But President Bush issued a memorandum stating that it was executive policy that U.S. states should implement the ICJ decision by affording further review of the affected death sentences. According to the Executive Branch, this executive policy, rather than the treaty itself, bound the state. The Executive Branch relied principally on *Garamendi*, which (it argued) stood for the proposition that if executive foreign policy conflicted with state law, the state law was preempted.[186]

182 These criticisms are developed and expanded in Denning & Ramsey, *supra* note 180, at 898–943.

183 *E.g.*, Ramsey, *Executive Agreements, supra* note 14.

184 *E.g.*, Clark, *supra* note 14; Michael P. Van Alstine, *Executive Aggrandizement in Foreign Affairs Lawmaking*, 54 UCLA L. REV. 309 (2006).

185 542 U.S. 491 (2008).

186 *See* Michael D. Ramsey, *International Wrongs, State Laws and Presidential Policies*, 32 LOY. L.A. INT'L & COMP. L. REV. 19, 34–7 (2010) (discussing the president's argument).

The Supreme Court disagreed, and in doing so substantially recast the decision in *Garamendi*. To allow executive policy to preempt state law, the Court said, would make the president a lawmaker, contrary to the Constitution's basic separation of legislative and executive powers.[187] This, of course, was what critics had said about *Garamendi*. But according to the Court, *Garamendi* was not to the contrary because it involved very limited circumstances: an Executive agreement on claims settlement, an area in which (per *Dames & Moore*) Congress had approved broad executive agreement-making authority.[188] That appeared to take much of the force from *Garamendi* and from sole Executive agreements, perhaps returning them to where they had been at the time of the Third Restatement: limited to a few areas of particular executive authority in which Congress had acquiesced to presidential agreement-making.[189]

The *Garamendi/Medellin* episode addressed only the domestic effect of sole Executive agreements. If Executive agreements lacked domestic affect beyond certain narrow categories, that limited their usefulness as a practical matter, but it did not limit their scope internationally. They still might constitute an effective and important tool of presidential diplomacy, and how much authority the president had to use them remained unclear. The Obama Administration at times implied a broad view of presidential power to conclude Executive agreements, suggesting that the president has independent power to undertake international obligations on behalf of the United States so long as those obligations do not require a change in domestic law.

But in the ACTA episode in 2011–12 Executive agreements suffered another blow. As discussed, the Obama Administration initially defended ACTA as a sole Executive agreement (on the theory that it did not require a change in domestic law), provoking substantial criticism. The administration ultimately withdrew its account of ACTA and substituted another: that ACTA had been implicitly approved by Congress.[190] Whatever the merits of that view, the administration's shift reflected a practical reality after *Medellin*. On one hand, the constitutionality of sole Executive agreements, outside of certain core categories of presidential power,[191] seemed suspect. On the other,

187 *Medellin*, 552 U.S. at 526. 188 *Ibid.* at 530.

189 *See* Ramsey, *International Wrongs*, *supra* note 186, at 36 (drawing this conclusion); Hathaway, *Presidential Power, supra* note 4, at 212 (noting limits on sole executive agreements and estimating that they constitute only about 10 percent of U.S. agreements.).

190 *See supra* nn. 7–9.

191 The president's power to conclude Executive agreements in areas of core presidential power, including recognition of foreign governments and on military matters such as Status of Forces agreements, retains a strong constitutional basis despite doubts about the president's power elsewhere. However, the JCPOA and Paris Agreement episodes, described *supra*

executive action might be justified on the basis of very opaque congressional action (or even, under *Dames & Moore*, inaction). Not surprisingly, in defending ACTA, the administration ultimately chose the implied-approval model. While the shift did not entirely satisfy critics, it held an important practical lesson. Although sole Executive agreements likely remain very common as instruments of everyday diplomacy, if they become important enough to be noticed they may quickly be described as something else.

3 Congressionally Authorized Executive Agreements

Thus we reach the numerical heart of modern U.S. diplomacy, at least as to binding agreements: Executive agreements claiming advance express or implied congressional (or treaty)[192] authorization. As with nonbinding agreements, it is hard to quantify them. Nearly all attempts to numerically classify modern U.S. agreements lump together sole Executive agreements and agreements with implied express or implied Congressional authorization. The ACTA episode illustrates that an agreement may arguably fit into either category, and indeed that the arguments in support may shift between them.[193] Still, an examination of current agreement-making practice suggests that most non-Article II agreements claim (or arguably claim, at least as much as ACTA) some sort of advance authorization.[194]

nn. 168–177 and accompanying text, reflect a retreat from an aggressive view of binding executive agreements. The Administration's insistence that the agreements were entirely or in all material respects nonbinding indicated a lack of confidence that the President could make binding agreements on the relevant topics without Congress' approval.

192 Although the most common source of authority for non-Article II agreements is Congress, the president also claims authority to make international agreements to implement or otherwise in connection with prior Article II treaties. For example, some of the many Status of Forces Agreements (SOFAs) and similar military agreements are based on prior security treaties. *See* R. Chuck Mason, *Status of Forces Agreement (SOFA): What Is It and How Has It Been Utilized?*, at 18–20 (Congressional Research Service, 2012), available at www.fas.org/sgp/crs/natsec/RL34531.pdf (discussing sources of authority for SOFAs and related agreements). Authority might also come from congressionally approved agreements: Congress' approval of the WTO agreements in 1994 can be read to implicitly delegate to the president authority to make additional agreements under the auspices of the WTO. *See supra* note 165 (discussing the 2013 Bali ministerial agreements).

193 The line between nonbinding agreements and congressionally approved agreements may also be difficult to identify. For example, although most commentators regarded the 2015 JCPOA with Iran, discussed *supra* Part III.C.1, as a nonbinding arrangement, at least two prominent legal scholars argued that it had been approved in advance by Congress and thus should be regarded as a binding Congressional-Executive agreement. *See* Ackerman & Golove, *supra* note 172.

194 *See* Hathaway, *Presidential Power*, *supra* note 4, at 155.

To give a sense of the numbers, review of the State Department reports for a random year, 2009, yields 233 agreements concluded outside Article II, Section 2, with only three of them receiving after-the-fact congressional approval.[195] (This does not include nonbinding agreements, which are not required to be reported.) In contrast, the State Department lists thirteen treaties taking effect in 2009, and only around one hundred treaties for the entire period 2001–2010 (most of them relating to tax or extradition).[196]

There are at least two ways of looking at these results. The first is as a story of enhanced executive power. Of 2009's 233 reported agreements, 230 of them were not approved by any part of the legislative branch in anything but the most general terms. That is not to say that the executive action was usually unapproved – only that it often occurred under broad delegation.[197] Yet at the same time, given the broad scope of modern Congressional legislation and modern treaties, an ambitious executive could find implicit approval for agreement-making on a wide range of subjects. Thus as a practical matter the president can claim support from the legislative branches while in effect pursuing an independent foreign policy. Ironically, then, the move to enhance Congressional agreement-making power vis-à-vis the Senate ended up shifting power to the Executive. Once it was established that Congress could authorize presidential agreement-making, and especially once it was established that that approval could be ex ante and implicit, the executive had an almost unlimited resource of Congressional actions in which to find implicit approval.

Another approach, though, is to consider the actual content of the agreements. A survey of the agreements reported in 2009 suggests that most are relatively minor efforts to implement a broader policy traceable to a statute,

[195] *See* U.S. Department of State, 2009 *International Agreements Other than Treaties Transmitted in Accordance with the Provisions of 1 U.S.C. 112b, as amended*, available at www.state.gov/s/l/treaty/caseact/2009/index.htm. The three agreements receiving after-the-fact approval were the free trade agreements with Peru and Oman, plus an agreement with India on trade in civilian nuclear materials. Some of these agreements entered into effect prior to 2009 (and likely there were 2009 agreements not reported in this list); the State Department does not always have immediately current information about low-level agreements or agreements made by other Departments.

[196] *See* U.S. Department of State, 2009 *Treaties and Agreements*, available at www.state.gov/s/l/treaty/tias/2009/ (listing four Mutual Legal Assistance treaties, four extradition treaties, one tax treaty, three multilateral treaties on weapons, and one multilateral treaty on trademarks).

[197] *See* Hathaway, *Presidential Power*, *supra* note 4, at 146 (noting that "once Congress delegates authority to the President to make the agreement, it usually plays no further role"); *ibid.* at 159–64 (listing representative authorizing statutes, typically giving approval in general terms); *ibid.* at 205–30 (criticizing presidential agreement-making under advance Congressional authorizations).

treaty, or core presidential power such as routine direction of the military and that many of them do not appear to impose material ongoing obligations on the United States.[198] To be sure, not all such agreements are routine; for example, the 2008 security agreements with Iraq (reported in 2009) established the basis for continuing U.S. military operations in Iraq.[199] But to return to a conclusion reached with respect to the nineteenth century, it is not clear that many such agreements would figure in an account of modern U.S. diplomacy. Although further study would be required for more detailed and definite conclusions, at minimum it appears that the volume of Executive agreements in modern practice is not matched by their importance.

IV CONCLUSION

In sum, the law of international agreement-making in the period following the Third Restatement defies easy categorization. It remains a fluid contest among the treaty and its rivals. A few general conclusions may be suggested, however.

First, the Article II, Section 2 process for approving treaties, as set forth in the Constitution's text, remains central to U.S. practice. It marks the decisive path for approval or rejection of most major international agreements aside from trade agreements. The U.S. president conducts treaty negotiations in the shadow of the need for the Senate's supermajority consent, as the

198 For example, the largest single group of agreements reported in 2009 consists of agreements regarding health care for military dependents, made with forty-two separate countries. Agreements to exchange technical or scientific information, or relating to military or cultural exchanges of personnel, take up another twenty-five agreements. Implementation of foreign assistance programs, in which the United States is disbursing development funds for particular projects, comprises at least twenty-seven agreements. Others involve such details as the implementation of a statute regulating the import of cultural artifacts and related protective measures (twelve agreements), implementation of prior trade agreements (four agreements), agreements on the payment of existing debts to U.S. agencies (nine agreements) and agreements on such specific matters as construction of embassy buildings in China and Kazakhstan, construction of a seismic monitoring station in Morocco, arrangements for Peace Corps volunteers in Togo, and the treatment of Americans on temporary duty in Panama (another thirteen or so agreements). *See* www.state.gov/s/l/treaty/caseact/2009/index.htm. Thus even a cursory review suggests that over 130 of the reported agreements are matters of routine diplomacy, and the true count is obviously much higher.

199 See Bruce Ackerman & Oona Hathaway, *Limited War and the Constitution: Iraq and the Crisis of Presidential Legality*, 109 MICH. L. REV. 447, 467–73 (2011) (describing the Iraq agreements). As with many executive agreements, the Executive Branch was vague as to whether the agreements were made under the President's constitutional authority or under an implied authorization from Congress arising from its approval of military action in Iraq. A number of senators sharply criticized the arrangement with Iraq for bypassing after-the-fact approval by either the Senate or Congress as a whole. *Ibid.*

Constitution's Framers anticipated. Yet the Senate's consent is not a mere formality, as the defeat of several presidential treaty priorities attests. The idea of "interchangeability" between Article II treaties and Congressional-Executive agreements, pursued by the Third Restatement and various academic accounts, has not come to pass. In modern practice, no one seriously thinks that a treaty blocked or voted down by the Senate could be resubmitted for majority Congressional approval without provoking furious debate. However, while there is a broad assumption that, generally speaking, major agreements (apart from trade agreements) will proceed on the Article II track, there is little theoretical explanation of how that category is defined or why this particular practice exists.

Second, the treaty has been wholly replaced by the Congressional-Executive agreement in one key area: international trade. Major trade agreements are submitted to Congress for ex post majority approval, not to the Senate for supermajority approval. Despite some academic opposition, this practice now seems thoroughly entrenched. But while there may be some substantial prospect of expanding this category by accretion – that is, by expansively defining what constitutes a trade agreement – there seems little prospect of adding material additional categories. And further, there is no satisfactory constitutional account of why trade agreements merit this particular treatment.

Third, the sole Executive agreement remains a viable option in some areas, particularly claims settlement agreements and matters related to recognition of foreign governments and diplomatic activities. Yet it seems unlikely to claim a broader role. Expansive Executive agreement authority provokes opposition in a way that Congressional-Executive agreements do not, as it seems profoundly destructive of separation of power values. In any event the president in many cases need not make such a dramatic claim for power because an alternate basis – implied approval – will often serve as well.

Fourth, the great numerical majority of U.S. international agreements appear to be of a different sort: agreements made by the president on the basis of some claimed authority, implicit or explicit, given by a prior statute or treaty. Typically these agreements are not of the importance of Article II treaties (although sometimes they are). This approach to making agreements has a number of advantages for the executive – most notably, no approval of the actual agreement is needed from any legislative body, and yet the president can plausibly claim not to be acting unilaterally but rather in pursuit of a goal expressed by Congress (or the Senate). Further, given Congress' tendency to draft broad statutes and the courts' willingness to find implicit approval not only from vague statutory language but also from other actions and inactions of

Congress, the president will often be able to plausibly claim such authority. Thus it is not surprising that this approach has come to dominate the ordinary agreement-making operations of the executive. The question for the future is whether this category, already the numerical leader, expands to include more important agreements, for which the Article II treaty and the ex post Congressional-Executive agreement (for now) remain the models.

But agreements in this fourth category face an important limitation: it is not clear to what extent they form part of domestic law. Unlike a potential fifth category, nonbinding agreements, they are binding as a matter of international law. To be full rivals to the Article II treaty or the ex post Congressional-Executive agreement, however, they need to have the same status in domestic law. Arguably they do, on the authority of *Dames & Moore* or by analogy to regulations issued by executive agencies under authority delegated by Congress. If that status is accepted as to such agreements generally, however, the practical effect would be a substantial increase in executive power that might become an irresistible rival to the treaty. Because the president will readily be able to claim at least implied authority in many circumstances, and because presidential lawmaking pursuant to implied power – validated by *Dames & Moore* and the concurring opinions in *Youngstown* – sounds less constitutionally suspect than unilateral presidential lawmaking, the practical shift of power to the executive branch could be of great magnitude. It remains to be seen if Congress, the Senate, or the courts will resist it.

8

Judicial Barriers to the Enforcement of Treaties

Roger P. Alford

Treaties serve a variety of purposes. Some treaties order relations between States and assume enforcement through political and diplomatic channels. Such treaties are horizontal and operate primarily on the international plane. Examples include military alliances, peace treaties, weapons conventions, and mutual assistance agreements. Other treaties order relations between private parties. These treaties are horizontal but operate at the domestic level. Examples include treaties that limit liability in the airline industry, require enforcement of foreign arbitral awards, or regulate contracts involving the international sale of goods. Still other treaties order relations between States and the nationals of other States with the object of securing reciprocal benefits for those nationals. These treaties are diagonal[1] and operate at both the domestic and international planes for the benefit of other States and their nationals. Examples include diplomatic and consular conventions, extradition treaties, bilateral investment treaties, dual taxation treaties, and treaties that coordinate transnational litigation. A fourth category of treaties coordinates relations between States and their own nationals. These treaties operate vertically by requiring the State to impose duties on individuals or legal persons or to guarantee individual rights. Such treaties typically operate at the domestic plane and often assume that the treaty will be brought into the domestic legal system through political processes and then enforced in individual cases by the judiciary. Examples include environmental, anti-corruption, and human rights treaties.

To the extent treaties operate at the domestic plane and assume judicial enforcement for their efficacy, one would expect the United States to empower the judiciary to enforce such international obligations. In many respects, the United States does this, particularly for transnational treaties that

[1] That is, they operate both horizontally and vertically.

coordinate relations between private parties. In other respects, it is less inclined to do so, particularly when a treaty orders the United States to do something it already is doing. Often when the United States breaches its treaty obligations, courts in the United States will refrain from reaching the merits of a claim arising from the breach. This begs the question: why? The answer is that courts have developed a number of doctrines that render judicial review of the merits of a treaty claim less likely, especially when the target of the claim is behavior by the U.S. government.

This chapter addresses the judicial barriers to the enforcement of treaties. One could choose any number of issues as the focus for such an analysis in the United States. This chapter focuses on four that are especially salient: (1) standing and private rights of action; (2) the last-in-time rule; (3) the political question doctrine; and (4) reservations, understandings, and declarations.[2] Each of these issues is addressed in the Restatement (Third) on Foreign Relations to one degree or another. Each undoubtedly will be addressed in the Restatement (Fourth) now underway.

Since the adoption of the Third Restatement in 1987, the United States either has continued to maintain judicial barriers then in place or has enhanced those barriers. In one sense this reflects a retreat from the internationalist agenda of many traditional foreign relations scholars. But it also reflects a rejection of the nationalist agenda of many revisionist scholars who call for still higher barriers.

I STANDING AND PRIVATE RIGHTS OF ACTION

In the international treaty context, the question of standing to assert a treaty claim elides with the question of whether a treaty creates a private right of action. Under traditional standing doctrine, a plaintiff must show an injury in fact, that is, "a concrete and particularized ... actual or imminent" invasion of a legally protected interest.[3] The federal government can create standing by passing laws that establish a legally protected interest. Treaties that have been implemented by statute or that are self-executing and that create judicially cognizable interests create standing for particular parties injured by the treaty violation.

[2] There are other procedural obstacles that are not dealt with in this chapter, such as the state secrets doctrine, the procedural default rule, and the act of state doctrine. Space limitations preclude a more comprehensive analysis of all the judicial barriers to the enforcement of treaty obligations.

[3] Lujan v. Defenders of Wildlife, 504 U.S. 555, 560 (1992). After nearly twenty-five years, *Lujan* remains the leading Supreme Court case on standing. The case relates to standing to assert a statutory claim, not a treaty claim.

The Third Restatement does not have specific provisions that address standing for treaty violations. There are, however, comments and Reporters' notes that allude to the issue.[4] The most important of these comments provides that "[i]nternational agreements, even those directly benefiting private persons, generally do not create private rights or provide for a private cause of action in domestic courts, but there are exceptions with respect to both rights and remedies."[5] Elsewhere the language is more positive toward the right of individuals to bring claims under international agreements. A Reporters' note to section 111 states that "there is no reason to treat claims arising under international law any differently from those arising under other federal law ... [h]owever, a case 'arises under' international law or an international agreement only if the law or agreement confers legal rights on the plaintiff."[6] The key question is whether an agreement creates such rights, and the Reporters recognized that "[t]reaties and other international agreements sometimes confer rights that would support a cause of action by private parties ..., but many agreements that may ultimately benefit individual interests do not give them justiciable legal rights."[7]

Prior to World War II, courts applied a presumption that treaties were self-executing and created private rights of action with respect to private law treaties that created traditional common law rights.[8] In the postwar period, a political backlash arose against public law treaties promoting international human rights, and that skepticism gave rise to treaty reservations and judicial interpretations limiting the domestic effect of public law treaties.[9] Consequently, before the Third Restatement, courts refused to recognize human rights treaties or other public law treaties as creating private rights of

4 *See, e.g.*, RESTATEMENT (THIRD) OF FOREIGN RELATIONS § 1, Reporter's Note 4 (1987) ("The jurisprudence of adjudication – principles as to jurisdiction, standing, mootness, ripeness, etc. – applies to foreign relations cases as to others").

5 *Ibid.* § 907, cmt. a (1987). 6 *Ibid.* § 111, Rptr. note 4. 7 *Ibid.*

8 *See, e.g.*, De Geofroy v. Riggs, 133 U.S. 258 (1890); Chew Heong v. United States, 112 U.S. 536 (1884); United States v. Percheman, 32 U.S. (7 Pet.) 51 (1833); Foster v. Neilson, 27 U.S. (2 Pet.) 253 (1829); Hopkirk v. Bell, 7 U.S. (3 Cranch) 454, 456–7 (1806); Ware v. Hylton, 3 U.S. (3 Dall.) 199 (1796); *see generally* Oona A. Hathaway, Sabria McElroy & Sara Aronchick Solow, *International Law at Home: Enforcing Treaties in U.S. Courts*, 37 YALE J. INT'L L. 51, 57–63 (2012). *See also* Ingrid Wuerth, "Self-Execution," Chapter 4 in this volume.

9 Among such treaties were the Convention on the Prevention and Punishment of the Crime of Genocide art. 1, Dec. 9, 1948, 102 Stat. 3045, 78 U.N.T.S. 277; Convention on the Prevention and Punishment of Crimes against Internationally Protected Persons, Dec. 14, 1973, 28 U.S.T. 1975, 1035 U.N.T.S. 167; International Covenant on Civil and Political Rights, *opened for signature* Dec. 16, 1966, 999 U.N.T.S. 171. *See generally* Louis Henkin, *U.S. Ratification of Human Rights Conventions: The Ghost of Senator Bricker*, 89 AM. J. INT'L L. 341, 348–50 (1995).

action.[10] But during this same time, courts granted standing and recognized private rights of action with respect to private law treaties, such as those affecting economic or commercial relations.[11] This distinction was based on a recognition that certain types of treaties regulating private behavior generally were self-executing, while others regulating public behavior generally were not.[12] This distinction – some treaties being deemed to be self-executing and some non-self-executing – was a source of controversy in drafting the Third Restatement, with Louis Henkin, the Chief Reporter, expressing the view that "lawmaking by treaty was to be an alternative to legislation by Congress" and that "the Framers intended that a treaty should become law *ipso facto*, when a treaty is made; it should not require legislative implementation to convert it into United States law."[13] But Henkin's personal views on this issue are not evident in the Restatement itself, which maintains the distinction between public law treaties and private law treaties.

In 2008 the Supreme Court in *Medellin v. Texas* articulated a general presumption against self-execution, finding that a treaty is not enforceable as domestic law unless there is implementing legislation or the "treaty itself conveys an intention that it be 'self-executing' and is ratified on these terms."[14] In the aftermath of *Medellin*, "instead of presuming that treaties that create private rights necessarily also create private rights of action, courts

[10] *See, e.g.*, Frolova v. Union of Soviet Socialist Republics, 761 F.2d 370, 373–4 (7th Cir. 1985); Mannington Mills, Inc. v. Congoleum Corp., 595 F.2d 1287, 1298 (3d Cir. 1979); Diggs v. Richardson, 555 F.2d 848, 851 (D.C. Cir. 1976); Dreyfus v. Von Finck, 534 F.2d 24, 30 (2d Cir. 1976). *See generally* David Sloss, *When Do Treaties Create Individually Enforceable Rights? The Supreme Court Ducks the Issue in* Hamdan *and* Sanchez-Llamas, 45 COLUM. J. TRANS. L. 20, 106–10; Hathaway, et al., *supra* note 8, at 68–70.

[11] *See, e.g.*, El Al Israel Airlines, Ltd. v. Tsui Yuan Tseng, 525 U.S. 155, 161–3, 176 (1999); Zicherman v. Korean Air Lines Co., 516 U.S. 217, 221, 231 (1996); Trans World Airlines, Inc. v. Franklin Mint Corp., 466 U.S. 243, 252 (1984); Sumitomo Shoji Am., Inc. v. Avagliano, 457 U.S. 176, 181, 189–90 (1982); BP Oil Int'l, Ltd. v. Empresa Estatal Petoleos de Ecuador, 332 F.3d 333, 336 (5th Cir. 2003); Delchi Carrier v. Rotorex Corp., 71 F.3d 1024, 1027–28 (2d Cir. 1995); Choi v. Kim, 50 F.3d 244 (3d Cir. 1995); Vagenas v. Cont'l Gin Co., 988 F.2d 104, 106 (11th Cir. 1993); Irish Nat'l Ins. Co. v. Aer Lingus Teoranta, 739 F.2d 90 (2d Cir. 1984).

[12] Hathaway, et al, *supra* note 8, at 63–5 (arguing that after World War II, the Supreme Court and lower courts considered treaties affecting economic or commercial relations between individuals as self-executing and adopted a skeptical posture for treaties regulating relationships between the state and individuals); David L. Sloss, Michael D. Ramsey & William S. Dodge, "Continuity and Change Over Two Centuries," in *INTERNATIONAL LAW IN THE U.S. SUPREME COURT: CONTINUITY AND CHANGE* 589, 593 (David L. Sloss, Michael D. Ramsey & William S. Dodge, eds., 2011) ("During the late twentieth century, the lower courts rarely invoked non-self-execution doctrine or the presumption against individually enforceable rights in cases between private parties, but they often invoked those doctrines to justify their refusal to enforce treaties against government actors").

[13] Louis Henkin, *supra* note 9. [14] Medellin v. Texas, 552 U.S. 491, 505 (2008).

now generally presume that they do not, regardless of the type of the treaty."[15] This change in the presumption diminishes the possibility that courts will recognize treaties as creating private rights of action, or even that a private party may use such treaties defensively to challenge a claim against it. This variant of non-self-execution precludes a private party from invoking the treaty as a basis for a claim or defense in court.[16]

A second development in party standing doctrine has also curtailed access to courts. In the non-treaty context, the standing doctrine has been an important limitation on public law litigation.[17] Public law litigation has focused on ill-defined cases or controversies and sought wide-ranging, prospective relief through judicial supervision over government policies.[18] Citizen standing was a key component of such litigation, allowing plaintiffs who suffered a legal wrong to challenge government action.[19] The Court in *Lujan* interpreted the standing doctrine to limit citizen suits, holding that courts cannot vindicate the public interest in the absence of individual harm to the plaintiffs.[20] Vindicating "the undifferentiated public interest in executive officers' compliance with the law" is, the Court concluded, "the function of Congress and the Chief Executive," not the judiciary.[21]

The international variant of citizen suits is transnational public law litigation under the Alien Tort Statute, a statute that has enabled suit for violations of either treaties or customary international law.[22] The Second Circuit's landmark decision in *Filartiga v. Pena-Irala*[23] interpreted the Alien Tort Statute broadly to empower aliens to sue for torts committed in violation of the law of nations or treaties. Such litigation became something of a cottage industry in

[15] Hathaway et al., *supra* note 8, at 71 (discussing *Mora v. New York*, 524 F.3d 183 (2d Cir. 2008)); *Gross v. German Foundation Industrial Initiative*, 549 F.3d 605 (3d Cir. 2008); *Gandara v. Bennett*, 528 F.3d 823 (11th Cir. 2008); *Toor v. Holder*, 717 F. Supp. 2d 100 (D.D.C. 2010).

[16] *See* Carlos Manuel Vázquez, *Treaties as Law of the Land: The Supremacy Clause and the Judicial Enforcement of Treaties*, 122 *Harv. L. Rev.* 599, 629–32 (2008).

[17] *See* Abram Chayes, *Public Law Litigation and the Burger Court*, 96 HARV. L. REV. 4 (1982); Abram Chayes, *The Role of the Judge in Public Law Litigation*, 89 HARV. L. REV. 1281 (1976) (discussing public law litigation).

[18] Chayes, *Public Law Litigation and the Burger Court*, *supra* note 17, at 5.

[19] *See, e.g.*, Bivens v. Six Unknown Named Agents, 403 U.S. 388 (1971); Ass'n of Data Processing Orgs. v. Camp, 397 U.S. 150 (1970); 52 U.S.C. § 702.

[20] Lujan, *supra* note 3, at 574–8.

[21] *Ibid.* at 576–7.

[22] *See generally* Harold H. Koh, *Transnational Public Law Litigation*, 100 YALE L.J. 2347, 2362 (1991).

[23] Filartiga v. Pena-Irala, 630 F.2d 876 (2d Cir. 1980). For a challenge to the suitability of applying the public law litigation model in the foreign affairs context, see Ann Woolhandler, *Treaties, Self-Execution, and the Public Law Litigation Model*, 42 VA. J. INT'L L. 757 (2002).

the 1980s and 1990s, with over 150 cases alleging an ATS violation.[24] For over two decades, interpretation of the Alien Tort Statute developed without the benefit of Supreme Court review.[25] Finally in 2004, the U.S. Supreme Court in *Sosa v. Alvarez-Machain* limited the scope of the ATS, but left the door ajar to further litigation, "subject to vigilant doorkeeping."[26] In *Sosa* the Court disagreed with lower courts that had held that the ATS created a private right of action. Rather, the Court concluded, the ATS permitted plaintiffs to bring only common law causes of action for torts committed in violation of the "present-day law of nations," provided those claims rested on accepted international norms and were defined with sufficient specificity.[27]

The Court in *Sosa* found that plaintiffs had statutory standing in that the ATS was a vehicle for pursuing a private right of action created elsewhere for international law violations arising from treaties or custom. But it avoided the question of whether the claimant had party standing in the *Lujan* sense of individualized harm.[28] Since *Sosa*, lower courts have struggled with the applicable standard to apply in assessing individualized harm for international law violations, particularly when the victim is deceased.[29] What they have not done is eschew the general standing requirements of individualized harm developed in the non-treaty context in favor of permitting citizen suits that seek redress for

24 *See* Jonathan C. Drimmer & Sarah R. Lamoree, *Think Globally, Sue Locally: Trends and Out-of-Court Tactics in Transnational Tort Actions*, 29 BERKELEY J. INT'L L. 456, 460 (2011); Michael Goldhaber, The Life and Death of the Corporate Alien Tort, LAW.COM (Oct. 12, 2010), www.law.com/jsp/law/international/LawArticleIntl.jsp?id=1202473215797&slreturn=20140016104130.

25 *See, e.g.*, Flores v. S. Peru Copper Corp., 414 F.3d 233 (2d Cir. 2003); Doe v. Unocal Corp., 395 F.3d 932 (9th Cir. 2002); Wiwa v. Royal Dutch Petroleum Co., 226 F.3d 88 (2d Cir. 2000); Beanal v. Freeport-McMoran, Inc., 197 F.3d 161 (5th Cir. 1999); Hilao v. Estate of Marcos, 103 F.3d 767 (9th Cir. 1996); Kadic v. Karadžić, 70 F.3d 232 (2d Cir. 1995); Siderman de Blake v. Republic of Arg., 965 F.2d 699 (9th Cir. 1992); Tel-Oren v. Libyan Arab Republic, 726 F.2d 774 (D.C. Cir. 1984).

26 Sosa v. Alvarez-Machain, 542 U.S. 692, 729 (2004).

27 *Ibid.* at 725. The Court stated that the modern-day international norms must be accepted by the civilized world and be defined with a specificity comparable to the features of the eighteenth century paradigms, namely violations of safe conduct, infringements of the rights of ambassadors, and piracy. *See ibid.* at 715 and 725.

28 With the holding that the violations alleged in *Sosa* were not tied to international law norms sufficiently universal, it was unnecessary to consider the extent to which the alleged harm was individualized.

29 *See, e.g.*, Bowoto v. Chevron Corp., 621 F.3d 1116, 1122–3 (9th Cir. 2010); In re Estate of Marcos, 25 F.3d 1467, 1476 (9th Cir. 1994); Estate of Cabello v. Fernandez-Larios, 157 F. Supp. 2d 1345, 1355–58 (S.D. Fla. 2011); Beanal v. Freeport-McMoran, 969 F. Supp. 362, 366–68 (E.D. La. 1997); Xuncax v. Gramajo, 886 F. Supp. 162, 169, 173 (D. Mass. 1995). *See generally* Alastair J. Agcaoili, *Wrongful Death and Survival Actions for Torts in Violation of International Law*, 50 SAN DIEGO L. REV. 383 (2013).

undifferentiated international public law violations.[30] This heightened standing requirement to establish individualized harm raises the threshold for judicial resolution of alleged breaches of international treaty obligations.

Thus, since the Third Restatement, there have been two developments relating to standing that have limited plaintiffs' access to courts. First, as Professor Wuerth explains in Chapter 4, the Court has rejected the presumption that treaties are self-executing without differentiating between public treaties and treaties regulating transnational activities of private parties. At the same time, courts have curtailed citizen suits by limiting party standing, thus requiring individualized harm for any legal violations, including treaty violations. The combined impact of these two trends has been to curtail access to judicial remedies for treaty violations.

II LAST-IN-TIME RULE

Pursuant to the Supremacy Clause, treaties and statutes have equal status.[31] The Supreme Court has consistently interpreted that equality to include the principle of *lex posterior derogat priori*, such that in the case of conflict between a treaty and a federal statute, the last in time will control.[32] The Third Restatement incorporates this principle, stating that:

> An act of Congress supersedes an earlier rule of international law or a provision of an international agreement as law of the United States if the purpose of the act to supersede the earlier rule or provision is clear or if the act and the earlier rule or provision cannot be fairly reconciled.[33]

The Third Restatement also recognizes the converse situation, such that "[a] provision of a treaty of the United States that becomes effective as law of the United States supersedes as domestic law any inconsistent preexisting provision of a law or treaty of the United States."[34]

30 *See* Baloco ex rel. Tapia v. Drummond Co., Inc., 640 F.3d 1338, 1343–4 (11th Cir. 2011); Beanal, *supra* note 29, at 367–70.

31 U.S. CONST. art. VI, cl. 2 ("This Constitution, and the Laws of the United States which shall be made in pursuance thereof; and all treaties made, or which shall be made, under the authority of the United States, shall be the supreme law of the land").

32 *See, e.g.*, Moser v. United States, 341 U.S. 41 (1951); The Chinese Exclusion Case, 130 U.S. 581, 600–2 (1889); Whitney v. Robertson, 124 U.S. 190, 194 (1888); Head Money Cases, 112 U.S. 580, 599 (1884); The Cherokee Tobacco, 78 U.S. (11 Wall) 616 (1870).

33 THIRD RESTATEMENT § 115(1)(a). However, this rule does not "relieve the United States of its international obligations or the consequence of a violation of that obligation." *Ibid.* at § 115(1)(b).

34 *Ibid.* at § 115(2). *See* Cook v. United States, 288 U.S. 102 (1933).

At the time the Third Restatement was drafted, academic commentary favored modifications to the last-in-time rule to give greater domestic effect to treaties. In particular, internationalists favored dispensing with the last-in-time rule so that later federal statutes would not supersede earlier treaties.[35] "Congress . . . has a constitutional obligation to implement the treaties which the President and Senate make," wrote Louis Henkin, so "it is anomalous to accord [Congress] power to disregard a treaty obligation, compel its violation, and put the United States in default."[36] Influential scholarship also employed historical and textual arguments to argue in favor of a more treaty-friendly version of the last-in-time rule.[37]

The Third Restatement proposed modifications to the last-in-time rule consistent with these interpretations. For example, one Reporters' note suggested that the last-in-time rule should not apply to "general international law established by a general multilateral treaty."[38] Nonetheless, the Third Restatement did not adopt that suggestion because such a distinction had not taken root in federal court jurisprudence.[39]

Since publication of the Third Restatement, there has been a fundamental change in academic commentary regarding the last-in-time rule. Prominent scholars have argued in favor of prioritizing federal statutes over treaties.[40] They also have argued that the last-in-time rule presumes treating statutes and treaties as equal in other areas, such that the federalism limitations imposed on statutes should apply to

35 Louis Henkin, *Treaties in a Constitutional Democracy*, 10 MICH. J. INT'L L. 406, 425–6 (1989); Jordan J. Paust, *Rediscovering the Relationship Between Congressional Power and International Law: Exceptions to the Last-in-time rule and the Primacy of Custom*, 28 VA. J. INT'L L. 393, 398–414 (1988); Peter Westen, *The Place of Foreign Treaties in the Courts of the United States: A Reply to Louis Henkin*, 101 HARV. L. REV. 511, 512, 516 (1987); Louis Henkin, *The Constitution and United States Sovereignty: A Century of Chinese Exclusion and its Progeny*, 100 HARV. L. REV. 853, 870–8, 853, 885–7 (1987); LOUIS HENKIN, FOREIGN AFFAIRS AND THE CONSTITUTION, 163–4 (1972).

36 HENKIN, *supra* note 35, at 164.

37 Jules Lobel, *The Limits of Constitutional Power: Conflicts between Foreign Policy and International Law*, 71 VA. L. REV. 1071, 1096–1101 (1985).

38 THIRD RESTATEMENT, at § 115, note 1 *citing* LOUIS HENKIN, FOREIGN AFFAIRS AND THE CONSTITUTION 163–4 (1972).

39 *Ibid*. Another note suggested that the last-in-time rule should apply to customary international law but conceded that courts are unlikely to give a later customary international law rule domestic effect in the face of an earlier federal statute. *Ibid*. at § 115, note 4.

40 AKHAL AMAR, AMERICA'S CONSTITUTION, 302–5 (2012); Vasan Kesavan, *The Three Tiers of Federal Law*, 100 NW. U. L. REV. 1479 (2006); John C. Yoo, *Laws as Treaties?: The Constitutionality of Congressional-Executive Agreements*, 99 MICH. L. REV. 757, 815–16 (2001); John C. Yoo, *Treaties and Public Lawmaking: A Textual and Structural Defense of Non-Self-Execution*, 99 COLUM. L. REV. 2218, 2243 (1999).

treaties.[41] These scholars also have defended the last-in-time rule based on historical and textual arguments, challenging internationalists who argue that treaties should have primacy over statutes.[42] This trend toward a less internationalist perspective on the last-in-time rule reflects the broader currents of revisionist thinking on the place of international law in our federal system.

While academic support for the ability of treaties to take precedence over subsequent federal statutes has waned, the judiciary has not altered its commitment to the traditional last-in-time rule. In *Breard v. Greene*, the Supreme Court cited old precedents in reaffirming the last-in-time rule and refusing to give effect to a treaty provision in the face of a subsequently enacted federal statute.[43] The consular rights conferred on Angel Breard pursuant to a treaty in effect since 1969 were subject to procedural limitations imposed by a federal statute enacted over twenty-five years after the treaty entered into force. The Court held that "an Act of Congress ... is on full parity with a treaty, and that when a statute which is subsequent in time is inconsistent with a treaty, the statute to the extent of conflict renders the treaty null."[44]

The Supreme Court and lower courts consistently have enforced this commitment to the last-in-time rule, which frequently results in the enforcement of subsequent statutes over earlier treaties.[45] With a few notable exceptions, the last-in-time rule is almost never applied to enforce a subsequent treaty over an earlier conflicting statute.[46] Courts also are at pains to interpret

[41] *See, e.g.*, Curtis A. Bradley, *Federalism and the Treaty Power*, 98 AMER. SOC. INT'L. PROC. 341, 342 (2001); Curtis A. Bradley, *The Treaty Power and American Federalism*, 97 MICH. L. REV. 390 (1998).

[42] Julian G. Ku, *Treaties as Laws: A Defense of the Last-in-Time Rule for Treaties and Federal Statutes*, 80 IND. L.J. 319 (2005).

[43] Breard v. Greene, 523 U.S. 371, 376 (1998) (*citing* Reid v. Covert, 354 U.S. 1, 18 (1957)).

[44] *Ibid.* at 376 (*quoting* Reid v. Covert, 354 U.S. 1, 18 (1957)).

[45] *See* Breard, *supra* note 43; Rainey v. United States, 232 U.S. 310 (1914); Chinese Exclusion Case (Chae Chan Ping v. United States), 130 U.S. 581 (1899); Head Money Case (Edye v. Robertson), 112 U.S. 580 (1884); The Cherokee Tobacco, 78 U.S. (11 Wall.) 616 (1870); Jamieson v. C.I.R., 584 F.3d 1074, 1075–6 (D.C. Cir. 2009); Port Authority of New York and New Jersey v. Dep't of Transp., 479 F.3d 21, 31 (D.C. Cir. 2007); Fund for Animals, Inc., v. Kempthorne, 472 F.3d 872, 874–77 (D.C. Cir. 2006); Kappus v. C.I.R., 337 F.3d 1053, 1057–60 (D.C. Cir. 2003); Havana Club Holding, S.A. v. Galleon, S.A., 203 F.3d 116, 124 (2d Cir. 2000); South African Airways v. Dole, 817 F.2d 119 (D.C. Cir. 1987). *See generally* Detlev Vagts, *The United States and Its Treaties: Observance and Breach*, 95 AMER. J. INT'L L. 313, 313–21 (2001).

[46] *But see* Cook v. United States, 288 U.S. 102, 118–20 (1933) (enforcing subsequent treaty); Greci v. Birknes, 527 F.2d 956, 959–61 (1st Cir. 1976) (same). Recently the United States has entered into numerous mutual legal assistance treaties (MLATs) to facilitate effective investigation and prosecution of criminal activities. These MLATs streamline the process of serving letters

a later-in-time treaty to avoid a conflict with an earlier statute.[47] The practical effect of these post-Third Restatement developments is to diminish the domestic effect of self-executing treaties, some percentage of which are not enforceable within the United States because of subsequent acts of Congress. Thus, in theory, statutes and treaties are on an equal footing, but in practice statutes routinely limit treaties, while treaties rarely limit statutes.

A new iteration of this issue, one that has produced a division among lower courts, has been determining which sovereign act counts for purposes of the last-in-time rule when treaties and statutes are repealed, updated, amended, and interpreted. Courts are bound to "construe and give effect to the latest expression of the sovereign will."[48] In ruling on which sovereign act counts for purposes of the last-in-time rule in these circumstances, the trend has been for courts to side with statutes over treaties, a development contrary to the Third Restatement.

For example, in *Kappus v. Commissioner of Internal Revenue*,[49] the D.C. Circuit held that protocols to the U.S.-Canada Tax Treaty enacted subsequent to a conflicting federal statute did not reflect the last expression of the sovereign will because the protocols were not the source of the conflict.[50] The protocols amended provisions of the original treaty other than those in conflict with the statute. Under these circumstances, such protocols neither revived the original treaty nor impliedly repealed the conflicting statute. The federal statute enacted after the original treaty but before the protocols was the last expression of the sovereign will.[51]

However, the Second Circuit has held that amendments to statutes are a different matter. In *Empresa Cubana del Tobaco v. Culbro Corp.*,[52] the court

rogatory and guarantee that the United States will provide greater legal assistance with respect to discovery requests by foreign governments for use in criminal proceedings abroad. These treaties are self-executing and conflict with an earlier statute, 28 U.S.C. § 1782, which grants federal courts significant discretion to deny discovery requests based on substantive protections relating to, inter alia, privileged evidence and foreign discoverability. In other words, discovery pursuant to the MLATs is direct and automatic, not indirect and discretionary as required under Section 1782. For cases according precedence to MLATs over § 1782, see, e.g., In re Premises Located at 840 140th Avenue NE, Bellevue, Washington, 634 F.3d 557, 567–71 (9th Cir. 2011); In re Commissioner's Subpoenas, 325 F.3d 1287, 1305–06 (11th Cir. 2003); In re Erato, 2 F.3d 11, 15–16 (2d Cir. 1993).

47 *See, e.g.*, Weber v. Finker, 554 F.3d 1379, 1383–84 (11th Cir. 2009); Blanco v. United States, 775 F.2d 53 (2d Cir. 1985); United States v. Trustees of Boston College, 831 F. Supp. 2d 435, 449 (D. Mass. 2011).

48 Whitney v. Robertson, 124 U.S. 190, 195(1888).

49 Kappus v. Commissioner of Internal Revenue, 337 F.3d 1053 (D.C. Cir. 2003).

50 *Ibid.* at 1057–60. 51 *Ibid.*

52 Empresa Cubana del Tobaco v. Culbro Corp., 399 F.3d 462 (2d Cir. 2005).

addressed whether a federal statute enforcing the embargo against Cuba superseded an earlier trademark treaty. The embargo against Cuba was enacted pursuant to federal regulations dating from 1963. The United States ratified the most recent iteration of the Paris Convention in 1970 and incorporated protections for famous marks in the Lanham Act. Subsequent events complicated the issue, as Congress reaffirmed and codified the Cuban embargo by federal statute in 1996 and also amended and updated the protections for famous marks under the Lanham Act in 1999. The Court held that the regulations imposing an embargo on Cuba were "reaffirmed and codified in 1996" by statute and that "any claim grounded in the Paris Convention that presented an irreconcilable conflict" with the embargo statute would be rendered null.[53] The fact that the amendments to the Lanham Act implementing the treaty protections took place after 1996 did not result in the treaty's being considered to be later in time than the embargo legislation.[54]

These cases suggest that amendments to treaties do not trump prior statutes unless those specific amendments are the source of the conflict. If the conflict does not stem specifically from the amendments, the treaty will not be deemed to be the last sovereign act. By contrast, statutory amendments often reaffirm and codify earlier statutes and are treated as the latest action for purposes of the last-in-time rule. In both cases, the result is the priority of statutes over treaties, a result contrary to the Reporters notes to Section 115 of the Third Restatement.

III POLITICAL QUESTION DOCTRINE

International law is an area fraught with ambiguity regarding the application of the political question doctrine. That doctrine declares certain subjects to be political questions that are not justiciable in domestic courts. The Supreme Court's articulation of the political question doctrine in *Baker v. Carr*, not a treaty case, recognized that "not every case or controversy which touches foreign relations lies beyond judicial cognizance,"[55] but provided little guidance as to which type of controversy is non-justiciable. The Court's plurality statement in *Goldwater v. Carter* amplified the confusion with a divided court in a denial of certiorari disagreeing as to the essential requirements of a political question and its applicability.[56] In the absence of guidance from the Supreme Court since *Goldwater*, lower courts frequently have applied the

[53] *Ibid.* at 481. [54] *Ibid.* [55] 369 U.S. 186, 211–12 (1962).
[56] 444 U.S. 996, 1002–3 (1979).

political question doctrine to limit judicial review in the foreign affairs context.[57]

The Third Restatement gives insufficient attention to the political question doctrine. It is briefly addressed in a Reporters' note to Section 1, but that note simply summarizes *Baker v. Carr* and *Goldwater v. Carter* and lists specific Executive actions courts typically treat as political questions.[58] Beyond that Reporters' note, the political question doctrine arises obliquely in a few instances but is otherwise omitted in sections where one would expect it to be included.

For example, there are several provisions in Part III of the Third Restatement dealing with international agreements where one would expect it to receive mention. Section 303 addresses Presidential authority to enter into Article II treaties, Congressional-Executive agreements, and sole Executive agreements. In each case, the Third Restatement concludes that the President has the authority to make such agreements subject to constitutional limitations. Justiciability is not expressly addressed with respect to the making of international agreements, but the implication is that the President's choice as to the form of agreement lies within the political domain and cannot be challenged in court.

With respect to the interpretation of international agreements, the Third Restatement stipulates that the President has the authority to interpret treaties in U.S. relations with other countries, but that courts have "final authority to interpret an international agreement for purposes of applying it as law in the United States."[59] In so stating, the Restatement advanced what Curtis Bradley subsequently has called a "rule of law" conception of treaty disputes. A Reporters' note to Section 326 states that treaty interpretation is not a political question.[60]

Finally, in discussing the termination of international agreements, the Third Restatement emphasizes that the President has the unilateral power to suspend or terminate international agreements.[61] A Reporters' note to Section 339 mentions the historical practice with respect to the President's

[57] *See generally* Ganesh Sitaraman & Ingrid Wuerth, *The Normalization of Foreign Relations Law*, 128 HARV. L. REV. 1897, 1925 (2014); MICHAEL D. RAMSEY, THE CONSTITUTION'S TEXT IN FOREIGN AFFAIRS, 322 (2007); K. Lee Boyd, *Universal Jurisdiction and Structural Reasonableness*, 40 TEX. INT'L L. J. 1, 12–16 (2004); K. Lee Boyd, *Are Human Rights Political Questions*, 53 RUTGERS L. REV. 277, 278–98 (2001); David J. Bederman, *Deference or Deception: Treaty Rights as Political Questions*, 70 U. COLO. L. REV. 1439, 1446–87 (1999).

[58] THIRD RESTATEMENT § 1, Rptr. Note 4 (among the issues treated as political questions are the recognition of states, sovereignty over territory, and presidential engagement in hostilities without Congressional authorization).

[59] *Ibid.* at § 326. [60] *Ibid.* [61] *Ibid.* at § 339.

authority to terminate Article II treaties and Congressional-Executive agreements, and discusses the Court's decision in *Goldwater*, in which four justices refused to reach the question of presidential authority to terminate a treaty on the basis of the political question doctrine.[62] The note expresses no opinion as to whether the presidential authority to suspend or terminate is justiciable.

Since the Third Restatement was adopted, the Supreme Court has not clarified the contours of the political question doctrine as it applies to treaties. Two cases are illustrative.

In a decision rendered just as the Third Restatement was being adopted by the American Law Institute, the Supreme Court in *Japan Whaling* addressed a federal statute that required the imposition of sanctions on a nation engaged in certain whaling practices. The statute allegedly diminished the effectiveness of a sole-Executive agreement regulating whaling.[63] In the agreement with Japan, the United States pledged not to apply sanctions against Japan despite the fact that Japan had exceeded its quota of whale capture. The Court concluded that, notwithstanding the political overtones of the case, the political question doctrine was not implicated; the Court was simply interpreting the President's compliance with a statute. All nine justices concurred that whether the sole Executive agreement was consistent with the statute was a justiciable question.[64]

Over twenty years later, the Court in *Boumediene v. Bush* indicated that whether the United States had de jure sovereignty over Guantanamo Bay pursuant to a treaty between the United States and Cuba was a non-justiciable political question.[65] But it resolved the case anyway, finding that the existence of *de facto* sovereignty was justiciable and was dispositive in resolving *Boumediene's* habeas petition. The case did not "turn on the political question doctrine," the Court concluded, because there was "scant support" for the "Government's premise that de jure sovereignty is the touchstone of habeas corpus jurisdiction."[66]

Neither of these cases squarely addressed fundamental questions about the justiciability of treaty accession, interpretation, or termination. So decades after *Goldwater*, we are still left with the *Baker v. Carr* criteria and the *Goldwater* gloss that the Third Restatement reporters struggled to comprehend. Under *Baker*, of course, courts apply a multifactor test to determine whether a case or controversy raises a political question. Courts are

62 *Ibid.* at § 339, Note 2.

63 *See* Japan Whaling Ass'n v. American Cetacean Society, 478 U.S. 221 (1986).

64 *Ibid.* at 225–20. Four justices dissented with respect to the question of the Executive Branch's compliance with the statute, implicitly concurring that the case was justiciable. *Ibid.* at 242–9.

65 Boumediene v. Bush, 553 U.S. 723, 753–5 (2008).

66 *Ibid.* at 755.

admonished to refrain from resolving cases based on constitutional text, judicial competence, coordinate branch respect, the need for univocal pronouncements, and the fear of political embarrassment.[67] Those factors are malleable enough to be invoked narrowly or broadly. Added to the mix is *Baker's* famous foreign affairs declaration that:

> . . . it is error to suppose that every case or controversy which touches foreign relations lies beyond judicial cognizance. Our cases in this field seem invariably to show a discriminating analysis of the particular question posed, in terms of the history of its management by the political branches, of its susceptibility to judicial handling in the light of its nature and posture in the specific case, and of the possible consequences of judicial action.[68]

In other words, justiciability determination requires the balancing of textual explicitness, historical practice, judicial competence, and political consequence.

The *Goldwater* gloss only highlights *Baker's* ambiguity. Four justices found that terminating a treaty with Taiwan was a political question because it was a foreign affairs matter pertaining to the legislature's power to negate presidential action, and there was no constitutional provision governing the termination of a treaty.[69] Justice Brennan found such reasoning to "profoundly misapprehend" the political question doctrine, which in his view restrains courts from reviewing political judgments that are constitutionality committed to a coordinate political branch, not "when a court is faced with the *antecedent* question whether a particular branch has been constitutionally designated as the repository of political decision-making power."[70] Courts must resolve that question as a matter of constitutional law, not political discretion.[71] Justice Powell shared Justice Brennan's skepticism, finding that "the question presented to us concerns only the constitutional division of power between Congress and the President."[72] Thus, the Court struggled to apply *Baker* in the treaty context and was deeply divided over the justiciability of the President's power to terminate treaties.

67 *See* Baker v. Carr, 369 U.S. 210, 217 (1962) ("Prominent on the surface of any case held to involve a political question is found [1] a textually demonstrable constitutional commitment of the issue to a coordinate political department; [2] or a lack of judicially discoverable and manageable standards for resolving it; [3] or the impossibility of a court's undertaking independent resolution without expressing lack of the respect due coordinate branches of government; [4] or an unusual need for unquestioning adherence to a political decision already made; [5] or the potentiality of embarrassment from multifarious pronouncements by various departments on one question").

68 *Ibid.* at 211–12.

69 *See* Goldwater v. Carter, 444 U.S. 996, 1003–5 (1979) (Rehnquist, J., concurring).

70 *Ibid.* at 1006 (Brennan, J., dissenting). 71 *Ibid.* 72 *Ibid.* at 999 (Powell, concurring).

In the years since the Third Restatement appeared, lower courts have tried to resolve some of *Baker's* ambiguity, but they have done so inconsistently and unpredictably.[73] Most notably, in 2001 the Eleventh Circuit in *Made in the U.S.A. Foundation v. United States* addressed whether NAFTA, a Congressional-Executive agreement with Canada and Mexico, was a treaty requiring Senate ratification. The Eleventh Circuit found that issue to be a non-justiciable political question.[74] Applying *Baker* and *Goldwater*, the Eleventh Circuit found a variety of factors counseled against judicial resolution of the question: (1) the constitutional text is silent on key issues and confers vast power on both political branches in regulating foreign affairs; (2) the Supreme Court has recognized the constitutional validity of some international agreements that do not constitute full-fledged treaties; (3) the delineation of which agreements are significant enough to require Senate ratification is unsuitable for judicial determination; (4) a declaration invalidating NAFTA would have serious repercussions for our nation's external relations and profound negative effects on its economy; and (5) judicial review of the process of negotiating international agreements would intrude upon the respect due to coordinate branches of government.[75] Thus, the Eleventh Circuit refrained from entering the debate about the interchangeability of treaties and other international agreements and ruled that the political question doctrine stood as a barrier to judicial enforcement of the Article II process with respect to NAFTA within the U.S. legal system.[76]

By contrast, in *Ntakirutimana v. Reno*, the Fifth Circuit went ahead to adjudicate a constitutional question similar to that in U.S.A. Foundation – whether a Congressional-Executive agreement rather than a treaty could be used to extradite an individual who was not a U.S. citizen. The Court did not pause to consider whether the political question doctrine barred it from

[73] *See, e.g.*, Beacon Products v. Reagan, 633 F. Supp. 1191, 1199 (D. Mass. 1986), *aff'd on other grounds* 814 F.2d 1 (1st Cir. 1987); Dole v. Carter, 569 F.2d 1109, 1110–12 (10th Cir. 1977).

[74] Made in the U.S.A. Foundation v. United States, 242 F.3d 1300 (11th Cir. 2001) *cert. denied* 534 U.S. 1039 (2001).

[75] *Ibid.* at 1312–8.

[76] *See generally* Oona A. Hathaway, *Treaties' End: The Past, Present, and Future of International Lawmaking in the United States*, 117 YALE L. J. 1236 (2008); Peter J. Spiro, *Treaties, Executive Agreements, and Constitutional Method*, 79 TEX. L. REV. 961 (2001); John C. Yoo, *Laws as Treaties?: The Constitutionality of the Congressional-Executive Agreements*, 99 MICH. L. REV. 757, 766 (2001); Laurence H. Tribe, *Taking Text and Structure Seriously: Reflections on Free-Form Method in Constitutional Interpretation*, 108 HARV. L. REV. 1221 (1995); Bruce Ackerman & David Golove, *Is NAFTA Constitutional?* 108 HARV. L. REV. 799 (1995).

reaching that question. *Ntakirutimana's* factual context was a request from the International Criminal Tribunal for Rwanda for the United States to extradite a *génocidaire* present in the United States.[77] Although the political question doctrine had been discussed by the district court[78] and briefed by the parties, the Fifth Circuit did not mention it.[79] Instead, citing a 1936 Supreme Court case recognizing the power to extradite by statute,[80] the Court concluded that far from reading "the treaty-making power out of the Constitution," Congressional-Executive agreements leave the treaty-making power "unaffected, because the President may still elect to submit a negotiated treaty to the Senate, instead of submitting legislation to Congress."[81] Accordingly, the Court concluded that it was permissible to surrender Ntakirutimana to the ICTR pursuant to an Executive-Congressional Agreement.[82]

Made in the U.S.A. Foundation and *Ntakirutimana* present starkly different perspectives on the extent to which the contours of the treaty power are appropriate for judicial resolution. Although *Ntakirutimana* dealt with extradition and *Made in the USA Foundation* dealt with foreign commerce, both presented the fundamental question of the interchangeability between treaties and Congressional-Executive agreements and whether that issue was to be resolved through adjudication. *Made in the USA Foundation* found that every *Baker* factor counseled against justiciability, and the court therefore refused to reach the merits of the constitutional treaty question. *Ntakirutimana* ignored the political question threshold inquiry and found that treaties and Congressional-Executive agreements are interchangeable in the context of extradition.

The Supreme Court's recent disposition of *Zivotofsky v. Clinton* may cast light on the conflict between the *Ntakirutimana* and *Made in the USA* approaches to the political question doctrine, though the dispute that gave rise to *Zivotofsky* took place outside the treaty context. The case concerned the constitutionality of a federal statute that required the Department of State, when registering the birth of a U.S. citizen born in Jerusalem, to identify the place of birth as Israel.[83] The Court stated that a controversy "involves a political question where there is a 'textually demonstrable constitutional commitment of the issue to a coordinate political department; or a lack of judicially discoverable and manageable standards for

77 Ntakirutimana v. Reno, 184 F.3d 419 (5th Cir. 1999).

78 *In re Ntakirutimana*, 1998 WL 655708 (S.D. Tex. 1998). 79 *Ibid.* at 424–7.

80 *Ibid.* at 424–6 (*discussing Valentine v. United States*, 299 U.S. 5, 9, 18 (1936)).

81 *Ibid.* at 427. 82 *Ibid.* 83 Zivotofsky v. Clinton, 132 S. Ct. 1421, 1427 (2012).

resolving it.'"[84] Noticeably absent from this new formulation were the prudential factors set forth in *Baker* and *Goldwater*.[85]

In applying the new formulation, the court in *Zivotofsky* found that all lined up in favor of justiciability. Regarding textual commitment of authority to the political branches, the Court said that the Judicial Branch properly exercises its authority in resolving the question of "whether Congress or the Executive is aggrandizing its power at the expense of another branch."[86] As for judicial manageability, the Court found that the arguments regarding the constitutionality of the statute "sound in familiar principles of constitutional interpretation" and that their analysis requires an examination of traditional canons of construction to assess whether the statute is constitutionally permissible.[87]

Zivotofsky suggests that the political question doctrine has been narrowed to two fundamental questions: constitutional text and judicial capacity. The prudential factors set forth in *Baker* of "expressing lack of the respect due coordinate branches of government," or the "unusual need for unquestioning adherence" to political decisions, or "the potentiality of embarrassment" had no part in *Zivotofsky's* delineation of the political question doctrine.[88] The majority appears to have jettisoned the prudential factors, but it did not do so expressly.[89] Only Justices Sotomayor and Breyer adhered to the view that these prudential factors "may counsel against a court's resolution of an issue presented."[90] Sotomayor argued that the "inquiry required by the political question doctrine [is] more demanding than that suggested by the Court."[91] The majority's failure to respond to the dissenting justices left uncertain whether prudential standards still have a place in the political question doctrine.

84 *Ibid.*, *quoting* Nixon v. United States, 506 U.S. 224, 228 (1993).

85 That is, the Court ignored the last three Baker factors. *See* Baker, *supra* note 67, at 217 ("[3] or the impossibility of a court's undertaking independent resolution without expressing lack of the respect due coordinate branches of government; [4] or an unusual need for unquestioning adherence to a political decision already made; [5] or the potentiality of embarrassment from multifarious pronouncements by various departments on one question").

86 Zivotofsky, *supra* note 83, at 1428.

87 *Ibid.* at 1430. After finding the matter justiciable, the Supreme Court struck down the statute specifying Israel as the place of birth as infringing on the Executive Branch's exclusive authority to recognize foreign states and governments. *Zivotofsky v. Kerry*, 135 S. Ct. 2076 (2015).

88 Zivotofsky, *supra* note 83, at 1427–30; Baker, *supra* note 67, at 217.

89 *Leading Cases*, 126 HARV. L. REV. 307, 313 (2012).

90 *Zivotofsky*, *supra* note 83, at 1432 (Sotomayor, J., dissenting).

91 *Ibid.* at 1432.

Following *Zivotofsky*, one would expect the political question doctrine to have declining significance in litigation regarding treaties.[92] One would expect to see an increase in judicial resolution of treaty formation and termination questions.[93] One also would expect the political question doctrine rarely to apply when adjudicating the balance of power between the political branches.[94] Thus far, these predictions have not materialized. In some cases, lower courts are citing *Baker's* multifactor test, but only applying the two *Zivotofsky* factors.[95] In others cases, lower courts continue to reference and analyze the prudential standards.[96] Most lower courts have yet to read *Zivotofsky* as fundamentally altering *Baker*.[97]

In sum, in the years since publication of the Third Restatement, lower courts have treated the multifactor test set forth in *Baker* and *Goldwater* as setting forth the framework for a political question analysis. This is an analysis that has presented threshold difficulties for adjudicating treaty claims. In contrast, *Zivotofsky* suggests that many questions pertaining to the competing authority of Congress and the President in the treaty realm can be resolved by typical separation-of-powers adjudication. To the extent *Zivotofsky* signals that *Baker's* prudential concerns have now been excised from the political question doctrine, and to the extent that *Zivotofsky* can be extrapolated to the

92 *See* Harlan Grant Cohen, *Formalism and Distrust: Foreign Affairs Law in the Roberts Court*, 83 GEO. WASH. L. REV. 380, 432–4 (2015); Ingrid Wuerth, Book Review, 108 AM. J. INT'L L. 116, 117 (2014) (reviewing Curtis A. Bradley, *International Law in the U.S. Legal System (2013)*; Sitaraman & Wuerth, *supra* note 57, at 1925–7; Carol Szurkowski, *The Return of Classical Political Question Doctrine in* Zivotofsky v. Clinton, 37 HARV. J. L. & PUB. POL'Y 347, 358–61 (2014).

93 For examples of how lower courts are interpreting the political question doctrine narrowly in light of *Zivotofsky* and outside of the treaty context, see, e.g., *Harris v. Kellogg Brown & Root Services, Inc.*, 724 F.3d 458, 465, 465–78 (3d Cir. 2013); *Kaplan v. Central Bank of the Islamic Republic of Iran*, 961 F.3d 185, 191–3 (D.C. Cir. 2013); *Republic of Iraq v.* ABB AG, 920 F. Supp. 2d 517, 534–5 (S.D.N.Y. 2013); *Alaska v. Kerry*, 972 F. Supp. 2d 1111, 1122–31 (D. Alaska 2013).

94 Chris Michel, *There's No Such Thing as a Political Question of Statutory Interpretation: The Implications of* Zivotofsky v. Clinton, 123 YALE L.J. 253, 261–2 (2013).

95 *See* Ministry of Oil of Republic of Iraq v. 1,032,212 Barrels of Crude Oil Aboard United Kalavrvta, 2015 Westlaw 93900 (S.D. Texas 2015); Republic of Iraq v. ABB AG, 920 F. Supp. 517, 534–5 (SDNY 2013).

96 Harris, 724 F.3d at 477–8; Kerry, 972 F.2d at 1122–31; Center for Biological Diversity v. Hagel, 80 F.Supp.3d 991, 1001–1011 (N.D. Cal. 2015).

97 *But see* Hourani v. Mirtchev, 796 F.3d 1, 8–9 (D.C. Cir. 2015) (discussing two factors presented in *Zivotofsky* without citing *Baker* or suggesting that other *Baker* factors are still relevant); Al Shimari v. CACI Premier Tech., Inc., No. 1:08-cv-00827-GBL-JFA, 2015 U.S. Dist. LEXIS 107511 (E.D. Va. June 18, 2015) (same); Starr International Co. v. United States, 121 Fed. Cl. 428, 2015 WL 5542545 (D.D.C. 2015) ("it is unclear whether factors three through six [of Baker] remain relevant after the Supreme Court's restrictive formulations in . . . Zivotofsky").

treaty context, then the balance of power between the political branches in future treaty disputes may result in judicial resolution, thereby lowering a procedural barrier to domestic enforcement of treaty norms, even in disputes that are politically charged. It remains to be seen, however, how *Zivotofsky* will be applied by lower courts.

IV RESERVATIONS, UNDERSTANDINGS, AND DECLARATIONS

The Third Restatement extensively addresses reservations but largely ignores understandings and declarations. Section 313 summarizes international law norms with respect to reservations, particularly the rule that reservations are permitted unless prohibited by the treaty or incompatible with the agreement's object and purpose.[98] Section 314 articulates post–World War II reservations practice in the United States, which requires the President to ratify a treaty subject to Senate reservations.[99]

The Restatement's treatment of understandings and declarations is relegated to comments, which focus on whether understandings or declarations so exclude, limit, or modify legal obligations that they effectively are reservations.[100] Section 314's one exception in this regard recognizes the President's obligation either to ratify a treaty subject to the Senate's understanding or not ratify it at all.[101] The comments also recognize the Senate practice of non-self-executing declarations and concede that there is "no accepted doctrine indicating limits on the conditions the Senate may impose."[102]

In the years after publication of the Third Restatement, the United States ratified several key human rights treaties with significant reservations, understandings, and declarations (RUDs) raising concerns of erecting obstacles to enforcement of the norms in these treaties.[103] These RUDs limited the

[98] Third Restatement, § 313. [99] *Ibid.* at § 314. [100] *Ibid.* at § 313, cmt. g.

[101] *Ibid.* at § 314(2). [102] Ibid. § 303, cmt. d; *see also ibid.* § 314, cmt. e.

[103] *See* U.S. Senate Resolution of Advice and Consent to Ratification of the Convention on the Elimination of All Forms of Racial Discrimination, 140 Cong. Rec. S14326 (daily ed. June 24, 1994); U.S. Senate Resolution of Advice and Consent to Ratification of the International Covenant on Civil and Political Rights, 138 Cong. Rec. S4783 (daily ed. Apr. 2, 1992); U.S. Senate Resolution of Advice and Consent to Ratification of the Convention against Torture and Other Cruel, Inhuman or Degrading Treatment or Punishment, 136 Cong. Rec. S17491 (daily ed. Oct. 27, 1990); U.S. Senate Resolution of Advice and Consent to Ratification of the Convention on the Prevention and Punishment of the Crime of Genocide, 132 Cong. Rec. S1378 (daily ed. Feb. 19, 1986).

domestic impact of human rights treaties through substantive and procedural reservations,[104] non-self-execution declarations, and federalism understandings. In a few cases, treaty ratification was accompanied by domestic legislation implementing the treaty.[105] In other cases, the RUDs rendered the human rights treaty of no force in domestic courts, but the substantive rights embodied in the treaty nonetheless were mirrored in domestic constitutional or statutory law.[106]

Some scholars have sharply criticized this practice of relying on preexisting and different domestic law in lieu of enacting specific implementing legislation.[107] Harold Koh has stated that:

> "[i]n the cathedral of human rights, the United States is more like a flying buttress than a pillar—choosing to stand outside the international structure supporting the international human rights system, but without being willing to subject its own conduct to the scrutiny of that system."[108]

Others strongly defend RUDs as a valid expression of the conditional nature of the United States' consent.[109] Jack Goldsmith, for example, writes that:

[104] Substantive RUDs limit the scope of the treaty obligation undertaken while procedural RUDs inform how the treaty obligation will be enforced within the U.S. legal system. *See* Brad R. Roth, *Under the "Understanding": Federalism Constraints on Human Rights Implementation*, 47 WAYNE L. REV. 891 (2001).

[105] *See* Torture Victim Protection Act, 28 U.S.C. § 1350 note; Genocide Convention Implementation Act of 1987, 18 U.S.C. §§ 1091–3.

[106] *See* Stewart, Chapter 6 of this volume; David P. Stewart, *United States Ratification of the Covenant on Civil and Political Rights: The Significance of the Reservations, Understandings, and Declarations*, 42 DEPAUL L. REV. 1183, 1206 (1993) ("The premise underlying most of the [RUDs] was the conclusion that existing U.S. law, even if not strictly in conformity with the precise language of the Covenant [on Civil and Political Rights], was acceptable and indeed preferable").

[107] *See* Catherine Powell, *Dialogic Federalism: Constitutional Possibilities for Incorporation of Human Rights Law in the United States*, 150 U. PA. L. REV. 245 (2001); Brad R. Roth, *Understanding the "Understanding," supra* note 104; Peter J. Spiro, *The States and International Human Rights*, 66 FORDHAM L. REV. 567 (1997); Thomas Buergenthal, *Modern Constitutions and Human Rights Treaties*, 36 COLUM. J. TRANSNAT'L L. 211 (1997); Louis Henkin, *U.S. Ratification of Human Rights Conventions: The Ghost of Senator Bricker*, 89 AM. J. INT'L L. 341 (1995); William A. Schabas, *Invalid Reservations to the International Covenant on Civil and Political Rights: Is the United States Still a Party?*, 21 BROOK. J. INT'L L. 277 (1995); Lori Fisler Damrosch, *The Role of the United States Senate Concerning "Self-Executing" and "Non-Self-Executing" Treaties*, 67 CHI.-KENT L. REV. 515 (1991); Louis Henkin, *Rights: American and Human*, 79 COLUM. L. REV. 405 (1979).

[108] Harold H. Koh, *A United States Human Rights Policy for the 21st Century*, 46 ST. LOUIS L.J. 293, 308 (2002).

[109] *See* Jack Goldsmith, *The Unexceptional U.S. Human Rights RUDs*, 3 U. ST. THOMAS L.J. 311 (2005); Curtis A. Bradley & Jack L. Goldsmith, *Treaties, Human Rights, and Conditional Consent*, 149 U. PA. L. REV. 399 (2000); Jack Goldsmith, *International Human Rights Law and the United States Double Standard*, 1 Green Bag 2d 365 (1998).

> RUDs ... reflect a sensible accommodation of competing domestic and international considerations ... [by] help[ing] bridge the political divide between isolationists who want to preserve the United States' sovereign prerogatives, and internationalists who want the United States to increase its involvement in international institutions.[110]

This compromise position on RUDs was succinctly expressed by Professor Louis Sohn, who served as an associate reporter for the Third Restatement. In 1998, he observed with respect to American conditional acceptance of human rights treaties, that "half a loaf is better than none, especially if you are hungry."[111]

The frequency of U.S. use of RUDs has grown since the 1980s. The typical effect of contemporary U.S. practice with respect to RUDs is to limit the judiciary's flexibility in interpreting treaty protections. In the human rights context, some RUDs deprive American judges of the ability to interpret the unmodified treaty and therefore from adding to "the emerging body of international law on the subject."[112] RUDs also can stand in the way of American judges considering judicial interpretations from other states party that have ratified without any RUDs. To the extent existing U.S. domestic law does not mirror the treaty's protections, RUDs deprive the victims of human rights violations of invoking judicial power to enforce international guarantees in the form in which they are enforced elsewhere.[113]

The impact of RUDs varies depending on the type of human rights treaties. There are, for example, certain treaties that are rarely referred to as human rights treaties but nonetheless afford significant substantive and procedural guarantees to foreign nationals. These treaties typically operate diagonally, with States agreeing to confer mutually reciprocal benefits on other States and their nationals. For example, the United States ratified the Vienna Convention on Consular Relations in 1969 without reservations.[114] The treaty grants detained foreigners the fundamental right of consular notification and access,[115] and this

110 Bradley & Goldsmith, *supra* note 109, at 402.

111 *International Law in a World of Multiple Actors: A Conversation with Louis Henkin and Louis B. Sohn*, 92 AM. SOC. INT'L L. PROC. 248, 257 (1998).

112 Buergenthal, *supra* note 107, at 221.

113 There are, of course, numerous instances in which international human rights treaties are more protective than domestic statutes. In those instances, the impact of RUDs in limiting the judicial enforcement of treaty law is highly significant. *See* Connie de la Vega, *Civil Rights during the 1990s: New Treaty Law Could Help Immensely*, 65 U. CIN. L. REV. 423 (1997).

114 *See* Vienna Convention on Consular Relations, Apr. 24, 1963, [1970] 21 U.S.T. 77, 100–101, T.I.A.S. No. 6820; Cong. Rec. 30997 (1969); Sanchez-Llamas v. Oregon, 548 U.S. 331 (2006).

115 Vienna Convention, *supra* note 114, at art. 36.

right is routinely adjudicated in U.S. courts.[116] Likewise, the United States ratified the Optional Protocol to the United Nation Convention on the Status of Refugees[117] and courts regularly adjudicate rights guaranteed in that treaty.[118] Such treaties implicate not only individual rights but also reciprocal protections that States afford to nationals of other signatory States. With respect to neither conferral of rights have RUDs been an obstacle to enforcement.

To the extent international treaties mirror domestic law, one should not overstate the importance of RUDs in impeding the enforcement of treaty rights. In the human rights context, RUDs often preclude the direct application of international law, but the United States nonetheless fulfills its international human rights obligations via domestic law.[119] "[W]hen a court issues an injunction ... prohibiting race-based discrimination, ... [it] is promoting compliance with U.S. treaty obligations ... even if the court never considers a treaty-based argument."[120] Moreover, some human rights treaties are implemented by statute.[121] With respect to treaties designed to protect individuals from the state, U.S. courts indirectly enforce human rights obligations all the time, even if they rarely do so directly. In other words, even if RUDs typically do not prevent enforcement of treaty norms, they do channel courts toward indirect rather than direct enforcement, with the result that to judges it may seem that they are enforcing domestic law rather than treaty law.

In the private law context, involving horizontal treaties that operate at the domestic plane, treaties are routinely enforced in court without obstacle.[122]

116 *See, e.g.*, Sanchez-Llamas, *supra* note 114; Medellin v. Dretke, 544 U.S. 660 (2005); Breard, *supra* note 43, at 371 (1998); Gandara v. Bennett, 528 F.3d 823 (11th Cir. 2008); Gomez v. Dretke, 422 F.3d 264 (5th Cir. 2005); United States v. Luna-Rodriguez, 242 F.3d 384 (9th Cir. 2000); Buquer v. City of Indianapolis, (S.D. Ind. 2011); United States v. Cisneros, 397 F. Supp. 2d 726 (E.D. Va. 2005); Standt v. City of New York, 153 F. Supp. 2d 417 (S.D.N.Y. 2001); Salazar v. Burresch, 47 F. Supp. 2d 1105 (C.D. Cal. 1999).

117 *See* United Nations Convention Relating to the Status of Refugees, July 28, 1951, 19 U.S.T. 6259, 189 U.N.T.S. 150, T.I.A.S. No. 6577.

118 *See, e.g.*, Sale v. Haitian Centers Council, 509 U.S. 155 (1993); I.N.S. v. Cardoza-Fonseca, 480 U.S. 421 (1987); I.N.S. v. Stevic, 467 U.S. 407 (1984); Annachamy v. Holder, 733 F.3d 254, (9th Cir. 2012); Garcia v. I.N.S., 7 F.3d 1320 (7th Cir. 1993); Chim Ming v. Marks, 505 F.2d 1170 (2d Cir. 1974).

119 David Sloss, *Domestic Application of Treaties*, in THE OXFORD GUIDE TO TREATIES, 367, 391 (D. Hollis, ed., 2012); David Sloss, *The Domestication of International Human Rights: Non-Self-Executing Declarations and Human Rights Treaties*, 24 YALE J. INT'L L. 129, 183–8 (1999); Stewart, *supra* note 106, at 1206.

120 Sloss, *Domestic Application of Treaties*, *supra* note 119, at 391.

121 *See* David Sloss, *United States*, *in* THE ROLE OF DOMESTIC COURTS IN TREATY ENFORCEMENT 504, 519 (D. Sloss, ed., 2009).

122 For a discussion of the judicial enforcement of such transnational treaties, see Paul Stephan, *Treaties in the Supreme Court, 1946–2000*, in INTERNATIONAL LAW IN THE U.S. SUPREME

That is, courts frequently enforce transnational treaties involving private parties who act across national boundaries. Examples include the 1929 Warsaw Convention, the 1958 Territorial Sea Convention, the 1958 New York Convention, the 1965 Hague Service Convention, the 1970 Hague Evidence Convention, the 1980 Hague Convention on Child Abduction, and the 1999 Montreal Convention. These treaties serve a coordination function between private parties and presume judicial adjudication of transnational activities. In such cases "the judiciary plays a central role in promoting compliance with transnational treaty provisions."[123]

Thus, whether U.S. courts confront procedural obstacles to treaty enforcement depends on the circumstances of each treaty. As a matter of international law, there is no general obligation of judicial enforcement of treaty guarantees.[124] "So long as the state achieves the substantive objective set forth in the treaty, the mechanism by which that compliance occurs is left to the state."[125] Many RUDs simply signal the procedural means by which the United States will abide by its obligations.[126] The role of RUDs typically depends on the nature of the treaty. With treaties involving horizontal relations between States, RUDs assign a significant role to the Executive Branch and a limited role for the Judiciary. With treaties that guarantee human rights, RUDs signal an indirect role for judicial enforcement through existing laws or treaty implementing legislation. But with treaties involving transnational relations between private parties, RUDs typically present few obstacles to either direct enforcement or indirect enforcement via implementing legislation.

V CONCLUSION

With developments in the law of standing, the push to enforce treaties through transnational public litigation via the Alien Tort Statute has waxed and now

Court, 317, 346–52 (D. Sloss & M. Ramsey & W. Dodge, eds. 2011); Sloss, *United States*, *supra* note 121, at 515–52; Sloss, *Domestic Application of Treaties*, *supra* note 119, at 376–9, 389–90.

123 *See* Sloss, *Domestic Application of Treaties*, *supra* note 119, at 388. There also are instances, of course, in which courts do not effectively enforce horizontal treaties that operate on the domestic plane. *See generally* Dubinsky, Chapter 3 in this volume (discussing *Aerospatiale* and the Hague Evidence Convention and *Schlunk* and the Hague Service Convention).

124 If States wish to require judicial enforcement of treaty obligations, they can so specify in the treaty. *See, e.g.*, New York Convention, art. 2(3); United Nations Convention against Corruption, art. 31(7).

125 Sean D. Murphy, Does International Law Obligate States to Open Their National Courts to Persons for the Invocation of Treaty Norms That Protect or Benefit Persons?, *in* Sloss, *supra* note 121 *The Role of Domestic Courts in Treaty Enforcement* 61, 63.

126 *See supra* note 105.

waned. The Court in *Sosa* recognized "statutory standing" arising from common law causes of action pursued through ATS human rights litigation. But the Supreme Court has been silent on party standing with respect to human rights litigation. Outside of the treaty context, lower courts have continued to require party standing based on traditional *Lujan* standards of individualized harm within the zone of interest intended for protection. There continues to be a dearth of cases applying *Lujan* in the context of allegations that U.S. behavior is inconsistent with treaty standards. If *Lujan* were applied in the treaty context, the result would be a substantial number of dismissals for lack of standing, thereby preventing courts from adjudicating the merits of the dispute.

With the last-in-time rule, courts typically apply that rule to negate the effect of international law obligations in the face of a later-in-time conflicting statute. Internationalist scholars have argued for a different last-in-time rule for multilateral treaties, one that accords primacy to treaties, but those efforts have been without success. The force of time, the frequency of legislative pronouncements, and the nature of statutory amendments all inure to the benefit of statutes and to the detriment of treaties.

Changes to the political question doctrine enunciated by *Zivotofsky* have the potential to expand the judicial role in adjudicating treaty disputes that previously would have been dismissed as political questions. It would seem that the Supreme Court, by ignoring (or rejecting) *Baker*'s prudential factors, envisions a greater role for courts in resolving disputes between the political branches over the negotiation, interpretation, and termination of treaties. However, lower courts thus far have not eschewed the prudential factors in *Baker* with the same ease as the Supreme Court. The result is a continuation of judicial abstention practices for many treaty questions.

With RUDs the change is not so much with respect to the law governing their application within the domestic legal system, but with the frequency with which RUDs are applied to canonical human rights treaties. With few exceptions, the United States has chosen to provide judicially enforceable protections for transnational treaties that regulate private party conduct but to rely on existing constitutional and statutory law to protect against the infringement of individual liberties. RUDs are the instrument to ensure that the level of protection is capped at domestic standards. To the extent RUDs limit rights enforcement in this manner, they undermine the efficacy and relevance of international human rights treaties within the U.S. legal system.

In the three decades since the Third Restatement appeared, on balance the trends in the United States – the narrowing of standing, the use of the last-in-time rule predominantly to give priority to statutes, and the proliferation of

RUDs – has been toward curtailing the judicial enforcement of treaty rights. The combined effect of (1) applying a presumption in favor of non-self-execution, (2) finding that a treaty has been superseded by a subsequent statute, (3) finding that a claim presents non-justiciable political questions, or (4) holding that the presence of one or more RUDs renders the treaty simply not enforceable by U.S. courts tends, as a practical matter, to preclude many individuals from vindicating treaty rights in U.S. courts. As a result, many treaty wrongs are without judicial remedy.

A Fourth Restatement on Foreign Relations should distill international and foreign relations law of the United States existing at the time of the Third Restatement's adoption. It should summarize the "rules than an impartial tribunal would apply if charged with deciding a controversy in accordance with international law."[127] In the quarter century since the Third Restatement was adopted, there have been numerous changes with respect to judicial enforcement of treaties. There also has been significant continuity. The current Reporters to the Fourth Restatement will no doubt wrestle with the question of whether to crystallize the changes or highlight the continuity.

[127] Third Restatement at 3.

9

Case Study No. 1

Exploring U.S. Treaty Practice through a Military Lens

Geoffrey S. Corn and Dru Brenner-Beck

Treaty practice related to the regulation of conflict provides a useful and comprehensive illustration of the interaction between treaties and U.S. law and policy. A body of international law termed the *law of armed conflict* (LOAC[1]) which establishes rules for the conduct of hostilities and treatment of war victims, is central to understanding the constitutional treaty power,[2] as LOAC treaties impact perhaps the most vital national security function of a government: employing military power to protect the nation. Ultimately, like so many other aspects of the relationship between international law and the pursuit of vital national security objectives, LOAC treaty practice reflects a continuous pursuit of balance between the two sometimes competing influences on national security policy – the effort to achieve the critically important objective of mitigating the suffering associated with armed hostilities while simultaneously providing sufficient flexibility and legal authority to engage in decisive military action – a balance at the core of the LOAC itself.[3] Ultimately, because LOAC treaties reflect a quintessential federal function, both their formation and the domestic responses of Congress, the Courts, and our constituent States to these core treaties can provide vital insight into U.S. treaty practice.

Striking an effective balance between mitigating the suffering in armed conflict and ensuring sufficient legal authority for decisive military action has

[1] U.S. Dep't of Def., Dir. 2311.01 E, DOD Law of War Program 2 (9 May 2006). The law of armed conflict, or LOAC, is the characterization for this branch of international law used in U.S. government circles. However, this branch of law is often also referred to as international humanitarian law, or IHL.

[2] U.S. CONST. art. II, § 2, cl. 2.

[3] GEOFFREY S. CORN ET AL., *Law of Armed Conflict Principles: The Foundation of Conflict Regulation, in* THE LAW OF ARMED CONFLICT: AN OPERATIONAL APPROACH 107, 115 (Vicki Been et al. eds., 2012).

long influenced the treaty development and implementation process. This chapter will illustrate how the three branches of the federal government have, over time, leveraged their constitutional roles in the treaty process to effect this balance. This pursuit of equilibrium is indeed an important trend reflected by LOAC treaty practice and has been manifested both through the checks and balances inherent in our Constitution's separation of powers and to a lesser extent through the division of power between the national federal government and the constituent states. This should come as no surprise, as our Founders intended that these separation of power and federalism frictions would influence U.S. treaty practice, even when that practice impacts the exercise of the war and foreign affairs powers.

This chapter will therefore provide a descriptive overview of LOAC treaty practice, and will also illustrate three themes that appear to run through this practice. First, the advice and consent and treaty implementation authority vested in Congress has and will continue to enable the legislature to significantly influence whether and to what extent the nation will commit itself to limitations on wartime prerogatives. From the close of World War II to the present, Congress has appeared to move from embracing extensive constraints on national military power to opposing such constraints in order to preserve U.S. flexibility for the use of such power. These efforts provide important examples of the tools Congress leverages to produce these effects. Primary among these tools is the power of the Senate to impose conditions on its advice and consent to ratification through the use of reservations and understandings circumscribing the president's ratification authority. Once a treaty is ratified, congressional enactment of implementing, or subsequent limiting, legislation provides another powerful tool to shape the scope and extent of U.S. obligations, particularly their domestic impact.

Second, this chapter highlights the important role played by the judicial branch in the treaty interpretation process, a role that complements – but may at times contradict – Executive interpretation. As will be discussed, the willingness of the judicial branch to exercise interpretive authority over complex issues implicating war powers is an important illustration of the scope and importance of judicial treaty interpretation despite the Constitution's explicit vesting of the war powers in the other two branches.[4]

Finally, although federalism constraints on national power have not recently produced any meaningful limits on the treaty power as it relates to wartime authority, the Supreme Court's revival of federalism concerns in

[4] *But see* Corrie v. Caterpillar, Inc., 503 F.3d 974, 984 (9th Cir. 2007) (invoking political question doctrine to avoid adjudication of case involving foreign relations).

Commerce Clause cases may augur some additional restrictions on treaty implementation. As shown in a recent case, *Bond v. United States*,[5] even treaties intended to regulate armed hostilities may implicate core federalism concerns. *Bond* also illustrates that even if federalism considerations have no impact on the power of the nation to bind itself to LOAC obligations, they may affect the implementation of those agreements domestically. Given the Founders' overriding concern to limit the States' interference with the fulfillment of national treaty obligations, it is ironic that federalism may be invoked in the twenty-first century to bolster such interference.

This chapter first provides a very general overview of the LOAC, and then considers how LOAC treaties provide a powerful indication of why treaties are and will remain essential to the development and implementation of international law. It then explores the role of the Senate in the creation and ratification of U.S. treaty obligations. It offers insight into how that role has subtly evolved since the end of World War II, particularly since the 1987 completion of the Third Restatement of Foreign Relations Law. The chapter then considers constitutional aspects of LOAC treaty implementation: first, the role of implementing legislation in fulfilling – or frustrating – the international obligations encompassed in these LOAC treaties; and second, the impact of federalism on LOAC treaty implementation. Finally, this chapter attempts to glean what minimal lessons are available from the limited judicial forays into the complex waters of LOAC treaty interpretation.

I TREATY CODIFICATION OF THE LAWS AND CUSTOMS OF WAR

A *The Law of Armed Conflict Generally*

One of the oldest branches of international law, the LOAC provides a detailed and surprisingly comprehensive framework to regulate armed conflicts. This law was historically divided between two branches: those governing the conduct of hostilities and humanitarian protection. While neither of these branches is truly isolated from the other (each branch imposes overlapping obligations), this general dichotomy provides a useful prism to facilitate understanding of the nuances of the law. Over time, this branch of international law evolved from customary in nature to a body of law dominated by treaties. This treaty

[5] Bond v. United States, 131 S. Ct. 2355 (2011); Bond v. United States, 134 S. Ct. 2077 (2014).

codification trend followed two general trajectories known as the Hague and Geneva traditions.[6]

The Hague tradition is derived from the Hague Convention IV and Annexed Regulations of 1907.[7] This treaty (a successor to the 1899 Hague Convention[8]) focused on the regulation of armed forces on the battlefield with a primary purpose of regulating the actual conduct of hostilities. The Geneva tradition is derived from the Geneva Conventions, treaties with a significantly different focus: protecting victims of war.[9] The first Geneva Convention,[10] adopted in 1864, focused on the protection of the wounded and sick in the field – a humanitarian objective immediately embraced by the international community. This first treaty blossomed into what are today four treaties, the 1949 Geneva Conventions. Each of the four Conventions focuses on ameliorating the suffering of a distinct category of war victim: (1) the wounded and sick in the field,[11] (2) the wounded, sick, and shipwrecked at sea,[12] (3) prisoners of war,[13] and (4) civilians in the hands of an enemy belligerent power.[14] In 1977, the Hague and Geneva branches of conflict regulation were effectively unified when the two Additional Protocols to the 1949 Geneva Conventions were opened for signature, as these two treaties combined elements of humanitarian protections and regulation of hostilities.[15] Today, the regulation of hostilities by multilateral treaty with origins in both the Hague and Geneva traditions is a ubiquitous

6 Geoffrey S. Corn et al., *History and Sources of the Law of Armed Conflict*, *in* The Law of Armed Conflict: An Operational Approach 33, 40–6 (Vicki Been et al. eds., 2012).

7 Convention No. IV Respecting the Laws and Customs of War on Land and Its Annex, Regulation Concerning the Laws and Customs of War on Land, Oct. 18,1907, 36 Stat. 2277, 207 Consol. T.S. 277 [hereinafter Hague IV]; *see also* Corn et al, *supra* note 3, at 41.

8 Convention (II) with Certain Powers Respecting the Laws and Customs of War on Land, July 29, 1899, 32 Stat. 1803, T.S. No. 403; Corn et al, *supra* note 3, at 41.

9 Corn et al, *supra* note 3, at 43.

10 Convention for the Amelioration of the Condition of the Wounded in Armies in the Field. Geneva, Aug. 22, 1864, 22 Stat. 940, TS No. 377.

11 Geneva Convention for the Amelioration of the Condition of the Wounded and Sick in Armed Forces in the Field, Aug. 12, 1949, T.I.A.S. 3362 [hereinafter Geneva I].

12 Geneva Convention for the Amelioration of the Condition of Wounded, Sick, and Shipwrecked Members at Sea, Aug. 12, 1949, T.I.A.S. 3363 [hereinafter Geneva II].

13 Geneva Convention Relative to the Treatment of Prisoners of War, Aug. 12, 1949, T.I.A.S. 3364 [hereinafter Geneva III or GPW].

14 Geneva Convention Relative to the Treatment of Civilian Persons in Time of War, Aug. 12, 1949, T.I.A.S. 3365. [hereinafter Geneva IV].

15 Protocol Additional to the Geneva Conventions of Aug. 12, 1949 and Relating to the Protection of Victims of International Armed Conflicts, June 8, 1977, 1125 U.N.T.S. 3 [hereinafter AP I]; Protocol Additional to the Geneva Conventions of Aug. 12,1949 and Relating to the Protection of Victims of Non-international Armed Conflicts, Aug. 6, 1977, 1125 U.N.T.S. 3 [hereinafter AP II].

aspect of planning and executing military operations.[16] Furthermore, because the United States is party to most of these LOAC treaties[17] – and attaches normative significance to many of the provisions of even those treaties to which it has thus far declined to accede – they provide a rich landscape for understanding the role of treaties in U.S. practice.

II TREATY FORMATION: ADVICE, CONSENT, AND RATIFICATION

The president "shall have Power, by and with the Advice and Consent of the Senate, to make Treaties, provided two-thirds of the Senators present concur."[18] As with other government powers constitutionally entrusted to both the executive and legislative branches, the treaty-making process was designed to restrain unchecked power in any one branch. Requiring Senate consent was intended "both to protect the rights of the states and to serve as a check against the president taking excessive or undesirable actions through treaties."[19] Involvement of the Senate, representing the legislative branch, was also essential because under the new Constitution, treaties automatically became "the supreme law of the land."[20] Because formation of law of war treaties is intertwined with another power shared between the Executive and Legislative branches – the war powers – the LOAC treaty ratification process is an especially important manifestation of this constitutionally required inter-branch interaction.

The Senate's advice and consent often reflects the impact of international and domestic politics as well as its effort to influence United States foreign policy. Thus, the Senate's decision to consent to treaty obligations will often fluctuate based on the broader national sense of geostrategic necessity. In some cases, as in the ratification of the 1949 Geneva Conventions, the

16 Geoffrey S. Corn et al., *Introduction*, *in* The Law of Armed Conflict: An Operational Approach xxv, xxvi-xxvii (Vicki Been et al. eds., 2012).

17 ICRC Databases on Int'l Humanitarian Law, Int'l Comm. of the Red Cross (last updated May 11, 2012), www.icrc.org/eng/resources/ihl-databases/index.jsp (the various treaties are signed by numerous state parties, but the four Geneva Conventions are the only ones universally ratified).

18 U.S. Const. art. II, § 2, cl. 2.

19 US Congressional Research Service, A Study Prepared for the S. Comm. On Foreign Relations, S. Prt. 106–71, Treaties and Other International Agreements: The Role of the United States Senate, 106th Cong. 2 (S. Print 2001) [hereinafter Senate on Treaties].

20 Senate on Treaties, *supra* note 19, at 28–9; *see also* David M. Golove & Daniel J. Hulsebosch, *A Civilized Nation: The Early American Constitution, the Law of Nations, and the Pursuit of International Recognition*, 85 *N.Y.U.L. Rev.* 932 (2010).

views of the Senate and the president merge with little disagreement.[21] In others, the president may set a course quite distinct from the Senate's position, as was the case with the two 1977 Additional Protocols to the Geneva Conventions (Additional Protocols I and II). In that case, President Reagan's concerns over the existing military-political realities resulted in the decision to reject Additional Protocol I (supplementing the law applicable to inter-state armed conflicts) even though the Carter administration had been instrumental in drafting this treaty. In contrast, President Reagan did seek advice and consent for Additional Protocol II (which supplemented the law applicable to noninternational armed conflicts and which was drafted at the same time as AP I), but the Senate exerted its power by failing to provide advice and consent. As a result, the United States remains a nonparty to these important treaties to this day.

In recent years, as geopolitical consensus between the president and the Senate has deteriorated, advice and consent for even seemingly uncontroversial treaties, such as the 1992 Chemical Weapons Convention has become fraught with controversy and disagreement. In the early 1950s, following the devastation of World War II and the emerging threat from the Communist bloc in the Cold War, bipartisan commitment to enhancing U.S. geostrategic interests through the use of the treaty power led to U.S. ratification of a number of vital treaties. During this period, President Eisenhower and both parties in the postwar Senate shared a world view in which a universal international law was seen as a bulwark against the nation's ideological enemies. As a result, the president and Senate (the two treaty-making bodies) were willing to accept binding restrictions in order to forge necessary alliances and impose limitations on the brutality of warfare, interests exemplified by the 1949 Washington Treaty establishing the NATO Alliance and the associated

[21] The Senate and a Bipartisan Foreign Policy: 1953–1960, 132 Cong. Rec. S4960–03, at 2, 1986 WL 791608 (Cong. Rec.) (In 1953 the two parties fundamentally viewed the world situation in the same way, and Eisenhower began his presidency with a broad national consensus on foreign policy and strong bipartisan support in the Congress). Indeed even prior to the 1950s, the Senate was intimately involved in treaty negotiation. Just after the completion of World War II, Senators Connally and Vandenberg accompanied the U.S. negotiating team at the U.N. Conference in 1945 and "were recognized as the authorities in the Senate on the Charter; they had been through all the negotiations, they knew the attitude of the Russians and the other delegates there. So there was no real problem getting it through the Senate." This further built on prior Senate practice – Senators Lodge and Underwood were delegates to the 1921 Washington Arms Limitation Conference. The value of Senate participating in negotiations was offset by the effect on Senate business caused by their absence. *See* Advice and Consent: The Senate and Treaties, 133 Cong. Rec. S5132–02, at 10 (Apr. 10, 1987), 1987 WL 949394 (Cong. Rec.).

NATO Status of Forces Treaty,[22] the defeat of the Bricker Amendments, and the ratification of the 1949 Geneva Conventions. However, by the late 1980s, this bipartisan foreign policy cooperation began to erode. The collapse of the Soviet Union further contributed to increased Senate resistance to binding restrictions posed by treaties.[23]

A *The 1949 Geneva Conventions: The United States as Standard Bearer for "Enlightened Practices of Civilized Countries"*

Against the background of the devastation of World War II as signs of the impending Cold War became apparent, the United States negotiated and signed the 1949 Geneva Conventions. These four treaties substantially amplified existing protections for victims of war. Although transmitted to the Senate in 1951, the Korean War led the Department of State to request the Senate defer consideration of the Conventions.[24] When the Senate finally took up ratification in 1955, issues concerning POWs – issues that arose both after World War II and during the conflict in Korea – were of particular concern.[25]

One issue that became especially contentious during the negotiations to end the Korean hostilities was the inherent tension between the obligation to repatriate prisoners of war (POWs) and the desire to allow Communist POWs to seek asylum.[26] The Soviet Union considered the repatriation provision of

22 The NATO SOFA (Status of Forces Agreement) Treaty, 4 U.S.T. 1792, T.I.A.S. 2846, 199 U.N.T.S. 67. Signed at London on June, 19, 1951, entered into force August 23, 1953.

23 *See* Martin S. Flaherty, *The Future and Past of U.S. Foreign Relations Law*, 67 LAW & CONTEMP. PROBS. 169, 179 (2004) ("[A] certain 'brand of anti-internationalism runs deep in the American political tradition.' However much this tradition ebbed and flowed beforehand, it seems clear that it receded for a sustained period in light of World War II, the Cold War, and the consensus for U.S. international engagement that the two conflicts fostered. It should therefore have come as no surprise that the end of the Cold War would have eroded that consensus and the dominant legal vision that sprang from it") (internal citation omitted).

24 *Geneva Conventions on the Protection of War Victims: Senate Report on Hearings Before Senate Foreign Relations Committee*, 84th Cong. 1, 4 (1955) [hereinafter Senate GC Hearings Rpt.], available at http://www.justice.gov/jmd/ls/legislative_histories/pl104-192/hear-060355-1955.pdf. One concern motivating this request was related to the requirement that prisoners of war be promptly repatriated.

25 At the end of World War II, the United States held over 425,000 prisoners of war in internment camps, a figure that would grow to over 4.3 million in U.S. custody worldwide by May 1945. Robert H. Cole, A Survey of United States Detainee Doctrine and Experience Since World War II, 1–2 (2006), available at www.dtic.mil/dtic/tr/fulltext/u2/a449746.pdf.

26 After World War II, the U.S. and other allied powers were faced with eastern bloc POWs who did not wish to be repatriated to their countries of origin. Although the Soviet Union was not

the Third Geneva Convention (the Geneva Convention Relative to the Treatment of Prisoners of War) as mandatory, with no possibility of asylum for POWs who did not wish to return to their countries of origin. In contrast, the United States concluded that POWs had a right to refuse to be repatriated to their country of origin and to instead seek asylum or repatriation to another country.[27] The United States considered this view to be in accord with the humanitarian object and purposes of the Geneva Conventions,[28] a view concurred in by the United Nations General Assembly.[29]

The uncertainty over this issue delayed the ratification process until 1955, after hostilities in Korea ended. By this point, the issues related to the Korean conflict had been assessed and incorporated into broader U.S. military policy,

a signatory to the 1929 Geneva POW Convention, at the February 1945 Yalta Conference, the United States and Soviet Union agreed to repatriate all citizens, not just POWs, at the end of the war and the United States initially agreed with the Soviet view that POWs would be sent back to their country of origin. However, the United States was soon faced with the Soviet practice of transferring repatriated soldiers to gulags and with mass suicides by prisoners after being informed they would be repatriated to the Soviet Union. Olivier Barsalou, *Making Humanitarian Law in the Cold: The Cold War, The United States and the Genesis of the Geneva Conventions of 1949* 38 (IILJ Emerging Scholars Paper 11, 33 (2008), available at www.iilj.org/publications/documents/Barsalou.ESP11-08.pdf. Stalin's Order 270 stated that every Red Army soldier who allowed himself to be captured alive would be considered as a traitor to the motherland. *Ibid.* at 38. This issue persisted into the Korean War. During the Korean armistice negotiations the most contested legal issue was whether the parties were obligated to compel prisoners to be repatriated against their will or whether the detaining power could in its discretion grant asylum to any prisoner who desired it. *See* Senate GC Hearings Rpt., *supra* note 24, at 22–4; *see also Text of Report to Defense Secretary by Advisory Committee on Prisoners of War*, N. Y. Times, Aug. 18, 1955, available at www.nytimes.com/learning/teachers/archival/19550818POW.pdf.

27 Barsalou, *supra* note 26, at 36–7 (U.S. legal advisors concluded that there was a firmly established principle of international law allowing a detaining state to grant asylum to POWs).

28 *Ibid.* at 37–8; *see also* Geneva Conventions for the Protection of War Victims, Executive Report No. 9, Report of the Committee on Foreign Relations, 84th Cong. 23–24 (1955) [hereinafter Senate GC Exec. Rpt. No. 9] (The committee unqualifiedly concurs [that article 118 does nothing to change accepted principles of international law under which asylum is applicable to prisoners of war] .... The interpretation ... is fully consistent with the great humanitarian purposes which underlie all four of the conventions").

29 *See* Senate GC Hearings Rpt., *supra* note 24, at 5 (the Senate was referring to a U.N. General Assembly Resolution adopted in 1952 that accepted the U.S. view that forced repatriation was not required by Article 118); *see* Int'l Comm. of the Red Cross, Commentary on the Geneva Convention III Relative to the Treatment of Prisoners of War 85 (Jean S. Pictet ed., 1960) [hereinafter Geneva III Commentary], available at www.icrc.org/ihl.nsf/COM/375-590104?OpenDocument; *see also* UN General Assembly Resolution a/res/610 (VII), Korea: Report on the United nations Commission for the Unification and Rehabilitation of Korea; U.N. Doc. A/Res/610(VII) (Dec. 3, 1952), available at www.un.org/en/ga/search/view_doc.asp?symbol=A/RES/610(VII)&Lang=E&Area=RESOLUTION; VOTE 54–5–1, and www.un.org/depts/dhl/resguide/r7.htm.

allowing the Department of State to request the Senate take up consideration of the 1949 Conventions.[30]

Against this backdrop of an advancing Communist ideology and the impending Cold War, officials within the U.S. government increasingly saw ratification as a means to defend the ideals of Western civilization through a universal system of international law.[31] In order to promote this ideological war, the Executive and the Senate were willing to accept the legal constraints imposed on the conduct of U.S. foreign policy by the Conventions,[32] "associat[ing] the preservation of the universality and unity of international [law] with the defense of its national interests in the rising world of the Cold War against the Soviet Union's anti-universalistic philosophy."[33] Accordingly, in 1955, the Executive, in seeking favorable consideration by the Senate, considered the four Geneva Conventions as:

> [a]nother long step forward toward mitigating the severities of war on its helpless victims … reflect[ing] enlightened practices as carried out by the United States and other civilized countries and they represent largely what the United States would do whether or not a party to the conventions.[34]

Delaying consideration of the Conventions by the Senate until after the lessons of the Korean War could be assessed was seen as necessary to allow a considered evaluation of their obligations. Furthermore, it also proved useful to assess their effect on actual military operations, particularly in the context of a war with a nonparty to the Conventions. According to the Senate Report:

30 Barsalou, *supra* note 26, at 38, 43–4; *see also* Senate GC Exec. Rpt. No.9, *supra* note 28, at 3 ("Not long after the treaties were received by the Senate, the Department of State indicated its desire that further action be postponed in view of developments in the Korean conflict. This suggestion seemed a wise course to pursue, since all parties to the Korean conflict had signified in one way or another an acceptance of the principles of the conventions, and there was every reason to believe that more careful and mature consideration could be given to their detailed provisions after, rather than in the midst of, armed conflict. In consequence, no steps were taken in the Senate to consummate ratification of the conventions. With the Korean conflict abated, it became possible to reconsider the matter of ratification").

31 "The United States has a proud tradition of support for individual rights, human freedom, and the welfare and dignity of man. Approval of these conventions by the Senate would be fully in conformity with this great tradition." Senate GC Exec. Rpt. No. 9, *supra* note 28, at 32; *see also* Barsalou, *supra* note 26, at 48–9 (In 1955, the Department of State and Defense prepared memorandum entitled Soviet Attitude Toward the Laws of War, in which the United States saw the Soviet Union as "a threat to the peace and security of the world and consequently, for the whole system of humanitarian law developed in the previous decades").

32 Barsalou, *supra* note 26, at 41. 33 *Ibid.*, at 50.

34 Senate GC Hearings Rpt., *supra* note 24, at 5.

> The experience of the Korean conflict emphasized the importance of the conventions. Our side, in fact, applied their humanitarian provisions and offered victims the protection these were designed to achieve. The enemy's ruthless behavior was exposed by their disregard of the Geneva rules. There is reason to believe that the moral acceptance of the conventions as a general norm did have some effect on the enemy. The Communists to some extent improved their treatment and eventually did repatriate a number of sick and wounded as well as numbers of other prisoners after hostilities. With further regard to the Korean conflict, our unified command, in giving effect through the Armistice Agreement to the principle of release and repatriation employed in the prisoners-of-war conventions, successfully confirmed that a detaining power has the right to offer asylum to prisoners of war and is not obligated to repatriate them forcibly. These fundamental points have been upheld by an overwhelming vote in the United Nations General Assembly.[35]

The Department of Defense's conclusion that "adherence to the standards embodied in the Conventions would not prejudice the success of our aims in battle" also reflected lessons of the recent brutal conflict in Korea, and was crucial to favorable Senate action. By urging ratification, the Department of Defense underscored that the Conventions merely require the treatment that the United States already accords[36] and that "fair and just treatment" of protected persons "contribute[s] to success in battle by providing those conditions of order and stability which permit a belligerent to devote its real efforts to the defeat of the enemy armed forces."[37] Pragmatically, the Department of Defense concluded that the "conventions give us the means of dealing with the problems we encountered in Korea and forbid those very acts which so outraged our conscience."[38]

35 Senate GC Hearings Rpt., *supra* note 24, at 5. The Senate was referring to a U.N. General Assembly Resolution adopted in 1952 that accepted the U.S. view that forced repatriation was not required by Article 118; *see* Geneva III Commentary, *supra* note 29, at 540–52; *see also* UN General Assembly Resolution a/res/610 (VII), Korea: Report on the United nations Commission for the Unification and Rehabilitation of Korea; U.N. Doc. A/Res/610(VII) (Dec. 3, 1952), available at www.un.org/en/ga/search/view_doc.asp?symbol=A/RES/610(VII)&Lang=E&Area=RESOLUTION; VOTE 54–5–1, and www.un.org/depts/dhl/resguide/r7.htm.

36 "In the first place, the conventions are largely but a statement of how we would treat, and have already treated the wounded, the sick, the shipwrecked, prisoners of war, and the civilian victims of war. One cannot help being struck by the close parallel which exists between many of the provisions of the conventions and the course of conduct we ourselves have pursued in recent wars." Senate GC Hearings Rpt., *supra* note 24, at 10 (statement of Wilber M. Brucker, Department of Defense General Counsel).

37 *Ibid.* at 10. 38 *Ibid.*

The Senate quickly recommended ratification, echoing the Executive position that the legal constraints imposed by the Conventions were constraints already present in the policies, practices, and values of the United States and its people, noting that,

> Our Nation has everything to gain and nothing to lose by being a party to the conventions now before the Senate, and by encouraging their most widespread adoption. As emphasized in this report, the requirements of the four conventions to a very great degree reflect the actual policies of the United States in World War II. [T]he practices which they bind nations to follow impose no burden upon us that we would not voluntarily assume in a future conflict without the injunctions of formal treaty obligations.[39]

The Senate also emphasized, as did the President, that the object and purpose of the 1949 Geneva Conventions reflected the values of the United States, particularly, that:

> these four conventions may rightly be regarded as a landmark in the struggle to obtain for military and civilian victims of war, a humane treatment in accordance with the most approved international usage. The United States has a proud tradition of support for individual rights, human freedom, and the welfare and dignity of man. Approval of these conventions by the Senate would be fully in conformity with this great tradition.[40]

Ratification of the 1949 Geneva Conventions was thus perceived by both branches as contributing to U.S. efforts "[t]o lead the free world and defend the interest of international law."[41] The United States viewed ratification of the 1949 Conventions as a critical step toward establishment of universal mandatory legal standards applicable to warfare,[42] standards that could be used in the ideological battle with the Soviet Union. Ratification of the Conventions reflected the U.S. view of the mandates of a universal international law of armed conflict and the U.S. leadership role in achieving it:

> Through its own conduct in previous wars the United States has been instrumental in encouraging the acceptance of standards of treatment which would preserve the peoples of all races and all nations from the

39 Senate GC Exec. Rpt. No. 9, *supra* note 28, at 32. 40 *Ibid.*

41 Barsalou, *supra* note 26, at 33.

42 Reservations by the Soviet Union and other Eastern bloc nations raised concerns in the U.S. State and Defense Departments, and the Senate on the possibility of future prisoners of war being subject to tribunals lacking any protections under international law. Moscow did not consider itself bound by the obligation to extend the application of the Convention to POWs convicted of precapture war crimes. *See* Barsalou, *supra* note 26, at 46–50; *see also* Senate GC Exec. Rpt. No. 9, *supra* note 28, at 28–29.

> savageries and barbarisms of the past. By adding our name to the long list of nations which have already ratified, we shall contribute still further to the ***world-wide endorsement*** of those high standards which the draftsmen at Geneva sought to achieve.[43]

The early 1955 consideration of the Geneva Conventions by the Senate was not done in isolation. Instead, the Senate evaluated their ratification in the immediate aftermath of Senator John Bricker's failure to amend the Constitution. As discussed in Chapters 5 and 10 addressing federalism and the treaty power, Senator Bricker led efforts from 1951 to 1954 to amend the Constitution to overturn the holding of *Missouri v. Holland*[44] and severely limit the treaty power. Also intertwined with the multiyear battle over the Bricker amendments was the Senate's consideration and ultimate approval of the NATO SOFA Treaty in July 1953. Ratification of the NATO SOFA Treaty without reservations was, for President Eisenhower, key to the entire U.S. military position in Europe and necessary to the "mutual security effort among the Nations of the Free World."[45] Its ratification, in the face of Senator Bricker's opposition, not only contributed to the ultimate defeat of his attempts to amend the U.S. Constitution but also underscored the Senate's willingness to accept significant domestic legal restrictions in order to support the successful integration of NATO defense forces.[46]

B The Ratification Process and Unilateral Actions: The 1977 Additional Protocols I and II to the Geneva Conventions and the Military Impact on Advice and Consent

The advice and consent process provides the Senate with an important ability to influence the nature of U.S. treaty obligations. However, this power has little meaning if the president never seeks ratification of a previously negotiated treaty. The way in which the Reagan Administration dealt with the 1977

43 Senate GC Exec. Rpt. No. 9, *supra* note 28, at 32 (emphasis added); *see also* Geneva P.O.W. Code Approved by the Senate, NY Times, July 6, 1955 ("Senator William F. Knowland of California, the Republican Leader, said the four international conventions drafted at Geneva in 1949 had established standards that 'any nation calling itself civilized will comply with.' . . . Another member of the foreign relations committee, Senator Alben W. Barkley, Democrat of Kentucky, said the conventions made an international standard of the 'humane practices the United States has followed over a long period of time'").

44 252 U.S. 416 (1920).

45 *See* Dru Brenner-Beck, *Federalism and the Treaty Power: Breaking the "Bond(s)"Between Nations, the Treaty Power and Status of Forces Agreements*, 5 AM. U. NAT'L SEC. L. BRIEF 1, 13 (2014).

46 *Ibid.* at 6–14.

Additional Protocol I to the Geneva Conventions of 1949[47] provides a somewhat unusual reminder that while the Senate can block the ratification of a treaty favored by the president, it has no power to influence the president's decision *not* to ratify a treaty.

In 1975 the International Committee of the Red Cross convened a conference to update and improve the 1949 Geneva Conventions. Two treaties emerged from this conference: Additional Protocols I and II (AP I and II).[48] AP I supplemented the law applicable to international armed conflicts (inter-state wars), while AP II supplemented the law applicable to noninternational armed conflicts (civil wars).[49] Each treaty included codifications of widely accepted customary international law, refinements of existing Geneva Convention obligations, and advancements in the law.[50]

The United States played a central role in the drafting of these treaties, which were signed by President Carter in 1977.[51] The Executive Branch then subjected the treaties to extensive review, including a comprehensive assessment by the Department of Defense.[52] The Pentagon's review was completed six years later, and identified a number of concerns with both Protocols – especially AP I; concerns shared by the Department of State.[53] Although the Department of Defense considered most of the treaty provisions either codifications of existing customary international law obligations or positive developments in the law, several provisions led the Pentagon to conclude that AP I reflected an unacceptable politicization of the LOAC. Most notably,

47 S. Treaty Doc. No. 100–2, at III-V (1st Sess. 1987).

48 Protocol Additional to the Geneva Conventions of Aug. 12, 1949 and Relating to the Protection of Victims of International Armed Conflicts, June 8, 1977, 1125 U.N.T.S. 3; Protocol Additional to the Geneva Conventions of Aug. 12, 1949 and Relating to the Protection of Victims of Non-international Armed Conflicts, Aug. 6, 1977, 1125 U.N.T.S. 3.

49 *Ibid.*

50 Michael J. Matheson, *The United States Position on the Relation of Customary International Law to the 1977 Protocols Additional to the 1949 Geneva Conventions*, 2 Am. U. J. Int'l L. & Pol'y 419, 420 (1987) [hereinafter Matheson]; Howard S. Levie, The Law of Non-International Armed Conflict: Protocol II to the 1949 Geneva Conventions (1987).

51 Gary Solis, The Law of Armed Conflict: International Humanitarian Law in War 132–33 (2010).

52 S. Treaty Doc. No. 100–2, *supra* note 47, at III-V. President Reagan noted that AP II, unlike Common Article 3, restricted its application to noninternational armed conflicts involving opposition forces capable of controlling a portion of national territory. Regarding these restrictions as unjustifiable, President Reagan affirmed that – consistent with the expansive humanitarian purpose of that original noninternational armed conflict regulatory provision – the U.S. would apply AP II to any armed conflict falling within the scope of Common Article 3.

53 *Ibid.*

the Protocol included "wars of national liberation" occurring solely within the territory of a state within its scope of applicability. This effectively transformed, for purposes of international legal regulation, inherently "noninternational" armed conflicts into "international" armed conflicts.[54] AP I also substantially diluted the requirements for POW qualification included in the Geneva Prisoner of War Convention, allowing insurgents to claim prisoner of war (and combatant) status so long as they showed their weapons immediately prior to attack (as opposed to the traditional requirement to "carry arms openly and wear a fixed distinctive symbol recognizable at a distance").[55] The Joint Chiefs concluded that the combined effect of these provisions incentivized terrorism and diluted key LOAC principles. As a result President Reagan did not transmit API to the Senate for advice and consent. In contrast, there were no significant concerns raised in relation to AP II,[56] which was transmitted to the Senate by the President for advice and consent in 1987.[57]

The wisdom of President Reagan's decision to reject AP I remains controversial.[58] Most U.S. allies, including almost all NATO allies, reached the opposite conclusion and ratified the treaty.[59] Many of these states shared the same concerns with specific provisions, but instead of outright rejection, addressed these concerns through reservations and understandings, an option that the Senate never had the opportunity to recommend.[60] The United States is today one of a handful of states not party to this treaty, which often complicates coalition operations because of disparate treaty obligations.[61] Although President Reagan transmitted AP II to the Senate recommending its

54 *Ibid.* 55 Matheson, *supra* note 50, at 420. 56 *Ibid.*

57 *Ibid.* In his transmittal letter, he indicated that the United States considered AP II a positive development in the law. However, in the same transmittal letter, President Reagan informed the Senate that he had decided not to transmit AP I for advice and consent. He explained that his decision resulted from his concurrence with the Joint Chiefs that AP I was "fatally flawed." *Ibid.*

58 George Aldrich, *Prospects for United States Ratification of Additional Protocol I to the 1949 Geneva Conventions*, 85 Am. J. Int'l L. 1, 20 (1991); *see generally* Curtis Bradley, *Unratified Treaties, Domestic Politics, and the U.S. Constitution*, 48 Harv. Int'l L.J.307 (2007).

59 ICRC Databases on Int'l Humanitarian Law, *supra* note 17. 60 *Ibid.*

61 "Interoperability" refers to the process of armed forces from a number of nations operating effectively within one overall combined command structure. This is a complex issue even without considerations of conflicting legal obligations. However, it is a common practice to integrate what are referred to as "national caveats" into the operational planning and execution process – legal and policy restrictions imposed upon forces by their own national authorities. When the United States is involved in such coalition operations – an involvement that will often take the form of coalition command – the impact of divergent positions on AP I can present challenges to mission allocation. *See* Geoffrey S. Corn, Harvard University, HPCR Working Paper Series: Multi-National Operations, Unity of Effort, and the Law of Armed Conflict 24–25 (2009), available at www.iihl.org/iihl/Documents/multi%20national%20ops.pdf.

ratification, a recommendation repeated by Presidents Clinton and Obama, the treaty remains in limbo.[62]

The U.S. failure to ratify the Additional Protocols illustrates the importance of the constitutionally required interaction between the president and the Senate in treaty ratification. As shown with AP II, even the most determined efforts of the Executive to bind the nation to an international obligation through a treaty are insufficient absent Senate support; conversely, as shown with AP I, no matter how much the Senate considers a treaty beneficial to the nation, Executive agreement is essential to both the making and ratification of the treaty. Finally, as will be discussed below, negotiation over reservations, understandings, and declarations (RUDs) is another key mechanism used between the Executive and the Senate not only to determine the legal effect of a U.S. treaty but also to leverage the resolution of other inter-branch disputes.

C The Chemical Weapons Convention ("CWC") of 1993: Bargaining, Horse Trading, or Extortion

Obtaining Senate consent to a treaty obviously requires political negotiation, and there is no guarantee that the Senate will agree to a treaty's goals, terms, or appropriate implementing measures even when the president believes it advances a critical U.S. interest. The four-year battle over the ratification of the CWC[63] – a process that was expected to be uncontroversial and largely uncontested – provides an especially useful illustration of the Senate's ability to influence both the international and domestic impact of a treaty through its use of RUDs and conditions attached to its resolution of advice and consent.[64]

Negotiated under U.S. leadership by both the Reagan and George H.W. Bush Administrations and signed by Secretary of State Lawrence Eagleburger in January 1993, the CWC enjoyed extensive bipartisan Congressional support. This treaty was a direct response to the ongoing fear of the widespread use of chemicals as a weapon of war, a fear that was very real throughout the Cold War. Although the 1929 Gas Protocol prohibited such widespread use, almost all state parties reserved the right to engage in retaliatory use of chemical

[62] *See* Col. Michael W. Meier, A *Treaty We Can Live with: The Overlooked Strategic Value of Protocol II*, *in* U.S. Dep't of Army, Pam 27–50–412 (2007), available at www.loc.gov/rr/frd/Military_Law/pdf/09-2007.pdf.

[63] John V. Parachini, *U.S. Senate Ratification of the CWC: Lessons for the CTBT*, 5.1 THE NONPROLIFERATION REVIEW 63 (1997) [hereinafter Parachini I].

[64] *Ibid.*

weapons.[65] As a result, militaries from both the Warsaw Bloc and NATO possessed massive stockpiles of chemical weapons and trained extensively for their use. In an effort to rid this weapon from any arsenal, the CWC prohibited not just use of chemicals, but also their manufacture and stockpiling.[66] In a clear effort to prevent the neutering of the treaty, the CWC prohibited reservations.[67]

The "reservation, understanding, and declaration" negotiating process took center stage in the final phase of the obtaining the Senate's advice and consent to the CWC's ratification. Because the treaty prohibited reservations, the focal point of this negotiation became understandings and conditions that would assuage the Senate's concerns related to the treaty. The Senate ultimately imposed three major categories of conditions: (1) those that reasserted the Senate's constitutional role in treaty-making; (2) those that imposed conditions on the Executive either prior to the deposit of the instrument of ratification or periodically, many of which purported to require presidential consultation with the Senate on foreign policy issues related to the implementation of the CWC; and (3) those that affected the operation of the Convention itself.[68] Of particular concern were the issues of whether search warrants

65 *See, e.g.*, Protocol for the Prohibition of the Use in War of Asphyxiating, Poisonous or Other Gases, and of Bacteriological Methods of Warfare, June 17, 1925, 94 L.N.T.S. No. 2138 (1929). Unsurprisingly, many state parties to this treaty, to include the United States, made such reservations especially in the form of preserving the right of retaliatory use of such weapons. *See* (State Parties) Protocol for the Prohibition of the Use in War of Asphyxiating, Poisonous or Other Gases, and of Bacteriological Methods of Warfare, June 17, 1925, www.icrc.org/ihl.nsf/WebSign?ReadForm&id=280&ps=P.

66 The broad definition of "chemical weapon" in the CWC was a result of the long history of attempted regulation of chemical warfare by treaty. *See* U.S. Dep't of State, Protocol for the Prohibition of the Use in War of Asphyxiating, Poisonous or Other Gases, and of Bacteriological Methods of Warfare (Geneva Protocol), Bureau of International Security and Nonproliferation, available at www.state.gov/t/isn/4784.htm. In recognition that prohibitions on use alone were insufficient to remove these weapons from the battlefield, the CWC banned the development, production, stockpiling and use of chemical weapons, contained an elaborate verification regime covering both military and civilian facilities, and established export controls and reporting requirements for precursor chemicals. The extensive verification regime was a new development in arms control treaties, and was designed to impede evasions of the CWC at local levels in every nation as chemicals were widely available and could be turned to wartime use with little effort. *See* Organization for the Prohibition of Chemical Weapons, Basic Facts on Chemical Disarmament, available at www.opcw.org/news-publications/publications/history-of-the-chemical-weapons-convention.

67 Article XXII, Convention on the Prohibition of the Development, Production, Stockpiling and Use of Chemical Weapons and on their Destruction [hereinafter CWC], Jan. 13, 1993, S. Treaty Doc. No. 103–219, 1974 U.N.T.S. 317.

68 Examples of the first category are condition one (the Senate's reassertion, even though not exercised in the CWC, of the right to include reservations in its advice and consent to ratification even though explicitly prohibited by the CWC); condition two (limitation on

would be required for challenge inspections of U.S. chemical plants (what would become condition twenty-eight), concern over possible trade-secret compromises (condition eighteen), and, most significantly, the issue of military use of riot control agents (RCA) (condition twenty-six).[69] The majority of the conditions imposed by the Senate did not result in an inherent conflict with the terms of the Convention. However, the condition imposed by the Senate related to U.S. authority to use riot control agents (RCA) during armed conflicts (which will be discussed in detail below), did seem fundamentally incompatible with the obligations imposed by the Convention.[70]

The treaty also included an obligation to eliminate existing chemical weapons and established a robust international inspection and verification regime. These aspects of the treaty benefited from widespread support by past and present military leaders, U.S. allies and trading partners, and the U.S. chemical industry.[71] Additionally, the CWC was expected to have little concrete effect on U.S. policy. It merely committed other nations to the same path the United States had adopted unilaterally in 1985 when Congress decided to destroy the U.S. chemical weapons stockpile.[72]

any payment or transfer without appropriation or authorization by Congress); condition six (statement that any amendment of the CWC required advice and consent of the Senate); and condition twelve (statement that nothing in the CWC authorized or required any action or legislation that violated the U.S. Constitution). In the second category, the Senate required numerous certifications by the President prior to depositing the instrument of ratification to address concerns of opponents of the treaty. CWC Case Study, *infra* note 69, at 21. Finally, the Senate also included conditions that affected the U.S. funding commitment to the Organization for the Prohibition of Chemical Weapons (OPCW) and the clarification of its understanding on the permissible use of riot control agents under the CWC. *See Summary of the Senate Resolution of Ratification*, on Arms Control Today, at www.armscontrol.org/act/1997_04/cwcanal.

69 Jonathan B. Tucker, Center for the Study of Weapons of Mass Destruction, Nat'l Def. Univ., Case Study Series 4: U.S. Ratification of the Chemical Weapons Convention 14–15 (Paul I. Bernstein 2011) [hereinafter CWC Case Study], available at www.ndu.edu/press/lib/pdf/CSWMD-CaseStudy/CSWMD_CaseStudy-4.pdf. The Senate drafted conditions requiring that administrative search warrants would be required for challenge inspections should the owner of the facility not consent to the inspection. It also drafted a condition prohibiting the removal of samples to international laboratories, raising a concern that if other nations followed the U.S. lead on this issue, the verification regime would be substantially weakened.

70 The CWC recognizes a party's right to withdrawal from the treaty; therefore, conditions purporting to require the president to consult with the Senate to determine if withdrawal is appropriate would not violate the Convention, even if controversial under domestic law. *See Summary of the Senate Resolution of Ratification*, *supra* note 68.

71 Michael Krepon, Amy E. Smithson, & John Parachini, "The Battle to Obtain U.S. Ratification of the Chemical Weapons Convention," The Henry L. Stimson Center, Occasional Paper No. 35, July 1997, at 7 [hereinafter Parachini II], www.stimson.org/images/uploads/research-pdfs/op35.pdf.

72 CWC Case Study, *supra* note 69, at 14–20.

The battle over ratification highlighted diametrically opposing views of the proper role of the United States on the world stage, and was also impacted by post–Cold War tension in the Senate between the internationalists, "who believe[d] that American leadership in world affairs is vital to the country and entails costs that are worth paying,"[73] and the more conservative "unilateralist and isolationist" wing of the party. For the internationalists, "failure to assume the appropriate leadership role [would] leave the management of world affairs to other states less able or inclined to uphold the political values and economic rights the United States deems important."[74] In contrast, the unilateralists believed that "the United States should shun international obligations ... when they may restrict U.S. freedom of action. For unilateralists, protection of American interests is best achieved without the encumbrances of working with other states in international bodies."[75] Senator Jesse Helms, a strong proponent of the isolationist wing of the party, and soon-to-be Chairman of the Foreign Relations Committee, opposed the ratification of the CWC.

The Clinton Administration did not submit the treaty for advice and consent until after the 1994 midterm elections, which shifted control of both the Senate and the House to the Republicans and resulted in Senator Helms becoming the Chair of the Senate Foreign Relations Committee.[76] Senator Helms leveraged his authority to control consideration of the treaty to obtain concessions from the Clinton Administration on other foreign policy questions. As a result, the CWC was not reported out of the committee to the full Senate for consideration until April 1996, with a vote scheduled for September 1996.[77] By that time, Republican opposition to the treaty made securing advice and consent uncertain. As the 1996 presidential election neared, the consideration of the CWC by the Senate became increasingly politicized. In the face of almost certain defeat, the Clinton Administration requested the Senate withdraw the treaty from consideration and re-refer it to the Foreign Relations Committee.[78]

On October 31, 1996, Hungary became the sixty-fifth country to ratify the CWC. This triggered the treaty's 180-day countdown to entry into force and a provision that required the United Staes to ratify the treaty by April 29, 1997, to become an original party to the Convention.[79] Failing to meet this deadline would have had significant consequences for the United Staes, including, *inter alia*, forfeiting a seat on the Executive Council overseeing execution of

[73] Parachini I, *supra* note 63, at 64. [74] *Ibid* at 64.

[75] *Ibid.*; *see also* CWC Case Study, *supra* note 69, at 7, 13 (describing the political divisions giving rise to the controversy).

[76] Parachini I, *supra* note 63, at 63–4. [77] CWC Case Study, *supra* note 69, at 9.

[78] *Ibid.* at 8–9. [79] *Ibid.* at 62.

the treaty, barring U.S. citizens from serving either on the Technical Secretariat (the primary verification body) and the international inspectorate (which administers the treaty regime), and the imposition of mandatory economic sanctions and embargos costing U.S. chemical companies over $600 million in business losses.[80]

Believing failure to ratify the treaty "would signal an American retreat from the world and undermine U.S. leadership in combating weapons proliferation, terrorism, and other transnational problems,"[81] the Clinton Administration began a major push for Senate consent. Secretary of State Madeleine Albright led the ratification effort.[82] Her testimony before the Foreign Relations Committee articulated the importance attached to the treaty's ratification, and her view of the leadership role of the United States:

> America is the world's leader in building a future of greater security and safety for us and for all who share our commitment to democracy and peace. The path to that future is through the maintenance of American readiness and the expansion of the rule of law. We are the center around which international consensus forms. We are the builder of coalitions, the designer of safeguards, the leader in separating acceptable international behavior from that which cannot be tolerated . . .This leadership role for America may be viewed as a burden by some, but I think, to most of our citizens, it is a source of great pride. It is also a source of continuing strength, for our influence is essential to protect our interests, which are global and increasing. If we turn our backs on the CWC after so much effort by leaders from both parties, we will scar America with a grievous and self-inflicted wound. We will shed the cloak of leadership and leave it on the ground for others to pick it up . . . By ratifying the CWC, we will assume the lead in shaping a new and effective legal regime. We . . . will be in a position to challenge those who refuse to give up those poisonous weapons . . . This treaty is about other people's weapons, not our own. It reflects existing American practices and advances enduring American interests.[83]

Substantively, the most controversial understanding related to the use of riot control agents (RCAs) by the U.S. military. The CWC prohibited the use of RCAs as a "method of warfare" because it was hard to distinguish between

80 CWC Case Study, *supra* note 69, at 9, 14; *see also* Chemical Weapons Convention: Hearing Before the S. Foreign Relations Comm., On the Congress, Senate, Committee on Foreign Relations, S. Hrg. 105–183, 105th Cong. 61 *et. seq.* (1997) (Statement by Secretary of State Madeleine K. Albright) [hereinafter CWC Hearings], available at www.fas.org/cw/cwc_archive/1997_SenateFRChearing105-183_1.html.

81 CWC Case Study, *supra* note 69, at 9.

82 Parachini II, *supra* note 71, at 19.

83 CWC Hearings, *supra* note 80, at 3–4.

nonlethal and lethal chemicals on the battlefield, creating the risk of inadvertent escalation."[84] This conflicted with existing U.S. policy, which allowed RCA use "in defensive military mode to save lives." In early ratification discussions in 1994, the Joint Chiefs of Staff had reluctantly acceded to the Clinton Administration's more "narrow legal interpretation of the CWC as banning any use of tear gas in situations where enemy combatants were present."[85] By 1997, in the face of Senator McCain's threat to vote against the treaty unless the option to use tear gas to rescue downed American pilots was retained (even if it violated the text of the treaty),[86] the Administration's representative agreed that the 1975 Executive Order allowing RCA use "in defensive military mode to save lives" would remain in effect.[87] Presented to the State Department as a fait accompli required to obtain Senate ratification of the treaty, this condition (number twenty-six) generated concern that a future president would be able to use RCAs in a manner prohibited by the CWC, undermining its object and purpose.[88]

As the ratification deadline approached, the Clinton Administration supported Senator Helms' desired reorganization of the foreign affairs agencies in order to move the CWC out of committee. This agreement resulted in a Senate vote five days before the CWC coming into force. The final proposed resolution of ratification contained thirty-two conditions, twenty-eight of which would by agreement not be subject to changes. The other five conditions, considered barriers to ratification approval,

84 *Ibid.* at 4.

85 *Ibid.* On June 23, 1994, the White House issued a statement from President Clinton to the Senate stating: "according to the current international understanding, the CWC's prohibition on the use of RCAs as a 'method of warfare' also precludes the use of RCAs even for humanitarian purposes in situations where combatants and noncombatants are intermingled, such as the rescue of downed air crews, passengers, and escaping prisoners, and situations where civilians are being used to mask or screen attacks." *Ibid.* In these situations, the administration argued, nonlethal weapons other than chemical agents could be employed that were fully consistent with the CWC. *Ibid.*

86 Convention on the Prohibition of the Development, Production, Stockpiling and Use of Chemical Weapons and on their Destruction, art. 1.5, Jan. 13, 1993, S. TREATY DOC. NO. 103–219, 1974 U.N.T.S. 317 [hereinafter CWC] ("Each State Party undertakes not to use riot control agents *as a method of warfare*" (emphasis added)).

87 CWC Case Study, *supra* note 69, at 16.

88 *Ibid.* Recall the CWC prohibited state reservations in hopes that the Convention would accomplish the goals of eliminating chemical weapons. Allowing reservations had resulted in the failure of the 1925 Gas Protocol to accomplish that goal. For the CWC, the White House also agreed to conditions prohibiting international inspectors from removing samples from U.S. industrial sites to overseas laboratories, heightening the risk that other parties to the Convention would impose similar restrictions and thereby weaken the international verification regime. *Ibid.*

remained subject to amendment by majority vote.[89] The White House continued to publicly push for ratification. After eighteen hours of floor debate, the five separate motions to remove each of the five killer amendments passed – leaving the agreed upon resolution of ratification with twenty-eight conditions to be voted upon by the Senate. In a dramatic floor vote, with Vice President Gore standing by as presiding officer of the Senate in case of a tie vote, the Senate voted seventy-four to twenty-six to ratify the Convention with the twenty-eight consensus conditions. It then took Congress another year to pass the CWC Implementation Act implementing the Convention domestically.[90]

The international negotiation of the CWC was seen as a major U.S. foreign policy success, creating a multilateral international regime to eliminate a heinous weapon of war – the first LOAC treaty to ban not only the use of an entire category of weaponry, but also production and stockpiling. However, in the four years after the U.S. signed the treaty, the bipartisan view of the wisdom of binding multilateral international legal obligations fell victim to the realities of politics and inter-branch frictions, and its ratification was made dependent on significant compromises to its object and purpose. The process of the ratification of the CWC with the resulting twenty-eight Senate conditions – most significantly the condition related to the assertion of authority to continue to use RCA – compromised the perception of U.S. commitment to the treaty. Perhaps more importantly, it raised significant questions as to the

89 CWC Case Study, *supra* note 69, at 16–17 (detailing the killer conditions).

90 During its consideration of the CWC, the Senate concurrently considered the CWC Implementation Act, to implement the CWC, if ratified. The Deputy Assistant Attorney General testified that both the CWC and the CWC Implementation Act "were painstakingly drafted to put in place an effective, verifiable ban on the development, acquisition, and use of chemical weapons, but none of their provisions in any way contemplates or permits conduct in contravention of the fourth amendment. Indeed, the inspection provisions were drafted to be fully consonant with the dictates of search and seizure law." *See* Constitutional Implications of the Chemical Weapons Convention: Hearings Before Sub-Committee on Constitution, Federalism, and Property Rights of the Senate Judiciary Committee, S. Hrg. 104–859, 104th Cong. 80 (1996) [hereinafter Senate CWC Constitutional Implications Hearing] (Statement by Richard I. Shiffrin, Deputy Assistant Attorney General, Office of Legal Counsel, U.S. Department of Justice). Some contentious issues resurfaced during the final consideration of the CWC Implementation Act after ratification of the CWC itself. This led to another round of negotiations between the President and Republican members of both houses of Congress, resulting in the insertion of a provision in the CWC Implementation Act, "authorizing a future President to block, on grounds of national security, an involuntary 'challenge' inspection of any facility on U.S. territory, declared or undeclared, that another member state believed was engaged in prohibited activities." This provision was seen as undermining another key element in the treaty's verification regime. CWC Case Study, *supra* note 69, at 23.

present and future willingness of the United States to commit to other weapon prohibition treaties.

III SELF-EXECUTION: NORIEGA AND THE MILITARY COMMISSION ACT

The domestic force and effect of the 1949 Geneva Conventions turns on application of the self-execution doctrine.[91] Adopted as a method of judicial treaty interpretation early in U.S. history, this doctrine draws a distinction between treaties that by their terms create discernible standards for judicial enforcement (those that operate of themselves), and treaties that commit the nation to perform some future legislative act.[92] Key to this determination is whether any given treaty provision can be enforced without additional legislative action. This distinction has been characterized as "one of the most confounding in treaty law."[93]

As this doctrine developed, courts looked beyond the text of the treaty, focusing on the treaty's object and purpose and the intent of the parties in order to determine if the treaty had immediate domestic effect. As a result, Senate action during the advice and consent process has often significantly impacted subsequent interpretation of the domestic effect of a treaty.[94]

[91] The legislative history of the ratification of the Geneva Conventions shows that the Senate carefully considered what further legislation, if any, was deemed "required to give effect to the provisions contained in the four conventions," and found that "very little in the way of new legislative enactments will be required to give effect to the provisions contained in the four conventions." Senate GC Exec. Rpt. No. 9, *supra* note 28, at 30. *See also* Hamdan v. Rumsfeld, 344 F.Supp.2d 152, 165 (D.D.C. 2004) ("it is quite clear from the legislative history of the ratification of the Geneva Conventions that Congress carefully considered what further legislation, if any, was deemed 'required to give effect to the provisions contained in the four conventions,' S. Rep. No. 84–9, at 30 (1955), and found that only four provisions required implementing legislation.").

[92] Louis Henkin, Foreign Affairs and the U.S. Constitution 199 (2nd ed. 1996) [hereinafter Henkin] (discussing Foster v. Nielson, 27 U.S. (2 pet.) 253, 314 (1829)); *see also* Carlos Manuel Vazquez, *The Four Doctrines of Self-Executing Treaties*, 89 Am J. Int'l L. 695, 700–701 (1995).

[93] United States v. Postal, 589 F.2d 862, 876 (5th Cir. 1979), *cert. denied*, 444 U.S. 832 (1979).

[94] Al-Bihani v. Obama, 619 F.3d 1, 13 (D.C. Cir. 2010), *cert. denied*, 131 S.Ct. 1814, 179 L. Ed. 2d 794 (2011) (Kavanaugh, J., in his statement to the denial of a rehearing *en banc*) (citing Medellín v. Texas, 552 U.S. 491, 128 S.Ct. 1346, 170 L. Ed. 2d 190 (2008); Sosa v. Alvarez–Machain, 542 U.S. 692, 124 S. Ct. 2739, 159 L. Ed. 2d 718 (2004)). According to Judge Kavanaugh:

> [S]tatutes and self-executing treaties are domestic U.S. law and thus enforceable in U.S. courts. By contrast, non-self-executing treaties and customary international law are not domestic U.S. law. Only when international-law principles are incorporated into a statute or a self-executing treaty do they become domestic U.S. law enforceable in U.S. courts.

Further complicating this already complex assessment is the common conflation of two distinct questions: first, whether the treaty operates domestically without further Congressional enactment; and second, whether the treaty confers a private right of action on an individual to enforce provisions of the treaty.[95]

Prior to the enactment of the 2006 Military Commissions Act (2006 MCA), few courts had struggled with the issue of whether the 1949 Geneva Conventions were self-executing, let alone whether they conferred a private right of action to enforce their provisions in domestic courts.[96] After the Supreme Court's 2006 *Hamdan v. Rumsfeld* decision, however, Congress passed section 5 of the 2006 MCA, which purports to dictate the resolution of these twin self-execution questions. In what can only be understood as an effort to bar Guantanamo detainees from invoking the Geneva Conventions in support of judicial actions challenging the legality of their detention, Congress included the following provision in the 2006 Military Commission Act:

> No person may invoke the Geneva Conventions or any protocols thereto in any habeas corpus or other civil action or proceeding to which the United

Ibid.; but see Committee of U.S. Citizens Living in Nicaragua v. Reagan (CUSCLIN), 859 F.2d 929, 938–942 (D.C. Cir. 1988) ("within the domestic legal realm, [an] inconsistent statute simply modifies or supersedes customary international law to the extent of the inconsistency").

95 Self-execution has two aspects: first whether the treaty operates domestically without subsequent congressional enactment, and second, whether the treaty provisions confer a private right of action. *See* Renkel v. United States, 456 F.3d 640, 643 n.3 (6th Cir. (2006) (citing Medellin v. Dretke, 544 U.S. 660, 125 S.Ct. 2088, 2103, 161 L.Ed.2d 982 (2005)(O'Connor, J., dissenting) ("Although related, 'the questions of whether a treaty is self-executing and whether it creates private rights and remedies are analytically distinct.' While a treaty must be self-executing for it to create a private right of action enforceable in court without implementing domestic legislation, all self-executing treaties do not necessarily provide for the availability of such private actions"); *see also* Hamdan v. Rumsfeld, 344 F.Supp.2d. 152, 164–5 (D.D.C. 2004).

96 A small number of judicial opinions have grappled with the self-execution question as it relates to the 1949 Geneva Conventions. In Hamdan v. Rumsfeld, Common Article 3 of the Conventions provided a treaty based authority for the Supreme Court to conclude that Hamdan's trial by military commission was unlawful. However, the Court did not resolve the question of whether the Geneva Conventions, *writ large*, were self-executing. Instead, the Court concluded that because Congress had incorporated the law of war into the Uniform Code of Military Justice (UCMJ) provision authorizing trial by military commission, the President was obligated to comply with this provision of the treaty, thus sidestepping the self-execution question. Hamdan v. Rumsfeld, 548 U.S. 557 (2006). Additionally, the prosecution, conviction, and decades later, extradition of General Manuel Noriega – whose antagonism of the United States culminated in the invasion of Panama in 1989 – also involved complex questions of self-execution of the Geneva Conventions. U.S. v. Noriega, 808 F.Supp. 791 (S.D. Fla. 1992); Noriega v. Pastrana, 564 F.3d 1290 (11th Cir. 2009).

> States, or . . . agent of the United States is a party as a source of rights in any court of the United States or its States or territories.[97]

Ironically, the first test of this statutory non-self-executing dictate arose in a case that had nothing to do with Guantanamo, but rather in the case of General Manuel Noriega's extradition.

General Manuel Noriega commanded the Panamanian Defense Forces and, after nullifying election results in 1989, took over all powers as the leader of Panama. Noriega was captured following the December 1989 U.S. invasion of Panama that led to the destruction of Noriega's military power base and the assumption of authority by the legitimately elected candidates Noriega had blocked. Noriega was brought to the United States to stand trial on preinvasion drug related indictments in the Southern District of Florida, but he quickly asserted that he was entitled to the protections of the Third Geneva Convention because he was a prisoner of war.

In one of the few judicial decisions addressing whether the 1949 Geneva Conventions were self-executing, the presiding district judge concluded in 1992 that Noriega was indeed entitled to POW status under the Third Geneva Convention. The court based its ruling on its conclusion that the POW Convention was both self-executing[98] and a source of enforceable individual rights. Furthermore, the court emphasized that only judicial action could ensure Noriega received the protections provided by the Convention. The U.S. government had asserted that Noriega was not entitled to POW status as a matter of law, but would be treated "consistent with" this status as a matter of policy. These assurances were rejected as inadequate by the district court judge.[99] After rejecting the government argument that the conflict in Panama was not "international" in nature and that Noriega was therefore not entitled to POW status, the court emphasized that allowing Noriega to invoke the protections of the Convention in a U.S. court was necessary to fulfill the object and purpose of the treaty. Accordingly, it concluded that Noriega, as a prisoner of war, was entitled to look to U.S. courts to protect his rights under the Convention:[100]

> In the case of Geneva III, however, it is inconsistent with both the language and spirit of the treaty and with our professed support of its purpose to find that the rights established therein cannot be enforced by the individual POW in a court of law. After all, the ultimate goal of Geneva III is to ensure humane

97 §5(a), 2006 Military Commissions Act. P.L. 109–366, 120 Stat. 2600, *codified at* 10 U.S.C. 948a *et seq.* (2006) [hereinafter 2006 MCA].

98 United States v. Noriega, 808 F. Supp. 791, 794 (S.D. Fla. 1992).

99 *Ibid.* at 796

100 *Ibid.* at 797.

> treatment of POWs – not to create some amorphous, unenforceable code of honor among the signatory nations. "It must not be forgotten that the Conventions have been drawn up first and foremost to protect individuals, and not to serve State interests." Commentary at 23.[101]

Unfortunately for Noriega, none of the enforceable rights in the Third Geneva Convention prevented his prosecution, conviction, or incarceration for preconflict crimes against the United States (although he did receive certain Convention-based conditions of confinement during his federal incarceration).[102]

Seventeen years later, upon completing his sentence, Noriega sought a different benefit from the treaty: a bar to his extradition to France. In 2007, France sought Noriega's extradition in order to try him for money laundering offenses that arose from his years of using France as a location to preserve his ill-gotten gains while he was head of the Panamanian Defense Forces. Noriega invoked the Third Geneva Convention to block the extradition, asserting that because France would not assure him POW treatment, the United States, as the Detaining Power, was barred from transferring him.

Noriega's effort to invoke the Third Geneva Convention to block his extradition ran headlong into section 5 of the 2006 MCA – the section in which Congress sought to eliminate any domestic enforceability of the Geneva Conventions. The Eleventh Circuit rejected Noriega's challenge, concluding that § 5 of the 2006 Military Commissions Act barred him from invoking the Geneva Conventions as an individually enforceable right in U.S. courts. The issue of self-execution was once again easily sidestepped, as the circuit court held that even if the Conventions were self-executing, Congress could eliminate their domestic applicability by enacting a subsequent statute contradicting their terms.[103] Specifically, the court noted that, "Congress has superseded whatever domestic effect the Geneva Conventions may have had in actions such as this."[104]

101 *Ibid.* at 799.

102 United States v. Noriega, 746 F. Supp. 1506, 1510–12 (S.D. Fla. 1990) (because members of the U.S. armed forces could have been tried in federal court for the same offenses alleged against General Noriega, his immunity as a POW did not shield him from criminal jurisdiction. Under art. 84: "A prisoner of war shall be tried only by a military court, unless the existing laws of the Detaining Power expressly permit the civil courts to try a member of the armed forces of the Detaining Power in respect of the particular offence alleged to have been committed by the prisoner of war.").

103 *See* Noriega v. Pastrana, 564 F.3d 1290, 1295–6 (11th Cir. 2009) (because it is within Congress' power to change domestic law, even if the law originally arose from a self-executing treaty).

104 *Ibid.* at 1296.

Although this conclusion could be criticized as Congress de-self-executing a valid treaty provision and invading the role of the judiciary,[105] it instead appears to be, at least for the Eleventh Circuit, a straightforward application of the rule of *lex posterior* which establishes that subsequently enacted statutes preempt prior inconsistent (self-executing) treaty provisions.[106]

Noriega sought Supreme Court review of this decision, creating the possibility that his case might have significance beyond the mere final disposition of a long-forgotten U.S. enemy. This hope was short lived, as the Supreme Court denied his petition for *certiorari*. However, Justices Thomas and Scalia dissented from the denial. In their view, the case offered an ideal opportunity to consider whether Congress is authorized to prohibit the courts from considering the provisions of a ratified treaty as it relates to an individual litigant seeking a remedy under that provision. For them, resolution of this issue "would provide much-needed guidance on two important issues with which the political branches and federal courts have struggled since we decided *Boumediene*": whether the Geneva Conventions are self-executing and judicially enforceable, and "the extent, if any, to which provisions like Section 5 affect 28 U.S.C. § 2241 [the federal habeas statute] in a manner that implicates the constitutional guarantee of habeas corpus."[107] They lamented the lost opportunity to "say what the law is" in a case unencumbered by classified information or issues relating to extraterritorial detention or the ongoing hostilities against al Qaeda.[108]

Unfortunately too late for General Noriega, the 2009 MCA significantly narrowed the bar to considering the Geneva Conventions by prohibiting only

105 *See, e.g.*, Steven I Vladeck, *Why Klein (Still) Matters: Congressional Deception and the War on Terrorism*, 5 *J. of Nat'l L. & Pol'y* 251 (2011) (arguing that provisions prohibiting reliance on Geneva Conventions may violate separation of powers principles).

106 Because treaties and statutes have equal status under the Constitution, in the domestic realm, inconsistencies between the two must be resolved by the rule of *lex posterior*. CUSCLIN, 859 F.2d at 936; *see also* Cook v. United States, 288 US 102 (1933) (self-executing treaty superseded prior statute to the extent of inconstancy with statute; and subsequent reenactment of statute did not abrogate treaty absent clear congressional expression of such intent); Tag v. Rogers, 267 F.2d 664 (D.C. Cir. 1959) (statute superseded prior treaty) (*quoting The Cherokee Tobacco*, 11 Wall. 616, 620–1 (1870) ("It need hardly be said that a treaty cannot change the Constitution or be held valid if it be in violation of that instrument. This results from the nature and fundamental principles of our government. The effect of treaties and acts of Congress, when in conflict, is not settled by the Constitution. But the question is not involved in any doubt as to its proper solution. A treaty may supersede a prior act of Congress, and an act of Congress may supersede a prior treaty").

107 Noriega v. Pastrana, *cert. denied*, 130 S. Ct. 1002, 1008–10 (2010) (Thomas, J., dissenting from the denial of certiorari).

108 *Ibid.* at 1003.

their use as a basis for a private right of action by alien unprivileged enemy belligerents,[109] perhaps reinvigorating the issue of the self-execution of the Geneva Conventions in the future. Perhaps most importantly, these cases demonstrate the powerful influence Congress may assert on the enforceability of what appears, absent such action, self-executing treaty provisions.[110]

Congress' non-self-execution mandate included in the 2006 MCA foreclosed Noriega's ability to invoke the Third Geneva Convention as the source of a judicial remedy. However, the statutory mandate, and its impact on the Eleventh Circuit, was unquestionably unusual. This is not necessarily because Congress provided its interpretation as to the domestic effect of these treaties, but because it did so in a completely distinct statute enacted decades after ratification of the Conventions. How other courts will interpret the impact of this provision is yet to be seen, and Justice Thomas' dissent in the denial of *certiorari* by the Supreme Court may provide ammunition for future opinions rejecting the ability of Congress to dictate a self-execution determination to the courts.

It is also important to note that a non-self-execution determination should not be equated with a conclusion that treaties are in some way insignificant. To the contrary, they remain central to the formulation of U.S. national security policies, and to the protection of individuals under U.S. control. Thus, while the statutory prohibition against individual invocation of the Geneva Conventions in U.S. courts has in large measure superseded questions of self-execution, how these protections, and other principles and rules of both treaty and customary law of war impact U.S. action remains a complex and important issue. Finally, even where treaty provisions are considered to apply to U.S. litigation as the result of statutory incorporation, the meaning, scope,

109 *Compare* 10 U.S.C. § 948b(e) ("Geneva Conventions Not Establishing Private Right of Action.—No alien unprivileged enemy belligerent subject to trial by military commission under this chapter may invoke the Geneva Conventions as a basis for a private right of action") *with* §5, 2006 MCA (No person may invoke the Geneva Conventions or any protocols thereto in any habeas corpus or other civil action or proceeding to which the United States, or . . . agent of the United States is a party as a source of rights in any court of the United States or its States or territories"), and § 3a(1), 2006 MCA ("Geneva Conventions Not Establishing Source of Rights.—No alien unlawful enemy combatant subject to trial by military commission under this chapter may invoke the Geneva Conventions as a source of rights").

110 Of equal note, § 6 of the 2006 MCA drastically limited the scope of the criminal liability provisions of the 1996 War Crimes Act by delimiting what offenses constituted grave breaches of Common Article 3, and prohibited the use of foreign or international sources of law to supply a rule of decision in the courts of the United States, in interpreting those prohibitions. *See* § 6, 2006 MCA, *supra* note 97; 18 U.S.C §2241(d).

and effect of these treaty rights continues to be a source of uncertainty and debate.[111]

IV INTERPRETATION: *YAMASHITA* AND *HAMDAN*

Like any other source of codified law, treaties will often be subjected to judicial interpretation. Indeed, interpretation of treaty obligations can have potentially profound consequences for U.S. national security. While cases involving judicial interpretation of LOAC treaties have been relatively infrequent, they provide important clarity for the military and have significantly affected the evolution of international law.[112] Two cases provide insight into this impact: *In re Yamashita*[113] and *Hamdan v. Rumsfeld*.[114]

111 Illustrative of the intense difference of opinion over the appropriate impact of international law on domestic U.S. law, the denial of a rehearing *en banc* in Al Bihani v. Obama, 619 F.3d 1 (D.C. Cir. 2010) provided the opportunity for several judges to extensively explain their views on the issue in the context of a habeas challenge arising after *Hamdan* and *Hamdi*. In that case, the law of war was again arguably relevant in interpreting the powers granted by Congress to the President in the 2001 Authorization for the Use of Military Force (AUMF). Although the majority of the Circuit's judges felt that determination of the role of international law of war principles in interpreting the AUMF had not been relevant to its disposition on the merits and was therefore not appropriate for *en banc* consideration, several judges nevertheless expounded extensively on the inapplicability of international law norms to limit the president's war powers absent incorporation of those standards into domestic law via statute, regulations, or self-executing treaties incorporating those limits. Rejecting the position that consulting international law sources as a method of statutory construction was valid, Judges Brown and Kavanaugh would limit the sources relevant to determine the powers granted by the AUMF solely to the significant body of legislation passed by Congress to prohibit certain wartime actions by the Executive and military. Judge Williams disagreed, reiterating his view that international law could properly serve as a source of information in interpreting Congressional statutes governing international matters. In his view, international law operated both prior to and after the Erie decision as a "source of interpretive guidance regarding statutes passed by Congress." Al-Bihani, 619 F.3d at 54. Pointing out that the plurality in *Hamdi* had used international law in this manner, *Ibid.* at 55, Judge Williams concluded "if the international laws of war 'can inform the powers that Congress has implicitly granted to the President in the AUMF, they logically can inform the boundaries of such powers.'" *Ibid.* at 54–5 (quoting Curtis Bradley & Jack Goldsmith, *Congressional Authorization and the War on Terrorism*, 118 HARV. L. REV. 2047, 2094 (2005)); *see also* Sosa v. Alvarez-Machain, 542 U.S. 692,729–30 (2004) (affirming that the domestic law of the United States recognizes the law of nations).

112 Geneva III Commentary, *supra* note 29; *see* Matthew C. Kirkham, *Hamdan v. Rumsfeld: A Check on Executive Authority in the War on Terror*, 15 TUL. J. INT'L & COMP. L. 707 (2007); *see also* Samuel Estreicher & Diarmuid O'Scannlain, *Hamdan's Limits and the Military Commissions Act*, 23 *Const. Comment.* 403 (2006); *see also* Sylvain Vite, *Typology of armed conflicts in international humanitarian law: legal concepts and actual situations*, 91, no.873 INT'L REVIEW OF THE RED CROSS, 69, 93 (2009).

113 In re Yamashita, 327 U.S. 1, 66 S. Ct. 340, 90 L. Ed. 499 (1946).

114 Hamdan v. Rumsfeld, 548 U.S. 557 (2006).

In *Yamashita*, the Supreme Court considered Yamashita's challenge to the legality of his trial and conviction by a U.S. military commission following his surrender at the end of the war with Japan. Yamashita qualified as a prisoner of war pursuant to the 1929 Geneva Convention Relative to the Treatment of Prisoners of War (1929 GPW).[115] He challenged both the validity of the finding that his conduct amounted to a war crime (in that there was no established precedent for prosecuting a commander for a war crime as the result of widespread war crimes committed by subordinates) and the nature of the tribunal used to try him. Specifically, he sought to invoke provisions of the 1929 GPW that required the United States to utilize the same trial process against him that it would have used to try a U.S. service member.[116]

Article 63 of the 1929 GPW provided that if a detaining power tried a POW for any offense, "sentence may be pronounced against a prisoner of war only by the same courts and according to the same procedure as in the case of persons belonging to the armed forces of the detaining Power."[117] The assumption seemed clear (although perhaps not completely valid): states will afford their own service members fundamentally fair military trials. Therefore, an obligation to use the same tribunals for POWs effectively ensures fair process for the enemy. Because the U.S. Army Articles of War prohibited the use of prosecution depositions and hearsay in trials by courts-martial for U.S. military personnel, Yamashita argued, use of such evidence at his military commission trial violated this treaty obligation.[118]

The Supreme Court rejected Yamashita's argument, concluding Article 63 was inapplicable to his case.[119] The Court based this conclusion on the nature of Yamashita's alleged misconduct. According to the Court, Article 63 applied only after the initiation of detention, *not* for precapture violations of the laws and customs of war subject to trial by military commission.[120] Thus, had Yamashita been tried for misconduct *as* a POW, his argument would have had merit. Because this was not the case, the Court concluded that use of

[115] Yamashita, 327 U.S. at 20–21. The United States ratified this treaty in 1932. See Convention Relative to the Treatment of Prisoners of War Ratification Dates, Int'l Comm. of the Red Cross (last updated May 11, 2012), www.icrc.org/ihl.nsf/WebSign?ReadForm&id=305&ps=P (last updated Aug. 8, 2012).

[116] Yamashita, 327 U.S. at 13–14. The Supreme Court reviewed Yamashita's trial and conviction by military commission pursuant to a writ of habeas corpus challenging a range of issues related to the trial. The Court's endorsement of a charge and conviction on a theory of vicarious command responsibility – even in the face of evidence that Yamashita lacked the capacity to communicate with or control most of his subordinates – is the most widely known aspect of the decision. However, Yamashita's procedural challenge was the aspect of the case that necessitated interpretation of the 1929 GPW.

[117] *Ibid.* at 20–1. [118] *Ibid.* at 6. [119] *Ibid.* at 21–3. [120] *Ibid.* at 22.

evidentiary rules different from those used for trial by court-martial did not violate the GPW.[121] This interpretation was consistent with that of several other state parties,[122] although inconsistent with that of the International Committee of the Red Cross.[123] It also produced a bifurcated approach to allocating the Convention's fair process protections that seemed inconsistent with the treaty's apparent objective: ensuring adequate process is used to ascertain whether the captive did in fact engage in the alleged misconduct. Indeed, this inconsistency between the ostensible objective of the Convention and the majority's interpretation generated a strong dissent.[124]

The *Yamashita* Court's interpretation of the 1929 GPW was consistent with how some other states interpreted this same provision at the time. Nonetheless, it also deprived individuals qualified for POW status of an important protection: the prohibition on use of tribunals utilizing different rules of evidence and procedure than those considered necessary for the fair trial of the detaining power's own armed forces. Indeed, as Justice Murphy noted in his vociferous *Yamashita* dissent, this interpretation could not be reconciled with the humanitarian objective of the treaty.[125] If these interpretations did nullify the objective of the treaty, it was a potential outcome that is inherent in any judicial treaty interpretation.

[121] *Ibid.* at 19–21; *see also* Johnson v. Eisentrager, 339 U.S. 763, 790 (1950) (adopting same interpretation of 1929 GPW Article 29 in habeas action challenging military commission conviction for precapture war crimes).

[122] Geneva III Commentary, art. 85, *supra* note 29.

[123] *Ibid.*

> The 1929 Convention contained no provision concerning the punishment of crimes or offences committed by prisoners of war prior to their capture. Although Articles 45 to 67 of that Convention do not specifically exclude such acts, it seems probable that the drafter actually had in mind only acts committed during captivity. At the end of the Second World War, this gap in the text of the 1929 Convention gave rise to much discussion until sentences were passed in most of the Allied countries. Among the prisoners of war who were nationals of the vanquished Powers were many persons who were accused of war crimes, and crimes against peace and humanity. During the ensuing trials, a number of the accused asked to be afforded the guarantees provided by the 1929 Convention in regard to judicial proceedings. The International Committee of the Red Cross . . . requested that the guarantees afforded by Articles 45 to 67 should be applied to them . . . In almost every case the courts of the Allied countries rejected the requests of the accused. The United States Supreme Court likewise rejected a request by General Yamashita of Japan on this point.

See Geneva III Commentary, art. 85, *supra* note 29.

[124] In re Yamashita, 327 U.S. at 26–7 (Murphy, J., dissenting) (Justice Murphy argued that strategic decisions to eliminate communication should not impute liability through the theory of command responsibility).

[125] In re Yamashita, 327 U.S. at 35 (Murphy, J., dissenting).

The interpretation of Article 63 that led to the *Yamashita* and *Eisentrager* decisions and divided the *Yamashita* Court was addressed directly in the 1949 revision of the GPW. Article 102 of the 1949 Convention addressed the same issue addressed in Article 29 of the 1929 Convention, specifically providing that "a prisoner of war can be validly sentenced only if the sentence has been pronounced by the same courts according to the same procedure as in the case of members of the armed forces of the Detaining Power, and if, furthermore, the provisions of the present Chapter have been observed."[126] Article 85 of the 1949 GPW eliminated all doubt as to the applicability of this provision to trials for precapture (pre-POW) misconduct, providing that "prisoners of war prosecuted under the laws of the Detaining Power for acts committed prior to capture shall retain, even if convicted, the benefits of the present Convention."[127] The associated commentary explains that this provision was included to ensure Article 102 applied to all POW trials, including those for precapture war crimes or even precapture crimes with no connection to the armed conflict.[128]

In *Hamdan v. Rumsfeld*, the Court considered the president's authority – acting in his capacity as commander in chief – to convene a military commission to try a captured al Qaeda operative for alleged violations of the laws and customs of war.[129] The Court would again interpret an important provision of the Geneva Conventions, one that did not even exist when *Yamashita* was decided: Common Article 3.[130]

126 Geneva III, *supra* note 13, art. 102.

127 *Ibid.* art. 85. The associated ICRC Commentary to this article explains:

> When the International Committee of the Red Cross undertook the revision of the 1929 Convention, it therefore gave immediate attention to introducing provisions which would afford certain guarantees to prisoners of war, even when accused of war crimes, and remove all ambiguity which had resulted from the earlier text.

See Geneva III Commentary, art. 85, *supra* note 29.

128 *Ibid.* The Soviet Union included a reservation to Article 85 stating: "The Union of Soviet Socialist Republics does not consider itself bound by the obligation, which follows from Article 85, to extend the application of the Convention to prisoners of war who have been convicted under the law of the Detaining Power, in accordance with the principles of the Nuremberg trial, for war crimes and crimes against humanity, it being understood that persons convicted of such crimes must be subject to the conditions obtaining in the country in question for those who undergo their punishment." See www.icrc.org/ihl.nsf/NORM/48D358FE7D15CA77C1256402003F9795?OpenDocument. This change to the GPW was noted by Justice Stevens in his Hamdan majority opinion addressing an analogous issue. *See* Hamdan v. Rumsfeld, 548 U.S. at 619–20.

129 Hamdan, 548 U.S. at 613–35.

130 In the case of armed conflict not of an international character occurring in the territory of one of the High Contracting Parties, each Party to the conflict shall be bound to apply, as a minimum, the following provisions:

Common Article 3 refers to an article included in all four of the 1949 Geneva Conventions. It was perhaps the most significant addition to the Conventions when they were revised following World War II, as it represented an extension of international legal regulation to noninternational armed conflicts.[131] This new category of conflict regulation was, at that time, focused on hostilities between state authorities and internal opposition groups – civil wars. Although the state parties were unwilling to extend the full corpus of the Conventions to these internal conflicts, they did ultimately agree that even in these primarily domestic affairs, international law required the humane treatment of any person not actively participating in hostilities.[132]

Accordingly, Common Article 3 requires the humane treatment of any person not actively participating in the hostilities and especially opposition

(1) Persons taking no active part in the hostilities, including members of armed forces who have laid down their arms and those placed 'hors de combat' by sickness, wounds, detention, or any other cause, shall in all circumstances be treated humanely, without any adverse distinction founded on race, colour, religion or faith, sex, birth or wealth, or any other similar criteria. To this end, the following acts are and shall remain prohibited at any time and in any place whatsoever with respect to the above-mentioned persons: (a) violence to life and person, in particular murder of all kinds, mutilation, cruel treatment and torture; (b) taking of hostages; (c) outrages upon personal dignity, in particular humiliating and degrading treatment; (d) the passing of sentences and the carrying out of executions without previous judgment pronounced by a regularly constituted court, affording all the judicial guarantees which are recognized as indispensable by civilized peoples.

(2) The wounded and sick shall be collected and cared for. An impartial humanitarian body, such as the International Committee of the Red Cross, may offer its services to the Parties to the conflict.

The Parties to the conflict should further endeavor to bring into force, by means of special agreements, all or part of the other provisions of the present Convention. The application of the preceding provisions shall not affect the legal status of the Parties to the conflict.

131 Geneva I, *supra* note 11, art. 3; Geneva II, *supra* note 12, art. 3; Geneva III, *supra* note 13, art. 3; Geneva IV, *supra* note 14, art. 3.

132 *Ibid.* Over time, the importance of Common Article 3 in the mosaic of humanitarian protections evolved substantially. In 1986, the International Court of Justice characterized this article as the "minimum yardstick" of protection in armed conflicts. *See* Military and Paramilitary Activities in and Against Nicaragua (Nicar. v. U.S.), 1986 I.C.J. 14, 104 (June 27, 1984). Then, in 1996 in response to the brutal conflict in the Balkans following the collapse of Yugoslavia, Common Article 3 emerged as a critical source of international criminal responsibility in noninternational armed conflicts. *See* Prosecutor v. Tadic, Case No. IT-94-1-AR72, Appeal on Jurisdiction (Oct. 2, 1995), at par. 70, *reprinted in* 35 I.L.M. 32 (1996). The United States also continuously emphasized the importance of respect for this critical humanitarian shield of protection, including it within the jurisdiction of the federal War Crimes Act (War Crimes Act of 1996, 18 U.S.C. § 2441 (1996)), and insisting that the scope of application of the 1977 Additional Protocol II (a treaty developed to supplement the law applicable to noninternational armed conflicts) apply as broadly as Common Article 3 applies (rejecting a more restrictive scope of application provision included in the Protocol).

"fighters" who are *hors de combat* (incapable of continued participation in hostilities) due to wounds, sickness, or capture.[133] Common Article 3 also enumerated a nonexclusive list of treatment that was especially prohibited, including murder, torture, cruel, inhuman, or degrading treatment, collective punishment, and failing to collect and care for the wounded and sick.[134] Also included on this list of enumerated prohibitions was "the passing of sentences and the carrying out of executions without previous judgment pronounced by a regularly constituted court affording all the judicial guarantees which are recognized as indispensable by civilized peoples."[135]

Based on Common Article 3's initial humanitarian focus, it was widely assumed that the term "noninternational armed conflict" was a synonym for internal armed conflict. As a result, a binary test of Geneva Convention applicability evolved: the full corpus of the four Conventions applied only during international (inter-state) armed conflicts, and the much more limited humane treatment rule applied during internal armed conflicts.[136] While the meaning of armed conflict was the subject of considerable debate prior to September 11, 2001, this internal versus international typology was not.

When the United States initiated its military response to the terrorist attacks of September 11, 2001, this binary paradigm became a source of major policy and legal controversy. What triggered this controversy was the widely condemned U.S. decision to invoke the expansive legal authorities of armed conflict[137] (most notably the authority to kill as a measure of first resort and to detain without trial) while disavowing any international humanitarian limits on that power. Thus the applicability of Common Article 3 became the focus of this storm.[138] This resulted from a two-part U.S. interpretation of the conflict and applicable law: first, because al Qaeda was not a state, the armed conflict was not "international" within the meaning of the Geneva Conventions, and the full corpus of the Geneva Conventions were not

133 Geneva I art. 3; Geneva II art. 3; Geneva III art. 3; Geneva IV art. 3. 134 *Ibid.*

135 *Ibid.*

136 Sylvain Vite, *Typology of Armed Conflicts in International Humanitarian Law: Legal Concepts and Actual Situations*, 91 *Int'l Rev. of the Red Cross* 69 (2009) (No. 873); *see also* Geoffrey S. Corn, *Hamdan, Lebanon, and the Regulation of Armed Hostilities: The Need to Recognize a Hybrid Category of Armed Conflict*, 40 VAND. J. TRANSNAT'L L 295 (2006).

137 Military operations conducted against al Qaeda involved the use of powers clearly derived from the law of armed conflict: attack with deadly force as a measure of first resort, preventive detention of captured "enemy belligerents," and trial by military tribunal for violations of the laws and customs of war.

138 *Text of Order Signed by President Bush on Feb. 7, 2002, outlining treatment of al-Qaida and Taliban detainees*, LawofWar.org, www.lawofwar.org/Bush_torture_memo.htm [hereinafter *Text of Order*].

triggered; second, because the armed conflict was not "internal," it failed to trigger Common Article 3.[139] Thus, prior to the Supreme Court's *Hamdan* decision, the articulated U.S. policy resulted in a critical protective gap for captured enemy belligerents who could not claim even the minimum protections of the Geneva Conventions encompassed in Common Article 3.[140]

Salim Hamdan challenged the legality of his trial by military commission by asserting, *inter alia*, that the procedures adopted for the military commission violated Common Article 3's humane treatment obligation.[141] The government responded by asserting that Common Article 3 did not apply to the armed conflict in which Hamdan was captured, and that even if it did, the procedures did not violate the prohibition against use of tribunals that fail to provide minimally acceptable process.[142] Each of these issues necessitated interpretation of Common Article 3: first, to resolve its field of application and, second, its substantive meaning.

The Supreme Court rejected the government's arguments and ruled in Hamdan's favor.[143] First, it held that Common Article 3 applied in "contradistinction" to Common Article 2, which dictates the applicability of the full corpus of each Convention to international armed conflicts.[144] By interpreting Common Article 3 to apply to any armed conflict that did not qualify as

139 Jay S. Bybee, Memorandum for Alberto Gonzales, Counsel to the President, and William J. Haynes II, General Counsel of the DoD, Re: Application of Treaties and Laws to al Qaeda and Taliban Detainees (Jan. 22, 2002), available at www.washingtonpost.com/wp-srv/nation/documents/012202bybee.pdf.

140 *Text of Order, supra* note 138. 141 Hamdan, 548 U.S. at 567. 142 *Ibid.* at 568–9.

143 *Ibid.* at 567.

144 *Ibid.* at 630–1. It is true that the Court held that the law of war was statutorily "incorporated" to trials by military commission by operation of Article 21 of the UCMJ, the provision pursuant to which the military commission was convened (the Court concluded that Article 21 represented a congressional delegation of authority for the President to convene military commissions in accordance with the law of war). Whether this interpretation, like Quirin's interpretation before it (interpreting the Articles of War predecessor to Article 21) is accurate, is questionable. Article 21 does not indicate a delegation of authority, but instead recognition of what the President asserted was a preexisting authority inherent in the function of commander in chief. However, because the Court did treat Article 21 as a delegation of commission convening authority, it provided a statutory basis for application of the law of war to Hamdan's commission.

This did not, however, resolve the Common Article 3 applicability issue. Instead, it merely framed that issue as one of both statutory and treaty interpretation. The Article 21 interpretation established the obligation to comply with applicable law of war rules related to trial by military commission. However, whether Common Article 3's fair process rules were included within that obligation required a second level of analysis, namely whether Common Article 3 applied to noninternational armed conflicts of international (as opposed to internal) scope. It was this issue that produced the most significant treaty interpretation aspect of the holding, which was equally significant as a rebuke to the President's interpretation of the same.

international within the meaning of Common Article 2, the Court closed the conflict regulation gap created by the Bush Administration interpretation of these two articles. This "contradistinction" interpretation meant the struggle against al Qaeda, because it was treated by the government as an armed conflict, had to fall within the scope of Common Article 3 as "noninternational."[145] The *Hamdan* Court then held that the procedures adopted for trial by military commission did not comply with Common Article 3's prohibition against "the passing of sentences and the carrying out of executions without previous judgment pronounced by a regularly constituted court, affording all the judicial guarantees, which are recognized as indispensable by civilized peoples."[146] This was because the process at issue – excluding Hamdan from his trial on request of the government – was not permitted in a court-martial, the standard the Court used as the touchstone for process that complies with Common Article 3.[147]

Some observers considered this outcome consistent with the true meaning of Common Article 3, while others viewed it as an exercise in unjustified judicial activism.[148] Critics of the Court's interpretation focus on both the text of Common Article 3 and its drafting context, and suggest it was understood, at least in 1949, to impose an obligation between States and opposition forces operating within a state's territory, not between a State and a transnational nonstate group.[149] Indeed, this was the justification for the D.C. Circuit's rejection of Hamdan's invocation of Common Article 3, although it must be noted that this interpretation was widely criticized as inconsistent with the meaning of Common Article 3 as it had evolved. However, many have also argued that Common Article 3 has evolved substantially since its adoption, and that as a matter of customary international law it must apply to any armed conflict, even one between a state and a transnational nonstate group.[150] But

[145] *Ibid.* [146] *Ibid.* at 630.

[147] *Ibid.* at 624–5. Congress responded to the decision by enacting the Military Commission Act of 2006, *supra* note 97, which substantially enhanced the process for trial by military commission, with further enhancements in the 2009 MCA. *See* P.L. 111–84, 123 Stat. 2190, 2574 *amending* 10 U.S.C. 948a *et seq.* [hereinafter 2009 MCA]. In fact, with few (albeit significant) exceptions, that process today is virtually analogous to the court-martial trial process.

[148] Brian M. Christensen, *Extending Hamdan v. Rumsfeld to Combatant Status Review Tribunals*, 2007 *BYU L. Rev.* 1365 (2007); Marko Milanovic, *Lessons for human rights and humanitarian law in the war on terror: comparing Hamdan and the Israeli Targeted Killings case*, 89, no.866 Int'l Rev. Red Cross, 373, 375–81 (2007).

[149] *Ibid.*

[150] Geoffrey S. Corn, *Hamdan, Lebanon, and the Regulation of Armed Hostilities: The Need to Recognize a Hybrid Category of Armed Conflict*, 40 Vand. J. Transnat'l L 295, 347, 49 (2006). See generally Michael Lewis et. al., The War on Terror and the Laws of

the Court did not rely on customary international law to reach its holding. Instead, the result was based exclusively on treaty interpretation. Thus, even if the outcome is considered by many to have been a positive development in the regulation of hostilities, it remains susceptible to criticism by those who contend that Common Article 3 was never intended to extend to this type of conflict.[151]

The conclusion that the process created by President Bush for trial by military commission violated Common Article 3 is equally susceptible to criticism. There is no question that the Court correctly noted the divergence between military commission process and court-martial process, a divergence that provided an alternate statutory basis for ruling in Hamdan's favor through Article 21's incorporation of the Uniform Code of Military Justice.[152] However, it is questionable whether these deviations indicate a violation of the humane treatment mandate, at least as it was understood in 1955 when the United States ratified the 1949 Geneva Conventions. Indeed, as Justice Thomas noted in his dissent, for trial process to be so defective that it violates this aspect of Common Article 3, something much more akin to summary execution is required.[153]

Nonetheless, the Court's interpretation of Common Article 3 produced a profound consequence that extended well beyond military commissions: as a matter of treaty obligation, the United States was required ensure the humane treatment of captured al Qaeda operatives.[154] This was a genuine "beginning of the end" to the debate over the permissibility of utilizing harsh interrogation techniques on captured unprivileged belligerents. These

WAR: A MILITARY PERSPECTIVE (2009) [hereinafter LEWIS]; see also Rogier Bartels, *Timelines, Borderlines and Conflicts: The Historical Evolution of the Legal Divide Between International and Non-international Armed Conflicts*, 91 no. 873 INT'L REVIEW OF THE RED CROSS 35 (2009).

151 LEWIS, *supra* note 150.

152 Hamdan, 548 U.S. at 619–25.

153 *Ibid.* at 716–18 (Thomas, J., dissenting). It is almost certain that at the time of ratification, Common Article 3's fair trial mandate aligned more closely with Justice Thomas' view than that of the majority. Part of the motivation for including the fair trial provision in Article 3 was the then-recent experience of summary justice in brutal civil wars like the one in Spain. Furthermore, the process adopted for trial by military commission, while inconsistent with contemporary courts-martial process, was much more similar to the version of that process provided for in the 1950 UCMJ. Thus, in 1955 when the United States ratified the Conventions, it is unlikely that the post-2001 commission process would have been viewed as inherently "inhumane" in violation of Common Article 3 at the time of the 1955 ratification of the 1949 Conventions.

154 Donna Miles, *England Memo Underscores Policy on Humane Treatment of* Detainees, GlobalSecurity.org (July 11, 2006), www.globalsecurity.org/security/library/news/2006/07/sec-060711-afps01.htm.

detainees were, following the Court's interpretation of Common Article 3, protected by this baseline humanitarian shield against abusive treatment, protection that foreclosed any treatment that came even close to torture.[155]

Taken collectively, although limited in number, these cases illustrate the significant impact judicial treaty interpretation may have on the execution of military operations.

V IMPLEMENTING LEGISLATION

Few treaties ratified by the United States are completely self-executing. Instead, it is much more common that treaties, or provisions thereof, are non-self-executing, thus requiring implementing legislation to give the treaty obligation the full force and effect of law domestically.[156] The process of treaty implementation in turn implicates the U.S. dualist theory of international law.[157] Ultimately, because the Supremacy Clause assigned higher priority to a later in time statute over a previously ratified treaty,[158] subsequently enacted implementing legislation takes priority over the prior ratified treaty. As a result, such legislation controls judicial resolution of any issues arising under the treaty and implementing statute in U.S. courts, even if the statute-based resolution is perceived externally as inconsistent with the terms of the treaty. Accordingly, while implementing legislation in no way alters the international obligation of the nation imposed by a treaty, it may, in a very practical sense, modify the *domestic* effect of the treaty obligations.

Statutory implementation of the war crimes repression provision of the four 1949 Geneva Conventions provides an iconic example of this practical domestic modification of a treaty obligation. In the wake of World War II, individual responsibility for the violation of the laws and customs of war emerged as perhaps the single most important development in the law.[159] Although there had been previous efforts to hold individuals accountable for violations of this

155 See James A. Barkei, *Legislating Military Doctrine: Congressional Usurping of Executive Authority through Detainee Interrogations*, 193 MIL. L. REV. 97 (2007); *see also* Exec. Order No. 13491 Ensuring Lawful Interrogations, 3 CFR 13491 (2009).

156 Senate on Treaties, *supra* note 19, at 76.

157 *See* RESTATEMENT (THIRD) OF THE FOREIGN RELATIONS LAW OF THE UNITED STATES (AM. LAW INST. 1987).

158 Senate on Treaties, *supra* note 19, at 75.

159 Henry King, Jr., *The Modern Relevance of the Nuremberg Principles*, 17 B.C. THIRD WORLD *L.J.* 279, 280 (1997); Nikolai Fedorovich Christiakov, The Nuremberg Trial and International Law (George Ginsburgs & V.N. Kudriavtsev, Law in Eastern Europe series No. 42, 1990); George Eckhardt, *Nuremberg – Fifty Years: Accountability and Responsibility*, 65 *UMKC L.* REV. 1, 1 (1996).

law, these had been largely ineffective.[160] During the revision of the 1929 Geneva Conventions, the absence of any individual accountability provisions in these or other LOAC treaties was recognized as a contributing factor to this ineffectiveness.[161]

In response, the drafters of the 1949 Conventions included penal provisions within each of the four treaties.[162] These provisions imposed an obligation on state parties to hold individuals criminally accountable for violating certain treaty obligations. More significantly, the Conventions imposed a mandatory prosecution obligation based on the concept of universal jurisdiction: all states parties accepted a responsibility to implement these penal provisions, even for violators with no nationality or territorial connection to the state.[163]

The Convention drafters clearly recognized that effective implementation of a penal sanction provision would require prosecution at the national rather than international level. Indeed, contrary to popular belief, the vast majority of post–World War II war crimes prosecutions were conducted by states, and although most prominent, the international military tribunals at Nuremberg and Tokyo represented only a small fraction of these prosecutions.[164] Accordingly, the drafters required that state parties "enact

160 Solis, *supra* note 51, 75–6.

161 Geneva III Commentary, *supra* note 29, art. 129–31; *see also* Marko Divac Oberg, *The absorption of grave breaches into war crimes law*, 91, no. 873 Int'l Review of the Red Cross, 163 (2009).

162 Geneva I, *supra* note 11, art. 49–51; Geneva II, *supra* note 12, art. 50–2; Geneva III, *supra* note 13, art. 129–31; Geneva IV, *supra* note 14, art. 146–8.

163 Geneva III, *supra* note 13 art. 129–31 ("The High Contracting Parties undertake to enact any legislation necessary to provide effective penal sanctions for persons committing, or ordering to be committed, any of the grave breaches of the present Convention defined in the following Article"). According to the ICRC Commentary:

> It is desirable that States which have ratified the Convention or acceded to it should take without delay the necessary steps to fulfill their obligations under Article 129 . This task of implementing the Conventions in penal matters is certainly a complex one and will often require long and thorough study. For that reason, the International Committee, when the four Geneva Conventions of 1949 were adopted, expressed the wish to draw up a model law on which the national legislation in various countries could be based and which would also have the advantage of creating a certain uniformity of legislation.

Geneva III Commentary, *supra* note 29, art. 129–31 (citations omitted). this obligation did not extend to all Convention articles. Instead, the drafters identified a limited number of articles imposing the most fundamental obligations related to the protection of war victims. Only violation of these articles – the most egregious violations – triggered the penal obligation. Such violations were designated as "grave breaches." Geneva I, art. 49; Geneva II, art. 50; Geneva III, art. 129; Geneva IV, art. 146. Other violations could provide the basis for penal sanction, but unlike grave breaches, state parties did not accept an *obligation* to enforce penal sanctions to repress such violations.

164 Solis, *supra* note 51, chapter 8.

legislation" to implement the mandatory penal response triggered by grave breaches. Article 129 of the Geneva Convention Relative to the Treatment of Prisoners of War (GPW) illustrates this methodology:

> The High Contracting Parties undertake to enact any legislation necessary to provide effective penal sanctions for persons committing, or ordering to be committed, any of the grave breaches of the present Convention defined in the following Article [Article 130 lists violations qualifying as grave breaches].
>
> Each High Contracting Party shall be under the obligation to search for persons alleged to have committed, or to have ordered to be committed, such grave breaches, and shall bring such persons, regardless of their nationality, before its own courts. It may also, if it prefers, and in accordance with the provisions of its own legislation, hand such persons over for trial to another High Contracting Party concerned, provided such High Contracting Party has made out a prima facie case.[165]

In contrast, other violations of the Conventions trigger a repression obligation, which differs from the mandatory prosecute or extradite obligation.[166]

Article 129 and its analogous versions in the other three Geneva Conventions represent perhaps as clear an example of a non-self-executing treaty provision imaginable. When the United States ratified the Conventions in 1955, the nation assumed the obligation to "implement this contract" by enacting the legislation called for by the treaty. Failure to do so would result in an unfulfilled treaty obligation.[167]

Article 129 establishes the expectation that states would enact domestic penal legislation criminalizing grave breaches of the Conventions. Alternatively, it permits a state party to meet its treaty obligation by extraditing an individual suspected of a grave breach to another state willing to prosecute.

165 Geneva III, *supra* note 13, art. 129.

166 *Ibid.* ("Each High Contracting Party shall take measures necessary for the suppression of all acts contrary to the provisions of the present Convention other than the grave breaches defined in the following Article").

167 In fact this requirement was recognized by the Senate in its consideration of the Geneva Convention, although the Senate concluded both that "the obligations imposed upon the United States by the 'grave breaches' provisions are such as can be met by existing legislation enacted by the Federal government within its constitutional powers" and that a "review of that legislation reveals that no further measures are needed to provide effective penal sanctions or procedures for those violations of the conventions." Administration witnesses also stated that there was not "intended that there be any enlargement of existing Federal power, which it was felt was already adequate for that purpose... and that the acts enumerated in [the grave breach provision] were already condemned by Federal and State criminal law." Senate GC Exec. Rpt. No. 9, *supra* note 28, at 27.

Known accordingly as the "prosecute or extradite" rule,[168] the extradition option might have offered the United States a case-by-case opportunity to avoid the perception that it failed to properly implement its Article 129 obligation. However, Congress did not act to implement the grave breach obligation by enacting domestic war crimes legislation until 1996. This was most likely based on the Senate's initial 1955 conclusion that acts condemned in the grave breach provisions were "already condemned by Federal and State criminal law."[169]

168 Int'l & Operational Law Dep't, The Judge Advocate General's Legal Center & School, The Law of War Deskbook 186 (2011).

169 Senate GC Exec. Rpt. No. 9, *supra* note 28. Interestingly, if the United States could prosecute grave breaches committed by individuals other than those subject to the Uniform Code of Military Justice (such as members of the armed forces), it was not Federal or State criminal laws that provided that jurisdiction. Instead, the UCMJ may have provided such jurisdiction. This is because universal jurisdiction for grave breaches may have been viable pursuant to a somewhat obscure provision of the UCMJ, Article 18. This article provides jurisdiction for "any person" (not necessarily a member of the armed forces or some other person "subject to the Code") who, by the law of war, is subject to trial by military tribunal – an apparent extension of General Court-Martial jurisdiction to any person who commits war crime. However, this provision was neither enacted to implement the Geneva Convention penal provisions, nor was it understood as providing universal jurisdiction at the time of ratification or any time thereafter.

Indeed, the false assumption that the UCMJ *did not* provide for such expansive jurisdiction was a major factor that finally led Congress to enact the War Crimes Act. *See generally* Major Jan E. Aldykiewicz & Major Geoffrey S. Corn, *Authority to Court-Martial Non-U.S. Military Personnel for Serious Violations of International Humanitarian Law Committed During Internal Armed Conflicts*, 167 Mil. L. Rev. 74, 91–101 (2001). Furthermore, at the time of the War Crimes Act was adopted, Article 18 had never been invoked to try anyone for war crimes not connected to an armed conflict with the United States, and whether such an individual could be subject to trial by a military court would itself raise complex constitutional questions. *See* Reid v. Covert, 354 U.S. 1 (1957). One thing is clear: even considering the UCMJ, there was no U.S. law that explicitly implemented the universal jurisdiction obligation imposed by the Conventions. *See War Crimes Act of 1995: Hearing on H.R. 2587 Before the Subcommittee on Immigration and Claims of the Committee on the Judiciary House of Representatives*, 104th Cong. (1996).

Congress did, however, correctly conclude that there was simply no basis to prosecute individuals suspected of committing grave breaches in Federal Court. The forum-enabling effect of the WCA was highlighted by Senator Helms, who perhaps came closest to accurately stating the real need for the War Crimes Act of 1996 when he said:

> Many have not realized that the U.S. cannot prosecute, in Federal Court, the perpetrators of some war crimes against American servicemen and nationals. Currently, if the United States were to find a war criminal within our borders – for example, one who had murdered an American POW – the only option would be to deport or extradite the criminal or to try him or her before an international war crimes tribunal or military commission. Alone, these options are not enough to insure that justice is done.142 Cong. Rec. S9648 (daily ed. August 2, 1996).

Four decades after the United States ratified the Geneva Conventions, Congress acted to fulfill its treaty obligation by enacting The War Crimes Act of 1996.[170] In doing so, Congress chose not to enact a universal jurisdiction war crimes statute that fully implemented the grave breach provision. Instead, the War Crimes Act provides federal criminal jurisdiction only when the grave breaches fall within the objective or subjective nationality principles of international jurisdiction: those circumstances where "the person committing such war crime or the victim of such war crime is a member of the Armed Forces of the United States or a national of the United States."[171] Thus, the act did not extend to foreign nationals committing grave breaches against non-nationals of the United States. This nationality requirement was inconsistent with the recommendations of both the State Department[172] and Department of Defense,[173] which both sought legislation that would fully implement U.S. treaty obligation by establishing universal jurisdiction for grave breaches.[174]

These jurisdictional limitations indicate that Congress chose not to *fully* implement the penal obligations accepted by the United States when it ratified the 1949 Geneva Conventions. The statute does not provide jurisdiction enabling the United States to bring "persons alleged to have committed, or to have ordered to be committed, such grave breaches . . . regardless of their

170 18 U.S.C.S. § 2441 (LexisNexis 2000). This law may have actually been enacted based on the misunderstanding that only members of the U.S. armed forces were subject to war crimes jurisdiction pursuant to the UCMJ, although this misunderstanding was actually pragmatically accurate.

171 *Ibid.*

172 H. Rep. No. 104–698, at 13 (1996), *reprinted in* 1996 U.S.C.C.A.N. 2166, 2178.

173 *Ibid.* at 2177–78:

> We believe . . . that the jurisdictional provisions should be broadened from the current focus on the nationality of the victims of war crimes. Specifically, we suggest adding two additional jurisdictional bases: (1) where the perpetrator of a war crimes is a United States national (including a member of the Armed Forces); and (2) where the perpetrator is found in the United States without regard to the nationality of the perpetrator or victim. *Ibid.* at 13 (statement by Judith Miller, General Counsel of the U.S. Department Defense, May 17, 1996, reference H.R. 2587, the precursor to H.R. 3680 (The War Crimes Act of 1996). The Department of Defense was focusing on broader jurisdiction than was proposed on H.R. 2587 or than was eventually passed in H.R. 3680. Additionally, the current version of the War Crimes Act of 1996 as amended in 1997, falls short of the expansive jurisdiction recommended by the Department of Defense.

174 The House Judiciary Committee, in addressing universal jurisdiction, stated:

> [E]xpansion of H.R. 3680 to include universal jurisdiction would be unwise at present. Domestic prosecution based on universal jurisdiction could draw the United States into conflicts in which this country has no place and where our national interests are slight.

H. Rep. No. 104–698, at 8 (1996), *reprinted in* 1996 U.S.C.C.A.N. 2166, 2173.

nationality, before its own courts."[175] Congressional concern that implementing the universal jurisdiction obligation might encourage other states to assert criminal jurisdiction over U.S. military personnel when the state lacked any nationality or territorial link to the alleged grave breach likely motivated this decision.

Congress took a step back from even this limited implementation when it amended the War Crimes Act in 2006. This amendment was incorporated into the Military Commission Act, and restricted the definition of a criminal violation of Common Article 3 subject to punishment pursuant to the War Crimes Act. This restrictive definition was linked to the scope of criminal jurisdiction vested in the military commissions established pursuant to the Act, allowing prosecution of alien enemy belligerents only for what the statute enumerates as "grave breaches" of Common Article 3 (exempting from the scope of criminal liability any violation that does not rise to that level as defined by the statute). However, this amendment to the War Crimes Act was almost certainly motivated by an effort to shield individuals who authorized and engaged in harsh interrogation techniques prior to the Supreme Court's decision in *Hamdan* from criminal liability under the statute, and not by a desire to synchronize commission jurisdiction with War Crimes Act jurisdiction. Accordingly, it was and remains the subject of criticism.

From a treaty implementation perspective, it does seem unfortunate that Congress chose to step back from the broad scope of federal criminal accountability for Common Article 3 violations previously established by the War Crimes Act. It is true that Common Article 3 falls outside the scope of the Conventions "prosecute or extradite" obligation because, contrary to Congressional declaration, a Common Article 3 violation cannot qualify as a grave breach within the meaning of the Conventions.[176] Accordingly, it is difficult to argue that limiting the scope of criminal liability for a violation is inconsistent with the express obligation established by the Conventions. Nonetheless, the apparent motivation for this restriction justifies concern that it is, at a minimum, inconsistent with the object and purpose of these vitally important treaties.

[175] Geneva I, *supra* note 11, art. 49; Geneva II, *supra* note 12, art. 50; Geneva III, *supra* note 13, art. 129; Geneva IV, *supra* note 14, art. 146.

[176] The "grave breach" provisions of each of the four Geneva Conventions are codified in articles that become applicable only during an international armed conflict as defined by common article 2 of the four Conventions. Accordingly, any conflict that falls within the scope of common article 3 will fail to trigger application of these grave breach provisions. SOLIS, *supra* note 51, at 94.

Regardless of the motivation, the War Crimes Act is a quintessential illustration of two important aspects of treaty practice in U.S. law: first, that accepting a treaty obligation by ratification is no guarantee of a prompt domestic execution of that obligation; and second, that even when Congress executes treaty obligations by statute, it remains Congressional prerogative to effectively qualify the legal impact of those treaties within the United States with a latter in time domestic law.[177]

VI FEDERALISM AND THE TREATY POWER: TESTING THE LIMITS

The Constitution clearly reposes the treaty power in the two political branches[178] and makes treaties the supreme law of the land.[179] What limits exist to cabin this power have been the subject of debate since the drafting of our Constitution. In addition to limits to the treaty power generally recognized as imposed by the Bill of Rights and other specific constitutional protections,[180] the questions of whether and if so to what extent the treat power is restrained by a subject matter limitation or the federalist structure of our government by operation of the Tenth Amendment remains unclear.

Debates over the subject matter limitations of the treaty power have existed since our founding, and continue to this day.[181] At its inception, the treaty

177 The Military Commission Act of 2006 again amended the War Crimes Act. Congress, in an apparent effort to align WCA jurisdiction with that of the military commission, established a distinction between those violations of Common Article 3 considered minor and those it considered serious. Accordingly, the WCA now criminalizes only what the amendment characterized as 'grave' breaches of Common Article 3 (an odd word choice, as grave breaches are not, as a matter of law, internationally cognizable in the context of a noninternational armed conflict). *See* P.L. 109–366, 120 Stat. 2600, *codified at* 10 U.S.C. 948a, at §6 (b).

178 U.S. CONST. art. II, § 2, cl.2 and art. I, § 8, cl.18.

179 U.S. CONST., art. VI, § 2.

180 "It is now settled, however that treaties are subject to the constitutional limitations that apply to all exercise of federal power, principally the prohibitions of the Bill of Rights." HENKIN, *supra* note 92, at 185. For example a treaty could not cede a State's territory without its consent (Art. IV., sec. 3, cl. 1) or modify the republican form of state government (Art. IV., sec. 4). *See also* Senate on Treaties, *supra* note 19, at 66 ("It seems clear from the Court's pronouncement in Geofroy v. Riggs that the treaty power is indeed a broad one, extending to 'any matter which is properly the subject of negotiation with a foreign country.' However, it is equally apparent that treaties, like Federal statutes, are subject to the overriding requirements of the Constitution").

181 In his later years, Thomas Jefferson construed the treaty power narrowly believing it limited to those subjects traditionally regulated by treaties between sovereign states and excluding those rights normally reserved to the states and further to exclude those subjects normally requiring participation by the House of Representatives. This narrow view, apart from rendering the treaty power a functional nullity, is not supported by the drafting history of the Constitution's

power was generally understood as a means to regulate the U.S. intercourse with foreign nations, with its exercise to be consistent with those external aims. As stated by James Madison in the Federalist No. 45, the treaty power, as a distinctly federal power, was to be exercised "principally on external objects, as war, peace, negotiation, and foreign commerce."[182] Yet, Madison also emphasized that precise definition of the power was undesirable because the treaty power was intended to be flexible to address future contingencies unknown to the drafters.[183]

This uncertainty was in the view of many resolved by *Missouri v. Holland*,[184] which seemed to foreclose any federalism argument limiting Congressional implementation of a valid treaty. In that case the Supreme Court rejected a Tenth Amendment challenge to legislation implementing the 1916 U.S./Canadian Migratory Bird Treaty. Prior to the treaty, the Court had struck down similar legislation as violating the Tenth Amendment.[185] In a concise opinion, Justice Holmes rejected the position that the Treaty and its implementing legislation were void as "an interference with the rights reserved to the states."[186] Echoing back to Madison's prescient description of the necessity of flexibility in the treaty power, Justice Holmes stated, "when we are dealing with words that also are a constituent act, like the Constitution of the United States, we must realize that they have called into life a being the development of which could not have been foreseen completely by the most gifted of its begetters."

treaty provisions during the 1787 Constitutional Convention, nor by historical practice following its ratification. *See* Senate on Treaties, *supra* note 19, at 27–9 (2001); *see also* Geoffrey Corn and Dru Brenner-Beck, *Exploring Treaty Practice Through a Military Lens*, 38 HARV. J.L. & PUB. POL'Y 547, 608–10 (2015); United States v. Bond, 681 F.3d 149, 157–8 (3d Cir. 2012) [hereinafter Bond II]; Golove & Hulsebosch, *supra* note 20; Jean Galbraith, *Congress's Treaty Implementing Power in Historical Practice*, available at http://papers.ssrn.com/sol3/papers.cfm?abstract_id=2275355; Erwin Chemerinsky, *Constitutional Law: Principles and Policies* 287 (4th ed. 2011); LOUIS HENKIN, FOREIGN AFFAIRS AND THE U.S. CONSTITUTION 191 (2nd ed. 1996); Brief of Amici Curiae Professors David M. Golove, Martin S. Lederman, and John Mikhail in Support of Respondent, Bond v. United States, 2013 WL 4737189, No. 12–158 (Aug. 16, 2013); EDWARD S. CORWIN, NATIONAL SUPREMACY, TREATY POWER, VS. STATE POWER, Forgotten Books 2012 (1913) [hereinafter NATIONAL SUPREMACY]; *contra* Curtis A. Bradley, *The Treaty Power and American Federalism*, 97 MICH. L. REV. 390, 395 (1998); Nicholas Quinn Rosenkranz, *Executing the Treaty Power*, 118 HARV. L. REV. 1867, 1875 (2005).

182 THE FEDERALIST NO. 45, at 289 (James Madison) (Clinton Rossiter, ed. 2003); *see* United States V. Bond, 681 F.3d 149, 160 n.11 (3d Cir. 2012).

183 Bond, 681 F.3d at 160.

184 Missouri v. Holland, 252 U.S. 416, 432 (1920). Tellingly, Congress itself sees Missouri v. Holland as dispositive of the issue of whether they have authority to legislate in support of a ratified treaty. *See* Senate on Treaties, *supra* note 19, at 66–7.

185 *Ibid.* 186 *Ibid.*

Evaluating the treaty power, the Court held, "[i]t is obvious that there may be matters of the sharpest exigency for the national well being that an act of Congress could not deal with but that a treaty followed by such an act could."[187] Recognizing that qualifications to the treaty-making power "must be ascertained in a different way,"[188] the Court determined first that the provision did not contravene any prohibitory language in the Constitution. The Court then queried further, "[t]he only question is whether it is forbidden by some invisible radiation from the general terms of the Tenth Amendment.[189] For Justice Holmes, that question could only be answered by considering what "this country has become in deciding what that amendment has reserved."[190] In upholding the Act, Holmes concluded, "[n]o doubt the great body of private relations usually fall within the control of the State, but a treaty may override its power."[191] What "invisible radiations"[192] exist to circumscribe the federal treaty power remains an open question.

Although federalism constraints on national power have not recently produced any meaningful limits on the treaty power as it relates to wartime authority, the Supreme Court's revival of federalism concerns in Commerce Clause and other cases may augur future federalism based restrictions on treaty implementation.[193] The recent case of *Bond v. United States*[194] indicates that even treaties intended to regulate armed hostilities may implicate core federalism concerns. *Bond* also indicates that even if federalism considerations have no impact on the power of the nation to bind itself to LOAC obligations, they may affect the implementation of those agreements domestically. What is certainly clear from the Court's *Bond* decision is that any such federalism concern will arise only if Congress clearly indicates its intent to intrude upon areas normally reserved to state power through a statute implementing a treaty. Absent such a clear statement, the Court will presume no such intrusion was intended, a presumption seemingly logical in relation to LOAC treaty implementation, as these treaties rarely address issues that implicate state authority.[195]

[187] *Ibid.* at 433. [188] *Ibid.* [189] *Ibid.* at 383–4, 434.

[190] *Ibid.* at 384, 434. *See also* David M. Golove, *Treaty Making and the Nation: The Historical Foundations of the Nationalist Conception of the Treaty Power*, 98 MICH. L. REV. 1075, 1258–65 (2000) (showing that Justice Holmes was both familiar with Corwin's work, NATIONAL SUPREMACY, TREATY POWER V. STATE POWER, and also paralleled its structure and analysis in the Missouri v. Holland decision, and concluding that the Civil War had resolved long-standing States' rights arguments in favor of national supremacy).

[191] *Ibid.* [192] Holland, 252 U.S. at 434. [193] *See* Bond, 681 F.3d at 158 n. 10.

[194] *See ibid.* at 160, 165 n.18; Bond v. United States, 134 S. Ct. 2077 (2014).

[195] In United States v. Bond, Carol-Anne Bond contested her prosecution in federal district court for use and possession of a chemical weapon in violation of the Chemical Weapons

A *The "Curious Case" of Ms. Bond and the Chemical Weapons Convention*

The two forays of Ms. Bond's appeal of her conviction to the Supreme Court resulted in two significant holdings. First, resolving a circuit split on the issue, the Supreme Court held that Ms. Bond had standing to raise the Tenth Amendment challenge to the treaty implementing legislation under which she was prosecuted.[196] In so doing, the Supreme Court explained:

> [t]he Framers concluded that allocation of powers between the National Government and the States enhances freedom, first by protecting the integrity of the governments themselves, and second by protecting the people, from whom all governmental powers are derived. [Because] federalism secures to citizens the liberties that derive from the diffusion of sovereign power, ... [f]ederalism also protects the liberty of all persons within a State by ensuring that laws enacted in excess of delegated governmental power cannot direct or control their actions ... Federalism secures the freedom of the individual.[197]

Thus, after the first *Bond* decision by the Supreme Court, persons injured by the application of treaty provisions or treaty-implementing legislation would have standing "to challenge a law as enacted in contravention of constitutional principles of federalism."[198]

On remand from the Supreme Court, the Third Circuit determined that under *Missouri v. Holland*'s "valid treaty equals valid implementing legislation" holding,[199] the Tenth Amendment posed no barrier to Bond's

Convention Implementation Act of 1998 and its associated criminal provisions. The permissible reach of this LOAC treaty was the central issue in this case, and it highlights the issues with which a court must grapple when faced with a federalism challenge to the Constitution's Treaty powers. The facts of Bond's case certainly exemplify the concern over the federal criminalization of conduct, which would otherwise have been considered local and left to the ministration of the State of Pennsylvania, involving a campaign of harassment using toxic chemicals by Ms. Bond against her romantic rival. Bond contested her ultimate federal prosecution for use of a chemical weapon, claiming it violated the principles of federalism embodied in the Tenth Amendment. See United States v. Bond, 581 F.3d 128, 132 (3d Cir. 2009).

196 Bond v. United States, 131 S. Ct. 2355, 2364 (2011) (holding that Bond had standing to raise a federalism challenge to the legislation, even absent the involvement of a state or state official).

197 *Ibid.* at 2364, 2407.

198 *Ibid.* at 2364–65 (citing United States v. Lara, 541 U.S. 193, 201 (2004), quoting Holland, 252 U.S. at 433).

199 Bond, 681 F.3d at 164, n. 18. The Court also rejected amici positions that the power under the Necessary and Proper clause regarding the Treaty Power was limited solely to the power to make treaties, not to implement treaties once they were agreed upon, determining the argument was foreclosed by Missouri v. Holland. Bond, 681 F.3d at 157, n. 9.

prosecution. Although acknowledging the various views on the appropriate scope of the subject matter of the treaty power,[200] the Third Circuit held that both that the CWC "falls comfortably within the Treaty power's traditional subject matter limitation,"[201] and that its Implementation Act was rationally related to the treaty.[202] Nevertheless, once again the Supreme Court granted certiorari to determine the merits of Bond's federalism challenge to legislation based on the CWC.

Despite anticipation (and extensive briefing from amici) that the *Bond* case would finally address the substance of the "invisible radiations" from the Tenth Amendment that Justice Holmes derided, provide guidance on any subject matter limitations to the Treaty Power, or address the scope of Congress's ability to legislate to implement a treaty, the Court instead reversed Bond's chemical weapons convictions, not on a constitutional basis, but instead on a statutory grounds, its analysis of § 229 of the CWC Act.[203] Avoiding the constitutional issue, the Court split the implementing legislation from its authorizing treaty: "we have no need to interpret the scope of the Convention in this case. Bond was prosecuted under section 229—and the statute, unlike the Convention—must be read consistent with the principles of federalism inherent in our constitutional structure."[204]

Analyzing the statute, the Court discovered an ambiguity in § 229 that arose from its context, created by the broad reach of § 229's definition of a "chemical weapon" and which existed solely because of § 229's broad potential impact on the traditional allocation of law enforcement between the Federal government and the States. This ambiguity led the Court majority to implement a "clear statement" rule, requiring Congress to clearly state its intent when drastically altering the traditional balance between State and Federal prerogatives when legislating to implement a treaty. Absent such a clear statement, purely local crimes were not reachable, at least in "this curious case,"[205] where

[200] Bond, 681 F.3d at 156–9 (discussing scholars conflicting work on the origin, scope, and historical practice of the Treaty Clause). The Third Circuit also rejected, as foreclosed *by Holland*, arguments that the Necessary and Proper clause in connection to the Treaty clause only authorized Congress to enact laws to enable the President to make treaties, not to implement that provisions of those completed treaties. *See* Bond, 681 F.3d at 157, n. 9. Justice Scalia, in his concurrence in Bond v. United States, adopted this argument, but in so doing, neglected the historical experience of the use of the Necessary and Proper Clause to enact legislation implementing treaty provisions. *Compare* Bond, 134 S.Ct. 2102 (Scalia, J. concurring), *with* Jean Galbraith, *Congress's Treaty Implementing Power in Historical Practice*, available at http://papers.ssrn.com/sol3/papers.cfm?abstract_id=2275355; Brief of Amici Curiae Professors David M. Golove, Martin S. Lederman, and John Mikhail in Support of Respondent, Bond v. United States, 2013 WL 4737189), No. 12–158 (Aug. 16, 2013).

[201] Bond, 681 F.3d at 165. [202] *Ibid.* [203] Bond, 134 S. Ct. at 2087–90.

[204] *Ibid.* at 2088. [205] *Ibid.*

there was no need for such drastic alterations with a Treaty that was instead focused on chemical warfare and terrorism. Thus, because Congress did not clearly state an intent to reach these "purely local crimes" in the CWC Implementation Act, Bond could not be prosecuted under that statute for her purely local assault.[206]

B Consequences of Bond

It is noteworthy what the *Bond* Court did not do: it made no attempt to analyze either the object or purpose of the CWC or its implementing legislation, avoiding the traditional tools of treaty interpretation altogether. It also did not address how federalism concerns are to be resolved with self-executing treaties, although it did imply that a different rule would apply.[207] As noted above, the Senate explicitly labeled the CWC non-self-executing, and its implementing legislation was drafted to accommodate other constitutional concerns such as the Fourth Amendment restrictions on searches. Federalism limits, however, were not seen as a relevant constraint after *Missouri v. Holland*,[208] and unsurprisingly Congress did not make any statement, let alone a clear one, on the federalism effect of the comprehensive CWC Implementation Act. In requiring Congress to make a clear statement in its treaty-implementing legislation, the Court also did not discuss how such a rule would apply when a self-executing treaty affected the traditional balance between the Federal and State governments.

This concern is far from illusory. A much more direct and potentially disruptive effect on the balance between federal and state authorities in our

206 Justices Scalia, Thomas, and Alito disagreed that there was any ambiguity in the statute, concluding that the language of § 229 was clear, and unambiguously reached Bond's local conduct. Bond, 134 S. Ct. at 2094–7. All three justices, therefore, wrote of their views of the Treaty power, with Justice Scalia adopting the most restrictive view. For Justice Scalia, Congress only had power under the Necessary and Proper clause to act to assist the President in "making" the Treaty. Accordingly, Congress had to rely on a separate Article 1 power in order to legislate to implement a treaty. Bond, 134 S. Ct. at 2098–9 (Scalia J. concurring in the judgment). It is worth noting that this theory was first formulated by George Nicholas in the State ratifying conventions in contrast to the views of Madison, Randolph, or Corbin. *See* Corwin, *supra* note 181, at 73 (citing Elliot, "Debates" (1836) III, 463–64). This view was not adopted nor subsequently followed in practice. *See ibid.* at 73 and Chapter 9.

207 Bond, 134 S.Ct. at 2088 ("[W]e have no need to interpret the scope of the Convention in this case. Bond was prosecuted under section 229 – and the statute, unlike the Convention, must be read consistent with the principles of federalism inherent in our constitutional structure").

208 *See, e.g.*, Senate on Treaties, *supra* note 19, at 67.

constitutional structure is produced by a different category of treaty related to military affairs: status of forces agreements (SOFAs). In 1953, shortly before ratifying the 1949 Geneva Conventions, the United States ratified the NATO SOFA.[209] This was only SOFA entered into as a treaty, as opposed to the much more common use of executive agreements to establish status of forces relationships. A core provision of the NATO SOFA is Article VII, addressing the allocation of criminal jurisdiction between the receiving and sending states. Article VII grants the sending (foreign) state primary criminal jurisdiction for official acts or for criminal acts between members of the sending force or their accompanying family members.[210]

Because the numbers of foreign soldiers present in the United States are relatively few in comparison to the numbers of U.S. soldiers overseas,

209 SOFAs address the legal status of military forces present in a foreign country with the consent of the receiving state, and in particular, "how the domestic laws of the foreign jurisdiction apply to U.S. personnel. US Congressional Research Service, Status of Forces Agreement (SOFA): What Is It, and How Has It Been Utilized? (RL34531; Mar. 15, 2012), by R. Chuck Mason, 1 n. 2 (depending on the terms of each SOFA agreement, "U.S. personnel can include members of the armed forces, DoD civilian employees, their dependent family members, and in some cases U.S. contractors accompanying the force) [hereinafter CRS SOFA Report]; available at www.fas.org/sgp/crs/natsec/RL34531.pdf. When foreign forces are present in the U.S., a SOFA addresses the applicability of U.S. federal and state law to those forces. The most common and central issue addressed in SOFAs is the delineation of criminal jurisdiction over a soldier. SOFAs typically use the term "member of the force" and "member of the civilian component" and "their dependents" rather than terms such as soldier or sailor. In addition to criminal jurisdiction, SOFAs also address claims and civil liability, force protection and use of deadly force to include authorization on carrying weapons, entry and exit requirements, taxation, customs and duties, vehicle registration/insurance/drivers' licensing, the authorization to wear military uniforms, and use of the electromagnetic spectrum for communications or other military operations – issues that also implicate federal-state divisions of authority *See* Int'l & Operational Law Dep't, The Judge Advocate General's Legal Center & School, U.S. Army, JA 422, Operational Law Handbook 122–4 (2012) [hereinafter 2012 Operational Law Handbook]; available at www.loc.gov/rr/frd/Military_Law/pdf/operational-law-handbook_2012.pdf.

210 Article VII of the NATO SOFA grants exclusive criminal jurisdiction where only the laws of one state are broken; in all other cases the NATO SOFA grants concurrent jurisdiction to both the sending and receiving state. In other words, if a service-member covered by the SOFA commits an act that violates the law of only one nation state, that state has exclusive jurisdiction. But in the much more common situation where the conduct violates the laws of both the sending and receiving state, jurisdiction is concurrent. Within these areas of concurrent jurisdiction, the SOFA allocates the primary right to exercise jurisdiction to the sending state for acts or omissions arising from the performance of official duties (for example, purely military offenses such as sleeping on guard duty or dereliction of duty, or espionage against the home country) or for *inter se* cases where "both the accused and the victim are members of the sending state." The receiving state is granted primary jurisdiction in all other cases. In cases of concurrent jurisdiction, either state may cede their right of primary jurisdiction to the other. *See* NATO SOFA Treaty, art. VII; 4 U.S.T. 1792; T.I.A.S. 2846; 199 U.N.T.S. 67.

the effect of these agreements on the federal-state division of power has been infrequently experienced and even more infrequently litigated.[211] Nevertheless, because of the criminal jurisdiction provisions of the NATO SOFA, the potential interference with a State's exercise of criminal jurisdiction over foreign soldiers and their families present in its territory is far-reaching and significant. The Senate provided advice and consent to the NATO SOFA in 1953 and it was then ratified by the United States The treaty, to include the criminal jurisdiction provisions in Article VII, were understood to be self-executing.[212] The framework contained within Article VII creates the potential for interference with state criminal proceedings in the two situations of concurrent jurisdiction where the foreign sending state has the right of primary jurisdiction: cases arising from official duty and *inter se* cases. Because these treaty criminal jurisdiction provisions remove the criminal jurisdiction over certain criminal actions of members of NATO sending states from a U.S. state entirely, their impact on the traditional allocation of state law enforcement is potentially extreme.[213]

211 The United States hosts over 7,000 military students from over 136 nations at 150 schools or installations nationwide under its International Military Education and Training (IMET) program, and at least two German units are permanently stationed in the U.S. at Fort Bliss in Texas and at Holloman Air Force Base in New Mexico. *See* Brenner-Beck, *supra* note 45, at 25–6.

212 Interestingly, in order to illustrate the potential interference with state's rights, the Senate explicitly discussed the impact of the NATO SOFA jurisdictional sharing provisions on a hypothetical foreign soldier in the U.S. involved in an automobile accident while on official duty resulting in injury or fatality to a U.S. citizen. The Senate fully understood that if ratified, Article VII would alter state criminal law under the Supremacy Clause, and further, it would regularly fall to the state courts to implement NATO SOFA obligations. Thus, the Senate envisioned a local court determining its own jurisdiction under the SOFA and the Supremacy Clause and dismissing any case in which the SOFA granted the primary right of prosecution to the foreign sending state. It is therefore clear the Senate understood the seriousness of this potential interference with state criminal jurisdiction. However, it also understood that permitting this interference was necessary to protect U.S. forces abroad from the plenary territorial sovereignty of allied receiving states, a trade-off certainly influenced by the expectation that U.S. forces would be affected by the SOFA far more frequently than allied forces in the United States. *See generally*, Brenner-Beck, *supra* note 45.

213 Evaluating examples of these cases highlights the tensions that can emerge between state and federal authorities when compliance with an international treaty or international agreement is at stake. Two hypothetical examples involving the German forces in Texas and New Mexico illustrate the potential for federalism concerns produced by the NATO SOFA. First, recall that the SOFA grants the sending state primary jurisdiction for official duty offenses. If an on-duty German military member kills an American citizen as the result of an automobile accident while driving an official German military vehicle off-post, the State of New Mexico or Texas would ordinarily have jurisdiction to charge the German driver with vehicular homicide. However, because the alleged criminal act occurred while the soldier was in an official-duty status, the German government (as the sending state) would have

The curious case of *Bond* thus indicates that even if federalism considerations have no impact on the power of the nation to bind itself to LOAC obligations, they may affect the implementation of those agreements domestically, potentially to the extent of placing the United States in breach of its international obligations. As many LOAC obligations are reciprocal, such potential breaches places U.S. military members at risk when they are deployed abroad to protect the nation.

VI CONCLUSION

As in any political system, voluntary international obligations assumed by a nation reflect the values and history of the nation acting on the international stage, both of which can change over time. In the United States, the policy objectives, views of the proper U.S. role in the world, and perception of U.S. values influence all three branches of government as they fulfill their constitutional roles in the formation, implementation, and interpretation of treaties. Although limited in number, because they implicate the core functions of the national government – foreign policy and national defense – LOAC treaties and the cases implicating them provide important insights into U.S. treaty practice. The role of treaties and international law influence all three branches' search for the equilibrium between national and international imperatives. Done against the background of their reverence for and commitment to the law of nations,[214] the Founders designed the Constitution to involve all three branches of the U.S. government in formulating and enforcing its international obligations. Although cases interpreting LOAC treaties are sparse in number, they provide evidence of the significant

a treaty-based right to assert primary jurisdiction for this offense. In the second type of case, a foreign military member might commit spouse- or child abuse case in their off-post residence. Assuming both the victim and the accused in this hypothetical are German citizens present in the U.S. under the provisions of the SOFA, this case is an "inter se" case, and again, under Article VII the Germans would have primary jurisdiction. It is easy to comprehend the sensitivities of local prosecutors and courts in cases involving these and other types of criminal misconduct committed in their jurisdiction. Nevertheless, a local court would be expected to analyze the provisions of the SOFA to determine the treaty-imposed limitations on the exercise of its jurisdiction, and in these cases, forgo prosecution or dismiss charges absent a German waiver of the right to exercise primary jurisdiction. If, however, the local court refused to defer to the German assertion of primary jurisdiction – the outcome mandated by Article VII of the NATO SOFA – the United States would be placed in breach of its treaty obligations by the actions of a local prosecutor or state judge, with significant consequences were Germany to then refuse to defer prosecution for American military members stationed in Germany.

214 *See generally*, Golove & Hulsebosch, *supra* note 20.

influence the judiciary has and will continue to have on the rules that regulate the use of U.S. military power.

Perhaps the nation has entered an era of a greater willingness by the judiciary to prioritize the object and purpose of relevant LOAC treaties over Executive interpretation. Such an interpretive perspective would certainly help explain decisions like *Hamdan* and *Noriega*. Whether this perception is justified or exaggerated, it is interesting that in the wake of the *Hamdan* decision, Congress sought to foreclose reliance on the Geneva Conventions as a basis for judicial relief. This provision of the Military Commission Act of 2006 was, ironically, challenged by none other than General Noriega when he sought to block his postincarceration extradition to France based on France's unwillingness to ensure respect for his rights as a POW. The District Court rejected his challenge based on this statutory ban on asserting the Geneva Conventions as a source of right in U.S. courts, a holding upheld by the Eleventh Circuit. None other than Justice Thomas questioned the validity of such a statute when he dissented in the subsequent denial of Noriega's petition for *certiorari* to the Supreme Court.[215] Ultimately, this merely reflects the ongoing ebbs and flows of influence asserted by each branch of our government on the treaty creation, implementation, and interpretation process as each seeks the appropriate equilibrium.

It is also possible that the nation is experiencing an era where Congress is taking a more narrow view of international law as a mechanism to restrict U.S. national power. This narrowing can be seen through Congress' role in LOAC formation: advice and consent, and statutory treaty implementation. In its approval of the 1949 Geneva Conventions, the Senate embraced the imposition of binding international standards governing armed conflict in large measure because it saw those standards as embodying the values and practices of the United States in the face of the emerging Cold War threat from the eastern bloc. In other cases, the Senate, and Congress more generally, resisted treaties they believed limited U.S. freedom of action in foreign affairs and war powers. Most notably, the Senate has leveraged the advice and consent process to compel Executive commitment to implement treaty obligations consistent with Senate will, and at times to even assert pressure on the President in relation to matters in no way connected to the treaty. The ratification struggle over the CWC illustrates both of these Senate practices, resulting in presidential concessions that were arguably inconsistent with the object and purpose of the treaty.

[215] Noriega v. Pastrana, 559 U.S. 917, 918 (2010) (Thomas, J., dissenting from denial of certiorari).

Limitations imposed by the U.S. federalist system of government are also now impacting the nation's implementation of LOAC treaty obligations. The *Bond* case demonstrates that individual citizens will have standing to contest the validity of implementing legislation or perhaps self-executing treaties in circumscribing their behavior in areas traditionally reserved to the states. Regardless, although not resolving Justice Holmes' "invisible radiations" from the Tenth Amendment, *Bond* establishes that implementing legislation will not be interpreted to interfere with the traditional division of law enforcement authority between Federal and State governments absent a clear statement from Congress of that intent. Given the central concern of the Founders during the drafting of the Constitution over the States' interference with the fulfillment of national treaty obligations, it is ironic that federalism may still have an impact on such an important function of the federal government in the twenty-first century.

Ultimately, while it is true that "war is a challenge to law,"[216] it remains an open question whether the law or war must adjust. Leveraging the nation's military power to advance vital national security interests while advancing the regulation of hostilities through the treaty power will, as it has in the past, impose pressures on the three branches of the U.S. government and on our federal system itself. Their actions in response will provide a lens into how treaties and international law itself will operate in U.S. practice in the future.

216 "War is a challenge to law, and the law must adjust." Al-Bihani, 619 F.3d at 882 (Brown, J., concurring).

10

Case Study No. 2
Private Law Treaties and Federalism
Can the United States Lead?

Paul R. Dubinsky

This chapter is concerned with the influence of federalism on U.S. treaty-making and treaty observance in private law[1] and private international law[2] (collectively "PIL"). Traditionally, both fields have been dominated by law-making at the state rather than the federal level. For much of U.S. history, the strong assumption was that this tradition of state dominance in PIL imposed constraints on federal power to enter into PIL treaties. But the period associated with the Restatement (Second) and the Restatement (Third) of the Foreign Relations Law of the United States (the "Second and Third Restatements") turned out to be unusual. The period from the early 1960s to the mid-1990s was one in which the federal government deployed the treaty power not only to enter into PIL treaties but also to take a leadership role in drafting those treaties. It did so largely free of the federalism-based constraints that for many decades had kept the United States out of such endeavors. Thus, from the perspective of American internationalists and proponents of broad federal power in all aspects of foreign relations, the Restatement years were a golden era. This was a time when ambitious projects in global PIL law-making seemed possible and U.S. delegations led such

A draft of this chapter was presented at the 2016 American Society of International Law workshop on International Law in Domestic Courts The author gratefully acknowledges the queries and suggestions made by participants.

[1] The unification of private law involves efforts to narrow differences among countries with respect to rules of contracts, torts, wills and inheritance, property, and other fields of law that predominate in transactions among nonstate entities.

[2] Rather than attempting to unify the underlying rules of private law, unification of private international law targets differences in national choice-of-law rules so as to make clear to transacting parties, *ex ante*, which substantive law will govern a given transaction.

projects with optimism that the Senate would ratify the instruments negotiated.[3]

It is now clear that in the decades after publication of the *Third Restatement* in 1987, the golden era lost some of its internationalist luster: The Restatement's provisions referring to PIL treaties have been cited by courts very rarely. PIL treaties and treaty proposals posing some prospect of federalizing state law, even tangentially, have received a cool reception from organizations devoted to the unification of state law in the United States. In treaty negotiations, the Executive branch has been cautious in pursuing positions that could draw fire from those opposing what they regard as federal incursion on the province of state lawmaking. During the Obama administration, the State Department was extraordinarily solicitous of state officials with respect to the implementation of new PIL treaties. A new stream of legal scholarship has been critical of traditional doctrines designed to support the supremacy of treaties within the domestic legal system – doctrines long regarded as foundational and beyond reconsideration.[4]

The pages that follow argue that a development long taken for granted – U.S. leadership of multilateral PIL treaty efforts – is very much in doubt as one looks to the future of global and regional efforts to unify PIL and strengthen international judicial cooperation. A decline in U.S. leadership in this realm

[3] *See* Hans Smit, *Recent Developments in International Litigation*, 35 S. TEX. L. REV. 215, 216 (1994) (characterizing a decade of rapid and unprecedented treaty-making activity as a key turn in "the modern history of international cooperation in litigation in the United States").

[4] Consider the *Charming Betsy* doctrine, first articulated by Chief Justice John Marshall in1804. *See* Murray v. Schooner Charming Betsy, 6 U.S. 64, 2 L. Ed. 208 (1804). Section 114 of the American Law Institute's Restatement (Third) of the Foreign Relations Law of the United States (1987) restates the traditional version of that doctrine: "Where fairly possible, a United States statute is to be construed so as not to conflict with international law or with an international agreement of the United States." In 1987, the doctrine seemed so unassailable as to require little commentary and few notes to §114. Shortly after publication of the Restatement, this long-entrenched perspective on the power of treaties to influence the meaning of federal statutes and thus indirectly preempt state law became the subject of rethinking. *See, e.g.*, Curtis Bradley *The Charming Betsy Canon and Separation of Powers: Rethinking the Interpretive Role of International Law*, 86 GEO L. J. 479, 483 (1998) (arguing that applying the *Charming Betsy* canon "is the same as creating a rule that the government regulatory scheme cannot violate international law") *quoting* Phillip R. Trimble, *A Revisionist View of Customary International Law*, 33 UCLA L. REV. 665, 675 (1986). Professor Bradley argues that the traditional justifications for the *Charming Betsy* canon have become inadequate and that, going forward, the canon "is best understood today as based on separation of powers considerations." *Ibid.* at 536. *See also* Curtis A. Bradley, *Chevron Deference and Foreign Affairs*, 86 VA. L. REV. 649, 685 (2000); Note, *The* Charming Betsy *Canon, Separation of Powers, and Customary International Law*, 121 HARV. L. REV. 1215 (2008); Jonathan Turley, *Dualistic Values in the Age of International Legisprudence*, 44 HASTINGS L.J. 185 (1993). *See also* Al-Bihani v. Obama, 619 F. 3d 1 (2010) (Kavanaugh, J., concurring in denial of rehearing *en banc*).

likely can be traced to several causes: the dispersion of global economic power, the rise of EU influence in global lawmaking, the relative absence of powerful U.S. domestic constituencies in favor of PIL treaty-making. This chapter focuses on an explanation that has received less attention: the resurgence of domestic U.S. federalism. In recent years, this resurgence has spilled over to the realm of treaty-making, treaty implementation, and treaty interpretation. This reemergence of federalism – one that either takes the form of a legal bar on U.S. entry into certain treaties or as a political constraint on congressional consent- has been one of several forces (some discussed elsewhere in this volume) that in effect tapped the brakes on the energetic pace of treaty developments that preceded the Third Restatement. That reemergence now calls into question whether the United States can continue to take a leading role in PIL treaty-making in the future.

I HISTORICAL BACKGROUND: FEDERALISM AND PIL IN THE UNITED STATES

The United States emerged from World War II with a robust economy that was dominant in manufacturing, that enjoyed breadth in its overseas markets, and that was in possession of a pool of capital that its citizens and businesses could invest abroad. Yet, the United States lacked a network of treaties capable of fully supporting these activities, notwithstanding decades of commentary by legal scholars pointing out the benefits of such treaties.[5] The United States was not a party to any treaty providing for the recognition

[5] *See, e.g.*, Simeon Baldwin, *The Comparative Results in the Advancement of Private International Law of the Montevideo Congress of 1888–89 and the Hague Conferences of 1893,1894, 1900, and 1903*, 2 AM. POL. SCI. ASS'N, 1905 Proceedings 73 (1906); Arthur K. Kuhn, *Should Great Britain and the United States Be Represented at the Hague Conferences on Private International Law?* 7 AM. J. INT'L L. 774 (1913); John Henry Wigmore, *The International Assimilation of Laws – Its Needs and Its Possibilities from an American Standpoint*, 10 ILL. L. REV. 385 (1916); John Henry Wigmore, *Problems of World-Legislation and America's Share Therein*, 4 VA. L. REV. 423, 423 (1917) (asserting that the route by which America could participate in the preparation of "world-legislation" was "the greatest problem of the future for our law"). There had been opportunities for the U.S. to enter into such treaties. Under the auspices of the Hague Conference on Private International Law, European countries in the early 1900s had entered into multilateral treaties harmonizing choice-of-law rules applicable to marriage, divorce, and guardianship. By 1909, fifteen countries had ratified the Hague Convention on Civil Procedure, which created a uniform set of rules for serving process, issuing letters rogatory, assessing litigation costs and addressing other aspects of transnational litigation. These early Hague Conference treaties, along with their ratification and accession information, can be found on the website of the Hague Conference on Private International Law, www.hcch.net/en/instruments/the-old-conventions.

of arbitration awards[6] nor any treaty on the recognition and enforcement of foreign court judgments.[7] The United States lacked judicial assistance treaties to expand the reach of U.S. civil procedure and evidence gathering.[8] It stood aloof from efforts to harmonize national approaches to conflict of laws,[9] and it had not participated actively in early efforts to unify national laws on international sales.[10]

This aloofness was accentuated by developments preceding and following World War II, a time when American experimentation in civil procedure[11] and

[6] Early in the twentieth century, the United States declined opportunities to shape the multinational regime for international arbitration. It declined to become a party to the Geneva Convention on the Execution of Foreign Arbitral Awards, *opened for signature* Sep. 26, 1927, *entered into force* Jul. 25, 1929, or the Geneva Protocol on Arbitration, *opened for signature* Sep. 24, 1923, *entered into force* Jul. 28, 1924.

[7] By comparison, networks of bilateral judgment recognition treaties had taken shape in Europe. *See generally*, Kurt H. Nadelmann, *Jurisdictionally Improper Fora in Treaties on Recognition of Judgments: The Common Market Draft*, 67 COLUM. L. REV. 995, 996–7 (1967). For a list of these treaties, *see ibid*. at 996, n. 16.

[8] Prior to World War II, Great Britain was a party to twenty-two bilateral treaties on service of process. *See* JOHN DAVID MCCLEAN, INTERNATIONAL CO-OPERATION IN CIVIL AND CRIMINAL MATTERS 21 (2nd ed. 2002).

[9] In contrast, France and Great Britain were party to many such treaties. *See* PETER HERZOG & MARTHA WESER, CIVIL PROCEDURE IN FRANCE 602–8 (1967); INTERNATIONAL COOPERATION IN LITIGATION: EUROPE 66–104, 119–70 (Hans Smit, ed., 1965).

[10] *See* Georg Cohn, "The *Beginnings of the International Assimilation of Commercial Law*,"*in* 11 *CONTINENTAL LEGAL HISTORY SERIES* 347 (1918) (essay first published in 1888) (summarizing late nineteenth-century international unification initiatives). Early studies of the differences in national laws relating to the international sale of goods can be found at www.unidroit.org/work-in-progress-studies/studies/international-sales/188-study-iv-international-sale-of-goods. After World War II, international sales law was among the first topics taken up by the Hague Conference on Private International Law. *See, e.g.*, Hague Convention on the Law Applicable to International Sales of Goods, June 15,1955; Hague Convention on the Law Governing Transfer of Title in International Sales of Goods, April 15, 1958; Hague Convention on the Jurisdiction of the Selected Forum in the Case of International Sales of Goods, April 15, 1958. The texts and ratification status of these treaties can be found on the website of the Hague Conference on Private International Law, www.hcch.net. The United States did not accede to any of these treaties but did become a party to the 1980 United Nations Convention on Contracts for the International Sale of Goods. *See* United Nations Convention on Contracts for the International Sale of Goods, April 11, 1980, 1489 UNTS 3, 19 ILM 668, 52 Fed. Reg. 6262 (1987) ("UN Convention on Sale of Goods") available at www.uncitral.org/uncitral/en/uncitral_texts/sale_goods/1980CISG_status.html.

[11] With the entry into force of the Federal Rules of Civil Procedure in 1938, American procedural law diverged considerably from that of even other common law countries. This was particularly so in regard to notice pleading and pretrial discovery. A divergence in conflict of laws resulted from the American "conflicts revolution." *See generally* SYMEON C. SYMEONIDES, THE AMERICAN CHOICE OF LAW REVOLUTION: PAST, PRESENT, AND FUTURE (2007); MATHIAS REIMANN, CONFLICT OF LAWS IN WESTERN EUROPE: A GUIDE THROUGH THE JUNGLE (1995).

conflict of laws widened the differences between the civil justice system of the United States and those of potential partners to judicial assistance treaties. By the 1960s, however, the orientation of the United States toward private international law institutions and treaties had changed. In a short period of time, and notwithstanding significant challenges, the United States went from being an outlier with respect to PIL treaties to being a central player.[12] Why was it not until the 1960s that the United States, a rapidly emerging economic power in the first half of the twentieth century, pursued PIL treaties? Why was there an aversion to PIL treaties in the first part of the century? And why, after an era of internationalism in PIL, has U.S. leadership in PIL treaty making now diminished?

Traditionally, the interaction between the United States and the judicial proceedings and laws of other countries was mediated not through treaties or statutes but through comity.[13] In their embrace of comity, state and federal courts from the late eighteenth century through the early decades of the twentieth century attempted to apply an imprecise concept[14] across a range of legal issues.[15] Crucially, the centrality of the comity principle during this

[12] The project that resulted in the Hague Evidence Convention, for example, was proposed by the United States in a 1967 letter to the Permanent Bureau of the Hague Conference on Private International Law. *See* Letter from Secretary of State William P. Rogers to President Richard Nixon (Nov. 9, 1971) at v, *reprinted as* appendix to Letter of Submittal of Hague Evidence Convention to the Senate of the United States (Feb. 1, 1972).

[13] *See* Hilton v. Guyot, 159 U.S. 113, 16 S. Ct. 139, 40 L. Ed. 95 (1895) (employing the principle of comity in determining whether to accord preclusive effects to a civil judgment from France and declining to do so in the absence of reciprocity). In a formulation that has been repeatedly cited, Justice Gray wrote that comity "is neither a matter of absolute obligation, on the one hand, nor of mere courtesy and good will, upon the other." *Ibid* at 162. Thus, the bedrock of American judicial cooperation for many decades was a doctrine with much built-in discretion. *See generally* Joel R. Paul, *Comity in International Law*, 32 HARV. INT'L L.J. 1, 9–12 (1991) (discussing ambiguities in *Hilton's* conception of comity).

[14] *See* Saul v. His Creditors, 5 Mart. (n.s.) 569, 1827 WL 1936 (La.), 16 Am. Dec. 212 ("[C]omity is, and ever must be uncertain"); Joseph Story, Commentaries on the Conflict of Laws §§ 18, 20, 23, 30, 33 (1834); Albert A. Ehrenzweig, *American Conflicts Law in its Historical Perspective: Should the Restatement Be Continued?* 103 U. PA. L. REV. 133, 137 (1954); *see also* William S. Dodge, *International Comity in American Law*, 115 COLUM. L. REV. 2071, 2086 (2015) (observing that Story's 1834 treatise *Commentaries on the Conflict of Laws* "cemented comity into the foundations of American conflicts law.").

[15] Examples included whether "the courts of one country will . . . sit in judgment on the acts of the government of another, done within its own territory" *see* Underhill v. Hernandez, 168 U.S.250, 252, 18 S. Ct. 83, 42 L. Ed. 456 (1897), whether U.S. courts will give effect to a marriage or divorce recognized in another country, *see, e.g.*, Kapigian v. Der Minassian, 212 Mass. 412, 413,99 N.E. 264 (1912) ("[I]t is a general principle of law recognized by international comity that every sovereign state has the right to determine the domestic and social status of those having their domicile within its territory"), and whether foreign litigants can be sanctioned for not obeying U.S. court orders that conflict with the laws of their own country. *See* Societe

period enhanced the power of state courts. Private law disputes touching upon significant aspects of foreign relations – the validity of foreign marriages and divorces, the administration of large multinational trusts and estates, the ability of foreign judgment creditors to seize assets in the United States – typically were adjudicated in state courts. State courts applied state-law principles of comity, there being no federal statutory or treaty law to apply[16] nor any duty to follow federal case law applying comity.[17] From a state court's perspective, its role in determining the validity of a foreign divorce (for example) was a natural extension of its role in the interstate recognition of divorces.

Until the 1960s, treaties were not a part of the American law of PIL. In applying comity when responding to requests for international judicial assistance, state courts engaged in unilateral acts of assistance rather than reciprocally imposed legal duties.[18] After *Klaxon v. Stenton* in 1940, state control increased, as the application of comity to choice-of-law and recognition of foreign-country judgments became governed by state law.[19] Thus, the baseline from which to evaluate the Third Restatement (that is, its place in the 240-year span of U.S. practice in PIL) is a period of more than 150 years in which the American law of PIL evolved by common law adjudication with the principle of comity at its core.[20] The volume of federal law, in the form of

Internationale Pour Participations Industrielles Et Commerciales, S. A. v. Rogers, 357 U.S. 197, 78 S. Ct. 1087, 2 L. Ed. 2d 1255 (1958).

16 In cases pertaining to public international law, courts applied "the law of nations" or customary international law. *See* The Paquete Habana, 175 U.S. 677, 694, 20 S. Ct. 290, 44 L. Ed.320 (1900) (explaining how comity can grow "by the general assent of civilized nations, into a settled rule of international law.").

17 *See, e.g.*, Johnston v. Compagnie Generale Transatlantique, 242 N.Y. 381, 152 N.E. 121(1926) (declining to follow *Hilton v. Guyot* and holding that recognition of foreign-country judgments by New York courts should not be conditioned on reciprocal treatment of U.S. judgments by foreign courts).

18 Before *Erie R. Co. v. Tompkins*, 304 U.S. 64, S. Ct. 817, 82 L. Ed. 1188 (1938), it was common for federal courts to apply their own comity analyses in diversity cases and not consider themselves bound by state court precedents.

19 *See* Klaxon Co. v. Stentor Elec. Mfg. Co., 313 U.S. 487, 61 S. Ct. 1020, 85 L. Ed. 1477(1940) (ruling that federal courts sitting in diversity must apply state conflict of laws rules). State law governed comity issues in both state and federal court. *See, e.g.*, Day & Zimmerman, Inc. v. Challoner, 423 U.S. 3, 96 S. Ct. 167, 46 L. Ed. 2d 3 (1975) (*per curiam*) (holding that federal court exercising diversity jurisdiction must apply Texas choice of law rule, even if that rule pointed to the law of a foreign country); Somportex Ltd. v. Philadelphia Chewing Gum Corp. 453 F.2d 435 (3d Cir. 1971), *cert. denied.*, 405 U.S. 1017 (1972) (applying Pennsylvania law, which at that time incorporated "principles of comity" to action seeking to enforce a foreign-court judgment in federal court").

20 *See generally* Donald Earl Childress III, *When* Erie *Goes International*, 105 Nw. L. Rev.1534, 1534–48 & 1535 (2011) (providing historical overview and arguing that the application of

statutes and treaties, was minimal for much of this period,[21] and federal judge-made law in the field did not preempt state law and did not impose legal obligations on state lawmakers or state courts.

The long stretch of time in which there was no specialized federal procedural law for transnational disputes is significant. This lengthy period fostered the view among state courts that private law and procedural law were presumptively state law, whether applied in an interstate setting or an international one.[22] This extended period of time adjudicating transnational disputes under state rules of civil procedure, evidence, and choice of law likely fostered the view among federal courts that PIL lay outside the scope of the federal statutory and treaty power.[23] So, when Secretary of State Hamilton Fish was invited by the Netherlands and Peru to attend intergovernmental meetings in the 1870s on unifying private law, he declined, citing federalism.[24] When

comity-based state law to private international law questions "thwarts" the "animating ethos" of the *Erie* doctrine).

21 There were occasional federal incursions and, in the nineteenth century, Congress enacted federal statutes that made it possible in a limited way for litigants in foreign proceedings to enlist the assistance of federal courts to obtain evidence located in the United States. *See, e.g.*, Act of Mar. 2,1855, ch. 140, § 2, 10 Stat. 630 (circuit court may appoint "a United States commissioner designated ... to make the examination of witnesses" on receipt of a letter rogatory from a foreign court); Act of Mar. 3, 1863, ch. 95, § 1, 12 Stat. 769 (authorizing district courts to respond to letters rogatory by compelling witnesses in the United States to provide testimony for use abroad in "suit[s] for the recovery of money or property"). In 1948, Congress substantially broadened the scope of assistance by eliminating the prior requirement that the government of a foreign country be a party or have an interest in the proceeding. *See* Act of June 25, 1948, ch. 646, § 1782, 62 Stat. 949 (June 25, 1948).

22 Under the Conformity Act, the rules of procedure applied in federal court were those enacted by the legislature of the state in which the court sat. Such rules applied in both diversity and federal question cases. *See* Conformity Act, 17 Stat. 196 (1872) *repealed by* Rules Enabling Act, 48 Stat. 1064 (1934).

23 In *The Treaty Power and American Federalism*, 97 MICH. L. REV. 390, 409–22 (1998), Professor Curtis Bradley marshals evidence that the prevailing view among the founding generation and the nineteenth century judiciary was that the treaty power was confined by subject matter. Professor Hollis largely agrees. *See* Duncan B. Hollis, *An Intersubjective Treaty Power*, 90 NOTRE DAME L. REV. 1415 (2015) (concluding that "the Third Restatement is wrong on the question of whether the Constitution imposes an affirmative subject matter limitation on the treaty power."). For a critique of Professor Bradley's account, see David Golove, *Treaty-Making and the Nation: The Historical Foundations of the Nationalist Conception of the Treaty Power*, 98 MICH. L. REV.1075, 1288 (2000).

24 *See, e.g.*, Letter from Hamilton Fish to Mr. Westenberg (June 4, 1874), *reprinted in* Papers Relating to the Foreign Relations of the United States 794–5 (1874):

> An[] objection in our uniting in a[n international] Congress like that referred to, is that, pursuant to the Constitution of the United States, the several States have reserved powers which it is not competent for this government to trench upon either by Act of Congress or by Treaty with a foreign power.

Charles Evans Hughes addressed the American Society of International Law in 1928 concerning Latin American efforts to unify procedural law, he echoed Fish:

> [I]f we attempted to use the treaty-making power to deal with matters which do not pertain to our external relations but to control matters which normally and appropriately were within the local jurisdictions of the States, then I again say there might be grounds for implying a limitation upon the treaty-making power that it is intended for the purpose of having treaties made relating to foreign affairs and not to make laws for the people of the United States in their internal concerns.[25]

This understanding of U.S. federalism and the scope of the treaty power persisted even after *Missouri v. Holland*.[26] In the decade after Justice Holmes in that case articulated a strong view of the treaty power, the Harding and Coolidge administrations took to the sidelines with respect to the first major

Just two years earlier, the Supreme Court had upheld federal exercise of the treaty power to carry out land deals with Native American tribes, but it had done so cautiously using a formula suggesting limits on the treaty power. *See Holden v. Joy*, 84 U.S. 211, 242–3, 21 L. Ed. 523 (1872) (stating that the treaty power was meant to extend to "those objects which in the intercourse of nations had usually been regarded as the proper subjects of negotiation and treaty, if not inconsistent with the nature of our government and the relation between the States and the United States"). The Court in *Holden* relied on *Holmes v. Jennison*, 39 U.S. 540, 569 (1840), a case striking down action by Vermont in extraditing an accused defendant to Canada in the absence of a U.S. treaty:

> The power to make treaties is given by the Constitution in general terms, without any description of the objects intended to be embraced by it; and, consequently, it was designed to include all those subjects, which in the ordinary intercourse of nations had usually been made subjects of negotiation and treaty; and which are consistent with the nature of our institutions, and the distribution of powers between the general and state governments. And without attempting to define the exact limits of this treaty-making power, or to enumerate the subjects intended to be included in it; it may safely be assumed, that the recognition and enforcement of the principles of public law, being one of the ordinary subjects of treaties, were necessarily included in the power conferred on the general government.

25 *See* Proceedings of the American Society of International Law, Twenty-Third Annual Meeting at 194 (1929). Hughes had served as chair of the U.S. delegation to the Sixth International Conference of Private International Law of American States in Havana. He opposed U.S. entry into the resulting treaty that 15 countries in the hemisphere eventually ratified. *See Convention on Private International Law*, Department of International Law (OAS), available at www.oas.org/juridico/english/sigs/a-31.html. For an overview of the work product of the Havana conference, see Report of the Delegates of the United States of America to the Sixth International Conference of American States 96–176 (1928), available at http://babel.hathitrust.org/cgi/pt?id=mdp. 39015070220986;view=1up;seq=7.

26 Missouri v. Holland, 252 U.S. 416, 40 S. Ct. 382, 64 L. Ed. 641 (1920) (upholding, against constitutional attack, a bilateral treaty and its implementing legislation pertaining to protection of migratory birds).

multilateral treaties on arbitration and the enforceability of arbitration awards.[27] After all, Holmes had characterized the treaty in *Missouri v. Holland* as pertaining to "a national interest of very nearly the first magnitude."[28] For decades after *Missouri v. Holland*, legal scholars were skeptical that PIL treaties met that standard. Their writings promoted the idea that the United States perhaps could keep up with Europe through state legislation, including uniform acts.[29]

After World War II, state and federal officials continued to articulate variations on this federalism-based skepticism toward PIL treaties.[30] During the 1950s, the United States continued to remain outside of multilateral

27 *See* Convention on the Execution of Foreign Arbitral Awards, Sept. 26, 1927; Geneva Protocol on Arbitration, Sep. 24, 1923.

28 *See Holland*, 252 U.S. at 435. Holmes did not articulate the national interest in that case that was "of nearly the first magnitude." He declined to take up Missouri's invitation to determine whether, by means of the treaty power and implementing legislation, the federal government could divest a state of ownership of natural resources located within its territory. Holmes brushed aside the state's Tenth Amendment argument by positing that "[w]ild birds are not in the possession of anyone" and, therefore, are not the property of the state in which they are found temporarily. *Ibid.* at 434.

29 *See, e.g.*, Kurt H. Nadelmann, *Ignored State Interests: The Federal Government and International Efforts to Unify the Rules of Private Law*, 102 *U. Pa. L. Rev.* 323, 359 (1954). In this way, the autonomy of state law would be preserved; there would be no federal treaty or implementing legislation to preempt state law. The problem with this approach was that for stretches of time there was little interest at the state level in such endeavors. For a detailed account of the reluctance of the National Conference of Commissioners on Uniform State Laws (NCCUSL) over a period of several decades to become involved in international unification of private law, see Peter Winship, *The National Conference of Commissioners on Uniform State Laws and the International Unification of Private Law*, 13 *U. Pa. J. Int'l Bus. Law.* 227 (1992).

30 *See Treaties and Executive Agreements: Hearings on S.J. Res. 1 Before a Subcommittee of the Senate Committee on the Judiciary*, *84th Cong., Sess.* 1, 183 (1955) (Secretary of State Dulles) (stating that treaties cannot regulate matters "which do not essentially affect the actions of nations in relation to international affairs, but are purely internal"); Joe C. Barrett, Report on the 1956 Barcelona and Hague Conferences on Unification of Law, 1957 Handbook Nat'l Conf. Commissioners on Uniform State Laws 299 (statement by former president of NCCUSL and commissioner from Arkansas arguing that U.S. involvement in the unification of private law "would present a head-on collision between Article 6 and Amendment No. 10 of the Constitution of the United States"). Professor Hans Smit, who served as reporter to the Commission on International Rules of Civil Procedure created by Congress in 1958, explained the decision of the Commission to focus on recommendations that could be implemented by statute rather than treaty, as follows:

> This decision was based not only on the view that internal reforms could obviate the need for international regulation, but also on the notion that regulation by treaty might invade areas traditionally covered by state law.

Hans Smit, *International Litigation Under the United States Code*, 65 Colum. L. Rev. 1015, 1015 (1965).

PIL developments even as European efforts pushed forward in the field of international sales,[31] and countries from many parts of the world came together to produce the 1958 New York Convention, which the United States did not ratify until 1970 because of initial concerns about its preemption of state law.[32]

In sum, federalism was an important reason why, for nearly a century, the Executive branch and Congress refrained from using the treaty power to align American private law and private international law with that of other countries.[33]

II FEDERALISM'S DECLINE AND THE GOLDEN AGE

The period from the late 1950s to the late 1990s witnessed a major departure from the tradition just summarized. A new U.S. receptiveness to PIL treaty-making coincided with the transition from the Eisenhower to the Kennedy and Johnson presidencies, a pro-treaty turn in American scholarly organizations,[34] and the long reign of J. William Fulbright as chairman of the Senate Foreign Relations Committee.[35] The Third Restatement, a high

[31] *See supra* note 10. The texts and ratification status of these treaties can be found on the website of the Hague Conference on Private International Law, www.hcch.net. Until the 1960s, the United States repeatedly declined invitations to become a member of the Hague Conference. *See* George A.L. Droz & Adair Dyer, *The Hague Conference and the Main Issues of Private International Law for the Eighties*, 3 NW. J. INT'L L. & BUS. 155 (1981).

[32] The U.S. delegation to the New York Convention negotiations recommended against U.S. ratification. *See* Official Report of the United States Delegation to the United Nations Conference on International Commercial Arbitration, May 20–June 10, 1958, *reproduced in* H.R Rep. No. 91–1181, 91 Cong., 2d Sess. (1970), *reprinted in* 19 AM. REV. INT. ARB. 91, 112 (2008) (expressing concern about Article II of the Convention's potential conflict with state contract law in the United States).

[33] *See* Stephen B. Burbank, *The Reluctant Partner: Making Procedural Law for International Civil Litigation*, 57 LAW & CONTEMP. PROBS. 103, 105 (1994) ("For years, the supposed requirements of U.S. federalism hindered international lawmaking through private international law treaties"). Federalism was not the only reason; *see, e.g.*, Paul Lansing, *The Change in American Attitude to the International Unification of Sales Law Movement and UNCITRAL*, 18 AM. BUS. L. J. 270 (first published 1980) ("The traditional attitude of the United States has been one of indifference toward all efforts at international cooperation in private and commercial matters").

[34] Important developments during this period took place at meetings of the American Branch of the International Law Association and the American Society of International Law. These are summarized in Kurt H. Nadelmann, *The United States Joins the Hague Conference on Private International Law*, 30 LAW & CONTEMP. PROBS. 302 (1965). Among the scholars most involved were David F. Cavers of Harvard and Elliott Cheatham of Columbia.

[35] Fulbright, an internationalist in the Senate, served in that position from 1959 to 1974. *See J. William Fulbright: A Featured Biography*, UNITED STATES SENATE, available at

point in U.S. engagement with PIL, came into existence during this period. Because the Third Restatement will serve as the baseline for evaluating the current position of the United States in PIL treaty-making, it is necessary to pause and sketch the milieu in which the Restatement was produced.

After nearly a century of being a bystander to early PIL treaty conferences, the United States became an initiator and leader of global treaty efforts in the field. The change came during a compressed period of time. In 1956, the United States became an observer at the Hague Conference.[36] Eight years later, it became a full member of the Hague Conference and a member of the Rome-based Institute for the Unification of Private Law (UNIDROIT). In 1968, it joined the United Nations Conference for International Trade Law (UNCITRAL).[37] The United States then acceded to the Hague Service Convention[38] in 1967 and to UNCITRAL's New York Convention in 1970.[39] It proposed the project that became the Hague Evidence Convention,[40] which it ratified in 1972. The Evidence Convention, a means for litigants to receive assistance in obtaining evidence located outside the forum state, entered into force the same year. As Professor Kurt Nadelmann put it, "A long policy of not collaborating in this kind of endeavor came, finally, to an end."[41]

Fresh from its success with the Evidence Convention, the United States set its sights on UNIDROIT. It pursued a project closer to the core of traditional state prerogatives: wills. The first multilateral PIL negotiations over which an American served as president made it possible for a single document to meet the validity requirements of multiple countries and thus function as an

www.senate.gov/artandhistory/history/common/generic/Featured_Bio_Fulbright.htm. Critically, Fulbright chaired the committee when it recommended U.S. membership in PIL organizations and in favor of the United States becoming a party to the Hague Service and Evidence Conventions.

36 *See* Letter from Secretary of State William P. Rogers to President Richard Nixon (Nov. 9, 1971), *reprinted as* appendix to Letter of Submittal of Hague Evidence Convention to Senate of the United States (Feb. 1, 1972). The sequence of events leading to that outcome is recounted in Nadelmann, *supra* note 34.

37 Unlike the Hague Conference and UNIDROIT, UNCITRAL is an international organization, not an intergovernmental one.

38 *See* Hague Convention on Service Abroad of Judicial and Extrajudicial Documents in Civil and Commercial Matters, Nov. 15, 1965, 20 U.S.T. 361, T.I.A.S. No. 6638 ("Hague Service Convention").

39 *See* Convention on the Recognition and Enforcement of Foreign Arbitral Awards (1958) (the "New York Convention"), 21 U.S.T. 2517, 330 U.N.T.S. 38.

40 *See* Hague Convention on the Taking of Evidence Abroad in Civil or Commercial Matters, Mar. 18, 1970 23 U.S.T. 2555, T.I.A.S. No. 7444 ("Hague Evidence Convention").

41 Nadelmann, *supra* note 34, at 291.

"international will."[42] The resulting treaty text, the Washington Convention, was completed in 1973.[43]

Thus, in one decade, the United States appeared to have shaken off a long tradition of opting out of global developments in PIL and did so with little domestic opposition.[44] Based on the traditional relationship between PIL and federalism, one would have expected these treaty developments to have attracted controversy. After all, the PIL treaties of the 1960s and 1970s imposed real requirements and limitations on state courts.[45]

42 *See* Kurt Nadelmann, *The Formal Validity of Wills and the Washington Convention of 1973: Providing the Form of an International Will*, 22 AM. J. COMP. L. 365 (1974); *Prefatory Note*, UNIFORM INTERNATIONAL WILLS ACT, available at www.uniformlaws.org/Shared/Docs/UIWA%201977%20Final.pdf. The president of the conference was Ambassador Richard Kearney.

43 *See* Convention Providing a Uniform Law on the Form of an International Will, 12 I.L.M.1298 (1973), available at www.unidroit.org/instruments/succession. There are 21 state parties at this writing. The United States signed the treaty in 1973. In 1986, Ronald Reagan, a president especially mindful of federal incursions on state lawmaking power, submitted it to the Senate. *See* President's Message to Congress Transmitting the Convention Providing a Uniform Law on the Form of an International Will, 1986 Pub. Papers 905–06 (July 2, 1986). The Senate gave its consent to the Convention in 1991, *see* 102d Cong., 137 Cong. Rec. S12131 (daily ed. Aug. 2, 1991), but the treaty has never been ratified. At the time of U.S. signature, Professor Nadelmann urged implementation by means of a new federal statute. *See* Nadelmann, *supra* note 42 at 375. This proposal had one main opponent. *See* Jerome J. Curtis, Jr., *The Convention on International Wills: A Reply to Kurt Nadelmann*, 23 AM. J. COMP. L. 119, 120 (1975) ("the Convention on Wills poses a threat to the reserved powers of the states to regulate the devolution of property within their borders or of their citizens"); *compare also* Jerome J. Curtis, Jr., *The Treaty Power and Family Law*, 7 *Ga. L. Rev.* 55 (1972–73). In the absence of U.S. ratification, 15 states have enacted legislation to align their laws with the Convention and with NCCUSL's Uniform International Wills Act (1977), available at www.uniformlaws.org/Shared/Docs/UIWA%201977%20Final.pdf. Professor Julian Ku characterizes this sequence of events as an example of "state control over international law" through the federal government's leaving implementation to the states. *See* Julian G. Ku, *The State of New York Does Exist: How the States Control Compliance with International Law*, 82 N.C. L. REV. 457, 503 (2004). Actually, from the complicated sequence of events from the early 1970s to the late 1990s over the course of six presidential administrations, it is difficult to infer that any deliberate decision was made at the federal level to leave implementation of the Wills Convention to state legislatures. And if that decision was made, then the result – implementation by just fifteen states (some by new legislation and some by amending the Uniform Probate Code) – has been unsatisfactory given that there is essentially no substantive opposition to the Washington Convention.

44 In contrast, the efforts culminating in moving federal-court practice from being beholden to state procedural law (via the Conformity Act) to being independent (via the Federal Rules of Procedure) transpired over a period of approximately three decades with heated disputes in Congress and among scholars. *See* Paul R. Dubinsky, "Harmonization and Voluntarism: The Role of Elites in Creating an Influential National Model, the Federal Rules of Civil Procedure" *in* CIVIL LITIGATION IN A GLOBALIZING WORLD (Xandra Kramer & Remco van Rhee, eds.) (2012).

45 The Hague Service Convention requires state courts to accept process served through mechanisms not authorized by their state legislatures. *See* Hague Service Convention, *supra* note 38, art. 17. It was thus the first treaty incursion into state procedural law in civil cases.

Notwithstanding these impositions on state courts, no significant opposition materialized in the 1960s and 1970s. The U.S. membership in UNIDROIT and the Hague Conference went forward with the support of the National Conference of Commissioners on Uniform State Laws ("NCCUSL")[46] and several state and city bar associations.[47] The joint resolution authorizing U.S. membership and funding easily passed without opposition in Congress.[48] Four years later, the Hague Service Convention received the consent of the Senate with the full backing of the American Bar Association ("ABA"),[49] NCCUSL,[50] and state and city bar associations.[51] At the Senate Foreign Relations Committee hearings, four witnesses testified in favor of the treaty. None spoke in opposition. One witness, from the State Department, characterized the Service Convention as part of a wider strategy to create a coherent federal approach to international judicial assistance.[52]

Witnesses at the Senate hearings on U.S. membership in UNIDROIT and the Hague Conference, and at subsequent hearings, assured senators that treaty-making would not change or reform existing U.S. procedural law.[53]

The New York Convention took adjudicatory power away from state courts, which are required to dismiss cases that lay within their statutory and constitutional jurisdiction. *See* New York Convention, *supra* note 39, art. II (3). The text of the Hague Evidence Convention can be read to curtail the authority of state courts to permit litigants to conduct discovery abroad using statutes and procedural rules enacted by state lawmakers, even if inconsistent with foreign law. *See* Hague Evidence Convention, *supra* note 40, art. 27(c) (permitting resort to non-Convention methods but only if permitted by the receiving State Party). The U.S. Supreme Court's 1987 Aérospatiale decision put such concerns to rest. *See* Société Nationale Industrielle Aérospatiale v. U.S. District Court, 482 U.S. 522, 107 S. Ct. 2542, 96 L. Ed. 2d 461 (1987). As applied by most state and lower federal courts, Aérospatiale rarely requires U.S. litigants to employ the Convention rather than availing themselves of state or federal discovery statutes or rules. *See generally* Patrick Borchers, *The Incredible Shrinking Hague Evidence Convention*, 38 TEX. INT'L L. J. 73 (2003).

46 *See* Letter from Joe C. Barrett to Senator J. W. Fulbright, Dec. 14, 1963, appendix to Sen. Rep. No. 781 (Committee on Foreign Relations), Dec. 16, 1963. The Joint Resolution authorizing an appropriation of funds for U.S. participation in these activities was also supported by the American Bar Association. *See ibid.* at 8–9.

47 *See* appendix to Sen. Rep. No. 781.

48 *See* H.J. Res. 778 (1963), H.R. Rep. No. 873 (Committee on Foreign Affairs) Oct. 29, 1963; Sen. Rep. No. 781 (Committee on Foreign Relations), Dec. 16, 1963.

49 *See* Hearings of the U.S. Senate, Committee on Foreign Relations (Apr. 11, 1967), at 11.

50 A former NCCUSL president, Joe Barrett, testified in support of the treaty. *Ibid.* at 3. During the hearing, the State Department Deputy Legal Adviser, Richard Kearney, asked that "special attention ... be paid to the support of" NCCUSL. *Ibid.* at 6.

51 *Ibid.* at 6–7. 52 *Ibid.*

53 In 1967, Deputy Legal Adviser Richard Kearny told the Senate Foreign Relations Committee that the representatives of other countries attending the Hague Conference sessions on the Service Convention "recognized that the United States had taken a giant leap forward in the field of international judicial cooperation and that this led them to adopt a very forthcoming

The main impact of such treaties, they said, would be for other countries to become as forthcoming with judicial assistance as the United States already was.[54] Thus, initial American forays into PIL treaty-making were presented to the Senate (and indirectly to the American Law Institute [ALI]), which was completing the Second Restatement[55] at the time, as "no-lose" propositions: the United States was making a commitment only to continue doing what Congress already had determined by statute was in the national interest. Congressional consideration of the Service and Evidence Conventions lacked discussion of these treaties' likely impact on state law and state courts.

How was it then that these groundbreaking steps in PIL provoked so little opposition? Several factors played a role. First, the congressional hearings and committee reports suggest that a favorable bipartisan vote with a wide margin was secured in part by supporters persuading the Senate that the Service and Evidence Conventions would bring U.S. norms of due process, judicial assistance, and civil litigation to Western Europe. A series of incomplete representations from the Executive Branch and others seems to have induced members of Congress to draw this conclusion.[56]

Second, the success of the Federal Rules of Civil Procedure (FRCP) in the 1940s and 1950s undermined the traditional view that matters of procedure were quintessentially the province of state lawmaking. After two decades of

attitude." Hearings, Senate Foreign Relations Committee, Apr. 11, 1967 (vol. 1), Testimony of Richard D. Kearny, at 5. With this testimony, and through written materials, the Executive Branch repeatedly told the Senate that the Service and Evidence Conventions were consistent with the 1964 International Judicial Assistance Act, Pub. L. 88–619, § 9(a), Oct. 3, 1964, 78 Stat. 997 (the "UIIPA") and that ratification posed no difficulties in terms of federalism and would not require a change in existing U.S. law.

54 *See, e.g.*, Statement of Joe C. Barrett, Hearings, Senate Foreign Relations Committee on the Convention of the Service Abroad of Judicial and Extrajudicial Documents in Civil or Commercial Matters (Apr. 11, 1967) at 13 ("[A] number of foreign countries will be radically changed by th[e] [Hague Service] Convention") and ("in and exchange for that [judicial assistance] we offer substantially nothing because we merely continue to do that which we are already doing"). Barrett was a member of the U.S. delegation to the Hague Conference on Private International Law during negotiations leading to the Service Convention.

55 *See* RESTATEMENT (SECOND) OF THE FOREIGN RELATIONS LAW OF THE UNITED STATES (Am. Law Inst. 1965).

56 *See, e.g.*, Statement of Joe Barrett, *supra* note 54; Statement of the Honorable Abram Chayes, State Department Legal Adviser, in Support of U.S. Participation in the Activities of the Hague Conference on Private International Law and the International (Rome) Institute for the Unification of Private Law (Dec. 16, 1963) *reprinted as* Appendix to Sen. Rep. No. 781 (representing that the United States would attempt to persuade PIL organizations to change their mode of operation and produce something more like model laws than treaties). There is no evidence that the United States ever pressed this approach vigorously with UNIDROIT, UNCITRAL, or the Hague Conference.

being applied, the Federal Rules began to exert an influence on state legislatures and state courts.[57]

Third, the new receptiveness toward PIL treaties coincided with the ascendancy in the academy of European *émigrés* who were expert in European approaches to private international law and the use of treaties as instruments of harmonization of law and judicial assistance.[58]

Lastly, the path to PIL engagement was paved by unilateral steps undertaken by the United States. In 1958, Congress created the Commission on International Rules of Judicial Procedure and a related Advisory Committee.[59] The Commission concentrated on recommending changes that the United States could make unilaterally rather than through treaty. Congress enacted many of these recommendations in 1964.[60] As a result of the Commission's work, much of the reorienting of the U.S. legal system toward

[57] *See* WILLIAM W. BARRON & ALEXANDER HOLTZOFF, FEDERAL PRACTICE AND PROCEDURE §9.1 (Charles Alan Wright ed., 1960) ("Among the most important consequences of the adoption of the Federal Rules of Civil Procedure has been the stimulus they have provided for procedural reform in the states"); Charles E. Clark, *Two Decades of the Federal Civil Rules*, 58 COLUM. L. REV. 435, 435–6 (1958) (reporting that "hardly a local jurisdiction remains unaffected" by the procedural reform wrought by the Federal Rules of Civil Procedure).

[58] Among these European-born scholars were Kurt Nadelmann (Harvard), Andreas Lowenfeld (NYU), Eric Stein (Michigan), Hans Smit (Columbia), Louis Sohn (Harvard), Louis Henkin (Columbia), Stefan Reisenfeld (Berkeley), Thomas Buergenthal (George Washington and elsewhere), and Detlev Vagts (Harvard). Nadelmann in particular was a strong advocate of a larger U.S. role in global PIL developments. *See* Nadelmann, *Ignored State Interests, supra* note 29, at 360 ("[T]he desirability of attaining internationally greater uniformity or better coordination for certain rules of law in the conflicts and commercial law fields is an actual and acute problem."). Hans Smit, who served from 1960 to 1969 as reporter to the U.S. Commission on International Rules of Judicial Procedure, was also a prolific and energetic advocate of greater U.S. engagement with European efforts at coordination in PIL. For a study of the influence of European *émigrés* in other university departments, see Gerhard Lowenberg, *The Influence of European Émigré Scholars on Comparative Politics, 1925–1965*, 100 AM. POL. SCI. REV 597 (2006).

[59] *See* Act of Sep. 2, 1958, Pub. L. No. 85–906, 72 Stat. 1743. This action flowed from calls from the practicing bar and academia for greater U.S. international cooperation. *See, e.g., Resolution Concerning Negotiation of Treaties of Judicial Assistance*, 45 ASIL *Proc.* 188–90 (1951); Hans Smit, *International Litigation under the United States Code*, 65 *Colum. L. Rev.* 1015, 1017(1965) (disparaging "abstract notions of sovereignty" in favor of the needs of litigants "to perform procedural acts in the most effective and efficient manner").

[60] *See* Act of Oct. 3, 1964, Pub. L. No. 88–619, 78 Stat. 995 (amending 28 U.S.C. to improve the processing of foreign letters rogatory and the receipt of foreign documents into evidence in U.S. courts). For an overview of the statute by a key participant in the process, see Philip W. Amram, *Public Law No. 88–619 of October 3, 1964—New Developments in International Judicial Assistance in The United States of America*, 32 J. BAR ASS'N D.C. 24, 28, 32 (1965). The UIIPA served as a model for a new generation of state long-arm statutes and other state legislation pertaining to international litigation.

international judicial assistance was accomplished by statute.[61] This legislation, which applied only in federal courts,[62] may have had the effect of defusing potential resistance to judicial assistance treaties by state authorities who were under the impression that the new treaties, like the 1964 statute, would have little impact on state courts.

Even before U.S. entry into PIL treaty-making, these unilateral developments were seen by some as beginning a new era in the transnational litigation of civil disputes.[63] But in two respects they accentuated existing problems associated with federalism. First, parts of the Uniform Interstate and International Procedures Act (UIIPA) were to be applied to both transnational and interstate litigation.[64] The statute thus continued a U.S. tradition of conceptualizing litigation that is transnational in scope as a merely variation on seemingly similar interstate litigation rather than as unique.[65] As a result, U.S. delegations to treaty conferences were hampered by the prevailing view conflating rather than illuminating important differences between the

[61] *See* Daniel J. Rothstein, *A Proposal to Clarify U.S. Law on Judicial Assistance in Taking Evidence for International Arbitration*, 19 AM. REV. INT'L ARB. 61, 68 (2009) (characterizing those portions of the 1964 legislation that were codified at 28 U.S.C. § 1782 as a "comprehensive revision of U.S. legislation governing international judicial assistance" and as addressing deficiencies in international cooperation in obtaining evidence, serving documents, and proving documents).

[62] In light of the Commission on International Rules of Judicial Procedure's study of international litigation and subsequent legislation that enacted the Commission's recommendations, it may have seemed reasonable to states and Congress that PIL treaties envisioned by the State Department would mainly involve persuading other countries to follow the new U.S. model rather than bringing changes to U.S. practice. This view can be found in Justice Stevens's majority opinion in Societe Nationale Industrielle Aérospatiale, v. U.S. District Court 482 U.S. at 542, concerning the Hague Evidence Convention.

[63] *See* Hans Smit, *The Uniform Interstate and International Procedure Act Approved by the National Conference of Commissioners on Uniform State Laws: A New Era Commences*, 11 AM. J. COMP. L. 415 (1962).

[64] For example, the model state long-arm statute did not distinguish between assertions of jurisdiction over out-of-state defendants and out-of-country defendants.

[65] *See generally*, Paul R. Dubinsky, *Is Transnational Litigation a Distinct Field? The Persistence of Exceptionalism in American Procedural Law*, 44 STAN. J. INT'L. 301 (2008) (summarizing that tradition). A few perceptive voices at the time pointed out important differences between interstate and international conflict of laws. *See, e.g.*, Eugene F. Scoles, *Interstate and International Distinctions in Conflict of Laws in the United States*, 54 CALIF. L. REV. 1599, 1599–1600 (1966), but those voices did not stop the conflation of the interstate and the international. *See* Uniform Foreign Judgment Recognition Act, Aug. 4, 1962, 13 U.L.A. 261 (1962) ("UFMJRA") (equating recognition of foreign-country judgments with judgments of sister states); *compare* Stephen B. Burbank, *The Reluctant Partner: Making Procedural Law for International Civil Litigation*, 57 LAW& CONTEMP. PROBS.103, 135 (1994) ("The Federal Rules represented a triumph over claims of federalism for the procedural law applied in federal courts" but as implemented "militated against special rules for international civil litigation").

international system for the litigation of civil disputes and the domestic one.[66] They were also hampered by the fact that the 1964 legislation unilaterally had given prospective treaty partners much of what they otherwise would have needed to seek through negotiation.[67]

Nonetheless, during this period, the United States ratified the Evidence Convention, acceded to the New York Convention, and joined the efforts to produce an international sales convention that culminated in the U.N. Convention on Contracts for the International Sale of Goods in 1980.[68] Long-standing federalism objections to exercising the treaty power in the realm of private law (like those voiced by Hughes in 1929) were faint. The conceptualizing, drafting, and vetting of the Third Restatement took place in the 1980s in this context.

III FEDERALISM AND THE THIRD RESTATEMENT

The dramatic shift described above took place just as ALI undertook for the first time the project of restating the foreign relations law of the United States. After a decade of analysis and drafting, ALI published the Second Restatement in 1965. Then, after 15 years of major PIL treaty developments, ALI began work on a Third Restatement, which it completed in 1987.

On the subject of federalism, §117 of the Second Restatement contained a cautious and narrow interpretation of *Missouri v. Holland*. There were, it said, preconditions to the exercise of the treaty power: The subject of the treaty had to be a matter of "international concern,"[69] and the treaty could not "contravene any of the limitations of the Constitution applicable to 'all powers of the United States.'" Neither §117 nor its comments and reporters' notes identified what the phrase "international concern" meant, nor did the Second Restatement deal explicitly with the overlap of federalism and private international law.[70] The notes and comments made no

66 *See* Dubinsky, *supra* note 65, at 309–12 (proposing the term "interstate equivalence" for this process).

67 *See* Burbank, *supra* note 65, at 113 (1994) (arguing that "many of the 1964 legislative amendments represented a unilateral grant of judicial assistance in aid of litigation abroad").

68 *See* UN Convention on the Sale of Goods, *supra* note 10; Paul Lansing, *The Change in American Attitude to the International Unification of Sales Law Movement and UNCITRAL*, 18 AM. BUS. L.J. 269, 270 (1980).

69 The phrase "international concern" echoed the position articulated by Charles Evans Hughes in 1929, see *supra* note 25.

70 Section 117 gave four fact patterns to illustrate the limits of the treaty power, but these tracked the facts of *Missouri v. Holland* and *De Geofroy v. Riggs*, 133 U.S. 258, 10 S. Ct. 295, 33L. Ed. 642 (1890) so closely as to be of little help in gauging where the law stood in the 1960s.

reference to developments in the 1960s, such as U.S. membership in PIL organizations.

Between the publication of the Second Restatement and the start of work on the Third, PIL treaty-making became quite fluid. The United States ratified a number of treaties negotiated under the auspices of UNIDROIT, UNCITRAL, and the Hague Conference on Private International Law.[71] The volume of scholarly writing on treaty law, federalism, foreign relations, and international law grew, and, unlike the drafting of the Second Restatement, the drafting of the Third was led by reporters who supported a broad scope of the treaty power.[72]

In its introductory comments, the Third Restatement observed that the period from the early 1960s to the late 1980s had brought forward a more systematic and treaty-based U.S. approach to PIL.[73] For reasons of timing, the Second Restatement had been unable to assimilate those developments. In the period before the Second Restatement's drafting process, case law and statutes on judicial assistance had been largely ad hoc.[74] The Third Restatement's solution was to depart from the Second's position on the narrow scope of the treaty power and the preemption of state law by PIL treaties. As to the former, the Third Restatement's comments[75] and reporters' notes[76] repudiated the international concern requirement.

The rationale offered in the comments and notes of section 302 of the Third Restatement stood in stark contrast to the representations made to the Senate by the Kennedy and Johnson administrations. It was odd that section 302 sought to effectuate such a major change in the scope of the treaty power and that the argument for doing so was vague and did not repudiate the Second Restatement clearly and compellingly. It was also odd for a vague explanation of such a major change to be tucked away in comments

71 *See* Section II, *supra*.

72 *See* Louis Henkin, *"International Concern" and the Treaty Power of the United States*, 63 AM. J. INT'L L. 272 (1969); Louis Henkin, *The Constitution, Treaties, and International Human Rights*, 116 U. PA. L. REV. 1012 (1968) (same); Andreas F. Lowenfeld, Book Review, *Foreign Affairs and the Constitution*, 87 HARV. L. REV. 494, 501 (1973); Detlev Vagts, Rudolf Bernhardt, Ulrich Beyerlin, Karl Doehring, and Jochen Abr. Frowein, Book Review, 86 AM. J. INT'L L. 608, 610 (1992).

73 *See* THIRD RESTATEMENT OF THE FOREIGN RELATIONS LAW OF THE UNITED STATES, Chap. 7, Intro. note (Am. Law Inst. 1987).

74 *Ibid.* ("Until the 1950s, no systematic attempt had been made to address the problems covered by this subchapter [on judicial assistance]").

75 *Ibid.* § 302, cmt c ("Contrary to what was once suggested, the Constitution does not require that an international agreement deal only with 'matters of international concern.'").

76 *Ibid.* rptr. note 6 (stating that § 302 "rejects the requirement that the subject of an agreement be of international concern").

and reporters' notes, where its significance could escape the reader's attention. Both facets of the change made section 302 vulnerable to criticism for lack of transparency.

As to supremacy, the Third Restatement's subchapter on judicial assistance provided that U.S. treaties take precedence over conflicting state law. Thus, state rules prescribing the manner of serving process on foreign defendants in some circumstances had to yield to treaty rules.[77] Authentication of documents in accordance with the Hague Convention on Abolishing the Requirement of Legalization[78] dispensed with the need to meet more onerous requirements imposed by state law.[79] So, contrary to the representations that the Executive branch had made to the Senate in the early 1960s, multilateral PIL conventions did trump state law (at least in part) through a combination of preimplementation[80] and self-execution.[81]

For several reasons, the foundation of the new PIL multilateralism rested on a foundation that was not as strong as appeared to participants at the time and that is weaker than the subsequent scholarly literature has acknowledged. The support of Congress, state bar associations, NCCUSL, the ABA, and others had been procured in part by the representation that the United States would reap the full benefits of its domestic reforms in procedural law by embodying the U.S. model in treaties to which other countries would assent.[82] Another weakness in the foundation was that neither courts nor state lawmakers were prepared in advance for the possibility that PIL treaties might conflict with state procedural law in subtle or not subtle ways. Finally, to the extent that section 302 was not the product of a well-aired debate, the

77 *Ibid.* § 472, rptr. note 5 ("precise conformity to [state] law in respect of manner of service is not required when service is made pursuant to the Convention"); *ibid.* ("the Convention prevails over state law").

78 *See* Hague Convention Abolishing the Requirement of Legalization for Foreign Public Documents, Oct. 5, 1961, available at https://assets.hcch.net/docs/b12ad529-5f75-411b-b523-8eebe86613c0.pdf.

79 *See* Third Restatement, *supra* note 73, § 473 rptr. note 9.

80 The 1964 amendments to 28 USC §1782 served to preimplement the new treaty's obligation for the United States to provide assistance to litigants in foreign proceedings seeking evidence in the United States.

81 The provisions of the Service Convention providing the details of service through the central authority mechanism became law in state courts without the need for a federal implementing statute or state implementing legislation.

82 The notes to § 474 of the Third Restatement allude to this in discussing reciprocity: "[A]showing of reciprocity is not required for execution of letters rogatory in the United States, since in adopting 28 U.S.C. 1782 Congress intended to take the initiative in rendering international judicial assistance." *See* Third Restatement, *supra* note 73 at § 474, rptr. note 3. *See also* note 1 (stating that the practice of the United States in responding to requests for assistance in obtaining evidence "is substantially the same under the Convention as apart from it").

results of which could be found in a prominent place in the Third Restatement, the claim that the "international concern test" had been buried or had never legitimately existed was a ripe target for subsequent revisionism, especially when proposed PIL treaty projects became more ambitious and in greater tension with state law.

IV THE REVIVAL OF FEDERALISM AFTER THE THIRD RESTATEMENT

In the 1980s, the Hague Conference took up a different sort of project, the transnational kidnapping of minors. The Conference addressed civil aspects of this problem in a treaty that had as its centerpiece a mechanism for returning children to the country of their habitual residence.[83] Under the Convention, which the U.S. ratified in 1988,[84] national courts in the country of habitual residence possess exclusive jurisdiction to adjudicate custody issues, regardless of any change in the residence of an abducting parent.[85] The role of courts in other Convention countries is limited to providing assistance designed to bring about the return of the child.[86]

This form of judicial assistance was new to the Hague Conference. For the United States, it raised federalism issues not encountered in the Service and Evidence Conventions. Consider a typical child abduction scenario within the scope of the Convention: A parent living outside the United States enters the United States accompanied by a child who has been taken from Country X without the consent of the other parent. In the absence of the Convention, a state court in the United States could exercise personal jurisdiction over both the child and the accompanying parent under the state's long-arm statute.[87]

83 *See* Hague Convention on the Civil Aspects of International Child Abduction, Oct. 25,1980, T.I.A.S. No. 11, 670, 1343 U.N.T.S. 49 ("Hague Abduction Convention"). Art.1 refers to the duty "to secure the prompt return of children wrongfully removed to or retained in any Contracting State" and ensure that "rights of custody and of access under the law of one Contracting State are effectively respected in the other Contracting States." The Supreme Court has referred to this as the Convention's "central operating feature." Abbott v. Abbott, 560 U.S. 1, 9, 130 S. Ct. 1983, 176 L. Ed. 2d 789 (2010).

84 The treaty was implemented in 1988 by the International Child Abduction Remedies Act (ICARA), 102 Stat. 437, 42 U.S.C. § 11601 *et seq*.

85 *See* Hague Abduction Convention, *supra* note 83, art. 16. In other words, subject to limited exceptions, one parent cannot change the national law applicable to custody issues by the unilateral act of taking the child to another country without the other parent's consent.

86 *Ibid*. at arts. 12 and 16.

87 For example, a statute authorizing the exercise of jurisdiction based on the physical presence of natural persons within the state's territory at the time of service of process. *See, e.g.*, Michigan Rev. Jud. Act § 600.701.

That court could then apply the state's family law (or the state's choice-of-law rules) in order to examine a range of legal issues[88] and order a range of remedies.[89] Under the treaty, however, the scope of the state court's inquiry and the range of its available remedies is limited. It cannot simply act in the best interests of the child, even if normally it would do so if Country X were not a party to the Convention. In terms of remedy, the forum court in this scenario only can order the child's return to Country X.

A second set of federalism concerns arise from the Child Abduction Convention. Prior Hague treaties had approached transnational problems either by prescribing choice of law rules to determine which country's substantive law would apply[90] or by creating a treaty-based substantive rule to supplant existing national law rules.[91] In contrast, the Child Abduction Convention is based on a third approach: when a court in Country Y receives a request to order the return of a child to Country X, the Convention designates the country in which custody issues must be adjudicated. Such issues must be resolved by courts in the country of habitual residence, the country from which the child was abducted. Rather than specifying the substantive law to be applied or the choice-of-law rules that govern, the Convention specifies the country in which treaty-based jurisdiction lies and requires that the child be returned to that country for resolution of custody and related issues.[92] The impact of this third approach on state law

88 The range of issues would depend on state statutory and common law but typically would include what constitutes the best interests of the child.

89 The range of remedies would depend on state statutory and common law but likely would include custody orders, orders of child support, or orders that the child not be removed from the United States without court approval.

90 This is the approach of arts. 4–6 of the Hague Convention on the Law Applicable to Products Liability, Oct. 2, 1973, available at www.hcch.net/en/instruments/conventions/full-text/?cid=84. The products liability convention resulted from a PIL treaty project proposed by the United States during the heady years just after U.S. entry into the Hague Conference. *See* Willis L.M. Reese, *The Hague Convention on the Law Applicable to Products Liability*, 8 Int'l Law. 606 (1974). Ultimately, the United States did not ratify this treaty.

91 The Service Convention, for example, requires each country to designate a central authority, which has a duty first to receive requests for service of process and, second, to effect service within its territory, provided that the request meets the criteria specified in the treaty. Ideally, all member-state central authorities apply the Convention in the same way and do not create exceptions unauthorized by the Convention. *See supra* note 38.

92 One may think of this as a choice-of-forum approach because the main goal of the treaty is to determine where the custody issues should be resolved and to limit the role of the courts of other countries to directing the parties to the courts of the appropriate country. Of course, with the Abduction Convention, there is no actual choice-of-forum clause in the sense of a contractual provision to which the disputing parties agreed voluntarily. Rather the parties are required to litigate in a specific forum by virtue of a treaty that their countries have ratified.

and state courts in the United States is different from the other two approaches.

The federalism implications of the three approaches can be analyzed by using what one might call a "hierarchy of intrusiveness." Choice-of-law treaties intrude least on prerogatives of state courts in the United States. Such treaties do not strip state courts of their nontreaty jurisdiction over parties or subject matter. Nor do they require state courts to transfer cases abroad or to stay their proceedings in deference to courts in other countries. Rather, choice-of-law treaties simply prescribe the law to be applied to a particular dispute. As a result, these treaties bring about little interference in the autonomy of state courts: treaties of this sort may require state courts to depart from their state's choice of law rules, but they do not interfere with their adjudicative jurisdiction or limit their remedial powers.

Treaties that incorporate uniform substantive rules are more intrusive than choice-of-law treaties. The former go beyond choosing the appropriate domestic substantive rules and require courts to apply treaty-selected rules, which courts must apply even when the treaty rules differ from the forum's substantive law. Thus, were a treaty pertaining to automobile accidents to prescribe the law of the place of the accident (a choice-of-law approach), it would displace the forum state's law some of the time but not all of the time. But a treaty that prescribed a uniform substantive rule of liability typically[93] would require forum courts to apply a liability rule different from the forum state's preferred rule.

The Child Abduction Convention adopts a third approach, which is more intrusive than either of the two approaches discussed thus far. Its rules are both jurisdiction-regulating and forum-specifying. Imagine that a parent resident in Country X files suit in a state court in the United States alleging that the other parent has transferred a child from Country X to the forum state in the United States. The treaty requires the forum court not to apply either the forum state's substantive law nor its choice-of-law rules. Rather, the forum court must select one and only one remedy; it must order that the child be returned to Country X.[94] By virtue of the Supremacy Clause, state courts in the United

This difference aside, the Child Abduction Convention functions as a forum-selecting mechanism by directing the parties to the one national court system with treaty-based jurisdiction to resolve the underlying custody dispute. The Convention does this reliably only if the courts of state parties interpret the Convention in the same way.

93 In some instances, the treaty's substantive rule can be the same as the substantive rule that results from applying the forum's choice-of-law rules.

94 This is the result assuming that none of the exceptions listed in the treaty applies. For example, the child need not be returned if he or she has been present in the United States (post-abduction) for more than a year.

States must supervise the execution of this remedy even if, under the substantive law of their state, the foreign country's custody order and law would be objectionable.

In light of the Child Abduction Convention's greater intrusiveness than the Service or Evidence Conventions, it was telling from a federalism perspective that the Child Abduction Convention did not provoke federalism-based opposition in Congress. In the years before the United States became a party to the Child Abduction Convention, state courts regularly exercised jurisdiction over minors found within the state and entered orders to further their best interests.[95] Notwithstanding this well-established practice of state court control over child custody, almost no federalism-based opposition to the Convention was voiced. The Convention was supported by state officials, state bar associations, and it gained easy passage in the Senate even though the Convention and its implementing legislation employs federal power to strip state courts of jurisdiction over custody determinations in international abduction cases.[96] In short, treaty provisions that in the eras of Hughes and Fish would have been dismissed out of hand, easily passed the Senate during PIL's golden era.

The relatively minor attention paid to preemption (raised in connection with implementing legislation) showed how strong the federalization of PIL had become by the mid-1980s. Late in congressional consideration of the implementing legislation for the Convention – the International Child Abduction Remedies Act or ICARA[97] – the Reagan Justice Department attempted to change the draft statute, from a concurrent jurisdiction regime allowing plaintiffs seeking a child's return to file suit in federal or state court, to an exclusively state jurisdiction regime. Though concurrent jurisdiction had been a common method of implementing prior PIL treaties,[98] matters were

95 This is still true with respect to abductions from countries that are not party to the Hague Child Abduction Convention. *See* Mezo v. Elmergawi, 855 F. Supp. 59 (E.D.N.Y. 1994).

96 The New York Convention, as implemented by the Federal Arbitration Act, also requires state courts to dismiss some cases that, in the absence of the treaty, would fall within their jurisdiction. Unlike the Child Abduction Convention, the New York Convention does this in deference to party autonomy; cases are dismissed because the parties bargained for a specific forum, not because the U.S. government entered into a treaty that requires that cases be sent abroad. *See* New York Convention, *supra* note 39.

97 *See* ICARA, *supra* note 84.

98 For example, concurrent jurisdiction had been the mode of implementing the New York Convention. *See* Federal Arbitration Act, Chapter 2 – Convention on the Recognition and Enforcement of Foreign Arbitral Awards, Pub. L. 91–368, §b 1, 84 Stat. 692, *codified at* 9 U. S.C.203 (providing for general federal question jurisdiction on a concurrent rather than exclusive basis).

complicated by the Reagan administration's promulgation of a far-reaching executive order on federalism that called for regulatory and lawmaking initiatives of the Executive branch to be implemented at the state level.[99] The Justice Department argued that in non-ICARA cases, child custody determinations had been made in state courts applying state law, reflecting a longstanding view of federalism[100] that should not be altered by treaty.

The proposed change never gained traction. It was voted down in committee, leaving concurrent jurisdiction in the bill that went to the House and Senate and that was enacted as ICARA.[101] This episode showed the weakness of federalism-based attacks on PIL treaties and implementing legislation at this time. In fact, the main impact of this episode seemed to be to allow PIL treaty advocates to make a record of arguments in favor of PIL treaty-making to be found in the transcripts of those who testified in favor of ICARA: concurrent jurisdiction had been common for PIL treaty adjudication in the past;[102] a world of difference exists between adjudicating custody issues and determining whether custody issues must be adjudicated by a foreign court, and the force behind federalism-based objections is at a low ebb when a treaty or

99 Exec. Order No. 12,612, 52 Fed. Reg. 41,685 (Oct. 26, 1987) stated in relevant part:

> In the absence of clear constitutional or statutory authority, the presumption of sovereignty should rest with the individual States. Uncertainties regarding the legitimate authority of the national government should be resolved against regulation at the national level.

Nothing in the Executive order suggested that it had been drafted with treaties and treaty implementing legislation in mind.

100 *See* Testimony of Stephen J. Markman, Assistant Attorney General for Legal Policy, U.S. Department of Justice, International Child Abduction Act, Hearing before the Subcommittee on Administrative Law and Governmental Relations of the Committee on the Judiciary, House of Representatives, One Hundredth Congress, Second Session on H.R. 2673 and H.R. 3971 (Feb. 3, 1988) at 48 (arguing that concurrent jurisdiction would require federal courts to adjudicate matters at the "heart of traditional domestic relations" with respect to which they had little experience); Letter to the Honorable Barney Frank from Acting Assistant Attorney General Thomas M. Boyd (Mar. 31, 1988) at 2, *reprinted* as appendix to Hearing (claiming that the proposed grant of federal jurisdiction "would represent a sharp departure from the longstanding policy, based on principles of federalism" of keeping domestic relations matters out of the federal courts).

101 H.R. Rep. No. 525, 100th Cong., 2nd Sess. 1988, 1988 U.S.C.C.A.N. 386, 1988 WL169798 ("Subsection (a)(2) of the amendment explicitly retains Federal court jurisdiction in those cases arising under the Convention").

102 *See* Testimony of Peter Pfund, Assistant Legal Adviser for Private International Law, International Child Abduction Act, Hearing before the Subcommittee on Administrative Law and Governmental Relations of the Committee on the Judiciary, House of Representatives, One Hundredth Congress, Second Session on H.R. 2673 and H.R. 3971 (Feb. 3, 1988).

statute is not actually moving some block of preexisting cases from state courts to federal courts.[103]

V PIL AND FEDERALISM IN THE SUPREME COURT (1987–88)

As the United States was ratifying the Child Abduction Convention, the Supreme Court was interpreting Hague Conference treaties for the first time. The issue in *Aérospatiale* (1987) was whether litigants need to pursue extraterritorial discovery via the Evidence Convention rather than through U.S. rules of civil procedure. In *Schlunk* (1988), the question was whether the Service Convention preempted state procedural rules permitting valid service on out-of-state parent corporations by serving in-state subsidiaries. In both cases, the Court found that the treaties were not broadly preemptive. Both left considerable room for litigants to utilize U.S. procedural law (including state procedural law), rather than applying the treaties.[104]

These cases signaled that state interests had a significant place in treaty interpretation and that the Supreme Court would not presume that Hague treaties and their implementing legislation were intended to federalize U.S. procedural law. In the *Aérospatiale* case,[105] Justice Stevens articulated a five-factor test for determining whether litigants need to pursue extraterritorial discovery through the Convention or, instead, can follow American procedural rules and statutes.[106] But neither the majority nor the dissent

103 *See* Abbott, 560 U.S. at 20 (2010) ("The Convention is based on the principle that the best interests of the child are well served when decisions regarding custody rights are made in the country of habitual residence").

104 *See* Volkswagenwerk Aktiengesellschaft v. Schlunk, 486 U.S. 694, 108 S. Ct. 2104, 100L. Ed. 2d 722 (1988).

105 *See* Societe Nationale Industrielle Aérospatiale v. U.S. District Court, 482 U.S. at 522 (1987). The U.S. Government's amicus brief in the Supreme Court was submitted by an administration acutely sensitive to states' rights and the need to check federal power. Nevertheless, the Reagan Justice Department's submission made no reference to the federalism issues associated with the Evidence's Convention's application in state and federal courts. *See* Brief for the United States and the Securities and Exchange Commission as Amici Curiae, Societé Nationale Industrielle Aérospatiale v. U.S. District Court (U.S. Supreme Court), 1986 WL 727504.

106 The Court's five factors are: (1) the importance to the litigation of the information requested; (2) the degree to which the discovery request is specific; (3) whether the information sought originated in the United States; (4) the availability of means other than through the Convention of securing the information; and (5) the extent to which noncompliance with the discovery request would undermine important interests of the United States, or compliance with the discovery request would undermine important interests of the country where the information is located. Aérospatiale, 482 U.S. at 544, n. 28.

considered whether the applicable test should be exactly the same in state and federal courts. One reason why it makes some sense to distinguish between the two in interpreting the Evidence Convention is that often state and federal rules differ with respect to extraterritorial discovery. Federal courts apply the Federal Rules of Civil Procedure and federal statutes. These reflect federal policies and are familiar to the State Department when it negotiates treaties.[107] State rules and statutes embody state policies; these are less familiar to U.S. treaty negotiators, with the result that pre-existing federal law is more likely to be consistent with a new treaty than is pre-existing state law because treaties tend not to be negotiated with state law in mind.[108]

That the Court in *Aérospatiale* did not distinguish between extraterritorial discovery in state proceedings and in federal proceedings has had consequences. Chief among them is that, post-*Aérospatiale*, state courts and lawmakers have enjoyed wide latitude in choosing to adapt to the Convention or not. Generally, they have declined to adapt. Since 1987, extraterritorial discovery in state courts largely has proceeded under state procedural law rather than via the Evidence Convention.[109] None of these state cases has been reviewed by the U.S. Supreme Court. That absence of close monitoring of how state courts interpret the Evidence Convention can be seen by state judges as granting wide berth to prioritize state policies on extraterritorial discovery. In short, although *Aérospatiale* does not address federalism directly, its imprecise five-factor test and the lack of Supreme Court review of state court decisions that decline to apply the Evidence Convention has allowed state courts to pay little heed to the federal interests advanced by requiring litigants to use the Convention.

The *Schlunk* case brought about a similar result: wide latitude for state authorities to diverge from federal treaty policy. *Schlunk* arose out of litigation in Illinois state courts against a German entity that had been served with

[107] In negotiating Hague conventions, the State Department receives input from the Department of Justice and other federal departments and agencies that routinely litigate in federal court.

[108] In addition, one would expect it to be rare for state lawmakers to pay attention to U.S. treaties when considering whether to amend state rules and statutes in civil procedure.

[109] Since 1987, commentators have reported that a majority of state and lower federal courts applying *Aérospatiale* have concluded that the parties need not pursue discovery abroad through the Hague Evidence Convention. *See generally* Borchers, *supra* note 45, at 82–5 (collecting cases); Gary B. Born & Peter B. Rutledge, International Civil Litigation in United States Courts 1052–7 (5th ed. 2011).

process in Illinois by delivery of the summons and complaint to the defendant's U.S. subsidiary. Applying Illinois law, which allowed out-of-state entities to be sued by service upon agents located within the state, the Illinois courts found service to be proper. The U.S. Supreme Court agreed, ruling that this method of service was a valid alternative to the Service Convention.[110]

Schlunk impairs the predictability and convenience that the Service Convention promises to foreign defendants.[111] Instead of being able to plan for just one method of service, foreign defendants must plan for several methods under different state rules that are potentially applicable. Thus foreign litigants experience a lack of predictability tied to the actions of state legislatures and courts,[112] which can shift convenience away from foreign defendants and toward in-state plaintiffs[113] by amending or reinterpreting state procedural law or laws on agency.[114] Federalism is also an important aspect of the *Schlunk* case. In bestowing its blessing on variations on the application of the Service Convention from one state to another, the Court in *Schlunk* frustrated the ability of foreign litigants to forecast their amenability to service in the United States by monitoring one body of law: federal case law interpreting the Convention.[115] Rather, because of *Schlunk*, such defendants are amenable to suit via a variety of state service rules, requiring them to monitor proposals to modify the

110 The Court held that the Convention did not apply to service on the U.S.-based subsidiary because, under Article 1, there was no occasion to transmit a judicial or extrajudicial document for service abroad. *See* Volkswagenwerk Aktiengesellschaft v. Schlunk, 486 U.S. at 707 ("Where service on a domestic agent is valid and complete under both state law and the Due Process Clause, our inquiry ends and the Convention has no further implications").

111 Had *Schlunk* been decided so as to require resort to the Convention's central authority mechanism, foreign manufacturers selling products throughout the United States would be able to plan on receiving U.S. pleadings in one standard manner – delivery in their home country, translated into their language, and in the manner customary in their country. They would not need to keep up to date on the procedural rules and laws on agency of more than fifty different U.S. jurisdictions. They would not need to train subsidiaries, agents, and individuals about what to do if served with process intended for the parent company.

112 Schlunk does not inconvenience foreign plaintiffs; like domestic plaintiffs, they can choose to proceed via the Service Convention or via U.S. rules on service.

113 Provisions such as the one in the Illinois statute at issue in *Schlunk* allow an attorney to serve process in the same manner, for domestic and international cases alike, without the need to become proficient in the operation of the Service Convention.

114 Subject to the constraints of the Due Process Clause of the 14th Amendment.

115 Similarly, in implementing the New York Convention, Congress conditioned the recognition of foreign arbitral awards on aspects of state contract law. *See* 9 U.S.C. § 2 (providing that awards shall be "valid, irrevocable, and enforceable, save upon such grounds as exist at law or in equity for the revocation of any contract").

procedural rules of state court systems.[116] Such modifications can even come about unintentionally.[117]

Another problem with the Court's first encounter with Hague conventions relates to forum shopping. Foreign defendants trapped in state court[118] must follow the discovery rules of the state in which the suit is pending. These rules can differ from those in federal courts in the same state. Litigants may have an incentive to forum shop in search of favorable discovery rules. In the aftermath of *Aérospatiale's* rejection of mandatory first use of the Evidence Convention, state case law interpreting *Aérospatiale* has in some states created a difference between the approach of state courts and that of federal district courts in the same state.[119]

In short, in the late 1980s, the Court interpreted PIL treaties with a spirit of deference toward state procedural law. Of course, one can regard this orientation as pro-treaty in that it smooths over potential conflicts between state procedural law and judicial assistance treaties. But the cost of this deference is substantial: the approach in *Schlunk* amounts to something of a clear statement rule in order for PIL treaties to trump state procedural law.

VI UNSUCCESSFUL ATTEMPTS AT A HAGUE JUDGMENTS CONVENTION

In 1992, the United States proposed that the Hague Conference take up the transnational recognition and enforcement of civil and commercial judgments.[120]

116 The court in *Yamaha Motor Co., Ltd. v. Superior Court*, 174 Cal. App. 4th 264, 94 Cal. Rptr. 3d 494, (2009), went a step beyond *Schlunk* in holding that the plaintiff could serve a Japanese parent by making service on the agent of Yamaha's California-based subsidiary. *See also* Kwon v. Yun, 2006 WL 416375 (SDNY 2006) (applying New York agency law).

117 In many states, rules on service of process do not distinguish between out-of-state defendants that are U.S. entities and those that are foreign. *See, e.g.*, Mich. R. Civ. P. 2.105. Thus, a revision to those rules intended by the legislature to make it easier for in-state residents to serve process on defendants in another U.S. state can have unintended international consequences.

118 Foreign defendants sued in state court are unable to remove the case to federal court if complete diversity and federal question jurisdiction are lacking.

119 If use of the Evidence Convention were mandatory, state/federal differences in discovery rules likely would not matter much to litigants with respect to foreign discovery. The most important factor would be the practices of the Central Authority in the foreign country.

120 *See* Letter from Edwin Williamson, State Department Legal Adviser, to Georges Droz (Secretary General of Hague Conference on Private International Law) (May 5, 1992), available at www.state.gov/documents/organization/65973.pdf.

That subject – the duty to recognize the judgments of the courts of other States – had been explored two decades earlier and had resulted in a 1971 Hague Convention that few countries had signed or ratified.[121] The United States neither signed nor ratified the 1971 treaty, and the United States was one of few Hague Conference member states that was not (and still is not) a party to any convention (multilateral or bilateral) on judgment recognition.

In proposing that the Hague Conference revisit the 1971 effort, the United States was walking on ground that was unsteady and was about to become more so. Not only had the 1971 Convention been a failure, but a separate attempt at a bilateral U.S.-UK treaty in the 1970s also had ended disappointingly, with both parties walking away from lengthy negotiations.[122] By 1992, the law in a supermajority of U.S. jurisdictions had evolved so as to be receptive to foreign-country judgments, even in the absence of reciprocal treatment of U.S. judgments by foreign courts.

For the U.S. delegation, succeeding in these new negotiations required giving careful thought to the history of judgment recognition and federalism in the United States in the decades since *Erie Railroad v. Tomkins*.[123] After *Erie*, state law supplied the substantive law regarding recognition of foreign-country judgments in both state courts and federal courts.[124] By the 1960s, a majority of states had adopted NCCUSL's 1962 uniform act on foreign money judgments.[125] Those states hardly could be expected to react enthusiastically to a federal treaty preempting that uniform act. Other states had adopted the Third Restatement of Foreign Relations Law or followed the Second Restatement of Conflict of Laws, both of which apply to non–money judgments as well as money judgments.[126] For other states,

121 Convention of 1 February 1971 on the Recognition and Enforcement of Foreign Judgments in Civil and Commercial Matters, available at www.hcch.net/en/instruments/conventions/full-text/?cid=78.

122 In 1976, the United States and the United Kingdom initialed a draft treaty, the Convention on the Reciprocal Recognition and Enforcement of Judgments in Civil Matters, U.S.-U.K., 16 I.L.M.71 (1977). A final version of that text never materialized, in part because the draft was highly unpopular in the U.K. The draft would have required recognition even when the jurisdictional basis under a U.S. long-arm statute was much broader than that exercised by British courts. *See* P.M. North, *The Draft U.K./U.S. Judgments Convention: A British Viewpoint*, 1 NW. J. INT'L L. & BUS. 219, 228 (1979) (describing general British reaction to the proposed convention as "hostile"). The project was abandoned in 1981.

123 *See* Erie R. Co. v. Tompkins, 304 U.S. 64 (1938).

124 *See* Ronald A. Brand, "The Continuing Evolution of U.S. Judgments Recognition Law" (Oct. 7, 2015), available at http://papers.ssrn.com/sol3/papers.cfm?abstract_id=2670866.

125 *See* UFMJRA, *supra* note 65.

126 *See* THIRD RESTATEMENT, *supra* note 73, §§ 481–6 and RESTATEMENT of the Law (SECOND) OF CONFLICT OF LAWS § 98 (AM. LAW. INST. 1971 & 1988 rev.).

foreign judgment recognition is controlled purely by common law. When the United States proposed the Judgments Project, transnational judgment recognition had been regulated by state law for over fifty years.[127]

Despite the extent of existing state law on judgment recognition, at the outset of the Hague Judgments Project, American federalism was not regarded as a significant obstacle to concluding a treaty. Other issues were of greater concern, chief among them being that U.S. courts had long recognized foreign judgments without requiring reciprocal behavior by other countries.[128] The 1962 Uniform Act, contained no reciprocity requirement. On the eve of the negotiations, studies showed that judgments emanating from Hague Conference countries typically were granted recognition in the United States.[129] This left the United States with the goal of persuading other

[127] *Erie* brought to an end the era of *Hilton v. Guyot*, 159 U.S. 113 (1895) in which the source of the legal rule regarding recognition of foreign-country judgments was the general common law, which federal courts could divine differently from state courts.

[128] Neither the 1962 UFMJRA nor the Third Restatement included a reciprocity requirement. *See* UFMJRA, *supra* note 65; *see* Third Restatement, *supra* note 73. Reporters' note 1 to § 481 of the Restatement correctly stated that *Hilton*'s reciprocity requirement over time had become a minority rule among U.S. states. *See* Third Restatement, *supra* note 73, §481, rptr. note. 1. Section§ 481 went beyond the 1962 UFMJRA in creating a rule of presumptive recognition not only for money judgments but for other judgments as well:

> [A] final judgment of a court of a foreign state granting or denying recovery of a sum of money, establishing or confirming the status of a person, or determining interests in property, is conclusive between the parties, and is entitled to recognition in courts in the United States.

See Third Restatement, *supra* note 73, § 481. Comment § 481 then overstated existing law in claiming that a foreign judgment "is generally entitled to recognition by courts in the United States to the same extent as a judgment of a court of one State in the courts of another State," a statement that ignored that foreign-country judgment recognition in UFMJRA states was limited to money judgments and by defences not available to judgment debtors in interstate recognition proceedings. *Compare* § 481, cmt. c, *with* § 482(2)(d) (stating that U.S. courts "need not" recognize a foreign- country judgment if "the cause of action on which the judgment was based, or the judgment itself, is repugnant to the public policy of the United States or of the State where recognition is sought."). In light of § 482, the comment to § 481 was especially conspicuous and seemed to be an effort to guide state courts and federal courts sitting in diversity toward interpreting the UFMJRA very liberally from the perspective of judgment creditors. Unlike recognition actions under the New York Convention and the FAA, actions to enforce foreign judgments do not arise under federal law. In order to be adjudicated in federal court, the latter must satisfy the complete diversity requirements and amount in controversy requirements of 28 U.S.C. § 1332.

[129] *See, e.g.*, Ronald A. Brand, *Enforcement of Judgments in the United States and Europe*, 13 *J. L. & Com.* 193 (1994). This was not surprising. By the 1990s, a supermajority of states had enacted the 1962 UFMJRA or had followed § 482 of the Third Restatement, or had adopted a comity approach that closely tracked *Hilton v. Guyot*. All three of these approaches were highly favorable to foreign judgment creditors. Section 482 of the Third Restatement

countries to become more receptive to U.S. judgments even though these countries had little need for a treaty ensuring enforcement of their judgments in the United States.

A second problem for the United States was that the Hague Permanent Bureau and a number of delegations favored a "double convention" – one that prescribed not only rules on judgment recognition but also rules regulating the assertion of jurisdiction by courts in the state party in which suit was initially brought (sometimes referred to as the "F1" state and this form of jurisdiction referred to as "direct jurisdiction").[130] Countries favoring a double convention worked for several years in the 1990s to create a restricted list of permissible bases of jurisdiction for F1 courts that also would produce judgments that other countries ("F2 states") would be required to recognize. This approach sought to replicate the Brussels and Lugano Conventions,[131] multilateral European treaties in force at that time that had been designed to limit the exercise of direct jurisdiction in any case to courts in just a handful of countries. Proponents of a double convention argued in favor of a treaty of this type because it would limit parallel litigation,[132] avoid costs associated with contesting jurisdiction, and increase the ability of potential litigants to predict

provided that although the 1962 UFMJRA did not apply to non–money judgments, that limitation was not especially problematic from the perspective of most judgment creditors, who seek to collect on money judgments. In contrast, in the 1990s and currently, U.S. judgment creditors face higher obstacles to enforcing U.S. money judgments around the world. *See generally* Samuel B. Baumgartner, *Understanding the Obstacles to the Recognition and Enforcement of U.S. Judgments Abroad*, 44 N.Y.U. J. INT'L L. & POL. 965 (2013); Samuel B. Baumgartner, *How Well Do U.S. Judgments Fare in Europe?* 40 GEORGE WASH. INT'L L. REV. 173 (2007).

130 *See* Prelim. Doc. No. 7, Special Comm'n on the Question of Jurisdiction, Recognition and Enforcement of Foreign Judgments, HAGUE CONF. ON PRIVATE INTL. LAW (1997) at ¶ 8 (Apr. 1997) available at https://asssets.hcch.net/docs/76852ce3-a967-42e4-94f5-24be4289d1e5.pdf (arguing that the Hague Judgment Project needed to be a double convention in order to enjoy the success of the Brussels and Lugano Conventions in Europe and to avoid the failure of the 1971 Hague Judgments Convention).

131 *See* Convention Concerning Judicial Competence and the Execution of Decisions in Civil and Commercial Matters, Sept. 27, 1968, 1262 U.N.T.S. 153 (the "Brussels Convention") which was mandatory for EEC (now EU) countries. The Lugano Convention, similar in substance to the Brussels Convention, included both EEC countries and EFTA countries (those belonging to the European Free Trade Area). *See* Convention of 16 Sep. 1988 on Jurisdiction and the Enforcement of Judgments in Civil and Commercial Matters (the "Lugano Convention") available at http://curia.europa.eu/common/recdoc/convention/en/c-textes/lug-idx.htm.

132 Parallel litigation occurs when proceedings over the same factual dispute take place in the courts of more than one country. Double conventions typically do not completely eliminate parallel litigation; courts other than F1 can adjudicate ancillary matters, such as requests for preliminary relief or requests for judicial assistance, such as those made pursuant to the Hague Evidence Convention.

in advance which national courts could exercise jurisdiction over a potential dispute.

With Special Commission[133] meetings focused on negotiating a double convention (and later a mixed convention),[134] federalism eventually emerged as a perceived negotiating constraint for the United States. Other delegations, especially those from Western Europe, urged the United States to relinquish practices in regard to direct jurisdiction that were regarded especially by civil law countries as "exorbitant." Such jurisdictional practices included doing-business jurisdiction,[135] tag or transient presence jurisdiction,[136] and other practices commonly found in state long arm

[133] Special Commissions are the bodies that perform most of the drafting and negotiations that lead to the final text of Hague Conference conventions. The final texts are voted upon at diplomatic sessions. *See* www.hcch.net/en/about.

[134] The mixed convention was the proposal of Professor Arthur T. von Mehren. *See* Convention of 30 June 2005 on Choice of Court Agreements Explanatory Report ("Explanatory Report"), at 16; *see also* Arthur T. von Mehren, *Enforcing Judgments Abroad: Reflections on the Design of Recognition Conventions* 24 BROOK. J. INT'L L. 17 (1998). The mixed convention proposal created three categories of jurisdiction by national courts: (1) jurisdictional bases on a "white list" that resulted in a duty of recognition by other countries; (2) jurisdictional bases that were "blacklisted," meaning that countries were forbidden by the treaty from exercising them, even if otherwise permitted to do so in domestic cases; and (3) "gray-list" jurisdictional bases that can be exercised at the outset but that result in judgments that other countries may, but need not, recognize. *See also* Arthur T. von Mehren, *Drafting a Convention on International Jurisdiction and the Effects of Foreign Judgments Acceptable World-Wide: Can the Hague Conference Project Succeed? ("Can Hague Succeed?")* 49 *Am. J. Comp. L.* 191 (2001). Professor von Mehren served on the U.S. delegation during the Judgments Convention negotiations and also later during the negotiations that led to the Choice of Courts Convention. He also served on U.S. delegations to prior conventions, including the Evidence Convention. *See* Jeffrey D. Kovar, *In Memoriam: Arthur T. von Mehren*, 119 HARV. L. REV. 1952 (2006).

[135] In the United States, doing-business jurisdiction is a form of general jurisdiction based on a defendant's continuous and systematic contacts with the forum. In 1998, the United States delegation submitted an analysis of doing business jurisdiction by courts in the United States in the context of the Hague Judgments Convention negotiations. *See* Paul R. Dubinsky, *The Reach of Doing Business Jurisdiction and Transacting Business Jurisdiction Over Non-U.S. Individuals and Entities*, Working Doc. No. 67, Special Comm'n on the Question of Jurisdiction, Recognition and Enforcement of Foreign Judgments, HAGUE CONF. ON PRIVATE INTL. LAW (1998).

[136] "Tag jurisdiction," based on an individual's physical presence within the forum at the time of service of process, is a form of general jurisdiction in widespread use in the United States and some other common law countries that employ power-based theories of jurisdiction. In *Burnham v. Superior Court*, 495 U.S. at 610, Justice Scalia held for a plurality that tag jurisdiction comports with Due Process, based in significant part on the finding that "among the most firmly established principles of personal jurisdiction in American tradition is that the courts of a State have jurisdiction over nonresidents who are physically present in the State."). Art. 3 of the Brussels Convention had barred the use of tag jurisdiction by British and Irish courts in Brussels Convention cases. *See* Brussels Convention, *supra* note 131, art. 3.

statutes.[137] Such U.S. jurisdictional bases stand in contrast to jurisdictional regimes in which the presence or not of jurisdiction turns on one or two specific factors, such as the place of performance of a contractual obligation.

Formal negotiations began in 1996 with many eyes on the United States to move things along by expressing a willingness to relinquish some jurisdictional bases (or at least their use in transnational cases) that had been employed by state courts for a very long time. This negotiating posture came at an inopportune time. At the very juncture that the U.S. delegation was engaging seriously on this point with other delegations, the federalism jurisprudence of the U.S. Supreme Court was changing. It took an unexpected turn away from nearly unlimited congressional power under the Commerce Clause toward federalism-based limits on congressional power. From 1992 to 1997, the Court struck down parts of four federal statutes as exceeding the

The United Kingdom and Ireland accepted this change to their domestic legal systems as part of becoming members of the EEC (now EU). At the beginning of the Hague Judgment Project negotiations, states party to the Brussels Convention did not anticipate that relinquishment of tag jurisdiction by the United States would be a problem, in part because of lack of familiarity with the role that tag jurisdiction had played in international human rights litigation in the United States since 1980 and in part out of lack of familiarity with the federalism dimensions of this issue. *See* Peter Schlosser, *Lectures on Civil-Law Litigation Systems and American Cooperation with Those Systems*, 45 U. KAN. L. REV. 9 (1996). Professor von Mehren's perspective on this was that the United Kingdom and Ireland had "accepted the Brussels Convention as part of a package deal in order to obtain the advantage of membership in an emerging economic and political union." von Mehren, *Can the Hague Succeed? supra* note 134, at 194. In contrast to the situation presented by British and Irish entry into the process of European economic integration, the sole carrot for U.S. participation in the Hague Judgments Convention negotiations was the prospect of more liberal recognition of U.S. civil judgments by foreign courts.

137 This label referred to jurisdictional practices that allow the existence *vel non* of jurisdiction in a national legal system to turn on the frequency and depth of a defendant's contacts with the forum, the extent to which activities (such as marketing or sales) are directed at the forum, or the defendant's receipt of some benefit from the forum. *See* Prelim. Doc. 15, "Informal Note on the Work of the Informal Meetings Held Since October 1999 to Consider and Develop Drafts on Outstanding Items," (May 2001) (containing, as annexes, proposals from Germany, Japan, and the United Kingdom designed to bridge the gap between U.S. "activity-based" approaches to jurisdiction and the approaches of most other parties to the negotiations) available at https://assets.hcch.net/docs/f76f699d-0e14-4e1a-aed9-cec296459e10.pdf; Prelim. Doc. 16, "Some Reflections on the Present State of Negotiations on the Judgments Project in the Context of the Future Work Programme of the Conference" at ¶ 5 (Feb. 2002) (listing main obstacles preventing the completion of the Judgment Project, including differences over "activity-based jurisdiction" and jurisdiction in the context of e-commerce), available at https://assets.hcch.net/docs/fc32c43e-22ac-4cb1-8f79-67688d66b282.pdf. The lack of a resolution of such issues led the Permanent Bureau to redirect negotiations toward producing what was to become the Choice of Court Convention. *See* Prelim. Doc. 25, Explanatory Report on the Preliminary Draft Convention on Choice of Court Agreements at ¶ ¶ 4–7 (Trevor C. Hartley and Masato Dogauchi, coreporters) (25 Mar. 2004).

Article I powers of Congress.[138] Though none of these cases involved the Article II treaty power, these rulings were a red flag to those seeking to create new federal law that would preempt state jurisdictional rules, especially rules with a long historical pedigree[139] Such state procedural rules included those employed to provide remedies to residents harmed, for example, by products manufactured abroad.[140] Though the Court's "new federalism" cases were an important indication of its willingness to revive judicial safeguards of federalism, these cases did not force U.S. negotiators at the Hague Conference into a straightjacket. None of the cases involved the treaty power. None dealt with state procedural law. None changed the fact that the Supreme Court had

138 *See* New York v. United States, 505 U.S. 144, 112 S. Ct. 2408, 120 L. Ed. 2d 120 (1992) (holding that Congress cannot require states to take legal ownership of and liability for radioactive waste within their territory as part of a federal program of waste disposal); United States v. Lopez, 514 U.S. 549, 115 S. Ct. 1624, 131 L. Ed. 2d 626 (1995) (striking down federal statute regulating the possession of firearms near schools); Printz v. United States, 521 U.S. 898, 117 S. Ct. 2365, 138L. Ed. 2d 914 (1997) (holding that federal government cannot compel states to administer a program of federally mandated background checks in connection with the purchase of firearms); City of Boerne v. Flores, 521 U.S. 507, 117 S. Ct. 2157, 138 L. Ed. 2d 624 (1997) (striking down the Religious Freedom Restoration Act as beyond congressional power to implement the 14th Amendment). A fifth case would come down soon thereafter. *See* United States v. Morrison, 529 U.S. 598, 120 S. Ct. 1740, 146 L. Ed. 2d 658 (2000) (striking down federal civil remedy provision of the Violence Against Women Act as beyond Congress' Article I powers and its authority to implement the 14th Amendment).

139 Justice Scalia's 1990 plurality opinion in *Burnham v. Superior Court* had stated that jurisdiction based on in-hand service of process within the territory of the forum state is consistent with the Due Process clause of the 14th Amendment because a long tradition supported the practice. *See* Burnham v. Superior Court of California, Cty. of Marin, 495 U.S. 604, 619, 110S. Ct. 2105, 109 L. Ed. 2d 631 (1990) ("The short of the matter is that jurisdiction based on physical presence alone constitutes due process because it is one of the continuing traditions of our legal system."). In 1984, the Court had reaffirmed that state long-arm statutes incorporating doing business jurisdiction could be constitutional. *See* Helicopteros Nacionales de Colombia, S.A. v. Hall, 466 U.S. 408, 104 S. Ct. 1868, 80 L. Ed. 2d 404 (1984) (citing *Perkins v. Benguet Consolidated Mining Co.*, 342 U.S. 437 (1952)). Since then, the Court has taken a narrower view of general jurisdiction, see Daimler AG v. Bauman, 134 S. Ct. 746 (2014); *Goodyear Dunlop Tires v. Brown*, 564 U.S. 915 (2011).

140 Subsequent to the suspension of the Judgment Convention negotiations, the Ninth Circuit's unanimous decision in *Tuazon v. R.J. Reynolds Tobacco Co.*, 433 F. 3d 1163 (9th Cir. 2006), illustrated this point. In *Tuazon*, the court upheld the assertion of general jurisdiction by a federal court in Washington state sitting in diversity with respect to an out-of-state tobacco corporation, even though none of the cigarettes that were the cause of injury were consumed by the plaintiff in Washington State. It is unclear which aspects of the analysis in *Tuazon* survive *Goodyear Dunlop Tires v. Brown*, 564 U.S. 915 (2011) (reducing the applicability of general jurisdiction over foreign corporate defendants in cases in which the defendant cannot be said to be "at home" in the forum state). To be clear, the relevant provisions of the 2001 Hague Interim Draft would have affected state jurisdictional practice only in transnational cases within the scope of the Convention. It was never proposed during the Judgments Project negotiations that the treaty would alter F1 jurisdictional practices in wholly domestic cases.

never held state procedural laws to be immune from preemption by Article II treaties.[141] Nevertheless, from 1998 to 2001, the United States devoted much effort to persuading other countries to accept a treaty text in which states in the United States retained the prerogative to exercise direct adjudicative jurisdiction over foreign parties pursuant to long-arm statutes that other delegations regarded as exorbitant.

In discussions at five informal meetings[142] among a subset of Hague Conference member states. U.S. negotiators also resisted key jurisdictional rules of the Brussels Convention, arguing that the Brussels Convention was "unconstitutional under United States standards."[143] The delegation presented itself as sharply limited in its ability to embrace a treaty that would regulate direct jurisdiction in the manner of the Brussels Convention which became the Brussels I Regulation as the negotiations were in progress. This was so, it said, because Supreme Court jurisprudence did not permit the federal government to commandeer state courts into adjudicating disputes that lay within the mandatory and exclusive jurisdiction provisions of the proposed convention when those provisions, in the U.S. context, went beyond the limits of the 14th Amendment. The delegation also expressed reluctance to accept treaty language that would change U.S. practices by barring state courts from exercising doing business jurisdiction and transient presence jurisdiction.

By 2001, the Judgments Project was in trouble. Nearly a decade had elapsed since the United States had proposed the endeavor. When U.S. negotiators, mindful of the new federalism, were unable to agree with their foreign counterparts, they advocated in favor of a "mixed convention" model, with the subjects of disagreement moved from a "black list" to a "gray list."[144] But the growing gray list was not in reality evidence of progress; it represented

141 Neither opinion in *Burnham* suggested that state legislatures are *required* to include in-hand-service jurisdiction in their long-arm statutes. According to the Scalia plurality opinion, tradition *permitted* state courts to exercise jurisdiction over people served while physically located in the state. Moreover, the Supreme Court never has held that the exercise of in-hand-service jurisdiction on *legal* persons comports with Due Process, nor has it upheld in-hand-service jurisdiction as used against a natural person who is not a U.S. citizen or permanent resident. Finally, though federalism overtones reverberate in *Burnham*, the Court has never said whether by Article II treaty and implementing legislation the federal government can prohibit a state court from exercising jurisdiction over a natural person served with process while voluntarily present within the state. Another gray area is whether an Article II treaty can deprive a state court of jurisdiction to determine title to real property located within the state.

142 For summaries of these informal meetings, see Prelim. Doc. No. 15, "Informational Note on the Work of the Informal Meetings held since October 1999 to Consider and Develop Drafts on Outstanding Items" (May 2001), available at https://assets.hcch.net/docs/f76f699d-0e14-4e1a-aed9-cec296459e10.pdf.

143 *See* von Mehren, *Can the Hague Succeed? supra* note 134, at 196.

144 *Ibid.*

more a kind of running tally of what non-U.S. delegations were unable to secure to improve the circumstances of nationals with respect to unpredictable U.S. jurisdictional practices. [145] The Special Commission's 1999 preliminary draft convention[146] became a text with many brackets and containing little that was a compelling reason why countries such as France, Germany, and Switzerland would be made better off by such a treaty.[147]

Demands that the U.S. relinquish "doing-business" jurisdiction[148] and "tag jurisdiction"[149] in cases within the scope of the new judgments convention became politically problematic for the U.S. delegation.[150] Some members of the delegation were unsure that a treaty impacting state-court jurisdiction would secure a two-thirds vote in the Senate's advice and consent process. Domestic constituencies in the United States that had

145 It was not entirely a U.S.-EU face off. There were interventions by Canada, Switzerland, and other Hague member states.

146 *See* Prelim. Doc. No. 11, Nineteenth Session of June 2001 of the Hague Conference on Private International Law, available at https://assets.hcch.net/docs/638883f3-0c0a-46c6-b646-7a099d9bd95e.pdf.

147 Special Commission debate over the 1999 preliminary draft led to a 2001 interim text, www.hcch.net/en/publications-and-studies/details4/?pid=3499, which was still far from reaching the major compromises needed to arrive at final agreement at a diplomatic conference.

148 Criticism of this form of jurisdiction was one of a set of stumbling blocks that was the subject of intense negotiations among a subset of Hague Conference countries from 1999 to 2001. Those negotiations did not yield a resolution. Ironically, the U.S. delegation was defending doing business jurisdiction abroad at a time when the practice was being questioned at home. *See, e.g.*, Mary Twitchell, *The Myth of General Jurisdiction*, 101 HARV. L. REV. 610, 633–43 (1988); Arthur Taylor von Mehren, *Adjudicatory Jurisdiction: General Theories Compared and Evaluated*, 63 *B. U. L. REV*. 279, 285–310 (1983); *see generally*, Paul R. Dubinsky, *Human Rights Law Meets Private Law Harmonization: The Coming Conflict*, 30 YALE J. INT'L L. 212 (2005).

149 Those defending the continued use of tag jurisdiction in at least some circumstances included human rights advocates concerned about the loss of a jurisdictional means of bringing civil actions against foreign human rights abusers. *See* Paul R. Dubinsky, *Proposals of the Hague Conference and their Effect on Efforts to Enforce International Human Rights Through Adjudication*, Working Doc. No. 117, Special Comm'n on the Question of Jurisdiction, Recognition and Enforcement of Foreign Judgments, Hague Conf. On Private Int'l Law (1998); Hague Conf. On Private Int'l Law, Report of Meeting No. 47, at 2 (Nov. 17, 1998); *see generally* Beth Van Schaack, *In Defence of Civil Redress: The Domestic Enforcement of Human Rights Norms in the Context of the Proposed Hague Judgments Convention*, 42 HARV. INT'L L. 141, 182 & N. 224. (2001).

150 *See* Schlosser, *supra* note 136, at 31 (observing that tag jurisdiction "is intimately associated with the power doctrine of jurisdiction which never penetrated civil-law countries.") Professor Schlosser participated in the negotiations that led to the United Kingdom acceding to the Brussels Convention in the 1970s. *Ibid.* In reference to those successful negotiations, he observed: "To our great surprise, it was no problem for the United Kingdom's delegates to accept that tag jurisdiction was no longer permitted under the [Brussels] Convention." *Ibid.* An inference to be drawn from Schlosser's comment (a prominent German scholar of procedural law) was that if the United Kingdom could relinquish power-based theories of jurisdiction in order to join the Brussels Convention, the United States should be able to do the same as part of an overall compromise leading to a Hague Judgments Convention.

supported Hague conventions in the 1960s with few rumblings of opposition based on federalism now, in the 1990s, had reason to reassess their pro-treaty posture with respect to PIL treaties.

The Supreme Court's new federalism jurisprudence could be understood as in tension with the Third Restatement's "one voice" view of the place of states in foreign relations law.[151] Thus the new federalism jurisprudence as applied to statutes in the 1990s increased the leverage of state constituencies with respect to the treaty approval process, a process in which the political safeguards of federalism are stronger (in terms of voting in the Senate rather than the House) than in the legislative process.

The so-called informal Hague meetings (attended by a smaller group of key players) did not work. Civil law countries wanted a convention that included both instances in which the exercise of jurisdiction was required and that also limited U.S. jurisdictional overreach in other circumstances.[152] They largely rejected U.S. pleas for activity-based jurisdiction.[153] The U.S. delegation, on the other hand, maintained that the proposed treaty would have to include some form of minimum contacts/activity-based jurisdiction in order to prevent state courts from acting contrary to the Due Process Clause. Domestic constituencies in the United States, however, had little interest in seizing upon the negotiations as a forum for reexamining U.S. jurisdictional law. The negotiations did not serve as an occasion to consider reforms that had been advocated domestically nor one to bring about harmonization between U.S. rules of jurisdiction and those of other countries.

The Judgment Project negotiations came to a halt not only over direct jurisdiction issues, but the sense that these issues had become intractable

151 *See, e.g.*, Third Restatement § 302, comment d, citing *Zschernig v. Miller*, 389 U.S. 429 (1968); *see also* David H. Moore, *Beyond One Voice*, 98 MINN. L. REV. 953, 953 (2014) (characterizing the one-voice doctrine as a "mainstay of U.S. foreign relations jurisprudence"). For post-*Restatement* criticism of the one-voice doctrine, see, e.g., Sarah H. Cleveland, Crosby *and the "One-Voice" Myth in U.S. Foreign* Relations Jurisprudence, 46 VILL. L. REV. 975 (2001); David H. Moore, *Beyond One Voice*, 98 MINN. L. REV. 953 (2014); Peter J. Spiro, *Foreign Relations Federalism*, 70 *U. Colo. L. Rev.* 1223, 1226 (1999); Edward T. Swaine, *Negotiating Federalism: State Bargaining and the Dormant Treaty Power*, 49 DUKE L. J. 1127 (2000).

152 Early in the negotiations, the Swiss delegation circulated a memorandum designed to call attention to jurisdictional overreach by courts in the U.S. *See* Prelim. Doc. No. 5, "A Case for the Hague," (June 1996).

153 *See* General Affairs Prelim. Doc. 16, Permanent Bureau, Hague Conference on Private International Law, "Some Reflections on the Present State of Negotiations on the Judgments Project in the Context of the Future Work Programme of the Conference," (Feb. 2002), available at https://assets.hcch.net/upload/wop/gen_pd16e.pdf; *see generally* Hague Special Commission on the Judgments Project, available at hcch.net/en/projects/legislative-projects.

clearly mattered. This need not have been so. The implicit, but rarely articulated, assumption of the U.S. delegation was that serious legal and political roadblocks lay ahead if it were to attempt to enhance the jurisdictional power of state courts using the federal treaty power. Thus when discussions focused on whether a treaty could require U.S. courts to assert jurisdiction in specific factual scenarios (e.g., tort cases in which the only nexus to the forum is the location of the harm), the U.S. delegation's response was that an attempt to accomplish this result by treaty would be unconstitutional.[154] That response, however, was not supported by a Supreme Court case with a transnational fact pattern directly on point. It was unclear in the 1990s how the Court would decide a case in which such an exercise of jurisdiction was mandated by an Article II treaty.[155] To the contrary, the Third Restatement had put forward

[154] Professor Ronald Brand, a longtime member of the U.S. delegation to the Hague Conference, expressed this view in a paper submitted to the Special Commission of the Hague Conference in 1998 and in a subsequently published article:

> U.S. objections to certain jurisdictional bases in a Hague Convention will many times not represent a judgment that a given basis is 'wrong' or 'bad,' but rather a determination that the Due Process Clauses of the U.S. Constitution protect a defendant from being subject to such a basis of jurisdiction. In this regard, the negotiators for the United States have no discretion.

See Ronald A. Brand, *Due Process, Jurisdiction, and a Hague Judgments Convention*, 60 U. PITT. L. REV. 661, 701–2 (1999). As the United States participates in the revived Judgment Project (see Section H, *infra*), this narrow-discretion assessment should be carefully reconsidered. In 2011, the Supreme Court revived the view that limitations on the personal jurisdiction of state courts originate not solely from the liberty interests of litigants but also from constitutionally imposed limitations on state sovereign power in an *interstate* context. *Compare* World Wide Volkswagen v. Woodson, 444 U.S. 286, 292 (1980) (stating that the concept of minimum contacts "acts to ensure that the States through their courts, do not reach out beyond the limits imposed on them by their status as coequal sovereigns in a federal system") *with* J. McIntyre Machinery, Ltd. v. Nicastro, 564 U.S. 873, 884 (2011) ("[W]hether a judicial judgment is lawful depends on whether the sovereign has authority to render it"), *ibid.* ("[I]f [a] State were to assert jurisdiction in an inappropriate case, it would upset the federal balance, which posits that each State has a sovereignty that is not subject to unlawful intrusion by other States"). *McIntyre* suggests that interstate jurisdictional intrusion is different from international jurisdictional intrusion, with the former having a U.S. constitutional constraint not applicable to the latter. Thus, a U.S. defendant in an interstate case is armed with two constitutional shields against judicial jurisdictional overreaching (the sovereignty interest and the liberty interest), whereas the foreign defendant may have only one. As a result, state courts may enjoy more constitutional leeway in exercising personal jurisdiction over foreign defendants than over nonresident U.S. defendants.

[155] Under Justice O'Connor's analysis in *Asahi*, the practical content of due process may differ depending on whether the context is international or interstate. *See* Asahi Metal Industry v. Superior Court, 480 U.S. 102, 114–16 (1987) (O'Connor, J. plurality) (referring to the "unique burdens placed upon one who must defend oneself in a foreign legal system" and finding that because of these burdens and other factors, exercise of jurisdiction would be

a robust view of the treaty power.[156] But in actual PIL negotiations, the Executive Branch self-judged the federal government's Article II powers conservatively.[157]

Rather than come to a halt, the general Judgments Project changed direction. The U.S. delegation asked the Hague Permanent Bureau to cancel a scheduled vote on the Interim Draft and suspend pursuit of the agenda for the Judgment Convention as originally planned.[158]

VII FEDERALISM AND THE HAGUE CHOICE OF COURTS CONVENTION

After a decade of negotiations, Hague Conference member states and the Permanent Bureau salvaged the project by greatly narrowing its scope. Put aside, for the time being, were fundamental disagreements over regulating

"unreasonable"). Although the third-party defendant in *Asahi* was the beneficiary of that interstate-international differential in terms of the defendant's liberty interest, *McIntyre* suggests, from an interstate federalism perspective, that foreign defendants should be more susceptible to personal jurisdiction than U.S. defendants.

156 *See* Third Restatement, *supra* note 73 at § 302. The extent to which the federal treaty power can be employed to abridge the procedural rights of foreign litigants in U.S. courts is a subject that has not been taken up much by Congress, U.S. courts, or scholars, though the notion that the treaty power can be used in this way is one with plausibility. If the government of Country X is willing to negotiate a treaty that would allow its nationals to be more amenable to the jurisdiction of U.S. courts than are U.S. citizens and residents, why should the Due Process Clause be read as prohibiting this differential? In the context of civil rather than criminal litigation, why should Country X not be able (within the bounds of international law) to negotiate for its nationals something less than full due process rights? One could imagine, for example, circumstances in which Country X lacks the resources or expertise to afford full judicial remedies and is in favor of adjudication taking place in the U.S. legal system or that of other countries.

157 *See* Duncan Hollis, *Executive Federalism: Forging New Federalist Constraints on the Treaty Power*, 79 *S. Cal. L. Rev.* 1327, 1332 (2006) (maintaining that "scholars have largely ignored executive efforts to self-judge when and how federalism limits U.S. treaty obligations").

158 *See* Letter from Jeffrey Kovar, Assistant Legal Adviser, U.S. Department of State, to J. H. A. van Loon, Secretary General of the Hague Conference on Private International Law (Feb. 22, 2000) (referring to "fatal defects in the approach, structure, and details of the text" in the context of negotiations among "extremely different legal systems"); von Mehren, Can Hague Succeed? *supra* note 134, at 192 (arguing that a diplomatic session under strict rules of procedure and based on the "majoritarian principle" does not "encourage the reaching of consensus through compromise). At the outset of the Hague Project, it was clear that the Hague Conference rules called for majoritarian voting during diplomatic conferences. At that point in time, approximately seven years had been spent engaging in negotiations and compromises. The problem was not the format; it was the influence of federalism on the delegation's negotiating positions.

jurisdiction in favor of focusing on areas of consensus.[159] Thus, the effort to create a far-reaching mixed convention morphed into negotiations in which the jurisdiction underlying judgments in search of transnational recognition would be the agreement of the parties to the dispute.[160] The duty of domestic courts to adjudicate certain disputes in the first instance and recognize the judgments of other domestic courts would arise from a choice-of-court agreement.[161] After four additional years of negotiations, the result was the 2005 Hague Choice of Courts Convention (CoCC),[162] which deals with only a modest subset of the issues in play from 1992 to 2001.

The duty to recognize national court judgments in countries party to the CoCC arises only when the jurisdictional basis underlying the foreign judgment is either a freestanding choice of court agreement or an agreement that is a provision in a wider contract.[163] The only court with jurisdiction over the dispute is the one on which the parties have conferred jurisdiction.[164] If an action is filed in courts in another country, contrary to the choice-of-court agreement, the courts of that other country must dismiss the action.[165]

Attention then turned to U.S. ratification, which then-Secretary of State Hillary Clinton identified as a priority for the United States.[166] The Obama

[159] *See* RONALD A. BRAND & PAUL HERRUP, THE 2005 HAGUE CONVENTION ON CHOICE OF COURT AGREEMENTS: COMMENTARY AND DOCUMENTS 3–10 (2008); Paul R. Dubinsky, *Adventures in Treaty Interpretation*, 57 AM. J. COMP. L. 745 (2009); Louise Ellen Teitz, *The Hague Choice of Court Convention: Validating Party Autonomy and Providing an Alternative to Arbitration*, 53 AM. J. COMP. L. 543 (2005).

[160] *See* Explanatory Report 16–17, *supra* note 134, at 16–17 (summarizing relationship between the original Judgments Project and the Choice-of-Court Convention that ultimately emerged).

[161] This is the term employed in the Hague Convention on Choice of Court Agreements. In the United States, the term more commonly employed is "forum selection agreement."

[162] *See* Hague Convention on Choice of Court Agreements ("CoCC"), June 30, 2015, 44I.L.M. 1294, available at https://assets.hcch.net/docs/510bc238-7318-47ed-9ed5-e0972510d98b.pdf.

[163] The broad reach and sometimes unpredictable nature of U.S. rules on personal jurisdiction do not come into play when parties have consented to the jurisdiction of a court in the United States. Also, what might be viewed as the rigid jurisdictional rules of the EU regime could be set aside because jurisdiction under the CoCC flows from the parties' choice of court agreement and not from the nature of the underlying action. Another source of stalemate during the Judgments Project negotiations, *forum non conveniens* dismissals in common law countries, also was defanged because such dismissals are rare in cases in which jurisdiction has been conferred by a forum selection clause.

[164] CoCC, *supra* note 162, art. 5. The Convention does not prohibit other courts, however, from exercising jurisdiction over requests for preliminary relief. *Ibid.* at art. 7. The presumption is that parties intend for such clauses to be exclusive. That presumption, however, can be overcome. *Ibid.* art. 3.

[165] *Ibid.* art. 6.

[166] *See* United States Department of State, Office of the Legal Adviser, White Paper (Apr. 16,2012), at 1, available at www.state.gov/s/l/releases/2013/211157.htm ("At the outset of the Obama Administration, the Secretary of State, Hillary Rodham Clinton, directed the

administration initially intended to follow the path taken with the New York Convention: sending the treaty to Congress along with draft federal implementing legislation intended to federalize some aspects of state law on jurisdiction.[167] Soon thereafter, the State Department made public its inclination to proceed in this manner. However, the tone of the discussion among stakeholders in the United States changed. At meetings of the Secretary of State's Advisory Committee on Private International Law and in other venues, several groups demanded that the CoCC be implemented through state legislation.[168]

In the seven years since this resistance to federal legislation surfaced, progress toward ratification of the CoCC has been stalled. In that time, neither the treaty nor proposed implementing legislation has been sent to Congress. A number of implementation strategies have been put forward during this time by different constituencies: federal agencies,[169] state executive branch officials,[170] state supreme court justices,[171] federal judges,[172] members of the

Legal Adviser to explore all avenues for securing implementation of the COCA under U.S. domestic law, with a goal toward securing advice and consent and domestic implementation of the COCA as soon as possible"). "COCA" refers to the Choice of Court Agreement or Convention.

167 *See* Memorandum of the Legal Adviser Harold Hongju Koh Regarding United States Implementation of the Hague Convention on Choice of Court Agreements (COCA) (Jan. 4, 2013) ("Koh Memorandum"), available at www.state.gov/s/l/releases/2013/206657.htm.

168 The idea of implementing a PIL treaty through state legislation was previously suggested by the Reagan Administration in connection with the UNIDROIT International Wills Convention and the Hague Child Abduction Convention. *See supra* Section D. The former treaty was not ratified, and the latter one ultimately was implemented by federal legislation.

169 *See, e.g.*, 2012 State Department White Paper, *supra* note 166, at I (referring to "interagency discussion" and emphasizing the importance of assuring U.S. compliance, providing certainty to transnational transactions, promoting transparency, and taking into account the views of treaty partners). The White Paper also referred to the "historical allocation of federal and state interests."

170 Those views have been formulated by committees of NCCUSL, such as the Committee on International Legal Developments. *See* http://uniformlaws.org/Committee.aspx?title=International%20Legal%20Developments.

171 *See* Conference of Chief Justices, Resolution 2, July 28, 2010, available at http://ccj.ncsc.org/~/media/Microsites/Files/CCJ/Resolutions/06282010-Urging-the-United-States-Government-to-Respect-State-Policies-and-Principles.ashx. CCJ is an organization addressing issues of common concern to state supreme courts across the country. Each state is represented in CCJ by the chief justice of its highest court.

172 *See, e.g.*, 2010 Report of the Proceedings of the Judicial Conference of the United States 14 (March 16, 2010), available at http://www.uscourts.gov/about-federal-courts/reports-proceedings-judicial-conference-us (stating that the Judicial Conference opposes the inclusion of a provision on removal jurisdiction in any CoCC implementing legislation and also

private bar engaged in transnational practice,[173] and legal scholars.[174] From 2010 to 2013, a concentrated effort was made to bridge differences by employing a cooperative-federalism approach to implementing legislation.[175]

Cooperative federalism, a common approach to implementing some federal statutory regulatory regimes, seemed to state participants in the CoCC implementation negotiations as a suitable model for sharing authority at the federal and state levels in implementing the CoCC.[176] State constituencies in these negotiations proposed that uniform state legislation be the sole source of substantive law governing the recognition of foreign judgments that would be within the scope of the CoCC. The Uniform Law Commission then drafted a Uniform Act along these lines, an effort completed in 2012.[177] This fait accompli complicated the federal government's efforts to insist on following a federal-legislation-only model; the State Department agreed in principle to implement the CoCC through parallel state and federal legislation with the details of the relationship between these two legislative tracks and issues relating to adjudicative jurisdiction to be worked out.

Concerned about potential lack of uniformity in the implementation of the CoCC,[178] the State Department then put forward two limiting conditions on

opposes that any recognition action brought pursuant to the convention automatically qualify for federal question jurisdiction).

173 The internationalist views of this constituency often have been expressed by the ABA, the Association of the Bar of the City of New York, the D.C. Bar, and at forums held under the auspices of the American Society of International Law.

174 *See, e.g.*, Stephen Burbank, "Federalism and Private International Law: Implementing the Hague Choice of Court Convention in the United States" (July 3, 2006), available at http://scholarship.law.upenn.edu/faculty_scholarship/97/; Julian G. Ku, *The Crucial Role of the States and Private International Law Treaties: A Model for Accommodating Globalization*, 73 MO. L. REV. 1063 (2008) (arguing against "reflexive nationalism" in treaty implementation).

175 *See* White Paper, *supra* note 166 at IIIA (observing, in 2012, that the cooperative federalism approach had been the basis of discussions on implementation between the State Department's Legal Adviser's Office and various stakeholders for "the past couple of years").

176 *See generally* William Henning, *The Uniform Law Commission and Cooperative Federalism: Implementing Private International Law Conventions through Uniform State Laws*, 2 ELON L. REV. 39 (2011).

177 *See* Uniform Choice of Court Agreements Convention Implementation Act, July 19, 2012, available at www.uniformlaws.org/shared/docs/choice_of_court/2012am_ccaia_approvedtext.pdf. Underlying this text was the assumption that a statutory variation on the *Erie* model should govern; in states enacting the Uniform Act, federal courts should be required to apply the Uniform Act and be bound by state-court precedent interpreting that Act. The logic of this approach was that under *Klaxon*, federal courts had applied state common law rules on conflict of laws since 1940. For elaboration, *see supra* note 19.

178 *See* White Paper, *supra* note 166, at II (stating as a central principle that implementation of the CoCC must be sufficient to "persuade transacting parties that choice-of-court provisions afford certainty and clarity that compares with or is superior to the arbitration alternative."). Uniform acts can be implemented differently by different state legislatures. They can be

the cooperative federalism approach. First, it demanded that state legislation be "as nearly identical as possible"[179] to the federal statute and that a state legislature's failure to meet this condition would result in federal preemption.[180]

Second, in the face of demands by the Conference of Chief Justices (CCJ),[181] the State Department rejected calls for exclusive state court jurisdiction over suits seeking recognition under the CoCC.[182] In the past, federal statutes implementing Hague Conventions had followed a concurrent jurisdiction model: actions could be adjudicated either in state or federal court.[183] The State Department insisted on sticking to this concurrent jurisdiction scheme and also insisted that all federal courts apply only the federal implementing legislation and not the Uniform Act, regardless of the state in which a federal court is located.[184] The State Department also demanded that the general federal removal statute (28 U.S.C. §1441) be made available so as to allow litigants to move CoCC suits from state to federal court.[185]

These proposed conditions launched further negotiations over federalism. From a state point of view, the combination of concurrent jurisdiction and easy removal to federal court likely would result in most CoCC actions being

interpreted differently by courts in different states. They can be amended so as to destroy uniformity over time and deviate from important federal policies that went into the treaty.

179 *Ibid.* at IIIA.

180 The State Department's proposal was for the federal statute to apply automatically in those states declining to enact the Uniform Act, in which case the pre-existing recognition law of those states would be preempted. *See ibid.* ("The federal statute will of course apply in those states that elect not to adopt the uniform law"). The federal statute would defer to state law in states adopting the Uniform Act but only to the extent that state law was consistent with the federal statute. *See ibid.* ("[I]f states adopt the uniform law but vary its text substantively, or if courts interpret state law so as to produce different results from those that would obtain under the federal law, state law will to that extent be preempted").

181 *See* White Paper, *supra* note 166, at IIIA.

182 *See ibid.*, attachment 3 (correspondence between State Department Legal Adviser and President of the Uniform Law Commission).

183 For example, ICARA, the implementing legislation for the Child Abduction Convention, was a federal statute that permitted concurrent jurisdiction. Suits relating to the New York Convention can be brought either in state or federal court. Similarly, an ALI project proposing the federalization of judgment recognition law by means of a proposed federal statute selected the familiar concurrent jurisdiction arrangement. *See* American Law Institute, Recognition and Enforcement of Foreign Judgments: Analysis and Proposed Federal Statute ("Proposed Federal Statute") (2006, Andreas Lowenfeld and Linda Silberman, co-reporters).

184 *See* White Paper, *supra* note 166 at III (A)(1).

185 *Ibid.* ALI's 2005 Proposed Federal Statute favored adjudication of recognition actions in federal court by making removal from state court available "without regard to the citizenship or residence of the parties or the amount in controversy" and with the ability of the federal court to exercise supplemental jurisdiction over related claims. *See* Proposed Federal Statute, *supra* note 183.

decided in federal court under the federal implementing statute. Application of the Uniform Act would be rare. CCJ responded to this concern by proposing that removal of CoCC actions be made less available to CoCC litigants than to other kinds of litigants availing themselves of the general removal statute, 28 USC. §1441.[186]

Negotiation of these federalism-related issues remains stalemated. Notwithstanding the designation of the CoCC as a priority treaty in 2009, the treaty was never sent to the Senate during the Obama administration. The federal government's willingness to import a domestic model of cooperative federalism into the realm of treaty implementation was "a very significant concession by those who would have favored the traditional approach of implementation through federal legislation only."[187] But this concession, a major departure from prior federal treaty practice, has been insufficient to secure state support for ratifying the CoCC. State constituencies demand that state law and state courts play a major role in transnational judgment recognition – demands fueled by the potency of federalism arguments in Congress and also perhaps by difficulties in securing Senate approval of Article II treaties during the Obama administration.[188]

The continuing lack of success in implementing the CoCC may signal a new era in the nexus between federalism and PIL, one in which federal power, both legal and political, to lead global treaty developments is contested at home. States' rights organizations may infer that this result is the product of a newfound clout that they possess in the international arena.[189]

186 *Ibid.* As with the Service and Evidence Conventions, many organizations made comments on the CoCC and its proposed implementing legislation. These included NCCUSL, the American Bar Association, the Secretary of State's Advisory Committee on Private International Law, various state and municipal bar associations, the Conference of Chief Justices, and legal scholars.

187 *Ibid.* at III (A)(1).

188 Despite much effort, the Obama administration was unable to secure Senate approval of the UN Convention on the Rights of Persons with Disabilities. For relevant documents, see www.foreign.senate.gov/hearings/convention-on-the-rights-of-persons-with-disabilities. Among the grounds cited by those opposing the Disabilities Treaty was its encroachment on state law, *See* Professor Curtis Bradley, *Testimony Before the Senate Foreign Relations Committee Regarding the UN Convention on the Rights of Persons with Disabilities* (Nov. 21, 2013) available at www.foreign.senate.gov/imo/media/doc/Bradley_Testimony.pdf (arguing that the proposed treaty was in need of "a well-crafted set of reservations, understandings, and declarations" in order for it not to conflict with the "constitutional values" of federalism). Similarly, the Law of the Sea Convention, the substance of which enjoyed support from many quarters, stalled in the Senate. For selected testimony and press statements, *see* www.foreign.senate.gov/treaties/103-39.

189 *See* Remarks by Michael Houghton at the 2012 Annual Meeting, 12 Quarterly Rep. of the Uniform Law Commission, available at http://uniformlaws.org/Narrative.aspx?title=QR%20Issue%2012%20%3E%20Message%20from%20the%20President (stating that the ULC "will

VIII BEYOND THE COCC: RETURNING TO THE JUDGMENTS PROJECT

After completing the CoCC, the Hague Conference revisited its 2001 decision putting on hold the broad Judgments Project envisioned in 1992. In 2001, the Conference had turned to the CoCC as a short-term and manageable alternative to the Judgements Convention with the intention of returning to pursue the original and broader goal after the CoCC's completion. The Hague Conference began this process in 2011 by constituting an Experts Group. The United States joined in this effort even though its ratification of the CoCC, the less ambitious treaty project, was uncertain.

In 2012, with input from the Experts group, the Hague Conference's Council on General Affairs and Policy appointed a small Working Group to lay the foundation for a draft convention to be taken up by a Special Commission.[190] The Working Group, in which the United States was represented, met five times from 2013 to 2015 and completed a draft (the "2016 Preliminary Draft Convention").[191] That draft was the basis for discussion and negotiation at the first Special Commission meeting in June 2016.

The 2016 Preliminary Draft calls for broadening and deepening the court-to-court relationships engineered by the CoCC and to do so by means of a new treaty that would require recognition of a range of foreign judgments in which a forum selection clause is not the source of jurisdiction. Among the underlying actions that would fall within the scope of the treaty would be common law claims (e.g., contracts, torts, property) as well as statutory claims (e.g., copyright, patent). This is significant; if the June 2016 document or something similar to it becomes the basis for a widely ratified treaty, such a development could establish globally influential rules on direct jurisdiction and recognition, legislative-type rules not based on the consent of the parties to the dispute.

For the United States, the June 2016 draft addresses some issues related to constitutional limits on state assertions of personal jurisdiction. For example,

be vigilant in the halls of Congress" and that "developing uniform laws to implement various private law treaties continues to be a very, very challenging task").

190 *See* Conclusions and Recommendations Adopted by the Council on General Affairs and Policy of the Hague Conference, (Apr.2011); Prelim. Doc. No. 14, Continuation of the Judgments Project (Feb. 2010).

191 This draft is the version that emerged from the Special Commission meeting held in June 2016. *See* Special Commission on the Recognition and Enforcement of Foreign Judgments, 2016 Preliminary Draft Convention ("Preliminary Draft",) *available on the secure portal of the Hague Conference website*; Council on General Affairs and Policy of the Hague Conference on Private International Law "Conclusions and Recommendations" (May 15–17, 2015), available at https://assets.hcch.net/docs/679bd42c-f974-461a-8e1a-31e1b51eda10.pdf.

the jurisdiction of F1 over contract claims would be governed by a rule that effectively is a hybrid of EU and U.S. law. Such contract disputes could be litigated in the place of performance (taken from the EU's Brussels 1 Regulation), provided that the "defendant's activities in relation to the transaction" constitute a "purposeful and substantial connection" to F1 (a U.S. due process approach). [192] When recognition is sought against a natural person whose principal place of business is in F1, recognition is to be granted provided that the "claim on which the judgment is based arose out of the activities of that business."[193] A judgment on a counterclaim is eligible for recognition "provided that the counterclaim arose out of th[e] same transaction or occurrence" as the initial claim.[194]

Notwithstanding these signs of progress, there are reasons to be skeptical that the current negotiations will result in a treaty that is broad in scope and that the United States will ratify. First, the negotiations have been bifurcated. The most difficult issues from a U.S. federalism perspective, such as regulation of direct jurisdiction and the prerogative to decline jurisdiction through tools such as forum non conveniens, have been postponed to an indefinite date in the future.[195] Second, on the eve of the second meeting of the Special Commission,[196] important provisions in the draft remained in brackets, and no binding votes had been taken. Third, in the United States any Hague Judgments Convention will require implementing legislation, and the dozen years that have passed without success for the CoCC on that front must be regarded as a strong cautionary note. Fourth, the United States has been engaged in treaty-making in this area for 25 years with little attention by Congress and without great support for harmonization of jurisdictional law among the bar or the academy. Fifth, the majority and concurring opinions in *Bond v. United States*[197] make clear that the Roberts Court, like the Rehnquist Court, is solicitous of state interests vis a vis Congressional power and not effusive in citing the Third Restatement's treaty provisions, another cautionary

[192] 2016 Preliminary Draft, *supra* note 191, art. 5(1)(g). [193] *Ibid*, art. 5(1)(b).

[194] *Ibid*, art. 5(1)(n)(1).

[195] *See* "Report of the Fifth Meeting of the Working Group on the Judgments Project (26-31 October 2015) and Proposed Draft Text Resulting from the Meeting," available at https://assets.hcch.net/docs/06811e9c-dddf-4619-81af-71e8836c8d3e.pdf.

[196] The present volume went to press before that second meeting of the Special Commission, scheduled for February 2017. The draft agenda for the second meeting can be found at https://assets.hcch.net/docs/4754306e-5287-450b-8073-c53fa58ca962.pdf.

[197] *See* Bond v United States, 572 U.S. _(2014); 134 S. Ct. 2077 (2014). For detailed analysis of *Bond*, see Margaret E. McGuiness, "Treaties, Federalism, and the Contested Legacy of *Missouri v. Holland*," Chapter 5 of this volume.

note as some provisions of the Hague draft appear to require exercise by the federal government of its treaty power and not solely its Article I powers.[198]

CONCLUSION

The renewed negotiations on a broad global judgments treaty are an opportunity for taking stock. The United States first proposed the Judgments Project in 1992. It did so shortly after publication of the Third Restatement, with its broad and preemptive understanding of the treaty power. In the intervening years, efforts to conclude a treaty on recognition of foreign judgments repeatedly have encountered obstacles associated with U.S. federalism. What is the likelihood that on a third try, the Hague Conference will produce a treaty that goes significantly beyond the CoCC in scope, that is ratified by the United States, and that becomes the basis for effective implementing legislation? Is the United States positioned to lead this effort and future PIL treaty projects?

The first question is among the most important in the field of PIL today. The effectiveness of civil justice systems around the world depends not only on fair, prompt, and efficient adjudication of disputes but also on the effectiveness of judicially ordered remedies. At a time when financial assets quickly cross borders, effectiveness means global effectiveness. The second question is closely connected to the success of the Judgments Project, an initiative the United States proposed in 1992 and then postponed. Answers to both questions depend on whether the Executive branch and Congress are willing to reexamine the bases on which the United States entered its golden age of PIL treaty-making and the background that is discussed in Section I of this chapter.

[198] *See* 2016 Preliminary Draft, *supra* note 191, at art. 1(d)(restricting duty to recognize judgments for which the exercise of jurisdiction over foreign defendants was based on the activities of their branches or agents to those instances in which the claim "arose out of the activities" of the "branch, agency or establishment"). This formulation means that where the presence of a foreign defendant's branches and agents in a U.S. state contributes to a finding of general jurisdiction over the defendant, the resulting judgment would not be entitled to recognition abroad in States parties to the treaty. The draft's formulation thus appears to be more restrictive of state-court jurisdiction than is the Supreme Court's formulation in *Goodyear Dunlop Tires v. Brown*, 564 U.S. 915, 919 (2011), which leaves open the possibility that branches and agents can contribute to a finding that a foreign defendant is "at home" in a U.S. state and thus within that state's 14th Amendment reach. The Hague draft thus would deny state courts in some cases the prerogative to assert personal jurisdiction in ways that are consistent with the 14th Amendment. *Cf.* Daimler v. Bauman, 134 S. Ct. 746, 759 (2014) Of course, however, it may be that *Goodyear Dunlop* not only signals the Supreme Court's narrowing of general jurisdiction but that in the future the Court will narrower it further, so as to eliminate any gap between the 14th Amendment power of U.S. state courts and their jurisdictional powers under any eventual Hague judgments convention.

There has been much consistency in U.S. behavior from era to era, during periods of U.S. internationalism in PIL treaty-making and during periods of relative isolationism. The main features of this behavior are: (i) an expectation that other legal systems will adjust their procedural law so as to be more like that of the United States, (ii) lack of judicial clarity and precision in the scope of the treaty power, and (iii) a tendency to regard PIL treaties as supplements to state and federal procedures instead of changes to or replacement of such procedures. The ramifications of this behavior and these assumptions have been far-reaching. They are at the heart of the majority opinions in *Aérospatiale* and *Schlunk*. They were a key part of the U.S. strategy in the CoCC negotiations and the Judgments Project. The mixed convention proposal resulted from a search for a treaty that, for the time being at least, would preserve existing U.S. jurisdictional practices. The gray list would have served perhaps as a mechanism for gradually marginalizing state long-arm statutes that employ doing business jurisdiction rather than negotiating the curtailment of such statutes in the context of a multilateral treaty.

The relatively cool reception that the mixed convention proposal received was an indication of a fundamental disagreement among Hague member states in terms of the basic nature of the Judgments Project. For many, the goal was similar to what had been accomplished by the 1968 Brussels Convention – creating a cooperative network of national courts with a similar culture in terms of jurisdiction and familiarity with other legal systems. For a smaller number of Hague member states, including the United States, a less ambitious goal was envisioned; the Judgments Convention was driven by producing a workable alternative to the New York Convention.

A long history of unilateralism, predating the Third Restatement, has hampered U.S. efforts to move forward on the Judgments Project and CoCC implementing legislation. Other countries already are beneficiaries of U.S. unilateralism: the UFMJRA, the Restatements, and state common law already confer U.S. recognition on the judgments of their courts. For these countries, coming away from the Hague negotiations with a treaty that does not curb U.S. jurisdictional practices is attaining very little. Early rounds of negotiations focused on jurisdiction, and early drafts had a double convention structure. The vetting of the Hague Judgments Interim Draft put U.S. states on notice that PIL treaties might involve federal encroachment on state procedural law. Over the next two decades, the states pushed back. This took the form of resistance to proposed treaty provisions, demands for state implementing legislation, arguments in favor of exclusive state-court jurisdiction, championing cooperative federalism, and exhibiting various levels of distrust toward federal negotiators. Implementation of the CoCC became a quagmire. The ability of interest groups marching under the banner of federalism to prevent the CoCC from going to the Senate put the United States in the position of being unable to ratify even though it had taken a leading role during the entire initiative. And these implementation problems with the CoCC followed on the heels of scaling back the original 1992 U.S. proposal.

These developments, all tied to federalism, present reasons for skepticism about future U.S. leadership over global treaty-making in private international law and private law. The United States has pursued a path of incrementalism. This was apparent in Congressional hearings in the 1960s, in the Supreme Court's interpretation of the Service and Evidence Conventions, in the protracted mixed judgment convention negotiations of the late 1990s, and in the CoCC implementing legislation impasse of the last decade. During all of these episodes, U.S. gradualism was the product of two brakes: (1) uncertainty about the meaning of *Missouri v. Holland* and judicially enforceable federalism-based limits on the treaty power, and (2) the political power of U.S. states as stakeholders in treaty negotiations requiring Senate approval. Both manifestations of federalism have complicated efforts by the Executive branch to exhibit flexibility in negotiations with other countries. Neither augurs well for future U.S. leadership in a context in which a significant number of countries are seeking to move beyond gradualism in PIL treaty-making.

In the years ahead, the political safeguards of treaty federalism are likely to become stronger, limiting the effective use of the treaty power in PIL. In the post-*Medellin* era,[199] an increasing proportion of treaties will require implementing legislation, with the result that federalism-based opposition to a treaty or its implementing legislation will be fertile ground for argument in the House of Representatives as well as the Senate. *Medellin* thus reinforces the growing leverage of state authorities in PIL treaty-making.

In light of these developments, the success of the Judgments Convention negotiations turns on American willingness to grapple with a complicated history. The United States entered the arena of PIL treaties with unrealistic assumptions about the extent of its influence and the willingness of other countries to follow its lead. U.S. delegations were uncertain regarding the extent of their constitutional negotiating power. Throughout the quarter century in which the United States has been negotiating jurisdiction and

199 *See* Medellin v. Texas, 552 U.S. 491 (2008) (invigorating the non-self-executing treaty doctrine with the result, going forward, that treaties typically will require implementing legislation). *Medellin* provides proponents of state interests vis a vis treaties with political leverage in the House as well as the Senate.

recognition of judgments in the Hague, it has pursued gradualism. Its basic posture has been to ratify (or not) proposed treaties that meet some specific need of its private sector or its governmental litigants. The United States has shown little interest in creating broad and deep relationships among national court systems.

United States leadership in PIL treaty-making efforts may turn on the ability to persuade other countries to accept gradualism on U.S. terms. More likely, it will turn on the ability of the United States to embrace some degree of unification of procedural law and to accept a conception of international judicial assistance that is mandatory and not supplemental. Success in these adaptations, in turn, will require U.S. negotiators to move forward with greater clarity about the scope of the treaty power, which at the present time remains unclear, notwithstanding the Third Restatement.

American leadership matters. It matters to U.S. citizens and businesses because in recent decades the United States has set a global PIL agenda that advances domestic interests. The Evidence Convention, the Wills Convention, the Judgments Project, and the Choice-of-Court Convention began with U.S. initiatives. American leadership matters to the rest of the world because, at its best, U.S. treaty leadership is effective. Traditionally, prompt U.S. ratification encourages other countries to proceed with ratification. And U.S. leadership matters to a global PIL regime. The increased effectiveness of that regime depends on better coordination among national courts and the avoidance of conflicts between legal systems, whether jurisdictional, evidentiary, or otherwise.

Conclusion

Treaties as the Law of the Land: Change and Continuity

Gary B. Born

The contributions in this volume explore an apparent paradox. Treaties are of fundamental, and increasing, importance to the United States. At the same time, ambivalence regarding treaties, and their domestic effects in the United States, is also deeply rooted, and, at least arguably, increasing. Is this paradox real or only apparent? If real, what explains it?

These themes are not new ones. The Framers and successive generations grappled with the same paradox, first breaking with British practice and granting treaties the status of the Law of the Land in Article VI's Supremacy Clause,[1] but soon thereafter fundamentally recasting that approach by classifying at least some treaties as non-self-executing,[2] while allowing for other forms of international agreements, with different domestic effects than treaties.[3]

The various contributions in this volume explore these historical and contemporary developments, identifying themes of both change and continuity. The contributions examine both the importance of treaties, and the ambivalence toward international obligations, in the United States, with a particular focus on the manner in which treaties have been implemented domestically over the past three decades. In doing so, this volume provides a variety of perspectives that reflect both the diversity of historical practice and contemporary attitudes towards treaties in the United States. That diversity offers valuable insights for exploring apparently paradoxical contemporary approaches towards treaties and for addressing the challenges that the inevitable use of treaties by the United States will present in the coming decades.

[1] *See* U.S. CONST. art. VI.

[2] *See* Foster v. Nielsen, 27 U.S. 253, 254, 7 L. Ed. 415 (1829).

[3] *See* U.S. Treaties: Contemporary Importance and Ambivalence, *infra* Section I. *See also* International Legal Research Tutorial, *What Are Treaties & International Agreements?*, DUKE UNIV. L. SCH. (last updated 2016), available at https://law.duke.edu/ilrt/treaties_2.htm.

I U.S. TREATIES: CONTEMPORARY IMPORTANCE AND AMBIVALENCE

The contributions to this volume leave no doubt regarding the exceptional contemporary importance of treaties to the United States. Although precise tallies are elusive, the United States has ratified or acceded to some 10,000 treaties within the meaning of Article II of the Constitution[4] and countless more international agreements of other forms.[5] These agreements deal with fundamentally important aspects of the nation's international trade and investment, security, environmental protection, and civil rights. They do so both in the form of multilateral agreements, such as the World Trade Organization Agreement, the North American Free Trade Agreement, the North Atlantic Treaty Organization Treaty, the U.N. Charter and the International Covenant on Civil and Political Rights, as well as in much more numerous bilateral agreements, including bilateral investment, judicial assistance, taxation, and defense treaties, as well as countless other types of international agreements.[6]

The contributions to this volume also make clear that treaties and other international agreements have become increasingly significant to the United States in recent decades. The pace of treaty-making by the United States accelerated substantially during the decades following World War II, particularly with respect to multilateral treaties.[7] At the same time, the terms and subject matter of international agreements concluded during this period have been increasingly significant to both the nation and its treaty partners – often involving comprehensive, detailed regulatory regimes among multiple states (like the WTO Agreement or ICSID Convention) and international organizations empowered to impose further obligations on contracting parties (like the UN, WTO, ICSID, and IMF).[8]

These developments leave no serious question that treaties and international agreements provide a more extensive, and more important, proportion

4 *See* Mark Janis & Noam Wiener, "Treaties in U.S. Law from the Founding to the Restatement (Third)," Chapter 1 of this volume. The United States is currently party to nearly 1,000 treaties and over 7,000 international agreements. U.S. Dept. of State, Treaties in Force (2013), available at www.state.gov/s/l/treaty/tif/. The most current information publically available is from 2013.

5 Treaties in Force, *supra* note 4.

6 *See* Michael Ramsey, "The Treaty and Its Rivals: Making International Agreements in U.S. Law and Practice," Chapter 7 of this volume.

7 *See* Janis & Wiener, "Treaties in U.S. Law from the Founding to the Third Restatement," Chapter 1 of this volume.

8 *See* Malcolm M. Shaw, International Law, 933, 938 (7th ed. 2014).

of the "Law of the Land" in the United States today than ever before. In ways that neither the Framers nor many later generations could have foreseen, much of today's Law of the Land in the United States is, in some fashion, international law, prescribed by agreements with foreign states. That trend appears unlikely to be reversed, as technology, culture, trade, and the character of human ills and needs continues to globalize.

These developments underscore the importance of the issues of treaty implementation and enforcement addressed in this volume. Given the central and increasing significance of treaties and international agreements to the nation, both the manner in which these agreements are implemented and the efficacy of their implementation are of vital importance to the United States and its treaty partners. That is particularly true because, as several of the chapters in this volume contend, the United States has manifested a wide, and increasing, range of doubts about treaties and other international agreements over the past thirty years. Indeed, a number of the contributions in this volume suggest that the period since publication of the *Third Restatement of the Foreign Relations Law of the United States* in 1987 has witnessed a materially increased ambivalence towards treaties and other international agreements in the United States.

At the core of this volume, and the subject matter it explores, lies an apparent paradox. The U.S. political branches have long regarded treaty-making as a vital tool of U.S. foreign policy and particularly in recent decades, the United States has frequently proposed and lobbied for major multinational and bilateral treaty projects. Nevertheless, the United States has long also mistrusted treaties, both internationally and domestically. In particular, during the past three decades, the United States has regularly failed to ratify, or sometimes even sign, major treaties, including agreements that it proposed.[9] More importantly for this volume, many of the treaties that the United States has ratified have received a lukewarm reception in the domestic U.S. legal system that has arguably become increasingly cool in recent years. As these developments suggest, therefore, the United States appears simultaneously both to value and to devalue treaties. Treaties are seen as essential, and increasingly essential, to addressing national and international challenges. But treaties are also seen as threats to critical values

[9] The United States failed to ratify, among others, the agreement to create an International Trade Organization (ITO) in the late 1940s, the Vienna Convention on the Law of Treaties, the Law of the Sea Convention, the two optional protocols to the 1949 Geneva Conventions, many of the instruments produced by the Hague Conference on Private International Law and, until just after the Cold War, virtually all human rights treaties, including the agreement in its own region, the American Convention on Human Rights.

of the domestic U.S. legal order – federalism, the separation of powers, and democratic law-making – and to the domestic laws that this order produces.

This apparent paradox provides the background for asking in what sense treaties today are the supreme "Law of the Land?" How capable is the U.S. domestic legal system of enabling the United States to use treaties as effective instruments of national policy? Is the U.S. legal order well-adapted to implementing and enforcing obligations that bind the nation as a matter of international law? There are a range of ways of addressing and answering these questions. Each of the chapters of this volume provides important perspectives on doing so.

In Chapter 1, Noam Wiener and Mark Janis provide a historical overview, from the eighteenth century until the publication of the Third Restatement, of the role of treaties in the U.S. legal system.[10] Their chapter illuminates early challenges to the supremacy of treaties *vis-á-vis* state law, together with the manner in which those challenges were overcome by the late 1800s. Wiener and Janis also trace the origins of the concept of non-self-executing treaties, while arguing that, in the early years of the Republic, treaties were generally assumed to be self-executing, with U.S. courts frequently applying treaty provisions without addressing the treaty's status as a matter of domestic U.S. law. Nor did U.S. courts during this period ask whether treaties created individual rights, with opinions by Justices Marshall and Story often assuming without discussion or explanation that treaty provisions were received whole into the domestic U.S. legal system, fully enforceable by private parties.[11]

By the time of the Third Restatement, however, U.S. courts rarely approached the domestic application of treaties in this fashion. *Foster v. Nielsen*'s distinction between self-executing and non-self-executing treaties provided the framework for treaty implementation for much of the twentieth century, an approach that was adopted by the Third Restatement.[12] In

[10] *See* Janis & Wiener, "Treaties in U.S. Law from the Founding to the Third Restatement," Chapter 1 of this volume.

[11] *See* Shanks v. Dupont, 28 U.S. 242, 7 L. Ed. 666, 249 (1830) (Justice Story wrote "[i]f the treaty admits of two interpretations, and one is limited, and the other liberal; one which will further, and the other exclude private rights; why should not the most liberal exposition be adopted?"); Owings v. Norwood's Lessee, 9 U.S. 344, 3 L. Ed. 120, 348 (1809) (Justice Marshall wrote "[e]ach treaty stipulates something respecting the citizens of the two nations, and gives them rights"); Oona A. Hathaway, Sabrina McElroy & Sara A. Solow, *International Law at Home: Enforcing Treaties in U.S. Courts*, 37 YALE J. INT'L L. 51, 53 (2012) (stating that there was a "background presumption in favor of finding treaties to confer private rights of action" before the *Medellin* case was decided).

[12] *See* THIRD RESTATEMENT OF THE FOREIGN RELATIONS LAW OF THE UNITED STATES, § 481 (1987) [hereinafter THIRD RESTATEMENT].

Chapter 4, Ingrid Wuerth describes both the Third Restatement's treatment of non-self-executing treaties and the subsequent shift, following 1987, to even more restrictive standards for self-executing status.[13] In particular, Wuerth details the Supreme Court's rejection, in *Medellin v. Texas*,[14] of the Third Restatement's presumption that treaties ordinarily possess self-executing status and, at least arguably, the *Medellin* Court's adoption of a reverse presumption.[15]

Wuerth shows that the presumptive status of treaties is critically important to the domestic effect of treaties in the United States. As the UN Charter provision at issue in *Medellin* demonstrated, treaties almost never address – either in text or *travaux préparatoires* – whether they are self-executing or not. *Medellin*'s rejection of the Third Restatement's presumption of self-executing status therefore has very significant practical consequences, providing a default rule that will likely be decisive in a substantial proportion of all cases. Moreover, *Medellin* effectively began and ended its inquiry into the domestic status of the UN Charter with treaty text – consulting neither the *travaux* nor materials surrounding the Charter's ratification in the United States. On one reading, *Medellin* thereby expanded the scope of the non-self-execution doctrine from that in the Third Restatement, arguably holding that, in the absence of express treaty text providing for self-executing status, a presumption against self-execution will rarely be overcome. That conclusion would appear to leave little of the Framers' declaration that treaties are the "Law of the Land."

Partially allaying such concerns, David Stewart shows in chapter 6 that legislative implementation of multilateral treaties has become the predominant practice in the United States in recent decades.[16] While providing a detailed study of treaty implementation in the United States– one of few contemporary works to do so – Stewart suggests that *Medellin* is not necessarily bad news for U.S. treaty compliance. Well before the Supreme Court's decision in *Medellin*, the U.S. Executive branch had pursued a practice of proposing implementing legislation on a wide range of international agreements, whether or not they might be considered non-self-executing. In reviewing this legislation – a process referred to as "preimplementation" – Stewart sees grounds for reassurance. Implementing legislation can have the virtue, in comparison to a self-executing treaty, of more specifically addressing the

[13] *See* Ingrid Wuerth, "Self-Execution," Chapter 4 of this volume.
[14] *Ibid.*
[15] *See* Medellin v. Texas, 552 U.S. 491, 506, 526–7, 128 S. Ct. 1346, 170 L. Ed. 2d 190 (2008).
[16] *See* David Stewart, "Recent Trends in U.S. Treaty Implementation," Chapter 6 of this volume.

integration of treaty obligations into the U.S. legal system.[17] As a series of Supreme Court decisions involving the Vienna Convention on Consular Relations makes clear, self-executing treaties rarely address directly the procedural routes by which treaty norms will be enforced in national legal systems, and pre- or postratification implementation of treaties can clarify and improve the domestic effects of international agreements.

Juxtaposed to Stewart's view that implementing legislation counterbalances the ascendance of the non-self-execution doctrine and ensures effective domestic implementation of treaties, are Paul Dubinsky's conclusions in Chapter 3 on treaty interpretation.[18] Dubinsky explores the canons of interpretation and interpretive models that have been employed by the U.S. courts in giving effect to treaties in U.S. courts. His chapter makes the important observation that, for much of U.S. history, the predominant models for treaty interpretation have been "treaty-as-contract" and "treaty-as-statute" models, both of which were recognized by the Third Restatement. Both approaches incorporate mechanisms for precluding one-sided, parochial treaty interpretation, and have proven reasonably effective in making U.S. treaty interpretation a judicially supervised, rule-of-law endeavor, albeit with important input from the political branches.[19]

As Dubinsky explains, however, the traditional models of treaty interpretation face a rival in the post–Third-Restatement era – the "treaty-as-delegation" model, which posits that courts are obliged to extend *Chevron* deference to Executive branch views as to the meaning of a treaty.[20] Thus, some scholars and courts have recently concluded that some categories of treaties (and implementing statutes) should be regarded as conferring on Executive branch officers and agencies primary authority to interpret treaty terms.[21] Giving executive agencies the leading voice in interpreting treaties does not necessarily mean that the United States will be less likely to comply with the treaty. Indeed, treaty compliance and enforcement might be enhanced by a greater Executive branch role in interpretation. Nonetheless, Dubinsky observes that this approach places treaty interpretation largely in the hands of Executive branch officials who are primarily concerned with the missions of their agencies and the interests of one treaty partner, and who may be less

17 *Ibid.*

18 *See* Paul Dubinsky, "Competing Models for Treaty Interpretation: Treaty a Contract, Treaty as Statute, Treaty as Delegation," Chapter 3 of this volume.

19 *Ibid.*

20 *Ibid.*

21 *See* Sanchez-Llamas, 548 U.S. at 378 (agreeing with the presumption that the "Executive Branch's interpretation of treaty provisions is entitled to 'great weight'"); Evan Criddle, *Chevron Deference and Treaty Interpretation*, 112 YALE *L.J.* 1927, 1930 (2003).

concerned with an objective interpretation of treaty terms or the United States' reputation for treaty compliance.

As Dubinsky shows, in a series of cases in the late 1980s and early 1990s, the Supreme Court ignored sections 325 and 326 of the Third Restatement and brought a unilateral interpretive perspective to bear on extradition, taxation, migration, and judicial assistance treaties.[22] Recent U.S. federal and state judicial decisions have also rarely referred to the Vienna Convention on the Law of Treaties or the customary international law rules that the Convention reflects. These developments suggest that the drafters of the Fourth Restatement may be required to reconsider the Third Restatement's treatment of treaty interpretation and that ambivalence about the role of treaties in domestic law has taken a variety of forms.[23]

Similarly, Roger Alford's chapter analyzes another aspect of treaty implementation which reflects increasing ambivalence regarding the role of treaties in the United States – the various procedural or prudential rules that bar access to U.S. judicial relief to particular categories of plaintiffs or claims. Some of these obstacles – standing, a private right of action and the application of state procedural rules – were touched upon only in passing in the Third Restatement (or not at all), but have subsequently been applied to a range of treaty claims by U.S. courts. In particular, as Alford explains, the past three decades have seen the crystallization of more restrictive standards for inferring private rights of action under treaties in U.S. courts and the development of higher hurdles to judicial enforcement of whatever private rights do exist.[24] Alford also concludes that the last-in-time rule has evolved so as only rarely to give precedence to a treaty over a previously enacted federal statute.

In chapter 5 of this volume, Margaret McGuinness summarizes recent expressions of judicial doubt about the scope of the federal authority under the tenth amendment to implement treaties.[25] As McGuinness describes, a majority of the Supreme Court declined, in *Bond v. United States*, to limit the expansive legislative authority to implement treaties provided to Congress by *Missouri v. Holland*[26] and embraced by the Third Restatement. The *Bond*

[22] *See* Dubinsky, "Competing Models for Treaty Interpretation: Treaty as Contract, Treaty as Statute, Treaty as Delegation," Chapter 3 of this volume.

[23] Thus far, the drafts of an ALI Fourth Restatement on the subject of treaties have not examined in depth how sections 325 and 326 of the Third Restatement have fared in the courts and in the Executive Branch.

[24] *See* Roger Alford, "Judicial Barriers to the Enforcement of Treaties," Chapter 8 of this volume.

[25] *See* Margaret McGuinness, "Treaties, Federalism, and the Contested Legacy of Missouri v. Holland," Chapter 5 of this volume.

[26] Missouri v. Holland, 252 U.S. 416, 433, 40 S. Ct. 382, 64 L. Ed. 641 (1920).

Court did so, however, without directly challenging the criticisms of three concurring Justices who urged the abandonment of expansive conceptions of federal authority to implement or even conclude Article II treaties.[27] McGuiness concludes by expressing doubts about the continued viability of *Missouri v Holland* and its view of the federal treaty power.

Criticisms of an exclusively federal role in negotiating, implementing, and interpreting treaties have been voiced at the state level as well. Among other things, federalism-based concerns about federal implementing legislation for private international law treaties appear to be diminishing the role of the United States in private international law initiatives. Mostly notably, federalism concerns related to the 2005 Hague Choice of Court Agreements Convention have frustrated efforts to forge a consensus on the character of implementing legislation for the Convention (federal, state, or some mixture of the two) for more than a decade, through two presidential administrations.[28]

Taken together, the various developments outlined in this volume arguably reflect a substantial shift in the treatment of treaties by U.S. courts over the past three decades – away from the Third Restatement's commitment to vigorous judicial implementation of U.S. treaties and expansive federal authority to implement treaties, towards greater skepticism about the wisdom of judicial implementation of international agreements and heightened checks on both such implementation and the treaty power itself. As suggested above, these developments might appear paradoxical: on the one hand, treaties and other international agreements have become increasingly important to the United States and its foreign relations over the past three decades, while such agreements have simultaneously become the subject of materially greater misgivings and increased limits on domestic judicial enforcement.

On reflection, however, the misgivings that have emerged in the United States regarding the making and domestic implementation of treaties during the past 30 years are neither surprising nor paradoxical. Given the materially increased number of treaties, and their importance to the nation since the end of World War II, it is understandable that these agreements would give rise to concerns and ambivalence. Indeed, it is precisely because treaties and other international agreements are so important – and are increasingly so important – to the United States that they provoke misgivings and doubts: if treaties

27 *See* Bond, 564 U.S. at 2109–10 (Scalia, J., Thomas, J., and Alito, J., concurring in the judgment).

28 *See* William J. Woodward Jr., *Saving the Hague Choice of Court Convention*, 29 U. PA. J. INT'L L. 657, 692 (2008).

were unimportant, or of declining importance, then they would occasion little or no controversy. But where major aspects of the nation's foreign commerce, defense, economic regulation, human rights safeguards, and criminal law are increasingly dependent, directly or indirectly, on treaties, it is neither surprising nor paradoxical that the treaty power would provoke concern and ambivalence.

II U.S. TREATIES: HISTORICAL CONTINUITY

It might also appear that the misgivings about use of the treaty power that the contributions to this volume describe as emerging over the past thirty years mark a departure from historic practice. In particular, the developments outlined in this volume's chapters might be understood as reflecting an increased ambivalence regarding treaties and other international agreements that has only emerged since the publication of the Third Restatement in 1987: this understanding might regard the Restatement as a high-water mark of the treaty-making power, with the ensuing three decades witnessing an unusual retreat, marked by a diminished commitment to the effective enforcement of treaties in U.S. courts, which broke with historical trends.

That thesis would be incomplete. On reflection, the ambivalence provoked by U.S. treaties and other international agreements is not a twentieth-first century innovation and is not an historical anomaly. Instead, misgivings of almost exactly the same sort have been a recurrent feature of U.S. law and politics since the earliest days of the Republic.

On the one hand, the Framers of the Constitution took the unusual step of embedding treaties as the "Law of the Land," making the international agreements of the United States coequal with federal legislation and granting them a privileged status in U.S. courts that treaties did not enjoy in most other eighteenth-century legal systems (notably Britain).[29] On the other hand, George Washington, Thomas Jefferson, and others abjured foreign "entanglements," while the Framers imposed an exceptional supermajority requirement on the treaty-making power, making it peculiarly difficult for the United States to conclude international agreements.[30]

Moreover, despite the Supremacy Clause's unqualified categorization of treaties as the Law of the Land, early U.S. Supreme Court decisions characterized some treaties as non-self-executing and not directly applicable in

[29] *See* Janis & Wiener, "Treaties in U.S. Law from the Founding to the Third Restatement," Chapter 1 of this volume.

[30] *See ibid.*

U.S. courts, thereby potentially undoing much of the effect of Article VI's inclusion of treaties as part of the Law of the Land.[31] Likewise, the absence of federal subject-matter jurisdiction over actions arising under treaties (and other rules of international law) for much of the nineteenth century materially restricted the interpretation and application of treaties by federal courts during this period.[32]

A similar ambivalence also prevailed in the twentieth century.[33] On the one hand, as noted above, there was a dramatic expansion in the number and importance of treaties following World War II. On the other hand, that expansion was accompanied by the Bricker Amendment debates, which presaged the recent rise of the "New Sovereigntists," challenging both the scope of the federal treaty-making power and the scope of federal judicial authority over other matters of international law, including customary international law.[34]

On reflection, this historical ambivalence about the treaty-making power is again unsurprising and, to a substantial extent, inevitable. It was precisely because the Framers' generation recognized that international law and treaty obligations had high importance for the nation, both internationally and domestically, that they were cautious both in fashioning the treaty-making power and in allowing unqualified judicial implementation of U.S. treaties and other international law obligations. Because of their importance, the formation and implementation of treaties were regarded as matters requiring careful consideration and involvement of the political branches. Seen from this perspective, the ambivalence about the treaty-making power that has emerged in the United States in the decades since the publication of the Third Restatement is of a piece with the concerns of the Framers and subsequent generations. Indeed, it is precisely because treaties have become increasingly important to the United States since World War II that misgivings about their binding effects and implementation have become more widespread and pointed in recent decades.

It might also appear that historic misgivings about the treaty-making power would produce only obstacles to the making and implementation of treaties, doing nothing more than undermining the ability of the United States to

31 *See* Foster, 27 U.S. at 254.

32 Congress did not enact a general federal question jurisdictional statute until 1875. The current version of that statute is codified at 28 U.S.C.A. § 1331.

33 Hathaway, *supra* note 11, at 57.

34 *See* Louis Henkin, *U.S. Ratification of Human Rights Conventions: The Ghost of Senator Bricker*, 89 AM. J. INT'L L. 341, 348 (1995); Arthur E. Sutherland, *The Bricker Amendment, Executive Agreements, and Imported Potatoes*, 67 HARV. L. REV. 281, 282 (1953).

implement and utilize international agreements. In fact, that conclusion is also inaccurate and would ignore both the vital role of international agreements in contemporary American affairs and important aspects of treaty implementation in the United States, both historically and over the past thirty years.

Thus, historic ambivalence regarding the treaty power has produced not only constraints on the exercise of the treaty power and the implementation of treaties within the domestic U.S. legal system, but also pragmatic solutions ensuring both expansive federal authority for the making of international agreements and reasonably effective, albeit nuanced, means for the domestic implementation of treaties. Likewise, although initial impressions might be otherwise, the contributions to this volume suggest that much the same treatment of treaties has often been adopted over the past three decades – namely, a pragmatic approach to the status and role of treaties in the American legal system which seeks to ensure effective implementation of international agreements in U.S. courts, but which also takes into account concerns regarding foreign entanglements and the domestic effects of international agreements. This approach to treaty implementation can be seen in a variety of developments that are addressed in this volume.

First, a pragmatic approach aimed at ensuring robust federal authority to conclude international agreements can be seen in early political and judicial conclusions that Article II's supermajority formula for "treaties" is not the sole means for the United States to enter into international agreements, and that instead, both Congressional-Executive and sole Executive Agreements can give rise to binding international commitments that are valid as "Law of the Land."[35] As Michael Ramsey points out in Chapter 7, this pragmatism has given rise to a wide variety and number of executive agreements, memoranda of understanding, and other instruments, all of which have been given effect by U.S. courts, functioning in a manner consistent with the intentions of the nation's political branches.[36]

These conclusions were not compelled by, and instead were difficult to reconcile with, the text of Article II and with the concerns that motivated Article II's supermajority protections, both of which suggested that Article II treaties were to be the sole avenue for undertaking international commitments, particularly those with direct domestic legal consequences.

[35] *See* United States v. Pink, 315 U.S. 203, 62 S. Ct. 552, 86 L. Ed 796 (1942); United States v. Belmont, 301 U.S. 324, 57 S. Ct. 758, 81 L. Ed. 1134 (1937).

[36] *See* Ramsey, "The Treaty and Its Rivals: Making International Agreements in U.S. Law and Practice," Chapter 7 of this volume.

Nonetheless, the resulting expansion in the scope, frequency, variety, and importance of the United States' international commitments became a central, and largely unchallenged, feature of U.S. foreign relations law in the twentieth century. And, as Ramsey's chapter details, nothing in the past thirty years has called into question this vitally important element of federal authority to conclude international agreements in ways other than through the Article II process.[37] On the contrary, U.S. courts have repeatedly given effect to international agreement not taking the form of treaties during this time.[38]

The same pragmatism can be seen in *Missouri v. Holland* and its progeny, which expansively interpreted federal legislative authority to implement Article II treaties. This conclusion, motivated by a realistic approach to the necessity that the United States engage in world affairs, also was not required by, and instead was again difficult to reconcile with, the text of the Constitution. This conclusion was incorporated in the Second and Third Restatements and, as *Bond v. United States* shows, remains intact today.[39]

Second, as observed above, one of the most notable examples of misgivings about the role of treaties in American law over the past thirty years was the Supreme Court's decision in *Medellin v. Texas*, which rejected the Third Restatement's presumption that U.S. treaties are self-executing: "if the Executive Branch has not requested implementing legislation and Congress has not enacted such legislation, there is a strong presumption that the treaty has been considered self-executing."[40] Indeed, although alternative interpretations of *Medellin* are possible, the Court arguably went further and also held that treaties are presumptively non-self-executing.[41]

At the same time, however, the past three decades have also witnessed contrary developments, where treaties have been given tangible effect in U.S. courts in ways other than through self-executing status and direct application in U.S. courts. Thus, the post–World War II era has been characterized

37 *Ibid.*

38 *See* Dames & Moore v. Regan, 453 U.S. 654, 657, 101 S. Ct. 2972, 69 L. Ed 2d 918 (1981).

39 That is true despite suggestions, noted above, by three Justices concurring in *Bond v. United States* that *Missouri v. Holland* was wrongly decided.

40 *See* THIRD RESTATEMENT], *supra* note 12, § 111, rptr. n. 5.

41 The Court's formulation suggests the need for textual evidence of an affirmative decision to make a treaty self-executing: "Our cases simply require courts to decide whether a treaty's *terms* reflect a determination by the President who negotiated it and the Senate that confirmed it that the treaty has domestic effect." *Medellin*, 552 U.S. at 521 (emphasis added). This conclusion has been followed by some lower courts. *See, e.g.*, ESAB Group, Inc. v. Zurich Ins. PLC, 685 F.3d 376, 387–8 (4th Cir. 2012); Safety Nat. Cas. Corp. v. Certain Underwriters at Lloyd's, London, 587 F.3d 714, 737 (5th Cir. 2009) (Clement, C.J., concurring in the judgment).

by a dramatic expansion of implementing legislation giving domestic effect to the nation's international agreements. As David Stewart observes, "for the United States, legislative implementation of multilateral treaties has clearly become the predominant practice;" and, tellingly, "the bulk of 'self-executing' treaties (extradition, mutual legal assistance, and tax treaties in particular) are in fact dependent on existing legislative structures for their operational effect, and overall they seem to be perceived as working reasonably well."[42]

These observations are vitally important to assessing the efficacy of U.S. implementation of the nation's international agreements and the broader consequences of the *Medellin* decision and similar developments over the past thirty years. If Congress generally implements U.S. treaties through the legislative process, the importance of the self-executing character of treaties is materially diminished: implementing legislation provides an alternative mechanism for ensuring that the nation's international agreements are given domestic effect. Where Congress implements an international agreement by legislation, U.S. compliance with treaty obligations is accomplished by means alternative to, and in some respects superior to, purely judicial implementation – provided, of course, that the implementing legislation fairly implements the treaty terms.

This role for implementing legislation is well-illustrated by the Supreme Court's decision in *Hamdan*,[43] which provides an important counterpoint to *Medellin*. In *Hamdan*, the Court held that the Uniform Code of Military Justice (UCMJ) incorporated the law of war and Common Article 3 of the Geneva Conventions, thereby imposing materially heightened international obligations on the U.S. military with far-reaching consequences both domestically and internationally. Given that conclusion, as Geoffrey Corn and Dru Brenner-Beck observe in Chapter 9, the question whether the Geneva Conventions are or are not self-executing has only secondary importance because the UCMJ is a viable source of relief for those harmed by violations of Common Article 3.[44] Despite *Medellin*'s retreat from the Third Restatement's presumption that treaties are self-executing, *Hamdan* substantially had reduced the significance of that issue in relation to the Geneva Conventions, while illustrating more generally the importance of implementing legislation in contemporary treaty application.

42 *See* David Stewart, "Recent Trends in U.S. Treaty Implementation," Chapter 6 of this volume.

43 *See* Hamdan v. Rumsfeld, 548 U.S. 557, 126 S. Ct. 2749, 165 L. Ed. 2d 723 (2006).

44 *See* Geoffrey Corn & Dru Brenner-Beck, "Case Study No. 1: Exploring U.S. Treaty Practice through a Military Lens," Chapter 9 of this volume.

Third, U.S. judicial decisions have also given domestic effect to U.S. treaty obligations in a variety of ways, in many cases adopting an alternative, albeit less direct and unqualified, means of judicial implementation than by holding the treaty to be self-executing. A prime example of this approach is the Supreme Court's decision in *Societe Nationale Industrielle Aerospatiale v. U.S. District Court*. In *Aerospatiale*, the Court held that the Hague Evidence Convention did not automatically preclude litigants from seeking extraterritorial discovery of materials located abroad (in a Contracting State to the Convention) pursuant to the Federal Rules of Civil Procedure, which Paul Dubinsky criticizes as an example of parochial bias in Supreme Court treaty interpretation. At the same time, however, the *Aerospatiale* Court also held that in some circumstances, principles of "international comity" require U.S. litigants to pursue discovery through the Convention rather than by application of the Federal Rules of Civil Procedure. The Court reasoned:

> [T]he concept of international comity requires in this context a . . . particularized analysis of the respective interests of the foreign nation and the requesting nation [, as well as] the particular facts, sovereign interests and likelihood that resort to [the Hague Evidence Convention] procedures will prove effective.[45]

Lower courts have applied these factors in a case-by-case manner – frequently permitting direct discovery under the Federal Rules, but applying the doctrine of international comity to often restrict the scope of direct discovery while also sometimes ordering discovery exclusively through the Convention.[46] Although the Court interpreted the Convention relatively narrowly in *Aerospatiale*, it also applied the doctrine of international comity broadly, to give effect to the Convention in a substantial set of cases as a matter of U.S. law and policy.

Likewise, the Supreme Court's decisions in *Scherk v. Alberto-Culver*[47] and *Mitsubishi Motors v. Soler Chrysler-Plymouth*,[48] relied in part on principles of international comity, together with the purposes of the New York Convention, to give broad effect to Article II of the Convention. In particular, while asserting the ability of the United States to apply Article II(3)'s non-arbitrability exception to claims under U.S. securities and antitrust legislation, the

45 *Ibid.* at 543–4.
46 *See* Gary B. Born & Peter B. Rutledge, International Civil Litigation in United States Courts 1040–41 (5th ed. 2011).
47 *See* Scherk v. Alberto-Culver Co., 417 U.S. 506, n.15, 94 S. Ct. 2449, 41 L. Ed. 2d 270 (1974).
48 *See* Mitsubishi, 473 U.S. at 629.

Court declined to do so, instead upholding the parties' agreement to arbitrate such claims. In *Mitsubishi*, the Court reasoned:

> The utility of the Convention in promoting the process of international commercial arbitration depends upon the willingness of national courts to let go of matters they normally would think of as their own. Doubtless, Congress may specify categories of claims it wishes to reserve for decision by our own courts without contravening this Nation's obligations under the Convention. But we decline to subvert the spirit of the United States' accession to the Convention by recognizing subject-matter exceptions where Congress has not expressly directed the courts to do so."[49]

Paralleling *Aerospatiale*, the *Mitsubishi* Court relied on principles of international comity to give broad effect to the New York Convention under domestic U.S. law, while holding that Article II of the Convention left U.S. courts free to reach a different conclusion in other contexts without violating the treaty. Adopting similar reasoning, the Supreme Court held in *Scherk v. Alberto-Culver* that claims under U.S. securities laws were arbitrable.[50] The Court reasoned:

> A parochial refusal by the courts of one country to enforce an international arbitration agreement would not only frustrate these purposes, but would invite unseemly and mutually destructive jockeying by the parties to secure tactical litigation advantages. In the present case, for example, it is not inconceivable that if Scherk had anticipated that Alberto-Culver would be able in this country to enjoin resort to arbitration he might have sought an order in France or some other country enjoining Alberto-Culver from proceeding with its litigation in the United States. Whatever recognition the courts of this country might ultimately have granted to the order of the foreign court, the dicey atmosphere of such a legal no-man's-land would surely damage the fabric of international commerce and trade, and imperil the willingness and ability of businessmen to enter into international commercial agreements . . .[51]

Moreover, in both *Mitsubishi Motors* and *Scherk*, the Court ordered arbitration of U.S. statutory claims in an international setting, even when the same claims would concededly not have been arbitrable in a domestic context at the

49 Ibid. at 653, n.21. *See also Ibid.* at 638–9 ("If [international arbitral institutions] are to take a central place in the international legal order, national courts will need to 'shake off the old judicial hostility to arbitration,' and also their customary and understandable unwillingness to cede jurisdiction of a claim arising under domestic law to a foreign or transnational tribunal. To this extent, at least, it will be necessary for national courts to subordinate domestic notions of arbitrability to the international policy favoring commercial arbitration . . . ").

50 *See* Scherk, 417 U.S. at 516–18.

51 *Ibid.* at 516–17.

time. In each of these cases, the Court also gave effect to a U.S. treaty, not by holding the treaty self-executing and directly applicable in U.S. courts, or by interpreting the treaty itself expansively, but instead by deriving implementing authority from domestic U.S. law and principles of international comity and by interpreting these principles expansively. This approach gave broad effect to the New York Convention, but also provided the Court with a degree of latitude in giving domestic effect to U.S. treaty obligations in U.S. courts, using principles of international comity or rules of domestic law as mechanisms to ensure that the judicial application of treaty provisions was consistent with the intentions of the political branches.

A comparable example of recent U.S. judicial implementation of treaties was *BG Group v. Republic of Argentina*,[52] where the Supreme Court confirmed an arbitral award against the Republic of Argentina in the United States under a bilateral investment treaty. Citing both international arbitral authority and international commentary,[53] the Court deferred to the jurisdictional decision of an investment arbitration tribunal rejecting challenges to the tribunal's competence giving domestic effect to both the treaty and the arbitral award.[54] Importantly, the Court did so through the application of domestic U.S. arbitration law (applying the Federal Arbitration Act), which it interpreted in light of the bilateral investment treaty and international commentary.[55] By taking this approach, the Court gave broad effect to the bilateral investment treaty, recognizing an award made pursuant to a treaty under U.S. law and, at the same time, giving domestic law a central role in its analysis and as an escape valve for future investment arbitration cases.

On close examination, the analysis in decisions like *Aerospatiale*, *Mitsubishi*, *Scherk*, and *BG Group* reflect the historic ambivalence of U.S. courts (and political branches) towards treaties and other international obligations. On the one hand, these decisions provide a mechanism for giving relatively expansive domestic effect to U.S. treaty obligations in U.S. courts. On the other hand, the approach adopted in these decisions allows U.S. courts, using principles of international comity or domestic law, to modulate the direct and unqualified application of treaty provisions, retaining a domestic escape valve for unforeseen cases. This approach may be less satisfying to proponents of the Third Restatement than direct judicial application of a

[52] *See generally*, BG Grp., PLC v. Republic of Argentina, 134 U.S. 1198, 188 L. Ed. 2d 220 (2014).

[53] *Ibid.* at 1218 (citing Daimler Fin. Servs. AG v. Argentine Republic, ICSID Case No. ARB/05/1, Award, 193, 194 (Aug. 22, 2012); Wintershall Aktiengesellschaft v. Argentine Republic, ICSID Case No. ARB/04/14, Award, 116 (Dec. 8, 2008); Gary B. Born, I International Commercial Arbitration 842 (2009).

[54] *Ibid.* at 1213.

[55] *Ibid.* at 1206.

self-executing treaty in U.S. courts, but the approach reflects, and is consistent with, an historic American ambivalence towards the treaty-making power.

Fourth, Paul Dubinsky's account of the increasingly unilateral method of U.S. treaty interpretation, often relying exclusively on the intentions of the U.S. political branches, instead of those of the United Sates' treaty-partners, describes a phenomenon that can be attributed in part to increasing skepticism and ambivalence about the United States' foreign entanglements during the past three decades.[56] At the same time, this phenomenon may also be attributable to other factors. It is understandable for treaties to be interpreted like regulatory statutes and agency regulations, rather than contracts, when the level of detail and the negotiating process of twentieth-century treaties often resemble those of statutes and administrative regulations. Contemporary international agreements frequently prescribe specialized, detailed regulatory regimes, in contrast to the much less detailed or comprehensive treaties, virtually always on a bilateral basis as was typically the case in the nineteenth- and early twentieth centuries. Judicial deference to the specialized expertise and experience of Executive branch officials is unsurprising in the context of litigation over treaties that deal with a highly technical subject matter and detailed regulatory regime.

Moreover, the "treaty-as-contract" metaphor, with only limited judicial deference to Executive branch views, continues to retain force, with regulatory, statutory, and contractual paradigms all being used in different settings. Thus, in *Mitsubishi Motors*, the Supreme Court declined to defer to the views of the Executive branch about the arbitrability of international antitrust claims under the New York Convention, and emphasized the importance of giving broad effect to the mechanisms established by US treaties.[57] Likewise, in *BG Group v. Argentina*, the Court rejected the views of the Executive branch and interpreted a bilateral investment treaty by applying traditional contract law principles, while also giving substantial weight to international arbitral awards interpreting similar treaties. That mode of analysis gave effect not only to the intentions of the parties to the treaty, in preference to contrary U.S. Executive branch views, but also to the holdings of independent international tribunals chosen by the parties, in keeping with the traditional "treaty as contract" metaphor. [58] Again, it is very difficult to reconcile these developments with a

[56] *See* Dubinsky, "Competing Models for Treaty Interpretation: Treaty as Contract, Treaty as Statute, Treaty as Delegation," Chapter 3 of this volume.

[57] *See* Mitsubishi, 473 U. S. at 658–60.

[58] That said, *BG Group* involved a treaty between the United Kingdom and Argentina, not a U.S. treaty, and the Court's decision did not directly implicate questions of deference to the U.S.

narrative that views the past three decades as a wholesale retreat from a robust approach to treaty implementation and interpretation.

Finally, in the same vein, the Third Restatement itself reflected a notable measure of ambivalence about the treaty power. Indeed, these features of the Third Restatement are among the most important aspects of post-1987 ambivalence towards the treaty power.

As both Roger Alford and Ingrid Wuerth explain, the Third Restatement introduced a presumption that treaties do not create private rights of action:[59] "[i]nternational agreements, even those directly benefiting private persons, generally do not create private rights or provide for a private cause of action in domestic courts, but there are exceptions with respect to both rights and remedies."[60] That presumption had not been recognized in either the *Second Restatement* or other pre-1987 sources of law, and appeared with little debate during the drafting process of the Third Restatement.

Despite the recent and relatively unheralded origins of this presumption against treaty-based rights of action, the presumption has established a very material limitation on the enforcement of treaty norms within the U.S. legal system, one no less significant than a presumption against the self-executing status of treaties. The presumption has been developed and extended over the past thirty years, most robustly in *Medellin*, but its origins lie firmly in the Third Restatement. Indeed, the post-1987 judicial development[61] of this presumption has arguably proceeded on a more nuanced, case-by-case basis, than suggested by the Third Restatement.

Similarly, the Third Restatement approached the process of determining self-executing status in a largely unilateral manner. It directed courts to the statements and views of the United States, specifically the President and Senate, rather than to the intentions of other parties to the agreement,[62] in order to determine whether a treaty is self-executing or not.[63] That approach has been followed in post-1987 U.S. judicial decisions, which have generally given little or no weight to indications of the intentions of foreign states in determining the self-executing status of treaties.[64] Again, the approach

political branches. The Court's approach in *BG Group* will nonetheless shape the interpretation of bilateral investment treaties to which the U.S. is a party.

59 *See* THIRD RESTATEMENT, *supra* note 12, § 907, cmt. (a).

60 *Ibid.*

61 *See* Sosa v. Alvarez-Machain, 542 U.S. 692, 124 S. Ct. 2739, 159 L. Ed. 2d 718 (2004).

62 *See* THIRD RESTATEMENT, *supra* note 12, § 325, cmt. (b) & rptr. nn. 1–2, 4.

63 *Ibid.* at § 111, rptr. n. 5.

64 *See, e.g.*, Frolova v. Union of Soviet Socialist Republics, 761 F.2d 370, 376 (7th Cir. 1985) (stating that the implementation of the provisions of the treaty is left to the discretion of the state); Islamic Republic of Iran v. Boeing Co., 771 F.2d 1279, 1284 (9th Cir. 1985) (relying on

adopted in the Third Restatement itself reflected, at least in part, the ambivalence historically displayed towards the treaty power and the concern to establish mechanisms for ascertaining that direct application of treaties in U.S. courts reflects the intentions of the U.S. political branches.

* * * * *

In sum, the past three decades have brought significant developments in the ways that Americans enter into treaties and adjudicate disputes arising from them. One of this volume's virtues is its presentation of a wealth of information and of competing conclusions that can be drawn about those developments. On the one hand, this volume presents evidence that the last thirty years may herald a significant departure from historic U.S. norms, with effective domestic implementation of U.S. treaties becoming increasingly rare and difficult. On the other hand, this volume also suggests a less pessimistic explanation for post–Third Restatement U.S. treaty law and behavior: that what we see is the continuing evolution of traditional U.S. ambivalence about the treaty-making power – an ambivalence that has deep roots and that reappears periodically. In the context of such ambivalence, U.S. courts during the past three decades, like Americans of earlier generations, have devised pragmatic and durable solutions to overcome obstacles to effective enforcement of treaty obligations and use of the federal treaty-making power. In the coming years of this century, we can expect these perennial misgivings regarding foreign entanglements to recur and that future generations will be required to develop new, hopefully equally pragmatic and effective, responses.

the intent of the President in making its determination on whether the treaty is self-executing); *see also* THIRD RESTATEMENT, *supra* note 12, § 111, cmt. (h) (stating that "[i]n the absence of special agreement, it is ordinarily for the United States to decide how it will carry out its international obligations").

Index

www.ingramcontent.com/pod-product-compliance
Lightning Source LLC
LaVergne TN
LVHW052213200926
848481LV00001B/93